FileMaker Pro 8

THE MISSING MANUAL

*The book that
should have been
in the box*

Other resources from O'Reilly

Related titles

iPod & iTunes: The Missing Manual

FrontPage 2003: The Missing Manual

Garage Band 2: The Missing Manual

Applescript: The Missing Manual

Adobe Encore DVD: In the Studio

Photoshop Elements 3: The Missing Manual

iPhoto 5: The Missing Manual

iMovie HD & iDVD5: The Missing Manual

Mac OS X: The Missing Manual, Tiger Edition

Mac OS X Power Hound, Panther Edition

oreilly.com

oreilly.com is more than a complete catalog of O'Reilly books. You'll also find links to news, events, articles, weblogs, sample chapters, and code examples.

oreillynet.com is the essential portal for developers interested in open and emerging technologies, including new platforms, programming languages, and operating systems.

Conferences

O'Reilly brings diverse innovators together to nurture the ideas that spark revolutionary industries. We specialize in documenting the latest tools and systems, translating the innovator's knowledge into useful skills for those in the trenches. Visit *conferences.oreilly.com* for our upcoming events.

Safari Bookshelf (*safari.oreilly.com*) is the premier online reference library for programmers and IT professionals. Conduct searches across more than 1,000 books. Subscribers can zero in on answers to time-critical questions in a matter of seconds. Read the books on your Bookshelf from cover to cover or simply flip to the page you need. Try it today with a free trial.

FileMaker Pro 8

THE MISSING MANUAL

Geoff Coffey and Susan Prosser

POGUE PRESS™

O'REILLY®

Beijing · Cambridge · Farnham · Köln · Paris · Sebastopol · Taipei · Tokyo

FileMaker Pro 8: The Missing Manual
by Geoff Coffey and Susan Prosser

Published by O'Reilly Media, Inc., 1005 Gravenstein Highway North, Sebastopol, CA 95472.

O'Reilly books may be purchased for educational, business, or sales promotional use. Online editions are also available for most titles (*safari.oreilly.com*). For more information, contact our corporate/institutional sales department: (800) 998-9938 or *corporate@oreilly.com*.

Editors:	Michele Filshie and Nan Barber
Production Editor:	Philip Dangler
Cover Designer:	Marcia Friedman
Interior Designer:	David Futato

Printing History:

September 2005:	First Edition.

RepKover™ This book uses RepKover,™ a durable and flexible lay-flat binding.

ISBN-10: 0-596-00579-2
ISBN-13: 978-0-596-00579-5

[M]   [2/07]

Table of Contents

Part Seven: Appendixes

The Missing Credits

About the Authors

Geoff Coffey has experience with all kinds of technical-sounding acronyms, but FileMaker Pro was his first true love—a fact his wife of ten years disputes. He's IT Director at Allegro Enterprises, an Internet retailer in Phoenix, where his team builds and manages FileMaker systems. He's been helping others use FileMaker for nine years, and occasionally gets a little philosophical about how it lets ordinary people use computers to solve their problems without a degree in Computer Science. (He's a little miffed he figured that out after finishing his own CS degree.) Away from the office, Geoff's a full-time dad to young daughters Isabel and Sophia. When he's not hanging out with the girls, he's always happy to get email from another FileMaker fans at *gwcoffey@gmail.com*.

Late one night, **Susan Prosser** dropped a stack of punch cards containing homework for a math course that inexplicably contained a computer science module. Instead of reordering the cards, she dropped the class and argued with the registrar: "Woodward and Bernstein don't use computers. I don't need this stuff for a journalism degree." Now a reformed journalist, Susan has stopped trying to bring new information to the people and helps them manage the data they already have using FileMaker. She scratches the journalism itch by writing curriculum and training other developers. To engage in Lance Armstrong vs Eddie Merckx polemic, discuss quilting as the perfect combination of left-brain/right-brain activity, or defend the use of globals to hold variable data in a script, please send a polite, well-reasoned email to *susanprosser@gmail.com*. Former guidance counselors or irate registrars should put "I told you so" in the subject line.

About the Creative Team

Nan Barber (editor) is O'Reilly's associate editor for the Missing Manual series and has worn every hat from copy editor to co-author. She lives in the Boston area and never doubted for a moment that both Macworld Expo and the Commissioner's Trophy would someday come back to town. Email: *nanbarber@mac.com*.

Michele Filshie (editor) is O'Reilly's assistant editor for the Missing Manual series and editor of four Personal Trainers (another O'Reilly series). Before turning to the world of computer-related books, Michele was all literature, all the time, and spent many happy years at Black Sparrow Press. She lives in Sebastopol and loves to get involved in local politics. Email: *mfilshie@oreilly.com*.

Sohaila Abdulali (copy editor) is a freelance writer and editor. She has published a novel, several children's books, and numerous short stories and articles. She is currently finishing an ethnography of an aboriginal Indian woman. She lives in New York City with her husband Tom and their small but larger-than-life daughter, Samara. Web: *www.sohailaink.com*.

Nonie Bernard (technical reviewer) is an independent information management consultant, director of curriculum development for FMPtraining, an instructor with the Maricopa Community Colleges, and co-author of Learn FileMaker Pro from Wordware Publishing. She has a degree in human resources and more than 20 years experience in training design and delivery. A lifelong artist and musician, Nonie has sung in an opera with Igor Stravinsky. Email: *innonievations@qwest.net*.

Jay Welshofer (technical reviewer) has been using one version or another of File-Maker Pro for almost 20 years, has had the pleasure of working for the company for 11 years, and is taught something new by customers every day. Jay is currently a member of a dedicated team of professionals creating future versions of File-Maker Pro. Email: *jlw@filemaker.com*.

Rose Cassano (cover illustration) has worked as an independent designer and illustrator for twenty years. Assignments have ranged from the nonprofit sector to corporate clientele. She lives in beautiful Southern Oregon, grateful for the miracles of modern technology that make working there a reality. Email: *cassano@highstream.net*. Web: *www.rosecassano.com*.

Acknowledgements

Picture this: My wife and I have two small children. I work full-time as a FileMaker consultant, and I'm in the thick of a two-year evening MBA program. One day over dinner, I casually mention that I'm considering writing a book about FileMaker for Pogue Press. I offer my sincerest gratitude to my sweet wife for not laughing, and even more for being so supportive despite her outlandish schedule. This book would have been impossible without her support.

I am also grateful to the outstanding engineers at FileMaker Inc. who have worked for years with no glory to develop the skills necessary to make FileMaker Pro easy so the rest of us don't have to work so hard. And I will always be indebted to Susan Prosser, who joined this team late in the game and pulled off a miracle to see this project to completion.

—Geoff Coffey

Thanks, Geoff, for the accolades and for asking me to work with on you on the book. As always, it's been great fun and hard work. I second your props to the good folks at FMI. Many of us have made good careers on the fruits of their labor; I'm very grateful that I can write a professional database using my airy liberal arts degree. And thanks to all the folks at O'Reilly, who've been so flexible on this unusual project. Nan, you've been a dream editor. Thank you for all your help and encouragement.

When my husband and I were talking about whether I should do the book, he got this rueful look and said, "It won't be like last time, will it?" Unless it was all those weeks when we didn't even start cooking dinner until after bedtime, I can't imagine what he meant. To be fair, it might have been the piles of languishing projects that didn't get cleared away: two(!) late baby quilts, plants needing repotting, pictures needing hanging, boxes needing unpacking, animals needing tending. Well, the piles were all waiting when the book was done, just like I suspected they would be. Thanks, Paul.

—Susan Prosser

The Missing Manual Series

Missing Manuals are witty, superbly written guides to computer products that don't come with printed manuals (which is just about all of them). Each book features a handcrafted index; cross-references to specific page numbers (not just "see Chapter 14"); and RepKover, a detached-spine binding that lets the book lie perfectly flat without the assistance of weights or cinder blocks.

Recent and upcoming titles include:

Mac OS X: The Missing Manual (Panther and Tiger editions) by David Pogue

Excel: The Missing Manual by Matthew MacDonald

iPhoto 5: The Missing Manual by David Pogue

iLife '05: The Missing Manual by David Pogue

GarageBand: The Missing Manual by David Pogue

iMovie 5 & iDVD: The Missing Manual by David Pogue

Google: The Missing Manual by Sarah Milstein and Rael Dornfest

Switching to the Mac: The Missing Manual by David Pogue

Mac OS X Power Hound, Panther Edition by Rob Griffiths

Dreamweaver MX 2004: The Missing Manual by David Sawyer McFarland

Office X for Macintosh: The Missing Manual by Nan Barber, Tonya Engst, and David Reynolds

Office 2004 for Macintosh: The Missing Manual by Mark H. Walker and Franklin Tessler

AppleWorks 6: The Missing Manual by Jim Elferdink and David Reynolds

Windows XP Home Edition: The Missing Manual by David Pogue

Windows XP Pro: The Missing Manual by David Pogue, Craig Zacker, and Linda Zacker

Applescript: The Missing Manual by Adam Goldstein

Photoshop Elements 3: The Missing Manual by Barbara Brundage

QuickBooks 2005: The Missing Manual by Bonnie Biafore

eBay: The Missing Manual by Nancy Conner

FrontPage 2003: The Missing Manual by Jessica Mantaro

Introduction

For many people, the word "database" conjures up an image of a computer, and a vast collection of information you can only access via a computer screen. But actually, databases are all around you—a phone book, a cookbook, and an encyclopedia are all databases. So is the stock page in your newspaper. In fact, if you look up the word "database" in a dictionary (which is a database, too) you'll probably read that a database is just a collection of information, or data.

Ideally, a database's information is organized so that you can easily find what you're looking for. For example, a Rolodex has information about people organized alphabetically, so you can find any person's card pretty quickly because you know approximately where it is, even though there may be *hundreds* of cards to look through. But physical databases like this example all have major limitations compared to those that are stored on a computer. What if you want to get a list of all your associates in California? A Rolodex isn't organized that way, so you have to look through every card one by one. That kind of tedium is one of the reasons so many Rolodexes are now at the bottom of landfills, and it's one of the biggest problems a computer *database program* like FileMaker Pro can help you avoid.

The term *database program* means a computer program designed to help you build a database. Lots of computer programs *use* a database in one way or another—for example, your email program tracks hundreds of email messages you've sent and received, but it isn't a database program. A database program lets you build your own database and customize it to meet your specific needs.

A database stored on a computer isn't much different in theory than one painstakingly collected on Rolodex cards or other forms of paper. It contains lots of information, like addresses, zip codes, and phone numbers, and organizes that info in useful ways (see Figure I-1 for an example). But because it's stored on a computer, you can organize the *same* information in numerous ways with ease—say, by name *or* by state. Computers also make searching databases a whole lot faster. In fact, a computer can often look through almost any amount of data in less than a second, which is a lot quicker than flipping through all your Rolodex cards to find everyone who lives in Kansas.

Figure I-1:
FileMaker Pro lets you do just about anything with the information you give it. You can use it like a Rolodex to simply store and retrieve information, or run your entire business with this one program. FileMaker's built-in number crunching and word processing tools let you track people, processes, and things, creating all your reports, correspondence, and collateral documents along the way. Here are two examples of real-world FileMaker databases created for very different kinds of businesses.

This book will teach you how FileMaker stores your information and how you can rearrange that information and get the answers to meaningful questions like which employees are due for performance reviews, who's coming to the company picnic and which amusement park has the best deal on Laser Tag for your top 50 performers. You won't have to learn to think like a programmer (or know the arcane terms they use), but you will learn how to bend FileMaker Pro's hidden power to your will and make it tell you everything it knows about your company, your stock portfolio or how much you've spent on the replacement parts for the '58 Bonneville Sport Coupe you're rebuilding.

Why FileMaker Pro?

If you're reading this book, you've already decided to use a computer databases instead of the mulched-up tree variety. *Choosing* a database program from the many options on the market is overwhelming. Some are enormously powerful, but take weeks to learn how to use. Others are easy to get started with, but don't offer much help when you're ready to incorporate some more advanced features. Here are a few reasons why FileMaker Pro is a great choice for most folks.

- **FileMaker Pro is the ease-of-use champion.** While other programs use funny words like *query, join,* and *alias,* FileMaker Pro uses simple concepts like *find, sort,* and *connect.* FileMaker is designed from the ground up for non-technical people who have a *real* job to do. It's designed to let you get in, get your database built, and get back to work.

- **FileMaker Pro can do almost anything.** Some other database programs are simple to use, but they're just plain simple, too—they can't do the kinds of things most businesses need to do. FileMaker Pro, despite its focus on ease of use, is very powerful. It can handle large amounts of data. It lets lots of people on different computers share data (even at different locations around the world). It even meets the needs of bigger companies, like integrating with high-end systems. And it's adaptable enough to solve most problems. If your home-based crafting business is taking off, and you need to figure out how much it costs you to create your top-selling items, FileMaker can do that. But if you're a large school district tracking dozens of test scores for more than 50,000 students in grades K-12 and you have to make sure those scores are tied to federal standards, well, FileMaker can handle that, too.

- **FileMaker Pro works on Macs or PCs.** If you or your company use both types of computers, FileMaker Pro makes the connection seamless. The exact same databases can be used on any computer, and even shared simultaneously without a hitch (see page 642).

- **FileMaker Pro is fun!** It may sound corny, but it's exciting (and a little addictive) to have such a powerful tool at your fingertips. If you get the bug, you'll find yourself solving all kinds of problems you never knew you had. You might not think that getting married is an occasion for breaking out a new database, but you'll be amazed at how helpful it is. You can make a mailing list for your invitations, track RSVPs, note which favorite aunt sent you a whole set of bone china (and which cheap cousin cheaped out by signing his name on his brother's gift card), and you can record what date you mailed the thank-you notes.

- **Everybody uses it.** Perhaps best of all, FileMaker Pro is very popular—more people buy FileMaker Pro than any other database program. And the program's fans love it so much they're actually willing to help *you* if you get stuck. You can find user groups, Web sites, discussion boards, chat rooms, mailing lists, and professional consultants all devoted to FileMaker Pro. This is one case where there's good reason to follow the crowd.

What's New in FileMaker Pro 8

FileMaker Pro is a single software package that serves two fundamentally different types of people: users and designers. Users are the folks who need a database to help them organize and manage the data they work with in order to do their jobs. Designers create the databases that users use. No matter which category you're in (and lots of people fall into both categories, sometimes popping back and forth dozens of times a day), you'll find that FileMaker doesn't play favorites. The features you need for both roles are equally accessible.

Day-to-day users appreciate features like the following, because they address the most frequently needed tasks:

- **If your boss down the hall needs a report, but he doesn't use FileMaker, you can still send him the data he needs.** Just create an Excel file from inside FileMaker with the Save Records as Excel command.

- But what if your boss doesn't even use Excel? No problem. **Export and email** the contents of any field–text, numbers, graphics, or even electronic files–without leaving FileMaker.

- **Maybe you don't want to give people the actual data you've painstakingly gathered, but you do want them to be able to see it.** You can make PDF files right from the menu to pass around the office or post on your Web site. No more fussing around with Adobe Acrobat or arcane print settings.

- When the sales data indicate that you've had a record month and you want to congratulate the entire marketing department, you could do that in older versions of FileMaker–if you knew how to write scripts. The new **email merge** feature lets you send batches of email **with a few, simple commands.**

- If you've got a warehouse full of paper products that have to be moved, you can find a list of all customers who've bought that product without even typing. Just find the first customer who bought item #456-234-WJ43. Highlight the item number, and then select **Find Matching Records.** Voila! You've got a list of customers without typing a single keystroke.

- **Auto-complete** settings work like type ahead in word processing programs. This setting can make data entry faster and more accurate.

- FileMaker's finicky about how you type a date. If you get the wrong sequence of numbers and slashes, the program complains until you get it right. Now, you can attach **calendar pop-ups** to any field. Just click the date you need and File-Maker pops it into the field without grouching at you.

- **Visual spell checker** highlights suspect words as you type, just like your favorite word processing program. You can correct your spelling as you speed type merrily along.

Some of the features listed above aren't completely new, as designers can tell you. They know, because in previous versions, designers spent lots of time making these tasks easy for their users. But now that FileMaker has built-in ways to send data as email or PDFs, designers can spend more time making other tasks easier and more reliable. Below are some new features that help you create databases (or improve the ones you already have):

- **Layout alignment tools** help you arrange fields so they line up and fit together better onscreen and for print. What would you do if somebody could give you back all the time you used to spend nudging and tweaking fields so they looked perfect?

- If you're combining data from other files, which is a major process if you're updating FileMaker files from versions prior to FileMaker Pro 7, the new **Table Import** feature is a welcome time and sanity saver. You can import data without defining tables and fields first. FileMaker creates the table for you before it brings your new data into your database.

- More than 20 **new functions** make your databases more powerful and efficient. If you're an old hand at writing calculations or creating complicated scripted processes, you'll love the power at your fingertips. If you're just starting to learn how to make calculations and scripts, you'll be out of the box faster.

- **Scripting variables** make designing scripts easier and more efficient because you don't have to create a bunch of extra fields to store data that's needed only for certain behind-the-scenes processes.

- Find out what happened to your data while you were running a script with the new option to attach a calculation to the **Exit Script step**.

- A powerful new **Go To Related Records option** lets you find all the records that match all the records you're already looking at. Say you're looking at a group of students and you need a list of all the students who have a class with any kid in your current list. In the old days, it was easy to find all classmates for a single student, but it wasn't so easy to get a list of more than one student's classmates at the same time. Now, you can do it with one script step.

UP TO SPEED

What About the Big Guys?

The word database is a little abused in the computer world. Both FileMaker Pro and MySQL–an open source database that you can use free, if you have the skills, manpower, hardware and know-how–are considered database programs, but they're about as similar as chocolate cake and dry flour. In reality, there are two kinds of database programs available. One kind is very powerful (as in, run-the-federal-government powerful) and *very* complicated. This type of database program just holds data, and computer programmers use these sophisticated, and expensive, tools when they build big systems for big companies.

The other kind of database program–sometimes called a *desktop database*–is less powerful and a lot easier, but it actually does a lot more. In addition to holding lots of data, these programs provide an *interface* to access, organize, and search the data. This interface includes the menus, graphics, and text that let you work with the data, much like any other computer program. In other words, you don't need a computer science degree to create a powerful database with a desktop program like FileMaker Pro.

The Very Basics

You'll find very little jargon or nerd terminology in this book. You will, however, encounter a few terms and concepts that you'll see frequently in your computer life. They include:

- **Clicking.** This book offers three kinds of instructions that require you to use the mouse or trackpad attached to your computer. To *click* means to point the arrow cursor at something onscreen and then—without moving the cursor at all—press and release the clicker button on the mouse (or laptop trackpad). Right-clicking works the same as clicking, but you use the right mouse button instead. (If you use a Mac and don't have a right mouse button, press the Control key as you click.) To *double-click,* of course, means to click twice in rapid succession, again without moving the cursor at all. And to *drag* means to move the cursor while keeping the button continuously pressed.

  When you're told to *Ctrl-click* something, you click while pressing the Ctrl key (the *Control* key on the Mac) on the bottom row of your keyboard. Such related procedures as *Shift-clicking* and *Alt-clicking* work the same way—just click while pressing the corresponding key.

Note: On the Mac, the key that does most of the Alt key functions is called the Option key. Macs also have an extra key called the Command key, which has a cloverleaf (⌘) on it. When the Mac keystroke is different than the one in Windows, this book gives it in parentheses (see page xxiii).

- **Menus** are the lists of commands that you pull down from the words at the top of the FileMaker window. (On the Mac, they're always in the bar across the top of the screen.) There are two equally valid ways to choose from these pull-down menus with your mouse: Click once to open the menu and then click again to choose a command, or click and *hold* the button as you drag down the menu and release when you get to the desired command. Use whichever method you find easier.

- **Keyboard shortcuts.** Every time you take your hand off the keyboard to move the mouse, you lose time and potentially disrupt your creative floow. That's why many experienced computer jockeys use keystroke combinations instead of menu commands wherever possible. Ctrl-P (⌘-P) opens the Print dialog box, for example.

  When you see a shortcut like Ctrl-Q (⌘-Q), which closes the current program, it's telling you to hold down the Ctrl (⌘) key, and, while it's down, type the letter Q, and then release both keys.

If you've mastered this much information, you have all the technical background you need to enjoy *FileMaker Pro 8: The Missing Manual.*

About This Book

FileMaker Pro comes with a printed manual, and an impressive online help system. These are actually pretty helpful resources…if you're a programmer, that is, or if you've been working with FileMaker for a while. Between the manual and the help file, you can figure out how FileMaker works. But you'll have to jump back and forth between page and screen to get the complete picture. And neither source does a great job of letting you know which features apply to the problem you're trying to solve.

This book is designed to serve as the FileMaker Pro manual, the book that should have been in the box. It explores each feature in depth, offers shortcuts and workarounds, and explains the ramifications of options that the manual doesn't even mention. Plus, it lets you know which features are really useful and which ones you should worry about only in very limited circumstances. Try putting sticky tabs in your help file or marking the good parts with a highlighter!

FileMaker comes in several flavors, and this book addresses them all. FileMaker Pro, the base program, takes up most of the book's focus. FileMaker Pro Advanced is an enhanced version of the program. Like the name promises, it contains advanced tools and utilities aimed at making development and maintenance of your databases easier. Its features are covered in Chapter 12 and 19. FileMaker Server lets you share your databases more safely and quickly than FileMaker Pro's peer-to-peer sharing. Learn about Server in Chapter 18.

About the Outline

FileMaker Pro 8: The Missing Manual is divided into seven parts.

- **Part 1: Introduction to FileMaker Pro.** Here, you'll learn about FileMaker Pro's interface and how you perform basic tasks, like entering data and then sorting through it again. You'll also find out how FileMaker Pro stores your data inside fields and then organizes those fields into units called records. You'll see how to define fields and make them do some of the data entry work for you.

- **Part 2: Layouts.** Just as your actual data is organized into fields and records, the appearance of your database is organized into layouts. FileMaker Pro provides a whole raft of tools that make creating layouts fast and powerful. You'll find out how to use layouts to make data entry easier and how to create layouts that list and summarize your data.

- **Part 3: Multiple Tables and Relationships.** When you're storing lots of different types of data in a database, it's helpful to organize types of data using FileMaker's tables. And when you have more than one table, you need to figure out how the information in one table relates to the information in another. You'll learn how to create, connect, and manage multiple tables and how to set up complex relationships that show you just the data you need to see.

- **Part 4: Calculations.** Most databases store lots of numbers, but the most important information in your database comes from performing some kind of math on those numbers. You'll learn how to use FileMaker Pro's 200+ functions to do the math for you. Surprisingly, you can also use functions on fields that don't contain numbers. For example there are functions for working with text, dates, and times. And some of the most powerful functions are the logical functions, which can perform tests on your data, and then give you results based on what the function finds out.

- **Part 5: Scripting.** Because there are so many things you have to do with a database that are repetitive, tedious, or just plan boring, FileMaker Pro provides a way for you to automate those tasks using scripts. You'll start with simple steps that teach you how scripting works, and learn how to make scripts for people to use. You'll see how to use scripts to work with fields and records, or with windows, or even with entire database files. And you'll explore more complex techniques, like making scripts pass information to one another and nesting scripts within other scripts.

- **Part 6: Security and Integration.** FileMaker knows your data's important enough to keep it safe from prying eyes. In this section, you'll learn how to protect your database with password and how to use privileges to determine what folks can do once they get into your database. This part also teaches you how to move data into and out of your database and how to share that data with other people. In the final chapter, you'll see the design and development tools provided in FileMaker Advanced to speed creation time and give you more control over how your database works.

• **Part 7: Appendixes.** No book can include all the information you'll need for the rest of your FileMaker career. Well, it could, but you wouldn't be able to lift it. Eventually, you'll need to seek extra troubleshooting help or consult the program's online documentation. So at the end of the book, Appendix A explains how to find your way around FileMaker's built-in help files and Web site. It also covers the vast online community of fans and experts: People are the best resource of all for fresh ideas and creative solutions. Appendix B lists FileMaker error codes.

Living Examples

Each chapter contains *living examples*—step-by-step tutorials that help you learn how to build a database by actually doing it. If you take the time to work through these examples at the computer, you'll discover that these tutorials give you invaluable insight into the way professional developers create databases. To help you along, online database files provide sample data for you to work with and completed examples against which to check your work.

You can get these files any time from the "Missing CD" page at *www.missingmanuals.com* (page xxiv). To download, simply click this book's title, and then click the link for the relevant chapter.

Macintosh and Windows

FileMaker Pro works almost precisely the same in its Macintosh and Windows versions. Every button in every dialog box is exactly the same; the software response to every command is identical. In this book, the illustrations get even-handed treatment, alternating between Windows XP and Mac OS X.

One of the biggest differences between the Mac and Windows versions is the keystrokes, because the Ctrl key in Windows is the equivalent of the Macintosh ⌘ key.

Whenever this book refers to a key combination, you'll see the Windows keystroke listed first (with + symbols, as is customary in Windows documentation); the Macintosh keystroke follows in parentheses (with - symbols, in time-honored Mac fashion). In other words, you might read, "The keyboard shortcut for saving a file is Ctrl+S (⌘-S)."

About → These → Arrows

Throughout this book, and throughout the Missing Manual series, you'll find sentences like this one: "Open your Home → Library → Preferences folder." That's shorthand for a much longer instruction that directs you to open three nested folders in sequence, like this: "In the Finder, choose Go → Home. In your Home folder, you'll find a folder called Library. Open that. Inside the Library window is a folder called Preferences. Double-click to open it, too."

Similarly, this kind of arrow shorthand helps to simplify the business of choosing commands in menus, as shown in Figure I-2.

Figure I-2:
When you read in a Missing Manual, "Choose View → Go to Layout → Customers" that means: "Click the View menu to open it. Then click Go to Layout in that menu; choose Customers in the resulting submenu."

About MissingManuals.com

At *www.missingmanuals.com*, you'll find news, articles, and updates to the books in this series. Click the "Missing CD-ROM" link to reveal a chapter-by-chapter list of the databases referred to in the book.

If you click the name of this book and then the Errata link, you'll find a unique resource: a list of corrections and updates that have been made in successive printings of this book. You can mark important corrections right into your own copy of the book, if you like.

In fact, the same page offers an invitation for you to submit such corrections and updates yourself. In an effort to keep the book as up-to-date and accurate as possible, each time we print more copies of this book, we'll make any confirmed corrections you've suggested. Thanks in advance for reporting any glitches you find!

In the meantime, we'd love to hear your suggestions for new books in the Missing Manual line. There's a place for that on the Web site, too, as well as a place to sign up for free email notification of new titles in the series.

Safari® Enabled

When you see a Safari® Enabled icon on the cover of your favorite technology book, that means it's available online through the O'Reilly Network Safari Bookshelf.

Safari offers a solution that's better than e-books: it's a virtual library that lets you easily search thousands of top tech books, cut and paste code samples, download chapters, and find quick answers when you need the most accurate, current information. Try it for free at *http://safari.oreilly.com*.

Part One: Introduction to FileMaker Pro

1

Your First Database

FileMaker Pro databases can be as simple as a phone list for the soccer team or as complex as a company-wide system for purchasing, sales, inventory, invoicing, shipping, and customer tracking. But they all have a few important aspects in common and essentially *work* the same way. This chapter gives you a tour of File-Maker's major features and gets you up and running on your very first database.

FileMaker's vast assortment of tools and options can make its window as intimidating as a jumbo-jet cockpit. But the program's menu commands, dialog boxes, keyboard shortcuts, and other options stay largely consistent across all databases, from the most basic to the most high-powered. Almost everything you learn in the next few pages applies to every database you'll ever use.

Note: Because a database usually solves a *problem* of some kind, some FileMaker experts call a database a *solution,* as in, "I can create an inventory solution for your bakery, but it's going to cost you some dough." Usually, *database* and *solution* mean the same thing, although the term *solution* sometimes implies a system of several connected databases (more on that in Part 3).

A Very Quick Database Tour

Every FileMaker Pro database has two things in common: One, it stores heaps of information; and two, it gives you the tools to manage that information. Whether you start from one of FileMaker's templates (page 6) or a completely blank slate (page 9), your new database starts out data-free. It's an empty vessel waiting to be filled. (It would be nice if the program could figure out what data you want and enter it for you, but that probably won't happen until FileMaker Pro 8008.) You have to take care of the data entry yourself. At first, all you see in the window are the tools—buttons, controls, and pop-up menus—that you use to fill the database up with data.

Every database window has the same basic structure. FileMaker provides a handful of special items around the window, as you can see in Figure 1-1.

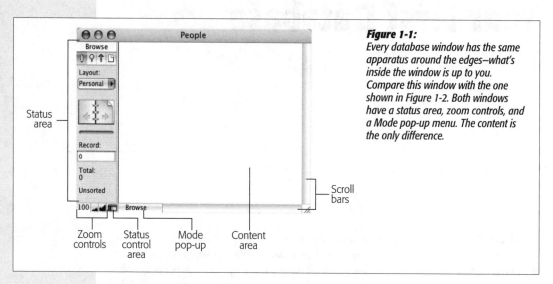

Figure 1-1:
Every database window has the same apparatus around the edges—what's inside the window is up to you. Compare this window with the one shown in Figure 1-2. Both windows have a status area, zoom controls, and a Mode pop-up menu. The content is the only difference.

Content Area

While some features like the status area, zoom controls, and Mode pop-up menu stay the same no matter which database you're using, what's inside the *content area* is the actual information (data) that makes each database unique.

When you create a new FileMaker database, you start with something that looks a little like Figure 1-1: plain and simple. That's because you haven't added any content yet. In Figure 1-2, you can see what your database will look like once you've started to fill it in. Depending on how you want to look at your information, you can use the controls described below to alter how your content appears onscreen.

Mode pop-up menu

This unassuming menu may not be the most prominent control in the window, but it's one of the most important. Each of FileMaker's four *modes* is a work environment unto itself, specially designed to help you view, edit, organize, or present your information in a specific way. Use this menu to switch modes depending on what you need to do.

- In stark contrast to rational expectations, you use **Browse mode** for more than browsing. In this mode, you can add, change, and view data in your database. Browse is the view shown in Figure 1-2, and it's where you'll spend most of this chapter.

- When you have a lot of data, looking through it all for a particular bit of info can be tedious. Use **Find mode** to let FileMaker do the looking for you. You tell FileMaker what you're looking for in Find mode; when it's done looking, File-Maker returns you to Browse mode and shows what it found. You'll see Find mode in action on page 23.

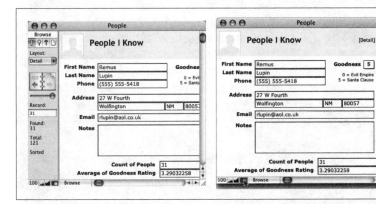

Figure 1-2:
Unlike the stark emptiness shown in Figure 1-1, this database is well underway, as you can see by the abundance of the content area. Left: The status area is part of all FileMaker databases, regardless of what they contain. Right: Maximize your view of the content area by hiding the status area with a simple click on its control.

- In addition to using databases (viewing, finding, sorting, adding, and changing data), you can use FileMaker to *build* databases. **Layout mode** is where you design the screens (or *layouts*) that present your database information to best advantage. Part 2 is all about Layout mode.

- Although computers make maintaining and manipulating mountains of information a breeze, there's still no avoiding paper. Eventually you'll want to print something out, like a set of mailing labels or a paper backup of all your records. If you're ever curious about how something will look when printed, switch to **Preview mode**. It shows a one-page-at-a-time view of your data exactly as it will appear when printed.

To use the Mode pop-up menu, just click it and choose one of the four modes. Your FileMaker window instantly switches to the new mode. You can also glance at the pop-up menu to see which mode you're currently in. (The Mode pop-up menu is the most popular way to mode-hop, but there are plenty more; see the box on page 8.)

Status area and the status area control

No matter what mode you're in, the *status area* (Figure 1-1, left) is your central command center. This slim panel lets you see how much information you've got in your database and your current position within it. It also has the controls you'll use most often for both adding information to your database and accessing it later. If you're like most people, at some point you'll come to resent the fact that the status area takes up so much space on your screen. Despite the fact that it usually contains just a few numbers and icons, it eats up a good inch of space along the entire left edge of *every* window. Luckily, you can easily conceal the status area when you don't need it, as shown in Figure 1-2.

A Tour of the Templates

FileMaker Pro's standard templates make it easy to perform routine tasks found in typical businesses, schools, and homes. Just choose a template and get right to work. Chances are one of the 40 templates built into FileMaker is set up to manage the kind of information you're working with, so you waste no time on setup. Here's an overview of the nine basic template categories:

- ·The **Business - Finance** set has the bean counters in mind. Track employee expenses and work hours (billable or otherwise), and generate purchase orders.

- ·The **Business - General** category is a mish-mash of useful templates from document management. With this category, you can keep track of computer files, create a searchable and printable product catalog, and more.

- ·If you need to keep track of real things—physical assets, customers, inventory, or just about anything else—use the **Business - People & Assets** category.

- ·Managers and planners can start in the **Business - Projects** category, where they'll find databases to help plan events, track problems, schedule people and other resources, and manage tasks and projects.

- ·See **Education - Activities** if you're organizing field trips or other events that require you to keep track of who's coming or who made a nice donation to the school boosters' fund.

- ·The **Education - Administration** set helps you administer your school's tasks. You can send emails to groups of people (to get a big turnout at your fundraising event), store notes about the research you're doing into how long sleepy students stay awake after lunch, or just keep track of student's names, addresses, and how to get in touch with their parents if they play hooky.

- ·**Education - Resources** is for collectors and those who keep track of collections. Librarians can manage a lending library, IT departments can make lists of its computer equipment, and anybody who needs to manage electronic assets, like graphics files or PDF documents, can do so right in FileMaker.

- ·The **Home - Collections** category includes databases to tell you whom you loaned that CD to and how many copies of The Princess Bride you have when you count up all the VHS and DVD formats.

- ·FileMaker is the people's database, so it's no surprise it comes prepared to tackle real problems. **Home - General** gives you a place to store Grandma's apple pie recipe, helps you send email invitations to the big family reunion picnic, and lets you keep track of who's allergic to bee stings.

Zoom controls

One of FileMaker's neatest features is the *zoom control*. No matter what you're doing, you can always zoom in for a closer look or zoom out for the big picture. This feature works no matter what mode you're in—even when you're previewing a printout.

To use FileMaker's zoom control, click the Zoom In button for a closer look (each click zooms in a little more). You can zoom in up to 400%, so that everything is four times bigger than normal. If you click Zoom Out, everything shrinks, as small as one quarter of its normal size. The Zoom Level shows your current level, and clicking it takes you back to 100%. Clicking the Zoom Level a second time returns you to the *last* zoom level you were viewing (see Figure 1-3).

Note: Since you probably don't need to examine the words and numbers in your database on a microscopic level, you'll probably use the zoom control mostly in Preview mode to fit the whole page on the screen, or to adjust the contents of your FileMaker window to the most easily readable size (depending on the resolution of your monitor).

Figure 1-3:
Clicking the Zoom Level button toggles you between 100% (left) and the zoom level you were just looking at (200%, right). Zoom in or out until you find a happy place, then click Zoom Level. Now click again. And again. And again. And again. This process can be a form of meditation—or procrastination, depending on your point of view.

Scroll bars

Every window has horizontal and vertical scroll bars that appear whenever you have more content than the window can display. (For an example, see Figure 1-3.) If everything in the content area fits in the window, you won't see scroll bars—after all, you don't need them. FileMaker's scroll bars work just like the ones in any other program, and you can use your keyboard to scroll up and down as well. Press Page Up to scroll up one screenful. Page Down scrolls the other direction. To scroll all the way to the top or bottom, use the Home and End keys respectively. (Don't toss out your mouse yet, though. There's no way to scroll right or left with the keyboard.)

If your mouse has a scroll wheel, you'll notice that it works a little differently in FileMaker. What you scroll through varies based on where you put your mouse cursor—a feature called *contextual* scrolling. The wheel scrolls through the *window* when the cursor is inside the content area of the window. It scrolls through the *records* in your database if you run the cursor over the Book icon in the Status area (page 5). And if you put your cursor over a field that has a scroll bar (page 156), the scroll wheel scrolls through the text in the field.

Note: Don't be alarmed when the menus across the top of your screen change a bit when you switch modes. That's just FileMaker being smart. Some commands aren't useful in some modes, so the program doesn't clutter up your screen—or your brain space—with menus when you don't need them. For example, the Insert and Format menus change from black to gray (meaning *unavailable*) when you enter Find mode. The Request menu, though, appears *only* in Find mode.

UP TO SPEED

Changing Modes

Switching between FileMaker's four modes is such a common task that the program actually gives you *four* ways to do it. The Mode pop-up menu (page 4) is just one way. You can also use the Mode tabs in the status area (shown here at left), or pick a mode from FileMaker's View menu (right).

The keyboard shortcuts are speediest of all:

- Press Ctrl+B (⌘-B) to switch to Browse mode.

- Press Ctrl+F (⌘-F) to switch to Find mode.

- Press Ctrl+L (⌘-L) to switch to Layout mode.

- Press Ctrl+U (⌘-U) to switch to Preview mode.

If you ever forget these shortcuts, check the View menu to refresh your memory.

FileMaker also gives you several ways to find out which mode you're *in*. The Mode pop-up always displays the current mode, and since it's always visible, it's the easiest place to check your mode. But the Mode tabs also reveal the current mode, and the View menu indicates the current mode with a checkmark. So when you return to FileMaker after checking email, you've got plenty of ways to reorient yourself.

View Menu   Mode Tabs   Mode Pop-up

Browse Mode ⏌   ⏌ Preview Mode
Find Mode ⏌   ⏌ Layout Mode

Creating a New Database

The best way to understand the concepts introduced in this chapter is to get some mouse-on experience. Fortunately, FileMaker Pro gives you a quick way to jump-start a new database.

Although a database can do just about anything, most people want to do a few of the same things (like keep track of their contacts). Accordingly, FileMaker Pro comes with dozens of prebuilt *templates*: sample databases that you can fill in with your own data and even customize as you see fit. A template is essentially a sample database, without any information filled in yet. Templates let you start up a database quickly, and as you go along, change or expand it to suit your needs. Almost any conceivable database can be built on one of these foundational layouts; see the box on page 6 for the full catalog.

Tip: if you're the DIY type, see Chapter 3 for instructions on designing your own database layout from scratch.

Since just about everybody in the world needs to keep track of people, a good place to start your FileMaker experience is with a Contact Management database, which does just what its name suggests: It keeps track of people and their various numbers and addresses. This is the template you might use if, for example, you volunteer for a local repertory company and need a place to store the names and addresses of all season-ticket holders. Once you've entered all the information, you can use the database to, say, print letters asking your subscribers for donations to provide new cup holders for the orchestra pit.

Choosing a Template

To start a new database from a template, you start by opening the template. Launch FileMaker Pro (by using the Start → Programs menu in Windows, for example, or clicking its Dock icon on the Mac) and choose File → New Database. The New Database dialog box appears, as shown in Figure 1-4.

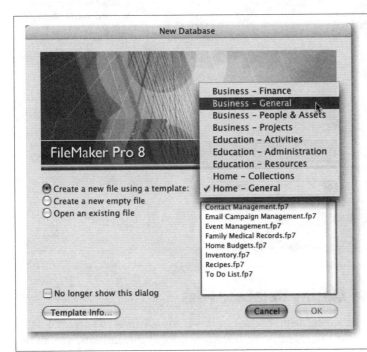

Figure 1-4:
To choose one of FileMaker Pro's built-in templates, click the pop-up menu and select from a list of categories (some templates appear in more than one category). If you don't want to use a template (you rebel, you!), just click "Create a new empty file," and then click OK. If you never again want to use a template, just turn on "No longer show this dialog." You can always turn it on again, as discussed in the box on page 6.

Note: Keyboard shortcut aficionados beware. If you're used to typing Ctrl+N (⌘-N) for a new document, you're in for a surprise. In FileMaker, that command makes a new *record*, not a new file. So when you really do want a new file, you'll have to resort to using the mouse and the menu.

To open the Contact Management template:

1. **In the New Database dialog box, select the Business – People & Assets category from the pop-up menu.**

    The list shows each template in this category. You can, of course, choose any template that looks like the database of your dreams, but in this example you're looking for Contact Management.

2. **In the Business – People & Assets list, select Contact Management.fp7, and then click OK.**

    FileMaker displays a standard Save dialog box.

3. **Name the new database and save it somewhere on your hard drive.**

    The new database appears onscreen, as shown in Figure 1-5.

Figure 1-5:
The Contact Management template is an ideal way to create a simple database that contains information about people, like their names, email addresses, and phone numbers. It can hold up to two addresses for each person, and you can even store a picture with each contact—a handy feature if you have trouble putting a face to a name.

Opening and Closing Database Files

Each database you create with FileMaker Pro is stored in a *file* on your hard drive—just like your Microsoft Word documents, Excel spreadsheets, and all the PowerPoint presentations you've ever created. This file contains all the information about how the database is structured, plus all the information stored inside it, which means you can open, close, copy, or back up a database as you would any other file. But if you need a bit more explanation, this section explains how to do those tasks, including some quirks that are particular to FileMaker files.

Opening a Database

To open a database that already exists, open FileMaker Pro and choose File → Open Database. Now select the file you want to work with (Figure 1-6). If you prefer, you can find the file using Windows Explorer (Windows) or the Finder (Mac OS X) and double-click its icon.

When you open a database, you'll see one or more windows on your screen. If you've opened the Contact Management Template you created on page 6, you have one database open, and that database has one window displayed.

Figure 1-6:
When you choose File → Open, you see the standard dialog box that lets you find the file you need. A drop-down menu lets you choose the specific type of file you're interested in opening. (As you can see, FileMaker can handle more than just its own files. You'll learn more about that in Chapter 17.)

Closing a Database

To close a database, close all of its windows in FileMaker: Choose File → Close or press Ctrl-W (⌘-W) When you have more than one database open, it isn't always easy to tell which windows go with each database.

If you're not sure what to close, there's an easy way to close all the windows in all the databases you currently have open. Hold down the Alt key (Windows) or the

Option key (Mac), then click the trusty File menu. In place of the Close command, you'll see the more powerful Close All. Choose it and FileMaker closes all its open windows, which also closes all your open databases.

WORKAROUND WORKSHOP

The *Other* New Database Dialog Box

If you don't see the box pictured in Figure 1-4 when you choose File → New Database, you may have told FileMaker to stop showing it to you (probably by turning on the "No longer show this dialog" checkbox also shown in that figure). To get the template-filled box back, follow these steps:

1. Click Cancel in the dialog box that did appear, if you haven't already. The imposter window goes away.

2. If you're on Mac OS X, choose FileMaker Pro → Preferences. If you're on Windows, choose Edit → Preferences. The Application Preferences dialog box appears automatically, with the General tab in front by. At this point, you can change a handful of settings that apply to the FileMaker Pro program itself.

Make sure "Show templates in New Database dialog box" is turned on.

1. Click OK. Bye-bye preferences.

2. Choose File → New Database again. Now the New Database window shows the full complement of templates.

If templates aren't your bag, you might find the New Database dialog box a bit of a drag, since you have to turn on "Create a new empty file" and then click OK *every* time you make a new database. Instead, just follow the steps above, but turn "Show templates in New Database dialog box" *off*. Now, when you choose File → New Database you'll see the template-free "Create a new empty file named" dialog box right away.

Saving Your Databases

Everybody knows that it's important to save files early and often, right? So you're working along in FileMaker entering information about your office birthday roster, and as good habit dictates, you type the keyboard shortcut that saves in practically every program in the known universe (that'd be Ctrl+S on Windows and ⌘-S on the Mac). Up pops the wrong dialog box. This one's asking you how you want to sort your data! What gives?

Don't worry, FileMaker has you covered. The program automatically saves all your work in a *cache*, which is part of your computer's RAM (Random Access Memory). Then, periodically, FileMaker transfers the information from the cache to your hard drive—where it's secure.

You can control how much work is held in cache before it's saved to your hard drive, as described in Figure 1-7. In Windows, choose Edit → Preferences, then click the Memory tab. On the Mac, choose FileMaker Pro → Preferences, then click the Memory tab.

Figure 1-7:
Specify the size of the FileMaker's cache and how often your work is moved from the cache to your hard drive. (Nerds call that flushing the cache.) A larger cache yields better performance but leaves more data in RAM. If you're working on a laptop, you can conserve battery power by saving cache contents less frequently. Just remember, in case of a power outage or other catastrophe, the work that's in cache isn't as secure as what FileMaker's saved to your hard drive.

Saving a Copy of Your Database

Chances are the data in your database is important (would you really go to all this trouble if it weren't?). Although FileMaker automatically saves your work as you go, what if the database file itself gets lost or suffers some digital harm? It's in your best interest to *back up* your database periodically. You can perform a backup by simply copying the database file. For example, you can copy it to a CD, email it to a friend, or duplicate it and tuck the copy away in another folder. The easiest way to make a backup is to choose File → Save a Copy As. You'll see the typical Save dialog box. Just make sure that "copy of current file" is selected as the Type option. When you click OK, FileMaker makes your copy in the background, then you can continue working in the original file.

But if you want to start working in the copy you've just made, select the "Automatically open file" option before you click OK. FileMaker makes the copy of your file, then helpfully opens it for you. FileMaker doesn't close the original file for you, so if you're finished with the original, choose it from the Window menu, then close it to avoid confusion. Now only your new copy of the file is open.

If you want to make a copy of your database to send to an associate in another office, chose the "Create email with file as attachment" option. FileMaker copies your file, then launches your email program, creates a new email, and attaches your newly minted file copy to it. All you have to do is provide an email address, type your message, and click Send. See page 619 to see how you can use similar options if you only want to send data to your associate in another format, like Excel or a PDF file.

Warning: You should always make sure a database is *closed* before you copy its file using any of the desktop methods (like Edit → Copy in Windows Explorer or the Mac's Finder, for example). If you copy the database file onto another disk while it's open in FileMaker, the copy you made may be damaged or missing information.

Saving a clone of your database

There's no ban on cloning in FileMaker. Clones are clean copies of your database, but without any of your valuable data. Clones are really useful, like when you've designed a killer database for running sales in your Dart and Billiards Supply Shop and you want to send the files to all your franchisees without giving away your store's sales data. Just make clones of your files and give them to your proud new owners. To make a clone, chose File → Save a Copy As, then make sure "clone (no records)" is selected as the Type option.

Adding Records to Your Database

When you first open a new FileMaker database (the Contact Management template in this example), it has everything you need to make a database except…well, data. Now that you understand the basic components of a FileMaker database, it's time to start adding your own content. Whether your database contains information about individual persons, objects, pictures, dung beetles, or whatever, FileMaker always thinks of that information in individual chunks called *records*. Each record contains everything the database knows about that person, thing, insect, or whatever.

Now, because you need to store many smaller pieces of information in each record (like a person's phone number, address, birthday, and so on), FileMaker can bestow each record with an almost infinite number of *fields*—the specific bits of data that define each record and make it unique.

For example, each person in a database of magazine subscribers gets her own record. Her first name, last name, phone number, street address, city, state, zip code, and the expiration date of her subscription are all examples of fields each record might include.

The techniques in this section work the same whether you're creating a new database for the first time (from the Contact Management template described on page 9, for example), or adding to an existing one (like the example file described on page 22).

Note: All records in a database must contain the same fields, but that doesn't mean you have to have to fill them all in. For instance, in a gift list database, if your boyfriend refuses to disclose his hat size, you can just leave that field blank in his record.

Refining Your Finds

When FileMaker looks for records, it expects them to match your find request *exactly*. For example, if you put "John" in the First Name field, and "Smith" in the Last Name field, FileMaker only finds John Smith. John Jones won't cut it, and neither will Sam Smith. FileMaker ignores any fields that are empty in your request, so it doesn't matter what John's title is because you didn't include a Title field in your find request.

Although FileMaker insists that every field in each found record matches each field in your request, the data *inside* each field doesn't have to be a perfect match. The next chapter explains how FileMaker decides when a match is good enough, and how you can change its decision-making process.

Finding the right records can be a real balancing act. Be too specific and you might not find anything at all; be too vague and you'll find more than you can handle.

Bear these in mind when you enter your find requests:

• Since FileMaker matches field values flexibly, you can often save typing and improve accuracy by being brief. For example, if you're looking for someone named "Rufus Xavier Sarsaparilla," just type *ruf* in the first name field and *sar* in the last name field. Chances are you'll find the right guy, and you don't have to worry about spelling out the whole name.

• Enter data only in fields you're sure you need. For example, even if you know Rufus lives in Montana, you don't have to put Montana in the State field in your find request.

• If you find more records than you wanted, just go back to Find mode and enter data in more fields to narrow the search. Better yet, read Chapter 2, where you'll learn about the many powers of Find mode.

Creating a Record

When you opened the template for your Contact Management database (page 9), it was blank and lacking in even a single record, so the first thing you need to do is create one. It's simple: Choose Records → New Record or press Ctrl+N (⌘-N). (Since you'll be creating lots of records in your FileMaker career, this is one keyboard shortcut you'll want to memorize.)

Note: When you're adding new records, you must be in Browse mode (see page 4).

Editing a Record

Now that you've created a record, you can enter information about the first person you want to keep track of. This is where those fields come in handy. To enter information in any field in a record, just point, click, and type. What to type? As Figure 1-8 illustrates, each field in this database has a label to its left, which indicates the type of information the field contains. Each field is also outlined in a light gray color.

Figure 1-8:
Fields can look like just about anything, but in the Contact Management database, they're pretty simple. When you click in the content area, the fields you can edit are indicated by dotted borders. The field you're currently editing gets a solid border.

UP TO SPEED

The Many Faces of a Field

Fields are inside the content area (see page 4), so don't be surprised if they don't always look the same. Unlike the status area, FileMaker Pro's content area is one place you can let your creative urges go wild. You can design your database to make them look almost any way you want. A field can have a label to the right of—or below or above—where you enter text, or no label at all.

A field can be white, blue, green, or any other color. The same goes for the border around a field. In fact, if mystery is your thing, you can make your field invisible—no label, no border, and no color. (But here's a tip: When designing your own databases, make sure folks can tell where the fields are and what goes in them.)

Usually, if you click in a blank space in the content area, all the fields appear with the dotted outline shown in Figure 1-14, but you can't count on this (you can turn this feature off, as described on page 139). So don't expect every field to look like those shown here.

See Chapter 3 for more detail on customizing and beautifying the fields in your database.

Moving between fields

To get from the field you're in to another where you can add or edit text, the most obvious way is to reach for the mouse, slide over to the new field, and click. Unless you're eager to burn that extra half a calorie, you may want to try a quicker, less exercise-intensive way, like the following:

 • Press the Tab key to move to the next field. If you're not in any field, the Tab key puts you in the first field.

 • Hold down the Shift key and press Tab to move to the previous field. This time, if you're not in any field, FileMaker puts you in the *last* field.

Note: If you're wondering who decides which field is *next* or *previous*, dig this: *you* do. When you design a database, you get to set the *Tab Order*, or the order FileMaker follows when you press Tab or Shift-Tab to move among fields. See page 228 for details.

UP TO SPEED

On the Record

To get *out* of all fields—so you're not in any field at all—press Enter, or click a blank spot in the content area. This process is called *committing* the record. No, you're not sending the record away for a little quiet time; rather, you're telling File-Maker you're ready to commit to the changes you've made. (If you don't want to commit to the changes you've made, you can choose Records → Revert Record to get out of all fields and discard those changes. This command is explained more fully on page 21.)

When you first click in a field, you've *opened* the record. If you imagine an old-fashioned file cabinet, you'd have to open someone's file before you could change something in it.

As long as you have a record open, you're *in* the record. You can be in only one record at any given moment, and that record is said to be *active*. Rounding out this nonsense, when you've committed the record, you're *on* the record but you're not *in* the record. Believe it or not, getting this terminology straight makes things easier later on.

Adding More Records

When you've filled in all the fields and you're ready to move on to your next subscriber, you must create an additional record to hold that contact, as each record can contain only one person's information. You've probably already figured out that you can just select Records → New Record again, and get another empty record to fill. You've also figured out you'll be creating records *a lot* as you enter all your subscribers. To speed things along, you can use the New Record keyboard shortcut: Ctrl+N (⌘-N).

Duplicating a record

While no two people are alike, it may not always seem that way from their contact information. For instance, if you want to include three people from the same company in your database, the data in the Company field is the same for each person.

Lost in the Wilderness

The database template you're using in this chapter has an assortment of *buttons* in its content area (they're all labeled here). They can look like tabs, text links, or just about anything else (a few even look like buttons). A click on one of these might show you things you're not familiar with—maybe even make you feel like you've lost your place.

To avoid an accidental left turn when you try to commit the record, avoid clicking a button by clicking somewhere in the empty white area around the fields (see figure below).

If you've already clicked a button, and now you're lost in the wilderness, finding your way back won't require a trail of breadcrumbs.

Just follow these steps, in order.

- If you see a button in the status area called Continue, click it. (If you don't see that button, don't worry—just skip to the next step.)

- If the Mode pop-up doesn't say Browse, click it and choose Browse from the menu that appears.

- In the status area, under Layout, you should see a pop-up menu. Make sure this menu reads "Form – Main Address."

You should now be back in your comfort zone. Phew!

Mysterious Click-able Things   Tabs   Links   Buttons

White Area: Safe Clicking

The Email and Phone fields won't be the same, but they might be close. It's time for a little organized laziness to kick in: Instead of making new blank records and retyping all that stuff, just choose Records → Duplicate (Figure 1-9). FileMaker displays a new record containing all the same information as the record you chose to duplicate. (FileMaker copied everything from the first record into a new one for you.) Now you can just edit the information that needs to be changed.

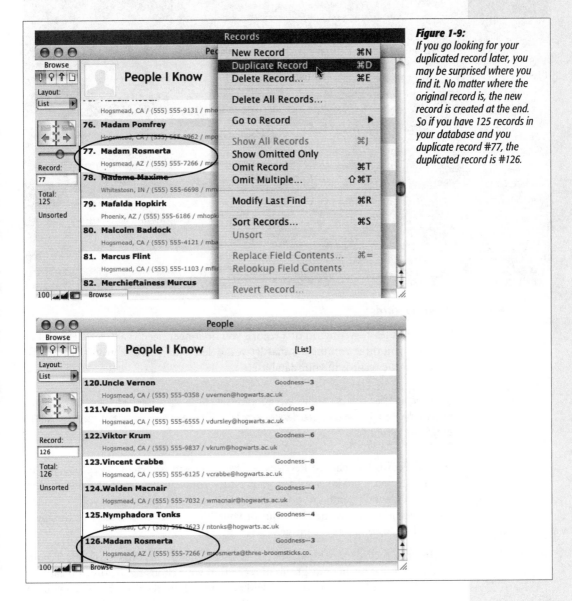

Figure 1-9:
If you go looking for your duplicated record later, you may be surprised where you find it. No matter where the original record is, the new record is created at the end. So if you have 125 records in your database and you duplicate record #77, the duplicated record is #126.

Tip: Be sure you don't accidentally leave in the first person's email address or phone number, lest a message or phone call get misdirected later.

WORKAROUND WORKSHOP

An Error a Day

When you create a database, FileMaker is nice enough to create the first record for you, so you can start typing right away. But when you start a database using a template, you're not so lucky. If you try clicking in a field, you're met with the first error message shown at top. Luckily, that error message tells you exactly what you need to do: Choose File → New Record first.

This minor annoyance is forgivable, since it's so easy to work around (and frankly, most databases don't stay empty for long). Unfortunately, another common error message is twice as annoying. If you try typing something *before* you've clicked in a field, FileMaker decides it better warn you with the box shown here. Apparently, the folks at File-Maker are afraid you'll type madly away before you figure out nothing's showing up onscreen.

So instead, you'll have to dismiss an error message every time you bump a key on your keyboard. This gets annoying quickly, but there's no way to get rid of the error message for good. Just remember that you have to be *in* a field before you can start typing.

Deleting records

Last but not least, getting rid of a record you no longer need is a breeze. FileMaker Pro gives you three commands that let you delete one record, a group of records, or even *all* the records in your database.

Warning: Deleting records can't be reversed. There's no Undo option, since FileMaker saves changes automatically (page 12). So when you delete a record (or all the records in a database), make sure you're ready to part with the data.

- **One record.** Just choose Records → Delete Record to delete the record you're currently on. FileMaker asks if you're sure you want to delete the record, lest you accidentally send, say, your aunt's address to the trash bin. If you've indeed written her—or anyone else—out of your life, simply click Delete in the message box to complete the purge.

- **Multiple records.** FileMaker has a neat command (Records → Delete Found Records) that trashes any group of records of your choosing. Before you can use this command, you have to tell FileMaker what those records are, which you do by using the Find command (page 25). In your FileMaker career, you'll often use the Find command to locate the records you want to act upon *before* you tell FileMaker what to do with them.

- **All records.** In some cases, you may want to delete all the records in a database. Maybe your friend wants an empty copy of your database for his own use. Or perhaps your database holds data you just don't need anymore, like test results you're about to reproduce. Complete record elimination is easily accomplished by way of two menu commands: Just choose Records → Show All Records, then choose Records → Delete All Records.

Tip: If you're feeling confident about a delete choice and want FileMaker to skip its "Are you sure?" confirmation message, hold down the Shift (Option) key while choosing Records → Delete Record.

Revert the record

Now that you know how to edit a record, and what it means to be in a record (see the box on page 17), you can learn about one of FileMaker's most overlooked features: the Revert Record command. Its purpose is simple: Choose Records → Revert Record and FileMaker throws away any changes you made since you first entered the record. This trick comes in handy when you accidentally modify a field by bumping into the keyboard, or realize you accidentally entered Uncle John's address in Aunt Ethel's record. Just revert the record and you can be confident that whatever you did has been forgotten.

But keep in mind that the Revert Record command is only available when you're in a record, *and* you've made changes. If you don't have the record open, or you haven't made any changes since you last committed the record, the Revert Record command is grayed out.

Note: Committing a record isn't exactly difficult: You just press Enter or click somewhere in the window and FileMaker dutifully saves the record without a peep. Once this happens, you can no longer choose the Revert Record command. (How's that for commitment?) If you want a little more control, you can tell FileMaker to ask you for confirmation before a record is committed. You'll learn how to do this on page 139.

Using the tools described so far for adding, deleting, and editing records in your database, you can quickly amass a large number of records. The next section explains how to find your way around this vast body of information.

Navigating Your Database

As exciting as it is to enter data into a database—well, the first time anyway—chances are you'll also want to look at those records again at some point. In fact, some might say that's the whole point of building a database. But first, you need to learn how to *navigate* around the records in the database, which this section explains. Fortunately, moving around a database isn't nearly as tough as following maps and highway signs in a foreign country. FileMaker makes it easy to skip from one record to the next, all the while keeping you abreast of where you are.

Tip: As you go through this section on navigating, it helps to have a database open in front of you so you can follow along and try some of these techniques. Since you probably don't have many records in the Contact Management database you just created, there's a sample one for you to download on the "Missing CD" page at *www.missingmanuals.com* (page xxiv).

Navigating Record by Record

In the Contact Management database, you can add as many records as you want. But you can view only one at a time in the window FileMaker displays. To tell File-Maker which record you want to look at, you have three options:

- The **book icon** lets you flip from record to record one at a time. Pretend your database is a book, with each record on its own page. To get to the next record, click the right-hand page. To go back, click the left-hand page. If you can't go any further in one direction, the appearance of the icon's "page" changes, as shown in Figure 1-10.

Figure 1-10:
The status area is the key to record navigation. In addition to displaying the controls for switching records, the status area indicates where you are in the database. This series of pictures, for example, shows the status area when you're on the first record in the database (left), a record in the middle of the database (middle), and the last record (right). Notice how the appearance of the Book icon and slider changes in each picture.

- The **slider** is kind of a turbo-charged version of the Book icon. Instead of clicking once for each record, you can advance through a bunch of records by dragging. If you know approximately where you want to go (like "around half way" or "about one-third from the end") then the slider is the quickest way to get there. The slider is most handy when you want to get to the beginning or the end of the database. In that case, just drag the slider as far as it will go in either direction.

- The **Current Record** indicator serves two purposes. First, it shows you which record you're on. Second, if you know which record you *want* to be on, you can simply type in the record number to jump to it. Below the Current Record, the status area also shows you how many records are in your database.

Keyboard Shortcuts

FileMaker also has a few keyboard shortcuts to make record navigation painless. If you haven't used a database program before, you'll notice that some keys act in ways you might not expect—like the Enter key, as described below. Still, spending a little time getting used to using these keystrokes will save you hours of time down the road.

- To go to the next record, press **Ctrl (Control)-Down Arrow.**

- To move to the previous record, press **Ctrl (Control)-Up Arrow.**

- If you press **Esc,** you'll jump immediately to the Current Record field, ready to type in a record number. (This shortcut only works when you're not in the record; see page 17.)

- Pressing the **Enter** key *commits* the record (page 17), rather than inserting a new line in a field, as you might expect based on what the Enter key does in other programs. To insert a new line in FileMaker, press the **Return** key.

Note: On some keyboards, there isn't a Return key—instead, two keys are labeled Enter. In this case, the Enter key that's near the number keypad commits the record, while the other (normal) Enter key enters a blank line in the field.

- Pressing the **Tab** key moves you from one field to another. (To indent a line you have to *type* a tab character into a field, by pressing Ctrl+Tab [Option-Tab].)

Finally, bear in mind that you can change these things on a field-by-field basis when you're designing a database, as you'll learn in Chapter 3. For instance, File-Maker lets you decide that Return—not Tab—should move you from field to field. If you make that choice, Tab types a *tab* into a field, and Return doesn't insert a blank line. There's unfortunately no way for you to tell which key does what by looking at a field—you just have to try some of these keys to find out.

Finding Records

When your database really gains some size, you'll realize that even keyboard short-cuts aren't the fastest way to get to the record you want. You need to *tell* File-Maker to pull up the record for you. For example, you have a season's ticket holder whose last name is Spinnet and who just renewed her subscription for a year. You need to find her record and make the update, and you don't have all day.

Suppose you have 126 records in your Contact Management database; it could take ages to find the one you want just by clicking the Book icon. Instead, switch to Find mode and tell FileMaker what you're looking for, and the program finds it for you. This section explains how to use Find mode to search for a record or group of records, and how to edit your search if you don't get the results you anticipated. (If you downloaded the example file discussed on page 22, you can open it and try out Find mode now.)

You can get to Find mode in four ways:

• Select Find from the Mode Pop-up menu.

• Choose View → Find Mode.

• Click the Find mode tab in the Status area.

• Press Ctrl+F (⌘-F).

The Mode pop-up menu, Mode tabs, and View menu all indicate what mode you're currently in. Once you're in Find mode, your window should look like Figure 1-11.

Figure 1-11:
The View → Mode menu indicates you're in Find mode, and every field is now empty, but everything else looks nearly the same. You can type information into fields, just as in Browse mode. You can even create requests, which look just like new records. The status area, though, looks slightly different, losing some record information and gaining a Find button.

Find mode looks just like Browse mode (where you've spent all your time up until now). The best way to tell that you're in Find mode is to look for clues in the Status area or Mode pop-up menu. Find mode also seems to work the same way—you can edit data in your fields and add, delete, or navigate through records. But don't be deceived: Find mode is very different from Browse mode.

Note: Another subtle clue indicates you're in Find mode: The borders around fields have a dashed-line appearance when the record is active. In Browse mode, active fields are bordered by a *dotted* line.

Even though it may seem like you're editing records in Find mode, you're actually not—you're editing *requests* instead. Requests describe what certain records look like, so FileMaker can find them for you.

Navigating Your
Database

UP TO SPEED

Numbers Sometimes Lie

When you first create a database, FileMaker numbers each new record as you add it—with a record number that appears in the book icon (see Figure 1-10). You may think that this number is a great way to locate a particular record later: "I need to call and wish Mom happy birthday. I remember I put her contact information in record #79. I'll just go to that number." Since record numbers may change as you add and delete records from a database, though, the record number isn't necessarily a reliable way to identify one particular record.

For instance, if you delete the first record in a database, every record below it moves up one slot. Now, what used to be record No. 2 becomes record No. 1, what used to be No. 3 is now No. 2, and so on. Your mom could have a few more candles on the cake before you find her number that way. If you want to assign every record its own number, and have that number stay with the record forever, then you want a *serial number*. They're discussed in Chapter 3.

You just need to enter enough information to tell FileMaker what you want. It then looks for records that have the same information you entered, much like searches you conduct using other programs.

Performing a Find

Say you want to find every person in your Contact Managements database whose last name is Spinnet. Here's what you would do:

1. **Choose View → Find Mode (or use any of the other methods described above to get to Find mode).**

    The window is now in Find mode, as you can tell by a quick glance at the Mode pop-up menu.

2. **Type *Spinnet* into the Last Name field.**

    This works just like Browse mode: Simply click to place your cursor in the field and then type. (Remember, you aren't editing a record—you're editing a *request*.)

3. **Click the Find button in the Status area.**

    (You can also choose Requests → Perform Find or simply press Enter.)

FileMaker then looks for any records that have "Spinnet" in the Last Name field. If the program doesn't find any, you see the message pictured in Figure 1-12. On the other hand, if FileMaker *did* find some records, you wind up back in Browse mode, presented with the records FileMaker found. (Technically, these records are called a *found set*. You'll learn much more about found sets in the next chapter.)

Figure 1-12:
If FileMaker can't find any records that match what you're looking for, you see the message pictured in this dialog box. If that's all you needed to know, just click Cancel and you'll wind up back in Browse mode as though you'd never performed a find. But if you realize you misspelled your search term or were a little too specific in describing what you wanted, click Modify Find. FileMaker sends you back to Find mode, where you can edit your request and click Find again.

After you perform a find, FileMaker displays the set of records that matched your find request (in this case, all the records with the last name Spinnet). You can see how many records you found by looking at the count in the Status area, as shown in Figure 1-13.

Although you're in Browse mode, you can't look through every record in the database—just the ones FileMaker found.

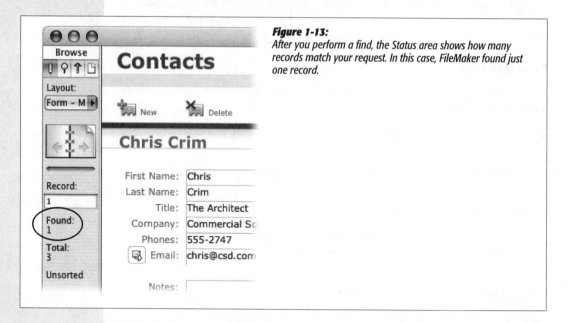

Figure 1-13:
After you perform a find, the Status area shows how many records match your request. In this case, FileMaker found just one record.

Tip: If your find didn't come out exactly the way you wanted, don't just return to Find mode. If you do, you'll have an empty request, and have to start all over again. Instead, choose Records → Modify Last Find, which takes you to Find mode and displays the request you used last. Now you can simply make any necessary modifications and perform the find again.

FastMatch

In the previous find examples, you had FileMaker search for records by telling it what to look for. But sometimes you're already looking at a record that has the right information in it—you just want to find more that match.

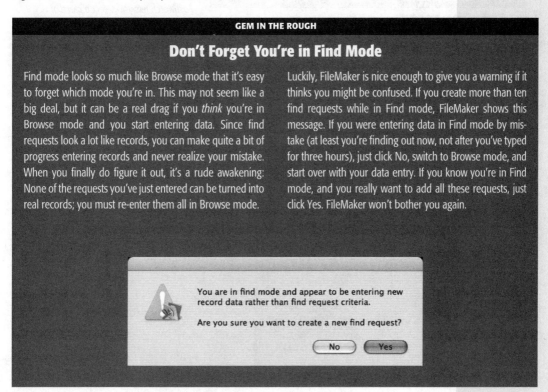

GEM IN THE ROUGH

Don't Forget You're in Find Mode

Find mode looks so much like Browse mode that it's easy to forget which mode you're in. This may not seem like a big deal, but it can be a real drag if you *think* you're in Browse mode and you start entering data. Since find requests look a lot like records, you can make quite a bit of progress entering records and never realize your mistake. When you finally do figure it out, it's a rude awakening: None of the requests you've just entered can be turned into real records; you must re-enter them all in Browse mode.

Luckily, FileMaker is nice enough to give you a warning if it thinks you might be confused. If you create more than ten find requests while in Find mode, FileMaker shows this message. If you were entering data in Find mode by mistake (at least you're finding out now, not after you've typed for three hours), just click No, switch to Browse mode, and start over with your data entry. If you know you're in Find mode, and you really want to add all these requests, just click Yes. FileMaker won't bother you again.

Say you need a list of everybody in the Contact Management file who has an email address from Hogwarts School. Flip to any record with a *Hogwarts.ac.uk* email address. Drag to select the word "hogwarts." You can do the whole *Hogwarts.ac.uk* if you're feeling vigorous, but "hogwarts" is enough to find the records you need. Right-click the highlighted text (Control-click on the Mac).

From the shortcut menu that pops up, select "Find Matching Records (Figure 1-14)." Bam! FileMaker shows you a found set of all your Hogwarts email contacts.

Same Database, Multiple Windows

So far, you've spent all your time in the same Contact Management window. If you're feeling a little claustrophobic, fear not. At any time, you can get yourself another window by choosing Window → New Window. What you get is an exact copy of the window you were just looking at. What's the big deal, you ask? The big deal is that you can switch to another record or do almost anything else in the new window, without affecting what's displayed in the first one.

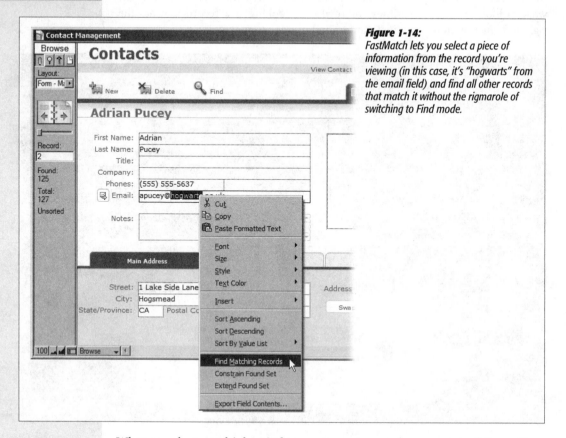

Figure 1-14:
FastMatch lets you select a piece of information from the record you're viewing (in this case, it's "hogwarts" from the email field) and find all other records that match it without the rigmarole of switching to Find mode.

When you have multiple windows open, you can change most of the settings you've seen so far for each window. For example, if you want to compare two contacts side-by-side, you can show one contact in each window.

You can even zoom one window in and another one out, or show the status area in one window but not the other (if that's your idea of fun). Another time multiple windows are useful is when you're working with one set of found records (page 26) but need to do another search. You can perform a find in a new window without disrupting your work in the original window. Say you've been fiddling with the Find command to come up with all your contacts who live in California, then suddenly need to find the phone number for a colleague in New York. Just create a new window and look up your East Coast colleague there (Figure 1-15). Your California group is safe and sound in the first window.

Note: If you have two windows open, both of them *are* connected in one way. If you edit the data in one window, the changes show up in the other window (or every window you have open, if you're working with multiple windows). Since FileMaker's windows just display the records in your database, a second window doesn't mean you have a second database—instead, both windows share the same data.

Figure 1-15:
In this example, the window in the back has a found set that includes all the California records in the database. But the window in the front shows a different set—just two guys from New York.

Automatically Arranging Windows

If you have a lot of windows on your screen and don't feel like rearranging them yourself, you can use one of several commands that arrange the windows for you—or at least try to. Using FileMaker's Window menu, you can choose one of three commands: Tile Vertically, Tile Horizontally, or Cascade. Each command rearranges the windows in a different manner, as shown in Figure 1-16.

The Window menu commands are a great place to start when you have so many windows open, you don't even know which one you're looking for! However, 99 times out of 100, these automatic rearrangements somehow seem to make every window the wrong size, and put each window in the wrong place. So use these commands with the understanding that you may *still* have to do some rearranging yourself.

Hiding Windows

If you have a window just the way you want it (for example, showing all the neighbors you need to hit up for Girl Scout Cookies), but it's in your way onscreen, you can opt to *hide* it instead of closing it. (When you close a window after using the Find command, your results disappear.) Hiding a window makes it disappear from your screen completely, but keeps the information stashed in a handy place in your computer so you can get it back if you want it. It's a neat timesaver when you're screen is crowded—or when you want to keep prying eyes away from your information.

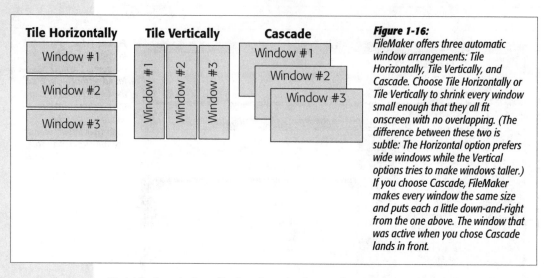

Figure 1-16:
FileMaker offers three automatic window arrangements: Tile Horizontally, Tile Vertically, and Cascade. Choose Tile Horizontally or Tile Vertically to shrink every window small enough that they all fit onscreen with no overlapping. (The difference between these two is subtle: The Horizontal option prefers wide windows while the Vertical options tries to make windows taller.) If you choose Cascade, FileMaker makes every window the same size and puts each a little down-and-right from the one above. The window that was active when you chose Cascade lands in front.

To hide the window displayed on the front of your screen, choose Window → Hide Window. To bring it back again, choose Window → Show Window, and pick the window you want back from the list. In order for this to work, you have to remember the *name* of the window you hid (its name appears in the title bar, across the top of the window).

Warning: You may be used to using your operating system's built-in features for dealing with windows, like minimizing them to the Mac OS X Dock. These techniques work just fine in FileMaker, but they might play havoc when a FileMaker *script* needs to control the same window. If you're using any of these little software robots to automate tasks, as you'll learn in Chapter 13, it's best to stick to FileMaker's own window commands.

Closing hidden windows

On page 11, you learned that the way to close a database is to simply close its windows. As with most rules, there's an exception: Even if you close all visible windows, the database itself may still be open—in a hidden window.

The easiest way to close all FileMaker's open windows, hidden ones included, is to press the Alt (Option) key and choose File → Close All. The ordinary Close command changes to Close All when you press that key.

POWER USERS' CLINIC

Record Locking

If you try editing a record in one window while it's showing in another window, you'll notice that your changes don't appear in the second window as you type. In order for the changes to appear, you must first commit the record (see the box on page 17). Once you do, the changes appear everywhere else.

Here's a hypothetical example. Suppose you start making changes to Auntie Marie's contact info in one window, but you're interrupted by a phone call before you finish. To help the caller, you need to look something up in the database. Since you're a savvy FileMaker guru, you make a new window and look it up there so you don't have to lose track of the changes you're making to Auntie Marie.

Unfortunately, by the time you finish the phone call, you've forgotten that you already started editing Marie's record. Now you go to Marie's record *in the new window* to make the changes. Bear in mind the record is already half-changed but uncommitted in the first window.

What happens if you start making changes now? Which set of changes wins?

To avoid the problem of which changes "win," FileMaker automatically performs *record locking* for you. If you try to edit a record that's already being edited in another window, you see this error message. Yes, it's frustrating to get this message, but just remember that automatic record locking really is your protection against major problems. (This is especially true when you have multiple users accessing your database at the same time—see Chapter 18.) This message is your friend.

Organizing and Editing Records

With all its advanced database options—like Find mode in this chapter and the relational database features covered in the later parts of this book—FileMaker is a pretty good deal for $279. But you're getting way more for your money than a powerhouse database program. FileMaker has many of the capabilities of a basic word processor built right in, so you can unleash your creative text-formatting urges using tools that look and feel quite familiar. What you can do with FileMaker is limited only by your imagination and willingness to plunge into a few dialog boxes.

Once you have even a few records entered into your database, clicking through them all whenever you want to make changes gets cumbersome. This chapter shows you how to pull up the records you want to work with. Then once you've got 'em, the real fun begins. You'll find out all the ways you can format text in FileMaker to get just the right look for your project, and how to print it out on paper.

Views

In the Contact Management database example, you learned how to add to and edit your new database with only one record onscreen at a time (page 17). This view is a common way to look at your information, but it's far from the only way. In fact, there are three possible ways to look at a database: Form view, List view, and Table view.

The one-at-a-time approach to viewing records you saw in Chapter 1 is called *Form view*. In *List view*, you see lots of records in, well, a list. If they don't all fit in the window, you can use the vertical bar to scroll through them. If you've used a spreadsheet program like Microsoft Excel, the *Table view* will look familiar—it looks a lot like a spreadsheet, with one row for each record and one column for each field.

To switch among views in any FileMaker database, use the View menu. Choose View → As Form, View → As List, or View → As Table. Figure 2-1 shows the same database in all three views.

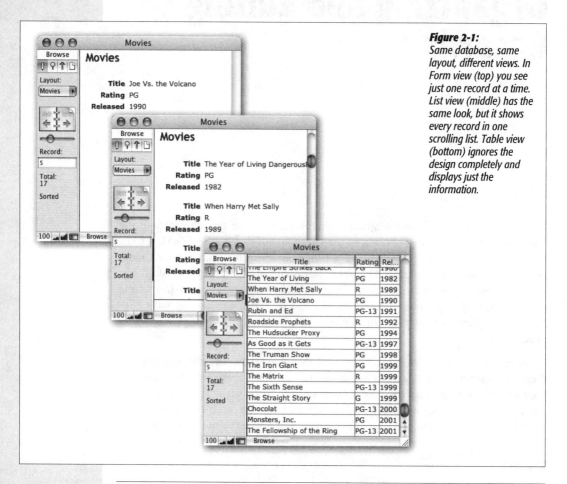

Figure 2-1:
Same database, same layout, different views. In Form view (top) you see just one record at a time. List view (middle) has the same look, but it shows every record in one scrolling list. Table view (bottom) ignores the design completely and displays just the information.

Note: When you design a database, you can add clickable buttons, tabs, or other handy means to switch among views. For example, the Contact Management database you used in Chapter 1 has View tabs built into the template (see Figure 1-5). You can even turn *off* certain views if you want. If your database holds mostly digital photographs and makes no sense in Table view, then you can make sure no one ever sees it that way. (You'll learn how in Chapter 5.)

Form View

In Form view, you see only one record at a time. If you want to see the next record, you must click the pages of the Book icon, press Control-down arrow, or use some other method of switching records (see page 22). Most of the database work you've done so far has been in Form view. You might use Form view when you have a lot of information to see about one record, or if you want to focus on just one record without being distracted by all the other records.

List View

List view works *almost* exactly like Form view. It shows your layout complete with its pretty design, but instead of limiting you to one record at a time, it shows you multiple records in a scrolling list. It also adds another element of feedback to the status area, as shown in Figure 2-2.

When you're working with a *group* of records—updating one field in several records or browsing through all your records in search of something—List view comes in handy.

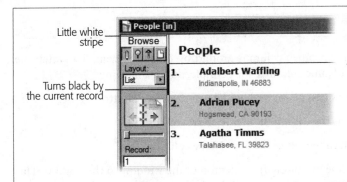

Little white stripe

Turns black by the current record

Figure 2-2:
The little white strip along the right edge of the status bar tells you you're in List view. Its job is to show you which record is currently selected. The strip is filled with black along the edge of the current record. In this example, the first record is selected.

Table View

If List view looks a lot like Form view, then Table view...well...doesn't. This view appeals to spreadsheet fans since it offers a consistent rows-and-columns design, the ability to sort with the click of a button, and the freedom to rearrange columns by dragging them around. Of course, like any self-respecting view, you can use Table view to add, edit, delete, and find records too.

When you put your layout into Table view, any graphical embellishments disappear. Instead, FileMaker displays the fields of your layout in a no-nonsense, spreadsheet arrangement (Figure 2-3).

Each column represents one of your fields, and the order of the columns matches the order you go through the fields when tabbing. For example, the first column is the field you wind up in if you press Tab for the first time. Another Tab takes you to the second column.

Headers

Figure 2-3:
In Table view, FileMaker ignores your layout's extra pictures, text, and other embellishments and shows you just the fields. Like a real spreadsheet, you can drag columns around to rearrange them. You can also click the header at the top of any column to instantly sort the records by that field. Table view shows the same vertical white strip that you see in List view.

In Table view, you can move columns around by dragging them. To switch the First Name and Last Name columns, for example, do the following:

1. **Point to the words Last Name and hold down the mouse button.**

   FileMaker darkens the column header to show you it's selected.

2. **Drag the column to the left of the First Name column.**

   You see a black line extending from the top of the window to the bottom. This line shows you where the column will land when you let go. All the other columns will shift around to make room. In this case, you want the black line to appear to the left of the First Name column.

3. **Let go of the mouse button.**

   FileMaker moves the Last Name column to its new home, swapping the columns.

The column headings also make it easy to *sort* your data, as shown in Figure 2-4.

Advanced Find Mode

In Chapter 1 you learned about using Find mode for simple searches—but you only scratched the surface. The more records you have in your database, the more you'll need advanced finding techniques to avoid wasting precious minutes clicking the Book icon 1,057 times in a row just to find the record or records you want to display, edit, or print. FileMaker's Find tools give you the power to track down the one record in 100,000 you need *right this minute,* or the five records with missing phone numbers that you created a week ago Tuesday.

Figure 2-4:
When you click a column header, FileMaker darkens that header and sorts the list. Here, for example, the list is sorted by Last Name. If you sort the records using the Records → Sort Records command instead, FileMaker doesn't try to figure out which column was used. Instead, it simply lightens all the column headers.

Finding by Omitting

If you know what you *don't* want better than what you do want, you can use the Omit checkbox. This feature comes in handy when the records you're looking for can best be described by what they aren't. For example, "every person who isn't from California" is a lot easier to say than "everyone from Alabama, Alaska, Arizona, Arkansas, Colorado…" In this case, you can get what you want by creating one find request, with California in the State field. Then, before you perform the find, simply turn on the Omit checkbox, which appears in the status area only when you're in Find mode (Figure 2-5). That's all there is to it. FileMaker starts with every record in the found set, then throws out all the records with "California" in the State field, so you're left with everything else.

Omit also works with multiple find requests (see the box on page 40). If *all* your requests have the Omit option set, then all the records that match *any* of your requests are thrown out. Whatever's left over goes in your found set. If you have a mix of requests with and without Omit set, FileMaker first finds all the records that match your normal requests. It then discards any that match an Omit request. You're finally left with a found set in which every record matches at least one of your requests, and doesn't match any of your Omit requests.

Constraining and Extending the Found Set

When you perform a find normally, it effectively throws away any found set you had before, searches through all the records in the database, and produces a *new* found set. But you can also tell FileMaker to *constrain* the found set (that is, search within your last find results) or *extend* it (add matching records to the current found set).

Constraining the found set

Suppose you've just created a great product, and want to send out some free samples to see how people like it. You can't afford the postage to send everyone in your database a sample, so you decide to start with a smaller sampling—just people named Smith.

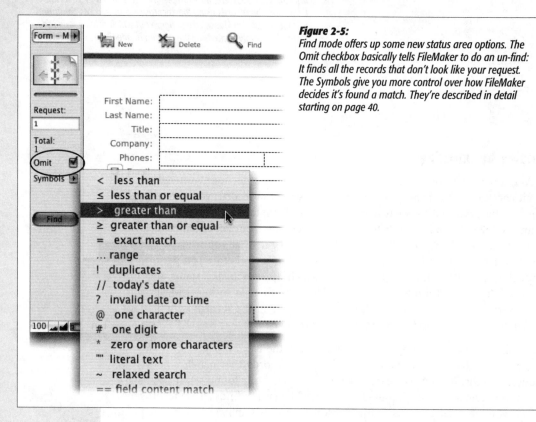

Figure 2-5:
Find mode offers up some new status area options. The Omit checkbox basically tells FileMaker to do an un-find: It finds all the records that don't look like your request. The Symbols give you more control over how FileMaker decides it's found a match. They're described in detail starting on page 40.

Problem is, your database has hundreds of Smiths. Some quick math in your head reveals that it's still too expensive. How about sending samples to just the Smiths in California? You *could* go back to Find mode and construct a request to find this criteria instead (by putting *Smith* in the First Name field and *California* in the State field), but there's an easier way. After all, you've already got all the Smiths in your found set. What you really want to do is search *inside this found set* for all the records with California in the State field.

Here's how the procedure goes:

1. **Switch to Find mode, type Smith in the Last Name field, and then press Enter.**

   FileMaker searches the database and, in Browse mode, shows you the records with Smith for the last name. You glance at the status area—678 records! You now need to search through these records for the ones whose state is California. That's *exactly* what the Constrain Found Set command does.

2. **Immediately switch to Find mode again using any of the methods described on page 24.**

In other words, don't choose Records → Show All Records, and don't do anything to tamper with the current found set (678 records, in this example). You're now in Find mode again, ready to enter a request.

Note: In Find mode, there's no way to see what your current found set is. You just have to remember that you last searched for Smith. If you need to *see* the found set, just switch back to Browse mode and flip through the records.

---

3. **Type California in the State field.**

Since the found set already has only Smiths in it, there's no need to repeat that information.

4. **Choose Requests → Constrain Found Set.**

FileMaker searches out the people from California, but this time it only looks in the current found set. In the end, you get what you want with less typing.

Warning: Once you're in Find mode, FileMaker is itching for you to perform a find. If you just press Enter, it assumes you want to throw away your last found set and make a new one. Once it's gone, there's no way to return to the old found set and constrain or extend it. Likewise, if you accidentally choose the wrong command from the Requests menu, there's no going back. If you want to constrain or extend, be sure you choose wisely or you'll have to start all over again.

Extending the found set

Extending the found set works similarly. This time, though, you're asking File-Maker to perform a new find (through all records in the database) and then *add* the records it finds into your found set. What you end up with is all the records you already had, plus any new ones that were found. Suppose you've already found the Smiths, and you want all the Johnsons as well.

1. **In Find mode, type Johnson in the Last Name field.**

So far, you're doing exactly what you would in every other find. You just have all the Smiths in your found set, even though you can't see that in Find mode.

2. **Choose Requests → Extend Found Set.**

This time, FileMaker looks through every record in the database for any Johnsons. Each time it finds one, it adds it to your existing found set. When it's done, you have all the Smiths *and* Johnsons in one found set.

Refining Searches with Find Symbols

Normally, FileMaker uses a pretty simple rule to decide whether a field value matches the field in your request (the *criteria*): If every word in the criteria appears at the *beginning* of any word in the field, FileMaker considers it a match.

Multiple Requests

It's rarely strictly necessary to use Constrain or Extend to get exactly what you want. To get the effect of a Constrain, just fill out multiple fields in your find request. Since a record has to match every field in the request, a computer geek would say you're doing an *AND search*. This odd term simply means you're asking for records where both the First Name is "John," for example, *AND* the last name is "Smith." Extend Found Set, by contrast, is analogous to an *OR search*, meaning it locates all the records that have *either* search term. An OR search is like saying, "Show me all the records where a student is either a 'Head Boy' or a 'Prefect.' Another way to get an OR search is with *multiple* find requests. Remember that a request is the Find mode equivalent of a record. When you're in Find mode, you're free to create as many as you want (choose Requests → New Request) and you can flip through them using all the same tools you use to flip through records. Here's how to make your own *OR* search using multiple requests:

1. Enter Find mode using any of the methods described on page 24. FileMaker opens a blank request.

2. Type *Smith* in the Last Name field. You're describing one kind of record—the kind with "Smith" in the Last Name field. If you add any more criteria to this request, you'll just be excluding some Smiths from your found set. So instead…

3. Choose Requests → New Request. FileMaker gives you a second empty request. The first request is still there, although you can't see it. Since requests work just like records, you can use the Book icon, the Slider, or the keyboard shortcuts to switch between them. Or you can switch the layout to list view.

4. Type *Johnson* in the Last Name field. You're describing the other kind of record you want. Since you have two requests, FileMaker treats them separately, finding all the Smiths, then finding all the Johnsons, and finally putting both lists into the found set.

Essentially, each request represents another extension of the found set. Many FileMaker Power Users, once they've mastered multiple requests, find they can perform them with fewer clicks and keystrokes than the Constrain and Extend Found Set commands. In the real world, though, the Constrain and Extend commands offer a more straightforward, intuitive approach to complex requests. In fact, even the pros constrain or extend the found set when a multiple request strategy fails. In the end, it usually comes down to preference.

Finally, there's no reason you can't mix these techniques, using Constrain and Extend *and* multiple requests at the same time. For instance, you could use multiple requests to find all your customers who live in Florida, Hawaii, and California, then use the Constrain Found Set command to find just the people named "Fred" who live in those three states.

For example, if you put "for" in the Note field in a find request, any of these notes would match:

• All for one and one for all.

• We will forever remember.

• Back and forth it went.

On the other hand, neither of these would match:

• Wherefore art thou, Romeo?

• Before there was art, there was an artist.

How do you tell FileMaker that you're looking for "for" *wherever* it appears in a word, not just at the beginning? You can use a special *symbol*—a character that has special meaning in a Find request—to stand for part of a word.

The Symbol pop-up menu, which appears in the status area when you're in Find mode, lets you add these special characters to your searches, thus gaining more control over FileMaker's decision-making process when it's looking for records. There are plenty more special symbols, and each is described below.

The Wildcard (*)

In the "Wherefore art thou Romeo" example, you would use the * wildcard symbol, which stands for "anything." It tells FileMaker that you don't mind if there's something *right before or right after* the "for." If you type **for** as your find criteria, FileMaker will display records that contain "wherefore," "before," "George Foreman," and so on.

Less Than (<), Less Than or Equal To (≤), Greater Than (>), and Greater Than or Equal To (≥)

These symbols tell FileMaker to use your criteria as a maximum or minimum rather than a direct match. For example, the criteria *<David* will find every person whose name comes before David alphabetically. *≤David* is just about the same, but it will include any Davids as well.

Note: In Mac OS X, the Less Than or Equal To symbol shows up as ≤, but on Windows, it shows up as <= instead. You can *type* the ≤ symbol on Mac OS X (hold down the Option key and press the comma key) but it works just as well to type <= as you would on Windows. The same thing goes for the Greater Than or Equal To symbol, which you can type as >=.

These symbols are smart enough to understand different kinds of information. *<10* in a field that expects numbers will find real numbers less than 10 (like 9). FileMaker performs the correct function with dates and times as well, in which case Less Than means *before* and Greater Than means *after*.

Exact Match (=), Literal Text (""), and Field Content Match (==)

The rule FileMaker uses automatically for determining a match is pretty loose. But sometimes you want exactly what you say: "Smith," not "Smithers" or "Smithey" or "Smithsonian." In this case, use the Exact Match symbol (=). In this example, type *=Smith* in the Last Name field, and perform your find.

If you want to exactly match *more* than one word, put the words in quotes instead. This Literal Text match is also good for criteria that contain punctuation, like "Mr. Smith."

Note: Like French fries, quotes come in two varieties: curly and straight. If you're someone who notices this kind of thing, you may wonder if it matters which kind you use. It doesn't. Usually FileMaker turns your quotes curly for you, but you can turn off smart quotes for a database in the File → File Options dialog box.

For the ultimate in specificity, use the Field Content Match symbol (==) instead. Exact Match requires that each *word* in your criteria match one or more words in the field. Literal Text only seeks to match whatever is in the quotes *anywhere* in the field. Field Content Match insists that the entire field matches the criteria text exactly. For example, =*Smith* matches "Smith," "Mr. Smith," and "Smith-Johnson." On the other hand, ==*Smith* matches only "Smith" in the field and nothing else.

Note: Literal Text doesn't actually match text *anywhere* in the field. The criteria text must match starting at the beginning of a word. For instance, a search for "Mr. Smith" would match "Mr. Smith" and "Mr. Smithers," but if you searched for *"r. Smith"* (no M) instead, you'd find no matches.

Range (...)

The Range symbol is like the Greater Than or Equal To and Less Than or Equal To symbols combined. The criteria "David...Michael" matches everyone from David to Michael, alphabetically speaking. Just like the other symbols, the Range symbol is smart enough to understand numbers, dates, and times, as long as the field expects them. (You'll learn more about field types in the next chapter.)

Duplicates (!)

The Duplicates symbol *(!)* can be hard to get the hang of. When you put *!* in a field in Find mode, FileMaker finds records with *duplicate data* in that field. In other words, it looks for records with the *same* value in that particular field. The same as *what* you ask? The same as *any other record*. Think of it this way: If you have only *one* person in your database from Idaho, and you perform a find with *!* in the State field, the person from Idaho won't appear. That's because—when considering the State field alone—the person from Idaho has no duplicates. On the other hand, if you have 11 people from Oklahoma, they'll *all* be found because they all have duplicates (each one has 10 others just like it, statewise).

Unlike most other symbols, the *!* symbol is always used alone in a field in Find mode. You would never put *!Smith* in the last name field. Instead, you'd just put *!* all by itself.

Advanced Find
Mode

POWER USERS' CLINIC

Finding Duplicate Records

Every database user eventually makes the mistake of entering the same data twice. Maybe you assume a person isn't in your database and add him, only to discover months later that he was there all along. The *!* symbol can help you hunt this sort of thing down.

If you want to find *whole records* that are exact duplicates, you'll have to put *!* in every field when you're in Find mode. But it isn't at all uncommon for "duplicate" records to be slightly different. Maybe you updated the phone number in one but not the other, for instance.

Or perhaps you misspelled the street name the first time you entered this person, and spelled it right the second time. Finding exact duplicate records wouldn't catch these kinds of so-called duplicates.

If you're looking for duplicate records, you're usually best off putting the *!* symbol in as few fields as possible. Try to pick fields that tend to be entered the same every time and stand a good chance of identifying an individual person. You might use just First Name and Last Name, for instance.

Today's Date (//) and Invalid Date or Time (?)

Like the *!* symbol, these symbols can go in a field in Find mode all by themselves. The double slash is convenient shorthand for the current date. If you're looking for all the payments due today, you can type // in the Due field more quickly than "September 15, 2005."

The Invalid Date or Time symbol (?) is another helper when it comes time to clean house. It's possible to end up with the wrong kind of data in fields that are supposed to hold dates or times (like "N/A," "Never," or "Next Week"). Put ? in the Due field, and FileMaker finds every payment whose date is not valid, giving you an opportunity to fix them. (You'll learn more about fields that hold special kinds of data in Chapter 3.)

Tip: You can mix and match these symbols in any combinations that make sense. For example, to find everything after today's date, just search for >// instead of >12/21/2003.

One Character (@), One Digit (#), and Zero or More Characters (*)

These symbols are like the wildcard characters you sometimes see in other programs. You already saw the Zero or More Characters symbol (*) at the beginning of this section. It simply tells FileMaker you're willing to accept some text—*any* text—in place of the * symbol. If you're not ready to go that far, you can instead permit just one character (letter, number, or punctuation) with the One Character (@) symbol. When matching numbers, you can be even more specific, permitting just one numerical digit with the One Digit (#) symbol. Here are a few examples:

- *smith* matches "Smith," "blacksmith," "Smithsonian," and "blacksmiths"

- *smith matches "Smith" and "blacksmith," but not "blacksmiths" or "Smithsonian"

- smith@ matches "smithy" but not "smithers"

- @*smith matches "blacksmith" but not "Smith" or "blacksmiths"

- smith# matches "smith1" and "smith2" but not "smithy"

POWER USERS' CLINIC

Finding Hot Dates

That heading got your attention, didn't it? Well, as long as you're here, you might as well read about some cool ways to get date fields to yield their secrets.

- If you need to find all invoices generated in September this year, type *5/2005*

- To find out who received large bonuses while the boss was on sabbatical last year, type *12/2004...5/2005*

- Keep tabs on payday sales by typing */15/*

- See if there's slow performance in the sales department on Monday morning by typing *=Monday* in a date field. You can even just type *Mon* if you'd rather not bother with those extra keystrokes.

- To find out if the lull lasts through Tuesday, type *Mon...Tue*

- Find those invoices generated just before the monthly incentive period closes by typing */{29...31}/2004*

Timestamp fields (see page 94) hold date and time information. You'd use a bunch of them to design a Time Clock Punching system. They also have some nifty search capabilities.

- Find out who clocked out between 4 p.m. and 4:59 p.m. today by typing *// 4 pm*

- See who your star performers and workaholics are (everybody in on any day between 6 and 7 a.m.), by typing *6 am*

- Find out who left work early to pick up their pre-order copy of *Harry Potter and the Half-Blood Prince* by typing *7/16/2005 3 pm*

- Check on anybody leaving after lunch any day in July by typing *7/2005 2 pm.*

Relaxed Search (~)

The last symbol, called Relaxed Search (~), only applies to searching Japanese language text. It instructs FileMaker to consider characters to match if they make the same sound, even if they aren't exactly the same character. Alas, in English, spelling always counts (you can't expect "~korn" to match "corn").

Refining a Found Set with Omit Commands

FileMaker provides a few menu commands to help you fine-tune your found set. Sometimes, after you've done the best find request you can, you still end up with a couple of records in the found set that you don't really want to see. FileMaker offers three commands that make tossing out misfit records as easy as pie.

FREQUENTLY ASKED QUESTION

Finding Special Characters

How do I find mrbill@microsoft.com when "@" means something special?

If what you're actually looking for includes one of these special symbols, you need to take extra precaution. When searching for mrbill@microsoft.com, the wildcard "@" symbol will match any character.

(Admittedly, that's not such a big deal in this case, unless you happen to have mrbillXmicrosoft.com in your database as well.) To prevent FileMaker from interpreting the @ as a special character, use the Literal Text symbols you learned about on page 41. In other words, putting the search text in quotes ("mrbill@microsoft.com") will do the trick.

Omit Record

Go to the record you don't want (using the Book icon, for example) and choose Records → Omit Record. This one-off command tosses the record out of the found set, reducing your found count by one. Don't confuse it with the Omit checkbox that shows up in the Status bar when you're in Find mode (page 38), which tells FileMaker to omit all the records that match your find request. The Records → Omit Record command just omits the single record you're sitting on.

Omit Multiple

If you have a whole stretch of records you don't want, use Records → Omit Multiple. It omits a contiguous group of records from the found set, starting with the current record. For instance, if you want to omit ten records in a row, navigate to the *first* record of the ten. Then choose Records → Omit Multiple and type 10 in the dialog box that appears. Click Omit and the job is done.

Tip: When you're done with your found set, and you want to see all the records again, choose Records → Show All Records.

Show Omitted Only

You might use this option when you're printing two separate lists—one of the California customers, and one of everyone else, for example. Once you've printed the California records, your found set happens to be exactly what you *don't* need. Choose Records → Show Omitted Only. This command effectively puts every record that's *not* in the found set into the new found set, and takes every currently found record out.

Here's how it works: Perform a find for the customers who have "CA" in the State field. FileMaker produces a found set of all California records for you, ready to print. After printing, choose Records → Show Omitted Only.

Now you have everyone *not* in California in your found set, and you're ready to print again.

Over-Omitted

If you try to omit more records than possible (for example, you're on the third-to-last record and you ask FileMaker to omit 12 records), FileMaker will complain with this message. But don't take offense: It's also nice enough to fix the problem for you. When you click OK, FileMaker returns you to the Omit dialog box and changes the number you entered to the maximum number possible. You only need to click Omit again to get what you probably wanted in the first place.

If you're looking at a record, and you know you want to omit it and every record after it, you might be tempted to look at the Record Number and the Found Count to figure out how many need to be omitted. But that's more trouble than it's worth. Just choose Records → Omit Multiple and enter something really big, like 999, or 9999999. When you click Omit, FileMaker will complain, do the math for you, and enter the right value.

This routine may sound contrived, but it's actually not all that uncommon among FileMaker pros. Imagine you're doing a direct-mail campaign and you can only afford to send 1200 post cards. Your find request, however, produces 1931 potential recipients. Rather than do the math, just go to record 1201 and use this Omit Multiple trick.

Tip: You can also use Show Omitted Only if you forgot to turn on the Omit box in your find request. Instead of going back to Find mode to fix your request, just choose Records → Show Omitted Only and you'll get the same effect.

Changing Multiple Records

Sometimes the whole reason you performed a find is to change something in several records. If one of the companies you work with changes its name, you may have several records that need to be updated. The first step to fixing them is to *find* them. Once your found set includes the people at that company, you could change the Company Name field one record at a time (especially if you're billing by the hour). But a better use of your time is to use the Replace Field Contents command. Here's how it works:

1. **Click in the Company Name field (it doesn't matter which record), and correct the company name.**

   You've just fixed one of the records. All the others in the found set need the same fix.

2. Choose Records → Replace Field Contents

   The Replace Field Contents dialog box appears (Figure 2-6). It has a handful of options that may not make sense to you yet. That's OK; just choose the first one: "Replace with." The new data you just typed is listed beside this option.

Figure 2-6:
The Replace Field Contents dialog box has three options: "Replace with," "Replace with serial numbers," and "Replace with calculated result." The first option is the only one you're concerned with right now. It replaces the contents of the current field in every record in the found set with whatever is in the current record when you click Replace. (You'll learn about serial numbers in Chapter 3 and calculations in Chapter 9.)

3. Click Replace

   FileMaker now updates the Company Name field in *every record in the found set* to match what you typed in the current record. When it's done, you're still sitting on the same record, but if you use the Book icon to click through the records, you'll see that they've all been changed.

Warning: The Replace Field Contents command can be dangerous. It really does change every record in the found set, even if that wasn't your intent. Make sure you're absolutely certain you have the right found set before clicking Replace. Once it's done, there's no Undo command.

Sorting Records

Your Rolodex may be limited to an alphabetical (by last name) arrangement, but a FileMaker database has no such limitation. You can sort the records in any order you want, as often as you want. You can even do a sort-within-a-sort, as you'll see later in this section.

The process always begins the same way: Choose Records → Sort Records. You'll see the Sort Records dialog box shown in Figure 2-7.

The Sort Records window lists all fields in your current layout on the left. Use the pop-up menu at the top of the list to switch to a list of all the fields in the table that are tied to the current layout. See page 317 for details on tables and layouts. You tell FileMaker what to sort by moving the field to the list on the right. For example, if you're in need of a short-term loan, you may find it useful to sort your contacts by annual income, so you'd start by clicking the annual income field.

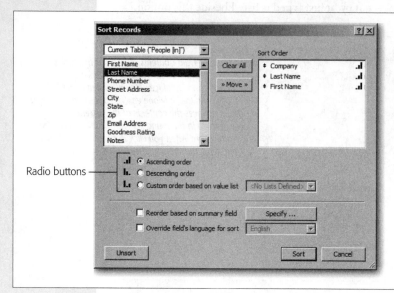

Figure 2-7:
The Sort Records dialog box offers a lot of options, but the two lists on top, and the first two radio buttons, are critical to every sort you'll ever do in FileMaker. In a nutshell, you pick the fields you want to sort by and the order they should be sorted. Then click Sort. That's the essence of any sort, from the simple to the most complex.

The steps below, though, show a more common example—sorting by Last Name:

1. **Choose Records → Sort or press Ctrl+S (⌘-S).**

   The Sort Records dialog box (Figure 2-7) appears.

2. **Select the Last Name field from the list on the left, and then click Move.**

   The field name appears in the Sort Order list on the right. You can save a little mouse-mileage by double-clicking a field on the left instead of selecting it, then clicking Move.

3. **Click Sort.**

   FileMaker sorts the records in the traditional alphabetical-by-last-name order. You can tell by flipping through the records or switching to Table view.

Each sort field has an *order* associated with it as well. Right now, you only need to worry about two of these orders: "Ascending order" and "Descending order." You can click one of these radio buttons *before* you click Move and the field will have the setting by the time it makes it to the Sort Order list. More often than not, though, you'll move the field over before you think about the order. In this case, just click select the field from the Sort Order list and then pick the order. Each field in the Sort Order list shows a little bar-chart icon representing the order assigned to it, which matches the icons next to each radio button.

Tip: If you change your mind about one of the fields in the Sort Order list, click it. The Move button changes to say Clear, and a click removes the selected field from the list. If you want to remove *every* field from the Sort Order list, click Clear All.

When you're all done, click Sort. If you change your mind, click Cancel instead and FileMaker will forget everything you've done while in this window. Otherwise, the next time you choose the Sort Records command, the dialog box will show the same settings you used most recently.

The status area lets you know if your records are sorted (no surprise there). Below the Record Count, it says "Sorted" if you've done a sort, and "Unsorted" otherwise. (See the box on page 50 to learn what "Semi-sorted" means.)

Multiple Sort Fields

FileMaker lets you pick more than one field to sort by, which comes in handy when you have lots of records with the same data in some fields. For example, if your People database gets really big, you might have several people with the same last name. If you just sort by last name, there's no telling in which order the like-named people will fall. In this case, it would help to sort by last name *and* first name.

When you use more than one sort field, the order the fields appear in the Sort Order list is important, because it determines which field FileMaker uses first. If you sort a list of family members by First Name, then Last Name, you might wind up records ordered like those shown at left in Figure 2-8.

If you sort by Last Name, then First Name, you'll get something like the window shown at right instead. In the first example, FileMaker sorts everything by First Name. When two people have the same first name, it then uses Last Name to figure out what order those two should be in. In the second example, the records are first sorted by Last Name instead. First Name is then used to figure out how to sort the folks with the same last name.

Figure 2-8:
Both windows show the same list of people, but are sorted differently. The one on the left was sorted by first name, then last name. Notice how all the Carolines are together. The data in the window on the right was sorted by last name, then first name. This time, the Fawcetts stick together.

Since the order of the sort fields is so important, FileMaker provides a convenient way to shuffle them around in the Sort Records dialog box after you've added them to the Sort Order list. Figure 2-9 sheds some light on how it works.

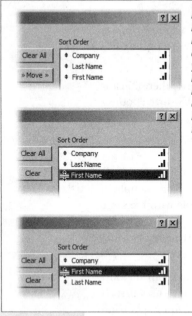

Figure 2-9:
Each field in the Sort Order list has a little double-headed arrow before its name (top). To change the order in which they're listed, first point to one of the arrows. Notice that your cursor changes shape (middle). FileMaker is letting you know that you can drag the item up or down in the list. Drag the item to its new position (bottom). If you prefer the keyboard, use the arrow keys to highlight the field you want to move. Then press the Ctrl (⌘) key along with the arrow keys to move the selected field. When you're done, and you click Sort, FileMaker will sort your records using each field in order, starting with the top field in the list.

If you do a multi-field sort and then discover you didn't get quite what you expected (because you had the fields in the wrong order), just choose Records → Sort Records again, move the fields in the Sort Order list to the right places, and then click Sort.

Sort of Sorted

When I haven't sorted my records, the status area says "Unsorted." What order is that, exactly? Is it completely random? Also, sometimes it says "Semi-Sorted." What in the world does that mean?

Remain calm. When the records are unsorted, they're in creation order. The first record you ever created (and haven't deleted yet) shows first, followed by the next one you created, and so on. Creation order is FileMaker's natural order for the records. Once you sort the records one way, they stay that way until you sort again or explicitly unsort them. (There's a button to do just that in the Sort dialog box, although why you'd want to use it is up to you.)

Now then: If the records are sorted and you add a new record, FileMaker doesn't put that record in its properly sorted place. Instead, it always goes to the end. So if you add Adam Aaronson to your sorted address list, he winds up after Zorba Zuckerman and the status area then reads "Semi-Sorted." For the most part, the data is sorted, but one or more records are out of place. Even if you then delete Adam Aaronson, it'll still say Semi-Sorted. FileMaker isn't smart enough to realize the data is back in sorted order until you tell it to sort again.

Editing What's in Your Fields

Once you've found the records you want to work on, it's time to learn timesaving and creative ways to revise and format your record text. FileMaker fields are a lot more capable than the little fields you're used to from dialog boxes. Each field is like a mini–word processor, with features that you're familiar with if you've ever written a letter on a computer. Of course you can do basic things like select text, and cut, copy, and paste. There's even a Find and Replace feature and flexible text formatting powers. Read on to find out what you can do.

Find and Replace

Like your word processor, FileMaker has a Find and Replace feature. And also as in your word processor, you can (and should) use Find and Replace tools as often as possible to automate your editing process and eliminate retyping.

Suppose one of your clients is called Anderson Consulting. For one reason or another, they decide to change their name to Accenture. Unfortunately, you have 27 folks in your database with the old name. You could look through your records one by one and fix them yourself, but you're never going to become a database guru that way. Instead, do a Find/Replace operation.

FileMaker fields can hold a lot of information, and it's not at all uncommon to put things like letters, emails, product descriptions, and other potentially long documents into a field. In cases like this, the Find/Replace command is just as useful as it is in your word processing program.

Since FileMaker has fields and records to worry about, though, its Find/Replace dialog box is a little more complicated that what you may be familiar with. Luckily, the concepts are simple, as shown in Figure 2-10. The Find/Replace dialog box lets you search a field, a record, or all records for a little snippet of text. It can also replace every occurrence of that text with something new—either one at a time, or all at once.

Note: Don't confuse Find/Replace with Find mode. Find/Replace is for finding *text* in one or more fields and one or more records. Find mode is for finding *records*. You'll probably use Find mode much more often than Find/Replace. For the full story, see the box on page 54.

Here's FileMaker's version of Find and Replace:

1. **Choose Edit → Find/Replace → Find/Replace.**

   The Find/Replace dialog box opens, as shown in Figure 2-10.

2. **In the lower-left corner of the dialog box, turn on "Match case" and/or "Match whole words only" to tell FileMaker how you want it to match the text you're looking for.**

   Turning on "Match case" ensures that FileMaker looks for an exact uppercase and lowercase match. For example, when "Match case" is turned on, "Kite" and "kite" don't come up as a match.

If you turn on "Match whole words only," FileMaker eliminates partial word matches. For example, "Drag" matches "Drag" and not "Dragon."

Figure 2-10:
In FileMaker, you use the same dialog box both to find text and to find and replace text. If you aren't replacing anything, don't click any of the Replace buttons. The text you're looking for goes in the "Find what" text box. If you're replacing it with something new, type that text in the "Replace with" text box. (If you want to replace some text with nothing, making it go away, leave the "Replace with" box empty.)

3. **Under "Search across," select either "All records" or "Current record."**

   You've just told FileMaker whether you want it to look through all the records in the found set, or only the record you're currently on. In a case like the Anderson/Accenture example, choose "All records."

4. **Under "Search within," select either "All fields" or "Current field."**

   "Current field" refers to the field you were editing when you opened the Find/ Replace dialog box. If you weren't editing one, FileMaker will let you pick Current field, but when you try to find, it will complain with an error message. You're allowed to select any combination of Search across and Search within. Here's how that shakes out:

   - **All records and All fields.** FileMaker looks through every field in the window for a match. When it's done, it moves on to the next record.

   - **Current record and All fields.** FileMaker looks through every field in the window, then tells you it's finished.

   - **Current record and Current field.** FileMaker looks only in the current field. When it reaches the end of the text in that field, it stops.

   - **All records and Current field.** FileMaker looks through the current field, then moves to the next record. It keeps looking through records for more matches, but it pays attention only to the current field.

5. **From the Direction pop-up menu, choose Forward, Backward, or All.**

The Direction pop-up menu controls which way FileMaker goes when it starts its search. To figure out what that means, imagine there's a long string running through your database. One end is tied to the first letter of the first field of the first record. The other end is tied to the *last* letter of the *last* field of the *last* record. This concept is pictured in Figure 2-11.

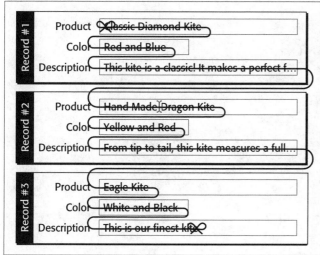

Figure 2-11:
The Find/Replace command expects you to give it a Direction. To decipher what that means, you have to do a little visualization. Here's a picture of the imaginary string, starting at the beginning of the first record, and stopping at the end of the last. When you click into a field, and the insertion point sits there blinking in front of a letter, it's marking a spot on the imaginary string. If you're not clicked into a field, FileMaker decides to mark the string right before the first letter of the first field of the current record. In this example, your cursor is sitting right there between "Made" and "Dragon."

- **Forward.** FileMaker starts looking at your current spot on the string, and moves *forward* (towards the end of the string). When it gets to the end, it beeps.

- **Backward.** FileMaker starts looking at your current spot on the string, and moves *backward* (towards the beginning of the string). When it gets to the beginning, it beeps.

- **All.** FileMaker starts off just like a Forward search. When it reaches the end of the string, instead of beeping, it skips to the start of the string and keeps looking. It finally beeps and stops when it gets back where it started.

Now that you're through setting all your Find/Replace options, it's time to decide which button to click:

1. **Click either Find Next, Replace & Find, or Replace All.**

Find Next starts FileMaker looking. When it finds a match, it highlights it right in the field. The Find/Replace window doesn't go away yet, though. This way, you can click Find Next as many times as necessary to find what you're looking for, then click Replace to change it to your replacement text. Click Find Next again to go to the next match.

Find/Replace vs. Find/Replace

You may be wondering how Find mode combined with Replace Field Contents is different from Find/Replace (discussed earlier in this chapter). In fact, they're very different, but deciding which to use can be confusing. Here are some guidelines:

- Find mode is significantly faster at finding things than Find/Replace. In Find mode, FileMaker uses something called an *index*, which lets it find ten matching records out of 293,000 in an instant. Find/Replace, on the other hand, looks through the fields the same way you would: one by one. It's faster than you, but it still takes time.

- Replace Field Contents always operates on one field across the entire found set. Find/Replace, on the other hand, also lets you replace across all fields in just the current record, as well as all fields and all records in the found set.

- Replace Field Contents always replaces the *entire* contents of the field. You can't replace every occurrence of "hte" with "the" for example. You can only give a new value that replaces whatever is in the field.

- Most important, Replace Field Contents assumes you've already found the records you want, and always modifies every record in the found set. Find/Replace adds a second layer of searching, as it scours the record or the found set looking for matches.

So why would you ever use Replace Field Contents? Sometimes you really do want to replace everything in the field every time, just like in the Company Name example on page 46. Also, Replace Field Contents is *significantly* faster at changing lots of records than Find/Replace. It takes just a few seconds to accomplish what Find/Replace would spend several minutes doing.

In general, if you want to find records, use Find mode, but if you want to find certain bits of text, use Find/Replace. Likewise, if you want to replace everything in a field in *every* record, use Replace Field Contents, but if you want to replace little bits of text, use Find/Replace. (If you want to replace little bits of text across thousands of records, study Chapter 7 first, or be prepared to take a vacation while your computer thinks about it.)

Finally, there's no reason you can't mix Find/Replace with Find mode. Since Find/Replace only searches records in the found set, you can establish a good found set *first* to make your Find/Replace go faster. (For example, if you're replacing "hte" with "the" in the Notes field, you may as well find all the records that have "hte" in their Notes field first, since Find mode is so much faster than Find/Replace.)

If you feel the need to work more quickly—say you've done Find Next and Replace a couple times and everything looks in order—click Replace & Find instead. It replaces the current match, and then finds the next one all in one step. Repeat as many times as necessary.

Finally, if you're sure you want *every* match replaced, click Replace All, and File-Maker will do the entire find-replace-find-replace dance for you. FileMaker always asks you if you're sure about Replace All first, just in case. For instance, if you have some clients whose last name is Anderson and others whose company name is Anderson, you may *not* want to use the Replace All option. You'll need to check each occurrence individually to make sure you don't accidentally change someone's last name to Accenture.

Get Out of My Way

Unlike the Find/Replace window in most other programs, FileMaker's won't politely step aside. If you try to click in your database window to switch back to it, FileMaker just beeps at you. In fact, you can't do *anything else* but find and replace unless you close the Find/Replace window first. You can always move the Find/Replace window around the screen by dragging it, but if your database window is big, or your screen is small, the Find/Replace window can really get in the way, keeping the very results it's finding hidden behind it. Here are a few pointers to help you cope:

Make sure the Find/Replace window is as small as possible by dragging the resize handle in the lower-right corner. Like most windows, it is resizable, but its smallest size is almost always big enough.

If you close the Find/Replace window (Click Close or just press Escape), FileMaker keeps the last-found item highlighted. Since FileMaker remembers all your settings, you can always open the Find/Replace window again and continue searching where you left off.

Wouldn't it be great if you could click the buttons in the Find/Replace window without having it open onscreen? Fact is, you can. In the Edit → Find/Replace menu, you'll see two handy commands: Find Again and Replace & Find Again.

Choosing these menu commands is just like clicking the Find Next and Replace & Find buttons in the Find/Replace dialog box.

FileMaker also offers one more convenient shortcut. If you have some text already in a field, and you want to find *the next* occurrence of the same text, you can choose Edit → Find/Replace → Find Selected. This one command does the same thing as copying the text, opening the Find/Replace window, pasting into the "Find what" box, clicking Find Next, and then clicking Close. All the other options in the Find/Replace window stay just as when you last used them.

Best of all, these handy commands all have keyboard shortcuts:

- To find the next occurrence (Find Again), just press Ctrl+G (⌘-G).

- To replace the currently selected text and find the next occurrence (Replace & Find Again), press Ctrl+Shift+G (Option-⌘-G).

To find other occurrences of the selected text, press Ctrl+Shift+H (Option-⌘-H)

2. **When you're done with the Find/Replace window, just click Close.**

Warning: Find/Replace can take a long time because it looks through the individual words in each field. If you're searching across all records, and you have lots of records, be prepared to wait a while as File-Maker does its magic.

Fields for Lots of Text

Click in the Notes field in the Contact Management database. Notice that when you do, a scroll bar appears on the right side of the field. If you type lots of notes, you'll be able to scroll through them. FileMaker fields can hold *a lot* of text. Technically, each field is limited to two gigabytes of data *per record*, which is a fancy way of saying "way more than you'll ever need." (When you design a database, you get to decide which fields have scroll bars, as discussed on page 156.)

You can enter text into a field in all the usual ways, like typing on your keyboard or pasting text you copied from another field or another program. You can also select text in one field and drag it into another. (In Mac OS X, in fact, you can drag text into a field from *any* other program.)

Note: Even if a field doesn't have scroll bars, you can still add lots of text. In this case, FileMaker just makes the field grow to hold whatever you type. When you leave the field, it shrinks back to its normal size, hiding anything that goes outside the edges. Don't worry, though, the text reappears when you click back into the field.

Drag and Drop Editing

In addition to copying and pasting, you can drag text from one place to another. But first, you have to turn it on in FileMaker's preferences, like so:

1. **On Windows, choose Edit → Preferences. On Mac OS X, choose FileMaker Pro → Preferences.**

   The Preferences dialog box emerges.

2. **Confirm that "Allow drag and drop text selection" is checked.**

   If you decide you don't like using drag and drop, just come back here and turn it off.

3. **Click OK.**

Now that dragging is turned on, here's how it works:

1. **Make a new record (Records → New Record).**

   Now you've got a nice clean work surface.

2. **Type *Editing text a is drag* into the Notes field.**

   Yes, it says "text a is." Type the mistake and all. Next you'll drag to fix it.

3. **Double-click the word "is."**

   The word is highlighted to let you know it's selected.

4. **Drag the selected word over between "text" and "a."**

Figuring out where dragged text is going to land can be tricky. If you look closely, you'll see that in addition to the text you're dragging, a little vertical line moves along under your arrow. You can see this in action in Figure 2-12.

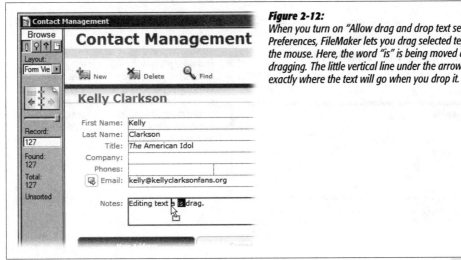

Figure 2-12:
When you turn on "Allow drag and drop text selection" in Preferences, FileMaker lets you drag selected text around with the mouse. Here, the word "is" is being moved after "text" by dragging. The little vertical line under the arrow shows you exactly where the text will go when you drop it.

You'll probably have to fix the spaces between words. Unlike most word processors, FileMaker isn't smart enough to figure out where they go for you.

Note: You can also drag text from one *field* to another. Instead of *moving* the text, FileMaker *copies* it. In other words, once you let go of the mouse button, the text will be both where it started *and* where you dropped it. If you want this behavior when dragging *within* a field, hold down the Alt (Option) key while you drag.

Text Formatting

Just like a word processor, FileMaker has commands to set the Font, Size, and Style of the text in a field. (Figure 2-13 shows a field with formatted text.) This feature comes in handy for many reasons. For instance, imagine you have some really important information about a customer ("NEVER PAYS HIS BILL") that you want to keep in the Notes field. To make sure it gets noticed, you can make it big, bold, and red. You can even use one of those fancy frilly fonts just to keep things interesting.

The formatting commands for font, font size, and type style are in the Format menu. But before you change anything, you'll notice that all FileMaker fields come with a preset (and pretty boring) standard formatting. (Part 2 of this book explains how you can change this automatic formatting.) Each of the formatting commands covered in this section lets you override the standard formatting for a field on a record-by-record basis.

Warning: Consider (and remember) the full implications of the paragraph above: *All* of the techniques described in the rest of this chapter pertain only to editing and formatting *individual* records. If you would like to change a field's formatting across the board, you need to make that change to your databases *layout*. For example, you might want all last names in your database to appear in boldface letters, or put a box around everyone's phone number. You'll learn how in Part 2 of this book.

Figure 2-13:
You can format the text in any field just like text in a word processor. FileMaker lets you assign fonts, sizes, styles, colors, and more. You can even adjust paragraph attributes like line spacing, indenting, and alignment. In this record (from the Contact Management database) every field but Email Address has had its contents stylized.

Font

FileMaker lets you pick from all the fonts you have on your computer (see More Fonts on Windows if you don't believe it). Using a font is a breeze if you're one of those FileMaker users who's heard of a computer. Just select the text you want to change, then choose the font you want from the Format → Font menu. (If you're the type who plans ahead, you can also choose a font *before* you start typing.)

Tip: As with all FileMaker's editing commands, if you make a mistake, just choose Edit → Undo. Or use your trusty Undo keystroke: Ctrl+Z (Windows) or ⌘-Z (Mac).

Size

Changing the size of text is equally easy. Like changing fonts, you simply select the text and pick a size, in points, from the Format → Size menu. (Again, you can pick the size *before* you type if that's your thing.) The Format → Size menu only lists a few standard sizes. If you need a size that's not listed, just choose Format → Size → Custom and FileMaker will let you enter any point size from one to 500. (See page 152 for more detail on font sizing.)

Immediately after Custom, one last size is listed. This one isn't separated from the rest just to be cute—it shows the last *custom* size you used. If you prefer 11 point, you only need to visit the Custom command once.

Once you've made the change, 11 will be listed at the bottom of the menu…until you decide that 13-point type is your new favorite, that is.

More Fonts on Windows

On Windows, the Font menu may not show the fonts you want—it normally only shows a few (on Mac OS X, the Font menu *always* displays all your fonts). To get to the rest, choose Format → Font → Configure/More Fonts to show the Configure Font Menu dialog box. Once here, you can do three things: Pick fonts that don't show in the menu, control which fonts *do* show in the menu, and change how they display.

- The Available Fonts list shows every font installed on your computer. If you want to choose a font that isn't in the Font menu, select it from the Available Fonts list and click Apply. Unlike every other Apply button you've ever seen, this one applies the new font selection *and* dismisses the window.

- To add a font to the Font menu, select it from the Available Fonts list and click Move to add it to the Appear in Menu list. If you want the menu to show *every* possible font, click Move All instead. When you select a font from the Appear in Menu list, the Move button changes to Clear, and a click removes the font from the list. As usual, you can double-click font names to mimic the Move or Clear buttons.

- FileMaker can show fonts in the menu *in their own typeface*. For instance, the words "Times New Roman" will actually be *in* Times New Roman in the menu. If you don't want this behavior, turn off Show Fonts in Typeface. This setting also affects the display of fonts in the Appear in Menu list right in this dialog box.

When you're finished configuring, click OK. Your selected text won't be changed, but the font menu will now list the fonts you put in the Appear in Menu list. If you want to change the font of the selected text at the same time, select the font and click Apply instead.

Style

Using styles is a snap. Pick the style from the Format → Style menu and start typing, or select some text and apply a style. In addition to the industry-standard Bold, Italic, and Underline styles, FileMaker adds a few less common options to the mix. Except where noted here, you can mix-and-match styles to your heart's content (see the Notes field in Figure 2-12).

- **Word Underline** underlines each word, but not the space(s) between them. Double Underline puts two lines under your text. Each of the Underline styles is mutually exclusive, meaning you can't have text that's double underlined *and* word underlined.

- **Condense** squishes the text together so it takes up less space. Extend does just the opposite, putting a little extra space between each letter. Since these choices are opposites, you can't use both at the same time.

- **Strike Thru** draws a line right thru…uh, *through* the middle of each line of text. Use it when you want something to look like it's been crossed out—perhaps you have some data in the Notes field that no longer applies, but you want it there anyway in case it's important later.

- **Small Caps** replaces all the lower-case letters in your text with uppercase letters in a slightly smaller size, for an effect like you often see on fancy lawyer's stationery or wedding invitations.

- **Uppercase, Lowercase,** and **Title Case** are handy for those times when you've already typed text and later realize that you capitalized it incorrectly. Maybe your Caps Lock key got stuck halfway through someone's name, or you realize that you forgot to capitalize every word of a street address. You can use these commands to repair the damage. Uppercase and Lowercase turn all selected letters to capital or small, respectively. Title Case makes the first *letter* of each word uppercase, and every other letter lowercase.

Note: Using one of these styles doesn't change the actual text in the field at all. If you type *Mr. President* into a field, then change its style to Uppercase, it will show as MR. PRESIDENT. But at any time, you can go back and remove the Uppercase style, and you'll get the original capitalization back unchanged.

- **Superscript** (Ctrl+Shift+plus sign or ⌘-Shift-plus sign) makes the text a little smaller and raises it up on the line, as in x^2. Subscript (Ctrl+Shift+minus sign or ⌘-Shift-minus sign) comes in handy when you're entering chemical formulas. (You *do* enter chemical formulas a lot, don't you?) You can't use superscript and subscript simultaneously on the same letter or number.

Note: The keyboard shortcuts for text styles in FileMaker are non-standard. While in most programs Ctrl+B (⌘-B) means Bold, in FileMaker it's *Ctrl+Shift+B* (⌘-Shift-B). The same goes for Italic and Underline. This change takes a little getting used to. Basically, take the keyboard shortcut you use in all your other programs, and add the Shift key.

Text Color

The mini–word processor wouldn't be complete without colors. The Format → Text Color menu gives you a handful of colors to choose from. If you don't like those options, you can select Other Color (located below all the little color squares in the menu) to pick any color you want, as described in Figure 2-14.

If you don't like the assortment of colors FileMaker provides, you can change them in the Edit → Preferences (Windows) or FileMaker Pro → Preferences → Layout panel (Mac). You get three choices: System subset, Standard system palette, and Web palette (see Figure 2-14). The normal palette (System subset) gives you 88 colors, which most FileMaker mavens find more than sufficient. It's also nice because it's small enough for you to remember what color you've been using ("the third red from the top").

If you find the System subset palette too limiting though, feel free to try one of the others. The Standard system option displays the color palette built into your computer's operating system—Windows or Mac. Since you've probably seen this color arrangement elsewhere on your computer, you may find it easiest to use.

Figure 2-14:
The Format → Text Color menu offers a handful of canned color choices. If you're not happy with the colors you see, you can pick from two other palettes in FileMaker's Preferences dialog box. Whichever palette you choose determines the selection of colors you get when you choose from the Text Color submenu. Choosing "Standard system palette" gives you the most colors to work with.

The Web palette lets you choose from the set of 216 colors commonly considered *Web safe*; that is, they're guaranteed to look pretty much the same in any browser on any computer. At one time, you needed to stick to only these colors if planning to publish your database on a Web site (Chapter 18), but the truth is you don't really need to worry about Web safe colors anymore. Every computer sold since, oh, about 1997 can display more colors than you ever dreamed of.

Note: The Format → Text Color menu is just one of several places where a color palette shows up in FileMaker. You'll see the others in Part 2. Just remember that if you change the color palette selection in preferences, the change affects the color palettes throughout FileMaker.

The Text Format Dialog Box

FileMaker provides one-stop shopping for all your text-formatting needs. Suppose you want to change a word to red 13-point bold-italic-underline-uppercase-condensed. That looks to be about seven trips to the Format menu. Instead, choose Format → Text to summon the Text Format dialog box (Figure 2-15). This one little window combines the Font, Size, Style, and Color menus described in the previous pages into one convenient place, turning seven menu commands into one. (Now if only it had a keyboard shortcut.)

Note: The Paragraph button reveals the Paragraph dialog box. It's covered on page 64.

Figure 2-15:
The Text Format dialog box (Format → Text) helps cut down your mouse mileage. It combines Font, Size, and Color (exact copies of their counterparts in the Format menu) with individual checkboxes for each style. As you make selections, the text in the Sample box reflects your changes.

Paragraph Formatting

Sometimes you put *lots* of information in a field. For example, suppose you decide to keep track of all your correspondence with your customers. You might make a database to store letters and emails so you can search them or print them out, as needed. In a database like this, you usually end up typing (or pasting) long blocks of text into a field, where you need to control more than just the font, size, style, and color.

Align Text

Text alignment is perhaps the most important aspect of your document's appearance. You can have text rigidly justified on both right and left, or with a loose right margin for a more casual look. If you use FileMaker to send party invitations to your contacts, you can use centered alignment for an attractive, social look. People may not think about text alignment much, but it really sets the whole tone of a document. FileMaker puts these settings right on the Format menu.

The Format → Align Text menu offers four useful choices:

- Choose **Left** to make every line of text start at the left edge of the field. As the text wraps from line to line, the right edge appears jagged.

- Choose **Center** to make every line of text center itself in the field. In this case, both edges are jagged.

- Choose **Right** if you want every line to end exactly at the right edge of the field. As you can probably guess, this options means the *left* edge is jagged.

- The **Full** text alignment (sometimes called Justified in other programs) tells FileMaker to take special care to make every line start on the left edge of the field and end on the right edge. It adds a little space between words and letters as necessary so that everything lines up.

Note: The Format → Align Text menu also has three perpetually disabled items: Top, Center, and Bottom. These items control *vertical* alignment of the text within the field. The reason they're gray is that you can choose them only when you're designing your layouts (Chapter 4), not when you're entering data.

Line Spacing

Format → Line Spacing lets you single- or double-space the text. Text is single-spaced normally, and if you choose Double instead, FileMaker spreads out your lines of text, giving them a little breathing room. This menu also has a Custom option, which is primarily just a shortcut to the Paragraph dialog box. As you'll learn on page 64, you can use the Paragraph dialog box to control several aspects of text formatting—including more fine-grained control of line spacing.

Note: Unlike the other format options, alignment and line spacing apply to an entire paragraph, not just the selected text.

The Text Ruler

A FileMaker field is much more than a mere container for plain text. Like a mini–word processor, you can set left and right indents and FileMaker makes sure your text stays between them. You can even set a first-line indent so the first line of each paragraph is automatically indented a little more (or less) than the rest of the text. Finally, you have complete control over tab stops: where they are and which direction the text goes when you tab to them.

The Text Ruler (View → Text Ruler) lets you set indents and tab stops for instant visual gratification. The ruler has an arrow icon for the Left, Right, and First Line indent settings (Figure 2-16), which you just drag to the spot on the ruler where you want the indent set. (For greater precision, you can also set indents in the Paragraph dialog box, as discussed in the next section.) You'll learn how to set tab stops on page 66.

When you turn on the Text Ruler, FileMaker adds a space along the top of the window to hold the ruler. When you're in a field, the ruler itself appears in the portion of this space that is directly above the field, with the zero point on the ruler lined up with the left edge of the field. (When you're not in a field, the ruler just measures the width of the content area.)

Figure 2-16:
Like most word processors, FileMaker has a text ruler that lets you position margin markers right where you want them. When you drag the Left indent arrow, it moves the First Line arrow with it, so first drag the Left indent arrow where you want it, then move the First Line arrow. If you want to move the Left Indent arrow without moving the First Line arrow, hold down the Alt (Option) key while you drag.

Detailed Formatting in the Paragraph Box

This multitalented window offers three groups of settings: Alignment, Line Spacing, and Indents. You can get to the Paragraph dialog box in one of two ways. Either choose Format → Line Spacing → Custom, or choose Format → Text and then click Paragraph. The dialog box opens, as shown in Figure 2-17.

Figure 2-17:
The Paragraph dialog box lets you define a paragraph's alignment, indentation, and a whole lot more. If the Single and Double options in the Format → Line Spacing menu seem lacking, you can use this dialog box to control line spacing precisely. Just enter any number you want in the Height box, and choose your units (lines, inches, centimeters, or pixels). You can also opt to add extra space above or below each paragraph by modifying the Before and After settings.

Warning: When you click Paragraph in the Text Format dialog box, FileMaker immediately applies any formatting settings you've made. To avoid unintentional reformatting, make sure you don't have any text selected when you choose Format → Text. (Better yet, bypass the Text Format dialog box altogether by choosing Format → Line Spacing → Custom instead.)

- The **Alignment** options are almost exactly the same as those found in the For-mat → Align Text menu. There is one small exception, though: Full alignment is called Justified, though it means the exact same thing. (Don't ask.)

- Next in line are the **Indent** settings. Here, you can specify how far the text indents from the left and right edges of the field. The Left setting applies to every line in the field, giving you the specified space between the left edge of the field and the beginning of each line. The Right setting works the same way, only it applies to the right edge of the field. The First setting, meanwhile, applies only to the *first* line of each paragraph. It tells FileMaker to insert more space before the first line, in addition to what's specified for Left indent.

Note: If you want a *hanging indent*, where the first line sticks out to the left of the rest of the paragraph, specify a negative value for the First indent option, and a positive value for the Left indent.

- The Paragraph window also gives you more fine-grained control over **Line Spacing**. For instance, you can give your text 1.5 line spacing instead of single- or double-spacing by entering 1.5 in the Height box and choosing "lines" from the popup menu beside it. The Above and Below options refer to spacing before and after each paragraph. Unlike the indent settings, the spacing options let you pick the units right in the dialog box. You can choose Pixels (little dots on the screen), Inches, or Centimeters from the pop-up menu.

When your text is positioned and aligned just the way you want it, you have two options: Click OK to make the changes and close the Paragraph dialog box, or click Apply to inspect your changes so far. The Apply button leaves the Paragraph box open, so you can peek at your database window and see how it looks, then continue tweaking. Click OK when you're satisfied.

Tabs

Since a field can hold just about any kind of text, you might eventually need to use tab stops *within* a field. For example, you could have a nice large field into which you paste rows of text from a spreadsheet. To make things line up properly, you can set tab stops for each column of text. To move the insertion point to the next tab, press Ctrl-Tab (Option-Tab). This is a special keystroke, obviously, because in FileMaker pressing Tab jumps you to the next *field*. See page 228 to learn how Field Controls make plain old tabs work the way you're used to.

Like most word processing programs, FileMaker provides two ways to create tab stops: the Text Ruler described on page 63, and the Tabs dialog box.

Setting tabs in the Text Ruler

To insert a new tab stop, simply click anywhere in the ruler. A small right-point-ing arrow appears where you clicked, representing a *left* tab stop. (The arrow shows you what direction text will go when you start typing.) FileMaker also supports other kinds of tab stops, but to get them, you have to visit the Tabs dialog box, described next.

TROUBLESHOOTING MOMENT

Units

In the pictures shown here, the Indent options are specified in Inches (you see "in" next to each text box). FileMaker actually has a setting for the unit used here and other places. FileMaker comes factory-set to inches, but it's nothing if not flexible. You can use inches, centimeters, or pixels—the choice is yours. If you're used to the Metric system, by all means tell FileMaker to use centimeters. Or choose pixels for *really* precise control over text positioning. Here's how to change how FileMaker displays measurements:

If the Paragraph dialog box is open, click Cancel. The remainder of these steps will work only if your database's main window is in front.

1. Choose View → Layout Mode. In this mode, the content area of the window changes somewhat. Don't be alarmed…and don't click anything in the window. (If you accidentally change something, that's OK. FileMaker will soon ask if you want to save).

2. Choose Layouts → Set Rulers to open the Set Rulers dialog box.

3. In the Units pop-up menu, choose Pixels. (If you'd rather use different units, you can select anything you like. You can always repeat these steps later to get things back.)

4. Click OK, then choose View → Browse Mode

You should be back where you started now. If you get a message asking if you want to save your changes, click Don't Save.

Setting tabs in the Tabs dialog box

The Tabs dialog box is a laborious way of setting tabs, but it gives you more options because you can control all aspects of each tab stop manually. Here's the drill:

1. **Choose Format → Text.**

   The Text Format dialog box appears.

2. **Click Paragraph.**

   The Paragraph dialog box makes its entrance.

3. **Click Tabs.**

   Ta-da! You found the Tabs dialog box (Figure 2-18).

Note: If the Text Ruler is showing (Figure 2-19), you can get to the Tabs dialog box quickly. Just double-click any tab stop in the ruler. The Tabs dialog box opens with the clicked tab preselected.

Figure 2-18:
The Tabs dialog box lists all the tab stops set for a field in the list on the right. You can also adjust a tab stop, delete it, or add a new one. Each stop has a Type, Position, and Fill Character. To change the settings for any stop, first select the stop, then edit the settings, and click Set.

To make a new tab stop, simply select the appropriate options as described below, and then click New. A new entry will appear in the list named after the Position you specified. You can create up to 20 tab stops, after which the New button becomes disabled. If you try to add a tab stop at a position where one already exists, the new stop simply replaces the old one.

Editing tab stops in the Tabs dialog box

Once you've created tab stops, you can change them anytime using the same Tabs dialog box. Select a Tab stop in the list to see its settings. The Type radio buttons, as well as the Position and Fill Character fields, change to reveal the settings for the selected stop. To change them, modify the values in any way, then click Set. To delete the selected tab stop, click Clear.

Finally, you've probably noticed that the Tabs dialog box has an Apply button just like the Paragraph dialog box, and it works the same way. Click Apply, and the tab stops showing in the list will be reflected in the current field. Sometimes it can be tough to position your tab stops in just the right place. Use the Apply button to see how things line up. When you're satisfied with the tabs, click OK.

Type. A Tab stop's *type* effects how text entry behaves when you tab to that particular stop. Figure 2-19 shows how these different tab stops look in action.

- A **Left** tab causes the next text you type to be anchored to the tab stop on its left side. As you type, the text moves to the right just like normal Left aligned text.

- A **Right** tab works in the other direction. When you tab to one, everything you type is anchored on the right, like right-aligned text. As you type, the text moves to the left, towards the beginning of the line.

- A **Center** tab causes the text you type to be centered at the point of the stop. As you type, the text moves in both directions.

• The **Align** on tab lets you specify any character (letter, number, or punctuation) to act as the point of alignment. For instance, if you specify a period for the alignment character, the period or decimal point you type will anchor to the tab stop. Any text you type before the period will be right aligned and any text after the period will be left aligned. You use this feature most often to line up lists of numbers by their decimal points.

Figure 2-19:
You have a lot of flexibility with your tab stops. This field has left, right, decimal-point aligned, and center-aligned tabs.

Position. In addition to a type, every stop has a *position*, which is measured from the left edge of the field, in the same units used for Indent settings (such as inches and centimeters). For example, if you're storing a little two-column list in a text field, you might set tab stops at .5 inches and 2 inches.

Fill Character. FileMaker also accepts a *fill character* for each tab. This character is repeated as many times as necessary to fill the blank space leading up to a tab. Most often you use a period for the fill character (as shown in Figure 2-20), but any character is allowed.

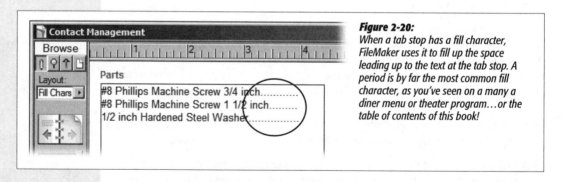

Figure 2-20:
When a tab stop has a fill character, FileMaker uses it to fill up the space leading up to the text at the tab stop. A period is by far the most common fill character, as you've seen on a many a diner menu or theater program…or the table of contents of this book!

Beyond Text: Container Fields

Words and numbers form the bulk of most databases. All these letters and figures convey important information, but they can be pretty boring. Increasingly, people are using FileMaker databases to store images, movies, and other bits of multimedia. For example, you can store a photograph of each employee right along with her personnel records. Or add product shots to your inventory database.

The Contact Management database has one field you may have been ignoring until now: Image. Unlike all the other fields in this database, the Image field doesn't expect (and won't accept) typed text. It's a special kind of field called a *container* field. Container fields can hold just about anything you want, including pictures, sounds, animation, music, and movies. You can even put any file from your hard drive into a container field, like a PDF file or a Word document. You can see container fields holding assorted things in Figure 2-21.

Figure 2-21:
Container fields can hold any file. If you put a picture into a container field, FileMaker shows you the picture. If you insert a sound file, FileMaker gives you a special speaker icon that plays the sound when clicked. Music and Movie files give you the typical play, pause, fast-forward, and rewind controls, just like movies on the Web. For other kinds of files, FileMaker just shows you the file's icon.

Whether you realize it or not, when you use container fields you're using File-Maker as *asset management* software. That's the industry term for elaborate, customized software that contains and catalogs huge numbers of images (for use in brochures, books, or Web sites, for example). These programs are essentially databases, and with FileMaker, you can also manage large numbers of the images and documents you use every day. The data in a container field falls into one of four categories: picture, QuickTime, sound, and file.

Pictures

A *picture* can be in any of more than a dozen formats, including the common kinds like JPEG, GIF, and TIFF, PICT, and BMP. FileMaker will also accept Photo-Shop and PostScript (.eps) files. When you put a picture in a container field, the field displays the picture itself.

The following methods for copying, pasting, and inserting pictures into container fields are the same whether you're inserting a movie, PDF, text, or other type of file. You see the same type of Insert dialog box for navigating your hard drive each time.

Copy and paste

The most obvious way to put a picture into a contained field is to paste it in. You can copy a picture from just about anywhere, then click once in the field and choose Edit → Paste (Ctrl+V or ⌘-V).

You can also copy data from the container field. Again, simply click once on the field, and choose Edit → Copy (Ctrl+C or ⌘-C) or Edit → Cut (Ctrl+X or ⌘-X). Whatever was in the field is now ready to paste into another field, record, or program.

Insert → Picture

If the picture you want in a container field is stored in a file, copy and paste doesn't do you much good. You'd have to open the file in some program first, and then copy it from there—and that's no fun. Instead, you can insert the file directly into the field without ever leaving the comfort of FileMaker. Here's how:

1. **Click in the Image field.**

   You've now entered the record, and the Image field in particular.

2. **Choose Insert → Picture.**

   The Insert Picture dialog box appears. This window looks almost exactly like a typical Open File dialog box in Windows or Mac OS X. You can use it to find the picture you want to insert.

3. **Click Open.**

   FileMaker grabs the picture and puts it in the Image field.

Tip: If you need to insert *lots* of pictures into a database, you can save yourself a lot of trouble by using the File → Import Records → Folder command. See page 631 for the full explanation.

QuickTime

QuickTime data includes anything supported by QuickTime Player, the multimedia software from Apple. FileMaker uses QuickTime to help it deal with multimedia files. The file types include QuickTime files (.mov); FLASH animations; video files like AVI, DV, MPEG, and MPEG4; virtual reality files (VR); and music files like WAV, AIFF, MP3, and AAC. Because FileMaker uses QuickTime, and QuickTime is frequently upgraded (*www.quicktime.com*), the exact list of formats FileMaker supports also changes. For the most part, QuickTime can handle most standard music, video, and animation formats.

When a container field holds a QuickTime file, you normally see the movie's *poster frame*, which is usually just the first frame of the movie. When you click the movie, a standard movie controller appears (like the one at the lower-left of Figure 2-21), so you can play, pause, fast-forward, and rewind it. The controller also has a button to adjust the volume and a little knob that shows you where you are in the movie.

POWER USERS' CLINIC

Store a Reference

When inserting a picture, QuickTime movie, or file (page 70), the dialog box includes an option to "Store only a reference to the file." When this option is turned off, FileMaker copies the actual file into your database. You can move or delete the original file and the data will still appear in the field, because the database now contains all the file's information within itself. If you turn on "Store only a reference to the file," FileMaker doesn't copy the file into the field at all. Instead, it just remembers the file you wanted. Each time you look at this record, FileMaker returns to the disk and finds the original file so it can display the data. In this respect, it works exactly like a shortcut or alias. If the file is gone (moved, deleted, or renamed), FileMaker will show you this message instead.

There's no simple rule for when you should store the actual file, and when you should store a reference instead. Most people decide to store the file itself, because it saves the trouble of keeping the files and database together.

This is especially true when multiple people are using the database from different computers. On the other hand, here are a couple of reasons you might want to store a reference instead:

- Storing many *large* files can make your database get big—really big—which can cause a number of problems. It's harder to back up and move a huge database file from one place to another. If you're trying to email the database to your home office, your ISP may not appreciate (or allow) a 3 GB attachment, for example. If the inserted files aren't critical to the record data, it may make sense to leave them out of the database so it's easier to work with.

- Sometimes you want to catalog files inside FileMaker even though they might change over time. For example, if you wanted to put promotional images into a database so they're easy to locate, you probably *don't* want to make editing those images difficult. If you store a reference to these images, you can still edit the originals any time. As long as you haven't changed their name or location, when you look in FileMaker, you'll see the latest edits.

Otherwise, when you're using your database day to day, it usually doesn't matter whether you've inserted a reference or the actual file. For the most part, both kinds work exactly the same. This book explains the differences as they come up.

Just as with a picture (page 70), you can copy and paste QuickTime movies or sounds into the container field or use the Insert → QuickTime menu command to select a QuickTime file from the hard drive.

Note: FileMaker lets you copy and paste either entire QuickTime files or sections of footage or sound that you've selected before copying. To do so, just open the file in QuickTime Player for Mac or Windows and use the movie controls to select the desired snippet.

Sound

A *sound* is a recorded bit of audio. FileMaker actually lets you record sounds right into the field. You can keep audio notes with a project record, or record your practice speeches and save them for when you're famous. When a container field holds a sound, it displays a little speaker icon; double-click it to hear the recorded sound.

Recording sound

The Insert → Sound command doesn't bring up the same dialog box as the other Insert commands. Instead, it shows the Record dialog box (Figure 2-22). If your computer has a microphone attached, you can record any sound directly into the field.

Figure 2-22:
FileMaker records sound from the sound input device you set up in your control panel (Windows) or System Preferences (Mac OS X). Most computers let you use more than just a microphone as the sound input device. For example, you can usually record sound from audio CDs in your CD-ROM drive or DVDs from your DVD drive.

The Record dialog box is simple, but capable. The speaker icon provides feedback about what the microphone's picking up, by showing little soundwaves indicating the sounds it's hearing. The more soundwaves you see, the louder the recording. In fact, the speaker icon lets you check for soundwaves even when you're *not* recording, so use it to do a quick sound check ("Testing, testing, 1, 2, 3"). If you don't see waves when you talk, make sure the microphone's plugged in.

When you're ready to record, proceed as follows:

1. **Click the Record button.**

   FileMaker immediately begins recording everything the microphone hears. As it does, the Recording Time progress bar fills slowly. When the progress bar reaches the end, you've recorded as much as you have room for.

2. **When you're done recording, click Stop.**

   At this point, you have some sound recorded. The length of the recording shows to the right of the Recording Time progress bar.

3. **To hear what you got, click Play.**

   Once the recording is playing, you can use the Stop or Pause button to stop it. Clicking Stop will stop it completely. (The next time you press Play, it starts over from the beginning.) Pause, on the other hand, lets you stop the playback momentarily. (Clicking Pause or Play again starts the playback right where it left off.)

4. **If you're satisfied with what was recorded, click Save to store the sound in the container field.**

If you click Cancel, FileMaker completely erases the sound you recorded with no warning…so be sure you click the correct button.

Tip: The Insert → Sound command is specifically for recording sound directly into the field. If you have a sound file of some kind already on your hard drive (an MP3 for example), choose Insert → QuickTime instead. In general, if the data you're putting in the field has a *time component* (meaning it happens over time, like video or sound), treat it like a QuickTime file.

File

A container field can also hold a *file*. Since FileMaker doesn't know what the file is supposed to be, it simply shows you the file's name and icon. Unfortunately, you can't do anything with a file like this while it's in FileMaker. You can't edit it. You can't even open it and view its contents. Rather, the Container field simply holds the file for you. (Soon you'll learn how to get it back out.)

GEM IN THE ROUGH

PDFs in Mac OS X

The ability to store pictures, movies, sounds, and files in your database can be useful for lots of reasons. For example, if you're a recruiter, you could store resumes in Microsoft Word or PDF format right in the database alongside the info about a particular candidate. In fact, the Adobe PDF format is so common that people often need to keep track of PDF files—the brochure, flyer, or documentation for each of your products, the prospectus for each of your investments, or a floor plan for each of your properties.

You already know you can use the Insert → File command to store the PDF document right in a container field (and get it back out again later to look at it). But if you're on Mac OS X, you can do one better. Choose Insert → Image and then select a PDF file. FileMaker then shows you the PDF (the first page of it, anyway), right in the container field. If your document has more than one page, you need to export the PDF out of the container field (page 75) to read the whole thing.

Or, try this unexpected twist: You can read multipage PDFs right in FileMaker if you use Insert → QuickTime instead (page 70).

This time, when you click the container field itself, the standard QuickTime movie controls appear, as shown here. Using these controls, you can flip through the pages in the PDF: Fast Forward goes to the next page, Rewind goes to the previous page. If you press Play, FileMaker flips through the pages one after the other until it reaches the end of the document.

If you need to search within a PDF file, try this. Open the PDF file, select all the text, copy it, then paste it in a regular text field. FileMaker can search the text field, but you can view the PDF in all its glory in the container field.

If you can't use the file in FileMaker, why put it there at all? Sometimes people need to keep track of lots of files. They might need to organize them in ways that make sense only to their business. Keeping all these files in a folder on your hard drive can be a real drag since they can be slow to search and hard to reorganize. With FileMaker, you can keep the files right alongside other important data. For example, you can store project specifications (in Microsoft Word format) and diagrams (in Visio format) in your database along with tasks, team members, and timelines.

POWER USERS' CLINIC

Getting the Most Out of Your Fields

The Edit → Export Field Contents command isn't limited to container fields. With very few exceptions, you can export the contents of *any* field to a file. By contrast, you can't export a sound you recorded in FileMaker and you can't export the contents of a field you can't click into. (To help understand why you can't click in some fields, read about field behavior in Chapter 6, and security in Chapter 16.)

Here are some examples of how to export to your advantage:

• Use Edit → Export Field Contents to create a file without having to retype what you've stored in File-Maker. But if you just whiz by the Export Field Contents dialog box without looking, you'll miss a couple of options that will save you buckets of time. If you want to watch a QuickTime video at a size larger than the skimpy container field, just click the "Automatically open file" option as you export the contents of your field. FileMaker creates a duplicate video file for you, then opens a QuickTime player for your viewing pleasure.

• In fact, FileMaker is smart enough to open the right program for whatever you've exported. You'll get a text editor for text, a PDF viewer for a PDF, or a graphics viewer for graphics. Best of all, you don't have to scramble around looking for a program that can handle your file, because FileMaker figures it out for you.

• If you want to spread the wealth around—let your colleagues know about a customer who always makes a big order at the beginning of the new quarter, say—then turn on the "Create email with file as attachment" option when you export your field contents. FileMaker makes a file (hey, that makes sense!), then launches your email program, starts a new email, and attaches your new file to the email. All you have to do is type in a name, subject, and some text, then send the email on its merry way.

Let FileMaker really impress you by clicking both options at once. You'll get a copy of the file open for reference and a fresh, shiny email nearly ready for sending. If you've got the screen real estate, you can look at both these little jewels while you're checking out the FileMaker record that spawned them.

The most common way to place a file into a container field is to use the Insert → File command. On Windows, you can also copy a file on the desktop and paste it into a container field. When you insert a file, FileMaker makes no effort to figure out what's *in* the file. If you choose a picture, you'll still get just the name and icon. If you want to *see* the picture itself in FileMaker, you must choose Insert → Picture, as described on page 70.

Exporting data from container fields

Inserting files into container fields is all well and good...but it's just as important to get them back out again. When you use the Insert → File command, all you get to see is an icon and file name. Copying the file from the field with Edit → Copy, doesn't even do you much good, since FileMaker can't *paste* files to the desktop where you might actually be able to open and read them. A better way is to use the Export Field Contents command. Just click in the container field in question, and choose Edit → Export Field Contents. FileMaker asks you where you want to put the file, and what to name it. Click Save, and FileMaker creates a new file that's an exact copy of the one you put in the container field.

Checking Spelling

Considering all the tools FileMaker provides for editing your records, it'll come as no surprise that it also has a full spell checker built right in.

Spell Checking in One Pass

Before printing out your database or otherwise sharing it with the greater public, you'll want to make sure your spelling is correct. If you've been typing new records at lightning speed, there are bound to be some typos. And nothing screams "amateur" louder than a date field that reads "Febuary 15." All the spell checking commands are found under the Edit → Spelling menu. Here you have three choices:

• Choose Edit → Spelling → Check Selection to spell check selected text only.

• To check the entire record, choose Edit → Spelling → Check Record.

• And finally, you might want to check spelling on many records at once. In this case, choose Edit → Spelling → Check All. When you choose this option, you're telling the spell checker to look at every field of every record in the current found set.

Tip: To check spelling in every record, make sure you have them all showing first. Just choose Records → Show All Records before running the spell checker

---

No matter how many records you're checking, FileMaker opens the same Spelling dialog box shown in Figure 2-23 as soon as it stumbles upon a misspelled word. At bottom, the Spelling window says Status: Questionable Spelling. The Word text box displays the word in question. There are a few different ways things can proceed from here:

• You can edit the misspelled word directly in this box. More often than not, though, the correctly spelled word appears in the list below. In this case, just click the correct spelling, then click Replace. (Alternately, you can simply double-click the correctly spelled word and save the trip to the Replace button.)

• If you don't see the right spelling, you can correct it yourself. Type the correct spelling into the Word box, right over the misspelled word. To confirm that your new spelling is correct, click Check; the status line changes to say Correct Spelling if you got it right. Otherwise, you'll be back where you started, with a misspelled word and a few suggestions below it.

• If you spelled it right originally, but FileMaker doesn't agree, you can Skip the misspelled word. Better yet, click Learn to teach FileMaker the word so it won't bother you about it in the future. (Clicking Learn adds the word to your current user dictionary, which is explained below.)

• If you change your mind and want to stop the spell checker, just click Cancel. When the spell checker has finished its work, the status line changes again, this time to say Finished Spelling.

Note: Clicking Cancel doesn't undo all the changes you've made in the spell checker. It simply stops any further checking. If you've already corrected some words, the corrections will stick around after you cancel.

Figure 2-23:
If by the magic of planetary alignment, you have no misspellings when you first run the spell checker, you'll still see the Spelling window but the status line will say it's Finished Spelling right away. This behavior is universally disorienting, so don't feel bad when you spend 10 minutes trying to figure out why nothing looks right before you notice that it's already finished. You'll also see that the Replace button now says Done; click it to make the Spelling window go away. In this figure, the spell checker found a typo: "quandrey."

Spell Checking as You Type

FileMaker's spell checker also works automatically as you type. This *visual* spell check is a per-database setting, so you control it from the File Options dialog box. Choose File → File Options, then click the Spelling tab. You'll find two options that you can mix and match to help you spell better, run faster, and jump higher. Well, you'll spell better, anyway.

The first option is "Indicate questionable spellings with special underline." If you miss your word processor, this one will make you feel right at home. You'll see that familiar red line underneath any word FileMaker doesn't like the looks of. Plus, if you right-click (Control-click on the Mac) on the underlined word, FileMaker offers a menu containing suggestions for spelling the word properly.

If red lines aren't annoying enough, you could turn on "Beep on questionable spellings" and FileMaker will make your computer beep when you type a space after a misspelled word. Unfortunately, it's just the same old alert beep that your computer makes in all kinds of other situations—so it can be easy to miss. But in combination with the red line, this pair could be a formidable reminder to spell better.

Tip: Use spell checking as you type with caution, because it's just bright enough to catch your errors, but not quite smart enough to know when you don't need it butting in. Lots of perfectly fine database entries aren't in the spelling dictionary, like inventory codes, abbreviations, or even email addresses. Most people (those who don't like being beeped at every seven seconds) turn these options on for typing long text passages, then turn them back off for other data entry tasks.

Managing Spelling Dictionaries

FileMaker comes with spelling dictionaries for various languages and choosing among them is easy. Just choose Edit → Spelling → Select Dictionaries. The Select Dictionaries window lets you choose the language to use for all spell-checking operations. You can see it in Figure 2-24.

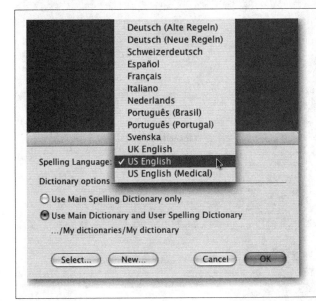

Figure 2-24:
The Select Dictionaries window lets you pick the spell checker language. You can also opt to use a User Spelling Dictionary (which happens automatically unless you come here and say otherwise). You can actually create as many user dictionaries as you want, and then select the one you want to use for a particular database.

User dictionaries

Remember from page 76 when you clicked the Learn button to teach FileMaker a new word? When you did so, behind the scenes, FileMaker actually added that word to the *user dictionary*, which is separate from the normal dictionary that comes with FileMaker.

In the Select Dictionaries window shown in Figure 2-24, you can choose whether or not to use the user dictionary. You can select an existing user dictionary (presumably, one you created previously), or create a new one. You can even have multiple user dictionaries for different purposes. For example, if you have two databases, one that tracks your apparel products and one that stores information about tools, it might make sense to keep two user dictionaries. The tools version might include words like "mm" and "pcs" while the apparel version would have "XXL" and "CottonPoly."

Tip: In reality, it's nine times easier to just use one user dictionary, so you don't have to worry about which one is selected. (It generally doesn't hurt to have *too many* words in your user dictionary, while not having enough makes spell checking much more time consuming. Nothing's worse than having to wade through a dozen correctly spelled words every time). Nevertheless, if you feel the need for more than one, the option is there.

POWER USERS' CLINIC

Rewriting the Dictionary

You've already learned how to add to your dictionary using the Learn button in the spell checker. Well, if you've ever wanted to just *tell* it what words you want it to skip, you can. Just choose Edit → Spelling → Edit User Dictionary to open the User Dictionary dialog box. Here you can add new entries to the dictionary (type the word and click Add), or remove existing entries (select the word and click Remove).

You can also export all the entries to a text file where you can edit them to your heart's content. When you click Export, FileMaker asks where it should save the export file. The file you get is simply a plain text file with one word on each line. You can then edit in a text-editing program.

If you already have a file that has words you want, you can Import those words into your User dictionary en masse. For instance, if you use a lot of technical terms, you might be able to download a list of terms from your industry and load them into a dictionary in one shot. The file has to have each word on its own line, so if it's in some other format, you'll need to clean it up first. (For example, use your word processor's Find & Replace function to turn a comma-separated list into one with a carriage return between each word.) Also, make sure the file is *plain text*.

A Microsoft Word file (.doc) or other special format won't work. (Making a plain text file on Windows is a breeze: Just use Notepad, the simple text-editor program in the Accessories folder in your Start menu. On Mac OS X, however, you need a little more care. You can use Text Edit—it's in your Applications folder—but you must tell it you want plain text. Just choose Format → Make Plain Text in Text Edit before you save the file.)

Using the Import and Export features together can be particularly useful. You can export your user dictionary, edit it manually in the text-editing program (where making lots of edits might be easier), then import it back in.

Printing and Preview Mode

All this talk about the wonders of an *electronic* database may leave you thinking FileMaker has nothing to do with paper, but that's not true. It's a cruel fact of life that eventually you'll need to put your data on paper. You might want mailing labels for all your customers in Canada, or a special printed form prefilled with patient information for insurance filing. Sometimes you just need your data with you when you're away from your computer. As you'll learn in Part 2, you can arrange the data any way you want in FileMaker, and make certain *layouts* that are particularly suitable for printing. But for now, remember that FileMaker lets you print *anything* you see onscreen (just choose File → Print). Its Print dialog box has a few special options, as shown in Figure 2-25. (In Mac OS X, you have to choose FileMaker Pro from the pop-up menu to see them.)

Figure 2-25:
FileMaker's Print dialog box gives you all the Windows (right) or Mac OS X (left) standard options, depending on what kind of computer and printer you're using. It also lets you decide which records you want to print (every record in the found set, or just the current record). To see the FileMaker-specific options on Mac OS X, you first have to select FileMaker from the unlabeled pop-up menu in the Print dialog box.

Pop-up menu

- **Records being browsed** tells FileMaker to print every record in the found set (page 26). If you want to print all your Canadian customers, choose this option.

- **Current record** will print just the current record, which comes in handy when you just want to print *one* thing: your doctor's contact information to keep in the car, perhaps, or maybe Aunt Edna's candied yams recipe.

- **Blank record, showing fields** causes FileMaker to print what's onscreen with no data at all. You can change the look of each field to a box or an underline if you want (just pick your choice from the pop-up menu shown in Figure 2-25). You would choose this option if you wanted to hand out pages for people to fill out with a pen (it's a kind of antique writing device), and later type their responses into the real database.

To see how the printout is going to look without committing trees to it, you can use *Preview mode* (Figure 2-26). You access Preview mode via the View menu, the Mode pop-up menu, or the Mode tabs.

Preview mode shows you what your database looks like as though it were printed on paper. For instance, you can see whether FileMaker's going to chop any information off to fit on the page (anything beyond the width of the page simply isn't printed). Preview mode also indicates the margins and lets you flip through the file page by page using the Book icon.

Figure 2-26:
In Preview mode, FileMaker reveals how your data will look when printed. You can't edit records in Preview mode—only view them. Also, the Book icon moves you a page at a time, instead of one record at a time, and the status area shows you the current page (not record) number and the total page count. The gray border around the page displays your page margin.

Note: When you first go to Preview mode, the page count says "?" instead of the number of pages. FileMaker actually doesn't know how many pages it's going to print until you force it to count them. To do so, just drag the Record Slider all the way to the right, which tells FileMaker you want to see the last page. On its way there, FileMaker counts the pages, too. The process may take some time but FileMaker will catch up eventually.

All the standard page-setup options (page 79) affect what you see in Preview mode. For example, if you change the paper orientation, Preview mode reflects the change right away. On some computers and printers, you can reduce the printout by a percentage.

When you reduce or enlarge in the Page Setup dialog box, Preview mode shows the page proportionately larger or smaller so you can see how the content area will fit on the page. (Which of these options are available to you depends upon the computer, operating system, and printer you're using.) The Zoom controls (page 6) work in Preview mode, too. If the full page is too big to fit on your screen, just zoom out a bit to see the whole thing.

Building a New Database

In Chapter 1, you jump-started your first database using one of FileMaker Pro's built-in templates. All FileMaker templates started out as blank databases. Some diligent FileMaker employees set up the fields and the formatting to get you started quickly, but there's no magic involved. With just a little knowledge and experience, you can create a database with all the power and fancy features of any File-Maker template. This chapter shows you how to build a contact management database from the ground up.

You really get FileMaker to work for you when you build your own databases. Lots of programs out there can help you keep track of one thing or another, but a database you build can think the way you do. You can design it to capture, organize, and display the information you need to know, when you need to know it—rather than making your business (or life) fit the software. It's time to learn how to custom-craft a database just for *you*.

Tables and Fields

So you're getting tired of your job, and you decide it would be exciting to get into the private investigator business. You found an office, ordered business cards, secured a phone line, and purchased some snazzy furniture. But have you thought about how you're going to *run* your business? Chances are, you could use some help from a database. And the first thing you need to think about when building a database is *what kind of information* it's going to track. For example, a private investigator might want to keep track of mostly people—names, phone numbers, aliases, passport numbers, and so on. Someone in retail, however, might want to track inventory—product names, descriptions, item numbers, prices, quantities, and similar details.

Tables: The Foundation of Your Database

You already know that whatever information you put in your database goes into fields—and that's where your database building begins. These fields in turn comprise a *table*. Tables are at the heart of the database, holding all the information and keeping it organized. Everything else in a database works in service of the tables in some way: letting you edit, extract, or view the information.

Conceptually, a table has rows and columns. The fields you define become the columns in the table. As you add records, you add new rows to the table. It's called a table because it stores information in a tabular form, just like the table of values in the back of a college math book. When you first start out with FileMaker, you may not even be aware that tables exist, but you have one anyway. FileMaker always creates one table for you when you make a new database, and that's where it puts all your information. It doesn't matter how your database *looks*—even if you never see any rows and columns, you still have a table inside where the data lives. See the box on page 83 for more on tables.

Note: In this chapter, you're going to build a database based on a single table. As you've probably guessed, a database can have more than one table. A database can also have no tables at all–instead, it can work with tables from other databases. You can even hook several tables together so they can share data and keep track of *relationships* between records. That's why FileMaker Pro is called a *relational* database program. In Part 4, you'll learn all about multiple table databases and hooking multiple databases together.

Figuring Out What Fields You Need

You decide the first thing your new business needs is a database to keep track of the people you deal with. Figuring out what fields your table should have is one of the most important decisions you'll make. To make the right choices, think carefully about *what* you need to track.

There's a lot of detail to consider when you plan a database. As you work, you may find it helpful to take some notes or even draw a picture. You'll learn more tips for this kind of planning in Chapter 7. For starters, use these guidelines:

- **Records** are *things*, like people, buildings, invoices, payments, products, or orders. If a single record holds information about more than one thing, you're probably making a mistake. For example, in the database you're building now, the records represent *people*. If you later want to keep track of the invoices you send to your customers, you don't want to add fields like Invoice Number, Amount, and Due Date to this table.

  Why not? Because if you did that, each person would only have room for one invoice. If the same customer makes another purchase, you'd have to create a new record for each invoice *and* enter the person's information all over again. Even worse, when the customer gets a new address or phone number, you'd have to change it individually in *every* record.

Note: If you have more than one thing to keep track of, there's a solution: Have more than one table: one for people and one for invoices, for example. If your business starts branching out, you may even need more than one database. You'll get into that in Part 4.

- **Fields** are *attributes* of the item in each record. First Name, for example, is an attribute of a person. Most things have lots of attributes, and that's why most records have lots of fields. Unfortunately, there's some gray area here. For instance, is Company Name an attribute of a *person* (the company he works for), or is it a separate *thing*? The answer depends on what you want to do with the Company Name information. Again, Part 4 will help you work through these tough issues. For now, a simple rule to follow is, if you're only tracking one attribute of a thing, it's usually safe to make it a field. For instance, if you just want to keep track of the company a person works for, and don't plan to use the company's main address, phone number, or Web address, then you probably need only a simple Company Name field on each record.

Think Table

When making a database, you need to understand the concept of a *table*. In a particular table, every record has the *same kind* of information. If you see a field called Email Address on one record, there's a place to put an email address on every record. If you want to record someone's birth date, you need to add a field for it. When you do, every record gets a birth date field, even if you only type it in on one record.

When you're deciding what fields to put in your database, it helps to imagine a real table, or a spreadsheet.

In a sense you have rows, which are the records, and columns, which are the fields. If you have a column in one row, it's obviously there for every row. If you add a new column, even after you've added 100 rows, that column is available to all the rows at once.

Name	Phone Number	Email Address
Harry Potter	+44 (020) 5555 7022	h.potter@hogwarts.ed.uk
Hermione Granger	+44 (020) 5555 2193	h.granger@hogwarts.ed.uk
Ronald Weasley	N/A	r.weasley@hogwarts.ed.uk
Vernon Dursley	+44 (011) 5555 9930	vdursley@grunnings.co.uk
Mr. Olivander	N/A	wandman27@hotmail.com
Stan Shunpike	N/A	stan@knightbusindustries.co.uk

So far, you know that your database will track people, and its fields will include any important attributes about a person. You might be tempted to have Name, Address, Phone Number, and Email Address as your fields—but you'd be making a mistake. What happens when you want to find all the people in Washington State? A search for Washington in the Address field will find them, as well as everyone on any Washington street and everyone in a town called Washington. Same goes for first and last name. You need a little experience and some careful thought to pick just the right fields. It's usually a bad move to have different bits of information in the same field. Instead, think about what elements—no matter how small—are important to how you'll search, sort, analyze, or otherwise access your records later. In database lingo, those bits of information are *individually significant*, and each one should get its own field.

For example, the first line of a person's address often contains several pieces of information: a street number, street name, direction (north, south, east, west), and an apartment, building, or suite number. Should these all be separate fields, or is one field enough to hold the whole street address? Are all these bits of data *individually significant*?

Usually, you can use just one field for the entire street address, since you never have reason to divide it into smaller elements and work with them separately. But suppose your work requires you to send different marketing materials to different people depending on which part of town they live in. You'd need to isolate people by street name (all the people on Hawthorne Street) or by ranges of street numbers (1000 to 1400 Elm). In this example, street name and house number are individually significant, and you'd want to create a separate field for each.

For your People database, you'll start off with fields to hold all the basics: Name, Phone Number, Street Address, City, State, Zip Code, and Email Address.

Defining Fields

As you know by now, every FileMaker database starts with a table. And since fields and tables are so fundamental to a database, FileMaker asks you to create them as soon as you start. FileMaker assumes your needs are pretty simple, and starts right off asking what fields you want in this single table.

1. **Choose File → New Database.**

   Up comes the New Database dialog box, just like the one in Figure 1-4. This time you're *not* going to start with a template. Instead, you're starting with a clean slate, so you can build a database that's all your own. (Can't you just feel the excitement?)

2. **Click "Create a new empty file," and then click OK.**

   FileMaker asks you what to name your new database and where to put it.

3. **Call this database *People* since that's what you're going to track.**

   In the Save As box (Mac OS X) or the "File name" box (Windows), type *People*. Then click Save.

   FileMaker creates the new file and automatically adds the .fp7 file name extension to your database name.

Note: That's not a typo. The extension .fp7 from FileMaker Pro 7 is the same for version 8. Good thing, too: It means people who still have version 7 can use your version 8 files just fine.

Just as promised, FileMaker asks you what fields you want—you see the Define Database dialog box shown in Figure 3-1. This little beauty is where you build and manage tables. There's a tab for the tables themselves, a tab for the fields in those tables, and a tab called Relationships, where you tell FileMaker how different tables work together. For now, you can simply ignore Tables and Relationships. Your one free table has already been created (it's called People, just like the database), and you're ready to give it some fields.

Column headers   Field list

Figure 3-1:
In the Define Database dialog box (File → Define → Database), the Fields tab is where you go to tell FileMaker about the fields in your database. The field list shows all the fields in the selected table.

Since you've already decided what fields you want, you need only to tell File-Maker. First, create a field to hold a person's first name:

1. **In the Field Name box, type** *First Name.*

   Every field has a name—you can choose almost anything you want. (For some guidelines, see the box on page 87.)

2. **In the Type pop-up menu, make sure Text is selected.**

   Every field has a *type*, which you'll learn about shortly. You're creating Text type fields right now.

3. **In the Comment box, type** *the person's first name.*

   Every field can have a comment to help you, the developer, remember what it's for. In this case, it's pretty obvious, so you could certainly leave the comment blank instead.

Note: Field comments don't show up when someone's *using* the database. They only show in this window. If you need extra information on the screen for the user to see, you'll want to *customize the layout* as explained in Chapter 4.

---

4. **Click Create.**

   FileMaker creates the First Name field and adds it to the field list.

Now that you've created the first field, the rest are a snap. Following the same steps as above, create Text fields with the following names:

- Last Name

- Phone Number

- Street Address

- City

- State

- Zip

- Email Address

When you're finished, the field list should look like Figure 3-2. (See page 103 to learn why your Zip field must be a text field.)

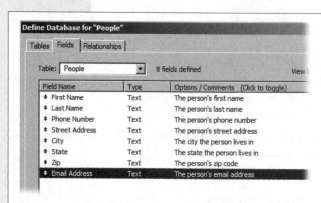

Figure 3-2:
Once you've defined the necessary fields, the field list should look like this example. You may not see the field comments in the third column—this column can show comments or options. To switch between these two possibilities, click the column header.

Changing a Field's Name

While you're here, you may as well try some more field-defining tricks. Say you want to change the name of the Zip field to Zip Code. It's very easy:

1. **Highlight the Zip field in the field list.**

   FileMaker fills in the Field Name, Type, and Comment boxes with the information about the Zip field.

2. **Change the field name to *Zip Code,* and then click Change.**

   When you have a field selected in the field list, the Change button becomes available. Instead of creating a *new* field called Zip Code, FileMaker just changes the name of the Zip field.

Duplicating a Field

The Duplicate button creates a new field that's an exact copy of what's selected in the field list. The new field's name says *Copy* at the end, which is the only difference.

Field Naming Conventions

I've seen databases with all kinds of funny field names. I've seen all caps, no spaces, lots of odd prefixes, and plenty of funny punctuation. How should I name fields?

People can get downright philosophical discussing the best way to name fields, and it seems everyone has an opinion. So how should you name your fields? Well, here are some of the common suggestions, as well as some discussion about why you would or wouldn't want to follow them.

Field names should have a prefix or suffix indicating their type.

FileMaker Pro developers often indicate the type of field in the field name. The reasoning is simple: You often have to pick a field from a list when you're building a database. All you see is its name, and you often want to know the type as well. In that spirit, people may name the First Name field something like "tFirst Name" where that "t" at the start means "text."

For most ordinary databases (in other words, not the really complicated stuff), you can usually figure out the type of a field by its name. For example, a field called Birth Date is probably a date field, while First Name is almost certainly text. You also don't often care about a field's type. For these reasons, you can usually ignore this advice and keep your field names prettier and more readable.

Field names should have a prefix or suffix indicating their purpose.

When a table starts to get a lot of fields, it can really be hard to keep track of which one does what. For example, a big database that keeps track of products might have dozens of fields.

Some would be about inventory levels (like Quantity on Hand, Quantity on Order, Quantity Desired, and Quantity Backordered). Others would be about pricing (like Base Price, Price for 10 or More, Price for 20 or More, Price for 30 or More, and so on). Some people like to come up with special codes to represent different types of information, to keep the field names more compact: QTY In Stock, QTY Order, QTY Desired, QTY Backorder, QTY Average. Again, for most databases this problem doesn't present itself very often. Usually the field names, if consistent, tend to develop their own English-language prefixes anyway (like all the Quantity fields). It's true, though, that field names can start to get long, and long names are more difficult to work with. In this case, abbreviations make good sense.

Some database programs aren't so flexible with names. To be safe, FileMaker field names should follow the same rules as everybody else.

This rule usually doesn't apply. Why settle for names like "FNAME" and "LNAME" when FileMaker happily accepts "First Name" and "Last Name" instead? If you actually need to create the same database in another program some day, you'll have a lot more to worry about than renaming the fields. You can just ignore this rule unless you simply prefer geeky-sounding names.

Fields can have many special options in addition to the name, type, and comment. You'll learn about them later in this chapter. Duplicate comes in handy when you want a second field with many options in common with the first. Just click Duplicate, and then change the new field's name.

Deleting a Field

As you define your fields, you may decide to name *all* your fields differently, say, or combine two fields into one. You may find it easier to delete some fields and start fresh than to painstakingly modify each one. Simply highlight the field you no longer want, and then click Delete.

Note: If you select a field and make modifications to any of the settings at the bottom of the Define Database window, FileMaker guesses you may want to click Change. If you then try to select *another* field (which would overwrite the changes you've entered), FileMaker asks if you want to Save first. Clicking Save is the same as clicking Change: It updates the selected field with the new settings.

Reordering the Field List

Now that you have several fields, you might decide you don't like the *order* they're listed in. Perhaps you want all the address fields first, or maybe you're a big fan of reverse-alphabetical lists. You can rearrange the fields in the field list any time you want.

To *manually* arrange the fields, just drag the little up-and-down arrows beside a field name. Figure 3-3 shows you how.

Figure 3-3:
This series of pictures shows how you can manually rearrange fields in the field list. When you mouse over the up-and-down arrows to the left of the word Email, the pointer changes to a new symbol that lets you know you can drag the item up or down (top right). As you drag, other fields in the list move out of the way to make room (bottom left). Use this maneuver to move all kinds of things in FileMaker.

If you'd rather let FileMaker order them for you, make a selection from the "View by" pop-up menu. This menu gives you four choices:

- **Creation order** is the order in which the fields were originally created. Sometimes you have a lot of fields, and you just can't remember what one of them is called. If you *do* remember that you created it relatively recently, you can view by creation order and look for it near the end of the list.

- **Field name** orders the fields alphabetically by name. This view is an easy way to find the field you want when you *do* know its name.

- **Field type** groups fields of the same type together. It puts the different types in the same order as they appear in the Type pop-up menu: text fields first, then number fields, then date fields, and so on. If you know you're looking for a calculation field (and that's all you know), View by type can help.

- **Custom order** is the order you put things in when you drag fields around in the list. Since you sometimes spend a lot of time getting the fields arranged in just the right way, you might be afraid to sometimes sort them by name instead, ruining your perfect custom order. But that's not the case. After viewing them by name, you can easily switch *back* to custom order and see your perfect arrangement again.

Warning: If you're one of those funny people who like to keep everything organized *just right*, beware this classic bugaboo: If you sort the field list another way (like by name) and *then* move a field manually, the *new* order becomes your custom order. You'll lose all your hours of hard work. Thus, once you've set up a Custom order just the way you want it, make sure you switch *back* to it before you move any fields.

You can also click the Field Name or Type column headers to sort the list by that column. If you want to *reverse* the sort order, click the Sort toggle button. This button is at the very right edge of the column headers, just above the scroll bar. Clicking the Options/Comments column header doesn't sort; instead, it switches what you see in that column. Normally FileMaker shows you the options for each field. Clicking the header shows you comments instead.

Printing Field Definitions

Finally, if you click Print, FileMaker prints all the details about the fields you've selected. The printout resembles the field list, except that it's expanded to make room for *everything* about a field. You might print such a list if you want to keep your field names and types handy while you're working with your database, or if you need to send a list of fields to an associate so she can send you the right information.

Tip: You have to select at least one field for the Print button to become clickable. Then, when you click Print, you'll get details for any field that's highlighted. To print just a few, Ctrl+click (⌘-click on the Mac) each field you want to print. If you want a printout of *all* the fields in the table, first select one field, then choose Edit → Select All. Now every field is selected, and the Print button prints them all.

GEM IN THE ROUGH

Use the Keyboard

You can get to almost everything in the Define Database window's Fields tab from the keyboard alone. If you are a speed freak, you can almost entirely avoid the mouse. You can do these things with the keyboard:

As usual, on Windows you can use the Tab key to move among buttons, text boxes, and pop-up menus. Unfortunately, FileMaker doesn't honor Mac OS X's Full Keyboard Access settings.

On Mac OS X, you can press the Tab key to move between the Field Name, Comment, and field list.

While the field list is active, the up and down arrow keys select the next and previous fields.

If you hold down Ctrl (⌘) while pressing the arrow keys, you move the selected field up or down in the list.

Each field type has a keyboard shortcut—look in the Type pop-up menu to see them—that you can use instead of selecting the type from the list.

To see the field options dialog box for the selected field, press Ctrl+O (⌘-O).

To delete the selected field, press the Delete key. In any of FileMaker's alert message windows, you can press the first letter of a button name to click that button. When it asks if you're sure you want to delete the field, press D.

Press the Escape key to close the Define Database window and throw away all your changes.

Now just click OK. FileMaker adds your fields to the database window. Congratulations! You've just built a database. It isn't pretty—as Figure 3-4 proves—but it works. The status area shows that your database has one record. Go ahead and edit this record and create some more, using any of the techniques you learned in Chapter 1. You can even find, sort, print, and Find/Replace in this simple database.

Field Types

Every field you create has a *type*, which determines what kind of information it holds. All the fields you just created are *text* fields—they're designed to hold text of any kind. You've also been introduced to container fields, which hold pictures, movies, sounds, and files. But FileMaker actually has eight different field types, each designed for something a little different. For just a moment, you'll step away from the database you're building to get a brief introduction to each field type. You'll actually use these field types in various databases throughout the rest of this book.

You specify the field type when you create a field by choosing it from the Type pop-up menu. The pop-up menu also shows handy keyboard shortcuts for each field type, so you can quickly define a series of fields without clicking the mouse.

Text

Text fields are the most common type—they hold any kind of text information like a name, phone number, or email message. A text field can store up to two gigabytes of information, so there's plenty of room for any realistic purpose. Whatever you type into a text field shows up just as you typed it, and you can use any of the formatting options described in Chapter 2.

Number

As if it isn't obvious, *number* fields hold numbers. Like a text field, you can type in just about anything you want, but as soon as you leave the field, FileMaker does its best to turn your data into a number, and that's what it shows you. What's not so obvious is that not all numerical values are numbers. Use a number field if you're going to be performing *math* with the numbers in your database. But for things like Zip codes and telephone numbers, use text fields instead. See the box on page 103 for the full explanation.

Numbers can be very large or very small, and they're *very* precise. The actual limits are thus:

- Numbers must be between 10^{400} and -10^{400}. If you're counting something reasonable—say, the number of protons in the universe—you'll be just fine.

- Numbers are precise to 10^{-400}. In other words, you can have 400 digits to the right of the decimal point.

- You get 400 significant digits in all. If you don't know what that means, ask a high-school student. They know everything.

- Only 400 digits are indexed in all, significant or otherwise. So if you're searching for numbers, you have a little less precision to work with.

FileMaker's number-handling capability is absolutely top-notch. If your work requires very precise mathematics, you'll be thrilled. For example, FileMaker is *much* more precise with numbers than, say, Microsoft Excel.

You can enter numbers in FileMaker as you would in most any program. Type the number and any symbols that define it, like a negative sign or a decimal point. You can also use *scientific notation*. For example, if you have a burning desire to count the air molecules in your living room, you can put 6.02E23 into a number field. That means 6.02 times 10^{23} and it's a lot easier to type than 60,200,000,000,000,000,000,000,000. Of course the exponent part (after the E) can be negative if really small numbers make your socks go up and down.

Date

At the risk of being obvious, a *date* field holds a date. FileMaker thinks of dates in numerical form by month, day, and year. You can put just about any punctuation *between* these numbers, but most people use a slash, a dash, or a period. For instance, 2/25/1975, 2-25-1975, and 2.25.1975 are all valid dates. If you type it in the wrong way, you see the error message in Figure 3-5.

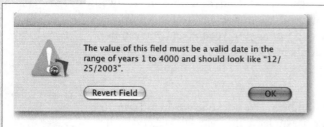

The value of this field must be a valid date in the range of years 1 to 4000 and should look like "12/25/2003".

Revert Field   OK

Figure 3-5:
If FileMaker doesn't like the date the way you entered it, it tells you so. The message ends with an example of a correctly formatted date.

Tip: If your date's in the current calendar year, you can save time by typing just the day and month. File-Maker fills in the current year for you. Don't add that second puntuation mark, though, or FileMaker will bark at you.

FileMaker accepts dates from the year 1 (AD) to the year 4000, but since most databases don't have *that* long a lifespan, the program lets you enter a two-digit year and takes its best guess as to which century you're talking about. Here's how it works: If you type a two digit year, FileMaker tries putting *20* in front of it. If that year is *more* than 30 years from now, FileMaker assumes you really meant 19-something and adds the *19* for you. Otherwise, it adds *20* for the first two digits. For example, if it's 2005 and you put *34* in for the year, you get 2034, but if you enter *36*, you get 1936. Confusing? Avoid all this runaround by entering four-digit years.

UP TO SPEED

System Formats

The way FileMaker wants to see numbers, dates, and times depends on how you've configured your computer. In Windows, you configure in the Date and Time control panel. In Mac OS X's System Preferences, you use the International pane. When you create a database, FileMaker notes what formats the computer is set for and remembers them. If you then open the same database on a computer that's configured differently, you'll get a message asking if you want to use the *system* format, or the format stored with the database.

If you don't want this message to appear, you can go to the File Options dialog box and pre-select your preference.

1. Choose File → File Options. This window lets you control a handful of settings for the current data-base.

2. Select the Text tab.

In this tab, the Data Entry section lets you control how the database handles varying format settings. The first two radio buttons prevent the message box from showing up. The third is for when you *want* FileMaker to ask every time.

FileMaker Pro

The date and time formats associated with "People" are different than the current system settings. What date and time formats would you like to use?

File's settings   System's settings

Time

You can probably guess what goes into a *time* field. Time fields actually serve two purposes, though. First, you can enter a time of day, like 4:30 PM or 1:27:03 AM. But you can also enter a *duration* instead, like 123:38:22 (meaning 123 hours, 38 minutes, 22 seconds). Even though this sequence isn't a valid time of day, it's an acceptable time value.

Times are easy to enter. They always go in like so: hours:minutes:seconds, and the seconds can also have a decimal part for fractions of a second. If you don't need seconds, you can just type in hours:minutes. Likewise, if you don't need minutes either, you can just enter a number of hours.

If you're entering a time of day, you can put an AM or PM after the time if you want, or you can use 24 hour notation. Either way, FileMaker can fix weird time entries, like 1:82:17, for you. In this case, you *can't* have 82 minutes because that's the same as 1 hour, 22 minutes, so FileMaker would change it to its more normal equivalent: 2:22:17. To have FileMaker check and repair time values, apply a time *format* to your time fields (page 240).

Note: When entering time values, you *always* start with hours. If you're trying to enter just 12 minutes, 37 seconds, you have to enter *00:12:37 or 0:12:37* so FileMaker doesn't think you mean 12 *hours*.

Time values are also quite precise. If you're recording track event times for your school, you can enter *00:00:27.180* for 27 seconds, 180 milliseconds. You can put up to six digits to the right of the decimal point.

Timestamp

A *timestamp* field is kind of like a date field and a time field combined. It holds *both* a date *and* a time. You use this kind of field to record when an event occurred, or when it will occur. If you want, you can create two fields, one for the date and one for the time. But FileMaker has all kinds of special abilities when it works with timestamp values that you'd have to otherwise try to figure out yourself. For example, it can figure out how much time has passed between two timestamp values with a simple calculation (End Timestamp – Start Timestamp). If you use separate date and time fields, the necessary calculation is anything but simple. If something happens on a specific date and time, you should use a timestamp field for it.

Timestamps support the same less-than-a-second accuracy as time fields. They show up as a date followed by a time with a space in between. All the rules for date and time entry apply: 2/25/1975 2:45 AM.

Container

You've already learned what a *container* field can do (page 68). It holds pictures, sounds, QuickTime multimedia files, and ordinary files. Containers can hold up to two gigabytes, just like text fields.

Calculation and summary

Unlike the other field types discussed so far, *calculation* and *summary* fields don't hold your stuff at all. Instead, they make up their own values based on the settings you give them. For calculation fields, you can specify a special *formula* that it uses to determine its value. For instance, if you had a field called Birth Date, you could create a calculation field that shows the person's age. The Age field automatically updates to stay correct as time goes by, so you don't have to change it. You'll learn all about calculations in Part 3.

Summary fields are the strangest of all. They aren't even associated with a record. Instead, their value depends on the values of other fields across some set of records. For instance, a summary field could show you the number of people in the database who are from California, or the total dollar value of all outstanding invoices for a customer. You'll learn about summary fields in Chapter 6.

Advanced Field Options

At this point your database is simple, but entirely usable. In fact, you could stop reading right now, and you'd be able to build super-simple databases to solve all kinds of problems. But FileMaker's Define Fields dialog box has lots more settings to make your database even smarter, easier to use, and more consistent.

Auto-Enter Options

All your fields are completely empty when you create a new record. Often, but not always, that's what you want—a completely blank slate. With FileMaker, you have a handful of other possibilities. Suppose most of your clients are from North Dakota, for example. It would be nice if FileMaker could put ND in the State field for you—you can always change it later. In fact, this situation is so common that every field has a group of *Auto-Enter* settings where you can tell FileMaker exactly what to put in the field for you (Figure 3-6).

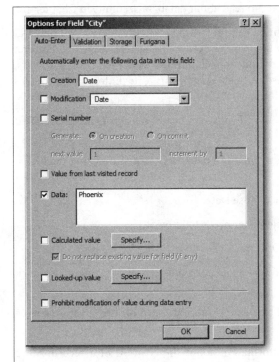

Figure 3-6:
FileMaker has several options for automatically entering information into a field. Most happen just once: when the record is created. The Modification, "Calculated value," and "Looked-up value" options, however, can automatically enter information in fields at other times as well.

When you first create a field, all the Auto-Enter options are turned off, so the field stays empty. To turn one on, follow these steps:

1. **Choose File → Define → Database.**

   The Define Database window appears.

2. **Click the Fields tab. In the field list, select any field and then click Options.**

   Even quicker, just double-click the field. The Field Options dialog box emerges.

3. **In this window, click the Auto-Enter tab.**

   Now you plainly see all FileMaker's Auto-Enter options.

Creation values

When a record is *first created*, FileMaker can enter some information about the circumstances under which it was created. You can record the date, time, or timestamp at the moment of creation.

The Name option refers to the name of the person who created the record. FileMaker gets this information from your operating system. On most systems, you must log into the computer before you can run programs. FileMaker uses the name of the system account you logged in with.

The Account Name, by contrast, refers to the FileMaker account you used when you logged into the *database*. You can read about database accounts in Chapter 16.

In your People database, it might be helpful to keep track of the date you first add each record, so you can tell how long you've been working with someone. You can even use this information in Find mode to seek out new customers, old customers, or customers you met on a Tuesday. FileMaker has an Auto-Enter option for this very purpose. Here's how to set it up:

1. **In the Define Database window's Fields tab, type *Creation Date* in the Field Name box.**

   Since the date the record was created is a piece of information being tracked, it needs to go in a field.

2. **From the Type pop-up menu, choose Date.**

   This field holds a date, and FileMaker needs to know it.

3. **Click Create, and then click Options.**

   The Create button adds the field to the list and selects it, so you can click Options right away.

4. **In the Field Options dialog box's Auto-Enter tab, turn on the Creation checkbox.**

   This setting lets you store information about the creation of a record. Since you're working on a date field, only the Date option is available in the associated pop-up menu.

5. **From the Creation pop-up menu, choose Date.**

   In this case, you want the date the record is created. Figure 3-7 shows the finished product.

Figure 3-7:
When you set the field options above, the dialog box shows you've turned on the Creation Auto-Enter option and selected Date. In English, that means you've told FileMaker to automatically record the date you add a new person to your database.

6. **Turn on the "Prohibit modification of value during data entry" checkbox.**

   Because this field *always* automatically gets the right value, you don't need to change it in Browse mode. Editing this data would probably be a mistake, so you can tell FileMaker not to allow it.

7. **Click OK, and then, in the Define Database window, OK again.**

   You're now ready to test your new field. The existing record won't have the current date in it, because it was created before you made the Creation Date field. Create a record and see how FileMaker automatically enters the current date.

Modification values

Sometimes you want to keep track of when you last changed the data in your records. FileMaker can track the same information when you *modify* a record as when you create one. So if you adjust an interest rate in your database, for example, you can tell how long ago the change occurred. Furthermore, because records can change often, more than once a day even, you may need to know what *time* a record changed, not just the date. The Timestamp field is just the ticket. Here are the steps:

1. **In the Define Database window's Fields tab, type *Modification Timestamp* in the Field Name box. From the Type pop-up menu, choose Timestamp.**

   Every field needs a name and a type, so you have to get those details out of the way first.

2. **Click Create, and then click Options.**

   The Field Options dialog box returns.

3. **In the Field Options dialog box's Auto-Enter tab, turn on the Modification checkbox.**

Now you can use the Modification pop-up menu.

4. **From that pop-up menu, choose Timestamp.**

As with record creation, you can have FileMaker enter any of several values when someone modifies the record. In this case, you want the program to make a Timestamp.

5. **Turn on the "Prohibit modification of value during data entry" checkbox.**

Just like before, you don't want this field edited manually.

6. **Click OK, and then, in the Define Database window, OK again.**

You're now ready to test your new field. Create a record and see how FileMaker automatically enters the current date.

Unlike the Data and Creation Auto-Enter options, the Modification setting affects the value of the field *after* you create a record. This option updates the value every time the record changes. In fact, if you don't select the "Prohibit modification of value during data entry" option, the Modification setting would overwrite whatever you type in your Modification Timestamp field, since the timestamp occurs when you commit the record (see the box on page 99).

Note: If it sounds strange that you can use the "Prohibit modification of value during data entry" checkbox on a Modification field, never fear. FileMaker's Auto-Enter mechanism isn't considered *data entry*. Other times when records can change outside of data entry are when you're importing records (Chapter 17) or setting fields via a script (Chapter 13).

Serial number

You learned in Chapter 1 that record numbers can change as you delete or sort the records. If you want to assign a unique number to your record that always stays the same, you can use the "Serial number" Auto-Enter option. In the Field Options dialog box, you can specify the "next value," which is the value FileMaker uses for the next record that you create. The "increment by" value tells FileMaker how to change the number each time someone creates a record. For example, suppose "next value" is 1, and "increment by" is 2. If you create three records, FileMaker numbers them 1, 3, and 5.

You can specify non-numerical values for "next value" if you want. For example, if your field is a text field, you can put INV00001 in the "next value" box. Your first record would then get INV00001, followed by INV00002 and INV00003.

The Generate radio buttons under "Serial number" control *when* the serial number is assigned. If you select "On creation," then as soon as you create a record, FileMaker puts the serial number in the field. If you then decide you don't want the record, and you delete it right away, that serial number value has been *used up*, and the next record you make will have a new value. If you instead select "On commit," the serial number doesn't show up in the field until you exit the record. In other words, you can delete before you exit without using up any serial numbers.

Embracing Commitment

The word *commit* refers to a semi-technical database concept. When you create a new record, you haven't actually added a record to the table yet. Instead, you get a blank record on the screen, and the information you enter is stored in a temporary working area in your computer's memory. When you *exit* the record, the information in that working area is *committed*—or written—to the database.

When you edit a record, the same principle holds: As soon as you enter the record, it's copied to the working area. While you edit it, you're actually editing this copy. When you exit the record, FileMaker puts your edited copy back in the table. In general, think of *committing* a record as the same thing as *exiting* a record. When you exit the record, you commit it.

You'll use serial numbers most often when connecting multiple tables (Part 4). Serial numbers also come in handy when the items in your database don't have a convenient name. In a database of invoices, it can be tough to talk about one particular invoice ("You know, that one we sent last Thursday. No, not that one, the *other* one"). People generally use serial numbers to clarify things.

Value from last visited record

For some databases, you need a lot of repetitive data entry. If you take a trip to Los Angeles, you might meet 12 people who should go into your People database. When you get home, you have to type them all in. Rather than type *Los Angeles* and *California* over and over again, you can tell FileMaker to automatically fill the City and State fields for you. If you turn on "Value from last visited record," you'll only need to type *Los Angeles* and *California* once. When you choose Records → New Record, FileMaker copies the city and state from the current record into the new record for you.

1. **Choose File → Define → Database.**

   The Define Database window reappears. If the Fields tab isn't selected, click it.

2. **Select the City field, and then click Options.**

   The Field Options dialog box puts in an appearance. With this window, you can tweak several options for each individual field.

3. **Click the Auto-Enter tab, if necessary.**

   You see the same window shown in Figure 3-6 above.

4. **Turn on "Value from last visited record."**

There are no additional settings for this option: Just turn it on. Here, you *don't* want to turn on the "Prohibit modification of value during data entry" option, because you want to keep the ability to change what's in the City field.

5. **Click OK. In the Define Database dialog box, select the State field, and then click Options.**

This time you want to auto-enter *California*. Make the necessary settings and click OK.

6. **Click OK again to dismiss the Define Database dialog box.**

You're back in your database. Notice that the City and State fields didn't get the new information, though. The Auto-Enter options tell FileMaker what to put in fields only when you *create* a record.

Now when you choose Records → New Record, the new record shows the correct city and state.

Tip: "Value from last visited" record is really cool when you're entering a bunch of records one right after another, but it can cause confusion if you poke around in your database before you start creating records. FileMaker thinks of your "last record" as the last record you *clicked in* or *opened*, not the last one you looked at. (See page 17 for the deal on opening records.) So make sure you open the record you want the value to come from just before you create a new record.

Data

This is the simplest Auto-Enter option. It puts some unchanging piece of information into the field every time you create a record. You can specify text, date, time, and timestamp values by entering the information just as you would type it in a field.

If 99 percent of your associates are from your home town, it makes sense to have your database automatically enter your city and state for you.

Calculated value

Sometimes you want to take advantage of the power of calculations, but you also want to be able to change the field if you need to. Since calculation fields always create their own (unchangeable) value, they don't work. Instead, you can create a normal field and have FileMaker automatically enter a calculated value into it. You can then change the value later if you want. You'll learn how to define calculations in Part 3.

Looked-up value

As you've already heard, FileMaker lets you connect multiple tables together in various ways. When you've done that, you can tell FileMaker to automatically fetch a value from some record in another table and plop it in the field. This feature is called *lookup*, and you'll learn about it in Part 4.

Prohibit modification of value during data entry

Usually, when you use an Auto-Enter option, it's just to save you some typing. You may end up needing to change the value to something else, though. But sometimes the value is automatically entered, and it should stay that way forever. The Creation and Modification options most often fall into this category. If you're trying to keep track of when the record was created, there's no reason to ever change the date field. If you turn on the "Prohibit modification of value during data entry" checkbox, FileMaker doesn't let you change the field's value at all.

Validation Options

Auto-enter options tell FileMaker to enter some things for you. *Validation* options sort of do the opposite: They tell FileMaker what *not* to let you put in a field. You decide what kind of information *should* go there, and FileMaker warns you when you enter something that doesn't look right. In your People database, you might want to make sure the Zip Code field always looks like a real Zip code.

1. **Open the Field Options dialog box for the Zip Code field.**

   You should be an expert at this by now. In the list, just double-click the field.

2. **Select the Validation tab.**

   As you can see in Figure 3-8, you have a lot of choices when it comes to field validation.

3. **Turn on the "Strict data type" checkbox, and from its pop-up menu, select Numeric Only.**

   These settings tell FileMaker to expect only numerals in this field.

4. **Click the "Maximum number of characters" checkbox and enter 5.**

   You can do better than just require numbers. The option tells FileMaker to accept no more than five digits in the Zip Code field.

5. **Turn on the "Display custom message if validation fails" checkbox.**

   FileMaker automatically shows a message when a value in a field doesn't match the validation settings, but it's often more considerate to give the message in your own words. That's what this setting does.

6. **In the text box below this checkbox, type** *The Zip code you entered doesn't look right. Are you sure that's what you want?*

FileMaker displays this message if the validation fails. (For a little guidance on what these messages should say, see the box on page 104.)

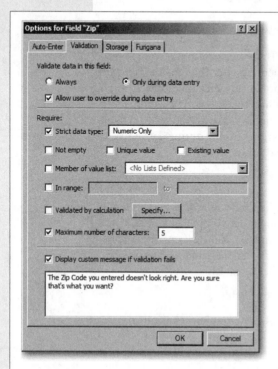

Figure 3-8:
The Validation tab in the Field Options dialog box lets you check for errors before placing information into fields. You can, for example, make sure only numbers are entered, or that the first name is no more than 30 characters. You can apply as many validation rules as you want, and FileMaker checks each one whenever someone modifies the field.

7. **Click OK and OK again.**

You're back in Browse mode and ready to test. Try entering too many characters into the Zip Code field, and you'll see your message when you exit the field, as shown in Figure 3-9.

Figure 3-9:
If you enter a bogus Zip code in your database, you'll see your custom message like this. Click Yes to keep the invalid Zip code. If you want to fix it, click No and you'll be back in the field. If you click Revert Field, the field value changes back to what it was before you started editing.

Note: It's true that the validation settings you selected in the previous tutorial aren't perfect. They don't allow Zip+4 codes (46077-1039), but they would let you enter something like *123,* which isn't a valid Zip code at all. To handle such nuances of the simple Zip code, you need to use the "Validate by calculation" option, which lets you set much more specific validation standards. You'll learn about FileMaker's calculation features in Part 3.

FREQUENTLY ASKED QUESTION

Numbers and Text

You have to set an awful lot of validation options to make sure people enter only Zip codes into a text field. Can't I just make the Zip Code field a number field instead?

No, you can't. Zip codes are numerical values, but they're not *numbers*, and that makes a big difference as far as File-Maker is concerned. For example, number fields don't recognize leading zeros—like the ones at the beginning of 00501 and scores of other perfectly valid Zip codes. If you enter *00501* in a number field, FileMaker thinks you meant to type the number *501* and helpfully removes those extra zeros when you exit the record. That's just not going to get your mail to Holtsville, New York anytime soon.

The Numeric Only validation option lets the field stay a Text field (which preserves all entered characters), but still accept only numerical digits on entry, which is exactly what you want for a Zip code.

Some people also assume that a phone number should be stored in a number field. Wrong again. Phone numbers contain not only numerals but also dashes, parentheses, and sometimes other special characters—all mere text to FileMaker. As a general rule, only make a field a Number field if you might have to perform some math with it. You'll learn all about using fields in calculations in Chapter 9.

Now that you know how to set them, you can tailor validation options to all kinds of situations. Here are your many choices in greater detail:

When to perform validation

The first two choices let you control when validation is actually performed. Normally, you only want to validate what you put into fields when you're typing in Browse mode. If you *import* data (more on that in Chapter 17) or enter information from a *script* (Part 5), FileMaker completely bypasses the validation step. If you want to be strict about it, select the Always radio button under "Validate data in this field." FileMaker does as promised: it *always* performs the validation, even during automated processes.

Overriding validation

In the Zip code example, you were given the option of accepting a bogus Zip code if you wanted to. FileMaker simply *warned* you that things didn't look right. It was up to you to decide if it should be fixed. If you uncheck "Allow user to override during data entry," FileMaker takes away the choice. Instead, it simply refuses to accept invalid data.

Validation Requirements

To validate a Zip code (page 101), you asked FileMaker to accept only numbers and allow only five digits.

UP TO SPEED

Validation Messages

Custom validation messages (like the one in Figure 3-9), give you a chance to communicate directly with whoever uses your database. If you don't provide a custom message, when you set up field validation, FileMaker uses a generic message of its own. This message dryly explains the validation option that's being violated, but may not be much help to whoever's using your database. Once you understand how FileMaker's validation messages work, try to improve upon them. You'll make your database a pleasure to use and give it professional quality.

For example, if you've turned on the "Allow user to override during data entry" option, FileMaker asks if the user wants to allow the value anyway (shown in the top image). Otherwise, it tells them to fix the field (shown in the bottom image). In either case, the message box includes a Revert Field button. This button takes away any changes someone's made to the field so that it returns to its previous *valid* value, but how's the user supposed to know that?

Instead, phrase the custom message as a question where Yes means "I want to keep what I've entered" and No means "I'll change it." When it shows your message, File-Maker automatically provides the Yes and No buttons, along with the Revert button.

If you turn off the ability to override the validation and you're showing a custom message, FileMaker replaces Yes and No buttons with just an OK button. In this case, the message should *not* be in question form. Instead, it should simply tell them what's wrong.

Finally, if the field value violates *several* validation options, the user must click Yes to a message about each one before FileMaker allows the value. Since all these error messages are annoying, you're better off using a custom message that explains all requirements.

But data type and character count are just two of the eight kinds of validations FileMaker has up its sleeve. In the Validation tab of the Field Options dialog box, there are six more checkboxes. Most of them work much the same way: They check what you type against some specific condition. But one option, "Validate by calculation," offers a completely flexible way to describe exactly what you're looking for. Unfortunately, to use it, you need to learn how to perform *calculations* (mathematical or logical formulas) with your FileMaker data. They're covered in Part 3. Until then, here's what the other options do:

Strict data type

This option lets you pick four specific validations. You've already seen Numeric Only, which insists every character in your text field be a number. 4-Digit Year Date tells FileMaker to expect a date value, and that the year must be four digits long (2006 instead of 06). This choice works with text, date, and timestamp fields.

Finally, Time of Day tells FileMaker that only time values that represent real clock times are acceptable. Since time fields can hold any number of hours, minutes, and seconds, you can enter something like *237:34:11* to mean "237 hours, 34 minutes, 11 seconds." But if the field is *supposed* to be the time of your lunch meeting, that value doesn't make sense. This option prevents its entry. It applies to text and time fields (Timestamp fields *always* require a time of day).

Not empty

If you insist on having *something* in a field, select the "Not empty" validation option. That makes FileMaker complain if you try to exit the record without entering a value. This option is the only simple validation option for container fields.

Unique

The "Unique value" option prevents you from putting the same thing in a field for two different records. For example, if you set this option for the First Name field in your database, you can't enter two people with the name "Bill." You would typically use this option for ID numbers, usernames, or other things that are supposed to uniquely identify a single person.

Existing value

"Existing value" is just the opposite of "Unique value;" it doesn't allow any value that isn't already in that field on some record in the database. This option usually doesn't make much sense unless you turn it on *after* you've entered a representative amount of information into the database. Otherwise, the first record you enter would dictate the field value for every record created thereafter.

Member of value list

You often have a field that can contain any one of a predetermined set of things. In your database, for example, you might want to ensure that the State field contains one of the 50 real states. This is where the "Member of value list" option comes in.

FileMaker lets you define something called *value lists*. These lists are, quite simply, lists of values: Red, Green, Blue; or Small, Medium, Large, for instance. You can make as many value lists as you want.

Note: You can see a value list in action in your Contact Management database. Just click the Address Type field. The items in this list let you mark the kind of address you're storing in each record.

---

1. **Open the Field Options dialog box for the State field.**

   Your mouse is probably able to get there by itself by now.

2. **On the Validation tab, turn on the "Member of value list" checkbox. Then, from the associated pop-up menu, choose Define Value Lists.**

   FileMaker shows you the Define Value Lists dialog box.

3. **Click New.**

   FileMaker creates a new empty value lists and shows it to you in the Edit Value List window (shown in Figure 3-10).

Figure 3-10:
A value list lets you specify exactly what entries a field can accept. This value list defines the 50 states in the U.S.

4. **In the Value List Name field, enter *States*.**

   Each value list has a unique name.

5. **Make sure the "Use custom values" radio button is selected, and enter state names in the list box under it.**

As usual, you'll need to ignore several available options for now, and focus on "Use custom values." Each item in a value list must be on its own line. You can paste into this box as well, so if you find a list of states on the Internet, you can save yourself a lot of typing.

6. **Click OK to close the Edit Value List window.**

The Define Value Lists window now shows your new value list.

7. **Click OK again to close the Define Value Lists dialog box.**

Back in the Field Options window, the value list you just created should now be selected in the "Member of value list" pop-up menu. If it isn't, select it now.

8. **Click OK to dismiss the Field Options and Define Database dialog boxes.**

You can now try entering a value in the State field that *isn't* in the value list. FileMaker will let you know you've messed up.

Note: Value lists are actually used for more than just validation. You'll learn how to create and edit them *outside* this dialog box in Chapter 6. You'll learn other uses for value lists throughout the book.

In range

"In range" lets you specify a minimum and maximum allowable value. FileMaker then protests if you enter a value outside this range. This method works for all the standard data types, since they all have a concept of order. For example, if you specify a range of *Adam* to *Johnson* for a text field, validation fails for *Schultz*. Range validation is most common, however, with number, date, and time values. You might require the Age field to be between 0 and 100, for example, or the Birth Date to be between 1/1/1900 and 12/31/2003.

Maximum number of characters

As previously mentioned, this option enforces a limit on the number of characters you can enter into a field. FileMaker fields can normally hold a huge amount of text. This option lets you keep things under control. You can use it to require specific kinds of information, like the five digit Zip code above, or to prevent abuse of the database (by, for example, limiting the First Name field to 30 characters so someone doesn't get carried away and paste *The Complete Works of Shakespeare* into it).

Storage Options

It's time to get a little technical. Sorry. In the Field Options dialog box (Figure 3-11), the Storage tab lets you control aspects of a field related to the nebulous concept of *storage*. Like a highly organized attic, FileMaker both holds onto your information *and* makes it easy to take out again. There are lots of details involved in how FileMaker compartmentalizes and maintains that information.

WORKAROUND WORKSHOP

Minimum Number of Characters

For some strange reason, FileMaker doesn't provide a simple validation option to enforce a minimum number of characters in a field. You often need to limit characters, but you have to dip into validation calculations to meet it. Luckily, the calculation to do it is really simple. Here's a validation calculation for requiring *at least* five characters in the field:

Length(Field Name) >= 5

To use this calculation, turn on the "Validate by calculation" option. In the window that appears, type this calculation. You'll have to change "Field Name" to the name of your field. If you want a number other than five, simply change it in the calculation. When you're done, click OK.

If you want *more than* five characters, change >= to simply >. If you want *exactly* five characters (no more, no less) then change >= to =. You don't need a lot of expertise for this calculation. (See Chapter 9 for much more on using calculations.)

You can actually tell FileMaker to store only one value in a field, no matter how many records you have, or to allow one field to hold *more than one value* in each record. Strange, but true. Also, you get control over *indexing,* as described in the next section.

Figure 3-11:
The Storage tab is where various behind-the-scenes field settings lurk. Here, you can make a field global so it has only one value for the whole table, or make it repeating so it has several values in each record. Usually, you'll set options like these when you're defining a database, not when using one day-to-day.

Global storage

"A field that uses global storage contains only one value that is shared across all records." So says the explanatory text in the dialog box, but what's that in English? When you use the "Use global storage" option, everything you learned about tables goes out the window. A *global field* isn't a column in the table at all. Rather, it's a single bit of storage that can hold one value, no matter how many records you have. In other words, if you change the contents of a global field on one record, FileMaker instantly changes it in every other record as well. Now every record has the same value for that field.

Suppose your company is planning a move or name change in the future, but you aren't ready to change your database just yet. In that case, you can make your company's name, address and phone number fields use global storage. You can even make a global container field and pop your company logo into it. Then, you'd just make your database's layouts display those *fields* instead of the actual company information. (See Chapter 4 for details on designing layouts.) When the company makes its move, you just place the new name, address, logo, and so on into your global fields, and *voila!* FileMaker changes them across the board.

If you use global fields for information that you might use throughout your database, you don't even have to remember every place you put the company information. When you update a global field, FileMaker finds every place that field shows up and makes the change consistently.

***

Note: There's an exception to everything, and indeed there's one situation where global fields don't instantly change everywhere for everybody. For details on how globals operate in shared files, see the box on page 654.

***

Repeating fields

A field can only hold a single value, right? Erm…well, not really. If you want to, you can turn any field into a *repeating field*. These fields can hold more than one value, each kept in a separate spot (and each shown in its own little field in the database window). In the Field Options dialog box, you specify the maximum number of values the field can hold. When would you want to use this limit? Almost never. See the box on page 110 for more info.

***

Note: The last tab in the Field Options dialog box applies only to Japanese text entry, and isn't covered in this book. Fortunately, should you ever need to add furigana to your kanji, you can read how right in the dialog box.

***

Indexing

Since you're reading this book, you're probably hoping FileMaker can help you search through volumes of information faster than you could do it yourself, especially as your database grows from a simple electronic Rolodex to a humungous mailing list. When you're looking for the three people out of 5,000 whose birthday is February 29, FileMaker can find them in an instant because it doesn't really look at the birthday field on each record one-by-one. Instead, it uses the field's *index* to skip straight to the appropriate records. It's much as you'd use a book's index to go directly to the pages that mention the topic you're interested in, rather than skimming every single page in the book. .

WORKAROUND WORKSHOP

Repeating Fields Aren't Your Friends

With very few exceptions, repeating fields cause more trouble than they're worth. The truth is, they only exist because years ago when FileMaker was a youngster, it wasn't a *relational* database. That means it didn't have any way to tie multiple tables together so that they can share information and make connections between things in each table. When you were learning about how to pick fields, you were introduced to the concept that you need a table for each kind of thing you're keeping track of. In a database that's not relational (called a *flat file database*), there's no good way to track lots of different kinds of things in one database, so FileMaker had repeating fields to let you store more than one thing in a single record. For example, you could have an Invoice table with one record for each invoice. The individual items on the invoice need a place to go too, so you would create repeating fields. That way, each individual invoice could hold, say, 20 items.

But this is the 21st century, and FileMaker's come a long way. Nobody in her right mind would build an invoice database that way anymore (they'd hook together two tables instead—see Part 4). Since FileMaker had repeating fields ten years ago, and since it's really friendly about supporting all your ancient databases, it still supports repeating fields today.

That said, repeating fields are *occasionally* useful when writing calculations (Part 3) and scripts (Part 5). Other than that, you should avoid them like the plague for a few reasons:

- Repeating fields are uniquely FileMaker. If you want to take data out of your database and put it in some other program (like a spreadsheet, or another database program) repeating fields could make an easy job one serious pain in the neck. Likewise for getting data from other programs *into* repeating fields.

- If your database is accessed by Web pages or other outside programs, repeating fields make everything more complicated.

Repeating fields are inherently limited: If you define a field to have 20 repetitions, you get 20 spots for data. If you need less, you're looking at empty fields all the time. If you need more, you have to modify your fields and make room in the window. A relational database, on the other hand, can grow and shrink as needed without modifying the database structure at all.

Note: FileMaker uses a field's index in other ways too. You need an index if you want to use the "Unique value" option in the field Validation screen. You also need indexed fields to create *relationships* in your data, as explained in Part 3.

FileMaker's indexing feature takes its own computerized notes on your fields *in advance*, so that when you enter Find mode (page 23), the hard work's already been done and your Finds go that much faster. To take a peek at what a field index might look like, see Figure 3-12.

Just like a book, you can have a field without an index. When FileMaker needs to find records based on what's in that field, it has to check every single record—a process that can take noticeably longer in big databases. On the down side, an index takes up space. If this book didn't have an index, it would be a fair bit shorter, and the same goes for a field's index. A database with indexed fields takes up significantly more space on your hard drive than one with no indexed fields. See the box below for more detail on this dilemma.

Figure 3-12:
You can see what's in a field's index right from Browse mode. Just click in the field and choose Insert → From Index. This command is designed to let you put a value in a field that you know is already in the same field on a different record. It shows you every value in that field for every record. In the window that appears, if you turn on "Show individual words," you'll see a list of the individual words in the index—every word in this field across all records. This option isn't very exciting in a last name field, where most entries are already individual words. It's most helpful in a lengthy field, like a note field.

FREQUENTLY ASKED QUESTION

The Dark Side of Indexing

If indexing makes searching faster, why not just index every field?

Indexes have disadvantages as well. First, an index is only useful if it's up to date. When you change a field value, File-Maker has to store that new value in the table. If the field is indexed, it *also* has to update the index so that it knows about the changes to the field. Updating the index takes time (not much time, mind you, but it does take time).

When you're editing records in Browse mode, you'll *never* notice because updating the index for a handful of fields takes FileMaker less time than it takes you to realize you've pressed Enter. But if you're entering *lots* of information (like when you're *importing* records, as discussed in Chapter 16), the index updating can slow things down noticeably.

Automatic indexing

The good news is you almost never need to think about indexing. FileMaker has a really smart way of dealing automatically with indexing: Every field starts out with no index at all, to save space and keep things as fast as possible. Later, while you're working with your database, if you do something that would be made faster with

---

an index, like use the field in a find request, FileMaker automatically turns indexing on for you. That first find is slow as FileMaker looks through records one-by-one and builds the index (showing a progress bar in really big files), but since the field is now indexed, subsequent finds happen quickly. You almost always want this automatic behavior.

Controlling indexing manually

In very large databases, there may come a time when you want to adjust indexing manually. For instance, if you never again plan to search for someone by Middle Initial, you can turn off that field's indexing to reclaim the space it's using. Click the None radio button to turn indexing off completely. If you want to be able to search efficiently in a field, turn on All instead. The third choice—Minimal—creates a smaller index for the field. This index has everything FileMaker needs for relationships and field uniqueness, but not enough for fast searching. If you *don't* need to search in a field, but you *do* need it indexed for other reasons, choose Minimal.

When None is selected, you can keep FileMaker's automatically-turn-it-on-when-I-need-it behavior by turning on "Automatically turn indexing on if needed."

Note: FileMaker uses the field index when you do a find from Find mode, but *not* when you use the Find/Replace command. The index points FileMaker to *records,* and since Find/Replace doesn't find records (as discussed on page 51), the index does it no good. Therefore, when you do a Find/Replace, you don't make FileMaker automatically index a field. Only two actions trigger indexing: using the field in a find request, and using the field in a *relationship.* You'll learn about relationships in Part 4.

POWER USERS' CLINIC

Put Automatic Indexing to Use

FileMaker's ability to automatically index a field when it becomes necessary doesn't just save you the trouble of thinking about all this stuff. You can also use it to your advantage in some situations. Sometimes people need to distribute databases full of information.

For example, suppose you have a large parts catalog that's stored in a database, and you want your distributors to be able to use the database themselves to find parts. You can make a real FileMaker database available on your Web site for them to download, complete with your 10,000 parts records.

If there's a lot of info about parts, that database is pretty big. To make the download more palatable, tell FileMaker not to index *any* of the fields. But leave "Automatically turn indexing on if needed" turned on, to make the database as small as possible when people download it. Once people get it, they can start performing finds. As they do, FileMaker automatically indexes fields, making searches faster, and ballooning the size of the database.

Indexing language

In order to keep its indexes as small and tidy as possible, FileMaker doesn't actually store all a field's text in the index. Instead, it performs a little cleanup on the field values first. Most notably, it gets rid of the notion of upper case and lower case letters: Bill and bill become the same entry in the index. It also splits the field value up into individual words and removes any characters that aren't generally part of a normal word. In order to do that, it needs to know what language the text in the field is in. For example, if your field holds text in French, then you wouldn't want searches for "la" to match find records with "là," (in French, the accent mark makes those two different words entirely). But when indexing in English, File-Maker ignores those markings, since they don't matter. Normally, all indexes assume the language is English. You can select a different language from the dialog box's Indexing section's pop-up menu. You also use the language setting when you sort records. FileMaker decides what order words go in depending on the text language.

Note: If the Language pop-up menu is unavailable, the field is probably not a text field. You can specify the language only for text fields.

POWER USERS' CLINIC

Unicode Indexing

One language option, called "Unicode," isn't a language at all. This setting tells FileMaker to forget everything it knows about languages and use the internal code numbers for each character as is. When indexing with this language option, FileMaker doesn't remove any special characters from the index, and it doesn't ignore upper and lower case letters.

A find in such a field is *case sensitive*. When sorting, File-Maker also uses the character code numbers. Whichever code is lower comes first in the sort order, so capital Z comes before lowercase A.

It's rare that you'll want your searches and sorts to be case sensitive, but if you do, you have the option. You're more likely to use Unicode indexing when you want to easily search for punctuation. For example, a field that holds text from a business-to-business EDI document might be well served by Unicode indexing so you can easily find the records that contain "~BIG."

Bringing It All Together

You've just finished learning a lot about the various options and settings in File-Maker's Define Database window. At this point, it would be a good idea to take them for a test drive by adding some more functionality to your database. While you're at it, you'll get a chance to add a new field to an existing database (something you haven't done yet) and see how FileMaker responds—see Missing Fields below.

A private investigator has to deal with all kinds of characters. You've decided you might need a little help separating the good guys from the bad guys. Of course, Mom always said there's some good in everybody, so what you *really* need is a field that holds a Goodness Rating: George Costanza gets a zero, Mrs. Cleaver gets a five, and everybody else gets something in between. You want to make sure the rating is between zero and five, and you'd like it to be three unless you manually change it.

1. **In the Define Database window, enter Goodness Rating in the Field Name box and, from the Type pop-up menu, pick Number. Then click Create.**

   You now have a field to hold the goodness rating.

2. **Click the Options button, which has now become available, and then select the Auto-Enter tab.**

   The Auto-Enter options appear. You might have to switch to the Auto-Enter tab, if it isn't visible.

3. **Turn on the Data checkbox. Then, in the text box next to it, type *3*.**

   Remember, this option tells FileMaker to place some fixed piece of information in the field when you first create the record. Since you're assuming people are generally a three, it makes sense to let FileMaker automatically fill in that value for you.

4. **Click the Validation tab, turn on "In range" and enter *0* to *5* for the range options.**

   This action tells FileMaker to expect goodness ratings between zero and five.

5. **Uncheck "Allow user to override during data entry."**

   You don't want to allow values outside the range *at all*.

6. **Turn on "Display custom message if validation fails."**

   A custom message makes this whole thing feel more personal somehow.

7. **In the custom message box, type *Please specify a Goodness Rating between 0 and 5.***

   You may as well give a message that is as meaningful as possible. Since the user can't override this validation, the message is a statement, not a question.

8. **Click OK, then OK again to close the Define Database window.**

   You're back in your database again, and ready to test the Goodness Rating.

That about does it. You now have a database that handily tracks people, including how good they are, and you can search it, sort it, print it, zoom it, and generally have a good time with it. In the next chapter, you'll learn how to gussy it up.

WORKAROUND WORKSHOP

Missing Fields

Normally, when you add new fields to a database, they show up automatically in the database window so you can work with them. However, you can tell FileMaker not to show them. If you do, it's your job to put the fields in the window yourself (which you won't learn how to do until the next chapter). If FileMaker isn't showing you the fields, you need to fix the preferences:

1. Open the Application Preferences and select the Layout tab. You can find the Application Preferences by choosing Edit → Preferences (Windows) or FileMaker Pro → Preferences (Mac OS X).

2. Make sure the "Add newly defined fields to current layout" checkbox is turned on.

When this option is turned on, fields automatically show up in Browse mode as soon as you create them. You won't see any fields you created before you turn this option back on, though. See page 143 to learn how to use the field tool to drag new fields onto your layouts. Eventually, you'll probably want to turn this option off and manage your layouts manually.

Part Two:
Layout Basics

2

Layout Basics

In the last chapter you created your first database, and it really works. Unfortunately, it doesn't *look* all that great. For example, the Street Address field is the same width as the State field, even though street addresses are usually much longer than state names. The Goodness Rating field is *much* longer than it needs to be. And unless you're a real minimalist, the whole thing just looks boring (see Figure 4-1).

Figure 4-1:
This database works, but it could work better. What if you want to see lots of people at once? What if you want to print address labels for all these people? What if you want to arrange these fields in logical groups so they're easier to figure out? This database can't do any of those things, but if you give it a few new layouts, you can do all of them—and lots more.

There are other things to worry about as well. There's no good way to see lots of people at one time—in a nice list, for example. A list would also be handy for printing. As it stands, you have to print a whole page for each person in the database if you want a hard copy.

The FileMaker concept of *layouts* solves all these problems and more. While the Define Database window lets you define the structure of your database (its fields and tables), layouts let you design the look and feel.

What Is a Layout?

If the tables form the heart of a database, layouts give it a face. When you design a layout, you feel like you're working in a graphics program: You can change the fonts, paste in your logo, make the background light fuchsia, and drag the fields around as though they're little onscreen Lego blocks. A single database may look like a White Pages, a "Hello! My Name Is" name tag, a glossy brochure, or a library card catalog index card. FileMaker displays the same information—but *how* it displays that information is up to you.

Better yet, a single database can contain as many layouts as you want; each shows the data in a certain way for a specific purpose. Figure 4-2 shows the People database with two layouts.

Figure 4-2:
This is the People database, too. It has the same fields and the same records (it's even the same file). Only the layouts have changed. Now it has two of them (one is shown in each window), and they've been gussied up a bit. The one in front is a detail layout. The other one is a list layout.

Types of Layouts

You can make layouts for just about anything. Most databases start off with a few common kinds of layouts for the most basic needs. Then, over time, you usually add more layouts to meet specific needs. When thinking about layouts, you should be thinking about how you'll want to see the data—what kinds of information should be onscreen at the same time, for example—and how you want to *print* your data (printable lists, name tags, special forms, envelopes, statements, reports, and so on). Here are some common kinds of layouts:

- **Detail** layouts show all (or nearly all) fields on the screen for one record at a time—a full employee profile, for example. You use detail layouts for most, if not all, of your data entry. If you have a lot of fields, you can even create more than one detail layout: Contact Info, Emergency Info, and Payroll Info, for example.

Tip: You've already encountered a detail layout. *Every* FileMaker database is born with one starter detail layout. It always looks like the one in your People database in the previous chapter—downright boring.

- **List** layouts show multiple records at one time, in a scrolling list. They usually show *less* information from each record than a detail layout so that more records can fit on the screen.

- **Table** layouts are designed to work best in Table view (see page 35). Like a list layout, they show lots of records at once, but unlike a list layout, it doesn't matter how the fields are arranged on the layout itself, since Table view always looks like a spreadsheet.

UP TO SPEED

Views and Layouts

FileMaker learners often confuse views and layouts. Both affect the way FileMaker displays your data. You can switch from layout to layout or view to view with ease. And you hear a lot about lists, tables, forms, and so forth when talking about either. So what's the scoop?

First of all, in every FileMaker window, you have a layout *and* a view selected at all times. Each layout is usually designed to work best with a certain view. Detail layouts are usually shown in Form view, while list and report layouts usually use List view. For instance, if you have a Client List layout, you typically use List view.

Most of the time, the layout tells FileMaker how each record should look on the screen: where different fields appear, what fonts, sizes, colors, and pictures show up, and how much space it all takes up. When you pick a layout, File-Maker uses it to decide how things look.

The view, on the other hand, tells FileMaker what to *do* with the layout. In Form view, it shows one record, using the layout to decide how that single record should look. In List view, it shows all the found records, each below the one before it. The layout dictates how each of those records should look, and you use the scroll bar to zip through them. In Table view, FileMaker ignores the layout almost entirely. It pays no attention to how fields are arranged, or what colors or pictures you've used to decorate things. Instead, it shows a clean, simple list just like a spreadsheet. The only say the layout has in how things look is in which fields you see, and how FileMaker formats each individual field.

- **Report** layouts are designed for printing (see page 79). They usually show multiple records in a list form, often with a title at the top and summary information at the bottom. Reports can even have groups of data and intermediate summaries or running totals (see page 262).

• **Envelope and Label** layouts format the data so that you can print it directly onto an envelope or a sheet of peel-and-stick labels. This layout makes addressing envelopes to people in your database a breeze. FileMaker can automatically create layouts for many envelope sizes and common label formats.

Very often, you create both a detail layout and a list layout for each table in your database. The list provides an easy way to scroll through records and find what you're looking for without getting data-overload. When you're ready to see *all* the data, you switch to the one-at-a-time detail layout.

Switching Between Layouts

The ever-helpful status area tells you what layout you're on *and* lets you switch to another one. The layout pop-up menu (Figure 4-3) is one of the most prominent elements of the status area. You can also see the same list of layouts in the View → Go to Layout menu.

Layout pop-up menu

Figure 4-3:
In the status area, click the layout pop-up menu to see a menu of layouts in the database. To switch to a layout, choose it from the list. The layout pop-up menu also shows you which layout you're using when you haven't clicked it.

Note: The layout pop-up menu doesn't necessarily show *every* layout. You can actually tell FileMaker to hide certain layout names in this menu. You'll learn how on page 137.

Your People database has only one layout, making for a poor demonstration. To get a feel for how layouts work, you can use the Contact Management database instead (you created this database from a template in Chapter 1).

1. **Open the Contact Management database.**

   It appears on the screen. If you need a sample database to play with, you can find it on the Missing Manual Web site (page xxiv), complete with sample data.

2. **If the status area isn't showing, click the status area control to show it.**

   You now see the status area. (The status area control is explained back in Figure 1-2.)

3. **From the layout pop-up menu, choose** *List View.*

Now that you finally understand the difference between layouts and views, the silly database has the nerve to name a layout "List View." Remain calm: The name just happens to be the best way to describe the layout (at least the developer thought so), because this layout is a List and it's displayed in list view.

The List View layout shows in the window. FileMaker remembers which view you last used with each layout.

Since the layout affects only how the data shows, your found set and current record stay consistent as you change layouts. The following two steps show how this layout works.

4. **From the List view layout, use the status area's book icon to switch to another record.**

Since you are viewing this layout as a list, as you change records, the little black line along the left edge of the window moves, as explained on page 35.

5. **From the layout pop-up menu, choose** *Form — Main Address.*

You're now viewing details of the record you selected when in list view. In other words, FileMaker stayed on the same record while you switched layouts.

Likewise, if you do a find on the Form — Main Address layout, and then switch to the List layout, you'll see just the found records in the list. Since FileMaker is all about making all your data easy to see, search, print, and otherwise use, switching among various layouts is a big part of the game.

Note: As you spend more time with your own databases, you'll probably discover that you switch layouts *a lot*. You may decide all those trips to the tiny layout pop-up menu are slowing you down. That's why most databases (the Contact Management template included) use *buttons* to make layout switching faster.

In Chapter 1, you learned how to click the tab graphics to switch between viewing record details, a list, or a table (page 18). Now you know these tabs simply switch between three distinct layouts. You too can create buttons to switch between layouts, and you'll learn how in Chapter 6.

What Makes a Layout

A layout is made up of layout parts—sections that each behave a little differently when displaying or printing multiple records. Even the simplest layout has at least one part, and each part has objects on it. One kind of object is a field, which you've seen plenty of so far in this book. Each field in your database has a little label beside it that tells you which field it is. These labels are another kind of object: they're text objects. It just so happens those objects all belong to a part called the body, and if you need to talk about your layout, you'd say they are *on the body*.

Parts tell FileMaker how to treat the objects inside them when it displays or prints the layout. One part might show just once at the top of the window, while another shows over and over again for each record. This section tells you exactly what each part type does and when to use it. Finally, you'll learn how they work together and how they behave in each mode.

Layout Parts

FileMaker has eight different kinds of parts in all. Every layout uses at least one of these parts, and often several—although not all databases need all eight kinds of parts. Most types can occur only once on each layout (like a header), while others can appear several times.

- **Title Header.** The Title Header part holds things you want to appear only at the top of the very first printed page. Use it for a descriptive title, larger column labels, a company logo, or you can even make it the height of your paper, and it acts as a cover page.

- **Header.** The Header part prints at the top of every page—unless you also use a Title Header, in which case the Title Header is on page one and the regular Header is at the top of all other pages. In Browse mode, the Header shows up at the top of the window. This part is where you might put a date and time, small title, smaller column labels, and anything else that you want on every page of the printout.

- **Leading Grand Summary.** This part prints below the header but above the records themselves. It's meant to contain totals and similar fields that add up, average, or in some way round up the results of your records, which FileMaker calls *summarizing*.

Note: Leading Grand Summary and all the other "summary" parts are how FileMaker creates *reports*. Reports, which help you compile and analyze your data, are nothing more than a special kind of layout, as you'll learn in Chapter 6.

- **Body.** The body shows the actual record information. In list view, or when printed, it repeats once for every record.

- **Sub-Summary.** These parts help you add things like subtotals to complex reports. You'll learn all about this layout in Chapter 6.

- **Trailing Grand Summary.** If you prefer totals and overall summary information at the *bottom* of a report, it would go in this part.

- **Footer.** The footer prints at the *bottom* of every page—unless you also use a Title Footer, in which case, the Title Footer appears on page one and the regular Footer appears on all other pages. The Footer also appears at the bottom of the window in Browse mode. The footer's a perfect place for page numbers, copyright notices, and anything that ought to appear at the bottom of every page of your printout.

• **Title Footer.** The Title Footer part shows at the bottom of just the first page. Use it for special footer info that only needs to show once.

Figure 4-4 shows a layout with seven parts—one of each type except sub-summary.

Form view

List view

Preview mode

Figure 4-4:
Each window shown here is displaying the same layout—one with seven parts. As you can see, the arrangement of the parts changes as you switch between form view and list view in Browse mode, or when you switch to Preview mode. When you're creating a layout, you can move parts around and make them bigger or smaller depending on what information you want to emphasize.

Parts in form view

When in Browse mode, and viewing the layout as a form, you see every part except sub-summary parts. As Figure 4-4 shows, the parts go in the same order as in the list on the previous page. In practice, you'll probably never use *all* these parts on a layout you plan on viewing this way. In fact, if you only ever want to view a layout as a form in Browse mode, you really need only a body part.

If the window isn't big enough to show every part, you get scroll bars as usual. In form view, the entire layout scrolls up and down, as shown in Figure 4-5.

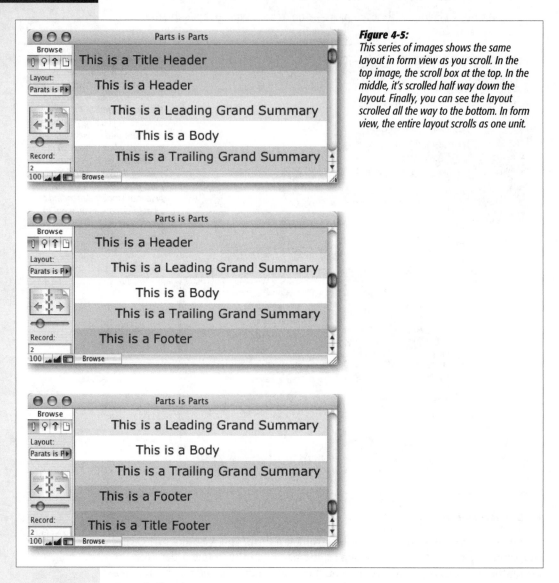

Figure 4-5:
This series of images shows the same layout in form view as you scroll. In the top image, the scroll box at the top. In the middle, it's scrolled half way down the layout. Finally, you can see the layout scrolled all the way to the bottom. In form view, the entire layout scrolls as one unit.

Parts in list view

In list view, the header is anchored to the top of the page and the footer to the bottom. When you use the scroll bars, the header and footer stay in place and the body part scrolls. If you resize the window, the footer moves with it so that it is always the same height, and always at the very bottom.

List view is a *list* because it shows several records at once. FileMaker accomplishes this magic by repeating the body part once for each record. The database in Figure 4-2 has three records, so in effect, the body part repeats three times.

The leading grand summary shows directly below the header, and before the body part's first appearance. The trailing grand summary, on the other hand, shows right after the last record's body part.

Scrolling in List view is altogether different from Form view, as shown in Figure 4-6.

Figure 4-6:
Like Figure 4-5, this sequence shows the same layout scrolled to various places. In this case, though, you're viewing the layout as a list. Notice that the header and footer stay put even when scrolling: They're always at the top and bottom of the window. The grand summary parts, on the other hand, scroll along with the body parts.

Parts in Preview mode

Figure 4-6 might lead you to believe that Preview mode shows only the title header and footer (exactly the opposite of list view) but that's not the whole story. Turn your eyes to Figure 4-7 for the whole story.

Figure 4-7:
In Preview mode, the title header and footer are at the top and bottom of the first page (left). Every page thereafter shows just the header and footer instead (right). If you don't have a title header, you'll get the regular header on the first page too (and the same goes for the title footer).

Just like list view, the grand summary parts place themselves before the first record and after the last record. Finally, scrolling in Preview mode just scrolls the current page. If you need to see other pages of your report while you're in Preview mode, use the Book icon to move around.

When to use 'em

While it's perfectly legal to put any parts on any layout, you can probably tell from the discussion above that some arrangements are more common than others:

- Detail layouts usually have just a body part, or some combination of header, body, and footer. These layouts may show only a single record, so there isn't much point to summary parts since there's no list of data to summarize.

- List layouts usually have a header and a body, and sometimes a footer. Occasionally, you want a trailing grand summary on your list layout as well, since it can show summary information after all the records without taking up precious space like a footer.

- Printed reports come in many forms. People often use all the parts shown above on a report: a large title header for the first page, and a smaller header for each additional page; a leading grand summary that shows below the title header and before the first record; a body part for each record; a trailing grand summary to show totals from all records, and a footer to show page numbers and the like.

- Envelope and label layouts often need headers and/or footers just to get the record data to align properly on the printed page. These parts are generally empty.

- You may have a list layout that you use to browse your records, but you often print it as well. Make the layout do double duty by adding a title header or title footer. They'll show only when you print, and you can save valuable screen real estate.

Layout Objects

Parts aren't so useful by themselves. They control how the items in your layout arrange themselves on screen or on the page, but they need to have *things* in them to be really useful. You call those things *layout objects*. Layout objects come in six flavors: Text objects, lines and shapes, images, fields, portals, and tab controls.

Note: Portals are all about relationships, and you won't learn about relationships—or portals—until Part 4. You'll take up tab controls a little sooner. Look for them in Chapter 6.

Text objects

Almost every layout ever created has included text objects: little blocks of text that are the same on every record displayed using that layout. Think about what happens when you move from record to record. The text labels for each field stay the same, even though the data inside each field changes with every record. Text objects give you one form of stability in the ever-changing world of database records.

When you design a layout, you can control every aspect of a text object, from the words in it to the font, size, style, color, line spacing, tab stops, and so on. (In fact, everything you learned in Chapter 2 related to formatting text in fields applies to text objects on layouts as well.)

Tip: FileMaker's spell checker works in layout mode too. Just choose Spelling → Check Layout. It looks and works just as it does in Browse mode—except that it checks text objects on the current layout. Also, the *visual* spell checking feature (page 76) works in Layout mode as well.

Lines and shapes

If you need simple graphic embellishments in your layouts, FileMaker has built-in tools. For example, you might want to put a box around a person's address information, and another around the Notes field, so they are visually separated. You can draw lines, rectangles, ovals, and round-cornered rectangles right on your layout. You can also control the line color, thickness, and pattern for lines and shapes; and the fill color and pattern for shapes.

Images

If simple shapes can't properly convey your artistic vision for your layout, you have recourse: You can paste any picture right on to the layout. You can also insert a picture from a file on your hard drive. Database developers often add icons, logos, and other decorations this way. For example, you might add your company logo to the top-right corner of your layout, or put a cute little envelope icon by the Email Address field. Just remember a little of this "eye candy" goes a long way. If you get carried away, you can actually create so much visual clutter that people using the program are confused, instead of enlightened.

Fields

A layout without fields is just a picture. Perhaps it's a very complex picture that changes as you switch from list view to form view, and has an entirely different effect when printed (thank you, parts!), but it's a picture nonetheless.

To get *data* into your layout, you add field objects. For instance, if you make a new layout in the People database, and you want to show the person's address, you can add the Street Address, City, State, and Zip Code fields to the body part of the layout. If the field is in the body part (the most common place), then it shows data from the current record (or each record when you view the layout as a list). In list view, fields in header, footer, or grand summary parts show the values from the first or last record in the found set. In Preview mode (or when printing), headers and footers show data from the first or last record on each page.

Note: You won't usually put ordinary fields in header, footer, and grand summary parts. These parts usually contain global fields, summary fields (see page 262), page numbering, dates, or just text and pictures.

With a firm understanding of layouts, views, parts, and objects, you're ready to get down to business. The next section shows you how to put all these ideas to work in your own databases.

Layout Mode

OK. It's time to dive into Layout mode and see what it's all about. You'll probably spend most of your time in Browse, Find, and Preview modes, but despite this fact, Layout mode has more options, more buttons, more menu commands, and more hidden features than any other mode. As you explore Layout mode in this section, you'll work with the People database you created in the last chapter, so to start things off, open that database and switch to Layout mode:

1. **Open the People database you created in Chapter 3.**

    The database appears on the screen, in Browse mode. If you don't have the People database, you can download a copy from the "Missing CD" page (page xxiv).

2. **Choose View → Layout Mode.**

   Whoa! Welcome to Layout mode…and you thought you had this FileMaker stuff figured out. (Figure 4-8 shows what you should see on your screen.)

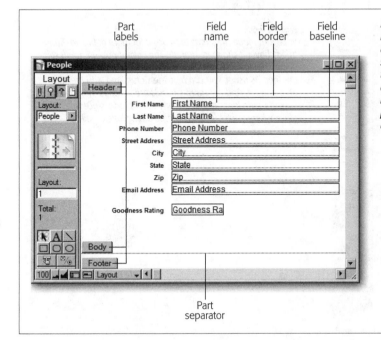

Figure 4-8:
In Layout mode, your database looks a lot different. Each field on the layout shows its name where the data used to be, has a black border, and a dotted line baseline. You can also see labels and separators for the three parts on this layout: header, body, and footer.

The Status Area

You don't have to look too closely to see that the status area has changed significantly (Figure 4-9):

- Instead of the current record number and record count, the status area now shows the current layout number, and the layout count. (You can't tell yet since you only have one layout, but the book icon now moves you through layouts rather than records.)

- A handful of tools—little square buttons with icons on them—appear. (Read on to find out what they do.)

- In the bottom-left corner of the window, a new control called the *part label toggle* has joined the usual zoom controls and status area control.

- The Mode pop-up menu and mode tabs now show that you're in Layout mode.

Note: It isn't just the status area that changes, though. Take a look at the menus. The Insert and Format menus, which are almost always gray in Browse mode, are fully functional now. And you have two new menus to help you design: Layout and Arrange.

Note: You may need to make your window taller to see everything the status area has to offer in Layout mode. In Windows, drag the top edge of the window up, or the bottom edge of the window down. In Mac OS X, drag the resize box at the bottom-right corner of the window.

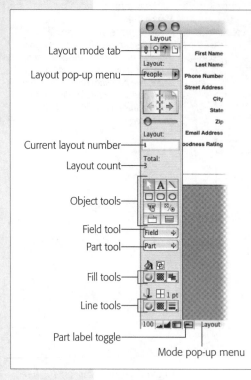

Layout mode tab

Layout pop-up menu

Current layout number

Layout count

Object tools

Field tool

Part tool

Fill tools

Line tools

Part label toggle

Mode pop-up menu

Figure 4-9:
In Layout mode the status area has a lot more going on. Some things haven't changed, though. The Layout pop-up menu still shows you layouts and lets you instantly switch from one to another. As usual, you can hide the status area with the status area control. And the zoom controls are perhaps more handy in Layout mode than they are in any other mode, since this is the place where you're likely to be fine-tuning little details.

View Options

Although Figure 4-9 shows how your database normally looks in Layout mode, FileMaker offers a host of options to change it. Each of these options has absolutely no effect on the finished look of your layout in Browse mode; rather, they help you while you're designing the layout. The View menu keeps those old standby commands (Browse Mode, Find Mode, Layout Mode, Preview Mode, and Go to Layout) right there where they belong. But you get choices that are more suitable for layout tasks.

Go to Layout

This hierarchical menu gives you an alternative to using the status area's Layout pop-up menu to move to all your layouts. In Browse mode, the Go to Layout submenu shows only those layouts that you've specified for inclusion in Layout menus. But in Layout mode, *all* layouts are listed, so you can switch quickly as you work.

Page margins

If you want a better feel for how your layout will look when printed, choose View → Page Margins (Figure 4-10). FileMaker shows a light gray border around your layout, representing your current page margins.

Figure 4-10:
In this picture, the graphic rulers, ruler lines, text boundaries, page margins, and sample data have been turned on; and field boundaries have been turned off. You can compare this illustration with Figure 4-8 to see how things have changed. You decide which settings you use, according to your personal preference. And you can turn any of them off or on with ease, so feel free to experiment.

Note: Remember that the parts *all* show in Layout mode, but in Browse mode or when printing, parts come and go. So even when you display page margins in Layout mode, the height of the *layout* doesn't directly translate to the height of the printed page.

Graphic rulers

Choose View → Graphic Rulers to get a handle on the actual size of the layout and the objects on it. When they're turned on, you see a ruler running up the left edge of the layout, and another across the top (see Figure 4-10). You can use this ruler to measure how big layout objects are and align things perfectly to a spot on the printed page, since an inch, centimeter, or pixels on the ruler matches the same unit when printed. Change the rulers' unit of measurement by clicking the square where they intersect. Units cycle through a series of presets: inch, centimeters, and pixels.

Text ruler

You might not care how tall your page is, but you do want to know how wide objects are. If so, choose View → Text Ruler. When you have no text objects selected on a layout, the text ruler looks just like the graphic rulers above, except there's no ruler along the left margin. You see text ruler in action when you have a text object selected. Then the ruler shrinks to the width of your object, and displays margins, indents, and tabs—an ideal tool for judging space when your trying to cram a lot of information onto a small screen.

POWER USERS' CLINIC

Configuring Graphic Rulers and Lines

You don't have to be content with the lines and rulers File-Maker gives you. If your rulers are in inches, for example, and you prefer to work in pixels, you can easily make the change. When in Layout mode, simply choose Layouts → Set Rulers. In this window, you can choose the units your ruler uses. If you choose Inches, FileMaker draws ruler lines one inch apart. If you choose Centimeters, your lines are one centimeter apart instead. When you set your ruler units to Pixels, the lines are 100 pixels apart (a line every pixel would probably be counter-productive).

If you have graphics rulers showing, you can avoid the trip to the Set Rulers dialog box. In this example, you can see that your current choice of units is in the top-left corner of the layout. If you click the unit label, it changes. Each time you click, the units change, rotating between all three options.

This dialog box also has a setting for grid spacing. See the box "Exercise Some Constraint" on page 163 for an explanation.

Ruler lines

Rulers running along the edge of the window may not provide enough visual alignment aid to suit your tastes. In that case, choose View → Ruler Lines. FileMaker draws dotted lines along your layout in a grid pattern. With this grid, you can more easily see how things line up on the layout, and get objects just where you want them on the printed page.

T-Squares

Choose View → T-Squares to show the T-Squares (Figure 4-11). When FileMaker shows you the T-squares, they always land aligned smack-dab in the middle of your layout. To move them where *you* want them, just drag them into place. Unfortunately, you have to move them one at the time. Practice your multiplication tables while you do this tedious task.

You can even use the T-Squares to line up objects on more than one layout. Align something to the T-Squares, and then switch to a different layout and align another object to them. Now, as you switch between these layouts, the two objects stay in the same place. So what, you say? Most often, the two objects are really two copies of the same thing, say a button you want in the same place on two different layouts. If these two objects aren't precisely aligned on each layout, you'll see a very distracting flash when you switch between those two layouts. Sure it takes a little time, but this kind of precision will give your database polish and a professional look.

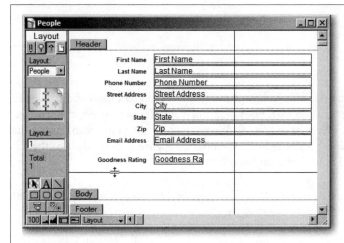

Figure 4-11:
T-squares are like little crosshairs you can move around on your screen. You can drag these lines anywhere on the layout, making it a breeze to align multiple objects. If you drag an object close to a T-square, it will "stick" to the T-square unless you hold down the Alt (Windows) or ⌘ (Mac) key.

Object size

This tiny window is a powerhouse of formatting options. See the box on page 161 for power users' secrets.

Buttons

Contrary to what you might think, View → Show → Buttons doesn't show or hide your buttons. Instead, this command puts a thick gray line around all objects you've defined as buttons. You haven't learned about buttons yet, so see page 246 for directions on how to make objects bend to your will and turn into buttons.

Sample data

As mentioned above, FileMaker normally shows the name of each field inside the field itself. If you yearn for something less useful (alright, differently useful), you can choose View → Show → Sample Data. FileMaker shows semi-random sample data in each field. Actually, this feature does have some limited value: It shows numbers in your number field, dates in your date fields, and so on. This feature can give you a visual clue about how these values are being formatted (you'll learn how to format data in fields shortly). Figure 4-10 also shows fields with sample data.

Text boundaries

Normally, text objects on a layout (like the field labels you see now) have no border around them. Sometimes, though, you can have a tough time visually lining text up since different letters have different shapes and sizes. If you choose View → Show → Text Boundaries, you see a tidy box surrounding each text object. When you line up these boxes, you ensure that the text inside them is lined up too.

Note: In case it isn't obvious, you can turn any of the above options *off* by choosing the appropriate command a second time.

Field boundaries

All the view options available in layout mode are turned *off* unless you turn them on yourself—except for this one. FileMaker normally shows a border around every field no matter how you have that field formatted. If you don't want to see this border, choose View → Show → Field Boundaries. Figure 4-10 shows how the layout looks with field boundaries turned off.

Note: Don't confuse field boundaries with text boundaries. Field boundaries show around field objects (of any type) while text boundaries show around text objects.

Sliding objects

This command places small, black arrows near the top of any item that's been set to slide during printing. See page 195 to learn how to make objects slide.

Non-printing objects

This command puts square black handles at the corners of any object that's set as non-printing. See page 231 to learn how to make objects non-printing.

Toolbars

You can find all FileMaker's toolbar commands in either the menus or on the status bar. But if the fascination of menus has lost its steely grip on you, you can show or hide any of FileMaker's toolbars at will. They come in four flavors:

- **Standard.** This toolbar contains the stuff you find in most application's toolbars. There are buttons for creating new files, for opening existing files, for saving, for undos and for cut, copy and paste, among many others.

- **Text Formatting.** Here you'll find the stuff you need to make your text look great. You can change fonts, sizes, styles, alignment and spacing.

- **Arrange.** These oddly marked buttons let you align objects, move them backwards and forward in layers, and rotate them.

- **Tools.** This powerful little bar gives you the strength to draw simple objects and to create those objects that make a database do what it does best. You can make fields, buttons, portals and tab controls, as well as insert parts into your layout. Any of those items mentioned here that don't make sense yet will make sense in due time, Grasshopper. Keep reading this chapter and the next one. Soon, you'll be ready to leave the temple and embark on your own journey of discovery and saving the world through better databases.

Tip: If the icons on these buttons don't immediately convey meaning to you, let your mouse pointer hover over each one. After a second or two, the button's name appears in a yellow field, called a *tooltip*. (If you have FileMaker Advanced, you can create tooltips of your own, as explained in Chapter 19.)

The first time you see these toolbars, they're anchored near the top of the screen, just under the menu bar. But they all have dotted gray lines at their left edges. Just use these lines to drag the toolbars wherever you want them. They are powerless to resist you and will stay where they're put. Use the close box to make them go away.

Status area

This is a menu-based choice for showing and hiding the status area. If you have to work on a laptop, or any other computer with a small screen, you'll be grateful for the extra pixels you can squeeze out by hiding the status area while you're designing your layouts.

Zoom in and out

The View menu also has options to zoom the layout in or out (View → Zoom In and View → Zoom Out). If the thrill of clicking the zoom controls in the status area isn't enough for you, you can alternate between zoom buttons below and zoom menus above. You do have some control over what area of the screen is magnified. If there's an object you need to see, select it before zooming in. FileMaker tries to keep that object centered as it zooms.

Layout Setup

Most of your layout work simply involves creating and adjusting layout parts, and filling them with things. But some important aspects of a layout aren't visible on the layout itself. These settings are tucked away in the Layout Setup dialog box (Figure 4-12) instead. You can call this window into action by choosing Layouts → Layout Setup.

With the People database open, switch to Layout mode. Now's a good time to set some options.

Figure 4-12:
The Layout Setup dialog box (Layouts → Layout Setup) gives you control over the layout's basic attributes. Under the General tab you can change the layout's name, for example. The "Show records from" pop-up menu controls which table the layout is connected to. Since your database only has one table, you don't have to worry about this option just yet. It's covered in full in Part 4.

Layout name

First up, suppose your People database holds all your clients. You might want to change the name of this layout to "Personal Details." This change clears the way for a "People List" layout down the road.

1. **Choose Layouts → Layout Setup.**

   The Layout Setup dialog boxs appears.

2. **In the Layout Name box, type *Personal Details.***

   You can give a layout just about any name you want, so long as it's no more than 100 characters long. You can even have more than one layout with the same name, if you're a fan of confusion. FileMaker keeps track of layouts using an internal ID number, so it always knows which layout is which. But you have to depend on the names you give your layouts, so name them wisely.

3. **Make sure the "Include in layout menus" checkbox is turned on.**

   Normally, each layout is listed in the Layouts pop-up menu, so that when you're using the database you can switch to that layout at any moment. In this case, you want to be able to check out client details at an instant's notice.

   Sometimes, you'll turn this checkbox off when a layout serves a special purpose: Perhaps it's a report that makes sense only after performing a special find and sort; or a search screen that works only in Find mode. In cases like these, you can turn off the "Include in layout menus" checkbox and use a script (Part 5) to go to the layout instead. When you do, the layout no longer shows up in the Layouts pop-up menu or the View → Go to Layout menu in Browse, Preview, or Find modes. *Every* layout shows in the Layouts pop-up menu in Layout mode, no matter how you set this checkbox.

4. **Turn off the "Save record changes automatically" checkbox.**

This way, FileMaker displays the message shown in Figure 4-13 whenever you try to exit a record after making edits to it using this layout. It's confirming that you want to save those changes when you commit the record.

If you leave this checkbox turned on, this saving happens quietly in the background. FileMaker's factory setting is to commit changes the moment you leave the record, as you learned on page 17. In this case, however, as your business grows, you're planning to hire a helper to edit and update client information. Until that person gets up to speed in FileMaker, you want to give him a chance to double-check his work.

Figure 4-13:
When the "Save record changes automatically" option is turned off, you see this message when you exit a record if you've made any changes. If you'd rather not keep the changes you made, click Don't Save. Click Cancel if you want to stay in the record, changes intact and un-saved. Click Save to exit the record and save the changes.

Note: Pay close attention to the fact that this is a *layout* setting. If you want to make sure record changes are always confirmed before being saved, you have to turn this setting on for every layout. There's a point to turning it on, though: Suppose you don't want to confirm changes to most of your fields, but you do want this behavior for the notes field. You can simply leave the notes field off the main layout, and create a separate notes layout. When you create this layout, you get the ask-before-saving feature for the notes field without the hassle for every other field.

5. **Turn off "Show field frames when record is active."**

The "Show field frames when record is active" option affects how FileMaker shows fields in Browse and Find mode. You've probably noticed that whenever you're in a field, every field on the layout has a dotted-line border around it. These borders help people figure out where the enterable fields are. Figure 4-14 illustrates the difference.

Using the tools in this chapter, you, O savvy database developer, can make your layout clear and user-friendly without the unsightly dotted lines, so turn them off.

You can always return to this dialog box (Layout → Layout Setup) if you ever get confused and want to use the dotted fields as a guide.

Now, if you switch to Browse mode, you see the new name in the Layout pop-up menu, and no frames when you click a field. Of course, without the field frames, your invisible fields look a little odd. You'll fix this problem shortly. But first, you need to learn about the tools you have in Layout mode.

Figure 4-14:
The window at the back shows the field frames FileMaker draws when you click into a record. In the window in front, this option has been turned off.

Layout Tools

The vast majority of new goodies in the status area are *tools*—like their real-world counterparts, you use tools to build things—in this case, your layout. You can see all the tools in Figure 4-15.

The drawing tools

The first set of tools in the status area is the *drawing tools*. These tools, for the most part, just let you draw decorations on the layout. They're the top two rows of the main tools panel, and you see them up close in Figure 4-16.

- The **selection** tool is active when you first enter Layout mode, and whenever you've finished using another tool, it immediately becomes active again. It's sort of the *default* tool in FileMaker—if you're not using some special tool, File-Maker assumes you want to use this one. Its only purpose in life is so you can select objects on the layout. Once an object is selected, you can do things to it (like move it, resize it, or adjust the way it looks).

• The **text** tool lets you put text on your layout. For the most part, this text is unchanging—it's the same no matter what record you're looking at. The most common example of text on layouts is field labels, which you've seen in every database you've used so far. See page 146 for the skinny on working with text on a layout.

Figure 4-15:
The layout tools come in three flavors. The drawing tools require just a click—once you select them, you can literally draw right on the layout. The field and part tools work like a post-it-note pad—just drag from the tool into the layout to peel off a blank field or part, ready to stick where you want. When you click one of the fill or line tools, you get a pop-up menu of choices.

Drawing tools

Field tool—Field

Part tool—Part

Fill tools

Line tools

Figure 4-16:
These are the drawing tools. In this picture, the selection tool is active (it has a darker background). To choose a different tool, click it. Once active, you can click or drag on the layout to draw a shape or add some text. When you release the mouse button, FileMaker automatically activates the selection tool again.

Text tool

Selection tool

Rounded rectangle tool

Rectangle tool

Button tool

Tab control tool

Line tool

Oval tool

Field/Control tool

Portal tool

• The **line, rectangle, rounded rectangle,** and **oval** tools. FileMaker has a built-in understanding of a few basic shapes. You can draw lines, squares and rectangles, circles and ovals, and *rounded rectangles* (rectangles or squares with round corners). Figure 4-17 shows a few ways people often use these shapes on layouts. On page 129, you'll get a chance to create some shapes and lines of your own.

Note: If you Find FileMaker's drawing tools limited, fear not. You can create icons, buttons, or any other elements in any drawing program, and then place these images on your layout. Find out how on page 163.

Figure 4-17:
You can use FileMaker's built-in shapes in lots of ways. Here, a line separates the header from the body of the layout. Circles make pretty buttons. And rectangles set apart blocks of related fields.

The control tools

The drawing tools let you gussy up your layout. But the control tools let the layout get down to business. With this fantastic four, you tell the layout where to put data and where it should go looking for that data. You can also create buttons to automate tedious or lengthy processes, and you can create tab controls, which make designing complex databases a breeze.

- The **Button** tool helps you create a button which, when you click it, tells File-Maker to do something interesting—create a new record, switch to a different layout, or even run a script. You'll learn how to create buttons in Chapter 6 and how to write scripts in Chapter 13.

- The **Field Control** tool lets you determine everything that's important about a field except what's inside it. You can control a field's placement on your layout, its shape and size, and even what it looks like. The first part of Chapter 5 is all about field control.

- The **Tab Control** tool gives you a major leg up on placing lots of fields on a single layout without clutter. Look to Chapter 6 for the full scoop on how tab control makes your life easier.

- The **Portal** tool creates portals—mysterious passageways to a different dimension. Wait…that can't be right. Portals actually show data from a *different* table right on your layout. You'll learn more in Part 4.

The field and part tools

The next tools in line are the Field and Part tools, which simply let you add fields and parts to your layout. To create a new field, drag the Field tool onto your layout. When you let go of the mouse, FileMaker draws the field and pops up the "Specify Field" dialog box. Click the "Create label" option if you need a field label. Click OK and your field is created.

The line and fill Tools

Next up are the fill and line attribute tools, shown more closely in Figure 4-18. When you click these buttons, you get menus from which to pick colors, patterns, line thicknesses, and other special effects, each of which you can apply to assorted objects on the layout. For example, when you have a shape selected, you can choose from the menu under the fill color tool and change the shape's color. You'll use these tools all throughout this chapter.

Figure 4-18:
The Fill and Line tools are labeled here. Each one controls a certain aspect of the look of an object on the layout. You can see the cumulative effect of the choices you make in the Fill Preview and Line Preview displays.

Fill color, pattern, and effect. When you select an object on the layout, the fill color changes the color of the object itself. You can also apply a repeating pattern to the object for that oh-so-80s look. If the early 90s is more your style, the Fill Effects tool lets you apply a simple drop shadow, an embossed effect, or an engraved effect. Figure 4-19 shows some rectangles with various fills.

Line color, pattern, and weight. The next three tools affect the outline of an object, rather than its fill. You can again control color and pattern. The Line Weight tool also lets you adjust the thickness of the outline itself. You can see some line settings in action in Figure 4-20.

Working with Parts

The first step to any layout design is to put the parts where they belong (or at least *approximately* where they belong; you can always tweak them later). In the beginning of this chapter you learned about the kinds of parts a layout can have, and it's your job to decide which ones you want for the layout you're building.

Figure 4-19:
This layout shows what happens when you apply various fill colors, patterns, and effects to a simple rectangle. You can use these same fills with other shapes, fields, and even whole parts.

Figure 4-20:
Here you can see the same rectangles with various line styles. When you adjust the line color, pattern, and thickness, you can get many effects, from no line at all to a dashed line, to a thick black line. You can apply line effects to shapes, lines, and fields with borders.

In your People database, your first job is simple—to pretty up the layout FileMaker created for you. It makes sense that such a layout would have a header part (where you can announce the layout's title) and a body (where you can put the actual fields). Figure 4-21 shows one person's idea of a nicer looking detail layout.

Figure 4-21:
Unless you're a real minimalist, you probably agree this layout looks nicer here than it did when FileMaker first created it. Here you can see the header part and the body part. Your first mission is to get these parts—and just these parts—on your layout.

Deleting a part

The quickest way to delete the footer part (which you don't need for this particular layout) is to click its part label and press Delete. (The part label is the little gray tag that says Footer.) Go ahead and delete the footer part now. Since this footer is completely empty, it simply goes away immediately. If a part has any objects in it at all, FileMaker asks you if you're sure before removing the part and everything in it.

Resizing parts

Your next job is to make the header a little larger. Just drag the part label straight down a bit. As you drag, a dotted line tells you where the part will land when you let go. For now, make it about double its original size.

Every part below the one you resize moves down to make room, which is *almost* always what you want. But suppose your overall layout size is just where you want it (perhaps it's designed to print on a special form, and the exact size is critical). In a case like this, if you want to resize the header, you probably *don't* want it to push other parts down. Instead, as the header grows, you want the body to shrink a little, so that the header eats into the body. To get this effect, hold down the Alt (Windows) or Option (Mac) key while you drag the part label. When you do, the border between parts changes, but the overall layout size remains the same, and the objects on the layout don't move at all.

Note: Unless you hold the Alt (Windows) or Option (Mac) key when making a part smaller, you can't drag the part boundary above the bottom-most object it contains. To get around this glitch, you must move the objects out of the way, delete the objects, or hold down the necessary keys while you drag.

FileMaker won't let you put objects *outside* a part, so sometimes as you're arranging things you get cramped for space. To make the rest of your layout work easier, go ahead and make the body part taller as well—you can shrink it back down later.

Coloring a part

The finished details layout should have a shaded header (Figure 4-21). Getting this effect is a breeze:

1. **Click the header part label to select it.**

   The label itself darkens to let you know it is selected.

2. **Click the Fill Color tool in the status area (it's shown in Figure 4-19).**

   A menu of available colors pops up.

3. **From the menu, select the color you want for the header.**

   The header part changes to match the selected color.

Note: You can apply a pattern to a part as well, but parts can't have fill effects.

Repeat the steps above, this time selecting the body part and a different color (like light gray). When you color a part, this color becomes the background color both in the database window and when you print. With this phenomenon in mind, you should probably avoid excessively dark or otherwise awful colors and patterns.

Adding and Editing Text

Figure 4-22 shows how your layout probably looks right now, and how it's going to look when you're done. Your next assignment is to put the text in the header. FileMaker's text tool makes it a cinch to click anywhere in a layout part and type away.

Adding new text

The first piece of text in the header should say "People I Know." This is a title for your entire database (in other words, your list layout will say the same thing on top). Here's how to do it:

1. **In the status area, click the Text tool (it has an "A" on it).**

   The Text tool button darkens to let you know it's active.

2. **Choose Format → Font → Trebuchet MS.**

   The text you're about to create will appear in this font.

3. **Choose Format → Size → 18 Point.**

   Now you're telling the text tool you want it to create larger text.

4. **Choose Format → Style → Bold.**

And finally, you want this title to be bold.

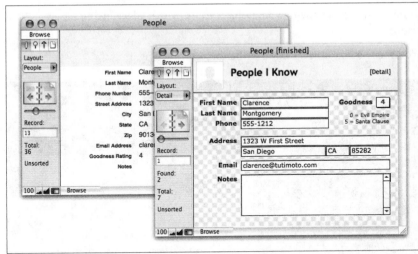

Figure 4-22:
The window in the back should look something like your database. Your ultimate goal is to make it look like the one in the front. You've still got a lot to do, and the next step is to add text to the header.

Note: You can dress up your text in any font, size, and style you like. But don't forget that the computer your database is *used* on must have the font installed. If you have fine-and-fancy $300 fonts on your computer, but your employees will be using the database on stripped-down PCs, you want to pick a font that comes standard with your operating system so everybody sees the same lovely letter forms.

---

5. **Click somewhere in the header.**

A new text box appears (Figure 4-23). This text box is FileMaker's way of saying "Go ahead and type."

Figure 4-23:
When you click with the Text tool, FileMaker shows a text box—you can type right in it. You can tell this text box is ready for typing because it has a dotted outline and a flashing insertion point. When you're finished entering text, just press Enter.

6. **In the text box, type *People I Know*.**

As you type, the words appear in the box.

7. **Press Enter.**

   The dotted outline and flashing insertion point disappear and you're left with a full-fledged text object. This object is automatically selected for you.

8. **If necessary, move the new text object to its proper place, using Figure 4-22 as a guide.**

   You move a text object like any other object: Just drag it.

POWER USERS' CLINIC

Locking the Layout Tools

After you create a text object with the text tool, the selection tool is automatically activated. FileMaker assumes you want just one text object, and saves you the trouble of switching back to the selection tool. If you anticipate creating several objects of the same type, give the tool icon a *double*-click instead of a single click. The icon on the button turns white to let you know the tool is now locked. With a locked text tool, you can create as many text objects as you want: Click to create the text box, type the text, click again for another text box, and so forth. When you're finished, click the selection tool again to make it active.

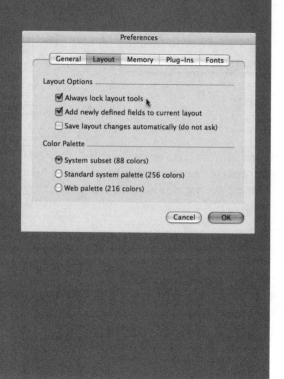

If, for some reason, you don't like FileMaker always switching back to the selection tool on your behalf, you can instruct it to lock the drawing tools automatically—so even a single-click keeps a tool active until you say otherwise. In Windows, choose Edit → Preferences. In Mac OS X, choose FileMaker Pro → Preferences. In the preferences window, select the layout tab (shown here) and turn on the "Always lock layout tools" checkbox. If you're like most people, you want to switch this checkbox off after trying it for about ten seconds; just revisit the Layout tab of the preferences window and turn this checkbox off.

As well as the main title, a header often also includes something to remind you (and the people who use your database) what layout you're looking at—the "[Detail]" text in this case. You already know how to do it:

1. **Using the text tool, click somewhere in the header part, being careful not to click the existing text object.**

   A new text box appears, ready for typing.

2. **Type *[Detail]*.**

   The text box reflects your typing, but the text isn't the right size or style.

3. **Press Enter.**

   Again, the signs of an editable text box disappear and FileMaker selects the new text object.

4. **Choose Format → Size → Custom.**

   The Custom dialog box pops up.

5. **Enter *11* in the "Custom font size" box, and then click OK.**

   The text you just created immediately changes size.

Note: Since 11 Point isn't normally in the Format → Size menu, you have to use the Custom size option instead. This option works the same in layout mode as it does in Browse mode (see page 51).

---

6. **Choose Format → Style → Plain Text.**

   The text object loses its "boldness."

7. **Move the text object to its proper place.**

   You can see it coming: Just drag.

Find and Replace Revisited

Layout mode retains some features you've already learned from Browse mode—albeit slightly modified to make sense to a database designer rather than a database user. For example, you might want to find and replace text on a layout, on occasion. Imagine you have decided to call the Zip Code field *Postal Code* instead, since you're planning a big drive into Canada. You can use Find/Replace to fix every field label on every layout in just one shot. When you're in layout mode, the Find/Replace command searches through text on the layout itself rather than search through the data in fields and records.

Here's the pared-down dialog box you see when you choose Edit → Find/Replace → Find/Replace in layout mode. Aside from a the lack of "Search across" and "Search within" options—which make no sense when you're not searching records and fields—it looks and works just like its Browse mode counterpart.

The other commands on the Edit → Find/Replace sub-menu—Find Again, Replace and Find Again, and Find Selected—also work exactly as they do in Browse mode. (See page 51 for details on the ins and outs of Find/Replace.)

Changing text font, size, and style

FileMaker created a handful of text objects for you when it made this layout—the field labels. You can change the font and style of each label to make them attractive and easy to read, and you can also adjust the size to make sure everything fits. Figure 4-22 shows 11-point Verdana—a simple style that looks tidy and readable on most monitors.

Tip: If you're designing a database on the Mac for use on PCs, you'll need to make all your text objects just a little larger than you think they need to be, because PCs display fonts larger than their Mac brethren do. It helps to check your layouts on a PC, because any text object that isn't wide enough will flow over onto another line, which probably isn't what you intended.

You've probably already figured out that to change something about an object, you first need to select it. You can select the first object, change its font, change its size, change its style; then select the second object and repeat...over and over until you're done or until you've torn out your last remaining hair. Or you can select *all* the field labels and change them in one shot. The box on page 151 describes several ways of selecting multiple layout objects, but the quickest way is often to *rubber band* them. That is, you drag to encompass the objects with your mouse. Here's how:

1. **With your mouse, position the selection tool just below and to the right of the Notes field label, and then click.**

   This spot is where you'll start your rubber band. Notice that as you drag around, a dotted rectangle follows you—that's the rubber band.

2. **Drag from this point up and to the left until the dotted rectangle completely surrounds the field labels.**

   Every object you want to select must be *inside* the rubber band—it can't hang out the edge—so be sure you go far enough to the left. You can see a picture of a rubber band in action on the next page.

3. **Release the mouse button.**

   You should see all the field labels selected. This process is easier to do than to explain, so the best way to learn how is to try it.

Note: To be sure you got what you want, make sure every field label has its own selection handles. If you missed one, just hold down the Shift key and click it—this action adds it to your current selection. Now that you have all the labels selected, you can start formatting them en masse.

---

4. **Choose Format → Font → Verdana.**

   Poof! All the labels change fonts.

5. **Choose Format → Size → 11 Point.**

   Poof again! All the labels change size.

Note: Since the *last* custom size you used was 11 Point (when adding the "[Detail]" text on page 148), FileMaker now lists it at the bottom of the Format → Size menu. (If it isn't there, shame on you for not following directions! Only kidding.) Choose Format → Size → Custom instead.

POWER USERS' CLINIC

Selecting Lots of Objects

Selecting objects on a layout is such a common task that FileMaker gives you several ways to do it. You can always click an object to select it, but you can use any of the following methods as well:

If you want to select more than one object (so you can operate on them all at once), select the first object, and then press the Shift key and click each additional object. As you click, each object joins the selection. If you accidentally select an object, Shift-click it again to deselect it.

To select *everything* on the layout, choose Edit → Select All or press Control-A (Windows) or ⌘-A (Mac).

You can even select every object of a certain type (every field, for example). First select one object of the type you want. Then hold down the Shift (Windows) or Option (Mac) key and choose Edit → Select All. FileMaker selects every object that is similar to the one you selected yourself.

If you have more then one object selected when you choose this command, FileMaker selects every object like any of the selected objects. For example, to select every field *and* every text object, select one field and one text object, and then choose this command.

Finally, you can easily select objects that are close together on the layout by *rubber banding* them, (see the figure below). Rubber banding takes a little practice, but the idea is simple: Click and hold any empty spot on the layout, and then drag diagonally. As you drag, a dotted rectangle follows the mouse. When you let go, any object completely inside this box is selected. If surrounding every object is too difficult, hold down the Control key (Windows) or the ⌘ key (Mac) and FileMaker will instead select any object the box touches.

See the box "Locking and Grouping below for a few more commands that help when you work with lots of objects.

Rubber Band — Text Object

The labels were already bold, so you don't need to change the style. Now you have labels that look right, but their positions are all out of whack. That's OK, though, 'cause you're about to move them all anyway—after one more text editing maneuver.

Text Format Dialog Box Revisited

If you've read Chapter 2, you know that you can choose Format → Text to summon the Format Text dialog box, a one-stop shop for all your text formatting needs. This handy window is fully accessible in layout mode as well (the Text command is just a little lower down in the Format menu). From here, you can adjust the font, size, and style in one shot if you prefer. You can also change text color and paragraph settings, both of which work just as well for text objects in layout mode as they do for field data in Browse mode.

For example, if you want to make the field labels bold, italic, red, 16-point Times New Roman, you can click the Format menu five separate times, choosing a different submenu each time. Or you can do the steps below. You get to decide which method to use. Ahhhh…choice.

1. Select the text object. As usual, you have to tell File-Maker *which* object to work with.

2. Choose Format → Text to open the Text Format dialog box.

3. From the Font pop-up menu, choose Times New Roman.

4. From the Size pop-up menu, choose 16 Point.

5. From the Color pop-up menu, pick a lovely shade of red.

6. Turn on the Bold and Italic checkboxes.

Editing existing text

If you compare the field labels you have now to those in Figure 4-22, you'll see you have a little more editing to do. The final layout has these field label changes:

- City, State, and Zip go away.

- Phone Number becomes Phone.

- Street Address becomes Address.

- Email Address becomes Email.

- Goodness Rating becomes Goodness.

Now you need to make these changes to *your* field labels.

First, get rid of the City, State, and Zip labels. Zapping them is a breeze: Select them all (using any of the methods described on the previous pages) and choose Edit → Clear or press the Delete or Backspace key. (If you're good with the mouse, you can use the rubber-band trick [page 151] to select them all, but it's probably just as easy to Shift-click each one.)

Now edit the remaining labels. Start with the Phone Number field:

1. **In the status area, double-click the text tool.**

   Your mouse pointer now has the typical text-editing I-beam shape. As an added bonus, the text tool is locked so you won't have to pick it again to fix the next field label.

2. **In the Phone Number label, double-click the word Number.**

   The text object turns back into an editable text box, with dotted outline and all.

3. **Press the Delete key twice.**

   The first Delete removes the word Number. The second wipes away the blank space after Phone.

Note: When you're editing a text object like this, you're free to use the mouse or arrow keys to move about the object. It works just like entering text in a field in Browse mode. You can even apply fonts, sizes, and styles to individual letters or words inside a text object. For example, you could make the "e" in Phone bold (if you really wanted to).

---

4. **Press Enter.**

   The label is now selected, and it says Phone, just like it's supposed to.

Three more labels need fixing: Street Address, Email Address, and Goodness Rating. Repeat steps two through four above to make the necessary edits. (Don't forget that you're just changing the field *label* here, not the actual field name [as you did back on page 86]. You can confirm this by looking inside the field in layout mode, or making a quick trip to the Define Database window. You can even give the same field different labels on different layouts.)

Note: By almost every measure, a field label is just like any other text object. But the labels FileMaker creates for you have one hidden property that makes them special: When you change a field's name in the Define Database window, its label automatically changes to match. As soon as you *edit* the text in a field label, though, this magical bond is broken. This break may be a good thing or a bad thing depending on your point of view. Some people edit their field labels manually so they can pick just the right name given the available space and the nature of the layout. Other people find that keeping their field labels and field names in sync helps them keep things straight in their heads. Thou mayest choose for thyself.

Figure 4-24 gives a quick sanity check. Your layout should look something like this.

Figure 4-24:
Here's how your layout should look after you've added header text; edited the text of the field labels; and formatted them with a new font, size, and style. To move those pesky field labels so they don't overlap your fields, select them and "nudge" them out of the way. You nudge objects pixel-by-pixel with the arrow keys on your keyboard. Tap the left arrow until the labels are clear of your fields.

POWER USERS' CLINIC

Locking and Grouping

Sometimes an object just keeps getting in the way when you try to work with another one. For example, you might paste a large picture as the background of your layout. Every time you try to rubber band some objects, you end up moving this picture instead, since it fills all the otherwise empty space. To put this problem to rest once and for all, just lock the offending object. First, select the object or objects you want to lock. Then choose Arrange → Lock. Now you can't move, resize, or otherwise edit the object. If you need to do any of these things to it, just click it once and choose Arrange → Unlock to bring it back to normal.

On the other hand, if you find you're working with a particular set of objects very often, you can group them (Arrange → Group) to make them act as one. Once grouped, anything you do to one of them happens to them all. If you move one, they all follow. If you delete one, they all go away. And if you change any attributes—like font size—all of them change. The only thing you can do to an individual item that is part of a group is edit its text—the text tool can cut right through the group and let you edit an individual object. When you're ready to treat them as separate objects again, just select the group and choose Arrange → Ungroup.

Formatting Fields

Before you get to arranging the fields on the layout, you need to make one more adjustment. In the previous section, you formatted the labels—the text that identifies your fields onscreen at all times. FileMaker also lets you control how text appears when someone *types* into those fields later.

Text formats

Formatting text fields works just like formatting field labels. The trick is to select the actual fields first. You can also give fields borders for emphasis or decoration. Here's how to give your fields the look shown in Figure 4-22:

1. **Click the First Name field to select it, and then hold down the Shift key (Windows) or the Option key (Mac) and choose Edit → Select Same.**

   All the fields are now selected.

2. **Hold down the Shift key and click the Goodness Rating field.**

   This field needs special formatting, and you'll get to that later in this chapter, so you don't want to change it now. When you Shift-click an already selected object, you remove it from the selection.

Now that you have the fields selected, your first job is to adjust the text formatting—the way text will look when someone types in Browse mode. You've done this with text objects already (page 57), and there's no difference here. Use the Format → Text command to bring up the Text Format dialog box, where you can choose 11-Point Verdana.

Other field type formats

If you've worked with numbers in other programs, like other databases or a spreadsheet program, you know that number formatting can save lots of keystrokes and help you organize numbers so they're more legible. Likewise, entering in Date, Time, and Timestamp fields can have their challenges when you're trying to get the data to look a certain way. See page 238 for details on formatting these alternate field types.

Field Control

You can get information into a database without typing. You can attach value lists to fields and format them as checkboxes, radio buttons, or menus for making data entry fast and accurate. And you can tell the field how decorative it ought to be by defining borders for it.

Field/Control setup

Up to now, you've been learning about formatting the text, or the stuff that's in a field. But now, you'll see that the field itself can be formatted with styles that have nothing to do with text. When FileMaker threw those first fields you defined out on the layout for you, it just made plain old fields, called Edit Boxes. But with Field/Control, you're in charge of how the field accepts information.

Control style. Take control with the Format → Field/Control → Setup command, which you can see in Figure 4-25. To see how it all works, you're going to turn your Goodness Rating field into a pop-up menu field and assign it a value list.

(And if you're wondering what all this talk of pop-up menus has to do with formatting, see the box on page 158 for an explanation.)

In the People database you've been working on so far, the Goodness Rating field works just like any other: You can type any number you want into it. But you've already decided it should only take whole numbers between zero and five. You want to prevent anyone (even if that's you) from messing up your database by accidentally (or nefariously) adding a bogus number—like 21.785 or 4E27.

The perfect solution is to make the Goodness Rating field a pop-up menu showing the choices 0–5. That way, anyone using the database can immediately see what the expected options are and choose one with a swift flick of the mouse. By providing only acceptable choices, a pop-up menu ensures that the right kind of information ends up in the field—and makes data entry easier to boot.

1. **Click the Goodness Rating field to select it.**

   It grows selection handles.

2. **Choose Format → Field/Control → Setup.**

   You see the Field/Control Setup dialog box. (You can see it in Figure 4-25, too.)

Figure 4-25:
The Field/Control Setup dialog box (Format → Field/Control → Setup) lets you control how a field presents itself on the layout. You can add scroll bars, control the display of repeating fields, and—most useful of all—turn ordinary fields into pop-up menus, checkboxes, or radio buttons. All of these advanced options are covered in detail in Chapter 6.

3. **From the "Display as" pop-up menu, choose *Pop-up Menu*.**

   The "Include vertical scroll bar" checkbox disappears and a new pop-up menu takes its place.

4. **From the "Display values from" pop-up menu, choose Define Value Lists.**

   The Define Value Lists dialog box swings into view. The details of creating value lists are explained in Chapter 3; flip back to page 106 if you need a refresher.

5. **Create a new value list with the values 0, 1, 2, 3, 4, and 5. Click OK when you're done to close the Field Format box.**

The Goodness Rating field now looks like a pop-up menu (a retro-80s pop-up menu, but a pop-up menu nonetheless). In Figure 4-26, you can see how it displays the value list you just created.

Figure 4-26:
A pop-up menu needs a value list to determine what choices it shows. Here, you're defining a value list called Goodness Ratings with values for zero through five. When you're done, click OK, and then OK again to return to the Field Format dialog box.

Field/Control borders. Next up are the field *borders*. In layout mode, your fields probably have black borders and baselines (see Figure 4-8), but in Browse mode, they're just floating bits of text. To give them a little more substance, you can put a true border around them, and then give them a nice engraved effect:

1. **Choose Format → Field/Control → Borders.**

   The "Field Borders for selected objects" dialog box appears. It's shown in Figure 4-27.

Figure 4-27:
The Field Borders dialog box lets you control more than just borders (go figure). If it's really borders you're after, make sure Borders is selected in the pop-up menu.

2. **Turn on the Top, Left, Bottom, and Right checkboxes.**

   The Sample area shows how your field will look with borders applied to all four sides.

3. **Click OK.**

   The Field Borders dialog box goes away. You probably won't notice any change since FileMaker normally shows a thin border around fields in layout mode, but your fields really do have borders now, even in Browse mode.

Formatting Different Field Types

Most people think of formatting as something you do to text—change the font, make it boldface, or whatever. That's also true in FileMaker when it comes to formatting *text*. But when you're talking about formatting *fields*, you begin by choosing the overall *style* of field you want in the first place. In FileMaker, that's called the *field setup*, which is why the Field/Control Setup dialog box includes options like Pop-up Menu and Checkbox Set. There you can apply various options and settings depending on the basic field format.

Chapter 6 goes into great detail about how these different field formats work and how to choose options for them. Here's a brief rundown:

- **Edit Box** is the fancy term for a plain old text field, like the ones that hold first and last names. You can type freely into this type of field.

- **Drop-down List** fields *look* just like Edit Box fields, but when you click or tab into one, it shows a list of choices below the field. You can either pick from the list, or click again and type something else. (The list of choices is defined by a value list, like those you created on page 106.)

- **Pop-up Menu** fields look and work like normal pop-up menus, forcing you to pick an item from a list. The Goodness Rating field in this chapter (page 156) is an example.

- A **Checkbox Set** is a block of choices, each with a checkbox beside it. You can turn items off and on at will, just like normal checkboxes. When you turn more than one item on, the field value is set to both items, each on a line by itself.

- A **Radio Button Set** looks a lot like a Checkbox Set, except you can pick only one item at a time.

- A **Drop-down Calendar** makes entering proper dates drop-dead easy. FileMaker is really picky about the data it's willing to accept in a date field. But if you attach a calendar to your date fields, you'll be able to just click on a date, and FileMaker pops that date right into the field for you. No muss, no fuss!

---

4. **In the status area, click the Fill Effects button (it has two blue squares on it), and choose Engraved.**

   FileMaker draws a beveled edge around each field.

   In addition, the notes field needs a scroll bar.

5. **Select the notes field, and then choose Format → Field/Control Setup and turn on "Include vertical scroll bar."**

   Click OK to close the Field Format dialog box.

The fields now look a little more like…well…fields. But you've unwittingly created a new problem: The fields are now too short. When you added the engraved effect, FileMaker put an extra border around each field. This extra border uses up one pixel on each side, reducing the vertical space *inside* the field by two pixels. These few pixels make a difference—look at the City field, for example, whose "y" has lost its tail.

To remedy this problem, you need to make each field a little taller. But how much taller? Luckily, FileMaker knows just how tall a field needs to be, and it's ready to help you out. When you resize a field with the mouse, FileMaker won't let it get smaller than it needs to be to properly show one line of text in the selected font and size. You just need to manually resize the fields, letting FileMaker do its thing. You can see the process in Figure 4-28.

Figure 4-28:
In this series of images, you can see the steps needed to get your field heights fixed. Start by grabbing the lower-right handle on one of the selected fields—it doesn't matter which field (one). Then drag straight down a little (two), and then back up (three). When you do, FileMaker doesn't let you make the field shorter than it needs to be to fit the text it contains. Release the button (four) and all the selected fields resize appropriately.

One

Two

Three

Four

You'll learn lots more about resizing, moving, and aligning objects in the next section.

Laying Out the Layout

You're finally ready to organize the fields on the layout. The goal of a layout is to present information in a clear and attractive manner—in this case, the details for the people in your database. Turn back to Figure 4-22 to remind yourself how this layout is supposed to look.

Right now, though, your window probably shows something of a mess. More like Figure 4-29, perhaps. To organize and beautify your layout, you need to move and resize your fields, and line things up, as described in this section.

Figure 4-29:
Here's how your database looks now. The field and label formatting is in place, but the layout itself is a mess. Some fields are too big for the data they need to hold, others aren't big enough. And this layout needs some pizzazz. It's time to tackle field arrangement.

Resizing objects

Turn on text boundaries (View → Show → Text Boundaries) and take a look at the labels you edited a few pages back. You see that some text objects are quite a bit longer than the text they contain. When you delete part of a label, the object itself doesn't get shorter. FileMaker doesn't let objects extend off the edge of a layout, so those long text boxes don't allow room to put the labels as far to the left as you want. You'll need to shorten them.

The first three fields are bigger than they need to be too. You can easily fix them all at once. Select each object (Shift-click or use the rubber band), and then resize one of them using its handles (it doesn't matter which one you resize). When you finish, every selected field changes size to match the one you dragged.

Tip: The trick above works great if all the fields start at the same size, but it gets squirrelly if they aren't equal sizes to start with. Use the Arrange → Resize to → Smallest Width command to resize fields that start out different sizes, but need to end up the same width. You can also resize fields by height and to the largest size instead of the smallest.

While you're at it, make the Goodness Rating field narrower too. It can be very small since it shows only one digit. Finally, make the notes field nice and tall so it can hold lots of notes.

Aligning objects

Most of the field labels on the finished layout are right-aligned against an imaginary line running down the layout, as shown in Figure 4-30. Only the Goodness label doesn't follow this rule, so for starters, move it to the right of the fields so it's out of the way.

POWER USERS' CLINIC

Super-Sizing

Dragging or using the Arrange menu aren't the only ways to resize objects. If you're a numbers person, you can use the Object Size palette instead. Use the View → Object Size menu command to bring up this tiny window. It shows information about the selected object—namely, its position (how far the left, right, top, and bottom edges of the object are from the top-left corner of the layout) and its height and width.

But the power of the palette doesn't stop there. You can also type numbers into the palette, and the selected object will move or resize appropriately. If you have two similar objects on two different layouts, and you want to make sure they're the same width on both layouts, the Object Size palette is the easiest way:

1. Select the first object. Note its width in the Object Size palette.

2. Switch to the other layout.

3. Select the second object.

4. Type the same width in the Object Size palette.

When you're done, you can be absolutely certain both fields are the same width. Of course, you can also use this technique to set an object's height. You can even change an object's position and both dimensions in the same trip. If your memory is good, remember all four numbers. If you're middle-aged, write them down, because you'll have forgotten at least one of the numbers by the time you switch to the second layout.

The Object Size palette uses the same units you have your graphics rulers configured to use. But don't waste a trip to the Layout → Set Rulers menu just to change it. Instead, you can click the units displayed on the palette. As you click, FileMaker cycles between the supported unit types—Inches, Centimeters, and Pixels— keep clicking until you find the one you want.

Size	
196	px
117	px
356	px
131	px
160	px
14	px

But in your layout as you have it now, the fields labels are all over the place. Your first order of business is to get them all lined up along the right edge: Select all the field labels except the Goodness label. Then choose Arrange → Align → Right Edges. They leap to attention, all with their right edges in line with the text object that had been farthest to the right.

Tip: If you have fields that are lined up vertically, but the spacing between them isn't even, use the Arrange → Distribute → Vertically command to make the spacing regular. There's also an Arrange → Distribute → Horizontally command to make your life a little bit easier.

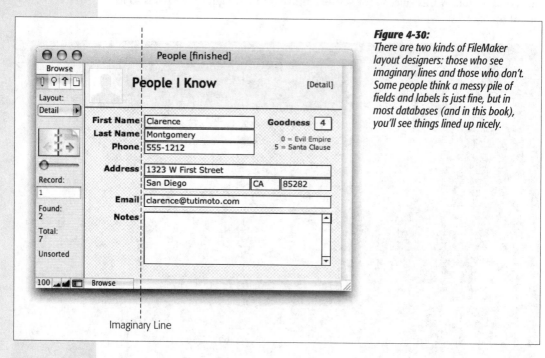

Figure 4-30:
There are two kinds of FileMaker layout designers: those who see imaginary lines and those who don't. Some people think a messy pile of fields and labels is just fine, but in most databases (and in this book), you'll see things lined up nicely.

Moving objects

Now that the field labels are lined up, you can move them to their final resting place. Just select them all and then drag them a little to the left. Hold down the Shift key to make sure they don't drift up or down while you drag. When you Shift-drag objects, FileMaker makes sure they only move in *one* direction: up and down or left to right.

Tip: You have to press the Shift key *after* you press the mouse button to start dragging. If you don't, File-Maker just sees a Shift-click, and deselects the object. Luckily, you can press the Shift key any time during a drag, and FileMaker will instantly snap the object to a perfect trajectory. You can even release Shift mid-drag if you decide you don't want constrained movement after all.

Using all the arrangement powers you now possess, it's time to line things up so the fields sit next to their labels. If you're using the Object Grids command (see the box on page 163) or you have very sharp eyes, you can probably just drag the fields next to their labels and get perfect alignment.

Tip: If you're having trouble getting perfect alignment, don't hesitate to turn on the T-Squares (View → T-Squares) or use the Arrange → Set Alignment command to ease your way.

Exercise Some Constraint

FileMaker developers often resize and move. Bearing this in mind, FileMaker has a few tricks up its sleeve to make things easier. You already learned how to hold down the Shift key to constrain mouse movement. Here are a few more goodies:

- Hold down the Control (Windows) or Option (Mac) key while creating or resizing a rectangle, rounded rectangle, or oval to make a perfect square or circle. When working with a line, this key makes it perfectly horizontal, perfectly vertical, or exactly 45° from one of these directions. If you drag an entire object with this key down, you get a copy of the object (the original stays put).

- With an object selected, press any of the arrow keys to move the object one pixel in the appropriate direction.

- Make a copy of an object by holding down the Ctrl (Windows) or Option (Mac) key while you drag it. Add the Shift key to the mix to make sure the object stays aligned with the original.

- Use the Duplicate command to create a new object that's 6 pixels to the right and 6 pixels below the original.

- Choose Align → Object Grids to turn another alignment feature on or off. Instead of moving with pixel-by-pixel freedom—which can make things nearly impossible to line up—things on the layout automatically align themselves to an invisible grid as you drag them. You can set the spacing of this grid by choosing Layout → Set Rulers and adjusting the "Grid spacing" value (see page 134).

As if that weren't enough, you can use the Object Size palette introduced above to move objects as well. If the palette says the left edge of an object is two inches from the ruler origin, you can type 4 instead to move it farther into the layout.

The City, State, and Zip fields don't have labels of their own. Instead, they line up side-by-side under the Street Address field. Make the City field about half the width of the Street Address field. Then place the State field next to it, and make it wide enough to hold two letters. Finally, drop the Zip field in place next to the State field. Chances are you can't align the Zip field perfectly with the right edge of the Street Address field. If necessary, use the T-Squares, the Object Size palette, and the arrow keys to bring things into alignment.

Lastly, put the Goodness label and its associated field in the right spot.

Adding images

The finished layout has a cute person icon next to the People I Know text. To add a picture to the layout, you can copy it from any other program, and then paste it directly on the layout. If the picture you want is in a file on your hard drive, use the

Insert → Picture command instead. When you do, FileMaker will ask you to pick a picture file, and then insert it on the layout.

Once the picture is added to the layout, drag it into position in the header. If necessary, resize the header to accommodate it, and move the People I Know text object out of the way.

Adding a Dividing Line Between Layout Parts

You may also want to add a line between the header and body parts. As you can see in Figure 4-30, this line helps break up the space in the window, and helps your eye locate the important information in the lower (body) part of the window. If you use a Mac, this line can serve as more than decoration, as discussed in Figure 4-31. (In Chapter 14, you'll learn more about how to deal with the differences between Mac OS X and Windows when working with multiple windows.)

1. **In the status area, activate the line tool.**

   The mouse arrow changes to a crosshair.

2. **With the Shift key held down, drag a horizontal line about the desired width of the layout.**

   As you drag, a dotted line shows you what your line will look like. When you release the mouse button, the line appears.

3. **Drag the new line as far to the right as it will go, and place it as close to the header part boundary as you can.**

   The Object Grids might prevent you from getting it right on the part boundary.

4. **Using the up or down arrow keys, nudge the line so that it covers the dotted part boundary perfectly.**

   The dotted part boundary line marks the *end* of the part above it, so this line is at the bottom of the header, not the top of the body.

5. **If necessary, resize the line so that it ends just a bit to the right of the [Detail] text object.**

   As you drag, hold the Shift key while you resize the line to make sure it stays perfectly horizontal. The line now marks the desired width for the layout.

Tip: If you're using the horizontal line as a device in Mac OS X to control the width of the window, but you don't actually want a line across your layout, you can make the line invisible. Just draw the line as described above, and set its thickness to None, using the Line Weight tool

---

Wrapping up

You only have a few last touches to complete your layout. First, add a text object to hold the Goodness Rating key and type into it, *0 = Evil Empire, 5 = Santa Claus.*

Tip: If you're like most people, your Font menu is half a mile long. It can be a real drag finding and selecting just the font you want. To save the trouble, duplicate one of your field labels and use that for the Goodness Rating key instead (Edit → Duplicate). Just edit it to show the correct text, and then change it to 9 Point and remove the bold style. You have an easier time duplicating an existing object than you do making a new one, since the duplicate picks up all the attributes you painstakingly set.

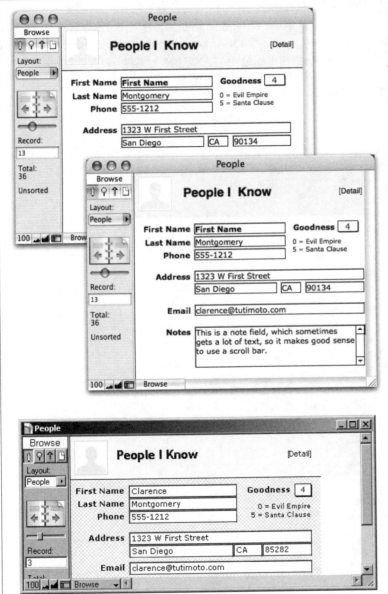

Figure 4-31:
When you click a window's zoom button in Mac OS X, FileMaker makes the window just big enough to hold the contents of the layout. With your layout as it is now, the edge of the "zoomed down" window bumps right up to fields (top front), which most people think looks funny. The solution is to add a line to the layout that's just a bit wider than the fields are across (top rear). See page 164 for instructions. If you're going to use the database only in Windows, you may want to leave the line out, since Windows can't easily resize a window to fit perfectly, and in fact the line may look odd in a wider window (bottom).

Just for added flair, go ahead and make the Goodness Rating field use a red text color. With the field selected, choose Format → Text Color and pick a red from the color menu.

The Goodness Rating pop-up menu looks nicer if you center its text. Select the field and choose Format → Align Text → Center.

You're ready to switch to Browse mode. When you do, FileMaker asks if you'd like to save your changes. Click Save. Now you see your new layout in action!

Phew! That was a lot of work. Designing a FileMaker layout is a very visual process. That's really good news since it makes the process pretty *obvious* once you learn the tools. This chapter may make it seem like a lot of work, but making a layout like this will quickly become second nature—you'll be able to crank one out in just a few minutes.

Creating Layouts

The last chapter introduced a lot of concepts, but you only had a chance to shuffle one layout around a bit. Now it's time to put everything you've learned to use. Your People database has a great detail layout, but what else could it use? For starters, a neatly arranged list of people would be nice. And how about a way to print mailing labels? You probably have some ideas about what *you'd* like your database to do, and FileMaker itself has some ideas of its own to help you along.

In this chapter, you'll learn the two main ways of designing and implementing your own layouts in FileMaker. You can create a unique new layout from scratch, say if you like to print all your worldly information on index cards (you know who you are). Or if your needs are more down-to-earth, you can let an assistant save you some time. Just answer a few questions, and the assistant plugs your answers into standard forms like mailing labels. You'll also learn about special FileMaker layouts called *reports*, which sort, filter, or summarize your data before presenting it.

The Lowdown on Layouts

Although you can create an infinite variety of layouts in FileMaker, they all boil down to a few basic types. You get a chance to try each of them as you proceed through this chapter. Here's a brief overview of each.

Standard Form

The "Standard form" choice creates a layout just like the one FileMaker creates automatically when you start your database—a simple detail layout (see page 84).

This time, though, you get to decide which fields to include. You also have some control over the fonts and colors. FileMaker calls these design controls "themes."

Columnar List/Report

If you want to show lots of records on the screen or page at one time, choose "Columnar list/report" instead. You still get to pick which fields to include and what theme to use, but FileMaker sets up the new layout as a list of records with one column per field, as shown in Figure 5-1.

Figure 5-1:
This "Columnar" List/ Report layout shows several people at a time in a space-efficient form. FileMaker plugs in the page title, date, and column headings automatically when you create the layout. (You'll find out how to adjust all these settings on page 189.)

Table View

When you select "Table view," FileMaker creates a layout much like "Standard form," but the layout is set to table view automatically. Actually, the pros (yourself included) know that you can choose View → View as Table in Browse mode to see *any* layout in table view (page 35), so you rarely need to create a separate layout of this type. But if you're new to this whole database thing and want a layout that looks and acts like the spreadsheets you're accustomed to, the Table view layout is your fastest way there.

Labels or Vertical Labels

If you ever need to print a sheet of peel-and-stick labels from your database—to make nametags for every attendee to your conference, or address labels for all those follow-up letters—the Labels layout type is your best friend (it's shown in Figure 5-2). FileMaker is smart enough to know how to set up a layout for any of the standard Avery label types. You just pick your type, and FileMaker does all the work. If you're not using Avery labels, you can plug in your own measurements.

Note: The "Vertical labels" type only applies to people with Asian language text in their database. This type rotates this kind of text to create *vertical* text labels.

Figure 5-2:
When you create a Labels layout, you can easily decide how all the field data mixes together to display as you want it. In this example, the First Name and Last Name are on the first line, with a single space between them. On the third line, City, State, and Zip have been combined appropriately.

Envelope

If you'd rather print right on the envelope than stick a label on it, use the Envelope type. FileMaker creates a layout specially designed to print on a Number 10 size envelope (Figure 5-3).

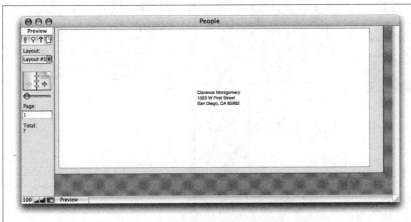

Figure 5-3:
You can address envelopes in a heartbeat to everyone with a layout like this one. Just find the people you want, load a stack of envelopes in your printer, and print them out.

Since every printer handles envelopes a little differently, the layout needs a little adjusting to print perfectly, though. Luckily, it's almost always a cinch to put things right. You can usually just delete the header part from the layout. On more persnickety printers, you may have to leave the header in place, and adjust its height. Getting things lined up always involves a few test prints, but once you've got it working, you never have to fuss with it again.

Blank Layout

The last type, called Blank layout, is both the simplest and the most flexible. You get a layout with a small header and footer, and a big body. It has nothing on it at all. If you like setting things up by hand, or your layout doesn't rightly match *any* of the types above, drawing a blank may be your best choice.

Use this option to create your first new layout.

Creating a Layout from Scratch

FileMaker's built-in layout types are nice for quick-and-dirty work, but if you want your database to look great *and* work exactly the way you say, you may need to do some heavy customization. In fact, you often find it easier to start with a blank layout and add exactly what you need than to try and slice'n'dice a standard form into the avant-garde arrangement you have in mind.

Adding a New Layout

However they may end up, all new layouts start the same way. Open a database, switch to Layout mode, choose Layout → New Layout/Report. You see the window shown in Figure 5-4—the New Layout/Report dialog box.

Figure 5-4:
The New Layout/Report dialog box (Layout → New Layout/Report) is the starting point for layout creation. Most importantly, you get to decide what type of layout you want. If you pick any type other than Blank layout, FileMaker does some of the initial busywork for you.

Note: As its name suggests, you'll see this dialog box again when you learn how to create reports, on page 187.

In this box, you tell FileMaker a few basic facts about the new layout you have in mind. (You can always tweak these settings later.) From top to bottom, here's how it works:

- **Show records from.** For now, you can just ignore this pop-up menu. (It lets you choose a table, but you have only one table so far.)

- **Layout Name.** Enter a name for your layout here. You can use any name you want, but you have to keep it to 100 characters or less.

- **Include in Layout menu.** Use this checkbox to tell FileMaker whether or not it shows up in the status area's Layout pop-up menu. Most new developers turn on this option for every layout, to make sure they can always find their work. As your databases get more advanced, you might have special layouts that you want people to access only under certain circumstances. When you get that fancy, you can turn this checkbox off so folks can't switch to the layout any time they want.

Note: *Every* layout shows in the Layout pop-up menu when you're in Layout mode. This checkbox controls what shows up when you're in other modes.

Right now, the most important decision you make in this window is the choice of items in the "Select a layout type" list. FileMaker asks you questions specific to the type of layout you ask for, and then creates the layout based on your answer. When you select a layout type, FileMaker shows a little graphic mock-up of what this kind of layout looks like, just to the right of the list.

To get a feel for how it works, you're going to create a layout in the People database like the one shown in Figure 5-5. Because this layout doesn't match any of the canned layout types in the New Layout/Report window, you'll start with a blank layout and build everything by hand. The goal is to see several people at once, so you'll tailor it with list view in mind.

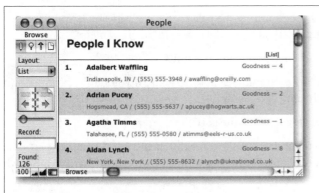

Figure 5-5:
The new list layout shows some information about a lot of people. As in all good list layouts, you can scroll through the records in the found set. Unlike your everyday, ordinary list, though, this layout doesn't have a strict "Columns design.

First, create the layout:

1. **Open the People database (see page xxiv for download instructions). In Layout mode, choose Layout → New Layout/Report.**

   The New Layout/Report window pops up.

2. **In the Layout Name box, type a fitting name, like *List*. Then, from the "Select a layout type" list, choose "Blank layout."**

   The Next button changes to Finish, since you don't have any more choices for a blank layout.

3. **Click Finish.**

   FileMaker returns you to your database, and shows you the new blank layout.

Set up the Header

This layout needs a header almost exactly like the one on the People layout. Unfortunately, you can't copy and paste the header part (page 124) itself, but you *can* copy everything on the header, and paste it on this new layout.

Before you do, you need to make this header the same size as the other so everything fits properly. As with many things in FileMaker, you have at least two good ways to perform this task. Which you use depends entirely on your personal taste.

Matching part sizes with the Object Size palette

If you're a numbers person, this method is for you. Using the Object Size palette, you can resize or reposition any layout object with pixel-perfect precision. To learn how to tackle it, you first check the exact size of the header part on the People layout, then adjust the new header so its size matches.

1. **Switch to the People layout.**

   You can switch using the Layout pop-up menu, or simply by clicking the left-hand page on the Book icon. When you do, you immediately see the People layout.

2. **If the Object Size palette isn't showing, choose View → Object Size.**

   You can have a hard time spotting the palette, since it's so small. You know it's there if you see a checkmark next to Object Size in the View menu.

3. **Make sure the palette is measuring in pixel units.**

   You should see "px" by each number in the palette. If you don't, click the unit you do see repeatedly until "px" shows.

4. **Click the Header part tag to select the part.**

   The Object Size palette updates to show measurements for the header part. The last field—with a double arrow pointing up and down—is the height. Jot down the height number you see there.

5. Switch to the new List layout, then select the header by clicking its tag.

The Object Size palette now measures this part.

6. Type the number you got in step 5 into the height field on the Object Size palette, and then press Enter.

The part doesn't move while you type; you have to press Enter to see your change take effect. When you do, the header part resizes, and now perfectly matches the header on the People layout.

If you prefer less typing and more mousing, you can use the T-Squares instead.

Matching part sizes with the T-Squares

In the last chapter, you learned about the T-Squares (page 134). These handy liner-uppers don't just help you keep objects on the layout straight. They can also help you make sure parts and objects are in the same place on *different* layouts. Start on the People layout, and then follow these steps:

1. If the T-Squares aren't showing, choose View → T-Squares.

The T-Square lines appear.

Tip: On a busy layout, the T-Squares can be hard to spot. If you know they're showing, but you can't *find* them, just turn them off and back on. When you do, they reappear smack-dab in the center of the layout.

---

2. Position the horizontal T-Square between the header and body.

The T-Squares float above everything else on a layout, so it covers the dotted part boundary line perfectly. If you add a black line between your header and body, you may not see the boundary. Just put the T-Square over your line instead.

Tip: If you're having trouble getting the lines to match perfectly, the Object Grids may be holding you back. Choose Align → Object Grids to tell FileMaker to let you move the T-square exactly where you want them.

---

3. Switch to the new list layout, and drag the header part tag into the right place, using the T-Square as a guide.

Since T-Squares stay in the same spot as you switch layouts, you can rest assured your new header is just the right size.

Now that the header is the right size, you can fill it with the necessary objects. You could drag objects into the header manually, just as you did in the last chapter when you built the People layout. But you've already done that work once. Why not take advantage of it here as well? You can easily reuse these items: Copy and paste them from the People layout. You use copy and paste *a lot* when you design layouts.

---

1. **Switch back to the People layout. Select the graphic, "People I Know" text, and "[Detail]" text.**

   You can Shift-click or use the rubber band. If you have a horizontal line on your layout, select it too.

2. **Choose Edit → Copy.**

   Nothing changes on the screen, but FileMaker copies the objects to your operating system's clipboard.

3. **Switch back to the list layout, then choose Edit → Paste.**

   The objects appear on the new layout, probably in the wrong place.

4. **Drag the objects (as a group) into their proper place in the header.**

   Since they're all selected, if you drag one object, the others follow.

Tip: If you're a stickler for details, you may want to use the T-Squares or Object Size palette to be sure everything's in the same place on both layouts. If you do, just check *one* of the objects. Since they were copied, pasted, and moved as a group, if one is in place, the others are too.

Adding the finishing touches

Your header part is nearly complete. To finish it, give it a colored fill (page 143). Finally, since you're not making a detail layout, it probably shouldn't say "[Detail]" in the header. Change that text object to say "[List]" instead, so it matches the name of the layout. Figure 5-6 shows how your layout should look now.

Figure 5-6:
Now that your header has been gussied up, this is how your layout looks. It has a nice-looking header, but the body could still use some work—it's empty right now. Since this is a list layout, you need to give it a short body without a lot of wasted space. This body appears once for each record in the found set, producing an attractive scrolling list.

Set up the Body

Now that the header is in place, it's time to work on the body—and learn a few new tricks. You add the first and last name fields to the layout, and make them flow nicely together. You'll also tell FileMaker to show the record number next to each person's name.

Making data flow with merge fields

Knowing what you know now, if you set out to build this layout yourself, you'd probably jump right for the field tool and start dragging new field on the layout. But look closely at Figure 5-7 first.

Figure 5-7:
The window at top uses normal fields, which are always in the same place on the layout, no matter what record you're on. Notice how the spacing between the contents of each field looks odd. By using merge fields, you can even out such awkward spacing for a more professional result, like the bottom window.

When you put a field on a layout, you're putting it *exactly* where you want it. No matter what record you're on when you look at the layout, that field value is in the same spot. Usually, that's where you want it to be, but sometimes—like in the new list layout—you want something a little more flexible. You want the Last Name field to start where the first name ends. Since some first names are longer than others, this spot changes from record to record.

In FileMaker, you solve this problem using *merge fields*. These work a lot like a mail merge in a word processing program. You create an ordinary text object on your layout (not a field object), and then tell FileMaker to merge different field values into the text. For example, to put the first and last names together on your new layout, you create a text object like this:

```
<<First Name>> <<Last Name>>
```

Merge fields always show up in Layout mode with angle brackets around their names, just like <<this>>. When you look at this text object in Browse mode, though, you see the value of the First Name field, then a space, then the Last Name field. Since all these values show up in a single text object, FileMaker sorts out the exact positions for you.

Merge fields have a downside, though: They're for display only. You need a real field if you want your users to be able to get into a field and change its contents. Your database already has a layout with real fields just for editing data (the details layout), so in this case, merge fields are just what the doctor ordered.

Putting merge fields into a text object is easy:

1. **In the status area, click the text tool.**

   FileMaker activates the text tool; it changes your mouse arrow to an I-beam, and darkens the text tool button. Now set up the font for the text object you're about to create.

2. **Using the Font, Size, and Style menus (in the Format menu) choose Verdana, 11 Point, and Bold. Then click somewhere in the body part.**

   A new editable text box appears, ready for you to type.

3. **Choose Insert → Merge Field.**

   The Specify Field dialog box appears, listing every field in your database.

4. **Select the First Name field, and then click OK.**

   FileMaker types <<*First Name*>> into the text object for you.

5. **Type a single space.**

   Since you don't want the first and last name *right* next to each other, you've just added a space.

6. **Choose Insert → Merge Field again. When the Specify Field dialog box returns, select the Last Name field, and then click OK.**

   FileMaker adds the Last Name merge field to the text object.

You now have a text object that shows the first and last names with a single space between them (you can switch to Browse mode and try it out if you want). You just need to put it into place.

The address, phone, and email information should also be in a merge field (study Figure 5-7 to see why—they all flow together in a nicely formatted line). In this case you want Verdana, 9-Point, Plain. You can also select a gray color (or any color you like) from the Format → Text Color menu. Repeat the steps above to build a text object like this:

```
<<City>>, <<State>> / <<Phone Number>> / <<Email Address>>
```

Tip: You can mix and match merge fields and normal text to your heart's content. When you were setting up the first and last name, you added a space between the merge fields. This time you add even more. After you add the City merge field, type a comma, and a space. After the State and Phone Number merge fields, type space-slash-space.

Using symbols to show important info

Merge fields aren't the only things FileMaker can squeeze into a text object on the fly. You can also insert a handful of special *symbols*—stand-in characters that you can replace with useful information when you view your database in Browse or Preview mode. For instance, notice in Figure 5-7, how each record in the list is numbered. You can accomplish this effect with the record number symbol.

Tip: FileMaker offers a host of other symbols besides the record number symbol. See the box on page 178 for full detail.

Since you're creating a *list* layout, it would be nice to show record numbers. That way you can easily see where you are in the list at any time, even if you've scrolled down from the top. You use the record number symbol to make it happen.

1. **Select the first and last name text object you just created.**

   If you just make a new text object with the text tool, you have to set the font, size, style, and possibly color. Instead, you can take a text object that already has *all* the attributes you want and use it as a starting point.

2. **Choose Edit → Duplicate.**

   A copy of the first and last name object appears.

3. **In the status area, click the text tool. Click anywhere in the new text object you're about to edit.**

   FileMaker outlines the text object and adds a flashing insertion point. Now select all the text in the object.

4. **Choose Edit → Select All, and then press Delete or Backspace.**

   The selected text disappears, leaving an empty text box.

5. **Choose Insert → Record Number Symbol.**

   "@@" appears in the text box.

6. **Type a period, then press Enter.**

   If you want a period after the record number symbol, you have to type it your-self. Pressing Enter tells FileMaker you're done editing the text object.

You now have a text object that contains "@@." But if you peek at it in Browse mode, you see that FileMaker actually puts the current record number in its place.

Other Symbols

FileMaker includes symbols for several special values you might want to show on a layout. You insert these symbols on the layout because you don't know in advance what they're going to be, such as the current date or record num-ber. Then, when you switch to Browse mode (or Preview mode), FileMaker replaces the symbol with the up-to-the-moment correct value. You can read about the record num-ber symbol on page 177. Here are the others:

- The date symbol (//) is replaced by the current date. People often include this symbol on printed reports so you can easily see when they were generated.

- The time symbol (::) is replaced by the current time.

- The user name symbol (||) is replaced by the cur-rent user's name. FileMaker takes the user name of whoever's logged into your computer. (That's two *pipe* symbols—Shift-backslash on most keyboards—typed side by side)

- The page number symbol (##) is replaced by the page number in Preview mode or when you print. Otherwise, it just shows as a question mark.

The Insert menu has three related options as well, but unlike symbols, these don't get replaced by anything in Browse or Preview mode. When you use the Insert → Cur-rent Date command, for instance, FileMaker simply adds today's date to the text object in Layout mode. It will show this same date forever in either mode.

You can use the Insert menu to place symbols where you need them, but it's faster and easier to type them in manu-ally. So once you've seen that "##" makes a page number, forget about mousing around and just type the two number signs.

Tip: You can apply the same formatting to date and time symbols as you can to regular versions of those fields. Just select the text block that contains your date symbol ("//"). Then select FormatDate and choose the formatting you want. Works for the time symbol ("::"), too.

Arranging the objects

Now that you've added three new text objects to the body part, you can arrange them on the layout. Using Figure 5-8 as a guide, use the techniques you learned on page 159 to move the text objects into a clear, attractive arrangement. Once they're in place, you just need to add the Goodness Rating field and make a few adjustments to the body part. You're almost done!

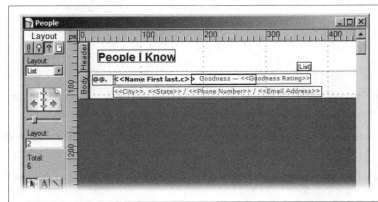

Figure 5-8:
Here's how to arrange your text objects on the layout. As you're dragging text objects around, you see a dotted line near the bottom of the item. That's an imaginary line called the baseline. You can use it to make sure your rows of data are neatly lined up.

Adding a field

The Goodness Rating is always a single-digit number, so unlike the First Name and Last Name fields, you don't need a merge field (page 175) to get its spacing right. You use an ordinary field object instead.

1. **From the status area, drag the Field tool onto the layout.**

   The Specify Field dialog box appears.

2. **Make sure the "Create field label" checkbox is turned on.**

   When this option is on, FileMaker automatically adds a text object to serve as a label for your field.

3. **Select the Goodness Rating field, and then click OK.**

   FileMaker adds the Goodness Rating field to the layout, along with a new text object that says "Goodness Rating."

Copying formatting with the format painter

Unfortunately, the new field and label aren't formatted properly. They have the wrong font, size, style, and color. Instead of fixing each object manually as you learned in Chapter 2, you can use the *format painter*.

This intuitive tool copies all the formatting from one object and applies it to another. Here's how to use it:

1. **Click the text object that shows City, State, Phone Number and Email Address to select it.**

   That object has the very formatting you want to copy.

2. **Choose Format → Format Painter.**

   Your mouse arrow changes to include a tiny paintbrush. The next thing you click with this special cursor takes on the copied format like a fresh coat of paint.

3. **Click the Goodness Rating label.**

   The label instantly changes to reflect the correct formatting. Also, it's already selected, so copying its formatting to the Goodness Rating field is a snap.

4. **Choose Format → Format Painter again, and then click the Goodness Rating field.**

   The field changes to the new formatting too. But it isn't exactly what you want—you want this field to be bold as well.

5. **Choose Format → Style → Bold.**

   The label now has just the right formatting.

The format painter is certainly easier than choosing each formatting option individually, but it seems to work for only one object at a time. There are actually a couple of ways to extend Format Painter's abilities. If the objects you want to format together are close enough, you can rubber band them with Format Painter and they all change together. Just like the regular rubber band, you have to fully enclose each object for the change to take place. But pressing the Ctrl (⌘) key lets you merely *touch* an object with the rubber band to get the same effect.

But maybe even that method doesn't work for you, because your objects are all over the place. Wouldn't it be nice if Format Painter were a button like the other tools? Then you could double-click it to lock it. Well, you're in luck, because that's just how it works.

1. **Choose View → Toolbars → Standard.**

   The Standard toolbar appears at the top of your screen.

2. **Select the object that has the formatting you want to copy**

   You've just copied a text block's formatting, but you can also use a field, a drawn object, or anything that has formatting.

3. **Double-click the format painter tool—the one that looks like a paintbrush, and then click each object you need to format.**

Double-clicking locks the tool, so you can use it over and over. You can even grab some rubber band selections if you want to.

4. **Click the Selection tool to let FileMaker know you're finished formatting.**

All good things must come to an end.

You now just need to make the Goodness Rating field smaller (just wide enough to hold one number) and put it in its place on the right side of the layout. Delete the word "Rating" from the Goodness Rating label, and then add a "-" to the end and position it just to the left of the field. Figure 5-9 shows where you're at.

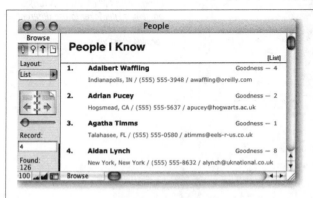

Figure 5-9:
With the Goodness Rating field in place, your layout is almost complete. In fact, you could stop here. But with just a few more steps, you can make your list much easier to scan and read. Simply add a gray background to every other record.

Alternating the body color

As Figure 5-5 plainly shows, the rows on this list layout are supposed to alternate between gray and white. FileMaker gives you this effect for free; you just have to turn it on. To do that, you pay a visit to the Part Definition dialog box via the Part Setup dialog box.

1. **Choose Layout → Part Setup.**

The Part Setup dialog box appears, as described in the box on page 183.

2. **In the Part Setup dialog box's list, select Body, and then click Change.**

This window lists every part in your layout. To select a part, just click its name. When you click Change, the Part Definition window opens (Figure 5-10).

Tip: There's a shortcut to the Part Definition dialog box: On the layout, just double-click the part tag. Turn on the "Alternate background fill" checkbox.

The Fill Color Menu and Fill Pattern Menu buttons, which had been grayed out, become available and ready for you to make a choice.

3. From the Fill Color Menu, choose a color to use for your alternate row color.

The Fill Sample changes to show your selection. Choose a color that's not too dark, or you'll have trouble seeing the beautiful layout you've created.

4. Click OK, and then Done.

Nothing changes in Layout mode, but if you switch to Browse mode, you see the new effect.

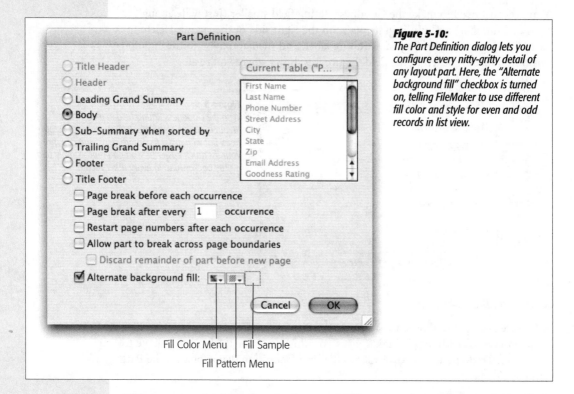

Figure 5-10:
The Part Definition dialog lets you configure every nitty-gritty detail of any layout part. Here, the "Alternate background fill" checkbox is turned on, telling FileMaker to use different fill color and style for even and odd records in list view.

When you use the "Alternate background fill" option, the settings you make in the Part Definition window apply to the even numbered records. You can still control the fill for odd numbered records by adjusting the body part fill right on the layout, just like you did with the header part. In this example, you tell FileMaker to color the even rows gray, and leave the odd rows white. You can use this feature any time you want to make it easier to see where one record ends and another begins, in a list.

Now all you need to do is resize the body part so it just fits its contents, using any of the methods described earlier in this chapter. When you've done that, your layout design is nearly finished.

Setting Layout View

Switch to Browse mode to admire your handiwork. If you're seeing only one record at a time, switch to list view (choose View → View as List). When you choose the blank layout template, you get complete freedom to make the layout look just the way you want. But one tradeoff is that you have to remember to tell the layout which view it's supposed to be in.

UP TO SPEED

Part Setup Dialog Box

When you choose Layout → Part Setup, FileMaker shows you Part Setup Dialog Box. This often-ignored box isn't just a slower way to get to the Part Definition window, though. From this one screen, you can create new parts and edit, delete, and rearrange existing parts. But, as you'll read on page 268, you can do most of this work more easily *without* this window, so you won't use it very often.

To add a new part, click Create. You're presented with the Part Definition dialog box, where you can decide what kind of part to create, and set various options. You can do the same thing by dragging the part tool from the status area or choosing Insert → Part.

To see the part definition for an existing part, select it and click Change. This maneuver too has a shortcut: Just double-click any part tag in Layout mode.

To delete a part, select it and click Delete. If the part contains any objects on the layout, FileMaker asks you if you're sure, because when you delete a part, you delete everything on it as well. You've already deleted parts without using this window, though, by selecting the part and choosing Edit → Clear. But if you hate menus, you can also just press Delete.

You can also rearrange parts using the same technique you use to order fields in the Define Database window. Just drag the arrow icon next to a part name. But some parts (most parts, in fact) have a padlock symbol instead of an arrow icon. This symbol tells you the part is *locked* in place and you can't move it. The reason is simple: It doesn't make sense to move most parts. For example, the header is always below the title header and above everything else. You really only need to rearrange parts when creating *sub-summary reports*, which the next chapter covers.

Since FileMaker always starts out showing form view, that's what you see until you tell the layout something different.

1. **Still in the People database, switch to Layout mode, then choose Layouts → Layout Setup.**

   Remember, Layout mode is the only place you can make changes to a layout. The Layout Setup box is where you work this particular piece of magic.

2. **On the Views tab, turn off Form View and Table View.**

You've just told FileMaker to make these two menu choices off-limits in Browse and Find modes. After all, they don't make much sense in a layout that's designed specifically to work as a list.

3. **Click OK to dismiss the dialog box.**

Honestly, you have to tell some programs *everything*.

Now, when you switch to Browse mode and look at the View menu, View as Form and View as Table are grayed out. FileMaker won't accidentally switch your list to a useless view of the data.

POWER USERS' CLINIC

Getting Table View to Mind Its Manners

Table view is a real boon if you want a quick and easy way to make your data look like a spreadsheet. With one command, your layout displays data in rows and columns, which you can rearrange and sort. But if you dig a little deeper, you find that you have a lot of control over how table view works. These controls lurk under the Layout Setup command. When you click the Views tab, you see that the Table View option has a button that leads you one dialog box deeper – into Table View Properties.

- With the **Grid** controls, you can show or hide table view's horizontal and vertical gridlines. Try switching off the Vertical gridlines to make rows more prominent. This way, it's easier to read across the data pertaining to a single record.

- With the **Grid Style** option come two familiar pop-up menus. You can choose a new color for the grids with the color pop-up or apply a pattern to them from the pattern pop-up menu. A sample swatch shows you the choices you've made.

- Under **Header and Parts**, you control the header, footer, and column heads. Headers and footers anchor to the top or bottom of the screen while the records scroll through long lists. Column heads are the field names at the top of each column.

- Headers and footers are normally suppressed when a layout's in table view. Choose **Include header part** or **Include footer part** to display those parts of the layout. (For obvious reasons, these options have no effect on a layout in which you don't have those particular parts.)

- Since the column heads tell you what information you're looking at, you don't often find a reason to turn off their display. But you can do it if you want to, by unchecking "**Include column headers**."

- More commonly, you might want to turn off some of the column headers' other features. Stop users from resizing columns by unchecking **Resizable columns**. Turn off **Reorderable columns** to keep folks from rearranging their order on the table. That way, nobody can move the First Name field so far away from the Last Name that the data loses its meaning. Nobody can sort records if you uncheck **Sort data when selecting column**.

- Choose **Use custom height** to set Rows to a specific height, and then select one of the measurement systems and type the height you want.

Creating Layouts for Reports

You've now knocked out two good layouts—a detail layout (Chapter 4) and a list layout (this chapter). Layouts like these meet many typical database needs: You've got your detail layout for finding and viewing individual records, and your list layout for rapidly scanning many records at once. You also want to do *reporting*, an equally important task in a typical database. A report's no different from any other layout as far as FileMaker is concerned. But report layouts are designed from the ground up to be *printed*. Almost no database gets by without some kind of a report layout, and most important databases have several, from straightforward lists to powerful snapshots of your data's important statistics, like sales by region or inventory by product category.

The People database needs a reporting layout, too. In this chapter you'll create a report layout for a simple purpose: printing a list of people. You can then file the printed list as a hard copy backup, take it with you on a trip, or mail it to an associate. But FileMaker's reporting powers go far beyond simple lists. The next chapter will introduce FileMaker's powerful data summarization and reporting capabilities.

Visualize the Result Preview Mode

First, you need a rough idea of how your layout should look. This step is especially important when you create a report, since the physical constraints of a piece of paper often dictate the working space you have. When you create a detail layout, you're free to make it large or small, tall or short, narrow or wide—whatever meets the needs of your data. Not so if you want to print your layout.

In the spirit of visualization, how about a picture? From the Preview illustration in Figure 5-11, you can get a pretty good idea of how this layout is going to come together. It has a header, body, and footer. The header includes a title, the date, and some column labels, and the footer has just a page number (these parts print on the top and bottom of each page). The body is the most important part: It has all the fields that show your information.

You can see the report in Layout mode in Figure 5-12. To see your layout in Preview Mode, choose View → Preview Mode.

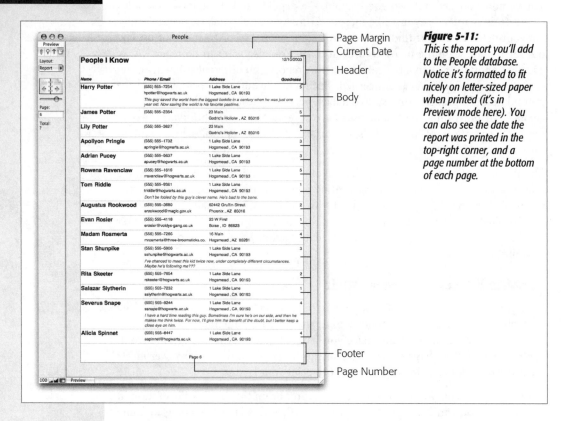

Page Margin
Current Date
Header
Body

Footer
Page Number

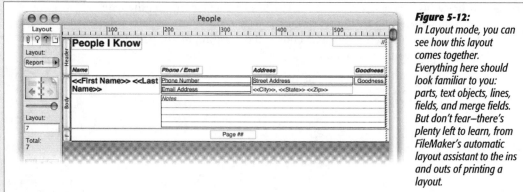

Figure 5-12:
In Layout mode, you can see how this layout comes together. Everything here should look familiar to you: parts, text objects, lines, fields, and merge fields. But don't fear—there's plenty left to learn, from FileMaker's automatic layout assistant to the ins and outs of printing a layout.

Creating a Report Layout with an Assistant

In the example in the previous section, you started with FileMaker's blank layout. Since blank layouts are always just blank, there were no more choices to make. This time, FileMaker does a lot more work for you. Before it does, it asks you a handful of questions. Your job is to answer the questions, click Next, answer some more, and so on. When FileMaker has all the information it needs, it changes the Next button to a Finish button. FileMaker then creates the layout according to your specifications. Here's how to proceed:

1. **In the People database, switch to Layout mode and choose Layout → New Layout/Report. Name the new layout** *Report*.

   You've been through these steps before (page 170). Next, select a layout type (Figure 5-13), so FileMaker knows which choices to offer you in the upcoming steps. Different layout types, different options.

Figure 5-13:
This is the first round of choices when creating a "Columnar list/report" layout. Here, you decide whether or not you want "grouped data" (you don't—more on that in Chapter 6). You also need to decide if you want FileMaker to make sure your layout fits the width of a piece of paper. As you make selections, the picture in the top-right corner shows a rough representation of what your choices do.

2. **Select the "Columnar/list report" radio button. While you're at it, turn on the "Constrain to page width" checkbox.**

   The picture in the top-right corner of the window changes to show that the layout won't extend past the width of a page.

3. **Click Next.**

   Now you see the window shown in Figure 5-14, where you tell FileMaker what fields to add to the layout.

4. **Click Move All.**

Every field in the "Available fields" list moves to the "Layout fields" list. Click Next.

Figure 5-14:
You pick the fields by adding them to the Layout Fields list. FileMaker adds them to the body part for you when it creates the layout.

5. **As shown in Figure 5-15, add the Last Name field to the "Sort order" list.**

In the "Report fields" list, click Last Name, and then click Move.

Figure 5-15:
Sometimes you want your reports sorted, so FileMaker offers to do it for you. In truth, it creates a script (Part 4) for you that sorts the records, switches to the layout, and goes to Preview mode—everything you do to view a typical report.

6. **In the same way, add the First Name field to the "Sort order" list.**

   The "Sort order" list now shows the Last Name field, then the First Name field. This arrangement tells FileMaker to sort first by Last Name, then by First Name. Click Next.

7. **From the "Layout themes" list shown in Figure 5-16, select Standard.**

   The picture changes to show a simple white background with black text. Click Next.

Figure 5-16:
Here's your chance to select a theme. As you make selections from the "Layout themes" list, the picture changes to show how the theme will look. Click all you want—it's pretty much guaranteed that none of them will match your business collateral. When you're done browsing, pick Standard for the example on these pages.

8. **From the "Top left" pop-up menu (Figure 5-17), choose Large Custom Text. When the Custom Text dialog box appears, type *People I Know*, and then click OK.**

   The "Top left" pop-up menu now shows that you've selected Large Custom Text.

9. **From the "Top right" pop-up menu, choose *Current Date*. Then, from the "Bottom center" pop-up menu, choose *Page Number*.**

   The pop-up menus' content changes to reflect your choices. Click Next.

10. **On the next screen, turn on the "Create a script" radio button. Then, in the "Script name" box, type *Report*.**

   As explained in Figure 5-18, you've just told FileMaker to add an item with this name to the Script menu. You can choose this menu command to run the report. Click Next.

11. **In the assistant's final screen (Figure 5-19), turn on "View the report in Layout mode."**

This tells FileMaker to deposit you in Layout mode after it finishes creating the report. Click Finish.

Figure 5-17:
Once you have a theme, you get to choose what to put in the headers and footers. You can add Page Numbers, the Current Date, the Layout Name, Custom Text, and Logos. And you can put these things in six different places: Top left, Top center, Top right, Bottom left, Bottom center, and Bottom right. FileMaker lets you put one thing in each spot.

Figure 5-18:
Almost done! Remember a couple steps back when you defined a sort order for this report? As you learned then, FileMaker can create a script for you to perform the sort and show the report in Preview mode. Now you get to decide if you want it to or not. If you turn on "Do not create a script," then the sort order you specified before does you no good—without a script you have to sort the records yourself.

Phew! You're finished at last. Your new report layout should look something like Figure 5-20.

Figure 5-19:
Time to make your last choice. You can opt to view the report directly in Preview mode, or you can view the new layout in Layout mode. Since you're going to need to make some adjustments to the layout, choose "View the report in Layout mode."

Figure 5-20:
The layout FileMaker creates for you looks like this. It has all the parts and pieces, but it needs a little cleanup. You can reorganize the fields in a way that makes more sense to you, and you can always change fonts, sizes, and styles to suit your taste. You can use any of the tools you learned about in Chapter 4 to modify these objects. You can even put a picture of your first-born in the header. After all, it's your database.

Print Margins

Before you begin arranging things on the layout, you need a feel for the amount of available space. Normally when you print from FileMaker, the page margins are set to the minimum size allowed by your printer. This arrangement provides the most usable space possible, but at a cost: The margins—and the printable area—change as you switch printers. For a report that you intend to print often, you don't want to deal with that kind of inconsistency.

Luckily, you can override this behavior and set explicit margins. Before you do, though, you need to make sure FileMaker is using units that make sense for page margins. Follow these steps to set the units and the margins:

1. **Choose Layouts → Set Rulers.**

   The Set Rulers window appears (page 133).

2. **From the Units pop-up menu, choose *Inches*, then click OK.**

   You're back on your new layout, where you've just told FileMaker to use inches for just about everything.

3. **Choose Layouts → Layout Setup, and then click the Printing tab.**

   The printing options associated with this layout appear, as shown in Figure 5-21. (This Layout Setup window is the same one you saw on page 137. This time, you'll explore a little more deeply.)

Figure 5-21:
These settings affect the way the current layout prints. For example, you can create a layout that prints in multiple columns (imagine printing sticky labels). You'll learn more about that in the next chapter. For now, draw your attention to the "Use fixed page margins" checkbox, which you need to turn on if you want this layout to have hard-coded (and consistent) page margins.

4. **Turn on the "Use fixed page margins" checkbox.**

   The Top, Bottom, Left, and Right text boxes start out grayed out. As soon as you turn on this checkbox, you can type into them.

Note: The numbers you see in these boxes (before you type anything into them, that is) are the margins associated with the printer you're hooked up to. That's why they probably look different from what you see in Figure 5-21.

5. **In each of the Top, Bottom, Left, and Right text boxes, type .5.**

   Don't forget to type the decimal point. Your goal is to set the margin on all sides to half an inch.

6. **Click OK.**

The Layout Setup dialog box disappears and you're looking at your layout again. If you have sharp eyes, you notice the page width has shrunk a bit, as shown in Figure 5-22.

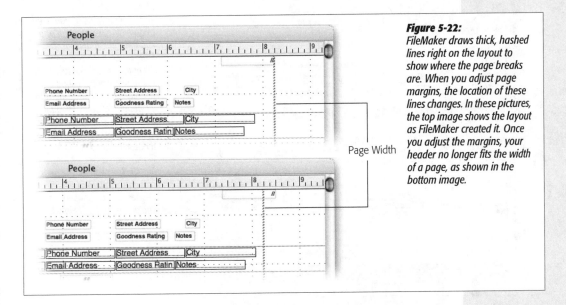

Figure 5-22:
FileMaker draws thick, hashed lines right on the layout to show where the page breaks are. When you adjust page margins, the location of these lines changes. In these pictures, the top image shows the layout as FileMaker created it. Once you adjust the margins, your header no longer fits the width of a page, as shown in the bottom image.

Tip: If you like working in pixels and don't want the bother of switching units, take heart. You can probably do the math in your head even faster. Remember, there are 72 pixels per inch: A one-inch margin would be 72 pixels and a half-inch margin would be 36. (If you like centimeters, figure there are 28 pixels per centimeter.)

Improving the Report Layout

Now that you've specified your page size, you can begin to lay out the report. File-Maker already created header, body, and footer parts. It already set the layout to list view. And it already added a title, date stamp, page number, column labels, and fields in the proper parts. As usual, it just isn't very pretty. (Remember, Figure 5-30 on page 203 shows how the finished product will look.)

Tidy up the header

Your first job is to clean up the header part. As shown in Figure 5-23 for guidance, your tasks involve mostly text formatting and dragging things around.

Rearrange the body

In Figure 5-23, you can also see before and after shots of the report's body. Again, you know everything you need to rearrange things. You want to replace the First

Name and Last Name fields with larger merge fields (page 175), rearrange the rest of the fields, and give them new font, size, and style formatting. This time, though, there are a few extra steps.

Figure 5-23:
To fix up the header, you need to do a little rearranging and change some fonts. For the look shown here, resize the "People I Know" title to 18-point. Simplify the column headings and change them to 11-point bold italic. Slide the date stamp (the "//" text object in the top-right corner) left so it doesn't extend off the page. Finally, add a 1-point black line the full width of the page along the bottom of the header. (Instructions for the line are in the box below.)

UP TO SPEED

Adding Straight Lines

You often see horizontal lines that cross the width of a page in printed reports. Many reports include a line between the header and the body of the page. (Technically, such a line is *in* the header part.) Creating these lines is a snap:

1. In the status area, click the line tool. The mouse arrow changes to a cross-hair icon.

2. With the Shift key held down, drag a straight horizontal line anywhere on the layout. Don't worry about getting the line in the right place. You can more easily move it later.

3. Drag the new line all the way to the left, so that its left end touches the left side of the layout. As you drag left, FileMaker won't let you drag the line past the edge of the layout.

4. With the Shift key held down, drag the selection handle on the right end of the line until it touches the vertical page break line. Again, since you have the Shift key down, the line stays straight.

5. Using the mouse or the arrow keys, move the line up or down until it's positioned properly.

Using these steps, you can be sure your line is straight and exactly the width of a page.

First, you can delete the First Name, Last Name, City, State, and Zip fields. In their place, add two new text objects. One—formatted as 14-point bold text—should hold merge fields for the First Name and Last Name fields, with a space between them. In the second, add City, and comma and space, State, another space, and Zip. Finally, change the font on the remaining fields to 10-point and italicize the notes field.

Once you've made these changes, you can rearrange the fields and objects using Figure 5-30 as a guide. (Don't worry about matching the example exactly. Periodically inspect your work in Browse mode and adjust the arrangement until it pleases your eye. Use your individual sense of style!)

With the fields in place, you have just one finishing touch to add to the body. It's hard to see in Figure 5-30, but there's a hairline-width line along the bottom edge. You can save some effort by duplicating the horizontal line you added to the header. Select the line and choose Edit → Duplicate. A new line appears just below the first. Move it into position, and use the Line Thickness tool to make it a hairline.

Tip: You can copy an object *and* position it in one quick move: Ctrl-drag (Option-drag) it. The Ctrl or Option key tells FileMaker to copy the object instead of move it. To constrain the movement, press *Shift* as you drag. Your new object stays right in line with the original.

Tweak the footer

Next up is the footer part. It's already almost perfect. But it would be nice if the report showed "Page 3" on the bottom of the third page, instead of the mysterious "3." Use the text tool to edit the page number text object ("##"), typing *Page* and a space before the page number symbol.

Sliding Layout Objects

Your layout is essentially finished; time to take a look. Choose Scripts → Report to run the script you told FileMaker to create for your report on page 189. As Figure 5-24 confirms, this report has one minor problem: It's not very paper-efficient. All that blank space beneath most items is the notes field, which may have lots of information, but usually doesn't. Wouldn't it be cool if you could tell FileMaker to slide the next record up if the notes field didn't need all that space? The engineers at FileMaker thought so too, and added a feature called *sliding*.

When to use sliding

Since the data in a field changes from record to record, the amount of space it takes up often changes too. Usually this behavior doesn't cause a problem. After all, you might *want* that empty space because you're printing onto a preprinted form, and everything needs to go in just the right spot on the page, or maybe your report design counts on consistent field sizes so things line up properly. But sometimes you can't get the effect you want without adjusting the layout based on the amount of data—usually when you're trying to tighten things up on the printed page to avoid wasted paper or excessive spacing around data.

Sliding does three things to help in this situation. First, it lets fields *shrink* to just the right size for their data. After a field has shrunk, any object on the layout can slide up or to the left to fill the space left behind.

Figure 5-24:
The report is looking better, but it sure wastes a lot of space. Only one record on this page has anything in the notes field, and even that is only two lines. But when you were arranging fields on the body, you told FileMaker to make the notes field about five lines tall, and that's how much space it reserves.

Finally, whole layout parts can shrink vertically to compensate for their shrinking contents. It's an idea that's much easier to see than to explain, so turn your attention to Figure 5-25.

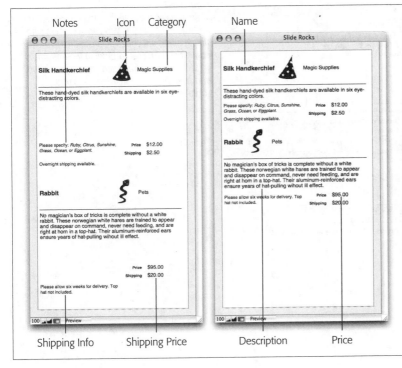

Notes   Icon   Category   Name

Shipping Info   Shipping Price   Description   Price

Figure 5-25:
These windows show the same thing: a page with two product records. The version on the left uses sliding to get rid of unsightly extra space. The width of the name field shrinks to fit its contents. The height of the description field shrinks to fit as well. The icon and category both slide left. The notes field, shipping info field, price field and shipping price field all slide up. Finally, the entire body part shrinks to fit its contents (notice how the second product record starts higher on the page in the right window).

Choosing the objects to slide

Object sliding in FileMaker is notoriously hard to figure out. It's a bit like that board game "Go." The rules take a minute to learn, but a lifetime to master. Here goes:

Sliding exists for only one reason: to compensate for changing field data. Therefore, unless you set at least one field to shrink, *nothing* on the layout moves. Unfortunately, you can't explicitly set a field to shrink. Instead, you set it to *slide*—and FileMaker makes sure it shrinks too. This seemingly simple principle is guaranteed to confuse you at least 36 times in the near future. You've been warned. Figure 5-26 shows how this field shrinking business works.

Once you've figured out which fields should shrink to fit their contents, you need to decide which objects should slide. What does that mean exactly? Normally, when you add an object to a layout, you specify exactly where it goes. But when the object is set to slide, its position is no longer fixed at an exact spot on the layout.

Instead, it moves up (or to the left) if other objects above it (or to the left of it) move or shrink. Figure 5-27 illustrates this concept.

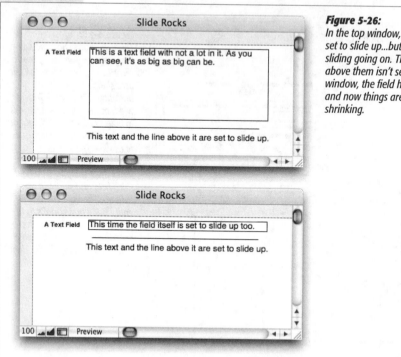

Figure 5-26:
In the top window, the line and text object are set to slide up...but as you can see, there's no sliding going on. That's because the field above them isn't set to slide. In the bottom window, the field has been set to slide up too, and now things are clearly sliding and shrinking.

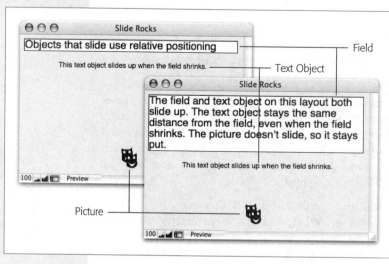

Figure 5-27:
Sliding objects (like the field and text object on this layout) position themselves relative to other objects on the layout. For example, since this field shrinks, and the text object slides up, the text object is always the same distance from the field. Its position on the page, though, changes from one record to another. The picture isn't set to slide, so it doesn't move at all.

Setting sliding options

Once you have a general idea of which elements need to slide (and which fields must shrink accordingly), you can start telling FileMaker.

FREQUENTLY ASKED QUESTION

Merge Fields vs. Sliding

Why should I bother with sliding? Isn't that what merge fields are for?

It's true that merge fields and sliding objects have some things in common. Both adjust the data shown on a layout, squeezing things together in the process. But they have some major differences:

- Merge fields work everywhere, even in Browse mode. Sliding objects, on the other hand, have no effect on Browse mode (or Find mode). Instead, they only do their thing in Preview mode and when printing.

- Any object on a layout, including pictures, can slide. There's no way to incorporate pictures into merge fields.

- Fields that slide act just like normal fields in Browse mode, in that you can edit the data in them. Merge fields are just text objects, and are only for display.

Bearing all these differences in mind, you can easily figure out which method to use. If you have a few fields that you want to display as a single block of text, use merge fields. If your needs are more complex (incorporating graphics, for instance), or you need to be able to edit data on the layout, use sliding objects instead.

Also, there's absolutely nothing wrong with using both on one layout. In fact, the layout you just created uses merge fields for the name and address, but you're about to add sliding to the notes field and hairline. You can even tell a text object containing merge fields to slide if you want. (Phew!)

The general process works like this:

1. **Select one or more objects on the layout.**

   FileMaker puts handles on the corners of each selected object.

2. **Choose Format → Sliding/Printing.**

   The Sliding/Printing window appears. (It's shown in Figure 5-28.)

3. **Make your selections.**

   Right now you're just getting comfortable, so feel free to choose whatever you want. For example, choose Sliding Left to make your selected objects slide to the left to get rid of excess space. Each option will be explained in the next section. Click OK when you're done to return to your layout.

4. **Click OK.**

   FileMaker returns you to your layout.

Since sliding affects the way your layout looks only in Preview mode and when printing, your layout won't look any different after you've made these changes. You can choose View → Show → Sliding Objects to identify the objects that will slide. With this option turned on, FileMaker draws tiny arrows on each sliding object, showing the direction it will slide.

Figure 5-28:
The Sliding/Printing dialog box is where you go to tell FileMaker how an object should slide, if at all. (You can also turn on "Do not print the selected objects" which does exactly what it says. Hence the "/Printing" in this dialog box's name.) You'll learn about all those other buttons soon.

Tip: Since setting sliding options requires a trip to a special window—and all those clicks—it can be tedious. If you have more than one object that will get the exact same settings, save yourself trouble by selecting them all first. If you plan ahead, you can usually set up even a complex sliding arrangement in just a few batches.

Now that you've *seen* the Sliding/Printing window, it's time to learn how to make sense of all those options.

The Sliding/Printing dialog box

The Sliding/Printing dialog box has several options to control just how the selected objects slide (and shrink if appropriate). In general, an object can slide left, up, or both.

If you want something to just slide left, you're in luck. Simply turn on the "Sliding left" checkbox and you're done. When you print or preview the layout, the objects slide to the left when field data isn't long enough to fill the full width of the field.

Objects that slide up, on the other hand, need a little more thought. To start, turn on the "Sliding up based on" checkbox.

When you turn this checkbox on, you make three more options available.

The "All above" and "Only directly above" radio buttons are hard to explain in words. Luckily, FileMaker gives you a picture to help you understand what they mean.

FREQUENTLY ASKED QUESTION

This Field Slides and That Field Shrinks

What if I have a field that should shrink but not slide? How do I do that?

Would you believe, "You can't?" Sadly, it's almost entirely true. This series of images shows the problem, and one workaround. Imagine you use FileMaker to keep track of the kinds of boards you sell. You record the material and the length, width, and height of the board. Sometimes you print this layout, and the first picture shows the result. It's not bad, but you decide you want the "ft" and "in" unit labels to slide left so they're closer to the numbers.

You remind yourself that the fields need to shrink for the sliding to work, and that shrink means slide. So you set the Length, Width, and Height fields, the "ft" text object, and the two "in" text objects all to slide left. The second image shows the result—not exactly what you had in mind.

What happened? Since the fields are set to slide, they did—right into one another. What you really want is for the fields to shrink but not slide. Alas, FileMaker has no such setting.

If you really want this to work, you have to get creative. The fields don't slide left if there's something in the way. Instead, they maintain their position relative to whatever is to their left. As shown in the third picture, you can put simple vertical lines next to the Width and Height fields. Since they're not set to slide, these lines act as little roadblocks for the slippery fields. To complete the effect, set the line thickness of the little lines to None. They disappear from the layout completely, but since they still exist, they still stop the sliding.

This workaround isn't perfect. It leaves invisible objects on your layout, which is always a recipe for trouble down the road ("Where is that line?!" or "What is this thing?"). But if you must have shrinking without sliding, a trick like this is all you've got.

Brad's Boards

Soft Pine
Material

12   ft   6   in   2   in
Length   *Width*   *Height*

Brad's Boards

Soft Pine
Material

12 ft   6 in   2 in
Length   *Width*   *Height*

Brad's Boards

Soft Pine
Material

12 | 6 in | 2 in
Length   *Width*   *Height*

Brad's Boards

Soft Pine
Material

12 ft   6 in   2 in
Length   *Width*   *Height*

Remember an object that slides up stays the same distance from the object above it. But which object? See Figure 5-29.

Finally, if you turn on "Also reduce the size of the enclosing part," the part the object is on shrinks to fit its contents. This setting is a little misleading, though. For example, imagine you have two sliding objects on the body part. One of these is set to reduce the body part, while the other isn't. How can the body both reduce and not reduce at the same time?

Address Field

Email Field   Do Not Contact Check Box

Figure 5-29:
Everything on this layout is "above" the Do Not Contact checkbox. But for the purposes of sliding, only two count. From FileMaker's perspective, the Address field is directly above it, while the email field is just above it. If the Address field and the Do Not Contact checkbox are both set to slide up, the "All above" or "Only directly above" choice becomes important. If you choose "All above," the checkbox never slides because the Email field doesn't. If you choose "Only directly above," it sticks with the Address field, even if that means sliding up alongside the Email field.

In truth, the "Also reduce the size of the enclosing part" setting only matters for the *lowest* object on the part. If that object wants the part to reduce, it will. If it doesn't, the part won't. Anything you set on any other object doesn't matter. The lesson: If you're trying to get your part to reduce, focus your attention on the bottom-most object on your layout.

Using sliding on the report layout

The report layout you've been working on provides a dramatic example of how sliding can both save space and produce a more attractive printout. You might have lengthy notes about some of the people you know, and no comment about others. Here are the specific steps for shrinking the notes field to avoid wasting space.

1. Select the notes field *and* the hairline below it.

   Both objects have selection handles, and the Format → Sliding/Printing command is no longer grayed out.

2. Choose Format → Sliding/Printing.

   The now-familiar Sliding/Printing window appears.

3. Turn on "Sliding up based on" and select "All above."

   You want the notes field to shrink vertically, and the line to slide up next to it, so *up* makes sense.

4. In this case, you're interested in sliding things *up*, so turn on the "Sliding up based on" checkbox. With this option selected, the notes field shrinks vertically to hold just its contents. The hairline also slides up, maintaining its distance from the notes field as it shrinks.

If you stop here, you won't quite have your problem solved. Even though the hairline slides up as much as possible, the body part itself doesn't shrink, and your report still wastes paper. To solve this problem, turn on "Also reduce the size of the enclosing part." When you're done, click OK.

If you view your report now (Scripts → Report), things should look much better. Figure 5-30 agrees.

Tip: If you need to rearrange the order of your layouts, choose Layouts → Set Layout Order. Like other elements lists in FileMaker, drag the double-arrow to reorder the list. You can also use the checkbox column to change which layouts display in the layout pop-up menu.

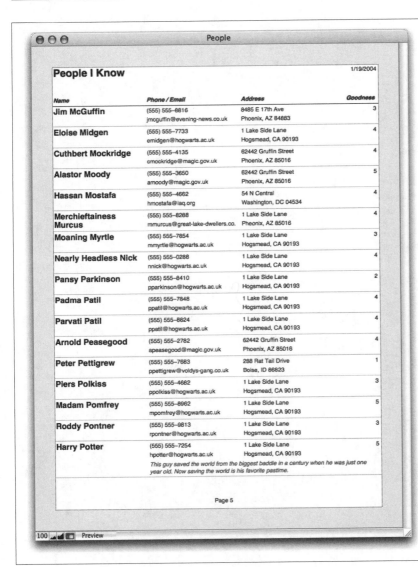

Figure 5-30:
Now each record in the People database is small and paper-efficient. When a record does have notes, like the last one here, FileMaker makes just enough room to hold them, with no wasted space. If you choose File → Print while viewing this report, you get a printout that looks surprisingly like what you see onscreen.

Advanced Layouts and Reports

Believe it or not, Layout mode has *even more* tricks up its sleeve. In the last couple of chapters, you've learned how to use the basic layout tools to position fields, create text labels, add graphics, and more. You've experienced stress-free layout creation with the layout assistant and seen reports in action. You even know how to design full-fledged layouts from the ground up.

Now, you're ready to learn the more advanced layout concepts: controlling how fields look and act, and adding buttons to perform customized tasks. You'll also learn how to develop massively powerful reports by using summary and sub-summary parts to add groups, subtotals, and grand totals.

Setting up Field Controls

You flirted a bit with the Field/Control Setup dialog box in Chapter 4, when turning the Goodness Rating field into a pop-up menu (page 114). Fields can be more than pop-up menus, though. The six main field styles are Edit Box, Drop-down List, Pop-up Menu, Checkbox Set, Radio Button Set, and Drop-down Calendar.

Each style (except Edit Box and Drop-down Calendar) lets you associate a *value list* with the field. Value lists limit the information you enter to a few, frequently used terms, numbers, dates or times. Using a value list, you can then easily enter a value from the value list into the field. You tell FileMaker how you want these choices presented, by selecting one of the field control styles.

Using a value list–based field control helps in two ways. First, you can more easily enter data into your database. If folks need to put a part number into a field, for example, they can just pick it from a list and avoid typing it exactly. Just as important, fields formatted this way help ensure *consistency*.

As your database grows, one of the toughest challenges you face is inconsistent data. For example, suppose you have two people entering addresses in your database. Cheryl is a fussbudget, and she *always* spells things out. Frank, on the other hand, is…ahem…keystroke efficient. He likes to abbreviate wherever possible. If all your customers are in central Arizona, you might wind up with some people in *Phoenix* and others in *PHX*; some in *Tucson* and others in *Tcsn*. Even worse, Frank, like most of his kind, can't even keep his own abbreviations consistent. He's got customers in *Chnd, Chndlr, Chand*, and (on a particularly bad day) *Ch*.

Even *horrendous* abbreviations may not cause a big problem to the human eye. After all, you can probably figure out where the person lives just by reading the City field. But what happens when you need to use FileMaker's find tools to find *all* the Chandler, AZ customers in your database? Searching for "Chandler" won't turn them all up. Instead, you have to try to think of all the different ways it could be abbreviated and search for each one. If you use a field formatted with a value list, however, you can make sure that everybody enters data the same way every time.

A value list has two parts. First, you decide which items appear in your value list. In this part, you're limiting the scope of the data your users can enter in a field. Creating value lists isn't technically a part of field control–you can define them at any time, using the Define → Value List dialog box (just like the one you first saw on page 114). But often, you create new value lists as you format a field with controls, so you'll learn how to define value lists first.

Once you've got your value list defined, you jump right back into Layout mode, and tell your field how to display the new value list—as a drop-down menu, a pop-up list, a Checkbox Set, or radio buttons. Here's the low-down on defining value lists.

Tip: If you don't need to create value lists, or if you want to provide a calendar for entering dates into a field, you can skip the next section. Go straight to page 213 and start setting up the field.

Creating Value Lists

Back in Chapter 3, you saw how to use a value list to validate information entered in a field. On page 114, for example, you created a simple value list to make sure folks can type values of only zero through five in the Goodness Rating field. Preventing database users from entering inappropriate information is all well and good, but why not be even more helpful? You use the true power of value lists when you make it easier for them to enter the correct information in the first place.

In this example, you can use a value list to translate those numbers into words anybody can understand without a legend. So, you define a new field—called Goodness Description, say—where you specify that a rating of five means "Angelic." While *you're* dedicated enough to type the full word out faithfully every single time, your teenaged son, who's helping out around the office after school, types *Angel* when he feels energetic and slips into *Ang* towards quitting time.

You don't have to adjust your son's Goodness Rating downward. Open your People database and make a value list. Then your son can just click a pop-up menu instead of doing all that exhausting typing. The Define Value List dialog box is shown in Figure 6-1.

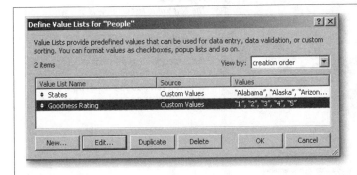

Figure 6-1:
The Define Value Lists window (File → Define → Value Lists) shows you every value list in your database. Here, you can add new lists, or modify those you've previously defined. You can use the "View by" pop-up menu to sort the list.

1. **Open your People database.**

   If you haven't been following along page-by-page, you can download a file with the fields listed in these steps from the Missing Manual Web site (page xxiv). (If you prefer to keep working in the file you created in Chapter 2, define a new text field called Goodness Description.)

2. **Choose File → Define → Value Lists.**

   The Define Value Lists dialog box appears. Notice that FileMaker's considerate enough to tell you the name of the file you're working in.

3. **In the Define Value Lists dialog box, click New. Then, when the Edit Value List dialog box opens (Figure 6-2), give your new Value List a name.**

   Since you already know that you're using this value list for the Goodness Description field, it's helpful to name it something that helps you remember that. You might just call it Goodness Description, but you can name it pretty much whatever you want.

4. **In "Use Custom Values" box, type the values you want to appear in your list.**

   Be sure to separate each item in your list with a line break (press Return at the end of each line). For your goodness scale, you might type: *Angelic, Role Model, Reliable, Somewhat Unpleasant, Approach With Caution,* and *Whiff of Sulfur.*

   If you want a menu divider in your list (between Reliable and Somewhat Unpleasant, perhaps), type a hyphen *and* press Return between those two values.

Tip: Don't leave stray line breaks in the middle of your list, though. They create blank lines.

5. **Click OK, and then OK again to close both dialog boxes.**

   You're back in your database.

Figure 6-2:
The Edit Value List window is also where you create new lists. Start by giving it a good, descriptive name. Then choose one of the three basic value list flavors. If you have some specific ideas for what should go in the field, create a custom value list, as shown here. You can also use values from an existing field or a completely separate file.

See page 213 for details on attaching your new value list to the Goodness Description field.

Note: You can also define a value list right there in layout mode. Select a field, then choose Format → Field/Control → Setup. Select Drop-down list, Pop-Up Menu, Checkbox Set, or Radio button set from the "Display as:" pop-up menu. You'll see the Define Value Lists dialog box and from there, you repeat steps 3–5 above.

Values from a field

The "Use values from field" radio button tells FileMaker you want your value list to automatically include data that's already in your database. It might sound strange, but this technique is pretty common. By the time you figure out that your assistant isn't following the data entry rules you've set down, there's already lots of data in your file. Put it to use by selecting the field's data for use in a value list.

When you want to use values from a field, simply click that option, and the Specify Fields for Value List dialog box appears (Figure 6-3).

Note: If you've already specified the field for this value list, and you want to change it later, return to the Edit Value List dialog box and click Specify.

POWER USERS' CLINIC

Using Tables for Value Lists

What if your database is so new that you don't have data in your fields yet? The "Use values from a field" method described on page 208 doesn't do you much good. So File-Maker lets you create a table for the sole purpose of hold-ing the values that *should* be in the list. Then you can put the data in the table just the way you need it.

But still, why create a whole new table just to hold a little ol' value list? Well, you may have people using your database who're perfectly capable of adding a record to a table, but don't have the training to make sense of the Edit Value List dialog box. A table lets them edit their own value lists while it protects your database's structure from mishaps.

To set up a value list table, you create a new table in your database and give it a main field to hold all the values that you want in your new value list. And to help your data entry people, you might even add a comments field that lets them make notes about the values they add. For example, "The value 'Angelic' is rarely appropriate in our business, but my sunny disposition requires me to include it here." Remember that one record in your table equals one item in your value list.

A word of warning: If your FileMaker database needs to share data with SQL or Oracle databases, be aware that a value list table may not translate perfectly.

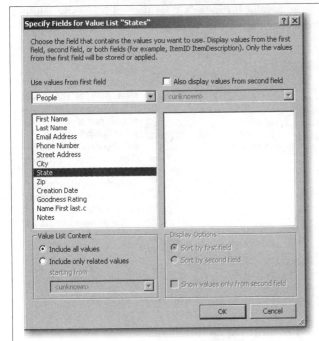

Figure 6-3:
When you create a value list using values from a field, you get to pick which field to use. You must first select a table from the "Use values from first field" pop-up menu. (In this case you have only one table—People.) The list below it then shows every field in that table. Simply select the field you want.

In the simplest case, just pick one field from the "Use values from first field" list. The value list goes and checks your old friend, the field's index, and then displays every value it finds in that field across all records. For example, if you choose the City field, the value list includes every city in your database.

Adding a second value field

Back on page 207, you created a value list for Goodness Description, and it's helped your son with his data consistency, but you really prefer the numbering system. You can use the values in the Goodness Description field to remind your son that five is the highest goodness rating and zero is no goodness at all, and still get the number you want entered in the Goodness Rating field. The secret lies in the "Also display values from second field" option:

1. **In the People database, choose File → Define → Value Lists. In the Define Value Lists dialog box, click New, and then name the new value list** *Goodness Ratings.*

   A descriptive name like this helps you remember what kind of information the list holds.

2. **Click "Use values from field."**

   The Specify Fields for Value List dialog box pops up (Figure 6-4). You can see the name you just gave your value list in the box's title, which is really helpful if you get called away from your database in the middle of your creative work.

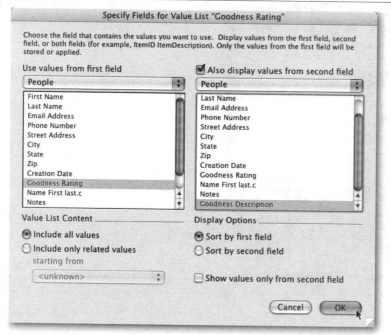

Figure 6-4:
A value list with two fields shows both field values side by side. Only the first value is actually part of the list: If you select "0 Whiff of Sulfur," only 0 goes in the field. The "Whiff of Sulfur" description just reminds you that the character you're rating has no character. (You learned how to make value lists appear in pop-up menus on page 156.)

3. **From the "Use values from field" pop-up menu, choose People. Then, in the field list, select Goodness Rating.**

Your new value list includes every item in the field's index. That is, the value list contains one instance of every value that you've entered in the Goodness Rating field. FileMaker sorts the list by the Goodness Rating field—unless you tell it otherwise. If you'd rather sort the list by Goodness Description, just turn on the "Sort by second field" radio button. The list works the same way, but File-Maker sorts it *alphabetically* by Goodness Description instead. See page 109 for details on field indexes.

4. **Turn on "Also display values from second field." Then, in the field list (at right), select Goodness Description.**

You've just told FileMaker to show your Goodness Descriptions in the value list.

5. **Click OK, then OK again, and then OK a third time to dismiss all the dialog boxes.**

You're now back in your database.

Sometimes you need to keep track of numerical data—like the Goodness Rating—but you think people using your database would find it confusing to see all those numbers cluttering up the value list. Solution: Hide the numbers. In the Specify Field for Value List dialog box (Figure 6-4), turn on "Show values only from the second field." This option suppresses the Goodness Rating number, letting only the Goodness Description show. But behind the scenes, FileMaker still puts the Goodness Rating number in the Goodness Rating field.

Note: Showing values only from the second field is most useful in conjunction with a Pop-up Menu (page 217), which always lets you see the contents of the second field. A Drop-down List, by contrast, displays the contents of the first field until you click it. Only then does it show the values of the second field like it's supposed to.

Value list from another file

If you have another database that already defines just the right value list, you don't have to recreate it here. For example, your People database can use a Zip code list containing all the Zip codes in your state from a different database. Instead of copying all that data into your People file, you can create a value list that simply goes and looks up the information in the other database—*refers* to it, in other words. If you later change the original value list (when the post office changes Zip codes, say), People reflects that change as well.

To define this kind of value list, you have to hook two databases together using a *file reference*. A file reference doesn't require anything fancy, like a relationship (something you'll learn much more about in Chapter 8). Instead, the file reference just remembers where the other file is. When you click a field that uses a value list

---

from another file, FileMaker can just hop over to the other file and grab what it needs without bugging you to find where that other file is stored. Here's how to reuse a list of information from another database:

1. **In the Edit Value List dialog box, turn on "Use value list from another file."**

   Now you can choose from a pop-up menu to the right of this radio button. (Right now the menu probably includes only two choices: Add File Reference and Define File References. If you've already added file references [page 361], each database you've connected to also shows up in this menu. If the database you want is already listed, choose it and skip the next two steps.)

2. **From the top pop-up menu, choose Add File Reference. When the Open File dialog box appears, select another database file, and then click Open.**

   The selected database's name appears in the pop-up menu, and the second pop-up menu lists every value list in that database.

3. **Select a value list from the second pop-up menu, and then click OK to seal the deal.**

   FileMaker creates a reference to the value list you specified.

Note: The value list you pick can be any of the three types explained in this section. In fact, if you *change* a referenced value list's type, your new value list still works fine.

Editing Value Lists

If your short list of approved part numbers changes, you need a way to edit your custom value list to reflect the new company policy. Choose Define → Value Lists, select the value list you need to change, and then click Edit.

When you're through editing a value list, just click OK. If you decide you don't want to change it after all, click Cancel instead. Either way, you wind up back in the Define Value Lists window. Just like Define Fields, if you instead click Cancel, *everything* you've changed is tossed out. The value lists go back to the way they were before you opened Define Value Lists. FileMaker asks you if you're sure first, since the Cancel button is precariously close to the OK button.

In addition to the New and Edit buttons, this Define Value Lists dialog box has a Duplicate button. It does just what you'd expect: creates a new value list that's an exact copy of one you already have. You can live a long, healthy life without ever using this button, because once you create a value list in FileMaker, you can use the same list over and over in a multitude of fields and databases. (But isn't it nice to know you have the option?)

The Delete button deletes the selected value list, after an appropriate warning. As usual, you can hold down the Shift (Option) key as you press Delete to skip the warning.

GEM IN THE ROUGH

Custom Sort Orders with Value Lists

Value lists play a part in so many database activities, it's a wonder they didn't call it ValueListMaker Pro. The Sort dialog box is another place Value lists show up. Suppose you have a database of clothing products, each with a size: Small, Medium, Large, X-Large. (If you want to follow along, you can find just such a database on the Missing Manuals Web site; see page xxiv.) If you sort these records by size, they show up in alphabetical order:

    Large
    Medium
    Small
    X-Large

Chances are, that's *not* what you want—you want them in order from smallest to largest, or largest to smallest. To arrange that, simply define a value list with custom values: each size in the proper order.

You can then tell FileMaker to sort the record by size, but to use the order of this value list instead of alphabetical order:

1. Choose Records → Sort Records. You see the Sort Records dialog box.

2. Clear any existing fields from the Sort Order list and add the Size field. Remember you can quickly add items to the list by double-clicking them.

3. From the Sort Order list, select Size. The radio buttons below the list are now clickable.

4. Choose the "Custom order based on value list" radio button. This option informs FileMaker to order the sizes according to a value list.

5. Select the Sizes value list from the pop-up menu. Here's where you pick which value list to use.

6. Click Move. The Size field moves to the Sort Order list. The little bar chart icon beside this field matches the "Custom order based on value list" icon.

7. Click Sort. FileMaker sorts the records according to size. This time, the records are in a good logical order

Adding Field Controls to Layouts

Plain old edit boxes are as popular as they are flexible. They're the kind of field that FileMaker automatically creates when you start a new database or use the field tool to drag a field onto a layout. Maybe a little *too* flexible: Just about anyone using your database can type just about anything into an edit box. If you're trying to

---

collect specific bits of information, though, you could apply some validation (page 101). Or for even more, well…*control* over what your database's users put in a field choose Format → Field/Control → Setup. In that dialog box, you find drop-down menus, pop-up lists, checkboxes, radio buttons, and pop-up calendars—just like the ones the pros use in databases and Web sites worldwide.

Figure 6-5 shows the Field/Control Setup dialog box, including the list of available formatting options.

Figure 6-5:
The Field/Control Setup dialog box (Format → Field/ Control → Setup) lets you pick one of six different field control styles. Control styles are like electronic schoolmarms who watch over data entry. Drop-down Lists and Pop-up Menus stand guard over your fields, tapping their rulers, to make sure the rules you set up are followed.

Edit Box

Most of the fields you've used so far have been *Edit Boxes*. These are the click and type variety that normal people call a *text box*. Distinctive as always, FileMaker has its own moniker.

When you select the Edit Box format, you have the choice of turning on the "Include vertical scroll bar" checkbox. You saw this option when you added a scroll bar to the Notes field on page 158. If you anticipate that a field will hold lots of information, a scroll bar can be a good idea, as Figure 6-6 shows.

Drop-Down List

This field type *looks* just like an Edit Box. But when you click into the field, a list of available choices appears just below it (Figure 6-7).

The items in the list come from a value list (page 114). When you pick the Drop-down List type, you get a "Display values from" pop-up menu. From this menu, choose the value list to use. You can also choose Define Value Lists to create a new one.

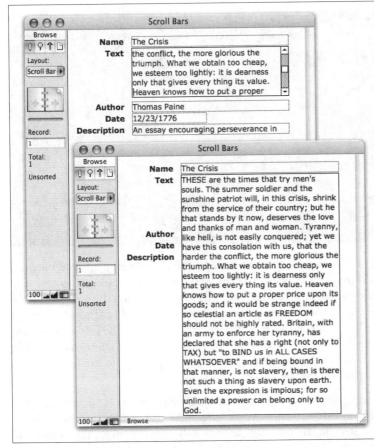

Figure 6-6:
FileMaker fields can hold a lot of text. In the top window, the Text field has more information than can fit in the field boundaries. Adding a scroll bar lets you know there's more. The bottom window shows what happens without a scroll bar. When clicked, the field expands to reveal its entire contents, covering anything below it. The field shrinks back down when you click out of it.

Figure 6-7:
A Drop-down List gives you a scrolling list of choices to save you the trouble of typing the one you want. Just click an item in the list and FileMaker enters it into the field. You can also use the up and down arrow keys to select an item in the list. Finally, you can type the first few letters of an item's name to select it. Once you have an item selected, press Enter (Return) to accept it.

Tip: If you don't apply borders to a Drop-down List, the show/hide arrow only appears when the field is active. Add field borders (page 157) to make the arrow a better visual cue.

Drop Down, Pop Up, Turn On

You may wonder how a Drop-down List differs from a Pop-up Menu. They're similar in purpose, but have three differences:

- A **Pop-up Menu** requires users to make a choice. With a Drop-down List, on the other hand, they can type directly into the field instead. When the list pops up, they can just click the field again to make the list go away, then start typing. From the keyboard, pressing Enter (Return) makes the list go away; Esc toggles the list on and off.

- **Drop-down Lists**, by contrast, can have *thousands* of items in them. Since the list scrolls, it doesn't much matter how long it is. Pop-up menus get very cumbersome with more than a dozen or so items.

- Finally, folks can make selections from a Drop-down List using just the keyboard, while a Pop-up Menu requires a trip to the mouse. Drop-down Lists' keyboard ability makes them preferable in most cases. Choose a Drop-down List unless you really don't want to let people type directly into the field.

Drop-down Lists look just like Edit Boxes until you click them or tab into the field. Then the list drops down for your data entry pleasure. But it could get annoying to have lists flashing at you just because you happen to be tabbing through the data in a record, so FileMaker lets you stop the list waving by choosing "Include arrow to show and hide list." Now the list is a little more polite. When the field is active, the list doesn't drop down until you click the arrow. If you make a choice from the list, the list disappears. Or, if you don't want to enter anything into the field after all, just click the arrow and the list goes back home.

Finally, turn on "Include 'Edit…' item to allow editing of value list" if you want your users to be able to easily modify the list of choices. When folks choose "Edit…" (always the last item in the list), the window in Figure 6-8 shows up so they can modify the value list.

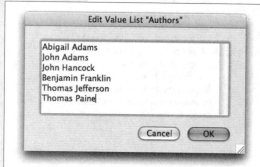

Figure 6-8:
You can include an Edit item in your Drop-down List. When folks choose it, this little Edit Value List box appears. From here, they can add new items, delete items, or edit items to the list-all by typing directly in the text box.

Pop-up Menu

When you format a field as a Pop-up Menu, the look changes significantly, as shown in Figure 6-9. Rather than type into the field, your users must click the menu and make a choice.

Pop-up Menu

Figure 6-9:
Here you can see a Pop-up Menu as it appears on the layout and when it's clicked. It works just like an ordinary pop-up menu: Just pick the item you want, and FileMaker puts it in the field.

Like Drop-down Lists, Pop-up Menus let mere mortals edit value lists, plus they up the ante by including an Other item. When your users pick "Other…" from the menu, they see the window in Figure 6-10. Entering a value in this window puts it in the field but *doesn't* add it to the value list. Turn on "Include 'Other…' item to allow entry of other values" to grant this power to the masses. (See the box on page 218 for advice on the ramifications of letting your users to edit or bypass your carefully crafted value lists.)

Figure 6-10:
If the Pop-up Menu, Checkbox Set, or Radio Button Set can't cover all the bases, you can include an Other item. Selecting "Other…" opens a dialog box that you can type into freely.

Checkbox Set

Figure 6-11 shows a field formatted as a Checkbox Set. With this format, database users can simply click each item to turn it on or off. As they do, the data in the field changes to reflect the checked items.

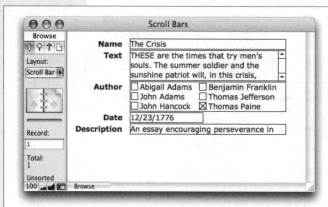

Figure 6-11:
When you format a field as a Checkbox Set, it looks like the Author field shown here. FileMaker adds one checkbox for each item in the value list, and arranges them to neatly fill the boundaries of the field. You can still apply borders, fills, and effects to a field like this—they affect the entire area the Checkbox Set covers.

A Cautionary Tale

Not even the most highly paid database developer can think of everything folks might want to enter in a database, and a Drop-down List with a handy edit option seems an obvious solution. But use it with caution. When some villainous or misguided soul chooses Edit, they're doing just that: editing your *value list* and potentially defeating the purpose for which you created it. Further more, if other fields in your database are formatted to use the same value list, *their* list of choices changes too, because the underlying value list itself has changed.

So remember that value-list-based fields serve *two* purposes: simplicity and consistency. If you make it easy for folks to add their own items to a value list, you're also making it easy for the value list to get inconsistent and disorganized.

Adding an Other item can undermine consistency even more, because it encourages quick-handed mousers to simply bypass the value list entirely.

If the primary purpose of your value list is to gain consistency, you should consider leaving the Edit and Other options turned off. You can always add new choices to the value list yourself at any time as the need arises.

Checkbox sets can include the Other item, just like a Drop-down List (page 214). If someone enters a value that isn't in the value list, FileMaker just turns on the Other checkbox to indicate the field has something more in it.

WORKAROUND WORKSHOP

Taming the Wild Value List

If your value list comes from a field index (page 109), you can't select the "Include 'Edit' item to allow editing of value list." But like so many things in FileMaker, there's a way or two around that little roadblock.

The value list you saw in chapter 3 was from an index of the field itself. Therefore, the index was a record of one instance of every value that's used in the record throughout the database. But if you click the field after the list has dropped down, you can type a new value into the field. It appears in the value list the next time you select it.

But if you make a value list that comes from another field (either in another table in your database (see page 209) or from another file, it's a little trickier. This value list is still from a field's index, but it's not from the field you're currently working in. They can still click through the list and type an entry that's not on the value list, but in this case, your users don't change the value list itself. To change the value list, they have to add records or edit the data in the *other* field.

Radio Button Set

A Radio Button Set (Figure 6-12) works much like a Checkbox Set. The only distinction is that your users can turn on only *one* item. If they try to turn another item on, FileMaker turns off items as necessary.

Figure 6-12:
This time the Author field is formatted as a Radio Button Set. Now you can simply click the right author to set the field.

Warning: Some users know they can shift-click to select multiple items in a radio button set. See page 424 to learn how calculations can control these users' urge to get around the system.

Just as with Drop-down Lists and Checkbox Sets, you can add an Other or Edit item to the Radio Button Set. (See the box on page 218 for more detail.)

GEM IN THE ROUGH

Checkboxes Behind the Scenes

The beauty of Checkbox Set fields is that they let folks click *more than one* checkbox. In other words, you can capture several values in one easy-to-use field. This method comes in handy when the things you're tracking in your database have fields like Available Sizes, Available Colors, Warehouses, or any other attribute of the *one or more* variety. But wait, you say—how can a single field hold *more* than one value?

Simple, if you're FileMaker. Just give each checkbox its own line. In other words, if you have a Checkbox Set showing colors, and you turn on Red, Green, and Blue, FileMaker actually thinks of the field like this:

    Red
    Green
    Blue

You can show the same field on another layout—or even the same layout if you want—without the checkbox formatting. If you do, you see the selected items: one on each line. This is called a "return-separated list". If you change what's in the field without using the checkboxes, you could end up with lines that don't match any of the value list items. In that case, the Checkbox Set turns on its Other item if it has one. (If not, the extra items simply don't show at all.)

A final note: Because Checkbox Sets need to be able to put several lines in the field, they're really suitable only for *text* fields. Other field types don't support multiline values.

Drop-down Calendar

In FileMaker, you can easily read date fields, and easily set them up. But actually typing dates into them is notoriously tricky. If you don't get just the right combination of numbers and separators, FileMaker gets all huffy and tells you the value you've just typed isn't valid. And if somebody swipes your desk calendar, how are you supposed to know what numbers to type in the first place? FileMaker Pro 8 can handle both these problems. It lets you give your date fields a nifty drop-down calendar where anyone can simply point and click to enter a date.

When you first format a field with a drop-down calendar, FileMaker doesn't give you any visual feedback letting you know a calendar's lurking there, waiting to drop down when you tab into the field. If you want to provide a visual clue, select "Include icon to show and hide calendar." Then you see a teeny, tiny calendar at the right side of your field (see Figure 6-13). Tiny as it is, the calendar icon still takes up some room, so you might have to make the field a little wider to display the entire date plus the new icon.

Tip: Like the show/hide arrow on Drop-down Lists, the calendar icon shows up in an inactive field only if the field has a border. If you're a minimalist on the field border issue, you can format your field with only a right border to force the icon to appear.

The calendar itself is a little dynamo. To enter a date, click the Month Year display at the top and you see a pop-up menu that lets you jump to a specific month in the current calendar year.

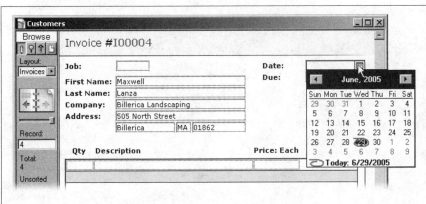

Figure 6-13:
The drop-down calendar makes entering dates a snap. It has some sweet controls, too. When the field's empty, the current date is highlighted when the field drops down. Or, if there's data in the field already, FileMaker highlights that date when the calendar appears.

Right-click anywhere on the calendar (⌘-click on the Mac), and the pop-up menu changes to read "Go to today." The calendar closes and plunks the current date into the field.

You can also change the month with the right and left arrows at either side. The left arrow icon moves you backward in time (careful, don't touch anything or you could change the course of human history!) and the right one moves you forward. The up and down arrow icons change the display of years. Finally, you can move the highlighted date with your keyboard's arrow keys. Tap the down arrow key a few times and you see how fast time flies.

But if you get carried away playing the controls (is my birthday on a Friday in 2015?), the calendar's footer always displays the current date. Just click that display to enter the current date, then drop the calendar down again. It reorients to today's date.

Auto-Complete

Auto-complete is a strong ally both for database designers who care about data consistency and for data entry folk who hate to type. Unlike the other Field/Control field styles, you can apply this little beauty to a regular Edit Box. Once you've turned on the option to "Auto-complete using previously entered values," the field gets ESP and tries to figure out what you want to enter. Where do these super-human powers come from? From that old friend, the field's index (page 109).

But Auto-complete behaves a little differently on Edit Boxes than it does on Drop-down Lists.

When Is Auto-Complete *Not* Useful?

With such a cool feature, one that seems to know what people want to type before *they* do, you may be tempted to add auto-complete powers to most of your fields. But there are cases when it just isn't very helpful.

Auto-complete depends on the index (page 109) to know what to show in its list. There has to be data in at least one field for FileMaker to have any entries in the index. And indexes add a lot of size to your files, so if you index a lot of fields so that Auto-complete works, you may find that the file size balloons. Remember, this feature comes with all of indexing's dark sides as a tradeoff for its power.

Another weakness: When someone types a letter that's not used much—like X, J, or Z—Auto-complete may not produce a Drop-down List.

This lack of a list doesn't mean Auto-complete's broken. It just means the index doesn't have any entries beginning with that letter. The index saves no time in such cases.

Auto-complete works best in larger databases where there are lots of records. And it's usually most effective if the records have a fairly wide range of data in them. For example, if a field is going to have only a few possible values (G, PG, PG-13, R, NC-17) then a drop-down menu or a pop-up list is a better choice than an Auto-complete Edit Box.

None of these cautions means that you shouldn't use Auto-complete. Just be aware of its limitations and the overhead it places on your file.

The differences are discussed in the following sections.

Auto-Complete in Edit Boxes

When you start typing into an Edit Box formatted with the Auto-complete option, FileMaker scans the field's index and drops down a list of matching entries. If you type *T*, for example, you see a list of entries that begin with the letter T. If you type *R* next, the list shortens to only words beginning with "TR." Once the list is short enough for you to find what you want, just click the list item to select it.

The Auto-complete list behaves just like a regular Drop-down List, so if you prefer you can highlight items with arrow keys and then press Enter.

Note: If there's only one item beginning with "Tr," the list's behavior can be confusing. It shortens to a single item and looks like the item's already in the field. You still have to click the item, or hit Tab or Enter, to complete the data entry, though.

Auto-Complete in Drop-down Lists

When you want to use Auto-complete in conjunction with a Drop-down List, you'll also need to specify a value list from which Auto-complete will draw its suggested entries.

WORKAROUND WORKSHOP

One or Many?

Strange as it sounds, Pop-up Menus and radio buttons both allow *multiple selections*, just like Checkbox Sets. Just hold down the Shift key while you select an item, and FileMaker dutifully turns it on without turning off the item that's already selected. Handy though it may be, however, chances are you don't want anyone to use this trick and choose more than one value—otherwise you use checkboxes to make it obvious that multiple choices are desirable.

Unfortunately, there's no direct way to turn this feature off. If you want to prevent your users from picking too many items, you have to get creative. Here's one way of doing so:

Chapter 3 introduced you to Auto-Enter calculations (page 100). They let you automatically change the value in a field, based on a *calculation*. You'll learn all about calculations in Part 4, so for now you just have to have some blind faith.

Here's how to limit your fields to a *single* value:

1. In the Define Database window, select the field you want to fix and click Options. The Field Options dialog box appears. If it isn't already selected, click the Auto-Enter tab.

2. Turn on the "Calculated value" checkbox. The Specify Calculation dialog box appears.

3. In the big free-entry box on the bottom half of the window, type *LeftValues (My Field ; 1)*. But instead of *My Field*, type the name of the field you're fixing. Otherwise, be sure you type this exact calculation. This calculation tells FileMaker you want to keep only the left-most—or *first*—value in the field.

4. Click OK. You're now back in the Field Options dialog box.

5. Turn off "Do not replace existing value (if any)" and click OK.

You're back in your database.

Now if you try to Shift-click a second item, FileMaker immediately throws it out. In practice, it *looks* like it simply doesn't let you Shift-click.

Use an existing value list or define a specific list just for Auto-complete. Just as with regular field entry, you can use a value list from:

- The field you're formatting with Auto-complete
- Another field in the same table.
- A field in a different table with the same file
- A field in another file
- A custom list

Remember, value lists based on fields depend on the field's index, but custom lists don't.

When you click into an Auto-complete Drop-down List that's formatted with a show/hide arrow, the list doesn't appear until you click the arrow or pres the Esc key. If you want the list to display as soon as the field is entered, then don't select the "Include arrow to show and hide list" option.

Note: Auto-complete works only with Edit boxes and Drop-down lists, so you'll have to stick with these two field controls to use that feature.

Repetitions

On page 109, you learned about repeating fields, which let you put several values in one field, with a separate Edit Box for each value. Remember, when you put a repeating field on a layout, you get to decide how many times it shows up. Even if a field has 200 repetitions, you don't *have* to show them all on the layout. You can elect to show just the first ten. Or just the last ten. Or numbers 37 through 118.

To control how repeating fields display, you use the same Field Format dialog box shown in Figure 6-5. This time, focus your attention at the bottom of this dialog box under Repetitions. Just enter the first repetition you want in the "Show repetitions" box, and the last one in the "through" box. You can't show noncontiguous repetitions here—you have to pick a range with one beginning and one end. But try this technique instead. Put multiple copies of the field on the layout, but specify that each copy displays a different range of repeats. You'll get much the same effect.

Note: If the "Show repetitions" and "through" options are grayed out, it probably means you didn't have a repeating field selected when you chose the Format → Field Format command.

Once you've figured out which repetitions to show, you get to pick an orientation. Your choices are Horizontal and Vertical, and Figure 6-14 makes sense of them.

Display Data From

So far, you haven't explored the right side of the Field/Control Setup dialog box, where there lives an incredibly powerful feature—the "Display data from" option. With this powerful tool, you can make one field display the contents of...another field. But why? While you ponder that Zen-like paradox, read the following example.

Say your layout has a series of similar fields—Email, Mail, and Phone—each of which indicates whether or not you have permission to contact a customer using that method. You format the Email field with a nice pop-up control and a value list with the custom values of Yes and No. You shorten it to just the right width and apply beautiful font formatting. Now, select Mail and Phone in turn and give them the same controls and text formatting. But that would take forever—twice!

Figure 6-14:
This layout shows two repeating fields, one with horizontal orientation, and one with vertical. (See the box on page 227 for further advice.) As you enter data in a repeating field, FileMaker numbers each repetition in a repeating field to let you know which one it is (bottom). The first repetition shows the full field name and–if there's room–the repetition number in brackets.

Instead, do the following: Delete the Mail and Phone fields, then copy the Email field, and paste it where the Mail field used to be. Next, use the Field/Control Setup dialog box to tell the duplicated Email field to display data from Mail instead. Paste again, change this copy to display data from the Phone field, and with a few quick clicks, you're done. You've just borrowed the formatting from one field to display the information from another. The moral of the story: Use "Display data from" to avoid doing work you've already done.

Field Behavior

The Field/Control Setup dialog box controls how a field looks and works. File-Maker has another dialog box, called the Field Behavior dialog box, that also influences how a field works, but in a different way. This time, you get to decide when (if ever) a person should be allowed to click the field, and how it handles certain special keystrokes. The Format → Field Behavior command shows this dialog box, and so does Figure 6-15.

Figure 6-15:
By "behavior," FileMaker means four things: Can you click the field? What happens when you do? How do you type into the field? And what do the special keys (Tab, Return, and Enter) do when in the field?

Field Entry

Sometimes you want to *show* a field value, but you don't want anyone *changing* it. If that's your fancy, select the field in Layout mode and choose Format → Field Behavior. Then simply turn off the "In Browse mode" checkbox (next to "Allow field to be entered").

Just because you don't want this field being *modified* on this layout doesn't mean you don't want to use it in a find request. If you leave "In Find mode" turned on, your users can still type into the field in Find mode. If you don't want that either, turn off "In Find mode." If you want to let people modify a field but not search in it, then turn on "In Browse mode" and turn off "In Find mode." For example, turn off Find if the field isn't indexed (page 109) and you don't want people stuck with slow finds.

Select Entire Contents of Field on Entry

If a field is formatted as an Edit Box or pop-up list, folks can click it to type a value. Normally, when they first click the field, a flashing insertion point marks the spot they clicked. If you prefer, you can instead have the field start out with all its content selected. For example, if the First Name field contains "Stacey," a single click on the "c" selects the entire name. To get this behavior, turn on "Select entire contents of field on entry."

Input Method

Unless you work for the UN, you probably never use the "Set input method" setting, but for the sake of completeness here's what it does:

In some languages, entering text isn't as simple as in English. For example, Japanese has many more characters than fit comfortably on a keyboard. To get the job done, a Japanese typist must use an *input method*—the set of rules and software interfaces used to get text into the computer. Unfortunately there isn't just one method, and FileMaker lets you pick which one you want. Normally, the "Synchronize with field's font" option is selected. This option just means FileMaker automatically picks the input method based on the font you've selected. If you want to override this behavior and specify a hard-coded input method, turn on this checkbox and, from the pop-up menu, choose the input method.

Borders Between Repeating Values

While you've got repeating fields on the brain, there's one more formatting choice worth talking about. You can put a border (page 157) around a repeating field just like any other field. But this border goes around the entire set of fields, not each individual repetition. You wind up with what looks like one big field, and it can be a surprise when you click it and discover those repetitions. Wouldn't it be nicer if you could format those repeating fields to look like a nice clear table, as shown here?

Nicer, yes. And possible too. Just select the repeating field in Layout mode and visit the Format → Field Borders window. If you look at this dialog box with a repeating field selected, you have one additional option: "Between repeating values." When this checkbox is turned on, you get your borderline *between* each repetition, as well as around the whole thing. You can even apply *different* color, pattern, and thickness to these lines if you want. For example, you can put a dark black border around the whole thing, and a paler gray line between each repetition if that suits you.

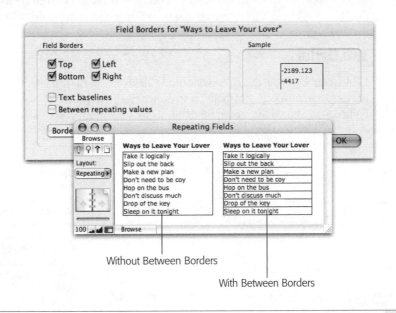

Without Between Borders

With Between Borders

Go To Next Field Using

Way back in Chapter 1 you learned to use the Tab key to move from field to field (page 17). It turns out you can actually change this behavior too: You can designate the Tab key, Return key, or Enter key to jump to the next field. You can select any combination of these three keys, including none of them.

Note: When one of these keys *isn't* assigned to go to the next field, its more normal behavior takes over: the Tab key inserts a tab into the field; the Return key inserts a new line into the field; and the Enter key exits the record.

You might want to change these settings for two reasons. First, if you have a field that *often* needs tabs typed into it (like a field that holds an ingredient list—quantity [Tab] unit [Tab] ingredient [Return]…), it can be annoying to have to press Ctrl+Tab (Option-Tab) all the time. You can turn off "Tab key" in the Field Behavior dialog box and make typing tabs easier. Since field behaviors are set for *each field*, you can give the Ingredients field this behavior, and keep the normal tabbing behavior for all the other fields on the layout.

The second reason comes down to the fact that humans are funny creatures. People are smart enough to put a man on the moon, but for some reason they *hate* to learn new ways to work. If you're creating a database for people whose old computer system used, for example, the Enter key to move between fields, you might decide to make FileMaker mimic that behavior to give their brains a break.

Tab Order

Whichever key you use to move among fields on the layout (as discussed in the previous section), it normally moves from the top left to the bottom right. Figure 6-16 shows the order fields go in as someone presses Tab (called the *tab order*).

Figure 6-16:
As the top window shows, each time you press Tab, FileMaker moves you to the next field to the right. When you get to the end, it starts down and left and starts moving through the next row of fields. This automatic tab order doesn't always make sense, though. The order shown on the bottom would be better for this database.

If the order FileMaker gives you isn't ideal for your layout, you can customize it. Your detail layout in the People database, for example, could benefit from a custom tab order. As it stands, the first time your users press Tab, they go to the First Name field, which is fine. But the next hit on Tab takes them to the Goodness Rating pop-up menu, while most people would expect the *Last* Name field to come next. To fix this annoying snafu, first choose Layouts → Set Tab Order. A few things happen onscreen, as shown in Figure 6-17.

Figure 6-17:
When you choose Layouts → Set Tab Order, the Set Tab Order window appears, and the database window's content area gets peppered with numbered arrows. Each of these arrows points to a field, and the number tells you where that field falls in the tab order.

The Set Tab Order window appears in the bottom-right corner of the screen (you can see it in Figure 6-17 as well). Here you have several options for changing the tab order to suit your needs, along with which of the objects on your layout you can include.

Since FileMaker automatically assigns a tab order to your layout, it assumes you simply want to modify what's already there—every arrow already has a number. If you click the Clear All button, all the arrows lose their numbers and you can start numbering from scratch.

Since the Goodness Rating field is a pop-up menu, and thus doesn't respond well to keyboard input, you probably ought to edit the tab order so it gets skipped when tabbing. The number inside each arrow is editable—just click the number to select it, and then type a new number. If you don't want the field in the tab order at all, remove the number from its arrow.

1. **Click the arrow pointing to the Goodness Rating field and delete the number.**

   The arrow pointing to Goodness Rating is empty.

   Also, your numbered arrows now skip 2—they go from First Name (1) to Last Name (3). Fear not. FileMaker's smart enough to figure out what you mean.

2. **Click OK in the Set Tab Order window.**

   If you switch to Browse mode and try out your tab order, you see that you can now tab right from First Name to Last Name.

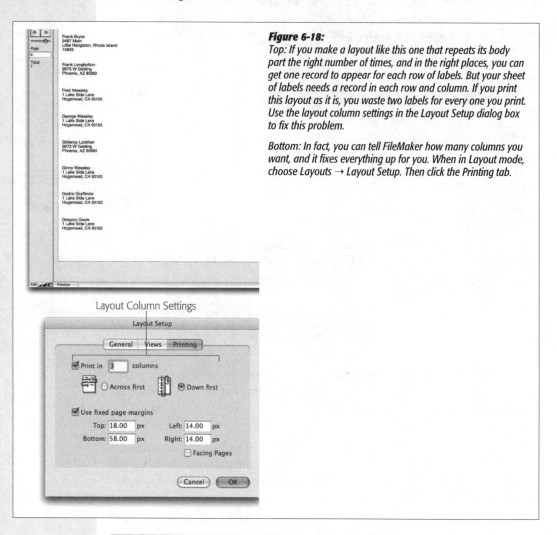

Figure 6-18:
Top: If you make a layout like this one that repeats its body part the right number of times, and in the right places, you can get one record to appear for each row of labels. But your sheet of labels needs a record in each row and column. If you print this layout as it is, you waste two labels for every one you print. Use the layout column settings in the Layout Setup dialog box to fix this problem.

Bottom: In fact, you can tell FileMaker how many columns you want, and it fixes everything up for you. When in Layout mode, choose Layouts → Layout Setup. Then click the Printing tab.

Note: To unlock the secrets of how the Set Tab Order dialog box can help you automate your database, see page 252. There you'll learn how to add buttons to a layout's tab order.

As long as you never choose the Set Tab Order command on a particular layout, FileMaker automatically manages the tab order for you. For example, if you add a Middle Name field to the layout, and place it between the first and last name fields, it automatically goes into the right spot in the tab order. If you switch the positions of the first and last name fields, Last Name becomes the first field in the tab order, and First Name comes next.

The first time you click the Tab Order window's OK button, though, FileMaker assumes you want full responsibility. If you add a new field to the layout, it just gets stuck to the *end* of the tab order, no matter where you put that field on the layout. If you move fields around so that the tab order makes absolutely no sense, FileMaker doesn't care. It keeps the tab order exactly as you had specified, even if it means the Tab key jumps you randomly around the layout.

GEM IN THE ROUGH

Tab Order and Repeating Fields

Each repetition of a repeating field is treated as a separate entity as far as tab order is concerned. It's perfectly legal to have the *last* repetition come right after the *first* if you're into aggravating your users. But it can be a real drag to have to click each and every one of those repetitions when you set the tab order. FileMaker has a nice feature to save you the trouble.

When you click the first repetition of a repeating field (while setting tab orders), FileMaker gives it a number—and the arrow begins to flash. If you click this flashing arrow *again*, FileMaker numbers that field's additional repetitions for you, in the logical order.

But the magic doesn't stop there: Suppose you have a series of repeating fields, as shown here. The standard tab order would go *down* each column before moving to the next one, but you'd prefer to tab *across* the rows first. For example, if you're sitting in the first Quantity field, you want to tab into the Product field, then the Price field. Then once you've completed a row, you want the next tab to take you to the next one.

FileMaker can automatically do this kind of numbering for you too. When setting the tab order, click the first Quantity field. It gets a number and begins to flash. Now click the first Product field, and then the first Price field, as pictured here. You notice that the arrow by the Quantity field continues to flash. Once you've done these three clicks, click the flashing arrow again. FileMaker now numbers all your repetitions properly.

In general, you click each repeating field in the order you want them tabbed to. When you're done, click the *first* one again to let FileMaker know. FileMaker fills out each row of repetitions matching this order.

(Of course you probably never actually build a database like this one. If you want to track line items on an order, read Part 3 of this book first.)

Print-Related Layout Options

Your layout needs are often different when viewing data onscreen versus on a printed page. For instance, you might want text blocks, fields or other objects to show onscreen, but to disappear completely when printed. Also, when printing, you're often concerned about wasted paper, but few people worry about using too much scrolling window. FileMaker gives you a handful of layout options to control how things print.

Non-Printing Objects

Sometimes you have something on a layout that you don't want to print, such as a layout that's designed to print over the top of preprinted invoice forms. When you view this layout in Browse mode, you want the appropriate boxes to show so your users know where to type. But when you print, you want only the field data.

You can tell FileMaker not to print *any* layout objects. First select the object (or objects). Then choose Format → Sliding/Printing. This brings up the Set Sliding/Printing dialog box, which you learned about in the last chapter (page 200). What you *didn't* learn about is the "Do not print selected objects" checkbox at the bottom of this window. Turn this checkbox on and the selected objects show in Browse, Layout, and Find modes, but not in Preview mode and not when printed.

Columns

Occasionally your printed page needs to spread records across several *columns*. For example, when you print on address label sheets, the sheets you buy usually have two or three columns of labels on one page. Even when printing a list or detail layout, if your data's narrow, you can save paper by printing two records side by side. How do you tell FileMaker what to do in special cases like this? Figure 6-19 illustrates the problem.

Figure 6-19:
FileMaker draws a dashed line through your layout to show you where the columns land (bottom). It also covers every column but the first with a dotted pattern. This pattern is its way of saying, "Don't expect anything you put here to print." Since every column is identical, you just have to lay out the first. FileMaker repeats it for the rest. Bottom: With the layout set to print in three columns, everything comes together (top).

When you turn on column printing for a layout, FileMaker does some pretty crazy stuff to your layout in Layout mode, as Figure 6-19 shows.

The column setting has no effect on your layout in Browse or Find modes. But if you print or switch to Preview mode, you can see the effect. Instead of repeating the body part just vertically, FileMaker *tiles* the body part both horizontally and vertically so that it fills the page.

Every column has to be the same width (this makes sense because every column contains the same kind of information). FileMaker automatically sets the column width so that the columns perfectly divide the page. But it bases its assumptions about the size of the page on the settings in the Print Setup (Windows) or Page Setup (Mac OS X) dialog box at the time you turn on columns. If you later switch to a different paper size or orientation, you probably want to resize the columns. To do so, just drag the first (left-most) dashed line on the layout. When you finish, FileMaker makes every column the same width as the first one.

Lastly, FileMaker gives you two choices for the way it arranges records in the columns. Choose "Across first" in the Layout Setup dialog box if you want the *second* record to be at the top of the *second* column. Choose "Down first" if it should be the second item in the *first* column. The flow arrows on the icons in the Layout Setup dialog box (Figure 6-18) show how the data flows onto the printout.

Format the Number/Date/Time/Graphic

All this talk about how fields look and work is well and good, but what if you want to change how the *data* inside them looks? A price and a weight both go in a Number field, but they are different types of values and should *look* different. FileMaker provides a series of formatting options for the data inside fields, giving you loads of control over how numbers, dates, times, and pictures look.

FileMaker has a special formatting dialog box for each kind of data a field can hold: Text, Number, Date, Time, and Container. (Timestamps are just a date and a time together, so you can format both parts separately.) You've already seen one of these dialog boxes—Text Format—in Chapter 4 (page 152). It's the thing you see when, in Layout mode, you choose Format → Text.

Below this menu command, you find four others, each of which accesses a dialog box specific to the type of information in your field.

Number Formatting

Select a number field and choose Format → Number to control how the number inside the field is displayed. The Number Format dialog box has a lot of options, as you can see in Figure 6-20. You can use most of these in any combination, so the possibilities are vast.

Note: As with most layout settings, if you choose this command *without* selecting a field, FileMaker lets you edit the *default* formats. In other words, the settings you pick apply to every number field you create on the layout thereafter.

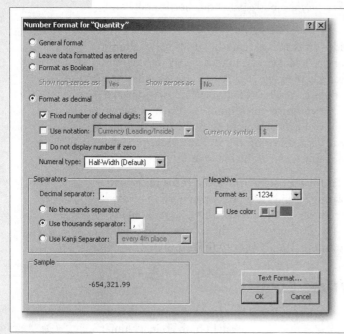

Figure 6-20:
FileMaker has four top-level number format settings: General Format, "Leave data formatted as entered," Format as Boolean, and "Format as decimal." If you choose either of the last two, you get still more choices. If you're looking for the kind of number formatting options you're accustomed to in a spreadsheet program, turn on "Format as decimal" and go to town. The sample at the bottom of the dialog box shows how a number looks with your settings applied.

General Format

If you don't tell it otherwise, FileMaker assigns the General Format to any new number fields you create. Usually, this format means, "show numbers the same way someone types them." But if your number has too many digits (either a very large number, or a number with lots of decimal places), FileMaker rounds the number or uses scientific notation to shorten it.

Leave data formatted as entered

If you don't want the automatic rounding and scientific notation you get with General Format, choose "Leave data formatted as entered" instead. FileMaker leaves your numbers alone, so they appear exactly as typed.

Format as Boolean

Sometimes you use a number field simply as a Boolean value. For instance, pretend you have a field that flags customers who get holiday cards. You could use a number field for this one, with a *1* in it if you want to send a card, and a *0* if you don't. But someone looking at the layout later might mistake all those 1's and 0's for so much computer gibberish (even if that someone is yourself).

For this reason alone, the Number Format dialog box has a choice called Format as Boolean. With this setting, a number field shows one of two text values. The first ("Show non-zero as") shows if the number field has any non-zero value. The second ("Show zero as") shows only when the field has a zero in it.

Format as decimal

The most flexible setting is called "Format as decimal." When you choose this option, you activate a host of new settings.

Fixed number of digits. Turn on "Fixed number of decimal digits" if you want to force every number to have the same number of decimal places. FileMaker also lets you say *how many* decimal places you want. If the number in the field doesn't have a decimal part, FileMaker just fills in zeros after the decimal point.

Notation and symbols. The "Use notation" checkbox lets you add currency symbols, units, or other labels to your numbers:

- Choose **Percent** to turn the number into a percent value. FileMaker automatically multiplies the number by 100 and puts a percent sign after it. That way, your users can enter *.1* for 10 percent, and you can later have your database multiply the percent value by another number. If the field held the value *10%* instead, you wouldn't be able to use that number to do any math.

- Choose one of the **Currency** options to format the number as a monetary value. When you do, you can supply an appropriate currency symbol as well. The four currency options in the pop-up menu have to do with *where* the symbol is placed, as explained in Figure 6-21.

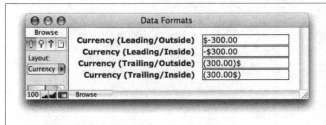

Figure 6-21:
FileMaker has four different currency options: Leading/Outside, Leading/Inside, Trailing/ Outside, and Trailing/Inside. Leading and Trailing determine on which side of the number the currency symbol should live. Inside and Outside matter only for negative numbers. As this picture shows, the currency symbol goes between the negative sign and the number with the Leading/Inside option, and before the negative sign with the Leading/Outside option. FileMaker also lets you put parentheses around negative numbers if you want. In this case, you get an Inside/Outside choice for trailing currency symbols too.

Do not display number if zero. Suppose you have a report with lots of numbers, where many of those numbers are zero. If you don't enter anything in a number field, FileMaker displays a value of zero—what else? But not every record needs every field filled in. In fact, it's quite common to have a lot of empty fields in financial databases, resulting in a teeming mass of meaningless zeros. So turn on the "Do not display number if zero" option, to make the zeros go away. Figure 6-22 shows a classic aging receivables report with and without zeros.

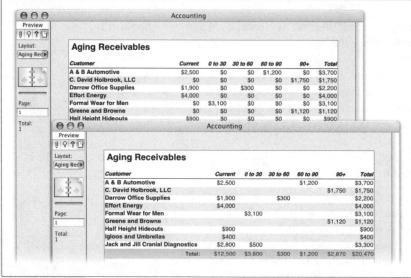

Figure 6-22:
These two windows show the same report, an Aging Receivables report just like you might get from your accountant. In the top window, all those zeros just get in the way of the real data. The bottom window shows how the report looks when each field has its "Do not display number if zero" option turned on (in the Number Format dialog box).

WORKAROUND WORKSHOP

Currency-ish

The currency symbol is, in a sense, just an expression of *units*. It isn't at all uncommon to want to put *other* unit labels on your numbers too. But FileMaker doesn't have an option for this variation. It seems hopelessly in love with currency.

But don't let the word *currency* in the "Use notation" pop-up menu get you down. Since you can type anything you want for the currency symbol, you're welcome to use one of the currency options for any other kind of unit too. In this picture, the Cost field is formatted with *normal* currency settings. The Height field uses the Trailing/Outside option with " cm" as the currency symbol, to display a number with centimeter units. Weight uses a similar approach, with a currency symbol of " lbs." (Note there's a space before the abbreviations here, so they don't crash into the field's actual number.)

The Part Number field shows another creative use of the currency formatting options. This time, "PN/" is inserted *before* the number value, using the Leading/Outside option. Every one of these fields really has *233* in it, but through number formatting they show very differently.

The currency symbol box accepts only up to five characters—and that includes the leading space if you want one—so it isn't perfect. But in many cases it gets the job done.

Separators. It's no surprise to you that numbers use special symbols to separate their parts. For example, you usually see a decimal point between the whole and fractional parts of a number, and a comma after the thousands place. FileMaker uses whatever symbols your operating system dictates for these special purposes, but you're free to override them if you want. For instance, you can use a space instead of a comma between each third digit.

In the "Decimal separator" box, type the character you want in place of a decimal point. The box accepts only a single character. FileMaker calls the comma between every third digit a "thousands separator" and you can opt to leave them out by turning on "No thousands separator." Turn on "Use thousands separator" if you want them, and feel free to enter something other than a comma in the associated box.

Formatting negative values. The last thing you get to control with the "Format as decimal" option is the way FileMaker represents negative numbers. In the "Format as" pop-up menu, you can choose any one of six negative number formats:

- *-1234* puts a negative sign before the number in the usual fashion.

- *1234-* puts the sign on the *end* instead, if that's the kind of thing that makes your socks go up and down.

- For that oh-so-financial look, choose *(1234)* instead. It puts negative numbers in parentheses.

- *<1234>* is similar, but it uses angle brackets instead of parentheses.

- If you're an accountant, hold onto your hat. The *1234 CR* option will make you feel right at home when crediting those accounts.

- The last choice, *(1234 with a black triangle before it)* puts that funny triangle before negative numbers. No idea what that's all about. If you know, more power to you.

To draw more attention to a negative number, you can have FileMaker automatically color it. Turn on "Use color" and pick a color by clicking the little icon button to its right.

Formatting a number's text. At the end of the day, a number is text too, really. It's made up of numbers and symbols using some font, size, style, and color. As such, you can choose the Format → Text command with a number field selected. If you're already in the Format Number dialog box and you want to format the text as well, the Text Format button serves as a shortcut to the Text Format dialog box.

Note: This window has two more choices—"Numeral type" and "Use kanji separator." These options are specific to Japanese numbers and aren't covered in this book.

Date Formatting

The Date Format dialog box works a lot like its number-oriented brother. This time, though, you tell FileMaker how you want *dates* to look. This date could be the value in a date field, or the date part of a timestamp field. For example, the date at the top of a letter might look best spelled out, while the due date on a list of 25 invoices might best be served by an abbreviated numbers-only format. Figure 6-23 shows the Date Format dialog box (no surprises here: just choose Format → Date).

Figure 6-23:
The Date Format dialog box gives you lots of control over how dates look. You get three primary choices ("Leave data formatted as entered," "Format as," and "Custom"), the last two with assorted settings. And you get a sample demonstrating your choices as well.

Leave data formatted as entered

When you choose "Leave data formatted as entered," FileMaker shows the date just *almost* the same way your users type it. If they type a two-digit year, the program changes it to four digits. Otherwise, it leaves the data alone.

Format as

If you choose "Format as" instead, you can pick from six common date formats in its pop-up menu, as shown in Figure 6-24.

Custom

For the ultimate in control, choose Custom. When you do, the mysterious unlabelled boxes, buttons, and pop-up menus to the right become usable. By selecting different parts of a date from the pop-up menus and adding your own text as appropriate to the boxes, you tell FileMaker exactly how you want the date formatted. You would use this option when none of the Format As formats (Figure 6-25) are exactly right. For example, if you're in the U.S., FileMaker suggests date formats that follow typical U.S. standards (month, then day, then year). But if people in England use your database, you might want to construct a custom format in line with their expectations (day, then month, then year).

Figure 6-24:
The "Format as" pop-up menu gives you six canned date formats to pick from. If you choose either of the first two, you can pick something other than "/" to go between each number by typing it in the "Numeric separator" box (it's covered by the menu in this picture). You can also add a leading zero or space to single-digit day and month numbers by picking from the Leading Characters area's pop-up menus.

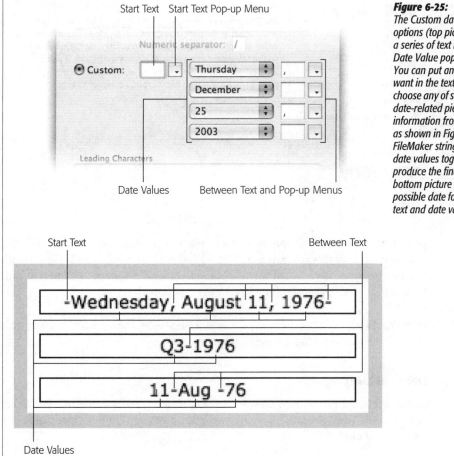

Figure 6-25:
The Custom date format options (top picture) consist of a series of text boxes and four Date Value pop-up menus. You can put anything you want in the text boxes, and choose any of several common date-related pieces of information from the menus, as shown in Figure 6-24. FileMaker strings the text and date values together to produce the final result. The bottom picture shows three possible date formats, with the text and date values labeled.

When FileMaker formats a date with the Custom option turned on, it assembles the final date value piece by piece according to your specifications. Whatever you type in the Start Text box comes first, followed by the first date value. FileMaker then adds the text from the top Between Text box. Next comes another date value and more between text. This process continues until the last text box is added to the result. By mixing and matching text and date values, you can make a date look any way you want.

If you don't want to use one of the date values, choose "<none>" from the relevant pop-up menu. Likewise, to skip a between text value, clear its text box. The pop-up menu buttons to the right of each text box give you a choice of common date-related symbols for easy picking. The have a "<none>" option as well, if you want to quickly clear the associated box.

In addition to "<none>", the date value pop-up menus all have identical choices, divided into four sections, as shown in Figure 6-26.

Figure 6-26:
The first group of three choices in this menu lets you show the day portion of the date. You can show the day-of-month number, or the day-of-week name as an abbreviation or full name. Next, you get the same three ways to display the month. If you're so inclined, you can add a quarter to your date in two ways. Finally, you can pick between a two-digit and a four-digit year.

As with the "Format as" option, you can use the pop-up menus in the Leading Characters area of this window to tell FileMaker how to handle single-digit month and day numbers. If you want them left alone, choose "<none>." To insert a leading space, choose Space, and for a leading zero, choose Zero.

Note: The "Display as" pop-up menu only applies to Japanese dates. And if you don't recognize these characters, you probably don't need to use this pop-up menu.

Time Formatting

Compared to dates and numbers, formatting time values is a breeze—FileMaker gives you just a few simple choices. Figure 6-27 shows the Time Format dialog box (Format → Time).

Leave data formatted as entered

This time, "Leave data formatted as entered" really means it. The time value shows exactly as you typed it.

Format as

The only other formatting option you get with time values is "Format as" and its related options. From the "Format as" pop-up menu, choose what time information you want to include:

- *hhmmss* tells FileMaker to show hours, minutes, and seconds.

- *hhmm* says you want hours and minutes, but no seconds. If your time value has seconds, FileMaker just ignores them.

- *mmss* limits the display to just minutes and seconds. If the time value has hours, the minutes are increased accordingly. For instance, if your field has *1:13:27* and you format it without hours, you see *73:27*—each hour adds 60 minutes.

- *hh* gives you a field that shows just the hours. Any minutes and seconds are left off.

- *mm* tells FileMaker to show the number of minutes. Again, any hours in the time value are counted as 60 minutes, and any seconds are ignored.

- *ss* shows a time as just a number of seconds. Every minute counts as 60 seconds, and every hour as 60 minutes. They're added up along with the seconds themselves to produce the final number.

Normally time values show a colon between each number. You can change this look if you want by typing something else in the Separator box. To leave out the separator entirely, clear the box. (This method lets you make military style times: 0730.)

International Super-Date

If people all over the world use your database, you quickly discover that date formats can lead to unending confusion. A date like 1/11/05 could mean January 11 or November 1, depending on your persuasion. To avoid all this confusion, consider a date format that strikes a nice balance between efficient display and unambiguous interpretation: 11-Jan-05.

To get this format, select a date field, choose Format → Date, and turn on the Custom option. Then configure it thusly:

• In the first pop-up menu, choose the number version of the day. (It's the number in the first group of options, right below <*none*>.)

• In the top text box, enter a hyphen (-).

• In the second pop-up menu, choose the abbreviated month name.

• In the next text box, enter another hyphen (-).

• In the third pop-up menu, choose the year (you can use either the two or four-digit version).

• Clear the contents of the two remaining text boxes and in the last pop-up menu, choose <*none*>.

Now click OK and switch to Browse mode. Your date field should show this svelte-yet-satisfying format.

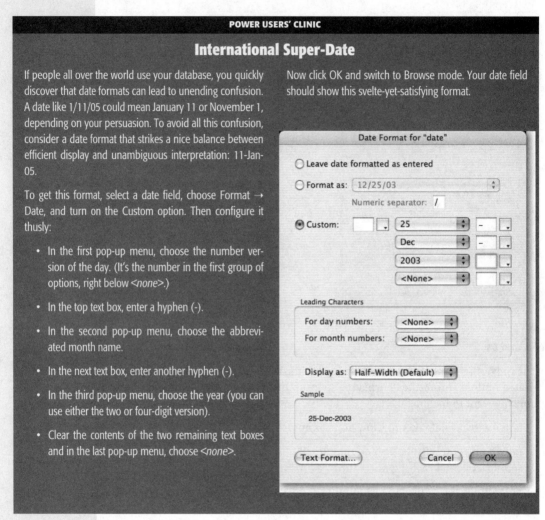

Note: As with date formatting (page 238), the pop-up menu between this box and its label lets you opt for a Japanese time separator instead.

When displaying clock time, FileMaker can use 24-hour or 12-hour notation. In other words, do you want to see *14:23* or *2:23 PM*? When you choose "24 hour notation," you can add some arbitrary text before or after the value (23:00UTC, for instance). When using 12-hour notation, you get to decide what text you want to represent a.m. and p.m. by typing in the "before noon" and "after noon" boxes.

You can choose from the pop-up menu to the right of these labels to put them on either side of the time value.

Like a date value, you get to tell FileMaker how to handle single-digit numbers. Again, you can leave them a single digit, add a leading space, or add a leading zero.

FREQUENTLY ASKED QUESTION

Formatting Fractional Seconds

I have times in my fields that have a decimal part in the seconds. Is there any way for me to control how these fractions-of-a-second show up in FileMaker?

For most people who actually care about fractions of seconds (you nerds know who you are) the visual appeal of your database is the least of your worries. But for the guy out there with a double major in nuclear physics and interior design, FileMaker has just what you need.

The Time Format dialog box doesn't give you options for fractional seconds, leading many people to believe you have no control over how these are formatted. In fact, you do have control.

Just select your time field, then choose Format → Number. Many of the number formatting options have no effect on a time field, but the "Fixed number of decimal places" and "Decimal separator" options work as expected. In other words, they let you control how many decimal places show and what character to use for your decimal "point."

There's an important caveat to this tip, though. If you have your time field set to "Leave data formatted as entered" in the Time Format dialog box, nothing you do in the Number Format window works. You must explicitly format the time value if you want to use number formatting on the seconds.

Timestamp Formatting

Although FileMaker has a timestamp *field* (page 94), there's no *Timestamp* option in the Format menu. Remember that timestamp fields really contain two values: a date and a time. So, you use the Format → Date command to control how the date part of a timestamp looks, and the Format → Time command for the time portion. Like time values, you can also use Format → Number to control decimal places and points in the seconds part.

In order for a timestamp field to show your settings, though, you have to format *both* the date *and* time parts. If either is set to "Leave data formatted as entered," the timestamp field just puts its hands over its ears and hums so it can't hear you trying to format it. Once you enter both the date and the time formats, the timestamp field straightens up and follows your formatting instructions.

You *do not* have to set the number format if you don't want to. If you don't choose a number format, FileMaker leaves the decimal part of your time values formatted as your users enter them.

Tip: Timestamp formats are a little tough to read because the date and time just kinda run together with a scrawny single space separating them. Make a custom format with " at" (that's *space*-a-t) in the last placeholder, and you get "Fri, May 6, 2005 at 12:30 pm." Much better.

Graphic Formatting

When your users want to put pictures or movies in a container field, they can use the Format → Graphic command to crop, scale, or otherwise control how it looks. If you'd like some control over how much formatting they can do, you can set some limits in the Graphic Format dialog box, as shown in (Figure 6-28).

Note: If someone puts a *sound* file in your container field (using Insert → File), you have no control over how FileMaker displays it. FileMaker automatically shows the appropriate icon and leaves it at that.

Horizontal Alignment Pop-up Menu

Scale Pop-up Menu   Vertical Alignment Pop-up Menu

Figure 6-28:
With the Graphic Format dialog box you can tell FileMaker to shrink and/or enlarge a picture to fit the field boundaries, or to crop it—showing only what fits. You also get to decide where the picture lives inside the field, or what part gets cropped. If you don't mind wildly skewed images, you can also tell FileMaker to stop keeping your pictures properly proportioned.

Basically, you're taking control of what happens when folks use FileMaker's usual image display commands. For example, when FileMaker shows a big picture in a container field, it normally shrinks it down so the whole thing fits inside the field. Smaller pictures are left at their normal size, and centered in the field. But this command isn't the only way to work it. Here are all the settings you can bend to your wishes:

Scale

The Scale pop-up menu lets you decide how FileMaker should handle pictures that aren't exactly the right size:

- Choose **Crop** if you want FileMaker to crop large pictures, showing only what fits. Figure 6-29 shows how this method works.

- Choose **Reduce** if you want FileMaker to shrink large pictures to fit, but leave small pictures alone. This setting is what you automatically get if you don't change it yourself.

- Choose **Enlarge** to *grow* small pictures so they fit the field but are as big as possible. Large pictures get cropped.

- Choose **Reduce or Enlarge** if you want FileMaker to shrink big pictures and grow small ones. This setting ensures that every picture in the field (on each record) is the about the same size.

Figure 6-29:
The back window shows a container field the way FileMaker creates them. The picture has been reduced to fit entirely in the field. In the front window, the field has been formatted to crop the picture. Now it shows only a small portion of the larger picture.

Alignment

If the picture is small and hasn't been enlarged, the alignment pop-up menus control *where* in the field the picture appears. For example, choose Right from the Horizontal Alignment pop-up menu and Top from the Vertical Alignment pop-up menu to nestle the picture in the top-right corner of the field.

If a picture has been reduced or enlarged so that it fills the field, it might still be smaller than the field in one dimension. In this case, the alignment pop-up menus tell FileMaker where to put the picture along this dimension. Figure 6-30 shows this process in action.

Note: When FileMaker reduces or enlarges a picture, it keeps the picture's aspect ratio the same. In other words, a picture that's four inches by six inches may not be that *size* in the container field, but its height *is* 2/3rds of its width. If you'd rather FileMaker make the picture *exactly* the size of the container field, even if it means distorting it, turn on "Maintain original proportions."

Figure 6-30:
When FileMaker reduces or enlarges a picture whose aspect ratio doesn't match the field, there's space left over. The top-left window has a tall picture reduced and aligned in the center. Below it, you see the same picture aligned to the left. The top-right window has a wide picture center-aligned. Below this one, the same picture has been top-aligned. In every case, the picture stays the same size, but moves within the field.

Cropping

Finally, when the picture is cropped, the alignment pop-up menus tell FileMaker which part of the picture to show. You can see the same cropped picture with each possible alignment in Figure 6-31.

Adding Buttons

The first FileMaker database you looked at (the Contact Management template on page 9) has a pretty slick system for switching between list and detail layouts. Instead of fiddling with the tiny Layout pop-up menu, you can just click tab graphics right on the screen. Each click magically transports you to a different layout. (Of course, at the time you didn't know it was changing layouts. You didn't even know what a layout was. But the buttons still made sense to you.)

You can easily duplicate this magic in your own databases. Just use FileMaker's Button tool, shown in Figure 6-32. But don't let the tool's name and appearance mislead you. You're not limited to the rectangular beveled buttons this tool creates. In fact, you can turn *any* object on a layout into a button—an imported graphic or even a field. When your users click the mouse button while pointing to such an object, FileMaker highlights it so they know they're about to perform some kind of action. When they let go, something happens. You get to decide what that *something* is.

Figure 6-31:
This window has nine container fields, all set to crop the same image. Each one has its alignment set differently. For example, the top-right field is set to align its picture in the top-right, and the center container has Center selected in both alignment pop-up menus. When an image is cropped, the alignment settings tell FileMaker which part of the picture you want to see. Top-right alignment tells FileMaker to show the middle of the picture, cropping out everything around it.

Button tool ———

Figure 6-32:
When you're in Layout mode, you find the Button tool in the status area, right about…there. It looks like a little button being poked in the face by its big brother…or being clicked…or something.

Creating Buttons with the Button Tool

You want to add a Go to List button to the detail layout in your People database, so open the database now and switch to the detail layout.

To add a button, first click the Button tool. Then *draw* the button on the layout as though you were drawing a rectangle. Figure 6-33 shows you where you might want to put it.

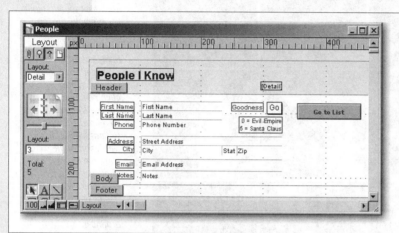

Figure 6-33:
You can put your button anywhere you want, and make it any size you want to. But if it's going to look like a button with the Go to List label, it should be close to the size of the button shown here.

When you release the mouse button, FileMaker immediately pops up the Button Setup dialog box (Figure 6-34).

Figure 6-34:
The Button Setup dialog box shows up whenever you create a new button. You get to pick one action from the Button Action list. Most actions require a little configuration. When you pick one, its options appear in the Options area. You can come back to this box and make changes to an existing button: just double-click the button in Layout mode (or choose Format → Button) to open it.

You want this button to switch to a different layout whenever someone clicks it, so find Go to Layout in the action list and select it (it's right under the boldface Navigation item). When you do, the Options area shows you a pop-up menu labeled Specify. You can pick any layout in your database from this menu. For this button, choose List.

If you're picky about such things, you can even control whether your button has square corners or slightly rounded corners. Choose the "Rounded button" option for an elegant, classy look. (If you don't make a choice, square is what you get.)

Something else changes when you select a button command: The "Change to a hand cursor over button" checkbox appears below the Button Style area. By turning this option on, you tell FileMaker to use a special pointing-finger cursor whenever someone mouses over the button. (The icon is similar to the one you usually see when you point to a link in a Web browser—the universal cue that an area is clickable.)

When you're done making choices, click OK. You can now switch to Browse mode and give your button a try.

Note: Buttons work in Browse mode and Find mode, but not in Preview mode (page 79).

Turning an Existing Layout Object into a Button

Buttons are handy, but they can be redundant. Often, there's already something on your layout—like a picture or even a field—that would make a perfectly good button. For example, if you've got your company's logo in the top-right corner of the layout, you can make it link to the main page of your Web site. A separate button reading "Go to Home Page" would be unnecessary clutter. (Incidentally, in this case you would use the Open URL button action; see page 532.)

Here's another common example: Now that you have a button that goes from the detail layout to the list layout (page 187), you might want to give folks an easy way to get *back* where they came from. Rather than add a button to the already full body part on the list layout, why not turn the person's name into a link of sorts? When you click the name, FileMaker shows you details on that person.

Turning one of a record's existing fields into a button capitalizes on the fact that FileMaker *always* selects a record when you click it in list view. And when you switch layouts, it always stays on the same record no matter which layout you use. This time you've added a button to the works, but the original behavior is unchanged: Clicking the list switches records, and the button switches layouts.

Here's how:

1. **If necessary, switch to Layout mode and to the list layout. Then, select the text object that holds the First Name and Last Name merge fields.**

   This is the object you want to turn into a button. You have to select it before you can work on it.

2. **Choose Format → Button Setup.**

   The Button Setup dialog box (Figure 6-35) makes its return. This time, though, you're not making a *new* button. Instead, you're turning the selected object *into* a button.

3. **Choose the Go to Layout button action. When the Options area shows the Specify pop-up menu, choose Detail.**

   This action tells the button *which* layout it should go to.

Figure 6-35:
Your list layout (in Browse mode) should look something like the top window. When you point to a name, your mouse arrow changes to the little hand icon, and when you click, the name highlights. After the button is released, you see the detail layout for the correct person, as shown in the bottom window.

4. **Click OK.**

   The window disappears and you're back on your layout. You don't see a change because you can't normally *see* if an object has been turned into a button. If you try the button now, it works fine, but it doesn't do your users much good if they don't know it's there. To make it obvious that the name links to the detail layout, why not make it *look* like a link.

Note: When you're in Layout mode, you can choose View → Show → Buttons. When this option is turned on, FileMaker outlines every button with a thick dotted line (it shows up only in Layout mode). Choose the same command again to turn it off.

5. **Using any of FileMaker's text formatting tools (page 150), turn the text blue and give it an underline (Format → Text Color and Format → Style → Underline).**

   Now your list layout looks like the one in Figure 6-35, and it works beautifully.

If you need a bunch of buttons on your layout, you can use the technique outlined on page 151 on several buttons at once. Just select all the objects that you want to button-ize before you choose the Format → Button command. FileMaker automatically groups the objects and turns the entire group into a button. These objects now act like any other grouped objects: Anything you do to one in Layout mode happens to all of them. If you later *ungroup* a grouped button, FileMaker warns you and removes the button behavior as well.

Warning: If you want four *different* buttons that do the same thing (so you can work with them individually), you have to button-ize them one at a time.

Making a Button not a Button

If you have a layout object that's already a button, and you don't want it to be a button anymore, you need a way to *turn off* its button-ness. It's easy to do but not very intuitive: Select the button and choose Format → Button Setup (or double-click the button). In the Button Action list (Figure 6-35), choose Do Nothing, and then click OK. Now the object isn't a button anymore.

Tip: Here's a faster way, even though it's cheating. Just click a button and choose the Arrange → Ungroup command (or better yet, press Ctrl+Shift+R or Shift-⌘-R). Even if the button *isn't* part of a group, FileMaker pops open a message box asking if you want to remove the buttons. Just click OK, and your object is no longer a button.

You can even remove the button action from the "real" buttons you create with the button tool (page 142). That's because, in reality, the button tool just creates a specially formatted text object and automatically turns it into a button. If you switch it to Do Nothing, you're just left with a fancy text object. (You might want to deactivate a button when you're troubleshooting your database…or for a little April Fool's Day fun.)

Button Actions

The Specify Button window has dozens of available actions, as you can see at the left side in Figure 6-34. In the previous section, you created buttons for the Go to

Layout action, but there are many more. As you scan through these commands, you probably notice that many of them repeat the same functions you find in File-Maker's menus. That's not just meaningless redundancy. By giving your databases buttons for lots of everyday commands, you can make FileMaker even easier to use than it already is. Design some icons (perhaps in your corporate colors), attach buttons to them, and you may find that you hardly have to train your colleagues at all, because the buttons and their labels help explain what they need to do to use the database.

POWER USERS' CLINIC

New Tab Orders

Buttons are user-friendly by their very nature. But you can make them even easier to use by including them in a layout's tab order (see page 228). When a button is in the tab order, your users can operate the button by tabbing to it, then tapping the Space bar or Return key to "press" it. As they tab, they can see which button is active by the double line around it. That means it's waiting for a press.

Be careful *where* in the tab order you put buttons, though. If you mix fields and buttons together without careful testing, your database may make people feel like they're held captive in a pinball machine. If your goal is to make users' lives easier, consider putting all your buttons together in the tab order, followed by all the fields, or vice versa.

Tab-able buttons take a certain amount of planning, so File-Maker doesn't take the liberty of putting them in the tab order for you. They don't appear in the order unless you specifically tell FileMaker that's what you want in the Set Tab Order dialog box (page 229).

Here's how the box's options work.

- The **Add Remaining** option lets you select a whole category of items to add to the tab order. The choices are Objects (both fields and buttons), Fields Only, or Buttons Only. Select the category you want, and then click the Add button. That tells FileMaker add to the tab order any object that doesn't already have a number in its arrow. Remember: FileMaker adds objects from top left to bottom right. If you want a custom order, click the arrows and type the number you need for each object.

- The **Remove** option lets you remove All Fields or All Buttons from the tab order. Make the selection you want from the pop-up menu, and then click the Remove button. This is most useful when you've got a messy order that needs some wholesale revision. If you've got buttons and fields all jumbled together, you don't have to hunt for each item individually. Just tell FileMaker which category you're looking for, click remove, and start fresh.

Here's a brief rundown on what some of these actions do.

Note: This section explains the button actions you're ready to use right now. Many available actions simply won't make sense to you until you've learned more about FileMaker. These buttons mimic the *steps* you can use when you write *scripts* to automate FileMaker procedures. (In fact, you can use *any* button action in a script.) You'll learn about scripts in detail in Part 5.

Go to Layout

Go to Layout is the action you used for the two buttons you created earlier in this chapter. It transports those who click it to another layout instantly. You get to pick which layout to visit (page 250).

Go to Record/Request/Page

The Go to Record/Request/Page action lets you switch to the Next, Previous, First, or Last record in the found set. If you're in Find mode, it navigates find requests instead. Despite the word "Page" in its name, it doesn't navigate pages in Preview mode because *buttons don't work in Preview mode.* (The reason it has this name is because you *can* navigate pages with a *script* in Preview mode. See Chapter 13 for more.)

Go to Field

Use Go to field if you want a button that delivers its clickers into a specific field. You get to pick the field by clicking the Options area's Specify button. For example, you could create a button that says "Back to Square One" that places the cursor in the first field in the tab order. (If you *don't* pick a field, this step goes to *no* field. In other words, it gets the user out of whatever field she's in.)

The Options area also has a "Select/perform" checkbox. For text, number, date, time, and timestamp fields, turn on this option if you also want FileMaker to *select* the contents of the field, so folks can just start typing to replace it. For container fields, this option tells FileMaker to *perform* the field contents. In other words, play the movie or sound, open the file, and so forth. This way, you could have a button that opens up a file (page 73), stored in a container field. For the Go to Field action to work, the target field *must* be on the layout.

Go to Next Field and Go to Previous Field

The Go to Next Field and Go to Previous Field actions have no options at all. They simulate the Tab and Shift-Tab keystrokes, bouncing to the next or previous field in the tab order.

Enter Browse Mode, Enter Find Mode, and Enter Preview Mode

The last three actions in the Navigation section—Enter Browse Mode, Enter Find Mode, and Enter Preview Mode—do just what you'd expect. Want a Find button on your layout? Assign it the Enter Find Mode action and you're done.

Note: The Enter Find Mode button has a "Specify find requests" option. You can use this power-user feature to preload the find requests and save your database's searchers a little time. You'll learn all about how to do this in Chapter 13.

Editing Actions

FileMaker has seven editing actions, whose names are largely self-explanatory:

- Undo

- Cut

- Copy

- Paste

- Clear

- Select All

- Perform Find/Replace

The Undo action takes no options at all; it simply runs the normal Edit → Undo menu command. Select All also has no options. It works exactly like the Edit → Select All command.

Cut, Copy, Paste, and Clear all let you optionally specify the field to act on. If you don't give a field, they act on the field your user is in when he clicks the button. You can also turn on "Select entire contents" for these actions if you want FileMaker to do a Select All before it cuts, copies, pastes, or clears. Again, if you don't, it works on whatever the user has already selected.

Perform Find/Replace lets you pop up the Find/Replace dialog box. You can click Specify to preload the dialog box with your own choices. And you can turn on "Perform without dialog" if you want it to perform your user's Find/Replace choices without showing the dialog box at all.

Note: The Editing section also has an action called Set Selection. You're not ready for this one yet, but it's covered in Chapter 14.

Field Actions

In the Fields section you find several useful and familiar commands.

Insert Text lets you stick predetermined text into a field. You can tell FileMaker *which* field to put it in, or leave "Go to target field" unchecked to have it land in the field the user's currently in. You also get a "Select entire contents" checkbox if you want the inserted text to *replace* whatever's in the field. Click the *bottom* Specify button to tell FileMaker what text to insert.

Several actions mimic the choices in the Insert menu (in Browse mode):

- Insert from Index

- Insert from Last Visited (Insert → From Last Visited Record)

- Insert Current Date

- Insert Current Time

- Insert Current User Name

- Insert Picture

- Insert QuickTime

- Insert File

For each of these, you can optionally choose the field to use, and whether or not to select everything in the field before inserting.

Finally, the Replace Field Contents action runs the Records → Replace Field Contents command. This time, you get to pick the field to replace into if you want. You can also predetermine what goes in the Replace Field Contents dialog box. If you turn on "Perform without dialog," your users never even see the dialog box. Instead, the replace *just happens*. You could use this action, for example, to add a Flag button to your layout. It would automatically flag every record in the found set by putting a *Y* in the same field on each of those records.

Record Actions

Use the New Record/Request action to make a button create a new record. To duplicate the current record instead, choose Duplicate Record/Request. To delete a record, use Delete Record/Request. This action has one option: "Perform without dialog." Turn this action on if you want your button to delete the record with no warning message.

Tip: Turn off the warning message only if the people using your database are very experienced (or very trustworthy). The Undo command can't undo a deletion, so there's no going back. Yet another reason for a good backup routine.

The Open Record/Request action locks the record without actually entering any fields. Chances are you *never* need to do this action from a button.

Use Revert Record/Request to mimic the Records → Revert Record menu command. This one has a "Perform without dialog" option as well.

To give folks an obvious Save button, assign it to the Commit Record/Request action. This action is just like clicking out of the record. It's useful, though. If you have your layout set to show a "Do you want to save…" message whenever someone edits the record, you can add a Save button to the layout, using this command with the "Perform without dialog" option turned on. Whenever anyone clicks the button, FileMaker saves the record straightaway without the annoying dialog box.

Found Set Actions

If you have certain finds that you perform a lot, you can create buttons to run them directly. Use the Perform Find, Constrain Found Set, and Extend Found Set actions to get the job done. Each action lets you specify what find requests you want them to use. See page 25 for an explanation of how to specify these requests manually.

For now, though, you can easily use them like this: First, perform the find you want the button to do (just go to Find mode, enter your criteria, and click Find). Then add the button to the layout and pick one of the find actions. Turn on "Specify find requests" and FileMaker shows you its complicated Specify Find Requests dialog box. But the box *already* has the requests you used last, so you can just click OK. Now your button performs the right find.

The last few actions work just like their counterparts in the Records menu:

- Modify Last Find

- Show All Records

- Show Omitted Only

- Omit Record

- Omit Multiple Records (This action has two options: how many records to omit, and the now-familiar "Perform without dialog.")

- Sort Records (This one also lets you predetermine the desired sort order, and avoid the dialog box if you want.)

- Unsort Records

Window Actions

Windows are, after all, where FileMaker displays your information, so it pays to be familiar with the button commands that control them. With these actions, you can adjust an open window so your data fits more comfortably, or even create a new window to navigate in while the form stays intact in the background.

- Use **New Window** to make a button that creates a new window. You can determine its name, size, and position, but it always shows the layout you're already on, so its usefulness is pretty limited. It's more typically used in a script.

- The **Select Window** action lets you switch to a different window if you know its name. Click Specify, choose Window Name, and type in the name of the window. (The Current Window option only makes sense when scripting.)

- **Close Window** simply closes the active window. You can also supply the name of *another* window, and FileMaker closes that window instead.

- The **Scroll Window** action gives the button rudimentary control over the window's scroll bars. Choose Home to scroll to the very top. If you choose End, a button click scrolls to the very end. Page Up and Page Down work like scroll bar clicks, moving it one screenful up or down.

  You can scroll a window while you're in a field. If you do, the field you're in may no longer be visible on the screen. The Scroll Window action's To

Selection option tells FileMaker to scroll the window so that the field you're in is visible.

- Use **Show/Hide Status Area** and **Show/Hide Text Ruler** to show or hide each embellishment. Your button can explicitly show or hide the item, or you can choose Toggle to have the button *switch* the setting with each click. The Show/Hide Status Area action also has a Lock checkbox. Turn this checkbox on if you want the Status Area control to become inactive when your button is clicked. With an inactive Status Area control, nobody can show or hide the status area without using your buttons.-

- The **Set Zoom Level** action lets you make your own Zoom buttons as well. This action also has a Lock option if you want to lock out the normal Zoom control. You also get a list of actions that perform menu commands:

  - **Adjust Window** lets you Minimize, Maximize, Resize to Fit, Restore (to its last size), or Hide the front most window.

  - **Arrange All Windows** gives you the Tile Horizontally, Tile Vertically, Cascade, and Bring All to Front options from the Window menu.

  - **View As** has an option for View as Form, View as List, and View as Table. You can also choose Cycle to have one button that cycles through all three views.

Note: The options to lock the status area and zoom controls might seem a little odd for button actions. Why would a person ever click a button to lock herself out of something useful? Actually, you'll usually use these options as part of a *script* (Chapter 13). You see them here since button actions and script steps always have the same options.

Print Actions

The Files section has two important actions: Print Setup and Print. These give you control over the File → Print and File → Print Setup or File → Page Setup commands. Optionally, you can preselect the options in each dialog box, and use the "Perform without dialog" checkbox to perform the action with no user intervention. You could, for instance, have buttons that switch to landscape and portrait page layouts, and a third button to directly print the current record.

Open Actions

The Open Menu Item section gives you button access to several common dialog boxes. You can add them to a layout to save people a trip to the menu bar…especially useful if they don't know where the menu bar *is*.

- Open Preferences
- Open File Options
- Open Define Database

- Open Define Value Lists

- Open Find/Replace

- Open Help

Exiting FileMaker

If you want a button that exits or quits FileMaker itself, use the very last action in the list: Exit Application.

Tab Panels

Dialog boxes are great examples of packing lots of stuff into a small space. Think about how the Layout Setup dialog box (Figure 6-18) works. When you first open the dialog box, you see a tab called General, which consolidates the most popular tools in one place. Two other tabs (Views and Printing) keep those categories of options out of your way until you need them. The Tab Panel tool and its controls help you use these same concepts to organize lots of objects on a single layout.

Creating a Tab Panel

If you want to add another set of fields to hold the work addresses of the contacts in your People database, you have to make the layout bigger in order to hold your new fields. But there are times when you just can't stretch a layout any farther. Maybe some of your employees have smaller monitors and you don't want them to have to scroll to see everything on the layout. Or you may feel you've already created a beautiful layout, with perfect proportions, and stretching it just to add a few more fields would ruin the design you worked so hard to create. Whatever the reason, if you don't want to make a layout bigger, you can organize lots more fields by adding a tab panel (Figure 6-36)

Here's how to use your existing detail layout (in the People database) to create a new layout using a three-tab panel:

1. **In the People database, go to detail layout and switch to Layout mode. Then choose Layout → Duplicate Layout.**

   An exact copy of the detail layout appears, which FileMaker names *Detail Copy*.

2. **Choose Layouts → Layout Setup. Change the layout's name to *Data Entry*.**

   The original detail layout was useful for printing, but this one helps you organize the fields for entering data. As your databases grow more complex, you could end up with dozens of layouts used for all different purposes, so painfully descriptive names like *Data Entry* make a lot of sense.

3. On the Data Entry layout, select everything below the Last Name field and drag it over to the right side of your layout.

You're clearing a space for your new tab control.

Figure 6-36:
You make a more space available on your layout by using tab panels to organize fields. These tabs are left aligned, but they can also be centered, right aligned or justified across the full width of the panel.

4. Click the Tab Panel tool (it looks like a file folder icon). Then, draw a tab panel like the one in Figure 6-36.

The Tab Control Setup dialog box appears (Figure 6-37). Here's where you tell the panel how many tabs it needs and what to name them.

Figure 6-37:
The standard settings for Tabs are left aligned, with rounded corners. But you can have square corners instead if you like them better. Left, center and right justified tabs are just wide enough to enclose the names you give them. But fully justified tabs stretch out and divide the space to fill the width of the entire panel.

5. In the Tab Name field, type *Address*, and then click the Create button.

In the Tabs list, the Address tab appears. Repeat this step for two more tabs: Contact and Notes.

6. When you're done, click OK to close the Tab Control Setup dialog box.

Your new tab panel, complete with three tabs, sits highlighted in place on your lay-out. Notice that there are four selection handles at each corner, and a dark box around each of the three tabs. Any changes you make to the tab panel now affects all three tabs.

Tip: You can change the tab panels individually if you want to. Click outside the tab panel to deselect it, then click the tab you want to change independently of the others. To reselect the whole panel, use the rubber band technique (page 151).

---

1. **Change the tab panels to a lighter gray, using the Fill Color palette.**

   You can also change the tab panels' font, font size, style and color if you wish.

2. **Click the Address tab to make it active.**

   You're getting ready to move the fields into place on the tab panel.

3. **Select the set of address fields you moved out of the way earlier and drag them onto the Address panel.**

   Repeat steps 2 and 3 to move the Phone and Email fields to the Contact panel and the Notes field to the Notes panel.

4. **Switch to Browse mode to test your panel.**

   Click the panels to see how the fields appear and disappear along with their panels.

There's plenty of room on the Address panel for another set of address fields to hold a separate work address. You can define them now, if you like, and place them on the Address panel. (See page 85 for a step-by-step tutorial on defining new fields.)

All the fields you've moved onto the tab panels are now firmly attached to those panels. If you move the panel, all the fields move along with it, so there's no need for fancy selection techniques. Just drag the panel to your new location, and you're golden. You can even copy the whole panel and paste it onto another layout. It works just as it did in the original location.

Warning: Tab panels are brand-new in FileMaker 8. Although earlier versions can open .fp8 files, some features, like tab controls, don't work in those versions. Folks using FileMaker 7 or earlier can't see your lovely tab panels, for example. Instead, they see a jumble of fields piled on top of one another.

Editing Tab Panels

You can edit a tab panel by double-clicking it to summon the Tab Control Setup dialog box.

- **Reorder** your existing tabs by dragging the little arrow that sits to the left of each tab. All the objects attached to the tab move along with it.

- **Add a new tab** by typing a new name and clicking the Create button. The new tab appears at the end of your list, but you can move it with the arrow. New tabs start out empty, but you can move any fields, buttons, or other objects onto the tab after you click OK.

- **Change a tab's name** by selecting the tab from the list. Type the new name, then click Change. Objects on the tab are unaffected.

- **Delete a tab** by selecting it from the list, and then clicking Delete. You delete any unlocked objects on the tab at the same time.

POWER USERS' CLINIC

Extra-Strength Tabs

As useful as they seem on the surface, tab panels have a few *hidden* secrets that you can use to your advantage.

- If you leave a tab active in Layout mode, that's the panel that's always active when you return to that layout. Try it on your People file. In Layout mode, click the Contact tab to make it active. Switch to Browse mode and click the Address tab. Now, if you switch to any other layout, then come back to Data Entry, the Contact tab is always the active one.

- Another way to go to a specific tab, without clicking the tab itself, is to make a button with a *Go to Field []* action. Make sure the field is on the tab you want to be active. Every time you click the button, the tab that contains the field in your *Go To Field []* action comes forward.

You can nest tab panels inside one another for even more space. So long as the new panel sits entirely *inside* an existing tab, it behaves just like any other object on a panel. It sits there quietly behind the scenes and doesn't make an appearance until you click its enclosing panel. Then, up the new panel pops, in all its tabbed glory. Download the file People Tab Panels from *www.missingmanuals.com/cds/fmakerprotmm/* to see this trick in action.

If you make a set of changes and realize you've made a mistake, just click the Cancel button. All changes you've made to the tab panel since you opened the dialog are swept away, even if you deleted some panels, added some and rearranged the furniture while you were in there. But once you click OK, your changes are written in stone—at least until you revisit the Tab Control Setup dialog box.

Deleting a Tab Panel

If you don't want a tab panel after all, just select it and choose Edit → Clear or tap Delete. FileMaker warns you that it's about to delete all unlocked objects on the tab panel as well (Figure 6-38). If that's the way you want it, click OK. If you need to keep fields or objects on the tab panels, though, click Cancel, then move the keepers off the panel (way to the right of your layout, perhaps) for safekeeping.

Figure 6-38:
If you try to delete a tab panel, FileMaker also deletes all the fields you've placed on the tabs, so it wants to make sure you really mean it. You can avoid this dialog box if you move all fields and buttons off each tab and onto another part of the layout first.

Reports and Summary Fields

A database excels at keeping track of things—itsy bitsy teeny tiny details about hundreds, thousands, even millions of little things. But people aren't so good at dealing with all that detail (hence the invention of the database). They like to see the *big picture*. If you want to understand your customer's music tastes, a report of 200,000 individual CD sales won't do you much good: The information is in there somewhere, but your feeble mind stands no chance of ferreting it out. But a report that divides that information into 25 *music genres*, each with sales totals, both in aggregate and by gender, helps you interpret all those reams of data at a glance. In other words, a well-designed report *summarizes* the data for you. FileMaker's not only fantastic at showing you information, it also excels at helping you see what it all *means*.

In Chapter 5, you learned how to create reports that show lists of records, but they don't include any so-called summary data. They only show the details. To get summary information, you need *summary fields*.

Summary Fields

In Chapter 3, you learned that a summary field isn't associated with records like the other field types (page 95). Instead, summary fields gather up and process data from several records. Creating summary fields is much easier than describing what they do, as you can see from the following example.

1. **In the People database, choose File → Define → Database.**

   You're about to add a field that counts up the people in your database. This action is one of the commonest ways to summarize database information.

2. **In the Define Database window, choose the Fields tab. Then, in the Field Name box, type *Count of People*.**

A summary field, like any other, has a name. You're going to use this summary field to count the people in your database.

3. **From the Type pop-up menu, choose Summary, and then click Create.**

The Options for Summary Field window appears (Figure 6-39).

Figure 6-39:
The Options for Summary Field dialog box appears when you make a new summary field. Unlike the field types you've used so far, a summary field has options that must be set for it to be usable, so FileMaker shows you those options right away. This window also shows up if, in the Define Database window, you select a Summary field and click Options.

4. **Choose the "Count of" radio button.**

A summary field can perform one of seven summary calculations. In this case, you want it to *count* things.

5. **From the Available Fields list, choose First Name.**

A summary field is always based on some other field in the database. For example, this field counts the First Name field. What does that mean? Simple: If a record has something in the First Name field, it gets counted, but if the First Name field is blank, FileMaker skips the entire record. Since every person has a first name, this field counts every record. But beware—if you forget to type somebody's first name in a new record, that person doesn't get included in the count.

6. **Click OK.**

FileMaker adds the new field to the field list.

You now have a field that helps you find out how many people are in the database. That piece of information is much more useful than it sounds; you'll be using it to find out interesting things soon. It would also be nice to be able to summarize the Goodness Rating information. In this case, an *average* makes sense.

---

1. **In the Field Name box, type *Average of Goodness Rating*.**

   Remember, field names can be about as long as you want.

2. **With Summary selected in the Type pop-up menu, click Create.**

   The Options for Summary Field dialog box makes its second appearance.

3. **Select the "Average of" radio button.**

   Since averages only make sense for *numbers*, FileMaker grays out any non-number fields in the Available Field list. In this example, that leaves only Goodness Rating, which is automatically selected. But if you had date, time or timestamp fields in your file, those would remain available, too, in case you wanted to do some math on them.

4. **Click OK to add the Goodness Rating field, and then OK again to dismiss the Define Database window.**

5. **FileMaker returns you to your database window.**

POWER USERS' CLINIC

Stop That

Normally when you add a field to the database, FileMaker automatically adds it to the layout you were just on. This feature is nice in the same way those child safety bottle lids are nice: It's probably good for kids. But big people like you find it terribly annoying.

First of all, FileMaker can't possibly know where you want the field, so it just sticks it at the bottom of the layout. This place might be the right one but it just as easily might not. If it isn't the right place you can just move it, but if the body part had to grow to accommodate it, you have to reduce it again.

What's more, it usually doesn't use the right font and formatting (your new notes field is probably formatted like the text under the Goodness Rating field shown on page 259: small, gray, and right-aligned). Putting it right is tedious. It's usually easier to duplicate an existing field and change it to show your new field.

This way, you get all the right formatting in one step. Finally, if you have several layouts in your database, you don't necessarily want the new field on the *current* layout—and its existence there is just something you have to go fix.

To teach FileMaker that you're a big boy or girl, just do this:

1. In Windows, choose Edit → Application Preferences; in Mac OS X, choose FileMaker Pro → Preferences. The Application Preferences window pops up.

2. Switch to the Layout tab. This tab is the place you set Layout mode preferences. You've already seen the Color Palette settings.

3. Turn off "Add newly defined fields to current layout."

If you someday decide to stop thinking for yourself, you can always turn the current layout setting back on.

If you squeeze these two fields onto the detail layout and have a look in Browse mode, you see something altogether unimpressive: the total number of people in the database (the status area already tells you this information) and their average goodness rating (OK, this number is *mildly* impressive). If you don't believe it, have a look at Figure 6-40.

Creating a Summary Report

This section began by talking about how useful it can be to summarize your data. It specifically mentions a report that shows sales by Zip code and genre for a music retailer. When you hear something like that, you're sure to think that a Summary field should have some kind of a "by what" option. In other words, how do you tell that Total Sales field to summarize *by Zip code*? You don't. There's no such choice in the Options for Summary Field dialog box.

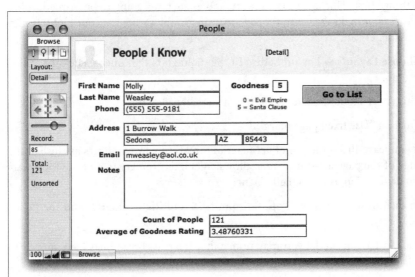

Figure 6-40:
Showing your new summary fields on the detail layout isn't terribly exciting. You don't need a field to tell you how many records you have (the status area does this job just fine). Next you see the average goodness rating of all people in the database, which is only mildly interesting. For the real power, see "Sub-Summary Reporting" on page 273.

A Summary field is, by nature, *abstract*. You tell it which field to summarize, and that's about it. You might have one that counts people, another that totals orders, and a third that shows the standard deviation of the Height field.

The way to tell reports how to summarize your data is to design your *layouts* to produce the specific groupings you want. For example, you can make that Total Orders field display totals *per customer* on one layout, *per product* on another, and *per month* on a third. This field gives you tremendous flexibility when asking your database questions, without the need to define different fields for the totals on each different report. You can even make a new layout that slices your data a brand-new way without ever revisiting the Define Database window. Once you understand this process, defining summary fields is easy. You usually need just a handful at most.

To help you understand how to tailor a layout to a report's best advantage, how about adding a new report to the People database that uses the new summary fields? Start by opening the database and switching to Layout mode.

1. **Choose Layouts → New Layout/Report.**

   The now-familiar New Layout/Report window returns.

2. **In the Layout Name box, type** *Summary Report, and* **then, in the "Select a layout type" list, choose Blank Layout.**

   You're going to build this layout by hand.

3. **Click Finish.**

   FileMaker creates its basic blank layout: empty header; empty body; empty footer.

First things first: This layout is a report, and as such it's going to be printed. A lot. In this case, it makes sense to fix page margins so the printed output looks as nice as possible.

1. **Choose Layouts → Layout Setup. In the dialog box that opens, click the Printing tab.**

   This panel should look familiar, if you've read page 230.

2. **Turn on "Use fixed page margins."**

   If you leave this option *off*, FileMaker automatically prints things as close to the edge of the page as your printer allows. When *on*, you get to edit the four margin boxes (Top, Bottom, Left, Right).

3. **In each of the boxes for Top, Bottom, Left, and Right, enter** *1*, **and then click OK.**

   Back in Layout mode, you may notice that the page break lines have moved to reflect the printable area considering the new margins.

4. **Choose File → Print Setup (Windows) or File → Page Setup (Mac OS X) and make sure the paper size is correct and the orientation is set to the normal** *portrait.*

   The page break lines may move once again to show the new size and shape of the paper.

Since your layout now has fixed margins, you might want to *see* them in Layout mode so you have a feel for how things fit on the page. Just choose View → Page Margins.

Note: Showing page margins in Layout mode is not a substitute for Preview mode. FileMaker doesn't attempt to show the page at the proper size. Instead, the margins in Layout mode help you get a feel for the space around your layout objects on the printed page. For example, without them, you might avoid putting text at the very top of the layout. But the margins remind you that this text will *actually* sit an inch below the top of the page. You can switch to Preview mode at any time for a more accurate look.

Now it's time to design the body part.

1. **Add a new field to the layout by dragging the field tool into the body part.**

   FileMaker instantly asks you which field you want.

2. **Select the First Name field in the Specify Field list, and then click OK.**

   The First Name field is now on the layout, although it may not be formatted properly. You're going to format it, and then use it as the basis for the rest of the fields in this layout—a great timesaving trick.

3. **Change the field's font to Verdana 10 point regular. Make sure the field content aligns to the left (Format → Align Text → Left).**

   The field now looks something like those in Figure 6-41. Now that the field is properly formatted you can copy it to produce the other needed fields.

4. **While pressing the Alt (Option) key, drag the First Name field to the right a few inches.**

   When you Alt-drag (or, on the Mac, Option-drag), FileMaker makes a copy of whatever you're dragging. See page 163 for more cool dragging tricks.

5. **Double-click the new copy of the First Name field. When the Specify Field window returns, choose the Last Name field from the list, and then click OK.**

   You now have a First Name field *and* a Last Name field on the layout.

6. **Repeat steps 4 and 5 six times to add these fields: Phone Number, Email Address, Street Address, City, State, Zip**

   You now have eight fields on the layout.

7. **Arrange the fields in the body part to match Figure 6-41.**

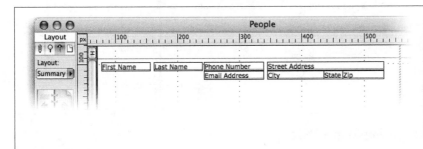

Figure 6-41:
The fields on your new layout should be arranged something like this. You'll add titles, page numbers, decorations, and so forth shortly. You also need to resize the parts and work your new summary fields in there somewhere.

If you stop and view this layout in Browse mode now, it looks sparse, but the data's there. You may notice, though, that the address portion is "spaced out" in an unpleasant way. You can fix this problem with sliding. (And if you don't remember what sliding is, see page 268.)

1. **In Layout mode, select these fields: First Name, Last Name, City, State, and Zip.**

   Remember to press Shift as you click to select more than one item. *All* these fields need to slide to the left.

2. **Choose Format → Sliding/Printing, turn on "Sliding left," and then click OK.**

Again, sliding only affects Preview mode and printing, so you don't see any change in Layout mode.

Next, you can add the summary fields to the layout. Since they summarize data, they really don't belong in the body part, which repeats for every record on every printed page.

Seen: Sliding

Is there any way I can tell which items have sliding turned on?

Yep. Choose View → Show → Sliding Objects. Every object that is set to slide gains a small black arrow pointing in the sliding direction. In this picture, you can see the arrows clearly on several fields, indicating that those fields slide left.

If that way's not your bag, there's another way. When you choose Format → Sliding/Printing, the Set Sliding/Printing window first appears with the settings that match the currently selected object. You can therefore find out how an object slides by selecting it and then choosing Format → Sliding/Printing.

Sliding Right Arrow

Adding a Summary Part

You need to show them only once—probably *after* all the data. There's a part type that does exactly this: Trailing Grand Summary. When you start with a brand-new layout, it has a body, a header, and a footer, but it doesn't automatically have any summary parts. You have to add them yourself:

1. **Choose Insert → Part. When the Part Definition dialog box appears, select Trailing Grand Summary, and then click OK.**

   FileMaker adds a trailing grand summary part to your layout, between the body and the footer.

Tip: If you prefer to have your summary information *before* the data in the report, use a *Leading* Grand Summary part instead, which appears between the body and the header. Whether you want your grand totals at the top of your report or at the bottom is purely a matter of preference.

2. **Add the two summary fields to the new part, along with meaningful labels.**

Refer back to page 143 for instructions.

Next up, you need to reduce the size of the body part so it shows a slim row, add a title and any lines you feel would look nice, and add a page number in the footer. You might also use separate title header and header parts so you can put a *smaller* header on every page after the first. You can see one way to format this report in Figure 6-42.

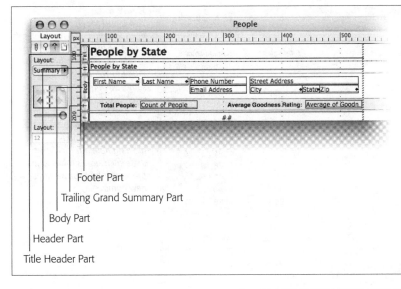

Figure 6-42:
This is one way you could lay out your report. The Count of People and Average Goodness Rating fields are in a trailing grand summary part, which shows just below the body. Switch to Preview mode and click the last page to see the summary fields in action.

Tip: If you use Find mode to find only a few records (you have to switch to the detail layout first), the summary fields change to reflect only the records in the found set. Of course the printed report also includes only the data in the found set.

Other Summary Field Types

The Options for Summary Field dialog box has several choices. The first decision you need to make when defining a summary field is which radio button to turn on. Here's what each choice does:

Total of

Use the "Total of" option to *sum* (add) number fields. For instance, you can make a summary field that shows total sales by turning on "Total of" and, in your Orders database, selecting the Order Amount field.

When you have this option selected, a "Running total" checkbox appears below the Available Fields list. When you use a summary field on one of those magical layouts (like the one you create on page 273) that produces grouping—total sales by Zip code, total sales by state, and so on—you normally see just the totals for each group in the report. If you turn on "Running total," FileMaker changes things slightly. Instead of individual totals for each group, the totals add up from group to group. Figure 6-43 shows just such a report.

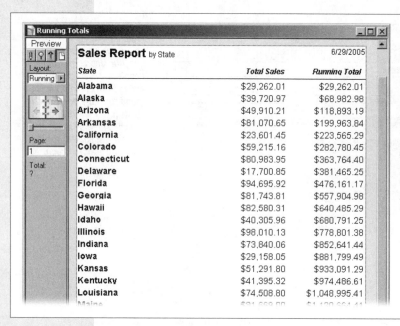

Figure 6-43:
This report shows summary fields in action. The Total Sales field uses the "Total of" option to add up sales numbers. The Running Total field is the same, but it has the "Running total" box turned on. As you can see, one shows totals for each individual state, while the other has a continually growing number. FileMaker adds each state's totals to the previous total to arrive at the new number.

Average of

Obviously, the "Average of" choice calculates the average of the values in a number field. This time, you see a "Weighted average" checkbox. When you turn it on, another field list appears (see Figure 6-44). From this list, you choose the field by which to *weight* your average.

You would use a weighted average when the things you are averaging have an associated quantity. For example, suppose your database has a record for each product sale. It records which product was sold, how many were sold, and the unit price. If you want a summary field that calculates the average sale price, you probably want to turn on the "Weighted average" checkbox. Imagine you have these sales figures:

- You sold three laptop computers for $2,500 each.

- You sold 18 more laptops for $2,200 each.

- You sold a single laptop for $2,800.

If you use a simple average, FileMaker tells you the average sale price for laptops is $2,500 ($2,500 + $2,800 + $2,200, divided by three). But that's not exactly right. You sold *18* of those laptops at just $2,200 each, but it only counts *once* in the calculation. In fact, you really sold 22 laptops in all, at three different price points. To calculate the correct average, you need to take quantities into consideration. In FileMaker, turn on the "Weighted average" checkbox and choose the Quantity field in the "Weighted by" list. Now it reports the correct average: $2,268.18.

Figure 6-44:
When you turn on the "Weighted average" checkbox, FileMaker adds a second field list—Weighted by—to the window, where you can pick another number field. FileMaker averages the data in the first field, and weights each record's input by the second field. If you're not a statistician, see the explanation on the previous page.

Count of

Choose "Count of" to *count* items without totaling them. Since this option doesn't involve actual math, you can pick *any* field type, not just numbers. FileMaker counts each record in which that field isn't empty. If it's empty, it simply doesn't contribute to the count. Choose a field that is *never* empty if you want to be sure you count *every* record. You can use this property to your advantage, though. If you wanted your count to reflect just the records that are flagged, count the Flag field instead. This option gives you a "Running count" checkbox. It works like "Running total" (page 270), but has an option that running total doesn't offer.

Say you want to know how many contacts in your People database live in each city. In your counting summary field, choose the "Restart summary for each sorted group" option. A new list of your fields appears, letting you determine how you want the restarted count to behave. Since it's the city you care about, choose the city field from the list that appears on the right. To see the restarted count in action, sort your list by city (Figure 6-45).

Minimum and Maximum

If you want to know the *smallest* or the *largest* value in a group, use Minimum or Maximum. Both are very simple: Just pick the number field you want to look at. No checkboxes, no extra lists. You might use these to see the largest goodness rating in your database, or the price of the least expensive product.

Standard Deviation of

If you're into statistics, use "Standard Deviation of." It gives you a field that calculates its namesake for the selected number field. It also has a "by population" checkbox, which is a little oddly named (it probably should be called "of population"). Turn this checkbox on if your records represent the entire population in your particular domain, and FileMaker uses the formula for the standard deviation of a population. Turn it off to calculate the standard deviation of a *sample*.

Note: If none of this makes sense to you, then rest assured you don't *need* to know what it means. If you're cursed with a curious mind, Google *define: standard deviation* and go to town.

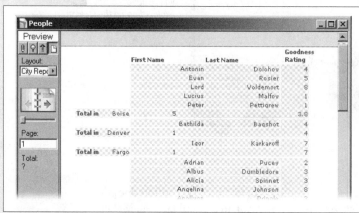

Figure 6-45:
When you turn on the "Running count" and "Restart summary for each sorted group" options for a "Count of" summary field, you get a nifty report that counts up each group individually. This report was sorted by the City field, so the people records are grouped according to city.

Fraction of Total

Fraction of Total is the most complex summary option. It looks at the total for the *group* you're summarizing, as well as the total for the entire database. It then reports what portion of the overall total the group represents, as a decimal number. If all your sales were in California, it would show *1*. If California only accounted for 5 percent of your sales, on the other hand, it would say *.05*.

The "Subtotaled" checkbox that comes along with this option is also a little confusing. When you turn it on, FileMaker lets you pick another field from a list called "When sorted by." The name of this list serves to inform you that you must *sort* the record by the selected field for this summary field to work. If you don't sort the records yourself before you view the report, the field stays empty.

Note: That problem's not as big as it might seem at first. As you'll see on page 274, you have to sort records to do a lot of things with summary fields.

FileMaker looks at the selected field, figures out which records have the *same* value in them as in the current record, and calculates the fraction based only on the total of *those* records. Figure 6-46 illustrates this concept.

Figure 6-46:
This report shows sales figures by region as well as by state. The Total Sales column shows the total sales in each region or state. Percent of Total shows each region's contribution to the total sales using the Fraction of Total summary type. The Percent of Region also uses Fraction of Total, with Subtotaled turned on and the Region field selected. Set up this way, it reports each state's contribution to the total sales for the region, rather than the grand total.

Summarizing repetitions

When you summarize a repeating field (page 109), you have another choice to make. Do you want *one* summary value that aggregates every repetition, producing a single value? If so, choose "All together." If you want a repeating summary value that aggregates each repetition individually instead, choose Individually.

Note: If you have sharp eyes, you notice that the "Summarize repetitions" radio buttons are available all the time, although they don't do anything unless you've selected a repeating field. Don't waste your time clicking them unless you're working with a repeating field. Just one of those FileMaker mysteries for the cocktail-party circuit.

Sub-Summary Reporting

The report you just created is nice, but it could be *even nicer* (imagine that). Wouldn't it be fantastic to know how many people in your database live in each *state*? The average goodness rating per state would be pretty telling as well. Since there are 50 possible states and two summaries, you need *100* summary fields, right? Nope: Here's where summary fields really start to shine. Since your new needs still involve just counting and averaging, you already have *all the fields you need*.

All you really need to do is *sub-summarize* your existing data by state. This process just involves adding a new part to your layout; a sub-summary part. You tell this part to use the State field, and any summary fields you put in it automatically operates on the correct subset of records.

Sub-summary parts

A sub-summary part shows summary information about a *subset* of the records in the found set. When you add a sub-summary part to a report, it acts like a cross between a trailing (or leading) grand summary and a body part. It doesn't repeat for *every* record, but it does repeat: It shows once for each *group* of records.

POWER USERS' CLINIC

Sub-Summary Power

You can actually put *two* sub-summary parts associated with the same field on a layout at the same time, as long as one's set to print above the records and the other below.

You can also put several sub-summary parts on the same layout with each associated with a different field. This way you can create nested sub-groupings, each with their own summarization data. When you create them, you need to be extra careful with the sort order. For sub-summary parts that print *above* the records, you should sort the fields in the order of the sub-summary parts themselves. If your sub-summary parts are *below* the records, you should sort first by the field associated with the *bottommost* part, and then by the next one up, and so on.

If you don't include a field in the sort order, FileMaker simply excludes the sub-summary part(s) for that field from the report. In this way, you can have a single layout that reports on data with different groupings based only on the sort order.

In the left window shown here, the records are sorted by state. In the right window, though, they're sorted first by city, *then* by state. Even though each window shows the same layout, you see very different results.

You can even make a layout with sub-summary parts, but no body part. A layout set up like this just shows group summaries, without individual record details. For example, if you remove the body part from the report you just made, you see the people count and goodness rating for each state in a simple list, but you don't see individual people.

Sub-summary parts are unique in two ways. First, they only show up in Preview mode. You never see a sub-summary part in Browse or Find modes. Second, they only show up when the data is *sorted* by the field they're associated with.

You tell a sub-summary part how to group records by associating it with a single field in your database. The part shows up once for each unique value in that field (you get to decide if it comes before or after the records in its group). But the magic doesn't stop there. If you put *summary fields* in a sub-summary part, the fields automatically summarize just the records in the associated group. In other words, you can put the *same* fields in *different* parts to see different results.

In the People database, for instance, you could add a sub-summary part to this report based on the State field and set to appear above the summarized records. The result would look something like Figure 6-47.

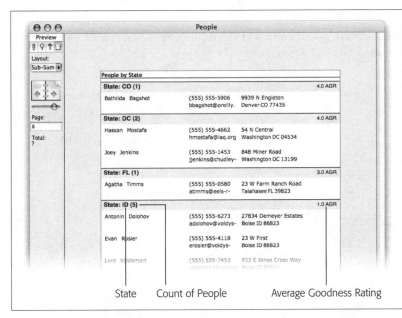

Figure 6-47:
This version of your report includes a gray-colored sub-summary part based on the State field. The part includes the State field itself, as well as the two summary fields. As you can see, the summary field values reflect just the group under them. In other words, they sub-summarize (clever, huh?).

State   Count of People   Average Goodness Rating

Creating a sub-summary part

Adding sub-summary parts to your layout is a breeze, since you already know how to create summary parts (page 268).

1. **In Layout mode, choose Insert → Part. Then, in the Part Definition dialog box, select "Sub-Summary when sorted by."**

   Now you can access the list of fields on the right side of this window. This is where you tell FileMaker which field you'll be summarizing by.

2. **Scroll down to State in the field list and click it.**

   You've just told FileMaker to use the State field to group records.

3. **Click OK.**

FileMaker asks if you want to print the part *above* or *below* the records it summarizes.

4. **To get the result shown in Figure 6-47, click Print Above.**

A new sub-summary part appears between the header and body.

5. **Add the State, Count of People, and Average of Goodness Rating fields to the new part.**

You can also decorate this part any way you see fit, using any of the methods described on page 146.

To see the results of your labors, sort the records by the State field and switch to Preview mode.

Part Three:
Multiple Tables and Relationships

3

Multiple Tables and Relationships

Up until now, you've been working with the simplest kind of database imaginable—it has just one table. In the real world, one table is almost never enough. In your private investigator business, for example, you probably need to keep track of more than just people. You need to record the time you spend working for your customers, the invoices you send them, and the payments you receive.

You can certainly create a separate database for each of these needs. But that's far from ideal, since you don't use each kind of information in isolation. You need all these different kinds of information to work in harmony, like a well-rehearsed orchestra. In database terms, what you need is a single, integrated file that keeps all your various lists, files, and records in one place, so you can arrange and rearrange them according to your needs—a *relational database*.

Relational Databases Explained

Before you dive head first into relational databases, it will be helpful to review some vocabulary. First, a *database* is a collection of tables, layouts, and other things that forms an organized system. A *table* holds information about one kind of thing, like people, orders, products, or suppliers. A *field* holds one attribute of something: the person's first name, the order date, the color of a product, or the supplier's address. (An *attribute* simply means an individual characteristic. For example, a bicycle might have several attributes: Color, Height, Style, and Price. In a database, each of these attributes gets its own field.)

In the previous chapter, you've created a database whose tables and fields track various attributes of people. You could repeat the process and build any number of individual databases for organizing your time, creating invoices, and logging payments. But that approach has real problems, like the following:

- When you log some billable work, you have to type in the customer information. Then, when you create an invoice, you have to type the customer information all over again in the invoice file. When you receive a payment, you have to type it a third time in the payment file. Since the databases aren't connected in any way, they can't share that information with one another.

- Suppose you want to see how much you've billed a customer over the years. You could use the Invoices database and run a summary report by, say, the customer's name. But duplicate names, misspellings, and name changes would render the information useless. You could use the People database instead. After all, the total amount billed (or outstanding balance) is, in some sense, an attribute of a customer. But to have that information ready when you need it, you'd have to create a field for it in the People database and retype the invoice information there every time. You know you have all the information somewhere, but because the system isn't integrated, it can't help you put all the pieces together.

Even if you could live with these limitations, you're certain to run into trouble when you try to create the Invoices database. An invoice typically encompasses information about two different entities: the *invoice* itself, and each *line item*. There's simply no good way to track invoices without involving at least two tables. Your solution to all these problems? Hook multiple tables together into one big database.

Note: Database developers use the word *entity* to mean "one kind of thing." *Person* is an entity, and so is *Invoice*. Remember, though, that one specific thing isn't an entity—Bill Gates isn't an entity, and neither is Invoice #24601.

Not only can you put more than one table in a database—and track more than one kind of thing in the process—but you can also tell FileMaker how the data fits together. You can say, for example, that invoice records have attached line item records; or that each payment record is associated with a particular customer record.

In database parlance, you define *relationships* among the data. A relationship is a connection from one table to another, along with the rules that define how records in the tables go together. For example, suppose you have two tables—Invoices and Line Items—as shown in Figure 7-1.

In order to figure out which line items belong to each invoice, you need to understand the relationship between these tables. Notice that the Line Item table has a field called *Invoice Number*. This field holds (surprise!) the invoice number for each line item. You can also show this relationship with a picture, just like the one in Figure 7-2. By defining this relationship, you've created a mechanism to hook together an Invoice record and a Line Item record.

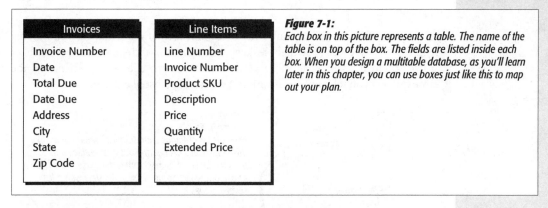

Figure 7-1:
Each box in this picture represents a table. The name of the table is on top of the box. The fields are listed inside each box. When you design a multitable database, as you'll learn later in this chapter, you can use boxes just like this to map out your plan.

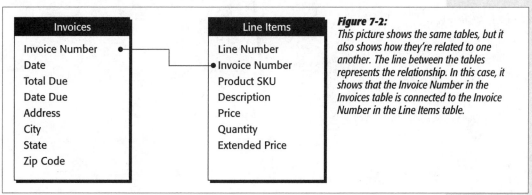

Figure 7-2:
This picture shows the same tables, but it also shows how they're related to one another. The line between the tables represents the relationship. In this case, it shows that the Invoice Number in the Invoices table is connected to the Invoice Number in the Line Items table.

Modeling Your Database

When you set out to design a relational database, you need to do a little upfront planning. You need to decide what entities you'll be tracking and which ones deserve a table, and how they relate to one another. It's easier to create the right tables and connections the first time than to go back and change them. You can create your own "blueprint" to follow as you build your database—what the pros call an *entity relationship diagram*.

Choosing Entities

Your first step in designing the database is deciding what tables you need and how they fit together. Since every table holds data about a single entity, you normally start by figuring out all the entities in your system. You probably won't be able to list them all in one shot. Everybody forgets some that are less obvious, so start with blank paper or a word processor, and list all the things the database will need to *do*. This list will help you identify entities.

Now's the time to stretch your mind and think of every possibility. What tasks do you do every day? What do you *wish* you could do—and what information do you need to do it? What do you want your computer to show you when you sit down first thing in the morning?

When your workflow hits a wall, what piece of information would get you moving again? What questions do people keep asking you—and how could FileMaker answer them for you? The more your initial plan matches your real needs, the more quickly you'll be up and running. You can see a list like this in Figure 7-3.

Figure 7-3:
Here's a list of things your database will do. A list like this helps you start figuring out your entities and possible tables. A more complex database could have a much longer list. Some big systems start with a list several pages long!

My Database:

• Keep track of the people I do business with and the jobs I do for them

• Track my time: what I did, for whom, and for how long

• Track expenses incurred while doing work for customers

• Create invoices

• Keep track of what I'm owed, and what's been paid

With this list in hand, you can start to figure out what *entities* your database needs to track. For each item on your list, think of all the *things* it involves. Figure 7-4 shows a possible list.

Most real-world problems have lots and lots of entities, so the second step is to figure out which ones matter. You'll use a process of elimination to remove extraneous items from your list. You might eliminate items for any of four major reasons:

• **They're already covered.** The list in Figure 7-4 includes Checks and Payments. A check is really just a kind of payment, so you don't need to track them separately in your database. Since a payment is more general than a check, you can eliminate Checks. Then, when you build your Payments table, you might add a field called Type and put Check, Cash, or Credit Card in that field.

- **They're too specific.** Sometimes you'll have things in your list that aren't general enough. This list shows Airline Tickets, Hotels, and Film. But you don't really need to track the details of each of these items. Instead, you're just interested in expenses in general—what they were, how much they cost, and what job they were for. To fix this problem, think of a more general word that encompasses all three things—something like Expenses. Add that to the list and remove the more specific versions.

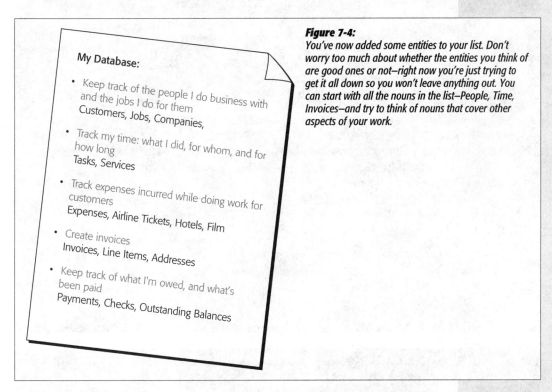

My Database:

- Keep track of the people I do business with and the jobs I do for them
  Customers, Jobs, Companies,

- Track my time: what I did, for whom, and for how long
  Tasks, Services

- Track expenses incurred while doing work for customers
  Expenses, Airline Tickets, Hotels, Film

- Create invoices
  Invoices, Line Items, Addresses

- Keep track of what I'm owed, and what's been paid
  Payments, Checks, Outstanding Balances

Figure 7-4:
You've now added some entities to your list. Don't worry too much about whether the entities you think of are good ones or not–right now you're just trying to get it all down so you won't leave anything out. You can start with all the nouns in the list–People, Time, Invoices–and try to think of nouns that cover other aspects of your work.

- **They're really just attributes of another entity.** Do you really need an entity called Outstanding Balances? You do need to know how much each customer still owes you, but do you already have that information somewhere else? A customer has an outstanding balance because one or more invoices are unpaid. So to see who owes you money, you really just want to look at the balance due on any unpaid invoices. Scratch Outstanding Balances off the list. For the same reason, you can also remove Companies—they're just attributes of a customer. (For more detail, see the box on page 284.)

Note: Just because you're crossing things off your list doesn't mean those things aren't important, or don't apply to your database. It just means they don't qualify as entities that need their own table. These things may show up as *fields* in other tables (like Company) or they may just be one *type* of a more general entity, like Check. Either way, you can still track these items in your database. See the box on page 288.

Many for One and One for Many

Relationships tell FileMaker which records in two tables go together. Conceptually, relationships come in three flavors: one-to-many, many-to-many, and one-to-one.

In a one-to-many relationship, one record in the first table relates to several records in the second. For example, one invoice record has several line items, so it's a one-to-many relationship. (Likewise, several line items belong to one invoice, so you could say that Line Items and Invoices have a many-to-one relationship. Since relationships work both ways, a one-to-many is *always* a many-to-one as well.) Figure 7-2 shows a one-to-many relationship, where one invoice has many line items.

A many-to-many relationship means something slightly different. Suppose you have a Products table and an Orders table. Each time you sell some products, you create a new order.

These tables have a many-to-many relationship: A person orders multiple products, and each product can be ordered many times.

Finally, you can have two tables that are locked in a one-to-one configuration. If your database held pictures of each product you sell, you might create a Pictures table. It would have one record for each product. But the Products record also has one record for each product. In fact, each product record is related to exactly one picture record, and vice versa.

You create any of these relationships with exactly the same steps in FileMaker. But each has its own set of considerations that affect the way you design your database. These concepts are discussed on page 285.

No Companies?

Why is Companies just an attribute of Customers? What if my customer is a company? Don't I need to be able to keep track of that?

Your decisions about entities depend on how you intend to use the database. In this database, you're assuming that *people* hire you. Even if they hire you on behalf of some business, you'll put the actual person you're working for in the database, along with the name of the company that employs her.

In a different database, you may decide Companies are important enough to be in their own table. If it were important to see all the people who work for one particular company, or to keep track of lots of people from each company, then you would probably want a Companies table.

• **They're not important enough to track in your database.** Suppose your list has an item called Services. These services are the kinds of things you do for your customers: Check into a cheating spouse, find a lost dog, recover a stolen computer, or whatever. You could create a Services table in your database, and put all these kinds of services in it. But what value would it add? Whichever service you're asked to perform, you have to keep track of how much time you spend and what you do. And what kind of information are you tracking about a service? Probably just its name. So, as an entity, leave out Services. Figure 7-5 shows an example of a well-edited entities list.

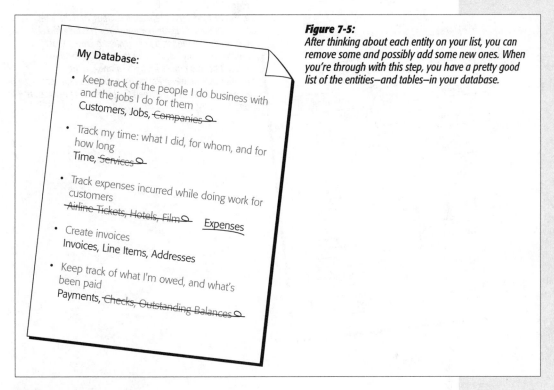

Figure 7-5:
After thinking about each entity on your list, you can remove some and possibly add some new ones. When you're through with this step, you have a pretty good list of the entities—and tables—in your database.

My Database:

• Keep track of the people I do business with and the jobs I do for them
  Customers, Jobs, ~~Companies~~

• Track my time: what I did, for whom, and for how long
  Time, ~~Services~~

• Track expenses incurred while doing work for customers
  ~~Airline Tickets, Hotels, Film~~ Expenses

• Create invoices
  Invoices, Line Items, Addresses

• Keep track of what I'm owed, and what's been paid
  Payments, ~~Checks, Outstanding Balances~~

Finding Relationships

Now that you have a list of entities, you need to figure out how they relate to one another. To get started, just pick two of your entities—Customers and Jobs, for example—and ask yourself how they go together (if you need some guidance, see the box on page 289.) You might come up with this answer: *A customer hires me to do jobs, and a job is done for a customer.* That sentence tells you two important things:

• Customers and Jobs are related.

• One customer has many jobs, but each job only has one customer.

By comparing different entities in this way, you can figure out how each relates to another, if at all. Your notes as you consider these relationships might look something like Figure 7-7.

You can easily translate most of the items on that list into database relationships. Each tells you about two entities in your list, and how they relate in each direction. You can usually translate these directly into database-ese, as shown in Figure 7-6. That picture is one example of a diagram representing each of these relationships.

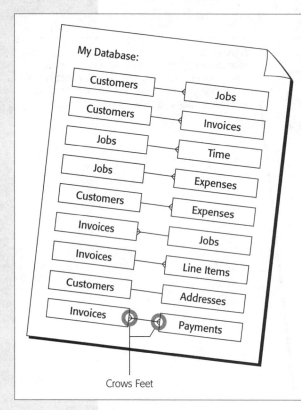

Figure 7-6:
In this picture, boxes represent entities, and the lines between them indicate relationships. The little forked end on the relationship lines (called a crow's foot) means "to-many" as in "one-to-many." If the line doesn't have a crow's foot, it's to-one. So the relationship between Payments and Invoices is many-to-many, while that between Customers and Invoices is one-to-many.

A glance at Figure 7-6 shows you how entities like Payments, Invoices, and Customers relate to one another, but the relationship with the Time entity isn't so obvious. Is "Time" plural? For that matter, if Time is an entity, then it must be a thing, so what is a *time*? You've just discovered one of the common challenges to good relational design—choosing good names.

You added *Time* to your list of entities because you spend time working on a job. That's a little ambiguous, though, so think about what exactly you'll be putting in the database. You'll be logging the time you spend working: what you're doing, when you started, and when you finished. You could call it a *work log entry* but that's pretty cumbersome. Because this kind of entity is quite common, database types have made up a name for it—*timeslip*. A timeslip is sort of like one entry on a timesheet. It says what you were doing for one period of time.

Using this language, your relationship description becomes clearer:

• A job has timeslips, and a timeslip is for a job.

Now it's a lot more obvious: This relationship is one-to-many.

> **My Database:**
>
> • A customer hires me to do jobs, and a job is for a customer.
> • A customer is sent invoices, and an invoice is sent to a customer.
> • A job takes time to do, and time is spent on one job.
> • A job has expenses, and an expense is for one job.
> • A customer is charged for expenses, and an expense is charged to a customer
> • An invoice is for one job, and a job is billed on invoices.
> • An invoice has line items, and a line item is on one invoice.
> • A customer has an address, and an address is where a customer lives.
> • An invoice is paid with payments, and a payment is applied to invoices.
> …

Figure 7-7:
Here's a list of relationships between entities on your list. (You may have worded things differently, or come up with some that aren't on this list.) If you follow the advice in the box on page 284, these sentences will usually exactly describe each kind of relationship.

One-to-many relationships

Most of the relationships in your diagram are one-to-many, which is normal. One-to-many relationships outnumber all other types by a large margin in almost any system. See the box "Many for One and One for Many" on page 284 for a description of the various types of relationships.

One-to-one relationships

Your list of entities and relationships shows a one-to-one relationship between Customers and Addresses. For the purposes of this database, one Customer can certainly have one Address, and vice versa. But if that's the case, are they really separate entities? In fact, Address is just an attribute of the Customer entity. That makes it a prime candidate for entity-elimination. Put the address *fields* in the customer table instead. You might argue that despite the conflict of interest, you *could* work for two people in the same household and would therefore have to type the same address twice in your Customer table if you didn't have an Address table. The best answer to an argument like that is: Big deal. This situation won't arise often enough to justify a more complicated database just to eliminate duplicating one or two addresses. Even without a separate Address table, you can still separately handle all other tasks for these two clients.

On the other hand, if you're managing a high-school, and it's important to know which students share a home, and which parents they belong to, then an Addresses (or more likely, Households) entity might make sense.

FREQUENTLY ASKED QUESTION

Only One Attribute

So, I'm supposed to eliminate Services as an entity because it has only one attribute (page 281). Is that another rule? Should I remove all entities that have just one attribute?

Not necessarily. There are times when an entity has only one attribute, but you still want to give it a table. For one thing, tables can help promote consistent data entry. Say your new database is going to track Jobs, among other things. A job may have just one attribute—the Job Name—so you could just put the job name on each expense, time entry, and invoice. But what if you misspell the job name? Then you'll have expenses that should go together but don't, because FileMaker sees different job names. By creating a Jobs table, you have a central place to enter job names and use it as a value list. With a Jobs table, instead of typing the job name everywhere, you simply choose it from a list.

Wait a minute. All you really need to do that is a list. Why have a table if it has just one column?

OK, wise guy. You could leave out the Jobs table and the job names themselves. Instead, you could just attach each expense, time log entry, or invoice to a customer. But what happens when the same customer hires you six different times? All those expenses, invoices, and entries are lumped together under that customer, and you lose the ability to track them back to the individual jobs. Sometimes a one-attribute entity exists because it gives your database greater powers of organization or categorization. (See the box on page 223 for more details—and a warning—about using a single-attribute table for a value list.)

In this case, the fact that two addresses are one and the same justifies your adding another table. As a general rule, unless you can articulate a good reason for its existence, a one-to-one relationship is just two tables where one would normally suffice. (For some clarification, see the box on page 291.) You'll almost always want to combine entities like people and their addresses into one table.

Many-to-many relationships

Many-to-many relationships pose a special challenge. Normally, FileMaker knows which records are related to one another because they have something in common. For example, the Invoice table and the Line Item table both have an Invoice Number field. But you can put only *one* invoice number in a Line Item record. Luckily, Invoices and Line Items have a one-to-many relationship. If they had a many-to-many relationship, you'd be in trouble.

To fix things, you need to chop your many-to-many relationships in half, turning each into two separate one-to-many relationships. You always need to add a new special-purpose entity in the middle. Your database has only one un-handled many-to-many relationship: Invoices and Payments. To split it up, you need to introduce a special entity. Since it doesn't have a decent name, just call it *Invoice Payment* (as in "This record represents one invoice payment—one payment on one invoice"). Now, instead of "An invoice is paid with payments, and a payment is applied to invoices," you can say these two things:

• An invoice is paid with invoice payments, and an invoice payment is applied to one invoice.

• A payment is divided into invoice payments, and an invoice payment is part of one payment.

UP TO SPEED

Think Relational

If you're dazed and confused trying to figure out how different entities relate, you're not alone. Understanding relational database design takes practice, plain and simple. Here are some ideas to improve your thought process:

• **Don't get hung up on technicalities**. At this point in your design, you shouldn't be thinking about database tools like primary keys, foreign keys, or join tables. Those are all *implementation details* that you can work out later. Right now, just focus on the kinds of things you're keeping track of and how they fit together.

• **Use familiar words**. If you're trying to figure out how customers and jobs should be related, say, "A customer hires me to do jobs," not "A Customer entity is related to a Job entity in a one-to-many configuration." As you get the hang of it, you'll discover that the simple sentences you use every day say a whole lot about relationships. For example, if a customer hires you to do *jobs* (note the plural), then you probably have a one-to-many relationship between customers and jobs.

• **Consider individual items first**. Don't think about what *customers* do. Instead, think about what *one customer* does. That will tell you whether a single customer has many jobs, or just one job. Then turn it around. Once you've decided a customer hires you to do jobs, ask yourself what a job has to do with customers. "I do a job for a customer." This process tells you that each job is connected to just *one* customer. By combining these results, you discover that a customer has many jobs, while a job has just one customer. That means Customers and Jobs have a one-to-many relationship.

• **One last tip**: Don't let the word "many" hang you up. It's just a standard term to help keep things simple. (Otherwise, you might have a *one-to-quite-a-few* relationship between Jobs and Invoices, a *one-to-a-handful* relationship between Customers and Jobs, and a *usually-just-one-or-two-to-rarely-more-than-three* relationship between Payments and Invoices. Yikes!) "Many" doesn't have to mean "lots." It might mean "exactly six" or "no more than three." The only time the relationship isn't one-to-many is when it's one-to-*exactly*-one.

Figure 7-8 shows the updated diagram.

The Entity-Relationship Diagram

Now that you have a list of entities and their relationships, you're ready to assemble your master plan: the entity relationship (ER) diagram. An *ER diagram* is a

---

picture that shows all the entities in your database and the relationships between them. Unlike the diagram you've already drawn (in Figure 7-8), each entity appears only once in an ER diagram.

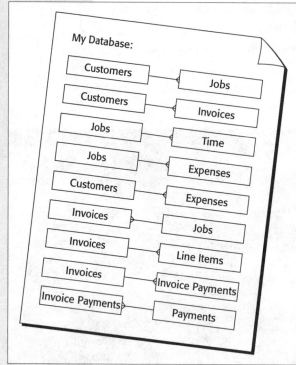

Figure 7-8:
In this updated version of the diagram, the Customers and Addresses relationship has been removed, and the Invoice Payments join entity has been added. Now you have only one-to-many relationships—perfect.

It has two purposes: to help you find relationships you missed, or relationships that don't belong, and to serve as a roadmap for your database. You'll use it when you actually create this database in FileMaker, and when you go back to make changes later. (Yes, you *will* get to use FileMaker again…pretty soon.)

Note: The diagram you're about to create isn't, in the most technical sense, a *real* ER diagram. The real kind deals with all kinds of technical details that simply don't matter in FileMaker. Nevertheless, some wisenheimer may chastise you for calling your beautiful picture an ER diagram.

Creating an ER diagram

When you assemble an entity relationship diagram, you must put all your entities and relationships together in one big picture. Your goal is to have each entity in the picture just *once*, and all the lines necessary to define the various relationships.

Your ER diagram is crucial to a successful database designing experience. You'll almost always find ways to improve your database when you put it in a picture. When you set out to actually *build* the database, the ER diagram guides you through the process. Finally, six years from now, when you need to add more to your database design, the ER diagram will bring you—or your successor—up to speed on how your database fits together.

You can start by making one box for each entity you've identified. Try to place the boxes on the page so that there's some open space in the middle where your lines can roam free. Then start drawing lines to represent each of the relationships you've come up with. For a simple database, you can usually get the lines in the picture without much difficulty. But creating a larger diagram without the right tools can be a real pain. If you work on paper, you end up starting half a dozen times before you get a good arrangement. If you use a typical drawing program (the drawing capabilities in Word, for example) then you spend copious hours reconnecting lines and entities, reshaping lines, and hand drawing crow's feet as you move things around. See the box on page 292 for some suggestions to solve this problem.

WORKAROUND WORKSHOP

When to Go One-to-One

When two things—like people and addresses—have a one-to-one relationship, it usually means you've got an entity you don't need (as in the example on page 288). There are exceptions to every rule, though. Here are some of the reasons you may see a one-to-one relationship in a database:

- FileMaker uses record locking to prevent two people from editing the same record at the same time. (Yes, Virginia, two people can use a database at the same time—see Chapter 18 to learn how.) Imagine you have a table of products and every time you sell something, you reduce the product's Quantity In Stock field by one. What happens if someone else is modifying the product description at the same time? FileMaker won't let you enter the inventory adjustment because the record is locked. Should you cancel the order? Allow the Quantity in Stock field to be wrong? Force your customer to wait while you ask your associate to get out of the record? A better solution is to put the inventory levels in a separate table. Each product has a Product record and an Inventory record, so two seemingly conflicting processes no longer lock each other out of your system.

- Sometimes you'll want to divide data you store about an entity among several tables. A database of stock photography might include high-resolution photographs in container fields. These photos make the database very large.

By putting the photos in one table, and the information about the photos in another, you make working with the information easier. You can back up the information to a CD, and the photographs to your high-capacity backup system. (This technique requires keeping each table in a separate file—something you'll learn about in the next chapter.)

- Imagine you have customers and employees. Employees don't place orders or make payments, and customers don't have a time sheet. But they both have addresses, phone numbers, and email addresses. What's more, you like to send Holiday cards to all of them every year. In a situation like this, you can create three tables: People, Customers, and Employees. The People table holds all the information that customers and employees have in common—names, addresses, and so forth. Information unique to an employee (Social Security number, Hire Date, and such) goes in the Employee table, and information only a customer could love (Referral Source, Membership Level, and so on) stays in the Customer table. You would have a one-to-one relationship between People and Employees, and another between People and Customers. When it comes time to send those cards, you can print envelopes right from the People table, and get customers and employees in one shot.

When you're done, you should have a single, unified diagram with each entity showing up only once, and every relationship indicated by a line.

It's All About the Tools

If you plan on doing this more than once, you're best off buying a proper diagramming program. Two excellent choices are Microsoft Visio for Windows and OmniGraffle for Mac OS X. These tools *understand* ER diagrams. They can hook entities together with ease, draw crow's feet on your behalf (lots of programs just don't understand crow's feet), and keep everything connected as you tinker with the arrangement.

If you give Visio a run, don't be tempted by its built-in database diagramming features—they're too complex for FileMaker work. Instead, create a basic diagram and use Rectangles and Dynamic Connectors from the Basic Shapes library. With the Format → Lines command, you can put crow's feet on your lines.

Both of these tools do more than you'll need for your ER diagrams, but the time you save is well worth the expense (about $200 for Visio and $70 for OmniGraffle). You can find free trial versions at *http://office.microsoft.com/visio*, and *www.omnigroup.com/graffle*.

If you're an unrepentant cheapskate, here's a tip: Write the entity names on a piece of paper and cut out each one. Then arrange them on paper, draw lines, and see how it looks. You can slide the entity scraps around a few times to find a decent arrangement, and then commit the whole thing to a clean piece of paper.

When you're thinking about relationships with just pairs of tables, you don't get the big picture. The ER diagram shows you how *everything* comes together, and when that happens, you often discover tangles of relationships just like those in Figure 7-9. Tangles like these aren't inherently bad; they're just usually completely unnecessary. Take the first tangled group—Expenses, Jobs, and Customers. The diagram tells you that customers have jobs, jobs have expenses, and customers have expenses.

But in point of fact, you don't need all those lines to understand all the relationships, and neither does FileMaker. It turns out that the line between Customers and Expenses is entirely superfluous. Even if it weren't there, you could still see all the expenses charged to a certain customer. Just find all that customer's *jobs* first (by following the line from Customers to Jobs). Once you've found those, you can look at the expenses for each job. Since customers only incur expenses by way of jobs, you'll get exactly what you want. In other words, if two entities are connected by a path along relationship lines—even *through* other entities—then they're related as far as FileMaker's concerned. It can show you the Expenses for a Customer just as easily as it can show the Jobs for that customer. Figure 7-10 illustrates this concept.

When you're thinking about these implied relationships, pay attention to the crow's feet. If, when moving from one entity to another along the relationship lines, you *ever* go through a to-many relationship, then the larger implied relationship is itself to-many. This isn't just a clever trick; it's actually intuitive. If a customer has more than one job, and each job has expenses, then clearly a customer can have more than one expense.

Figure 7-9:
This diagram (created in OmniGraffle) doesn't look all that bad—except for one thing. The area labeled Rat's Nest has a lot of lines between just a few tables. Expenses, Customers, and Jobs are all interrelated—there is a relationship between Jobs and Customers, another between Customers and Expenses, and a third between Expenses and Jobs. If you look closely, the same situation exists for Customers, Jobs, and Invoices. In both cases, there's a better way.

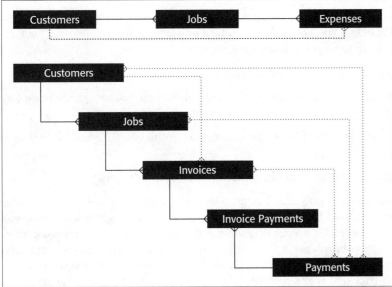

Figure 7-10:
In this picture, the solid lines represent relationships you've defined among the entities. The dotted lines show relationships you don't have to define—they are implied. As long as there is a path—any path—from one entity to another, they are related. You don't have to have a direct path.

When you make your ER diagram, you should get rid of redundancy in your relationships. In other words, remove lines that show direct relationships when the relationship is already implied by other entities and relationships. In your diagram, you can remove the relationship between Customers and Expenses. You can also axe one between Customers and Invoices because Customers can find their Invoices by way of Jobs. With this revision, the ER diagram now looks like Figure 7-11.

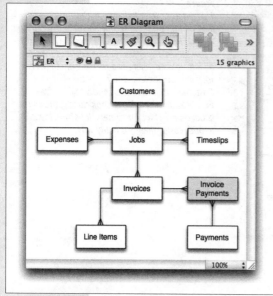

Figure 7-11:
Here's the final ER diagram that you'll use as the roadmap for creating your database. Notice that every entity is related to at least one other entity in some way. Stray, unrelated entities are so rare in a real database system that if you see one in your diagram, you should check to make sure everything belongs.

Next, you need to figure out what fields your tables need to make the relationships work. But before you get to that step, take one last chance to look over your ER diagram. Keep these points in mind as you check for errors:

- You should have no undivided many-to-many relationships.

- If you have any one-to-one relationships, make sure you can justify them (see When to go One-to-One on page 291 for some ideas).

- Make sure you don't have any unnecessary entities hanging out all by themselves.

- Be certain you don't have any unnecessary lines or rat's nests.

If you discover an entity that has no relationships, you may not need it in your database at all. Read back on page *281* and see if that item might belong inside one of the other tables. Or if your diagram has two or more groups of related entities and no relationships *between* the groups, you might've forgotten to draw in a relationship, or again, you might have one or more entities that your system doesn't need. Go back and make sure you're clear on your one-to-many and many-to-many relationships.

Keys

In a diagram, you can show relationships by simply drawing a line. FileMaker, however, knows what records are related only because they have some data in common. It's time to look more closely at how that works. Take, for example, the typical Invoice table and its little brother, Line Items. The Invoice table probably contains fields like Due Date, Balance Due, and Terms; all attributes of the invoice itself. Then there's *Invoice Number* field. Unlike the other fields, it's a made-up number. It does one thing—identify an invoice—and does it very well. Without it, you and your customers might have conversations like this: "I need a refund on one of my invoices…you know, the big one…yeah, in February…right, with three items…no, the other one…." As soon as someone mentions an invoice number, though, everybody knows exactly which invoice to look at. More important, File-Maker knows which invoice it is.

The invoice number can do its job as a key field because it has three important characteristics:

- **It's unique.** No two invoices will ever have the same invoice number.

- **It's unchanging.** Invoice #24601 is #24601 today and it will be tomorrow, and the next day, and the next day.

- **It's consistent.** All Invoice records have an Invoice number.

Since it's a unique number, if you're talking about invoice #24601, and your customer is talking about invoice #24601, there's no question that you're both referring to the same invoice. Since it's unchanging, you can go back weeks, months, or even years later and find the invoice every time. And since it's consistent, you'll never have lonely Invoices hanging out there without an identifying number. In database terms, the invoice number is called a *key*. A key is a field whose value uniquely, unchangingly, and consistently identifies one record.

As far as FileMaker's concerned, any field that you use to link one table to another is a key field. Although FileMaker doesn't differentiate between key types, in the larger world of database theory there are two types of keys: primary and foreign. Understanding how the two types of keys work helps you choose appropriate ones for your databases.

Primary keys

When you tell FileMaker how two tables are related, you need a way to identify each record: You need a key. On the "one" side of a one-to-many relationship, this key field is called a *primary key*. Invoice Number is the primary key in the Invoices table. Like the Invoice Number in your database, a primary key is most often a made-up number. You can add a new field to your table, and tell FileMaker to make up a unique value for it each time you create a record. This kind of primary key, based on purely made-up data, is called a *surrogate key*.

Note: Unless you generate the value in your database, it's not a surrogate key.

Occasionally, your table will have a real value that meets the requirements for a key. For example, if your Product database has a field for your internal Inventory Control Number, you may be able to use that field as the primary key. If you use your Inventory Control Number to relate tables, then it's a *natural key*.

FREQUENTLY ASKED QUESTION

Going Natural

Should I try to find natural keys for the tables in my database if I can?

Good question! In fact, it's right up there with Coke or Pepsi, Tastes Great or Less Filling, and To Be or Not To Be. Some of the smartest people in the world of database theory say, "Absolutely." Unfortunately other equally smart ones say, "Absolutely not." The general arguments run like this:

Natural Keys are hard to find and once you pick one, the data in that field should be hard to change. If you discover later on that the natural key you chose really does need to change sometimes, you'll be forced to work through the challenges of dealing with it. A surrogate key, on the other hand, will never need to change because it has no meaning. Your boss will never pop into your office and say, "You know what? Invoice numbers do change after all." It happens more often than you think. Suppose you work for a company that assigns an Employee ID to each employee. You're building a database to keep track of employee stock options. Just like Social Security Number, Employee ID is a surrogate key to somebody but it's a natural key to you. You decide to make it your primary key. Then you discover that you need to track stock options for employees even if they quit and then return to the company. When they do this, their Employee ID changes, and your database can't track them properly without some inconvenient upkeep. If you had used your own surrogate key instead, this wouldn't be a problem.

On the other hand, surrogate keys don't mean anything. If you're looking at the data in the Stock Options table, you might have a field called "Employee Key." If you need to put the Employee ID on an Options Exercise form to turn in to HR, your Employee Key won't do you any good. Instead, you have to look him up in your Employees table and find the correct Employee ID. If you had used a natural key instead, you'd save the extra step. In other words, meaningful keys make your life a little easier. But FileMaker's work gets a little harder. If you use surrogate keys, FileMaker always has to visit another record in another table to show any meaningful related data. With a natural key, at least one piece of useful data is stored right in the current record, as a foreign key. Although the difference is very small, natural keys can make your database run a little faster.

If you're not yet persuaded, do more research and make your own choice. A Google search for "Surrogate and Natural Keys" will bring up a wealth of pages full of arguments for either side. Just remember, the penalty for choosing an unsuitable natural key is stiff. At minimum, you risk losing the relationship between your tables in a few records. At worst, you'll spend enormous amounts of time tracking hundreds of broken relationships and rebuilding your database using a more reliable primary key.

You might be tempted to use a birth date or a Social Security number as a natural key. But remember, in order for a natural key to be reliable, it must be unique, unchanging, and consistent. Social Security numbers are supposed to be unique and unchanging—but duplicate numbers and identity theft have put a big dent in that theory. And you can't even rely on everybody in your database *having* a Social Security number. While most Americans have one, you'll have to redesign your database the minute your company wants to do business with a customer who doesn't live in the US.

In practice, you'll almost never find a suitable natural key. Natural keys almost always originate from surrogate keys in another database system. For instance, your database might track invoices created—and numbered—by a separate accounting system. If those numbers are unique, unchanging and consistent, you can use them as a natural primary key. (See the box on page 296 for more perks and perils of natural keys.)

Foreign keys

If the Invoice Number field in the *Invoices* table is the primary key, what is the Invoice Number field in the *Line Items* table? It's not a primary key because it isn't unique—lots of line items could have the same Invoice Number. In this case, it's called a *foreign key*. A foreign key is simply the primary key from another table, and you'll find it on the "many" side of a one-to-many relationship. A table has only one primary key, but it can have lots of foreign keys (or none at all).

But where do you *put* these foreign keys? In the Invoices database, how did you decide to put the Invoice Number field in the Line Items table? Why not create a Line Item ID field in the Line Items table, and put it in the Invoices database? Wouldn't that accomplish the same thing? At first glance, it might seem like both methods would produce an identical relationship. After all, they sure *look* the same in a picture (Figure 7-12).

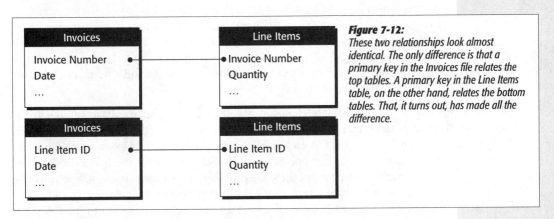

Figure 7-12:
These two relationships look almost identical. The only difference is that a primary key in the Invoices file relates the top tables. A primary key in the Line Items table, on the other hand, relates the bottom tables. That, it turns out, has made all the difference.

Think about what a primary key means. Each value identifies one, and only one, record in the table. If you build a relationship based on Line Item ID, then each invoice can have only one line item. If it had two, there would be two line items with the same line item ID. When you have a one-to-many relationship, you must put the foreign key in the table on the *many* side. Luckily, keeping this information straight in your head is a breeze. Since foreign keys belong on the to-many side of a relationship, just remember this rule: When you see a crow's foot on your ER diagram, you need a foreign key in the table to which it's attached. (But if you're getting confused, the box below should clear things up.)

Note: When you see a field name like Line Item ID, think *primary key*. ID, in this sense, means the field *id*entifies a record. Primary keys in a database are often called IDs.

Composite Keys

A key value doesn't necessarily have to be stored in just one field. Sometimes you can get the value that uniquely identifies a record by combining several field values into one. This kind of key is called a *composite* key. Suppose you have a database of photographs you've taken. Your Photographs table holds the photo itself, as well as some information about each photo: Date and Time Taken, Roll Number, Shot Number, and Film Speed. If you wanted to use a natural key, you could combine Roll Number and Shot Number. No two rolls have the same number, and you'll never take the same shot twice on a single roll, so this combined value is always unique.

If you choose to use a composite key, you'll have to add *multiple* fields to each related table that needs to store the foreign key. For example, if you sell your photographs, and you want to relate the Photographs table to an Order Line Items table, you'll have to put both the Roll Number and the Shot Number in the Order Line Items table. When you do, it will be the combination of these two fields that forms the foreign key. See page 369 to learn how to link tables with a multi-key, or composite, relationship.

You can have as many fields in a composite key as you need.

Join Tables

A many-to-many relationship is more complicated than its one-sided brethren. Imagine your database tracks payments from your customers. A customer could easily send a check to cover *two* invoices. On the other hand, another customer might send a check to cover just *part* of an invoice, with the promise to send another later. So an invoice can have multiple payments, and a payment can be for multiple invoices: many-to-many.

How do you build a relationship like this? If you put the Payment ID in the Invoices table, then a payment can be applied to more than one invoice (just put the same Payment ID in each invoice record). But an invoice can have only one payment since it has just one Payment ID field. If you put the Invoice Number in the Payments table, you get the same problem in the other direction. You might be tempted to try putting a foreign key field in *both* tables. In other words, add a Payment ID field to the Invoice table, and an Invoice Number field to the Payments table. Dig a little deeper and you'll see that this has a whole *host* of problems:

- An invoice now has a field called Payment ID, but that field *doesn't* identify the payments for that invoice. To find the payments for an invoice, you have to open the Payments database and use the Invoice Number Field. That's just plain confusing.

- Instead of one bidirectional relationship, you have two unidirectional relationships. The Payment ID in the invoice matches the Payment ID in the Payments table, but this only tells you which invoices belong to each payment. You need the other relationship (based on Invoice ID) to figure out which payments belong to each invoice. If you connect a payment to an invoice by putting the invoice number in the payment record, you also have to put the Payment ID in the invoice record. If you forget, your data is no longer valid.

Luckily, there's a better way to accomplish a many-to-many relationship. You need something called a *join table* (see Figure 7-13). A join table doesn't usually represent a real entity. Instead, each record represents a relationship between two records in the related tables.

Figure 7-13:
A join table's main job is to facilitate a many-to-many relationship. This one holds foreign keys for Invoice Number and Payment ID. If you want to attach a payment to an invoice, add a new record in the join table, with the correct Invoice Number and Payment ID. Once the record is added, the payment and invoice are properly connected in both directions. Since you can add as many records as you want to the join table, you can flexibly relate multiple invoices and payments.

If it helps, think of join tables this way: Invoices and Payments both have a one-to-many relationship to the join table. So one invoice can connect to many join records, each of which connects to one payment. Likewise, one order can connect to many join records, each of which connects to one invoice. So you get many related records in both directions. A join table always contains *two* foreign keys, one from each table it's joining. If your database has many-to-many relationships, you may have to create a join table to hold just these two keys, but sometimes your database may already have a real table that can act as a join table. Figure 7-14 shows an example.

Other times, you can use a join table to hold fields that don't quite belong in any other table. Suppose you wanted to record what portion of a payment was applied to each invoice. For example, if a customer hands you a check for $100 and you have two outstanding invoices for that customer, for $80 and $30, you might want to decide how to allocate the payment. Perhaps you apply $80 to the first invoice and $20 to the second. This dollar amount applied to each invoice can't be stored in the Invoice table because an invoice might have several payments. It can't be stored in the Payment table because you have *two* amounts and only one payment record. The best place for it is right in the join table itself.

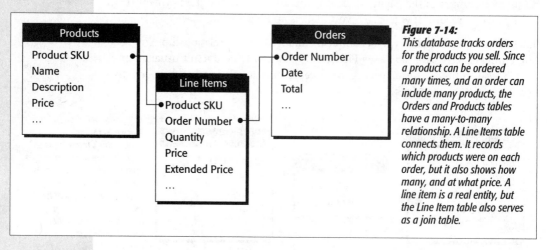

Figure 7-14:
This database tracks orders for the products you sell. Since a product can be ordered many times, and an order can include many products, the Orders and Products tables have a many-to-many relationship. A Line Items table connects them. It records which products were on each order, but it also shows how many, and at what price. A line item is a real entity, but the Line Item table also serves as a join table.

At this point, you have a good ER diagram, you've eliminated many-to-many relationships by adding join tables, and you understand what foreign keys you'll need to make it all work. You're (finally) ready to actually build your database.

Creating a Relational Database

The tedious planning is finally over. Now comes the fun part—actually making the database. And believe it or not, this part will go *much* more smoothly with your plan in place. You create a relational database in three steps. First, you tell File-Maker what tables you want. Then you define the fields in each table. Finally, you add relationships. Don't be alarmed if you forget a table or miss a field: You can go back at any time and make changes—even six months from now when your tables are loaded with data.

Relational databases start out like any other. Go to FileMaker and choose File → New Database. Name your new database, pick the folder to save it in, and click Save.

***

Note: If you see an option to "Create a new file using a template," choose "Create a new empty file" and click OK. Then you'll be able to name and save your new database.

***

Defining the Tables

When you first create a database, FileMaker shows you the Define Database window's Field tab (you first saw this on page 84). Without your knowledge, it has already created a table for you with the same name as the database itself. FileMaker assumes you just want one table, and it's ready for you to add fields to that table.

UP TO SPEED

Relationship Types and Key Types

As this picture shows, the position of the primary and foreign keys in a relationship determines its type. In a one-to-many relationship (or its identical counterpart, many-to-one), the foreign key belongs on the *many* side. Since a primary key guarantees uniqueness, there can be only one record with a particular key value. But a foreign key doesn't have to have unique values, so you can have as many matching records as you want.

In the rare case that you define a one-to-one relationship, you'll be matching two primary keys together. In this case, both tables *share the same primary key*. The uniqueness ensures that you have only one matching record in each table.

This time, though, you *don't* want just one table, so click the Tables tab (you can see it in Figure 7-15). Your first job is to remove the table FileMaker added for you since it doesn't match one of the entities in your ER diagram. Just select the table in the table list, and then click Delete.

Now that you've deleted the starter table, you're ready to add your own carefully planned tables. Grab the ER diagram and create a table for each entity. The diagram has eight tables in all, so make sure you create all of them.

Warning: Deleting a table is a *dangerous* operation. Right now there's no risk because you're working in a brand-new database. But imagine you come to this window two years from now. If you accidentally delete a table, you lose *all* the data in it. You'll also have a lot of work to do putting your relationships and layouts back together. FileMaker warns you before it lets you delete the table, but it's worth an extra measure of caution.

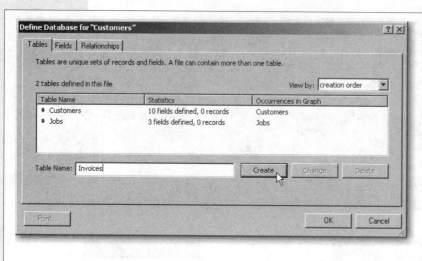

Figure 7-15:
The Define Databases window's Tables tab lists all the tables defined in your database. It works a lot like the Fields tab: To add a table, type its name in the Table Name box, and then click Create. If you want to change a table's name, select it in the table list first, then type the new name, and click Change. To delete a table, select it in the list and click Delete.

Defining the Fields

With the tables defined, you're ready to add fields. Click the Define Database window's Fields tab (see Figure 7-16). You choose which fields to add to each table the same way you learned to in Chapter 3, with one caveat: key fields. *Every* table needs a primary key. In this database, you'll be using surrogate (made-up) keys in each table.

Adding primary keys

To keep things consistent, each primary key field will match the name of the entity, with the word "ID" added to the end. For example, the primary key in the Customers table should be called Customer ID. This technique is so common, in fact, that you can often spot the primary keys in any database by looking for the letters "ID."

The easiest way to make a surrogate key in FileMaker is to use a *serial number*. The process is simple:

1. **Click on the Fields tab in the Define Database dialog box, if necessary. Then, from the Table pop-up menu, select Customers.**

   You're now ready to add a field to the Customers table. You'll start with the primary key.

2. In the Field Name text box, type *Customer ID*. In the Type pop-up menu, make sure Text is selected.

Key fields can be any type, but text is a good choice because you have the most flexible formatting options.

Figure 7-16:
When you have multiple tables defined, they all show up in the Tables pop-up menu. When you choose a table from the menu, its fields show in the field list. When you add a field, it gets added to the selected table. You can also double-click a table in Tables tab to jump straight to its field definitions.

3. Click Create.

FileMaker adds your new field to the field list. But so far all you have is a normal text field.

4. Click Options, and make sure the Auto-Enter tab is selected, as shown in Figure 7-17.

To be a good primary key, this field needs a unique value on every record. That sounds like a job for a computer:

5. Turn on the "Serial number" checkbox.

When you tell FileMaker to auto-enter a serial number, it automatically makes up a new unique number every time you create a record. It sets the field to a number one bigger than the *last* value it created. Since the number always grows, it never repeats.

6. Make sure the "On creation" radio button is turned on.

When you make a field a serial number, you get to choose when the serial number gets entered. It can happen when you create the record, *or* when you commit it. In other words, FileMaker can automatically put the serial number in the field for you right away, when you first create the record, and most of the time, that's exactly what you want. (As you'll see on page 327, FileMaker lets you set

your layout up so that you can create related records automatically while editing a record; you need the serial number for that to work.)

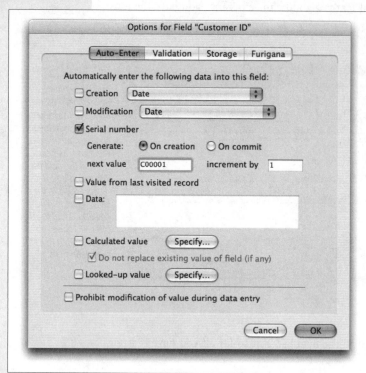

Figure 7-17:
*Here's the Field Options window's
Auto-Enter tab, in case you've
forgotten what it looks like. Pretty
slick, huh? In the next few steps, you'll
be setting up those "Serial number"
options.*

Alternatively, you can have FileMaker wait until you finish entering data and
actually commit the record. You might choose "on commit" if, for instance,
you have a complex, automated database that adds new people to your database from lists you get from other offices. You can have the database add a person record *first*, and then see if it's a duplicate before committing the record.
That way, you don't skip serial numbers. (And if you know how to do that, you
probably should be the one *writing* this book.)

7. **In the "next value" text box, type *C00001*. Make sure the "increment by" box
reads "1."**

You've just established your starting serial number and told FileMaker how to
continue. Your first customer record will have the Customer ID C00001, your
second will be C00002, and so on.

8. **Select the "Prohibit modification of value during data entry" option.**

Since key fields provide the links between your tables, relationships would break
and other database disasters could ensue if key values got changed. When you
turn on this option, you prevent that unhappy fate.

Click OK to return to the Define Database window. You'll get a chance to test that serial number field in a few minutes. First, though, you need to follow those steps again for each table. You can, of course, add any field to any table at any time, but here you'll create tables, then primary keys, then foreign keys, and finally other fields. It's not the quickest way, but creating a relational database requires lots of steps, and you don't want to forget anything, so an organized approach pays off.

INCREDULOUSLY ASKED QUESTION

Serial *Text?*

I'm telling FileMaker to put a serial number into a text field, but my serial number isn't a number at all. Is this OK?

As funny as it sounds, not only can you auto-enter serial numbers into text fields, but the values themselves can contain text. FileMaker looks at the text you've specified for "next value" and tries to find a number in it somewhere. When it comes time to generate a new value, it pulls that number out, increments it, and stuffs it back in its place.

Say your "next value" is C000LX and "increment by" is set to 10. The first record you create will get C000LX. The second will get C010LX, and then C020LX, and so on. When you get to C990LX, FileMaker doesn't just give up. Instead, it makes more room: C1000LX.

If your "next value" has more than one embedded number (C000LX22, for example), FileMaker uses the last number only. Likewise, if you don't have a number at all, it simply adds one to the end.

When you set your serial number options, use a different letter in the "next value" for each table. For instance, use *E00001* as the starting value in the Expenses table, and *IP00001* in the Invoice Payment table. That way, whenever you see a serial number, you'll have a clue table it belongs to. You don't *have* to name your serial numbers that way, but it might come in handy. Sometimes you take data out of FileMaker to put it into other programs (like Microsoft Excel, so you can make charts). When you do, you'll lose your field names and just see lists of data. Although most data is easy to identify (phone numbers look like phone numbers, for example), primary keys can be a mystery. Having a textual primary key like these can eliminate just a touch of mystery, should you ever be in this situation.

Note: Strictly speaking, you don't need to add an Invoice Payment ID field to the Invoice Payment table. Since you're making a simple join table, it's going to have two foreign keys, one for the Payment ID and one for the Invoice ID. A record in this table represents the *connection* between an Invoice and a Payment, so you can just use these two foreign keys together as the primary key (a composite key, as you remember from the box on page 298). You'll never have one payment on the same invoice twice, so the combination of these two values will be unique. That said, lots of people add surrogate keys to their join tables anyway, and it certainly won't hurt.

Adding foreign keys

Adding foreign keys requires a little more thought than the primary keys, but not much—you already did the hard part by creating an ER diagram (page 294). To decide where the foreign keys go, just look for the crow's feet. Figure 7-18 offers a refresher.

Figure 7-18:
Each crow's foot in your ER diagram indicates the need for a foreign key. Each table with a crow's foot stuck to it needs a foreign key inside it. What should the field be called? Simple: Find the other end of the line. That's the entity the foreign key points to, so name it appropriately. For example, the Line Items table needs a field called Invoice ID.

Since your primary key fields are all Text fields, your foreign key fields should be too—after all, the foreign keys hold primary key values. Following the crow's feet, you come up with these foreign keys (remember that a foreign key is always just a primary key from another table):

- In the Expenses table, add a field called Job ID.

- In the Jobs table, add a field called Customer ID.

- In the Timeslips table, add a field called Job ID.

- In the Line Items table, add a field called Invoice ID.

- In the Invoices table, add a field called Job ID.

- In the Invoice Payments table, add two fields: Invoice ID and Payment ID.

Go ahead and add the foreign keys now.

Note: Because these are foreign key fields, they don't need to be unique. They're just plain old text fields. If you turn on Auto-Enter serial number options for foreign key fields, you can get some squirrely results.

Defining the Relationships

With tables and keys, you have everything you need to define some relationships. In other words, you tell FileMaker how the tables in your database fit together by matching up keys. As usual, FileMaker manages to make a tricky task seem kind of fun. You get to work with a visual, intuitive picture of the relationships between your tables—the *Relationship Graph*. In the Define Database window, click the Relationships tab, which is reproduced in Figure 7-19.

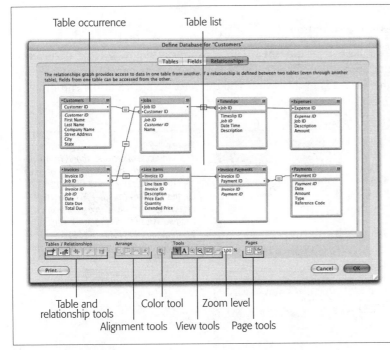

Figure 7-19:
The Define Database window's Relationships tab is a stark departure from the other tabs. Gone are the list, Create button, Change button, and Delete button. Instead, you get a relationship graph where you can draw your relationships. FileMaker also gives you a myriad of tiny tools to help you lay out the graph. The boxes in the graph are called table occurrences. (There's a reason why they aren't called tables in this case; see page 344.)

Your table occurrences (TOs) may not be in precisely the same order as Figure 7-19; they appear in the order you created them. If you want to move them around, just drag them. Or you can drag right through a table occurrence that's in your way. (Later on, you'll see how the Relationships Graph's tools work to help you manage the graph further.) To create relationships, you simply drag in the Define Relationships window.

1. **Point to the Customer ID field in the Jobs table occurrence and press your mouse button.**

    The field name highlights and the mouse arrow changes shape indicating you're about to join (relate) two tables together.

2. **With the mouse button held down, drag the arrow over the Customer ID field in the Customers table**

   As you drag, FileMaker draws a line starting from the first Customer ID field. When your cursor is over the second Customer ID field, it too highlights.

Tip: If you make a mistake and start dragging the wrong field, just point to some empty space in the graph before you let go of the mouse button. That way, you haven't actually defined a relationship, and you can just start over.

---

3. **Release the mouse button.**

   Poof! You have a relationship. The Customers and Jobs table occurrences change in appearance slightly: FileMaker adds a new panel to each box, and shows the key fields in this space. You can see each step, and the end result, in Figure 7-20.

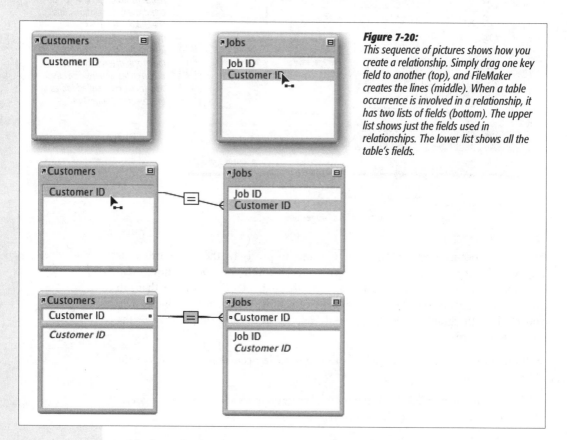

Figure 7-20:
This sequence of pictures shows how you create a relationship. Simply drag one key field to another (top), and FileMaker creates the lines (middle). When a table occurrence is involved in a relationship, it has two lists of fields (bottom). The upper list shows just the fields used in relationships. The lower list shows all the table's fields.

With the technique mastered, you can now define the rest of your relationships. You can refer to your ER diagram at this point, or use this handy cheat sheet:

- Drag Expenses::Job ID to Jobs::Job ID.

- Drag Invoices::Job ID to Jobs::Job ID.

- Drag Line Items::Invoice ID to Invoices::Invoice ID.

- Drag Invoice Payments::Invoice ID to Invoice ID.

- Drag Invoice Payments::Payment ID to Payments::Payment ID.

- Drag Timeslips::Job ID to Jobs::Job ID.

DON'T PANIC

Lost and Found Again

You may not see table occurrences in the Relationships Graph for all the tables you create. Remain calm. You have all the right table occurrences; you just can't see them all at once. Chances are you just need to scroll the graph to the right. Unfortunately, it can be tricky to drag between two fields if you can't get them both on the screen at once. (You can do it, mind you. When you approach the edge of the graph while dragging, FileMaker automatically starts scrolling. It's just a little tedious.)

If you have a big enough computer screen, you can simplify things by making the entire window bigger by dragging the bottom-right corner. If you still can't fit everything in, even when the window is as big as it can get, you can zoom out on the window. Click the Shrink to Fit button (shown here) and FileMaker shrinks everything so it all fits on the graph at once. In this reduced view, you can still drag relationships. When you're ready to see things full-size again, just type 100 in the Zoom Level box and press tab.

(Don't press Enter or Return after changing the zoom level or FileMaker will think you meant to click the OK button and make the Define Database window go away. If you do close it accidentally, just choose File → Define Database again.)

You can zoom in on certain parts of the graph with the Zoom In tool. First, click the tool, and then click anywhere in the graph. Use the Zoom Out tool instead if you want to zoom back out again. Unlike the Zoom controls on a database window, these controls don't let you zoom in past 100%, but you can zoom way out—to 1% if you want. At that level, your tables are reduced to undifferentiated goo in the corner of the graph.

When you're done zooming, be sure to choose the Selection tool again so you can drag relationships or table occurrences.

Zoom out
Zoom in

Selection   Shrink to   Zoom
fit   level

When you're done, you can spot-check your work by counting the lines in the relationship graph. Including the one between Customers and Jobs, you should have seven, and the graph should look like the one in Figure 7-21.

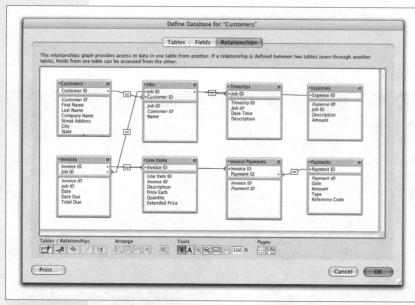

Figure 7-21:
Here's how your Relationship Graph looks with all the relationships defined on page 294. These relationships work OK, but the graph is now a little hard to read. First, there's no logical order to the tables. Even worse, there are lines running under table occurrences (the line connecting Timeslips and Jobs, for instance). You can do a little manual rearranging and fix this up.

FREQUENTLY ASKED QUESTION

FileMaker's Sixth Sense: Crow's Feet

I haven't done anything to tell FileMaker what kind of relationships I created. How does it know where to put the crow's feet?

You never have to tell FileMaker about the types of relationships because it doesn't really matter. The work FileMaker performs to deal with a one-to-many relationship is no different than what it does for a one-to-one, so it doesn't care about the distinction.

However, it's useful to you as the database designer to know what kind of relationships you have. (It helps you decide whether an invoice should have room for one line item or a whole list of them, for example.) FileMaker tries its best to figure out where the crow's feet go, as a special service to you. It assumes every end of every line needs a crow's foot unless it finds evidence to the contrary.

Such evidence includes:

- The field used in the relationship is a serial number.

- The field used in the relationship has the Unique validation option turned on.

A line that connects to a field that meets either of these conditions will *not* have a crow's foot. Since all your primary keys are serial numbers, FileMaker has no trouble figuring out where to leave off the crow's feet.

Cleaning up the Relationship Graph

Although this relationship graph is small and easy to understand, chances are it will grow as you power up your database by adding more tables, layouts, and fields. As it grows, your graph can easily get messy and hard to decipher. To make your graph manageable, first get rid of unnecessary information. Right now your graph shows *every* field in each table occurrence (in fact, it shows some fields *twice*, and a healthy dose of empty space too). But you don't need to see every field here—that's what the *Fields* tab is for. Figure 7-22 shows how to reclaim the wasted space.

Little Button

Figure 7-22:
Each table occurrence in the graph has a little button in the top right corner. When you click it, the format of the table occurrence changes. The first time you click, the bottom section disappears, leaving only the fields used in relationships. Another click makes all the fields disappear. Click a third time to return to the original format. (The button itself changes to show the selected format, which is a screaming example of redundancy. There's a much easier way to see how a table occurrence is set—look at it.)

To make your graph more efficient, switch every table occurrence to show only the fields used in relationships (one click should do it). Now a lovely graph is just a few drags away: You can move the table occurrences around so they form a pleasing arrangement that's easier to understand than the mess you had before. Figure 7-23 shows the result.

Instead of closing up the table occurrences, you can resize them. Hover the mouse over any of a table occurrence's four edges and the pointer changes to a double-headed arrow. Drag with the arrow to resize.

Tip: If you have a stray table occurrence (named the same as the database itself) on your Relationships Graph, just select it and hit Delete. It's a useless artifact from the table you deleted when you first defined this file. Since this table occurrence is not part of your ER diagram, you can safely ignore FileMaker's protestations that deleting it will break things.

Arrange the graph

The table occurrences in the graph behave a lot like layout objects in Layout mode. You can Shift-click or drag across more than one table occurrence to select them all. You can even press Ctrl+A (⌘-A) to select *all* the table occurrences. Just click into empty space on the graph to deselect. Once you have some selected, you can use the Arrange tools to line them up. Figure 7-24 shows them close up.

Figure 7-23:
It's amazing what a little straightening up can do. Now you can clearly see every relationship. The table occurrences are arranged in logical groupings (Invoices, Line Items, and Payments; Customers, Jobs, Timeslips, and Expenses).

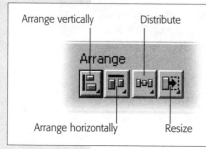

Arrange vertically   Distribute

Arrange horizontally   Resize

Figure 7-24:
When you select more than one table occurrence, the Alignment tools become available. Each tool has a tiny triangle in the bottom right corner to show that you get to make a choice about how that tool does its work.

Once you've dragged a few table occurrences around on your graph, it can look pretty sloppy. Here's how to use the tools to inflict some order on the graph:

• The **Arrange vertically** tool lets you choose whether to align the left edges, centers, or right edges of any highlighted table occurrences.

• The **Arrange horizontally** tool lets you align the top edges, centers, or bottom edges of the highlighted table occurrences.

• The **Distribute** tool makes the space between selected table occurrences uniform. You can choose horizontal or vertical distribution.

- The **Resize** tool makes short work of getting those manually resized table occurrences back in parade dress. Select some table occurrences, then click the Resize tool to tell FileMaker whether you want all the highlighted table occurrences resized to the smallest width or height, the largest width or height, or even the smallest or largest width and height.

Color your table occurrences

You can also change the color of the selected table occurrences. This won't affect the database's behavior at all. It's just there to help you organize your graph (you could make all the occurrences of the Invoice table blue, or all the join tables green, for example). Just select one or more table occurrences, then use the Color tool as explained in Figure 7-25.

Figure 7-25:
When you click the Color tool, FileMaker shows a menu of color choices, just like you see in Layout mode. Pick a color and all the selected table occurrences change to match it.

Adding notes

To notate your graph, select the Note tool, then drag on the graph to create the note. The Edit Note dialog box appears. There you type the text of the note and set its font, size, text and background colors. If you want to edit a note, double-click it and the dialog reappears, ready to do your bidding (Figure 7-26).

Printing the graph

Last but not least, FileMaker offers some tools to help you print the graph. Since the graph is a roadmap to your tables, some people like to print it and tape it up beside the computer for quick reference while building layouts. Figure 7-27 shows how to lay out the graph so you can print without surprises.

Deleting relationships

If you accidentally connect the wrong fields, or later decide you don't want a relationship you already created, you can easily delete it. Just click the relationship line itself to select it. Then click the Delete Relationship button or press the Delete key on the keyboard. You can see a selected relationship and the button in Figure 7-28.

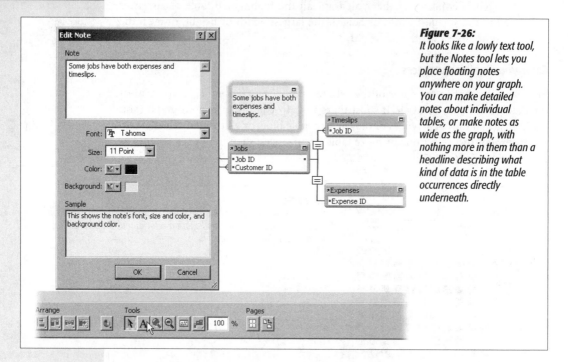

Figure 7-26:
It looks like a lowly text tool, but the Notes tool lets you place floating notes anywhere on your graph. You can make detailed notes about individual tables, or make notes as wide as the graph, with nothing more in them than a headline describing what kind of data is in the table occurrences directly underneath.

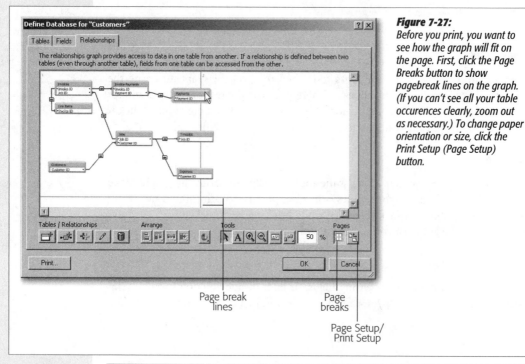

Figure 7-27:
Before you print, you want to see how the graph will fit on the page. First, click the Page Breaks button to show pagebreak lines on the graph. (If you can't see all your table occurences clearly, zoom out as necessary.) To change paper orientation or size, click the Print Setup (Page Setup) button.

Page break lines

Page breaks

Page Setup/ Print Setup

Finishing the Field Definitions

Now that your relationships are defined, you can add the rest of the fields to your tables. Since you already know how to define fields, there's no need to bore you with the gory details. Below is a list of all the fields needed to complete this database.

Figure 7-28:
Selecting a relationship line can be tricky because the line is so thin. It's easiest to click the "=" in the middle of the line, and it works just as well. You can tell you have it selected because its line is thicker and its equal sign is highlighted (like the relationship between Invoices and Line Items here). When a relationship is selected, you can delete it with the Delete Relationship button, or the Delete key on the keyboard.

Tip: To save time, you can find the completed database with all fields defined on the "Missing CD" page at *www.missingmanuals.com*. If you choose the ready-made option, you can skip ahead to page 317 and start learning how to use a relational database.

Customers table fields

Create the following fields in the Customers table:

- A text field called First Name.
- A text field called Last Name.
- A text field called Company Name.
- A text field called Street Address.
- A text field called City.
- A text field called State.
- A text field called Zip Code.
- A text field called Phone Number.
- A text field called Email Address.

Jobs table fields

In the Jobs table, you need only one more field: a text field called Name. Of course, you could call this field Job Name, so that at a glance you could tell what table it comes from. But in FileMaker such redundancy is unnecessary. Almost everywhere the program shows field names, it includes the table occurrence name as well—*Jobs::Name*, for example. The exception, inexplicably, is Layout mode, where related fields look like this—*::Name*. You can always double-click a field to see where it comes from, but that gets boring after about the 79th time. To spare yourself the tedium, you have permission to change any field names listed here.

Expenses table fields

The Expenses table needs three new fields:

- A text field called Expense.

- A number field called Amount.

- A text field called Company Name.

Timeslips table fields

Timeslips also needs three fields:

- A timestamp field called Date Time.

- A number field called Duration.

- A text field called Work Description.

Note: You might be tempted to call the Date Time field *Date and Time* instead, but if you try to do it, FileMaker sternly warns you against putting the word "and" in a field name. You can create fields that break the naming rules, but you'll have to jump through hoops to use them in calculations (Chapter 9). It isn't usually worth the hassle: pick a safe name instead.

Invoices table fields

The invoices table is easy too; just three new fields:

- A date field called Date (as in the date of the invoice).

- A date field called Date Due.

- A number field called Total Due.

Line items table fields

Add four new fields to the Line Items table:

- A text field called Description.

- A number field called Price Each.

- A number field called Quantity.

- A number field called Extended Price.

Payments table fields

The payments table is easy too; just three new fields:

- A date field called Date (as in the payment date).

- A number field called Amount.

- A text field called Type.

- A text field called Reference Code (this will hold a check number, direct deposit transaction number, Credit Card transaction ID, or other appropriate value).

Click OK in the Define Database window, and FileMaker shows you your database. After all that work, the result is wholly uninspiring—it looks exactly like the single-table database you already created. But take a peek at the Layouts pop-up menu (or Figure 7-29). Surprise: FileMaker has made *several* layouts for you—one for each table occurrence on your relationship graph. At this point, everything you know about using a FileMaker database still applies. The only difference is that each layout is attached to a different table.

Figure 7-29:
When your database has multiple tables, FileMaker still makes ugly layouts for you...it just makes more of them. Remember, you can always review Chapter 4 for advice on beautifying layouts.

Relational Databases

The essence of a relational database is its multiple tables. But every database you've worked with up to this point has had just one table. Now you need to learn how multiple tables affect the FileMaker concepts you're familiar with: Editing records, finding records, and building layouts.

One Table Occurrence, One Found Set

The most important thing to understand when using a multi-table database is that each layout sees the entire database from a different perspective. You'll want to do a little exploration to see this concept in action. A layout is attached to an occurrence on the graph, and that's how it sees the world. This means when you're looking at a record on the Customers layout, you're seeing a customer. If you switch to table view (View → View as Table), you'll see a list of customers. You won't see payments at all. To see those, you need to use the Layout pop-up menu (or choose View → Go to Layout → Payments) to switch to the Payments layout.

Since each table holds different data, the concept of a found set changes a little as well. Whenever you initiate a Find, the layout you're on determines which table FileMaker searches. Your newfound set is associated with that table occurrence too. Just like when you had only a single table, the found set stays the same until you perform another find, or you tell FileMaker to show you all the records for that table occurrence (Records → Show all records).

For example, if you find the six customers from Texas, then switch to the Expenses layout, you won't have six records in your found set anymore. Instead you have a separate *Expenses* found set. Switch back to Customers and you'll see the six Texans again. FileMaker remembers one found set for each table occurrence. It also remembers the *current record* for each table occurrence, so if you switch to a different layout, then come back, you'll still be on the same record that was active when you left that layout.

Of course you can have more than one layout attached to the same table occurrence—Customer List and Customer Detail, for example. The found set and current record are associated with the *table occurrence*, not the layout, so a find on the Customer List layout will affect the found set on the Customer Detail layout.

Tip: If you want more than one found set or current record in the same table occurrence, you can use multiple windows, just like you learned in Part 1.

If you want to see two kinds of records side by side, you can create a new window (Window → New Window), then switch one of them to a different layout.

Viewing Related Fields

Having each table occurrence completely segregated from the rest on its own layout is a good starting place, because you will probably want separate lists of all your entities, but it's hardly ideal for a fully functional database. After all, if you wanted to view everything separately you could have created individual databases and saved yourself all the trouble of making an ER diagram.

So think of the layouts FileMaker made for you as starting points. It's time to put those relationships to work. For starters, you'd like to show the customer name when you view a Job record. But the Job table doesn't have a customer name field. Instead, you'll use the fields from the Customer table and let FileMaker find the correct *related* data using the relationships you defined.

1. **In the Jobs layout, choose View → Layout Mode.**

   So far everything looks familiar. You've certainly seen Layout mode before (page 131).

2. **In the status area, use the Field tool and drag a new field onto the layout, somewhere below the existing fields.**

   As soon as you release the mouse button, FileMaker asks you what field you want.

3. **In the Specify Field dialog box, click the Table Occurrence pop-up menu (see Figure 7-30).**

   Here's where you venture into unfamiliar waters. This menu lets you pick any table occurrence on your graph.

Table Occurrence Pop-up Menu

Specify Field

Current Table ("Jobs")

Job ID
Customer ID
Name

☑ Create field label

Cancel   OK

Figure 7-30:
The Specify Field window has always had a Table Occurrence pop-up menu; you've just been told to ignore it until now. This menu shows a list of all the table occurrences on the graph. FileMaker is smart enough to know which ones are related from the current layout's perspective. It breaks the list into two groups: related tables and unrelated tables. Right now you don't have any unrelated tables because the entire graph is connected in one group.

4. **Choose Customers from the pop-up menu, then, from the field list, select the First Name field. Click OK**

   FileMaker adds the Customers::First Name field to the layout. It just says "::First Name" on the layout, but it does belong to the Customers table occurrence.

Tip: If you forget which table occurrence a field comes from, just double-click it. The Field/Control dialog box reappears, and you can read the source table from the "Display data from" bit. Just make sure you dismiss the dialog box without making any changes. To be safe, click Cancel.

---

5. **Change the field label FileMaker created for the new field to Customer First Name. Then, add the Customers::Last Name field to the layout too.**

Change its name, too, so you can remember what these fields are for.

When you're finished, switch back to Browse mode, saving your layout changes when prompted.

Adding or Editing Data

In Browse mode, the new field doesn't look all that impressive yet. That's because you don't have any data in your database. You'll really see the magic of relationships once you add some, starting with some customers. Open your database and go to the Customers layout.

1. **If the status area shows there are no records, choose Records → New Record**

FileMaker creates one record for you automatically, but only in the first table you added. Unless you happened to create this table *first*, you will need a new Customer record.

2. **Name this customer *Kesuke Miyagi* by filling out the First Name and Last Name fields. Then, create a second customer record with the name *Daniel LaRusso*.**

Notice that FileMaker has already filled in the Customer IDs for you—*C00001* and *C00002*. Time to add a job or two.

3. **Switch to the Jobs layout, and, if necessary, create a new record. In the Name field, enter Paint the Fence.**

Now you have one job record, but it isn't attached to a customer yet, so the Customer First Name field is empty.

Note: If you try clicking in the Customer First Name field right now, you'll get another surprise: FileMaker won't let you click in the field. It *looks* like a field, it *smells* like a field, but it doesn't *work* like a field. You're seeing the First Name field from the related Customer record, but there is no related customer record. No record, no field: No click.

---

4. **In the Customer ID field, type *C00001*, and then press Tab.**

Presto! As soon as you leave the Customer ID field, FileMaker goes to work finding the correct Customer so it can show you his name. Like magic.

Editing Related Data

To see how editing works in a relational database, add another Job record. Using the same steps as above, name it "Wax the Car," and attach it to Customer C00001 as well. It should then show the same customer name. Now try this:

1. **Change the value in the Customer First Name field to Mister.**

   Now the Wax the Car job is attached to "Mister Miyagi." But who's the Paint the Fence job attached to? Kesuke Miyagi or Mister Miyagi?

2. **Switch to the first Job record using the Book icon in the status area.**

   Drum roll… Paint the Fence is Mister Miyagi's too.

3. **Switch to the Customers layout and then switch to the first record.**

   Ta da! The customer record itself *also* now says Mister Miyagi.

If you don't think that's cool, you need your geek level adjusted.

Now you've seen a *relational* database in action. From a Job record, you can view data from the related Customer record. You can even edit that customer data directly from the Job record. The power of a relational database is all about working with related data like this.

Tip: If you want to protect your data so it doesn't get changed out of context, set the related field's behavior so that it can't be entered in Browse mode. Switch to Layout mode and choose Format → Field/Control → Behavior (page 225).

Showing multiple related records

Adding the customer name field to the Job layout makes good sense because a job is attached to exactly *one* customer (it's a to-one relationship). But what if you want to go the other way? Suppose you put the Job::Name field on the Customers layout. How would that work since a customer can have more than one job? (In fact, Mister Miyagi has *two* jobs right now.)

There are two answers to this question. The less interesting answer is that you can go right ahead and put that field on the Customers layout if you want. It will work fine. Since FileMaker can't show two values in one field, it just shows the *first* related record—in this case, Paint the Fence. (You can try for yourself if you want.)

The more interesting answer is *portals*. A portal is a layout object that makes viewing, editing, and even deleting multiple related records possible. The portal shows a list of records from a related table right on the layout. It can show as many rows (records) as you want, and you can even add a scroll bar so you can scroll through lots of related records in a small space. You can also edit related field data right inside the portal. When you add a portal to your layout, you get to decide which records it shows, how they're sorted, and what the portal looks like. For example, you can add a border to your portal, or change the background color of each row.

(See the box on page 326 for details on all the options available for portals.) The Customers table has a to-many relationship to Jobs, so it's a perfect candidate for a portal.

Portals are easy to create. The following steps take you through an example in the Customers database:

1. **In the Customer layout, switch to Layout mode. Drag the body part a few inches down.**

   The Customers layout is a full one. You'll need more room for your portal.

2. **Click the Portal tool in the status area.**

   You can see what it looks like in Figure 7-31.

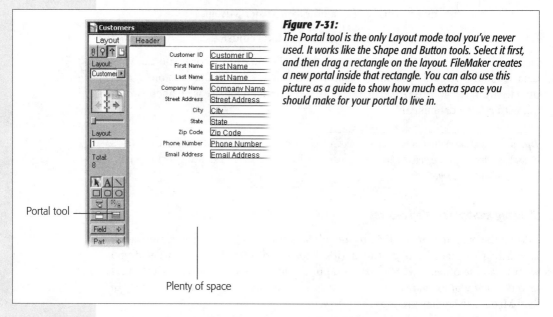

Portal tool

Plenty of space

Figure 7-31:
The Portal tool is the only Layout mode tool you've never used. It works like the Shape and Button tools. Select it first, and then drag a rectangle on the layout. FileMaker creates a new portal inside that rectangle. You can also use this picture as a guide to show how much extra space you should make for your portal to live in.

3. **Drag a large rectangle in the space below the Customer fields (you can use Figure 7-31 as a guide, but don't worry too much about the size; you can always resize the portal later).**

   When you release the mouse, FileMaker displays the Portal Setup dialog box. It's displayed in Figure 7-32.

4. **Make sure the "Show related records from" pop-up menu is set to Jobs.**

   You're telling FileMaker to show data from the Jobs table occurrence—in this case all the Jobs for the customer.

5. Turn on the "Sort portal records" checkbox. In the Sort dialog box that appears, add the Name field to the Sort Order list, and then click OK.

When FileMaker shows Job records for a customer, they'll be sorted alphabetically by job name.

Figure 7-32:
In the Portal Setup dialog box, you can choose which table you want to show records from and how those records should be sorted. You can also decide which related records to show and adjust the look of the portal. See the box on page 326 for details on all these options.

6. Turn on "Allow deletion of portal records."

With this option turned on, you can delete records in the Jobs table right from the Customers layout, saving yourself a trip to the Layout pop-up menu.

7. Turn on "Show vertical scroll bar."

A portal has a fixed size on the layout. If you have more records than fit in the allotted space, two things can happen. It can either ignore the additional related records, or you can put a scroll bar on the portal. With a scroll bar, you'll be able to view all the related jobs, no matter how many exist.

8. Turn on "Reset scroll bar when exiting record."

If you've scrolled way down in a lengthy list of related records, the first records don't show up anymore, naturally. By selecting this option, you're telling the portal to go back to the first record anytime you click out of (or exit) a portal record.

Note: Some people really hate seeing the portal pop back up to show the first record. They want the portal to stay scrolled even if they click out of that related record. To appease these folks, leave the option turned off. But be ready to reassure these malcontents that sometimes FileMaker has no choice but to redraw the data in the portal, and when that happens, the portal pops back to related record number one. That's just how it is.

---

9. **Click OK.**

The Add Fields to Portal window take the Portal Setup window's place. From here, you get to pick which fields from the job table should be displayed in the portal.

10. **From the Available Field list, select the Name field, and then click Move.**

FileMaker adds Jobs::Name to the Included fields list. Click OK again.

Your layout now has a portal. It looks just like the one in Figure 7-33.

Figure 7-33:
Portals are much more involved than any other layout object. They live in a rectangle on the layout like any other object, but they have intricate parts within them. Every portal is made up of rows. The more rows a portal shows, the more related records you can see at one time. A row can have any other layout object inside it. In this example, the portal row has just one field. Each portal also shows what table occurrence it's associated with, and which rows it shows. Finally, if you ask for it, a portal has a scroll bar so you can scroll through lots of related records.

Editing fields through a portal

Switch to Browse mode to see your portal in action. If you look at Mister Miyagi's record, you'll see both his jobs listed in the portal. Like any related field, you can click into either Job Name field and edit the data therein. When you do, the Job record itself is updated.

You can also delete records through the portal. Click the Paint the Fence row in the portal. When you do, you'll either enter the field itself, or select the portal row. Figure 7-34 shows the difference.

When you're on a portal row, the Delete Record command takes on new meaning. If you have an entire portal row selected, FileMaker assumes you want to delete the *related* record—the one you've selected—not the record you're sitting on. If you're in a field on the portal row when you choose the command, FileMaker instead asks you which record you want to delete: The Master record or the Related record. Figure 7-35 shows each message.

Figure 7-34:
When you click a portal row, one of two things happens. If you click onto an enterable field, you'll go right into that field. You would say you're on the first portal row, and in the Jobs::Name field. If you click in a portal row somewhere other than on a field, you select the portal row instead—the entire row highlights. You're still on the first portal row, but you're not in any field this time.

— In the field, on the portal row

— Selected portal row

Figure 7-35:
Top: If you select a portal row, the Delete Record command deletes the related record.

Bottom: If you're in a field on the portal row when you choose the command, you get this message instead. This time you get to pick which record is deleted. Click Master to delete the Customer record, and Related to delete the Job record.

If you're not on a portal row, the Delete Record command works exactly like it does on a layout that has no portals.

You've covered a lot of ground in this chapter. You now have a full-fledged relational database, and a good idea of how it works. But manually typing arcane customer numbers into foreign key fields and bouncing from layout to layout to add a job is probably not your idea of efficiency. In the next chapter you'll learn how to harness *all* the power of the FileMaker features you've learned so far: Value lists, field formats, buttons, and additional relationship options all combine to make data entry a breeze, even in a complex database with several tables.

Portal Power

In Figure 7-32, you learned a little about how the Portal Setup dialog box works. Now it's time to dig a little deeper.

To see the settings for your portal, select it in Layout mode and choose Format → Portal. (A double-click on the portal itself will get you there, too.) Portals work a lot like repeating fields. The main differences are:

- Portals work with related data, which is the way God intended multiple values to be stored. In other words, portals aren't evil like repeating fields.

- Portals can have a scroll bar. Got 326 items on that invoice? No problem.

- Each row in a portal can hold more than one field. In addition to the Job Name, you could show the Job Start Date if you had one. Adding objects to a portal is a breeze: Just drag them into the first row in Layout mode. When you add a field, FileMaker will show its correct value on each portal row. You can also add lines, shapes, pictures, and even buttons. You'll do some of this in the next chapter and you'll learn how to troubleshoot when the data isn't showing up correctly.

In addition to these differences, portals have more options affecting the way they look and work. As you've already seen, you can tell FileMaker to sort the records in a portal. Whenever you view the Customers layout, for example, the job list is sorted alphabetically.

This has no effect on the sort order of the records on the Jobs layout. It just sorts the Jobs portal in the Customers layout. You can even put another Jobs portal on a different layout and set it to use a different sort order.

You can also assign an "Alternate background fill" to a portal. This works just like its counterpart in the Part Setup dialog box. When you turn it on, every even-numbered portal row will have a different background color and pattern. You can make every other row green, for example. The *odd*-numbered rows will have whatever background color you assign to the portal itself on the layout.

Finally, portals have the same partitioning power as repeating fields. Normally, a portal starts with the first related record (which record that is, exactly, depends on the sort order assigned to the portal). If you change the "Initial row" value, though, the portal will skip some rows. For example, if you put *5* in this text box, the portal will show rows five through 14 instead of records one through nine.

If it suits your needs, you can put the same portal on your layout more than once, and give it different initial rows. Your layout could show the first five jobs in one column, and jobs six through ten in a second column, for instance.

Advanced Relationship Techniques

FileMaker 8 was built to work with related data and make it seem easy. Related fields, for example, work just like ordinary fields. Not only can you put them on layouts, but you can use them in Find mode and the Sort dialog box too. When you do, it *just works* exactly the way you'd expect.

Now you're ready to learn how to take advantage of FileMaker's relational capabilities to make the best database system possible. You can make data entry a breeze, minimize double-entry, show data from different tables side by side, and easily move from one kind of data to another. You can also give each relationship you create special powers given it to make creating, deleting, and displaying related records easier. This chapter shows you how to do all these things.

Creating Related Records

The first thing you probably notice with the database you worked on in Chapter 7 is that getting the records to relate is a tedious affair. To add a job record, for example, you go to the Customers layout, copy the Customer ID, and then go to the Jobs layout, add the record, and paste in the ID. That's a pain. Since FileMaker is all about relieving the pain of working with databases, it gives you a better way—a couple, in fact. In the last chapter you learned how to use a portal to *display* related records. Here you'll learn how a portal can also *create* related records. But first, you'll learn how to use a value list to help you enter appropriate data into a key field.

Value Lists Based on Fields

You've already seen value lists based on field values—on page 210, you attached a value list to the State field to make sure folks enter only valid state names. In a relational database, valid data entry is even more critical, since relationships work only when the key fields in each table match. Similarly, you can use a value list in the table on the "to-many" side of a relationship to make sure that the key field in table on the "one" side of the relationship only accepts valid key values. When you make this change to your layout design *once,* you save hours of data entry work down the line. Good database design is all about this kind of up-front work. In the Customers database, for example, you may want to create a value list that ensures the entry of valid Customer ID numbers. Just follow the steps below:

Tip: You can download this sample database from the "Missing CD" page of MissingManuals.com (page xxiv).

1. **In the Customers database, choose File → Define → Value Lists, and then click New.**

   Name your new value list *All Customers.* You want this list to automatically show all the customers in the Customers table.

2. **Turn on the "Use values from field" radio button.**

   When you click this radio button, the Specify Fields for Value List window immediately appears. (You can see an example in the box on page 329.)

3. **In the pop-up menu under "Use values from first field," choose Customers.**

   Way back in the dark ages, when you had only one table, FileMaker put that table in the pop-up menu for you. Now that you have multiple tables, you get to choose which table you want.

4. **In the list of fields, select Customer ID.**

   When you use this value list, you want to be able to choose a Customer ID for the job record, so you're basing the value list on this field.

5. **Turn on the "Also display values from second field" checkbox. Then, from the right-hand field list, choose First Name.**

   Since you're trying to avoid having to remember Customer IDs, you display another field value too, so that you can more easily find the Customer ID. In this case, the value list shows the first name and the customer ID.

Note: Of course, showing first *and* last name is the best way to find the right customer but the dialog box lets you pick only one field.

6. **Turn on the "Sort by second field" radio button.**

   After all, you'd probably prefer a list of customers in alphabetical order to one ordered by ID.

7. **Click OK, then OK again, and one more time.**

   It took three clicks to get here, so it takes three more to get back out.

UP TO SPEED

Field-Based Value Lists

A value list doesn't have to be a simple list of canned values. In the Edit Value List dialog box (page 208), you can also tell FileMaker to "Use values from field." When you do, you see the window shown here. You get to decide whether the list includes values from every record in the entire table, or only the related records.

First and most important, you need to choose *which* field the value list is based on. The pop-up menu under "Use values from first field" lets you pick a table occurrence. When you do, the list below it shows all the table's fields. Simply select the field you want.

You can also elect to show a *second* field in the value list. The field you choose has no effect on the actual value File-Maker inserts when you pick an item from the list. It just helps you decide *which* item to pick. To show a second field, just turn on "Also display values from a second field" and pick it from the list (see step 5 on page 328). You can choose a field from any table occurrence—if the second value isn't from the same table as the first field, FileMaker uses the value from a related record.

Once you've chosen what fields to show, you get to choose which records to use. If you turn on "Include all values," FileMaker puts the field's value from *every* record in the value list. When "Include only related values" is turned on, FileMaker looks at only the records related to the one you're sitting on. For this method to work, FileMaker has to know which table occurrence you're coming *from*. In other words, if you ask for only the related Jobs, do you mean jobs related to the Customer record or to the Invoice record?

You make that choice in the pop-up menu below these radio buttons. (When you define a value list like this, it works properly only when it's attached to a field on a layout associated with the same table occurrence selected in this menu. If you try to use it on a different layout, FileMaker doesn't know which record to start from and the value list won't show the right values.)

Display options let you choose how the list should be sorted: by the first field or the second field. Finally, you can tell the list to display values from only the second field—an ideal use for a Pop-up Menu.

Now that you've defined the value list, you can attach it to the Customer ID field on the Jobs layout. And to do *that*, you need to go back to the layout:

1. **Switch to the Jobs layout, and then go to Layout mode. Select the Customer ID field, and then choose Format → Field/Control → Setup.**

   The Field/Control Setup dialog box appears.

2. **In the "Format field as" pop-up menu, choose Pop-up Menu.**

   You want to let your employees pick the customer ID from a menu. (You could use a Drop-down List instead if you want, as discussed on page 214.)

3. **From the "Display values from" pop-up menu, choose *All Customers*.**

   In other words, choose the value list you just created.

4. **Click OK, then switch back to Browse mode.**

Now, when you click the Customer ID field, you get a list of customers to choose from. You can see it in Figure 8-1.

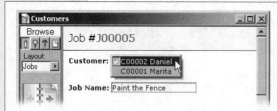

Figure 8-1:
Here's the Jobs layout after a little prettying up. To attach a job to a customer, you can now select the customer from a pop-up menu. When you do, FileMaker places the ID of the customer you choose in the Jobs::Customer ID field for you. The name is just there to help you pick the right one.

Creating Related Records Through a Portal

As the database designer, you have to think about how data gets entered and where (what layout) it makes sense for that data to go. Sometimes choosing a related record's primary key from a menu doesn't make sense. The Invoices and Line Items tables illustrate this scenario. To use the pop-up menu like you just created in Jobs, you'd have to add it to the Line Items layout. This process is how you'd create an invoice:

- Create the invoice record.

- Go to the Line Items layout.

- Add every line item, choosing the correct invoice ID each time.

Again, FileMaker has a better way. You need to edit your relationship so that it lets the program create new records; then you add a portal to the Invoice layout.

Preparing the relationship

When you first drag a relationship into existence in the relationships graph, it starts off pretty plain vanilla. But there are three special properties that you can set to make your workflow more efficient. You get to set whether a relationship lets FileMaker create or delete related records and whether it sorts those records before it displays them. To make these changes, you need to visit the Edit Relationship dialog box:

1. **In the Customers database, choose File → Define → Database. If necessary, click the Relationships tab.**

   FileMaker remembers which tab you were in the last time you were here, so Relationships may already be selected.

2. **Select the relationship between Invoices and Line Items table occurrences.**

   Click the = signs in the middle of the line for an easy target.

3. **Click the Edit Relationship button (see Figure 8-2).**

   The Edit Relationship dialog box is now on your screen, as shown in Figure 8-3. (You can also double-click a relationship to open this box, saving the trip to the button.)

Edit table occurrence
or relationship

Tables / Relationships

Delete table occurrence
or relationship

Print...

Add table
occurrence

Add/Edit relationship

Figure 8-2:
The buttons at the lower left of the Define Database window open dialog boxes where most of the relationship work in this chapter gets done. You can always back out of your mistakes...er, experiments by clicking the trash can (Delete) icon.

4. **In the set of checkboxes under Line Items, turn on "Allow creation of records in this table via this relationship."**

   Now if you put the Line Items::Description field on the Invoices layout, File-Maker lets you type in the field even when there is no related Line Item record. When you do, FileMaker immediately creates a new Line Item record for you and automatically enters the correct value in its Invoice ID field to make the two records related.

Tip: Since a relationship goes in two directions, you get to pick from the same three options for *both* table occurrences involved in a relationship. If you need a portal to display records through that relationship, then that's going to be the side that needs to allow record creation.

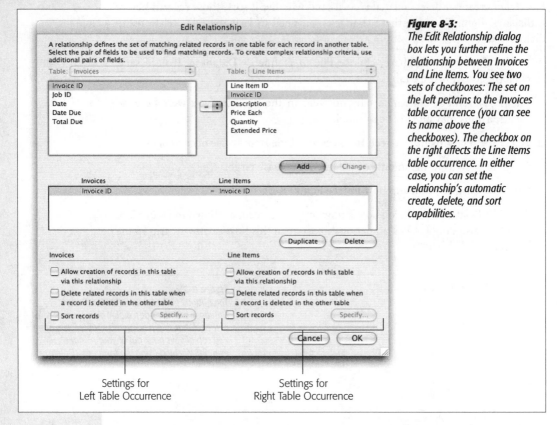

Figure 8-3:
The Edit Relationship dialog box lets you further refine the relationship between Invoices and Line Items. You see two sets of checkboxes: The set on the left pertains to the Invoices table occurrence (you can see its name above the checkboxes). The checkbox on the right affects the Line Items table occurrence. In either case, you can set the relationship's automatic create, delete, and sort capabilities.

5. **Again, in the checkboxes under Line Items, turn on "Delete related records in this table when a record is deleted in the other table."**

   With this option turned on, if you delete an Invoice record, FileMaker automatically deletes all the related Line Item records for you. This step is what you want, since a Line Item without an Invoice is meaningless.

6. **Click OK a couple of times to dismiss the Define Database window.**

Adding a portal to a layout

In the last tutorial, you edited the relationship to allow FileMaker to create records from Invoices to Line Items. Now you're ready to fix up your Invoices layout to use that edited relationship. You're set to build a portal to display the Line Items from the relationship you've just edited.

UP TO SPEED

Cascading Deletes

The "Delete related records" option can be dangerous for a couple of reasons. First, if you turn it on accidentally, you can find yourself in an odd situation: Records keep disappearing for no apparent reason. You'll get frustrated if you don't realize how this option works.

But even if you *want* it on, keep this fact in mind: FileMaker can't bring back a record you delete. It's one thing if someone accidentally deletes a Jobs record—you just have to look up the Job Name and enter it again, being careful to give the job the same ID it had before.

It's something else entirely if you also have Delete turned on in the Jobs-to -Customers relationship, and the Customers-to-Invoices relationship, and again in the Invoices-to-Line Items relationship. You've set up the Towering Inferno scenario called "cascading deletes." Because now, when you delete one job record, perhaps thinking that the job is finished and you don't need the record anymore, FileMaker also obeys your "hidden" instructions and deletes the Customer record attached to that Job record, *all* the Invoices attached to the Customer and *all* his line items, too!

Some people decide it's not worth the risk and leave the delete option off even when it *should* be on. For a better solution to the cascading deletion problem, read up on security in Part 6.

In the Customers database, you want to create a portal on the Invoices layout. Switch to Layout mode. Then, using the portal tool (Figure 8-4), drag out a large portal on the layout.

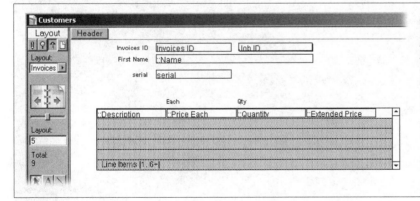

Figure 8-4:
This layout shows a portal like the one created in the steps on page 322. It needs to be wide enough to hold four fields, and tall enough to show several rows.

After you draw a portal, FileMaker shows the Portal Setup dialog box so you can specify which data to show in it. Proceed as follows:

1. **From the "Show related records from" pop-up menu, choose Line Items.**

   Your new Invoice record needs some Line Items, so that's the table you'll display in this portal.

---

2. **In the Portal Setup window, turn on "Show vertical scroll bar" and "Allow deletion of portal records." Click OK when you're done.**

Turn them both on, since you never know how many items you'll add to an invoice—or take off.

The Add Fields to Portal window appears.

3. **Add the fields *Description*, *Price Each*, *Quantity*, and *Extended Price* to the "Included fields" list.**

Notice the pop-up menu under Available fields. Because you selected the Line Items relationship three steps ago, FileMaker assumes that's where the fields are, too.

4. **Click OK.**

FileMaker adds your portal to the layout, and divides the available space among the four fields.

You don't get field headings to help you see which field is which, and you may need to tweak the relative widths of your fields, but FileMaker's done the bulk of the work for you.

Tip: The "Alternate background fill" option in the Portal Setup dialog box lets you add color and/or a fill pattern to every other row of your portal. A subtle color really helps make it easier to read across each line. Test colors on a variety of monitors and light conditions first, so you don't end up making your data harder to read, instead of easier.

FREQUENTLY ASKED QUESTION

How Do I Know Where to Sort?

In the last chapter I set the sort order for a portal when I was adding it to my layout. Now you're saying I can set the sort order in the relationship. What's the difference? Does it matter?

When you set a sort order in the Edit Relationship dialog box (page 332), it applies to the relationship itself. Any time you use that relationship, the sort order applies: in portals on any layout, when showing a single related field, and when finding a set of related records (that's covered in the next section).

A portal's sort order (page 323), on the other hand, applies only to the portal itself. If you don't tell the portal to sort, FileMaker uses the relationship's sort order—if any—instead.

If you know that every time you look at your related data, it should be shown in a specific order, set the relationship to sort. But if you think the related data ought to be sorted different ways in different contexts (and thus in different portals), don't sort the relationship because you add some overhead. FileMaker has to sort the records for the relationship, then sort them a different way for your portal. (You don't see this process happening, but FileMaker's doing it behind the scenes.) So when you're planning on viewing data in lots of different orders, rely on sorted portals instead of sorted relationships.

Adding records in a portal

Now that you've edited a relationship to allow the creation of related records, and provided a portal on the Invoice layout for viewing the records, you're ready to try out some Auto-creation goodness:

1. **On the Invoice layout, switch to Browse mode.**

    The portal is empty right now because you have no line items. You probably don't have an invoice record yet either.

2. **If necessary, create a new record.**

    Once you have a record, you see that the four fields in the portal are ready for a click. There isn't a related record yet, but FileMaker is offering you the chance to create one.

3. **Click the first (left-most) field in the portal and type** *Waxing the old yellow car.*

    As soon as you start typing, a *second* row of fields appears in the portal. That second row is FileMaker showing you that it's ready to make another new record for you. Figure 8-5 explains.

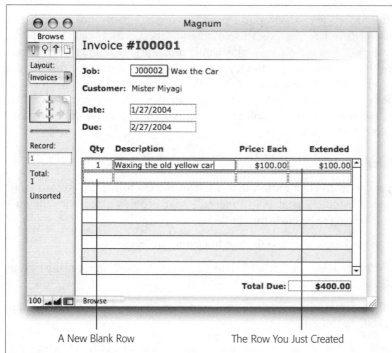

Figure 8-5:
In this picture, someone's just typed a description for the first line item on an invoice. As soon as you fill out any field on the first portal row, a second row appears. In Auto-creation, FileMaker stays one step ahead of you, always ready with a new blank portal row.

A New Blank Row   The Row You Just Created

You can fill out the remaining fields if you feel up to it. You can even add more line items: Just keep clicking into the last portal row. You can test your auto-deletion setting that you added in step 5 on page 332 by deleting the invoice you just created. When you do, the line item records should also go away. If you still have both windows open, you see this action happen live.

Note: The last portal row is *not* a new record until and unless you type something in it. (See page 99 for a refresher on committing records.)

Of course, the Invoices to Line Items relationship isn't the only relationship in your database that can benefit from the use of portals. For an exercise in thinking like a designer, take a look at your relationships graph and think about where else you could put portals to make data viewing and record creation easier. There's no real right or wrong answer. That's the beauty of FileMaker—you can use its tools to create virtually any system your business needs.

Navigating Between Related Records

With pop-up menus and auto-creating records, adding data to your new database is now a joy. But you still do some serious work navigating around the system. For example, if you're looking at an invoice and you want to see details about the related customer, you have to note the Customer ID, switch to the Customers layout, and then find the customer. That's three steps too many.

Simplify this process with a button (see page 246) on the layout—one that uses the *Go to Related Record* command. This command (affectionately called GTRR by FileMaker gurus) does the obvious, plus a little more. It goes to the related record to be sure. But it also changes the layout appropriately, and it can find all the related records and sort them too. It can create a new window, too, while it's at it. That's a lot of work for one little command. Since there are so many ways to use this little powerhouse, you can look at a couple of different sets of options—with and without the use of a found set.

Go to Related Record

Here's one way to create a button that activates the Go to Related Record command. In the Customers database, you already have people's names showing on a layout—just waiting to be made into buttons.

1. **Switch to the Jobs layout and then go to Layout mode.**

   You've already added the related field Customers::First Name on this layout (page 319).

2. **Select the Customers::First Name field, and then change the text color to blue and its style to Underline.**

   Now this field looks like a link on a Web page. This configuration is how you can tell later on that it's a button.

3. **With the field still selected, choose Format → Button Setup.**

   The Button Setup dialog box appears.

Auto Creation Without a Portal

You don't have to have a portal to get automatic creation of related records. It works when you type in *any* related field as long as the relationship is set up to allow it. Suppose you have a one-to-one relationship with one table for photographs and another for photo information. Both tables have a Photo ID field, but only the Photos::Photo ID field is a serial number. Finally, you tell FileMaker to allow creation of related Photo Information records.

You might wind up with a database that looks like the one shown here. There aren't any portals in sight. (Who needs them with just a one-to-one relationship?)

But since the relationship is set to auto-create Photo Information records, you can add a new photo record, and then just type a name right in the Quilt field. FileMaker creates the related record for you. If you type in the Type or Size field, it doesn't need to create a record because it can use the one that already exists.

If you don't have Auto-creation turned on, you can't click into the Quilt field. FileMaker shows the dotted field outline, but doesn't let you in.

4. **From the Navigation section of the list, select the Go to Related Record script step. When the Options section of the window appears, click its Specify button.**

   The Go to Related Records Options dialog box appears (Figure 8-6).

5. **From the "Get related record from" pop-up menu, choose *Customers*.**

   When you pick a table occurrence, you determine which record the button goes to. Notice that FileMaker shows you only the layouts that use the table occurrence you just selected.

---

6. **From the "Show record using layout" pop-up menu, choose *Customers*.**

If you're going to a related record, it's usually from a different table occurrence. Your current layout can't show you related data, because it doesn't have the required fields. So you need to tell the button which layout it can use.

Figure 8-6:
Go To Related Record options pack a powerful punch. If you turn on "Show in new window," FileMaker leaves your current window alone and shows the related record(s) in a new window.

7. **Click OK, then OK again to return to your layout.**

Now give your creation a trial run: Switch to Browse mode. First make sure you have a customer related to this job. If you don't, click the Customer ID field to choose one. When you assign a customer, your button works. Click the Customer First Name field and you're transported directly to that customer's record. Figure 8-7 shows what it looks like.

Figure 8-7:
When you click the Customer First Name (shown here at the top of the background window), FileMaker shows you that customer (front window). Give thanks to the Go to Related Record command.

Tip: The "Use external table's layout" option applies only when you're linking multiple *databases* together. You'll learn about that later in this chapter.

GTRR with a found set

If you're looking at a customer record, you can see all that customer's jobs because they're right there in the Jobs portal. But what if you want to see those jobs (and only those jobs) in a sorted list on the Jobs layout? It would take a bunch of steps if you had to do it manually. But the Go to Related Record command does all those steps for you—when you add a few new options to the mix.

1. **On the Customers layout, switch to Layout mode, and then select the Jobs:: Name field.**

   It's the one in the jobs portal.

2. **Choose Format → Button Setup. In the Button Setup dialog box, select the Go to Related Record command from the list, and then click Specify.**

   The Go to Related Record Options window pops up.

3. **From the "Get related record from" pop-up menu, choose *Jobs*. From the "Show record using layout" pop-up menu, choose *Jobs*.**

   You need a layout that shows you meaningful data from the Jobs table. So far, this process is just like creating a related record button without a found set. The next steps make all the difference.

4. **Turn on "Show only related records."**

   When you turn on "Show only related records," FileMaker changes the found set, showing just the related records. You land on the desired record, and you have all the other records in the found set. If the relationship has a sort order, FileMaker sorts the found set, too.

   For now, leave "Match current record only." (Selecting "Match all records in the current found set" lets you a new feature called *Enhanced GTRR*. See the box on page 341 for more detail.)

5. **Click OK, and then OK again.**

   You're looking at your layout again.

6. **For good measure, make the Jobs::Name field blue and underlined as well, using FileMaker's editing tools (page 152).**

   It's good to provide some kind of clue that the field is clickable. Anybody who's ever surfed the Net knows that blue underlined things take you to faraway places.

Now you have a Go to Related Record button *in* a portal. Switch to Browse mode to see what happens. First, use the book icon to navigate to a customer record that

---

has more than one related job. Click the *second* portal record. Because you're on the second row, the button takes you to the second record in your found set, not the first one. Then click the Customer name button again.

Note: If you don't have any customers with multiple jobs, just switch back to the Jobs layout and fix it: Attach a few jobs to one customer. Then come to the Customers layout again and find that customer.

As you switch back and forth, you can see another difference: the portal changes the button's context (Figure 8-8). That is, the records related in a portal are already a set, unlike the single field you made into a button in the previous tutorial. In other words, when you click the GTRR button on the Jobs layout, you expect to see only the single Customer that's related to your job. When you click the button in the Jobs portal, you get a found set of only the job records that you just saw in the portal.

Figure 8-8:
The Go to Related Record command notices you're on the second portal row (top), and takes you to the second record accordingly (bottom). To see the customer's other jobs, just use the Book icon.

Table Occurrences

In Chapter 7, you learned that a relationship graph doesn't really depict tables—it shows *table occurrences*. They're really just graphical representations of the underlying table. Because these occurrences are representations, you can make new occurrences of a table without duplicating it (and all its data). FileMaker's not trying to confuse you; it's actually helping you relate to the same table in different ways.

GTRR On Steroids

With the "Show only related records" option, you can use Go to Related Record to display a found set of records (from a related table) in a portal. But what if you want to something really cool and complicated, like find a couple of customers, who don't have anything in common other than not having paid their invoices yet, and somehow see their customer records in a set without performing a complicated search?

GTRR shows its juice in a new-to-FileMaker 8 feature called *Enhanced Go to Related Record* (eGTRR). Here's how it works: Make a button on your Invoice layout and give it a GTRR step that goes to the Customers table occurrence using the Customers layout.

Then, in the Options window, select "Show only related records" *and* "Match all records in current found set" (the second option is the enhanced part). Do a regular find to show Invoices from just Daniel and Ali—they're always late payers. You could just omit Mr. Miyagi, who pays as soon as he gets his invoice, thank you very much. Click the eGTRR button to see a new found set in the Customer table that shows only Daniel and Ali's records.

Apply eGTRR liberally throughout your database, and your users won't need to do as many complicated searches to find the data they're looking for.

When you create a very simple database, you have only one Table Occurrence on the graph for each table, so it's tempting to think of them as the tables themselves. But as you add new and more powerful features to your databases—and the relationships to make them work—sooner or later you need to graph the same table multiple times so you can keep everything straight.

Understanding Table Occurrences

There are few databases that can manage all their tasks without multiple occurrences of the same table. Your Customers database is no exception. Here's an example: Your database has Expenses to record what you buy to service your customers. It also has Line Items to record what you charge your customers for. Right now these are connected only by way of jobs. Figure 8-9 illustrates how your tables are currently related.

You can do better than connecting expenses and line items via jobs, however. When you do connect them this way, it means you don't know *which* line item is actually billing for a particular expense—so you can't be sure you've actually billed for that expense yet. In other words, when you look at a line item, you can't tell which expense it's billing for.

Of course you can type this information into the Line Items::Description field, but this does nothing to help FileMaker know how these are connected. What you really need is a whole new relationship—one that directly connects Expenses and

Line Items. This new relationship lets you use Go to Related Record commands to toggle between expenses and invoices, for example.

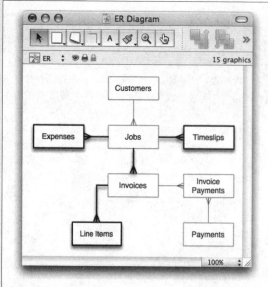

Figure 8-9:
In this version of the ER diagram, the Expenses and Line Items tables have been emphasized, along with the relationships that connect them. The only relationship between an expense (which you need to be reimbursed for) and a line item (which allows for reimbursement) is through the Jobs table and the Invoices table.

Tip: Later, when you learn more about calculations (Part 4) and scripting (Part 5), you can use this relationship to have FileMaker tell you exactly what has and hasn't been billed.

One-to-one relationships are fairly rare birds. One example you've seen in this book is a table of photographs and a table of their captions, with a one-to-one relationship between each. Each image file had one corresponding description. This new one-to-one relationship—expenses to line items—is even rarer, in that it connects two completely different *types* of data. It's also unusual in that it's not integral to your database's structure. Unlike the other relationships in this database, you could delete it and your system would work just fine. This relationship exists for one purpose only: to give your database a new level of ability.

As Figure 8-10 explains, however, when you add that relationship to the existing graph, you create ambiguity in FileMaker's digital mind. You can relate Line Items to the Expenses table, but to avoid interacting with existing relationships to Line Items, you need to create a new occurrence of that table.

To create this relationship and really make it work, you need three things:

- A new primary key (page 302) to hook the two tables together.

- A way to represent the new relationship in your relationship graph without throwing the whole thing into disarray. That's right—a new table occurrence.

- New fields on one of your layouts (the Expenses layout in this case), to use the newly related data.

To put these new database elements into play, you need to acquire some new skills and learn new twists on some old ones. The next section covers the entire process.

Figure 8-10:
This revised ER diagram now includes a relationship between Expenses and Line Items. It's a one-to-one relationship because an expense is billed only once, and a line item bills only for one expense. Notice, too that you now have two relationships between Expenses and Line Items—one direct, and one through Jobs and Invoices. FileMaker can't deal with that kind of ambiguity, which is why you create a new table occurrence to represent the relationship (page 344).

Relationships with Table Occurrences

FileMaker doesn't require you to follow a set order when you create new table occurrences, relationships, and layouts. Sometimes you create a new layout, thinking it's just for displaying a set of data and only later realize you need a new relationship—and a new table occurrence—to make it work. Fortunately, FileMaker makes it easy to switch modes so that you move freely from one part of the program to another creating and arranging various bits and pieces to make your new features work. In this section, you'll create a new key field and a new table occurrence, and then you'll add fields to a layout so you can assign invoice items to the proper expense item. The following sections take you through the process in one possible, and logical, order.

Adding a new key field to a table

Before you can hook up table occurrences in a new way, you've got to make sure both tables have the proper key field for the new relationship. In this case, the Expenses table needs a Line Item ID. (See the box on page 344 for more detail.)

In the Customers database, choose File → Define Database and switch to the Fields tab and the Expenses table. Create a new text field called Line Item ID, and click OK when you're done. This new field is how you relate the Expenses table to Line Items.

Note: You may be tempted to create your new relationship now by dragging the new Line Item ID field to the Expenses table. In fact, you may have already tried that—and gotten a confusing error message. To find your way out of that conundrum, see the box on page 347.

FREQUENTLY ASKED QUESTIONS

Putting New Keys in New Key Fields

I need to add a new key field to a table, but it's already got a lot of records in it. Since my serial numbers are created only when I create new records, am I stuck?

No, you're not. Lots of people need to "retrofit" key fields and add serial numbers after the data's already in a table. First, create a new field and give it the Auto-Enter serial number option. Put it on a layout that's tied to one of that table's table occurrences. If you have only one table occurrence for that table, so much the better—you don't have to make a choice.

Choose Records → Show All Records to make sure that all your records get a value in the key field. Then click in your new key field and choose Records → Replace Field Contents. Select the "Replace with serial numbers" option. FileMaker figures that you'll have to do this stuff pretty regularly when you're designing, so the values in the "Initial Value" and "Increment by" fields are already set correctly for this task. Select "Update serial number in Entry Options?" then click the Replace button. FileMaker does the hard work of giving each record a unique serial number. It even updates the serial number so that the next *new* record you create has its own serial number. (See page 302 for the full story on creating key fields.)

Adding a table occurrence

You need to make a new relationship between the Expenses TO and the Line Items TO using your new Expenses::Line Items ID key field. Since you want to access Line Item details while you're on the Expenses layout, you create a new TO for the Line Item table. In general, it's the information that you're using in a new way (the Line Items data in this case) that gets the new table occurrence. The Expenses table is fine as it is. (See the box on page 346 for more detail on how to make that decision.)

Figure 8-11 shows a picture of what that relationship might look like with the new Line Items TO. With the new graph in mind, here's how to create that additional TO in your Customers database.

1. **On the Relationships tab of the Define Database dialog box, click the Add Table Occurrence button.**

   You see the Specify Table dialog box (shown in Figure 8-12).

2. **Select the Line Items table from the list, and then, in the Name of Table Occurrence box, enter *Expenses Line Items*.**

Tip: If you don't see the Line Item ID field, it may be because your table occurrences (TOs) are collapsed and they show only fields used in relationships. Click the little button in the upper-right corner of the TO to expand it. Since the TO cycles through three states, you might have to click twice before you see all the fields.

Figure 8-11:
This diagram uses a new table occurrence to achieve the new relationship between Expenses and Line Items, while you avoid the problem of ambiguity shown in Figure 8-10. This shows you how you set up this relationship in FileMaker's relationship graph. Although you have only one Line Items table, you tell FileMaker it has two meanings: a line item on an invoice, and a line item that bills for an expense.

Figure 8-12:
Clicking the Add Table Occurrence button (shown back in Figure 8-2) opens the Specify Table box, so you can tell FileMaker which table to make a new occurrence of. You also get to give the new occurrence a name. You can then drag fields to the new TO to create relationships as usual.

3. You want a descriptive name so you can pick it out of a lineup later. When you click OK, FileMaker adds the new occurrence to the graph and selects it for you.

4. **Drag the Expenses::Line Item ID field to the Expenses Line Items::Line Item ID field.**

FileMaker creates the relationship.

UP TO SPEED

Deciding Which Table Needs a New Occurrence

Once you know that you need a new table occurrence, as in the Expenses – Line Items example, you immediately face another challenge: Of which table do you make a new occurrence? To answer that question, ask yourself this one: Which table has the information I need? Here are the three possible scenarios: See which one you think makes the most sense.

- If you create a new occurrence of the Line Items table, you're giving that table a new meaning in the relational structure of your database. You can access this new TO—Expense Line Items—from any table occurrence in the system. In particular, you can add Expense Line Item details to the Expenses layout. (You *can't* put fields from Expenses on the Line Items layout because that layout is attached to the Line Items table occurrence, not the Expense Line Items occurrence.)

- If you decide to create a new occurrence of the Expenses table instead, then the opposite is true: You can't view Line Item information from the Expenses layout, but you *can* view Expense information from the Line Item layout. In this case you've given Expenses a new meaning (Billed Expenses, perhaps).

If you want, you can create new occurrences of *both* tables. If you do, you can see Expense information from a Line Item *and* Line Item information from an Expense. But unless you plan to use your data that way, you're only creating more work for yourself.

Now that you have both relationships defined, you can switch the table occurrences back to their just-the-key-fields modes if you want, and arrange the graph however it suits you. When you're done, click OK to dismiss the dialog box. Now it's time to add fields from your new table occurrence to the Expenses layout. If no fields on at least one layout access the table occurrence you just created, it's not going to do you a bit of good.

Adding fields for new table occurrences

To put your new relationship to work, switch to Layout mode and go to the Expenses layout. As discussed on page 343, you want to add a couple of fields that let you view invoice line items and assign them to the corresponding expenses. That's the whole point of all the trouble you've gone to these last four pages.

Tip: Adding the fields using the Expense Line Items is like adding any other fields, but make sure you're using the Expense Line Items table occurrence, not the original Line Items.

When Dragging Doesn't Do It

When you first learned to create relationships, it was by dragging fields on the relationships graph (page 307). Since there's a clear path from the Expenses table to the Line Items table, you may be tempted to drag the Line Item ID field to connect them. You may have already tried it—and gotten the nasty message shown here.

FileMaker's not trying to be difficult. It's just letting you know that what you're trying to do doesn't work, and even going out of its way to suggest a solution. It's offering to create a new Line Items occurrence right now. FileMaker makes this choice because you dragged *from* Expenses *to* Line Items. (If you had dragged the other way, it would be suggesting a new Expenses occurrence instead.)

In the Name of Occurrence box, type *Expense Line Items* and click OK. Whenever you see this message box, you can click Cancel and try to figure out how your ER diagram conflicts with FileMaker's relationships graph, or just let FileMaker create the new TO. A new TO may not be what you had in mind, but you can rest assured that FileMaker's doing what it needs to do to make your desired relationship work.

FileMaker adds the new occurrence—which you can move to a less intrusive place on the graph—and creates the relationship.

Add Relationship

There cannot be more than one relational path between any two tables in the graph. Another occurrence of one of the tables must be added to the graph.

Name of Occurrence: Hansel and Gretel

[Cancel]   [OK]

Here's how to add the fields that do the trick:

1. **Drag a new field onto the layout. When the Specify Field dialog box appears, in the pop-up menu at the top, choose Expense Line Items.**

   The fields from the Line Items table appear (remember, this is an occurrence of the Line Items table, just like the Line Items occurrence itself).

2. **Choose the Invoice ID field from the list, and then click OK.**

   This field lets you view the Invoice ID on which this expense was billed.

3. **Add the Expenses::Line Item ID field to the layout as well.**

   And this field lets you assign a line item from that invoice to the expense. Again, make sure you pick the Expenses::Line Item ID field, *not* the Line Items::Line Item ID field.

If you switch to Browse mode, you can start entering expenses. Make some expense records, and put the ID of a line item in the Line Item ID field. You see the associated invoice number through the relationship. (If you haven't created invoices yet, make a few, or else the fields can't show you any data.)

Managing Data with Data Tunneling

In the first part of this chapter, you learned how to manage data that's in a table only one relationship away from your source table. For example, earlier in this chapter, you learned how to create line items through a portal in an Invoice record. (Remember from the graph in Figure 8-10 that the Invoice table occurrence is directly connected to the Line Items table occurrence.)

But you can also manage data that's stored farther away on the graph. For example, your Invoice table occurrence is also related to the Expenses table occurrence all the way at the other end of the graph because there's a continuous line of table occurrences connecting them through their respective relationships (Figure 8-13). Even though they aren't directly connected, you can still work with data that's several TOs away from your current table.

Database nerds like to use the term "data tunneling" to describe how you can manage data that's multiple hops away on your relationships graph. This concept means that you don't have to navigate over to a layout based on the table where your data's stored, to create or display it. If there's a path to the table occurrence you need on the graph, you can stay right where you are and tell FileMaker to tunnel through your graph and bring you back the data you need. In this section, you'll learn how to create layouts and arrange table occurrences to bridge the distance between where you are and the data you need.

How to Use Data Tunneling

Relationships like the one between Expenses and Line Items you created in the last section are *functional,* but they aren't very easy to work with yet. You can create a value list that lets you choose from all your invoice line items and connect them to expenses (page 210), but as your database grows, so can the problems. First of all, your database could have *thousands* of line items. And even if it doesn't, line items don't have a very good name—their descriptions aren't unique and their IDs aren't very meaningful.

It would be better if you could type in an Invoice ID *first*. After all, you're used to throwing invoice numbers around. Then it would be easy to pick from a list of items on just that one invoice. A new layout (like the one shown in Figure 8-14) uses data tunneling to let you manage line item data from the Expenses table.

Figure 8-13:
You can use the select tool to learn more about the structure of your relationships graph. The Line Items table occurrence is selected, and then the Select tool highlights the Invoice table occurrence, which is one "hop" away from it. Use the Select tool again to highlight table occurrences two hops away. The Line Items table is three hops from the Expenses table occurrence.

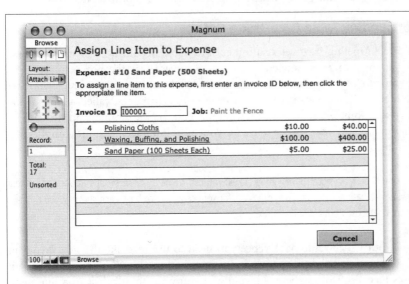

Figure 8-14:
This layout provides a nice interface for assigning line items to an expense. First, you fill out the Invoice ID field. Then, from the pop-up menu (it only shows line items on the invoice you ID'd), you choose a line item. You can download a real live copy of the database from the "Missing CD" page at www.missingmanuals.com. Use the file to see how the finished process works and as a reference as you go through the exercises that create your new layout.

What you need in your data tunneling interface

The Assign Line Items layout provides a special set of tools, or an *interface* to expedite a certain *process*. In this case, the process is matching line items records to expense records so you *can* track whether or not they've been billed. For the new interface to work, you need a few basic supplies. They're listed here to avoid confusion as you start creating them, and you learn more about the role each item plays as you build the interface. You need:

- **A field to type in the Invoice ID.** Since this field doesn't hold information about any particular entity in your database, it's a good candidate for *global* storage. Global fields, as you remember from page 109, have the same value across every record of their table.

Note: The Assign Line Items layout needs fields to show the job name and line item description as well, but you can create them any time. In this example, you add them last (see Figure 8-14).

- **A value list that shows line items on that invoice.** Value lists based on fields come in two forms: those that show *all* records, and those that show *related* records. Since you don't want to pick from every line item in the database, you need the second type.

- **A relationship for the value list.** This relationship needs to show the line items that match the Invoice ID in the new global field.

To get these three major elements to work together, you first have to revisit your relationship graph and decide which table occurrences to connect. Read on.

Understanding Table Occurrence Groups

Since data tunneling involves relating existing table occurrences in multiple new ways, you can easily get tangled in a mass of arrows (see the box on page 353). Since you can create as many occurrences of each table as you want, FileMaker makes it easy to create an entirely *new* group of occurrences, called a *table occurrence group*, somewhere *else* in the graph. You can assemble and wire these together in any way that makes sense for your new interface, without complicating the existing group.

Note: Remember, table occurrences aren't tables. You can create as many groups as you like without making your database any bigger. The groups are for your convenience only, each showing you a "snapshot" of your database from a different angle.

To figure out which table occurrence you need to use to make the new layout in Figure 8-16 work, think about what you need it to do. You're looking at an expenses record on the Expenses layout and you want to attach it to a line item.

You need to get to the new Assign Line Items layout—via a button, perhaps. After you choose the line item (quite easily with the help of the new layout), FileMaker puts a value in the Line Item ID field—right there on the original expense record. Every step of the way, the interface takes place from the viewpoint of an expense record.

Tip: FileMaker mavens prefer the term *context* to refer to the viewpoint of a layout. Just so you know.

Since your new layout is all about modifying an expense record, you must attach it to an occurrence of the *Expenses* table. The other tables you need are Jobs, Invoices, and Line Items. As shown in Figure 8-15, those tables already have relationships to all the other tables in your database. There's no problem in creating new relationships to the Expenses table, too—at least not for FileMaker. But if you start dragging to create those relationships, you need 3-D glasses to ever make sense of your relationships graph again (see the box on page 353).

Figure 8-15:
You can use your ER diagram to figure out which tables you need in your new group, and how they go together. In your new group, you recreate just the highlighted portion of the diagram.

Instead, you can create new TOs for that entire group of tables, and position it off to the side, as shown in Figure 8-16. This graph lets you work separately with the two distinct "sets" of relationships. Since the two groups share no relationships, FileMaker can put the relevant table occurrences in the Expense Assign group, and separate everything else in the unrelated tables group.

Note: There is a downside to this approach. Since each layout is attached to a single table occurrence, if you create a new group, you need a new layout to use it. A small price to pay for the added simplicity.

Figure 8-16:
In this illustration, a new group of table occurrences will handle a new set of data entry and management tasks. More table occurrences may seem to clutter up the graph, but take a look at the organization in the Specify Field dialog box. More TOs can actually reduce the overall confusion because now they aren't lumped together in a long list. They're grouped by Related and Unrelated Tables (note though, that this dialog box should really say "Table Occurrences).

Building a Data Tunneling Interface

Now that you know how the relationship graph for this interface works, it's time to start the actual construction. Start with the new global field. It's an easy place to begin, and you need the global field for all the next steps.

Creating a Global Field

Since the context of your interface is the Expenses table, that's where you add the field. Open the Customers database and proceed as follows:

1. **Choose File → Define Database and switch to the Fields tab. From the Table pop-up menu, choose** *Expenses.*

   FileMaker shows the fields in the Expenses table.

2. **In the Field Name text box, enter** *Global Invoice ID,* **and then click Create.**

   The new field appears in the field list. (See the box on page 354 to see why you've put the word *global* in this field's name.)

3. **Click Options. Then, in the Field Options dialog box, click the Storage tab.**

   FileMaker shows you the field storage options. You first saw these on page 108.

(page 108)

UP TO SPEED

The Importance of Being Organized

You can easily get so carried away with new table occurrences and new relationships that you make an illegible, illogical graph. This window illustrates a common mistake that can create havoc in a database: no consistent naming system to the table occurrences, and no visual grouping to show how the relationships operate. The database may work just fine, but if it ever does need troubleshooting or updating, any developer (even if that's *you*) would have a hard time figuring out what's going on.

First of all, the relationships graph is about as easy to navigate as a bowl of spaghetti. Even worse, since every table occurrence relates to every other, the table occurrence menus would be useless. And the table occurrence names, though marginally descriptive, don't help you find the TO you need. If you do a little planning before you go throwing your new TO creation skills around, you can steer clear of these rocky shoals.

4. **Turn on "Use global storage (one value for all records)," and then click OK.**

   FileMaker creates the field, and it now appears in the Field list.

You use this new global field as a key field in the next section.

Creating a New Table Occurrence Group

Since the Assign Line Items layout has to be tied to an occurrence of the Expenses table, you need a new one of those. You also want to be able to show the line item attached to that expense, so you need a new occurrence for that table, too. Finally, you'll use the global field you just defined to hook up to another new table occurrence that will hold an invoice ID. With it, you'll access the following information:

- The job name of the job associated with that invoice.

- The line items attached to that invoice.

A quick glance back to Figure 8-16 reveals all the new table occurrences you need to create.

One (Global) Field to Rule Them All

You know that fields set with global storage have the same value across every record in the table that holds them. Since they're so different from other fields, many database designers give them special names so that the fields stand out in a list. That way, it's less likely that they'll get used inappropriately—say in a context where they don't have much meaning, or plopped down on a layout where someone can edit the values when they should stay static.

You can just preface the names of all your global fields with the word "global," like you did in the exercise on page 352. But in the real world, people commonly just use a lowercase "g" as a prefix. With this scheme, you can name your global field "gInvoice ID" and save a few keystrokes. Plus, you look like a guru.

The steps are simple if you take it one table at a time:

1. **If necessary, click the Relationships tab of the Define Database window.**

   You need to see your existing relationship graph.

2. **Click the Add Table Occurrence button (see page 331). When the Specify Table window appears, select the Jobs table.**

   It's always good to give TOs a descriptive name. When you're data tunneling, it's even more important. When you create relationships, the names help you keep the various tables and groups straight.

3. **In the Name of Table Occurrence box, enter *Expense Assign: Global Invoice Job*, and then click OK.**

   The Expense Assign bit says that this new table occurrence was created especially for the process of assigning expenses. "Global" says you're planning to use the new TO in global relationships and the "Invoice Job" part helps you remember which other TOs you plan to hook up to it.

When you click OK, FileMaker adds the new table occurrence to the middle of the graph. Move it out of the way to get ready for the next steps.

1. Add an occurrence of the Invoices table called *Expense Assign:Global Invoice,* an occurrence of the Expense table called *Expense Assign:Expenses,* and an occurrence of the Line Items table called *Expense Assign:Global Invoice Line Items.*

   You now have the three table occurrences on your graph. Since the names are so long, you might have to stretch your new TOs so you can tell them apart. See page 311 for tips on resizing TOs.

2. Create a relationship between Expense Assign: Global Invoice::Invoice ID and Expense Assign: Global Invoice Line Items::Invoice ID.

   You drag and drop; FileMaker draws the lines.

3. Create another relationship, this time between Expense Assign: Global Invoice: :Job ID and Expense Assign: Global Invoice Job::Job ID.

   The necessary relationships are now in place. Your new graph looks something like Figure 8-17.

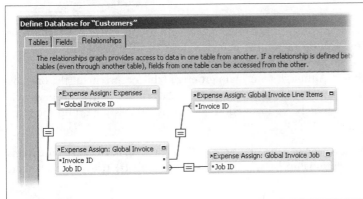

Figure 8-17:
With the Expense Assign: Expenses table occurrence in the picture, you can start to clearly see how this new layout works. When someone puts an invoice ID in the Global Invoice ID field, it instantly matches one Invoice record. You can then show fields from the Expense Assign: Global Invoice table occurrence on the layout, and you see the right invoice. Of course, you can also follow the additional relationships to show line items and the job.

Now that the occurrences and relationships are in place, you can move them to a new spot on the graph where they have some breathing room. FileMaker gives you nearly infinite space down and to the right, so pick a spot that you like.

Tip: Remember, if you like things lined up nice and neat, you have Arrange tools in the Relationships graph that let you resize and align a selected group of TOs together (page 307).

Adding new table occurrences to a group

You're partway through creating the new table occurrence group that supports the Assign Line Items layout. You've created some of your new TOs and arranged them on the graph. It's time to take stock. The purpose of that layout is to select an invoice based on a global field, and then show the job name and a list of line items. But this group of table occurrences simply defines the relationships between Invoices, Line Items, and Jobs. You already know the layout will be tied to an occurrence of the Expenses table, so you need to make sure that from that layout, you have a relationship that pinpoints the invoice you're interested in. In other words, you need a relationship from the Expenses table to the Invoices table, based on the global Invoice ID field. Figure 8-18 shows this connection.

Figure 8-18:
This graph shows the final table occurrence group. It has an Expenses occurrence to anchor the layout to, and all the right tables (Invoice, Job and two occurrences of Line Items) to show the necessary data.

You need one last table occurrence to complete your group. Once you pick a Line Item ID from the pop-up menu, the Expenses::Line Item ID field gains a value. It would be nice to show you information *about* the line item you just selected, to reinforce the choice. Although your main group of table occurrences (the one you created in the last chapter) knows how expenses relate to line items, this new table group doesn't. Fortunately, you can add new TOs to an existing group the same way you create any other TO:

1. **Add a new occurrence of Line Items called Expense Assign: Expense Line Items and create a relationship between the two Line Item ID fields in each table occurrence.**

   Fastest way: drag the Line Item ID field in one TO to the Line Item ID field in the other. (It doesn't matter which direction you drag—just do it.) You can see the result in Figure 8-19.

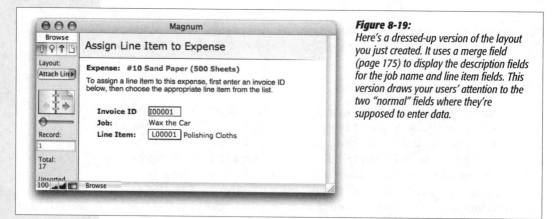

Figure 8-19:
Here's a dressed-up version of the layout you just created. It uses a merge field (page 175) to display the description fields for the job name and line item fields. This version draws your users' attention to the two "normal" fields where they're supposed to enter data.

Building a Global Field Layout

Now that you've finished the new table occurrence group and hooked up its relationships, you're ready to create the Assign Line Item layout you first saw way back in Figure 8-14. With the graph defined, this process is surprisingly simple. First, create a new, blank layout that's based on your Expenses Assign: Expenses table occurrence, and call it Attach Line Items. See page 170 if you need a refresher on creating layouts.

Now add these fields to the layout:

- Expense Assign: Expenses::Expense.

- Expense Assign: Expenses::Global Invoice ID.

- Expense Assign: Global Invoice Job::Name.

- Expense Assign: Expenses::Line Item ID.

- Expense Assign: Expense Line Items::Description.

Note: Remember, this layout is associated with the Expense Assign: Expenses table occurrence. When you choose fields for the list above, in the Specify Field dialog box, from the top of the pop-up menu, select *Current Table*.

Using a global pop-up field to change the display in a value list

By definition, a global field has the same value in all its tables' records.. Therefore, you can change the data in a global field without affecting any of your "real" data for those records. When your global field is used in a relationship, and you change the value in the global field, the relationship changes and so do the records that are related to your current record

You use this technique to create a value list that's based on the global relationship between your new Expenses TO and the new Invoice TO. When that global relationship changes, FileMaker tunnels in the new table occurrence group from Expenses to Invoices to Line Items to get the line item that's related through the value in your global. Refer to your relationships graph to refresh your memory on how those TOs hook up, if this technique doesn't make sense without a visual aid.

This advanced technique is just like searching for records, without all the hassle of going to Find mode and actually performing a search.

To make the Line Item ID field into a pop-up menu, double-click it to see the Field/Control Setup dialog box:

1. **From the "Display as" pop-up menu, choose** *Pop-up Menu.*

    The "Display values from" pop-up menu appears, with <unknown> displayed.

---

2. From the "Display values from" pop-up menu, choose *Define Value Lists.*

   You need a new value list based on the values in the Line Item ID field from the Expense Assign: Global Invoice Line Items table occurrence you made a few pages back.

3. Click New and type *Expense Assign: Global Invoice Line Items* as the value list name.

   Even though you're about to assign your new value list to a field, you want the name to be descriptive, so you can remember your thought process later on.

4. Turn on the "Use values from field" radio button and choose *Expense Assign: Global Invoice Line Items* from the Specify Fields window's the drop-down list. Then click the Line Item ID field.

   This field's data shows up in your new value list.

5. Under Value List Content, select "Include only related values starting from" and, from the drop-down list, choose *Expense Assign: Expenses.*

   The idea is to keep your users from assigning an expense to a line item from the wrong invoice, or from assigning an invalid Line Item ID. This option tells the value list to display only line items that are related to the invoice that matches the value in your Global Invoice ID field. Since that field's on the Expense Assign: Expenses TO, then that's where the value list relationship is "starting from." To understand how this works, remember the concept of context (page 350).

6. Turn on the "Also display values from second field" checkbox and, from the list, choose the *Description* field.

   Since a Line Item ID by itself isn't very meaningful, you show the description too.

7. Turn on the "Sort by second field" radio button and click OK until the dialog boxes are gone.

   You're back on your Attach Line Items layout and your Line Item field is formatted with your new value list.

Switch to Browse mode and try out your new layout. If you type *I00001* into the Global Invoice ID field, you should be able to pick a line item from the pop-up menu. When you do, the Expense Assign: Expense Line Item::Description field should show the selected line item's description. Figure 8-19 shows how you might format this new layout.

Connecting Databases

In FileMaker, you can make two databases work together as easily as you work with any other multiple tables. Using the data tunneling techniques discussed in the previous section, you connect tables from another file (often called an *external database*) without the overhead of copying all that data into your file. You simply put a table occurrence from your external file onto your relationship graph, which defines its perspective in relation to all your other tables.

POWER USERS' CLINIC

Naming Table Occurrences

When you create a new group of interrelated table occurrences, it's helpful to choose good names. There are many places in FileMaker where you see a list of occurrences on your graph. Although the list is always in alphabetical order, it gets lengthy once you start duplicating TOs, and it can be hard to find what you're looking for. It's extra confusing when you have several occurrences of the same table with similar names—"Which *Line Items* am I supposed to use here?"

A good way to keep things straight is to give the same prefix to every table occurrence in a group. The prefix makes them sort together in the list, and serves as a clear reminder of which occurrences go together. It's even better if the prefix also tells you what the group actually *does*. If you compare the two lists shown here, you can easily see the advantage of this technique. As helpful as long, prefixed TO names are in the *list*, they're not as much help in the *graph*, where FileMaker often cuts them off. Nothing's more confusing than three occurrences named "Expense Assign: ...." Also, since you can name a table occurrence anything you want, it can be hard to remember *which* table it's an occurrence of.

Luckily, FileMaker has good solutions to both these problems. First, you can easily resize any table occurrence. No matter how the table occurrence is configured, you can drag the right or left edge to make it wider or narrower. If it's set to show all its fields, you can also drag the top or bottom edge to change its height. A table occurrence that's too short to show all its fields has little arrow icons above and below the field list. Click these arrows to scroll the list. (When a table occurrence is set to show just the key fields, or no fields at all, its height is fixed.)

To see which table an occurrence represents, just point to the arrow icon to the left of the occurrence name. FileMaker pops up an information window that tells you everything you need to know. And if long names and pop-up tips aren't enough, you can use the note tool (page 313). Use the note as a reminder about the purpose of your new table occurrences that's more detailed than a naming prefix. Notes behave themselves, staying in the background behind all your TOs, so some designers make large notes that enclose a new TO group to visually unite them on the graph.

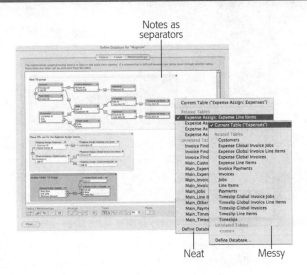

Notes as separators

Neat   Messy

For example, suppose you want to connect the People database you created in Chapter 3 to your new system. You'd like a portal on the Customers layout to show all the people in the People database who live in the same state as that customer. After all, you never know when one of your leads will come in handy.

Adding a Table Occurrence from Another File

Creating a cross-database relationship is as easy as adding a table occurrence. Once you have the People table on the relationships graph (in the Define Database dialog box), it begins to act like a first-class citizen in its new environment: You can define relationships to it, attach layouts to it, and just about anything else you can do with the tables in this database. Here's how:

1. **In the Customers database, bring up the Relationships tab of the Define Database window. Click the Add Table Occurrence button.**

   The Specify Table dialog box appears.

2. **From the File pop-up menu, choose Add File Reference.**

   A standard Open File dialog box appears—just like you see when you're opening a database. To use a table from another file, you have to add a *file reference*. A file reference is just a way to tell FileMaker where you store the external databases it needs to interact with.

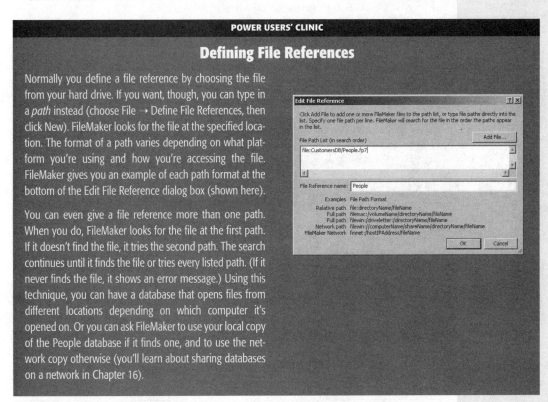

POWER USERS' CLINIC

Defining File References

Normally you define a file reference by choosing the file from your hard drive. If you want, though, you can type in a *path* instead (choose File → Define File References, then click New). FileMaker looks for the file at the specified location. The format of a path varies depending on what platform you're using and how you're accessing the file. FileMaker gives you an example of each path format at the bottom of the Edit File Reference dialog box (shown here).

You can even give a file reference more than one path. When you do, FileMaker looks for the file at the first path. If it doesn't find the file, it tries the second path. The search continues until it finds the file or tries every listed path. (If it never finds the file, it shows an error message.) Using this technique, you can have a database that opens files from different locations depending on which computer it's opened on. Or you can ask FileMaker to use your local copy of the People database if it finds one, and to use the network copy otherwise (you'll learn about sharing databases on a network in Chapter 16).

3. **Browse to the People database, select it, and click Open.**

   The Specify Table dialog box now shows tables from the People database (it has only one).

Tip: File references aren't dynamic. That is, if you move the files from the location in your file reference, then you need to manually update the reference for the new location. Just choose File → Define File References and double-click the file reference to edit it.

---

4. **Select the People table and click OK.**

FileMaker adds the new occurrence to the graph. As Figure 8-20 attests, you can tell at a glance that it's an occurrence of what FileMaker calls an *external* table because it shows you the table occurrence's name in italics.

Figure 8-20:
External tables' names display in italics. To find out which database it comes from, point to the little arrow to the left of the name to show the information window. FileMaker displays the source table's name as well as the source file's name.

Empty Lookups

Lookup options give you some control over what happens when there's no matching related record. Normally, if File-Maker tries to find a related record to look up data from, and it can't find one, it just leaves the lookup field alone.

That's what happens when you choose "do not copy" in the "If no exact match, then" group of radio buttons. Here's what the others do:

- The "copy next lower value" option looks at the closest *lower* related record. For example, if you turn it on for the Invoices::Street Address field, and there's no matching related customer, FileMaker copies the address of the customer with the next lower Customer ID alphabetically. In this case, it makes absolutely no sense.

But what if you were looking up price information based on quantity? If the customer orders 38, but you have pricing for 30 or 40, you might want to get the price for 30 items: the next lower value.

- The "copy next higher value" option works just like its similarly named counterpart. It just copies the value *from* the next higher related record instead. People don't use these two options a lot, but they sometimes come in very handy.

- The "use" option lets you specify any value you want to substitute for a missing related value. For example, if you're looking up customer age information, and you don't have an age for one person, you can tell FileMaker to use "N/A" instead.

Tip: You can double-click the People table occurrence and change its name to Other Leads to better reflect its meaning in this table occurrence group.

5. **In the relationship graph, drag the State field from the People table to the Cus-tomers::State field.**

Now that the People table is in the graph, attaching it to the Customers table works just like every other relationship you've ever defined.

You can use this relationship like any other. For example, you could create a portal, as described in Figure 8-21.

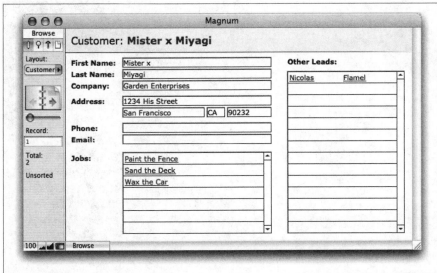

Figure 8-21:
Using the new table occurrence for a portal also couldn't be easier. Just switch to the Customers layout in Layout mode and add a new portal. Choose the Other Leads table occurrence, turn on the vertical scroll bar, and tell the portal to sort by Last Name, then First Name. Finally, add the First Name and Last Name field.

Lookups

Since you have a relationship between the Jobs and Customers tables (page 307), you don't have to enter customer information on each job record. Instead, File-Maker shows the same customer fields for each related job. If you update the customer's first name, the new name automatically shows on the Jobs layout. This dynamic updating of related data is the essence of a relational database. However, many times you *don't* want a piece of information to change; you want FileMaker to remember the way it was at a certain point in time. Lookup fields, which use relationships as a source for a sort of one-time copy and paste action, let you take a piece of data from a table *and* protect it from future updates.

Take a look at the Invoices table, for example. When you create an invoice, you attach it to a job. The job is in turn attached to a customer. When it comes time to mail the invoice, you can easily put the address fields from the Customers table occurrence on the Invoice layout and see the customer's address. This method is a bad idea for two reasons:

- **It doesn't allow for special circumstances.** If a customer tells you he's going to be in Majorca for a month and to please send his next invoice there, you have no way to enter an alternate address on just one invoice. You have to change the address in his customer record, send the invoice, and then change the address back.

- **It destroys relevant information.** When you *do* update the customer record with his original home address, you lose any record of where you sent the invoice. If you go back to the special-case invoice two years from now, it will *look* like you sent it to his home address. But that's not correct.

Systems with More than One Database

Even if you're building a brand-new system from scratch, there's no rule that says every table has to be in the same database. In fact, you have many good reasons to divide your system across multiple files. The last chapter talked about one of those reasons: You might be storing large images or other files in your database. You can keep these files in an external table so the database file itself isn't so large. Then you can back up, copy, and email the information about the images without including the images themselves.

Here are some other reasons to use more than one file:

- You can create a database for each kind of interface you need. For example, if you need to track sales, you can create a database with the tables you need to store the actual data: Orders, Line Items, Customers, Shipments, Products and so forth. You can use this database in two ways, though: Sales Entry (creating and managing orders) and Reporting (daily, monthly, and quarterly sales reports, trend and promotion analysis and so on). To keep your system as simple as possible, you can create these separate interfaces as two distinct databases. Since they share the tables from the central Sales database, the reporting data stays up-to-date as FileMaker processes new sales. .

But since they're in two databases, the layouts you need for order entry don't get in the way of the reporting layouts, and vice versa

- One company usually has many database needs. You might have Sales, Marketing, and Engineering departments in your organization. Each of these departments has unique needs and wants a database to match them. But the Marketing department might be very interested in sales data, and the Sales department needs access to engineering information. You can create a separate database for each department, but share some tables between systems. This way you get an interface tailored to each group, but the important data is shared.

- When you can use external table occurrences, you have a very flexible design metaphor. A database-or file-can hold interface elements (layouts, scripts, value lists) or data (tables and fields) or both. You can construct the database in almost any way you see fit: one file for each table, all tables in one file, or tables in logical groupings; all the interface in one database, or several databases to break things up. A FileMaker file is a very flexible unit of organization: Use it as you see fit.

These problems arise because invoice data is *transactional*—an invoice represents a single business transaction at one point in the past. But your customer record doesn't represent a single transaction with your customer. Instead, it represents an association you have with that customer. In general, transactional data should *never* change once the transaction is complete. Lookup fields solve the problem of saving transactional data.

Lookups

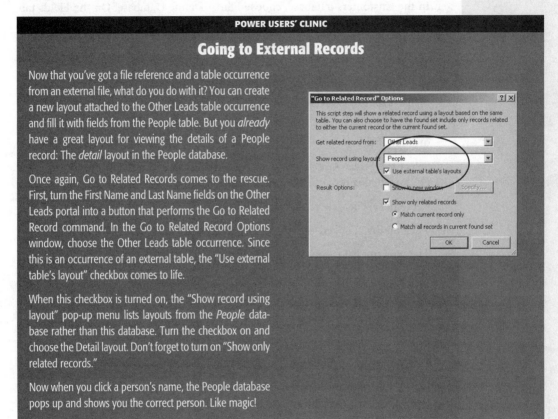

Going to External Records

Now that you've got a file reference and a table occurrence from an external file, what do you do with it? You can create a new layout attached to the Other Leads table occurrence and fill it with fields from the People table. But you *already* have a great layout for viewing the details of a People record: The *detail* layout in the People database.

Once again, Go to Related Records comes to the rescue. First, turn the First Name and Last Name fields on the Other Leads portal into a button that performs the Go to Related Record command. In the Go to Related Record Options window, choose the Other Leads table occurrence. Since this is an occurrence of an external table, the "Use external table's layout" checkbox comes to life.

When this checkbox is turned on, the "Show record using layout" pop-up menu lists layouts from the *People* database rather than this database. Turn the checkbox on and choose the Detail layout. Don't forget to turn on "Show only related records."

Now when you click a person's name, the People database pops up and shows you the correct person. Like magic!

While related fields automatically show new data, lookups use a semi-automatic approach. If you change a customer record, it *won't* affect the fields in the Invoices record at all. But if you change the Job ID on an *invoice* record, the lookup triggers again, and FileMaker fetches the new customer's data. Additionally, you can *change* the data in a field formatted with Auto-Enter lookup at any time—for a one-time address change, for example. This semi-automatic approach to updating data turns out to be just the right thing for transactional data like address fields on invoices: When you change the *transaction* record, its fields update appropriately, but when you change *source* records (the address fields in your Customer record), FileMaker leaves the transaction alone.

Creating Lookups

To create a lookup, you define a field normally but add an Auto-Enter option called *Looked-up value.* You can also add a lookup to an existing field. Simply click the field in the fields list, then click the Options button. The following steps explain how to define a new lookup field:

1. **In the Customers database, choose File → Define Database. On the Fields tab, from the Table pop-up menu, choose Invoices.**

   You see the fields in the Invoices table—and you're ready to add a new one. You start by adding a lookup field for the customer's street address.

2. **In the Field Name box, enter *Street Address* and make sure the Type pop-up menu is set to Text. Click Create.**

   FileMaker adds the new field to the field list. Right now, though, it's just an ordinary field.

3. **Select the Street Address field in the field list and click Options. In the Field Options dialog box, click the Auto-Enter tab.**

   Remember, FileMaker automatically enters a lookup field's value for you.

4. **Turn on the "Looked-up value" checkbox.**

   The Lookup dialog box appears (Figure 8-22).

Figure 8-22:
Imagine you have a table of currency exchange rates. Some of the currencies didn't have data available the day you gathered the rates, so those rate fields are blank. If you use a lookup to refresh exchange rates in your Products database, you don't want to wipe out the existing exchange rate in this case. Instead, you'd rather keep last week's value, so you turn on the "Don't copy contents if empty" option.

5. **Make sure the "Starting with table" pop-up menu is set to Invoices.**

It almost certainly is set, because in this case, the context is clear. You're defining a field in the Invoices table, so that's the field's perspective. If you have a table on the graph multiple times, you might have to change the "Starting with table" pop-up, and doing so will influence how the lookup finds related data.

6. **From the "Lookup from related table" pop-up menu, choose Customers.**

As soon as you choose a table, the "Copy value from field" list is populated with all the fields in the Customers table. You're interested in the Street Address field's value.

7. **In the "Copy value from field" list, choose Street Address. Turn off the "Don't copy contents if empty" checkbox.**

If you turn off "Don't copy contents if empty," FileMaker dutifully copies the empty value, wiping out data in the lookup field. If you turn this option on instead, FileMaker leaves the lookup field untouched—its value before the lookup remains in place.

8. **In the "If no exact match, then" group, turn on the "use" radio button and leave the associated text box empty.**

If there is no customer record, the street address field should be *blank*. If you leave this set to "do not copy," any existing address (for a different customer perhaps) is left in the field. (See the box on page 362 for other "If no exact match, then" options.)

You're done. Click OK three times to back out of all the dialog boxes. Now switch to the Invoices layout and add the new field to it (page 143). When you choose a job from the Jobs table, the Invoices address field now looks up the appropriate address from the Customer table, provided you've entered addresses for your customers.

Note: If you're not using the version of this database that's pre-populated with data from the Missing Manuals Web site (page xxiv), and you want to see this in action, give one of your customers some address information and a job.

To finish your Invoices improvements, add lookup fields for the following customer information. Use the same options as in the steps on the previous pages, or to save clicks, duplicate the Street Address field, change its name, and then just change the field from which it looks up. You get all the other lookup settings for free. When you're done, you can arrange your Invoices layout like the one in Figure 8-23.

- Company Name.

- First Name.

- Last Name.

- City.

- State.

- Zip Code.

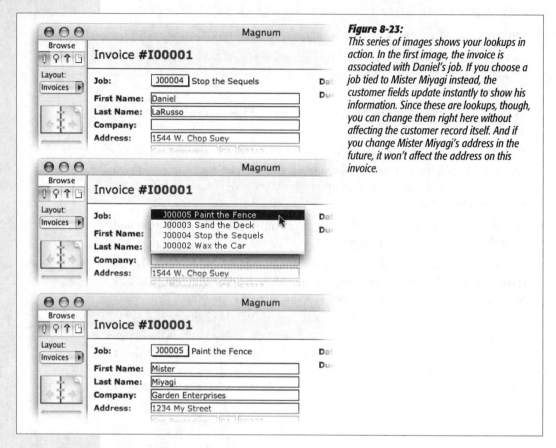

Figure 8-23:
This series of images shows your lookups in action. In the first image, the invoice is associated with Daniel's job. If you choose a job tied to Mister Miyagi instead, the customer fields update instantly to show his information. Since these are lookups, though, you can change them right here without affecting the customer record itself. And if you change Mister Miyagi's address in the future, it won't affect the address on this invoice.

Triggering a Lookup

Normally you *trigger a lookup* whenever you change the data in the key field on which the relationship is based. That's why changing the Job ID field makes File-Maker look up the address information again.

Sometimes you have a reason to cause a lookup to occur *without* changing the key field. For example, suppose a new customer hires you. You do work for her for three months, but never receive payment—despite sending three invoices. You finally decide it's time to ask her what's up, and that's when you discover you've been sending them to the *wrong address*. You mistyped her address in the Customers layout and now all your invoices are incorrect too.

She agrees to pay you as soon as you mail the invoices to her correct address. You can correct her address in the Customers table, but that doesn't affect the old invoices. Luckily, you can easily fix them, too—with the Relookup Field Contents command. To use it, you first click the field that normally triggers the lookup—the Job ID field in this case. Then you choose Records → Relookup Field Contents command. You see the message shown in Figure 8-24.

Figure 8-24:
When you run the Relookup Field Contents command, FileMaker shows this message. It's careful to let you know just how many records you'll be updating. That's because you can't undo this action. If you lookup new address information into old invoices accidentally, you lose historical data. If you're sure you want to proceed, click OK.

Tip: To get into the Job ID field, just click it and be sure to choose the job that's already selected. After you make your choice, the Relookup Field Contents command works as expected.

Advanced Relationships

In this chapter and the previous one, you've only created simple relationships with one rule and keys that match exactly, but you can create relationships that go far beyond those basic concepts. And even if you don't have a very complicated database, you need to know how these advanced relationships work.

For example, you might have a table of Student Test Scores that contains all the tests for every kid in your school. You can view a classroom's scores on a specific test by making a relationship that matches two key fields: the Classroom ID and the Test ID. You can also find all the kids who're failing by matching every test score that's less than 70 points. Sure, you can perform a search in your Test Scores table and add some summary fields to a report to do the same tasks, but you're limited by the fact that the subsummary parts and their fields don't show up in Browse mode, and by the need to perform the search again every time you want to see the data. With the techniques below, you can make this data available with just the switch of a layout or a Go to Related Record command (page 336).

Relationships with More than One Criterion

First, you can assign more than one rule to a relationship. For instance, you already added a relationship between Customers and People that matches based on state. Suppose you want to be more restrictive: You want to show only people who live in the same *city* and state.

It's easier than it sounds:

1. **In the Customers database, go the Define Database window's Relationships tab (page 307), and select the relationship line between Customers and People.**

   The easiest way to select a relationship is to click the "=" box in the middle of the line (it provides a nice big target). When you select the relationship, the line gets slightly thicker and the box highlights.

2. **Click the Edit Relationship button (page 331).**

   You can also just double-click the relationship. Either way, you see the Edit Relationship dialog box, as shown in Figure 8-25.

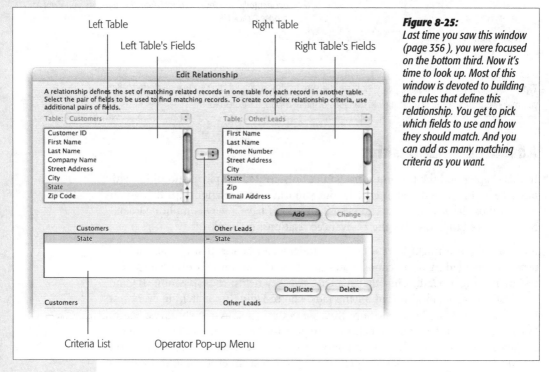

Figure 8-25:
Last time you saw this window (page 356), you were focused on the bottom third. Now it's time to look up. Most of this window is devoted to building the rules that define this relationship. You get to pick which fields to use and how they should match. And you can add as many matching criteria as you want.

3. **In the left table's field list, choose *City*.**

   The City field highlights.

4. **In the right table's field list, choose *City*.**

   You've now described a new criterion for your rule: *Customers::City = Other Leads::City*

Note: The Edit Relationship dialog box tries to mimic the layout you've created on your Relationships Graph. That is, if your Customers TO is to the left of your People TO in the graph, that's how they'll appear in the dialog box. If two TOs are on top of one another (vertically aligned), then the table on top appears at the left of the dialog box. The order shown in these lists has no effect on how the TOs relate to one another, but if you're having trouble reading this dialog box, close it, rearrange your graph, and reopen it.

5. **Click the Add button.**

   FileMaker adds this criterion to the criteria list. You now have *two* criteria for this relationship:

   ```
   Customers::State = Other Leads::State
   AND
   Customers::City = Other Leads::City
   ```

6. **Click OK.**

   FileMaker uncovers the relationship graph.

You've just defined a relationship with *two* criteria, sometimes called a *multi-key relationship,* for the obvious reason that it uses two key fields. In order for two records to relate, they must meet *both* criteria. In other words, a person must be in the same city *and* the same state as a customer to show up in his portal. Figure 8-26 shows the new relationship in the graph.

Figure 8-26:
When a relationship is based on more than one criterion—like this one between Customers and Other leads—FileMaker forks the relationship line on each end. From this line, you can see that City matches City and State matches State. The = sign in the box in the middle of the line tells you these fields must match exactly.

If you test your Other Leads portal now, it shows only people living in the customer's city.

Other Relationship Operators

In addition to adding *more* rules to a relationship definition (by defining multiple criteria), you can also base relationships on different *kinds* of rules. Each relationship in your ER diagram for your database mandates that the fields on either side match exactly. This type of relationship is called an *equijoin,* in honor of the = sign that defines it. Sometimes, though, you want to relate records without an exact match. When you make a non-equijoin relationship (don't you just love technical terms?), you use FileMaker's other comparative operators:

- **Equals** (=). The keys on both sides of the relationship match exactly.

- **Not Equals** ( ).All records but those with matching keys relate to one another.

- **Less Than** (<). Keys in the table on the left side of the dialog box must be less than keys in the table on the right side.

- **Less Than or Equal To** (≤). Keys in the table on the left side of the dialog box must be less than or equal to the keys on the right side of the table.

- **Greater Than** (>). Keys in the table on the left side of the dialog box must be greater than keys in the table on the right side.

- **Greater Than or Equal To** (≥). Keys in the table on the left side of the dialog box must be greater than or equal to the keys on the right side of the table.

- **Cartesian Join** (x). All records in the table on the left are related to all records in the table on the right, regardless of the value in their key fields.

As you work with your database, you might decide you need a quicker way to find invoices. You often want to see every invoice in a specified date range, and sometimes only those that are above a certain total amount due. Using relationships, you can create a new layout that makes it easy for you to see the invoices you want. You enter a start date, end date, and minimum amount into global fields. A portal displays every matching invoice.

Creating the Invoice Finder

To set up your new relationship, you need three new global fields (page 352). Since the global fields aren't associated with any particular table, you can create a *new* table to hold them. You also need a new relationship that matches fields in the Invoices table with these global fields. This job is the sort that benefits from its own table occurrence group, as you saw on page 354. Call this group *Invoice Finder*.

To get the portal to show the right invoices, you need a relationship that uses your new global fields, and it'll have slightly more complicated rules than you've seen before:

```
Invoice Finder: Globals::Start Date ≤ Invoice Finder: Invoices::Date
AND
Invoice Finder: Globals::End Date ≥ Invoice Finder: Invoices::Date
AND
Invoice Finder: Globals::Minimum Amount ≤ Invoice Finder: Invoices::Amount
Due
```

These rules say that an invoice should match if its date is *on or after* ( )the global start date, *on or before* (≤) the global end date, and its amount due is *more than* (>) the minimum amount global field.

Below are the steps for creating a new table, defining some global fields in that new table and then using your creations in a new table occurrence group.

FREQUENTLY ASKED QUESTIONS

Globals and Relationships

I don't get it. I thought relationships were supposed to hook different records together, but a global field isn't associated with any record at all. How come you keep using global fields to create relationships?

When you set out to design your database in Chapter 7, you learned how to organize your information into tables and construct the relationships that make them work together. But relationships can do a whole lot more.

As the Invoice Finder example (page 372) and the Expense Assignment example (page 354) illustrate, relationships can be part of an overall interface (or layout) that performs a specific task. For example, when you use a global field in a relationship, it works just fine. Put an ID in the global and FileMaker makes a match one or more records on the other side.

This kind of relationship doesn't define a connection between records—rather, it just gives you temporary access to related records.

Since global fields can't be indexed, the relationship doesn't work in the other direction. As the picture here shows, FileMaker doesn't connect the relationship line in the graph directly to the global field. This picture is a visual cue to let you know this relationship works only one way.

One last point: If you want to use a global field from another table, you don't need a relationship at all. Since global fields aren't associated with any record, you can view and modify them from anywhere. For example, you can put the Global Invoice ID field on any layout in the entire database, and it works just fine.

Not Quite Connected

You've done most of this stuff before in other tutorials, so although there are a lot of steps, they should all be pretty familiar already:

1. **In the Customers database, go to the Define Database window's Tables tab. Create a new table called Invoice Finder.**

   FileMaker adds the new table to the table list.

2. **Click the Fields tab. Then, in the Field name box, enter** *Start Date.* **Make the field a Date type, and then click Create.**

   This field holds the starting date you're searching for.

3. **Click the Options button. When the Field Options dialog box appears, click the Storage tab and turn on the "Use global storage" checkbox. Click the OK button.**

   Since this field isn't holding data about an entity, it makes sense to use a global.

4. **Repeat steps 2–3 to create two more global fields. One, a global date field, should be called** *End Date.* **The second is a global number field called** *Minimum Amount.*

   You've finished creating your three global fields.

5. **Switch to the Relationships tab. Double-click the Invoice Finder occurrence FileMaker made for you and change its name to** *Invoice Finder: Globals.*

   Now this occurrence has the prefix you want for the new table occurrence group.

6. **Add a new occurrence of the Invoices table called** *Invoice Finder: Invoices,* **and a new occurrence of the Jobs table called** *Invoice Finder: Jobs.*

   Since your portal shows invoices and the job associated with each invoice, you need these tables in your group as well.

7. **Drag the Invoice Finder: Invoices::Job ID field onto the Invoice Finder: Jobs:: Job ID field to create a relationship.**

   You've just told FileMaker that the Job ID field relates these two tables. Now you'll use that field to complete the relationship.

8. **Click the New Relationship button (Figure 8-27) to open the Edit Relationship dialog box. From the left table pop-up menu, choose** *Invoice Finder: Globals.* **Then, from the right table pop-up menu, choose** *Invoice Finder: Invoices.*

Add/Edit relationship

Figure 8-27:
You haven't used the Add/Edit Relationship button before because you've always used the drag-and-drop method to define relationships. But if the relationship you're creating is more complex, this button skips the drag altogether and goes straight to the Edit Relationship dialog box, so you don't have to delete or edit the equijoin relationship that FileMaker creates when you drag.

The left list is filled with the global fields you created in the earlier steps; the right list shows the fields from the *Invoice Finder: Invoices* table occurrence. Next, you select the two key fields and tell FileMaker how to relate these TOs together.

9. **From the left table field list, choose Start Date. From the Operator pop-up menu (it's between the two field lists), choose ≤ (Mac OS X) or <= (Windows).**

    This symbol tells FileMaker you want the field on the left to match when it's *less than or equal to* the field you select on the right side.

10. **From the right table field list, choose Date, and then click Add.**

    The Date field tells the relationship what value to compare to the Start Date in the Globals table. In other words, you want the relationship to match only when the Start Date is *before* the Invoice Date.

    Later on, you'll create a portal that uses this relationship to display only certain records. The criteria you chose tell the portal to show only Invoice records that are dated on or after the date entered in the global Start Date field.

11. **Repeat the steps, but this time, from the left table field list, choose the End Date field. From the right table field list, choose the Date field, and from the Operator pop-up menu, the ≥ or >= option.**

    When you click Add, FileMaker adds the second criteria to the list. This part tells the portal to display records that are on or before the date in the global End Date field. The relationships between the Start Date and End Date fields together determine the range of records the portal displays.

12. **Repeat steps 9 through 10 again, choosing Minimum Amount from the left table, Amount Due from the right table, and ≤ or <= for the operator. Click OK when you're done with the third criteria.**

    The third part of this complex relationship system lets you type a minimum value in a global field to further restrict the display of related records in the portal.

    FileMaker returns you to the graph. It should look like Figure 8-28.

To test your new relationship, create a new layout and attach it to the Invoice Finder: Globals table occurrence. Add the three global fields and a portal based on the Invoice Finder: Invoices relationship. As you put values in the three global fields, the portal updates to show the matching invoices. You can see it in action in Figure 8-29.

Note: The Invoice Finder table has no records. Since it has only global fields, you'd think this lack of records wouldn't be a problem, but it is. Portals don't work properly when you have no records. To clear this problem up, just create a new empty record.

So what has all this work gotten you? As a designer, this technique of using global fields in a complex relationship to populate a portal has improved your understanding of relationships and tested your skill in applying that knowledge. People who use your database benefit most practically. Now they can see a group of invoices at a glance, without having to do a search, then go to a list view of their data. In the next section, you'll learn some techniques that you can apply to make this layout even handier. You'll learn how to create a calculation field that summarizes the value of the invoices in your portal (page 395).

Figure 8-28:
Your latest relationship (between Invoice Finder: Globals and Invoice Finder: Invoices) connects three fields to two. The box in the middle of the line now has an X instead of an = sign. This just means you're using multiple operators in your relationship.

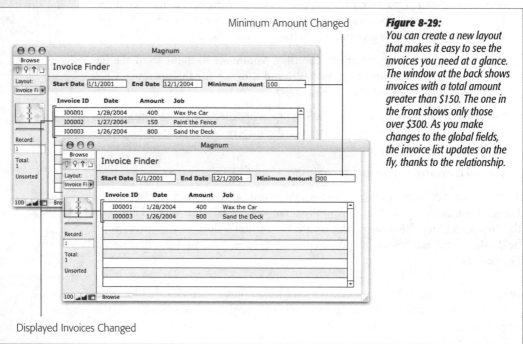

Minimum Amount Changed

Displayed Invoices Changed

Figure 8-29:
You can create a new layout that makes it easy to see the invoices you need at a glance. The window at the back shows invoices with a total amount greater than $150. The one in the front shows only those over $300. As you make changes to the global fields, the invoice list updates on the fly, thanks to the relationship.

Part Four: Calculations

4

Introduction to Calculations

Fields and layouts form the basis of every database: You can't have a FileMaker database without them. Using just what you know so far, you can build all kinds of useful systems that store data, from an address list to a catalog of products.

But if you want to do the really useful stuff with your data—total an invoice, analyze trends, compare figures—you need specific tools. For those tasks, File-Maker provides *Calculation fields* and a whole drawer full of functions that let you examine, compare, and combine field values. And calculations aren't just limited to number-crunching tasks. You can use them to find out about the computer your database is running on, track who's logged into the system, monitor their privileges, and then perform logical tests based on what you find. You'll start by learning how FileMaker handles calculations, and then you'll see how some common functions can take your database up to a new level of power.

Understanding Calculations

A calculation is a mathematical formula: It shows how different things combine to come up with an answer. But even if you hated algebra class, don't close the book yet! Instead of the Xs, Ys, and Zs of the math world, FileMaker lets you use your own fields to supply your formula with data—a much more intuitive approach.

FileMaker calculations can also do more than just math. For starters, you can do calculations on time, date, timestamp, container, and text fields, too. (See the box on page 383 for an example.) Way back in Chapter 3, you learned that FileMaker can create *calculation fields* (page 94). Calculation fields work just like any other

FileMaker field, except that you can't type data into them. Instead, they use a calculation to determine their own value.

You can use a calculation field just like any other field: Put it on a layout, use it in Find mode, and even use it in *other* calculation fields. But as a calculation field, its value always stays up-to-date automatically. If the price or quantity changes, the calculation updates the data in your field without your doing anything. Figure 9-1 shows where calculation fields could benefit your invoices layout.

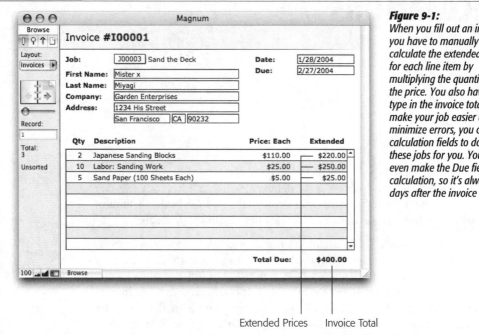

Figure 9-1:
When you fill out an invoice, you have to manually calculate the extended price for each line item by multiplying the quantity times the price. You also have to type in the invoice total. To make your job easier and minimize errors, you can use calculation fields to do both these jobs for you. You can even make the Due field a calculation, so it's always 30 days after the invoice date.

Furthermore, calculations aren't limited to working inside fields. Once you understand the basic concept of calculations, you gain all kinds of new FileMaker skills. For example, you can use calculations with the Records → Replace Field Contents command (page 46). Instead of replacing the data in every record with the *same* value, the calculation can produce a unique value for each record. You can start using the Auto-Enter Calculation and Validation Calculation field options, making those features much more powerful. Scripts, as you'll learn in Part 5, use calculations a lot. And finally, if you're using FileMaker Advanced, you can use calculations to create custom menus and custom menu commands (page 686).

Creating a Calculation

A simple example speaks more loudly than several pages of explanation, so you start off by adding a *calculation* to an existing number field to the database you built in Chapters 7 and 8. As your database now stands, when you add line items to an invoice, you have to type the quantity, price for each item, *and* the extended price, as shown in Figure 9-1. But since the extended price is always the price times the quantity, why not let FileMaker handle the repetitive work while you do the creative stuff?

Note: To work through the examples in this chapter, you can download the Customers database from the "Missing CD" page at *www.missingmanuals.com*.

Here's how you add a calculation to a number field:

1. **In the Customers database, choose File → Define Database, and make sure you're on the Fields tab. From the Table pop-up menu, choose Line Items.**

   That's the table with your Extended Price field in it.

2. **In the field list, select the Extended Price field. From the Type pop-up menu, choose Calculation; then click Change.**

   FileMaker warns you that when it converts the field, it changes (read: deletes) any information already in the field. See Figure 9-2.

Figure 9-2:
This warning is serious. Your new calculation overwrites existing data. But even if you write a calculation, there's a way out, so long as you haven't OK'd the Define Database dialog box. Just click its Cancel button and you'll get the chance to discard all the changes you've made in the dialog box.

3. **Click OK.**

   As shown in Figure 9-3, FileMaker asks you what calculation you have in mind.

4. **In the Calculation Box, type *Price Each * Quantity*.**

   The calculation box holds the calculation itself. In this case, you've just added a brand-new calculation that multiplies the contents of the Price Each by the contents of the Quantity field.

5. **In the Define Database window, click OK, and then OK again.**

   You're now back in your database. Switch to the Invoices layout and add a line item. You see that the Extended Price field updates *automatically* to reflect the proper price.

Tip: If FileMaker complains about not being able to find a field when you click OK, check the spelling of your field names.

Table Pop-up Menu   Table Occurrence Pop-up Menu   Function Type Pop-up Menu

Figure 9-3:
Whenever you edit a calculation, you see a window just like this one. There's a lot going on here, including the fundamental step of typing your calculation in the box. You'll learn how to use all these options in the rest of this chapter.

Result Type Pop-up Menu   Calculation Box

Field List   Operators   Function List

The Structure of a Calculation

If you accidentally mistyped or misspelled a field name in the example above, you already know that FileMaker is a little picky about how you create a calculation. Clearly, syntax (the order of elements and the punctuation in your calculation) matters. Still, a calculation is really just text, arranged in a specific order. Here you learn the basic parts of a calculation through a couple of examples.

Tip: Calculations are often called *calcs* for short, or formulas. Although there are some slight differences between a calculation and a formula, people usually use the terms interchangeably. Note: Sometimes, a formula is so useful, or common, that FileMaker defines it as a reusable formula, also known as a *function* (page 400).

A calculation can be short and simple:

```
Pi * Diameter
```

Or it can be more complicated:

```
Case (
    Shape = "Circle" ; Pi * (Diameter/2) ^ 2 ;
    Shape = "Rectangle" ; ShapeLength * Width ;
)
```

Note: FileMaker won't let you name a field the same thing as an existing function. The field containing the length of a rectangular object has the unwieldy name "ShapeLength" to avoid confusion with File-Maker's Length function. The field name "Width" is fine, because there's no Width function.

FREQUENTLY ASKED QUESTION

Text **Calculations?**

Aren't calculations just for numbers?

Many people, when first learning FileMaker, see the Define Database window's Calculation field type and assume it's for numbers. Too bad, because calculations can do all this:

- Calculations can pick apart *text* and put it together in different ways (in the next chapter, you'll use a calculation to make a Web address that links to a customer's address map). You can even modify fonts, sizes, colors, and styles (turn every occurrence of the word "FileMaker" to bold text, for instance).

- You can do math on *dates, times,* and *timestamps.* You can find out how old someone is based on their birth date; figure out how long you worked on a job; or see which payment came first.

- Using calculations, you can use summary values (page 262) without switching to Preview mode.

- If you've stored a reference to a file in a *container* field, you can use a calculation to retrieve the *path* to the original file.

You can even convert one kind of value into another when you use calculations. For example, if you have a text field that contains *12/29/2001,* you can use a calculation to turn that date into a proper date value.

So you see, calculations can do much more than add a few numbers together.

In fact, calculations can be *really* long and complicated if you need them to be—up to 30,000 characters. Practically speaking, the only limit on the complexity of a calculation is your patience for creating it.

Regardless of its complexity, a calculation, or formula, is made up of three different elements: *field references, constants,* and *operators.* In the first example, "Pi" is a constant, "*" is an operator, and "Diameter" is the name of a field. The second example uses a function, called a case statement. In that example, "Shape" and "Diameter" are field references, "Circle" and "2" are constants, and "=," "*," and "^" are operators.

Field references have *values* that FileMaker replaces in the formula once it goes to work on your formula. First, all the values are replaced, then the operators tell File-Maker what to do to those values, and finally, FileMaker returns a *result* in your field.

You'll see these terms again in the next few chapters. Here are some helpful definitions:

- **Field References** are just what they sound like. They refer FileMaker to data that's in the field you're referring to. Since the data inside those fields may change on each record in your database, the values that get replaced in each record are different and may yield a different result.

- **Constants** stay the same each time FileMaker does the calculation. See page 385 for details.

- **Operators** tell FileMaker how to treat the values in the calculation. See page 386 for a listing of operators and what they do.

- FileMaker has more than 180 defined **Functions** that you can use as shortcuts when you create your formulas. You learn about some of the most common functions later in this chapter. Chapter 11 introduces you to more advanced functions, and in Chapter 12 you learn how FileMaker Advanced lets you create your own reusable functions, called Custom Functions.

- Each calculation has a **Result**. This result is, in a sense, the "answer" to the calculation. The result of the first calculation above is the circumference of the circle. The second calculation is a little more complex: Its result is the area of a circle *or* a rectangle, depending on the value in the Shape field. (Don't worry if this calculation doesn't make sense to you. It will before too long.)

The result of a calculation has a *type* (just like every field has a type). The type can be any of the standard field types—Text, Number, Date, Time, Timestamp, or Container—or a type called *Boolean*. A Boolean value has only two possible results: yes or no. (Chapter 10 goes into more detail about calculations and data types.)

Note: Sometimes people call a Boolean value "True or False" or "One or Zero" instead. Which term you use doesn't matter much if you just remember that there is a yes-like value and a no-like value.

Fields

The most exciting thing about calculations is learning all the new things you can do with the fields that hold all your data. But the underlying principle is simple: When you reference a field in a calculation, FileMaker takes the data stored in the field and uses its value when it determines the calculation's result. For example, if a field has this calculation:

```
First Name & " " & Last Name
```

When FileMaker performs (or *evaluates*) the calculation, it replaces the First Name and Last Name field names with the person's first and last names from a given record. The field type determines the value's type: A number field has a number value; a text field has a text value; and so forth.

Note: FileMaker uses the value *stored* in (not displayed in) a field. So if you have a number field with 3.1415926 as the stored value, and you've formatted the field on the layout to display only two decimal places, FileMaker uses all seven digits of the stored value to do its math. If you don't want it to use all those digits, use the *Round* function (page 398).

POWER USERS' CLINIC

Evaluating Calculations: Now or Later

When you use a calculation, you're asking FileMaker to do something with your fields, constants, and operators and come up with a result. In technical lingo, FileMaker *evaluates* the calculation. *When* the evaluation takes place depends on *where* in your database FileMaker encounters the calculation. Sometimes FileMaker evaluates right away, as when you're calculating an Extended Price. As soon as you type in either a Price or a Quantity, FileMaker tries to multiply out the value. But because one of the fields is empty, the Extended Price calculation has a result of zero (because any value times zero equals zero). When you provide the second value, FileMaker immediately does the math and shows you your result.

If you define a new calculation field after you already have data in your database, FileMaker spends some time updating the calculation as soon as you go to the Define Database dialog box and click OK.

You may see a progress bar if you have a slower computer and a lot of records.

When you run the Records → Replace Field Contents command, for example, FileMaker evaluates the calculation you specify once for every record as soon as you click OK. As above, this might take a couple of seconds, but it's happening just as soon as FileMaker can plow through your found set.

- Validation calculations evaluate whenever you change the field, or exit the record (you get to decide). See page 405 for more on these.

- Calculation used in scripts evaluate whenever you run the script. Part 5 of this book is all about scripts.

Constants

As handy as it is to refer FileMaker to a field to find the values in your calculations, you don't want to have to store everything in fields just to use it in a calculation. When a value is going to be the same for every record, it's time to call in a constant. You simply include that value right in the calculation.

Number constants

Sales tax is one of the most common constants. If you need to add sales tax to your order, you can just type the percentage right in the calculation, since it's the same for everybody:

```
Order Total * 1.0625
```

You can enter numbers in any of the formats supported by number fields:

- 37

- .65

- 28.3

- 6.02E23

Text constants

You can also use a constant to have FileMaker plunk some text in with your results. If you want a text value instead of a number, put it in quotes:

```
Age & " years old"
```

Everything within the quote marks is a *text constant* (some people call it a *string* as in "string of characters"). Those quote marks are very important (see box "Quotes in Quotes"). Suppose you have a field called First Name, and a calculation like this:

```
"This is my First Name"
```

The quote marks enclose the text that is also a field name, so the result of this calculation is always (*constantly*) "This is my First Name." FileMaker makes no connection whatsoever between the First Name field and the words "First Name" in the text, because the text is in quote marks.

Forgetting quote marks around a text string, or putting them in the wrong place, can make FileMaker whiny. If you make the following calculation:

```
"This is" my First Name
```

FileMaker throws up a warning message that says, "The specified field could not be found," when you try to click OK to close the Define Database dialog box. The characters "my First Name" are highlighted in your calculation so you can tell exactly which part of the calculation confuses FileMaker. Move your quotes appropriately, and FileMaker stops telling you that it can't find your field reference. Here's the correct answer:

```
"This is my " & First Name
```

Operators

If a calculation could only contain one thing, it wouldn't be much good: How often do you want to calculate a field value, number, or text value you already know? The power of calculations comes from their ability to combine different values to come up with a new and interesting value. This situation is where *operators* come in. An operator takes the values on either side of it (the *operands*) and *does something* (operates) with them.

A special symbol or word stands for each operator. This calculation uses the + (addition) operator:

```
3 + 2
```

In this case, the + operator is given 3 and 2 as operands. When the calculation evaluates, the operator and its operands combine to produce a single value.

Operators come in three flavors:

- **Mathematical and logical operators** combine two values into one. The + operator is a good example; It takes two number values and adds them together. Its resulting value is the sum of the two numbers.

- **Comparison operators** compare two values. For example, the = operator tells you if two values are exactly the same. This kind of operator always produces a Boolean value.

- **Parenthesis** operators are used to group parts of a calculation together. Remember your 8th grade math teacher carrying on about the "order of operations"? FileMaker remembers too, and it uses those same rules to figure out how to evaluate calculations. If the rules don't work for you, parentheses let you take more control.

FREQUENTLY ASKED QUESTION

Quotes in Quotes

You're saying that I should use quote marks to incorporate a word or phrase into the results of a calculation. But what if I want to put a quote mark inside my text?

You're out of luck.

No, just kidding. Just put a backslash ("\") in front of the quote mark, and FileMaker pretends it doesn't exist when it analyzes your calculation. When a quote is preceded with a backslash, you say it's escaped, and "\" is called the escape character. When you put the escape character in front of another character, it tells FileMaker to ignore any special meaning that character might have and treat it as ordinary text. It looks like this:

"My line was, \"There's a lady with slacks on lying in the gutter! Who does she belong to?\" Can you believe that?"

This calculation is just one long text constant. The two quote marks inside it are escaped.

If you're a real troublemaker, your next question is, "What if I want to put a real backslash *and* quote mark inside my text constant?"

Luckily, that's easy too. Just escape the backslash and then escape the quote:

```
"I really want this: \\\" inside my text"
```

This calculation evaluates to:

```
I really want this: \" inside my text
```

Note: Two buttons in the Operators section of the Specify Calculation window aren't really operators at all. The ¶ is a special character that tells FileMaker you want a new line in your calculation result and the quote marks are for entering text values, as explained in the box above.

Mathematical operators

The most obvious use for a calculation is to do a little math. Maybe your database of products includes fields for dimensions (Length, Width, and Height) and you want to know the volume. This calculation does the trick:

```
Length * Width * Height
```

It consists of three field values and two copies of the * (multiplication) operator. The result is just what you'd get if you used a calculator to multiply the three field values together.

FileMaker includes operators for basic math:

- + for addition

- - for subtraction

- * for multiplication

- / for division

- ^ for exponentiation ("to the power of" a value)

The concatenation operator

While the mathematical operators combine numbers, the & (concatenation) operator works with text. It hooks together two text values:

```
Length & " inches"
```

If the Length field contains 36, the result of this calculation is *36 inches*.

Tip: FileMaker is such a good friend that it can mix numeric values and text together in the same calculation. If you use a number value or field in a place where FileMaker is expecting text, it just converts the number into text and gets on with its business.

Comparison operators

You often need to compare two values to learn about them. For example, you may need to add an additional shipping charge if the total weight of an order is more than 20 pounds. All comparison operators result in a Boolean value (page 234).

FileMaker can compare things in several ways:

- = tells you if two values are the same.

- ≠ or <> tells you if the two values are different.

- > tells you if the first value is bigger than the second.

- < tells you if the second value is bigger than the first.

- ≥ or >= tells you if the first value is bigger than or equal to the second.

- ≤ or <= tells you if the second value is bigger than or equal to the first.

Logical operators

The logical operators evaluate values and come up with a Boolean (Yes/No) result (page 234). Unlike the other operators, most of them are recognizable words.

- The *and* operator tells you if both values are Yes. The calculation below uses the *and* operator. It evaluates to Yes if the length is more than 3 *and* the height is more than 5.

```
Length > 3 and Height > 5
```

- The *or* operator tells you if *either* value is Yes. The *or* calculation below evaluates to Yes if the length is more than 3 *or* the height is more than 5.

```
Length > 3 or Height > 5
```

- The *xor* operator's function is as offbeat as its name. It stands for *exclusive or.* The *xor* operator tells you when *only one* of your two choices is Yes. Put another way, if you find yourself thinking, "I want one of two things to be true, but *not both* of them," then *xor* saves the day. For instance, you may want to track whether you've billed a customer *or* you've marked her character rating below 3. That formula would look like this:

```
Invoice Sent = Yes xor Character Rating < 3
```

Note: If you can't think of a use for *xor*, don't worry. Most of the time when you need an "or" calculation, you can handle it with plain old *or* and not *exclusive or.*

- The last logical operator, *not*, stands alone: It only works on one value, not two like every other operator. It simply reverses the Boolean value that comes after it. So the calculation below would evaluate to Yes if the length is *not* more than 3.

```
Not Length > 3
```

Note: The comparison and logical operators are usually used with the *logical functions*. Those are covered in Chapter 10.

The ^ Operator

The last—and probably least used—operator is the exponentiation, or ^ operator. This lets you calculate exponents:

```
Pi * Radius ^ 2
```

This calculation uses the exponentiation operator and squares the value in the Radius field.

Parentheses

FileMaker uses standard mathematical rules to decide in what order to evaluate things. The order of evaluation is exponentiation, then multiplication/division, then lastly addition/subtraction. If you need FileMaker to do part of your calculation *first*, before moving onto any other operators, put it in parentheses. The parentheses tell FileMaker to treat everything between them as a single unit.

In the calculation below, FileMaker multiplies 3 and 2 before adding 4, and gives you a result of 10.

```
4 + 3 * 2
```

Even though the + operator comes first in the calculation, FileMaker follows the order of calculation. If you want to add 4 and 3 before multiplying, you need to use parenthesis:

```
(4 + 3) * 2
```

Thus, it sees that it needs to multiply 2 by the value of (4+3). You can see the value of parentheses in calculations like the one below, which calculates the interest on the sum of the balance and service charge. Without the parentheses, FileMaker would calculate the interest on only the service charge and then add that to the balance due, with an entirely different result:

```
(Balance Due + Service Charge) * Interest Rate
```

Note: If you have trouble remembering (nay, understanding) the order of calculation, just use parentheses when in doubt. It certainly doesn't hurt to be *too* explicit.

Functions

Values, fields, and operators alone make for a pretty powerful combination. But if you stop there, you've only scratched the surface. The meat of calculations is found in the Function list (which you saw back in Figure 9-3). A *function* is simply a predefined formula, and FileMaker's list covers most common calculation purposes. If you find a function that already does what you want to do—like average all invoices over a specific time period—use it. When you add these tried-and-true formulas to your calculations, you save time and even help prevent errors.

For example, if you didn't know about functions, you could find your average with a series of fields. First, you'd need to define a calculation field to total all the invoices in your found set. Then you'd need another field to count the invoices in the set and a third one that divides the first field by the second. It would work, but it'd be clumsy and inefficient, since you've created at least two fields that you didn't really need.

Because you often need to find averages, FileMaker gives you a *function* that handles the math in a given field. All you have to do is tell FileMaker *which* field you want to average. The function takes care of figuring out the total of the found set and how many records there are. It looks like this:

```
Average ( Invoice Total )
```

The word "Average" is the function's name. "Invoice Total" is a reference to a field. This field reference is called a *parameter*. Parameters tell the function how to perform its specific calculation. The Average function has only a single parameter, but many functions have two or more.

Parameters are always enclosed in parentheses. (A few functions—most notably, Random—don't need any parameters, so you leave the parentheses off all together.) When there's more than one parameter, they're separated by a semicolon, as in the Date function below:

```
Date ( Month ; Day ; Year )
```

FileMaker has more than *180* functions, divided into 16 groups, as described below. Later in this chapter, you learn how to use some of the more common functions. (Functions come into play in Chapters 10 and 12, as well.)

Note: FileMaker has a lengthy help file (Ctrl-? Or ⌘-?) that lists each function and some sample uses. If you want to explore a function that isn't covered here, open Help, then type in the function's name.

Text functions

Dozens of *text* functions let you work with text values. You can compare them; convert them into other types (like numbers); split them up in various ways; count the number of letters, words, or lines; change case; and replace parts of them with new text values. If you're trying to slice, mix, or examine words, look here first.

Text formatting functions

Text formatting functions let you adjust the font, size, style, and color of all or part of a text value. For instance, you could make the account balance for a customer turn red if it's over $100.

Number functions

Number functions do everything with numbers—from the mundane (rounding) to the esoteric (combinatorics). In between, you can get rid of the decimal part of a number, calculate logarithms and square roots, convert signs, generate random numbers, and perform modulo arithmetic.

Date functions

Date functions make working with dates a breeze. You can safely create date values without worrying about the computer's date settings. You can also pick date values apart (for example, get just the *month* from a date), convert day and month numbers into proper names, and work with weeks and fiscal years.

Time functions

Time functions are few: They create time values from hours, minutes, and seconds, and split times up into the same parts. You use these values most frequently when you're trying to find out how long something took. For instance, if you bill your services hourly, you can create Start Time and Finish Time fields. Then, in a Duration field, you can subtract Finish Time from Start Time to find out how long you worked on a project.

Timestamp functions

There's only one *Timestamp* function: It lets you build a timestamp value from a separate date and a time. If you're creating your own data, you already know that FileMaker needs both a date and a time for a valid Timestamp field and you've planned accordingly. But you may receive data from an outside source in which the date and time aren't already in a single field. No problem, just use the Timestamp function.

Aggregate functions

Aggregate functions calculate statistics such as average, variance, and standard deviation. They can also count things, sum things, and find minimums and maximums. By definition, aggregate functions *gather up* multiple values and find results based on the group as a whole. (See the box below for more detail.)

UP TO SPEED

Aggregate Functions

Usually when you perform a calculation on a group of related records, you use an Aggregate function. These functions take multiple values and combine them in some useful way:

    Sum (10 ; 20 ; 30 ; 40)

But if you refer an aggregate function to even one related field, FileMaker aggregates that field's values from *every* related record:

    Sum (Line Items::Extended Price)

Finally, you can also reference a single repeating field. When you do, FileMaker combines each repetition into a single value.

This special behavior for related or repeating fields works only if you use a single parameter. You can't, for example, sum two sets of related fields as one like this:

    Sum (Line Items::Extended Price ; Line
          Items::Shipping Charge)

If you refer to more than one field in a Sum function, it only looks at the *first* related value or repetition for each field. Of course, if you did want to total two related fields, you could do so by calling Sum twice and add their results:

    Sum (Line Items::Extended Price) +
    Sum (Line Items::Shipping Charge)

Summary functions

There's only one *Summary* function—GetSummary. Its sole purpose is to let you use the value of a summary field (page 262) in your calculations. In the olden days, before FileMaker was the robust relational database it is now, the GetSummary function was the best way to sort and summarize certain kinds of data. Now that FileMaker is relational, you use calculations through table occurrences to do that work, as you saw in the last chapter.

Note: GetSummary is included in FileMaker 8 so that files created in older versions still work. Nowadays, though, GetSummary serves primarily as a way for one FileMaker developer to ridicule another as in, "Get a load of that guy. He thinks he's a hotshot, but his database is spilling over with GetSummary functions."

Repeating functions

Repeating functions work with repeating fields, and some of them work with *related* fields as well (see Part 4). You can make non-repeating fields and repeating fields work together properly in calculations, access specific repeating values, or get the *last* non-empty value. Since repeating fields have limited uses in these days of related tables within files, so do these functions. However, there are a few valid uses, as you'll learn in Chapter 11.

Financial functions

Financial functions make the MBAs in the audience feel right at home. Calculate present value, future value, net present value, and payments. Non-MBAs could calculate the cost of competing loans with these functions.

Trigonometric functions

Trigonometric functions, on the other hand, bring back terrible memories from high school math. If you're making a business-related database, don't worry; you don't even have to look at these functions. But engineers and scientists will know what to do with this bunch: sine, cosine, and tangent. They can also convert between radians and degrees. And because everybody has trouble remembering it, you get Pi out to 400 decimal places.

Logical functions

Logical functions are a powerful grouping. These functions can make *decisions* based on calculated values (if the due date is more than six months ago, double the balance due); functions to evaluate *other* calculations inside your calculations; functions to figure out if fields are empty or contain invalid data; performance-enhancing functions to define and use variables (page 451); and functions to perform lookups inside calculations (page 447). Chapter 11 is where you learn when and how to use these big dogs of the function world.

Get functions

Get functions pull up information about the computer, user, database, or FileMaker Pro itself. They make up the largest group (70 in all). You can, for example, find out the computer's screen resolution, the current layout's name, the computer's network address, the current user's name, or the size of any database window. This list just scratches the surface, though. If you're looking for information about the current state of FileMaker, the computer, or the user, you can probably find it with a Get function.

Design functions

Design functions tell you about your database's structure. You can get a list of tables, fields, layouts, or value lists; or details about any of these items. You won't need most of these functions until you become an advanced database designer indeed. But one notable exception is ValueListItems, which gives you a list of the values in a value list, separated by paragraph breaks.

Custom functions

If you have FileMaker Advanced, you can create your very own *custom* functions and have them show up on the list. Once you have them, you (or anyone you let define fields in your database) can choose them just like the built-in functions. (See Chapter 12 for details on creating and using custom functions.)

External functions

If you're not using plug-ins or FileMaker Server, your *External* functions category is empty. If you've installed any plug-ins ("mini-programs" that add extra features to FileMaker), they probably brought along some functions for their own use. File-Maker stores them in this category. FileMaker Server also uses plug-ins, ironically to help you update your third-party plug-ins. (External plug-ins are covered on page 464.)

Expressions

Expression is a fancy name for a subsection of a calculation—one or more fields, functions, or constants, each connected with operators. When you made the first calculation in this chapter (page 380), you multiplied the contents of the field called Price Each by the contents of the field called Quantity. That's a calculation, but it's also an example of an *expression*.

An expression always reduces to a single value when you combine its individual values according to the operators. If you can't boil it down to a value, it's not an expression. That's an important point, because it means you can use expressions as function parameters (page 399) just like any individual values—fields and constants. When used in a function, these expressions are called *sub-expressions*.

Here are some examples of expressions:

The following is a simple expression, which reduces to the value 6.

```
3 + 3
```

Below is a more complex expression. It might turn into something like "Miller, Thomas J."

```
Last Name & ", " & First Name & " " & Middle Initial & "."
```

The following calculation is a function *and* it's an expression, because it reduces down to a single value.

```
Average(L1 * W1 * H1 ; L2 * W2 * H2 ; L3 * W3 * H3)
```

But if you look at just the stuff in parentheses, you have this:

```
L1 * W1 * H1 ; L2 * W2 * H2 ; L3 * W3 * H3
```

That's *not* an expression because it doesn't reduce down to one value. It has three expressions in all, each separated by a semicolon. Each expression reduces to a single value—three values in all—which become parameters passed to the Average function.

You can put *any valid expression* in place of a parameter in a function. In the trade, that's called *nesting* expressions. For example, the expression 3 + 3 above could be rewritten like this:

    (1 + 1 + 1) + 3

In this case, the sub-expression (1 + 1 + 1) has replaced the original value 3. The whole thing is a new expression, and it contains one sub-expression. This idea comes in particularly handy when you work with functions. Instead of using individual fields or constants in a function, you can pass along whole expressions. You can even nest functions within other functions (page 455).

Creating a Calculation Field

The invoice line items now calculate their extended prices automatically, because you created a calculation at the beginning of the chapter to handle that. But you still have to add up the extended price of each line item and enter the total amount due on the invoice itself. Another calculation solves this problem.

1. **In the Customers database, choose File → Define → Databases and go to the Fields tab. From the Table pop-up menu, choose Invoices.**

   The field list shows all the fields in the Invoices table.

2. **Select the Total Due field in the list.**

   The Field Name, Type, and Comment at the bottom of the window update to show information about this field.

3. **From the Type pop-up menu, choose Calculation, and then click the now-highlighted Change button. When FileMaker asks if you're sure you want to make this change, click OK.**

   The Specify Calculation dialog box pops up. (See page 382 for details on its many features.)

4. **From the "Evaluate this calculation from the context of" pop-up menu, choose Invoices.**

   The Invoices table has multiple occurrences on the graph, but Invoices is the one that models your ER diagram. And it's the one that's directly attached to the line items you're totaling up. (See page 350 to learn about a context.)

5. **From the View pop-up menu (above the function list), choose Aggregate Functions.**

   The function list now shows just the functions FileMaker uses to calculate various kinds of totals and averages. You're looking for the Sum function.

6. **Double-click the "Sum (field {; field…})" function in the list.**

   FileMaker copies the full function example into the calculation box. To save you an extra step, it even selects everything between the parentheses. The next thing you type or click becomes the first parameter to the function.

Tip: Anything within curly braces in a function is optional. In the Sum function above, you could reference several fields that all get summed up into one glorious total. But that doesn't make sense when you're trying to summarize line items on an invoice, so you're just replacing all the highlighted material with a single field reference.

---

7. **From the pop-up menu above the field list, choose Line items. Then, in the list of line item fields, double-click the Extended Price field.**

   FileMaker adds this field to the calculation, placing it between the parentheses that surround the parameters to the Sum function. Your calculation should now read:

   ```
   Sum ( Line Items :: Extended Price )
   ```

Tip: If you prefer the keyboard, you can use the Tab key to move from the calculation box to the field list, then the operator list, then the function list. Once you're in one of these lists, use the up and down arrow keys to select an item (or type the first few letters of the item's name). Finally, press the Space bar to add the selected item to the calculation box.

---

8. **From the "Calculation result is" pop-up menu, choose *Number*.**

   This calculation is based on number fields and produces a number too.

9. **Click OK.**

   If you've done everything right, the Specify Calculation window disappears.

Your Total Due field should now work perfectly. Since you modified an existing field that's already on your layout, you don't need to do anything else. Every layout that shows the Line Items::Extended Price now shows the new calculated value.

Switch to the Invoices layout to try for yourself. As you change the Price Each or Quantity fields on a line item, the Extended Price field changes automatically to reflect the correct total.

The Specify Calculation Dialog Box

As you saw in the steps on the previous pages, whenever you create a new calculation field, FileMaker shows the Specify Calculation window (Figure 9-4). This window is where you tell it what calculation to use. This window is loaded with options, making it seem a bit daunting—but all those buttons are there to help you. FileMaker shows you the table occurrences, fields, operators, and functions, and all you have to do is point and click to build any calculation you have in mind.

Once you learn how this box works, you can write calculations like a pro without memorizing complicated functions and or typing out long field names. The following pages give you a guided tour of each element in the window.

Figure 9-4:
The Specify Calculation window appears whenever FileMaker expects you to enter a calculation. When you need to change the calculation definition for a field, just select it in the Define Database window's Fields tab, and click Options. Since it doesn't make sense to give calculation fields Auto-Enter or Validation settings, this dialog box's options are for storage only. Note the button says "Storage Option...".

Table occurrence context

This pop-up menu lists every occurrence of the current table—the one you're adding a field to—on the relationship graph. In the last chapter, you learned that File-Maker sees your entire database from the perspective of one table occurrence at a time. This list is where you tell FileMaker how to view the database when it evaluates this calculation. (If the calculation doesn't reference any related data, you can skip this menu.)

Field list

Since most calculations include fields, and field names are often long and hard to remember, FileMaker lets you pick field names from a list. The Table pop-up menu shows every table occurrence in the graph. The list below it shows the fields in the selected table occurrence. A calculation can refer to any field in the database: FileMaker follows the appropriate relationships if you use related fields.

TROUBLESHOOTING MOMENT

Think Like a Machine

If you've jumped right in and started making perfect calculations every time, you can skip this bit of arcana. But if File-Maker throws up a warning dialog box every time you try to make a halfway complex calculation, or if the syntax seems fine, but you just aren't getting the math to work out right, you might have to try thinking like FileMaker thinks. To understand how fields, constants, functions and operators come together to produce a single result, you have to think very logically and in a straight line that inexorably leads to the end of a problem. When FileMaker evaluates a calculation, it looks for something it can do to simplify it-fetch a field value, perform a function, or evaluate an operator.

The calculation shown here has a function (Average), several operators (* and &), a constant ("cubic inches") and six fields (L1, W1, H1, L2, W2, H2). You might think the Average function is the right place to start, because it comes first. But you quickly realize that you can't compute the average until you figure out what its parameters are by performing the multiplication. The * operators multiply values on either side to produce a new value-but FileMaker needs to replace these fields with their values before it can do anything else.

In Step #1, FileMaker identifies six fields. Step #2 shows how the calculation looks once FileMaker replaces them with values.

Now the * operators are all surrounded by values, and File-Maker is ready to do some multiplication (Step #3). Step #4 shows the calculation once all the multiplication is finished.

At last the Average function has two parameters (Step #5), which is just what it needs, so FileMaker performs this function and the new calculation looks like Step #6.

There are no more fields to replace and no more functions to perform, but there's one last operator. The & operator takes two text values and puts them together, but this & operator has a number on one side. FileMaker notices this fact in Step #7 and fixes it in Step #8. Finally, the & operator is evaluated and Step #9 shows the calculation result.

If you apply the concepts outlined here to your problem calculations-find the answer to each step, then plod along to the next one-you can always figure out where your calculation has gone astray.

Start	Average (L1 * W1 * H1 ; L2 * W2 * H2) & " cubic inches"
Step #1	Average (L1 * W1 * H1 ; L2 * W2 * H2) & " cubic inches"
Step #2	Average (3 * 5 * 4 ; 7 * 2 * 3) & " cubic inches"
Step #3	Average (3 * 5 * 4 ; 7 * 2 * 3) & " cubic inches"
Step #4	Average (60 ; 42) & " cubic inches"
Step #5	Average (60 ; 42) & " cubic inches"
Step #6	51 & " cubic inches"
Step #7	51 & " cubic inches"
Step #8	"51" & " cubic inches"
Step #9	51 cubic inches

If you want to put a field in the calculation itself, just double-click its name in the list, and FileMaker does the typing for you. See step 7 on page 396 for a prime example of when *not* to type a long field name.

Note: When you double-click a field from the list of table occurrences, you create what FileMaker calls a "fully-qualified field reference," which contains the Table name, two colons, and the Field name (Invoices:: InvoiceID). Because you might have similar field names in several tables, a fully-qualified name makes sure you reference the right one.

Operators

To help you remember all those operators, FileMaker shows them in the Operators area. Eight buttons represent the most common operators—just click one to insert it. Other operators appear in a scrolling list, which requires a double-click.

Function list

Some functions are so short and sweet that it's faster to type them than to hunt through this very lengthy list. Or you may come to memorize the functions you use most often. But you can't beat the Function list for convenience. It shows every function FileMaker understands *and* all the parameters each function expects, in the right order. (See the box on page 398 for more detail.)

As usual, double-click a function to add it to the calculation. If you don't fancy an alphabetical list of every function, you can narrow down your choices using the View pop-up menu. You can pick a specific function type and see a list of just those functions. The pop-up menu also includes three special categories. The first, "all functions by type" reorganizes the functions in the list. You can see the effect in Figure 9-5.

Figure 9-5:
When you choose to see "all function by type" in the function list, FileMaker groups the functions by their type, and sorts them by name in each group. The type itself is shown in bold above each group. This method is the easiest way to explore the list of functions when you're not quite sure what you're looking for.

Tip: You can always switch back to "all functions by name" to see every function in one alphabetical list. This choice comes in handy when you know a function's name, but not its category.

UP TO SPEED

The Function List

The function list doesn't show just a list of meaningless names—it also shows an example of how to use the function. The example includes everything you need to call the function in a calculation: name, the necessary parentheses, and a placeholder for each parameter. You just need to replace the placeholders with fields, constants, functions, or expressions.

Most functions are simple, and have a simple example to match:

```
Date ( month ; day ; year )
```

This function, called Date, expects three parameters, a month, a day, and year. (If you're curious, it returns a date value based on the three numbers passed to it. See Chapter 10 for more details.

Many functions aren't quite so simple. Some functions don't have a predetermined number of parameters. The Average function needs *at least* one parameter, but you can pass as many as you want. It looks like this in the Function list:

```
Average ( field {; field...} )
```

The first "field" parameter shows that you must specify at least one value. The second one is inside curly braces, meaning it's optional. And it's followed by "..." meaning you can add more copies if you want.

The Case function shows up like this:

```
Case ( test1 ; result1 {; test2 ; result2
; ... ; defaultResult} )
```

This shows that you can add additional test and result parameters, and you can put a final defaultResult parameter on the end if you want.

Finally, a few functions actually accept more than one value for a single parameter. The Evaluate function is an example:

```
Evaluate ( expression {; [field1 ; field2
;...]} )
```

It always expects one parameter, called an expression (see page 394).You can also specify a field to go with it. The brackets around the field show you that it can take two parameters, but the second can be a bracketed list of multiple values. In other words, you can call this function in three ways:

```
Evaluate ( "<some expression>" )
Evaluate ( '<some expression>" ; A Field )
Evaluate ( "<some expression>" ; [Field 1
; Field 2 ; Field 3] )
```

In the first case, it receives only one parameter. In both the second and third cases, you're passing *two* parameters. In the third case only, the second parameter is actually a list of values. Functions like this are rare, but a few exist.

Result type

Just as you specify field types when you define fields (page 91, you also specify result types for your calculations. You use the Result Type pop-up menu to tell FileMaker what kind of data this field holds. You can easily figure out result type. If you're using a text calculation, your result is probably going to be *text*. If it's a number calculation, the result type is *number*. Surprisingly though, you can also make calculations that are *container* types (page 436).

Calculation box

Your calculation itself goes in the Calculation box in the middle of the window (it has the field name above it as a label). You can type right into the calculation box if you're a codehead, but mere mortals usually use the field list, operators, and function list and let FileMaker assemble their calculations for them. When you're getting started, you probably mostly point and click, but as you get more familiar with formulas and functions, you start typing more often. Most people end up using a hybrid of typing and clicking to create their calculations.

Tip: You can also copy and paste into the Calculation box. If you have a calculation in another table file that's the same or similar, you can paste and then update it for its new home, saving yourself some typing.

Result Type

Why do I have to tell FileMaker my calculation has a number result? I'm multiplying two numbers together, so isn't it obvious?

You're right; FileMaker can figure that out for itself. In fact, in a calculation where you're performing simple math, the field always has a number result. But the ability to set the result type for a field gives you a good measure of control.

For one thing, you and FileMaker may have different ideas about what type a result *should* be. Take this calculation, for example:

    1 & 1 * 3

Because you're mixing concatenation (&) and math (*) operators, it's not terribly obvious *what* that calculation will produce—a number? Or just a numerical text value? So File-Maker lets you say what you *want* it to produce. If it doesn't do what you expect, you can easily fix the calculation, but at least you don't have to wonder what type of field you have.

Furthermore, setting the type explicitly prevents FileMaker from changing it later. Imagine if a simple change to your calculation accidentally changed the result type from number to text. If you tried to reference this field in a calculation or relationship, you'd get strange results. And it might take you a while to figure out that the problem is due to File-Maker calculating a text value rather than a number, rather than a mistake in your calculation.

If you've set a result type and your calculation doesn't naturally produce the correct type, FileMaker converts it for you before it stores the final result. Thus, you can always tell exactly what type the field is just by looking at Result Type pop-up menu.

Repetitions

Like any field, a calculation field can be a repeating field (page 109). FileMaker provides this option for the rare occasion when you need to calculate repeating fields. Suppose you have a repeating field that holds five quantities, and another with five prices. You can write a calculation that multiplies the two fields, and turn on this box. FileMaker takes care to match all the repetition numbers for you, so the third repetition of the calculation multiplies the third price and the third quantity, for instance. (You're more likely to have related tables, and use a standard single calculation to do the totals, but the option to calculate on repetitions is there if you need it.)

Do Not Evaluate if All Referenced Fields are Empty

When you define calculation fields (like the Extended Price and Total Due fields in this chapter), you may notice a long-winded checkbox labeled "Do not evaluate if all referenced fields are empty." FileMaker always turns this option on when you first specify a calculation. Here's what it does:

Say you create a new invoice record. It's completely empty, no line items yet. If the Total Due field's "Do not evaluate when all referenced fields are empty" checkbox is turned on, that field is also completely blank, as shown here. After all, there are no referenced fields (line items), so FileMaker skips the calculation, as the checkbox says.

To be perfectly accurate, however, the value of total due isn't a blank oblivion, it's zero dollars and zero cents, or $0.00. And indeed, if you turn the "Do not evaluate" option off, FileMaker goes through the calculation even when the invoice's fields are empty. For a newly created invoice, File-Maker shows the correctly formatted Total Due result—$0.00. You're free to choose whichever result you prefer.

There are other types of calculations where you'd want File-Maker to keep its paws off empty fields, though. Suppose you had a calculation like this:

```
Height & " inches"
```

If FileMaker evaluates that calculation and the Height field is empty, the result is " inches," which is pretty meaningless. In cases where something is worse than nothing, the "Do not evaluate if all referenced fields are empty" option saves you from worry.

Auto-Enter Calculations

Calculation fields are fantastic—they save time and ensure error-free results. But they have one serious limitation: You can't *change* their values. Of course you can adjust the calculation itself, but sometimes a field needs the capacity to override its calculated value on a record-by-record basis.

For example, it would be nice if your invoice's Date Due field automatically showed a date 30 days after the date of the invoice itself. But sometimes you might want to make an invoice due earlier or later, based on special circumstances (like a holiday). If you make the Date Due field a calculation field, you don't have this flexibility. The solution is to use a normal Date field with an *Auto-Enter calculation* (see box on page 404).

Like all the Auto-Enter options (page 95), an Auto-Enter calculation automatically fills in a field's value, but leaves it changeable. You can get all the accuracy and time savings of a calculation field, plus the power to change your mind. Here's how to put it to use:

1. **Bring up the Define Database window and switch to the now-familiar Fields tab. From the Table pop-up menu, choose Invoices.**

   The fields from the Invoices table appear.

2. **Select the Date Due field in the list and click Options.**

   The Field Options dialog box makes an appearance.

3. **On the Auto-Enter tab, turn on the Calculated Value checkbox.**

   The Specify Calculation window appears. It looks just like it did before, but this time you're *not* creating a calculation field. Instead, you're specifying the calculation used to determine the auto-enter value.

4. **Create the calculation *Date + 30*.**

   You can use any method you want to build this calculation: Click the field and operators, or type them. Notice that the calculation result is set to Date, and there's no pop-up menu to allow you to change that. Your calculation must resolve to a valid date, or FileMaker will squawk at you.

5. **Click OK three times to dismiss all the dialog boxes.**

   You return to the database itself.

Now you can create a new invoice and test out your field. When you enter a Date for the invoice, the Date Due field updates instantly with the date 30 days from now. Notice that you can still *change* the Date Due field if you want.

Validate Data Entry with a Calculation

In Chapter 3 you were introduced to several ways to validate data entered into a field. But what if the Validation tab in the Field Options dialog box doesn't have a checkbox to meet your needs? For example, you might want to use validation on the Zip Code field in the Customers table. A valid Zip Code has *either* five characters *or* 10 characters (in other words, it can look like this: 90210, or this: 90210-1100). The closest validation option you'll find is "Maximum number of characters"—close, but not right.

This situation is just the kind where the "Validate by calculation" option comes in handy. Your job is to create a calculation with a Boolean result. It should return True when the data is valid, and False otherwise. Here's how it works:

1. **View the field definitions for the Customers table (In File → Define Database). Select the Zip Code field and click Options.**

   The Field Options dialog box pops up.

2. **Click the Validation tab, and turn on "Validate by calculation."**

   The Specify Calculation window appears, ready for you to enter your validation calculation.

POWER USERS' CLINIC

Do Not Replace Existing Value

Auto-Enter calculation fields don't act *exactly* like other calculation fields. If you *change* the invoice date, the due date doesn't update to reflect the change. Instead, it keeps its original value, as in the example on the previous page. That's normally the way Auto-Enter calculations work: Once the field gets a value, the calculation never changes it. It only acts when the field is empty.

Often, though, you don't want this behavior. Instead, you want it to change the field value every time any field used in the calculation is changed, just like a normal calculation. You can easily get this modified behavior by turning off the "Do not replace existing value of field (if any)" checkbox in the Field Options dialog box (shown here). When you turn this checkbox is *off*, FileMaker dutifully updates the field value whenever the calculation evaluates—in other words, when any field it uses changes.

Which option you should choose depends on the situation. For the Date Due field, you probably want to turn this option off. After all, if you're changing the date of an invoice, it's reasonable to assume you want to rethink the due date as well.

But suppose you have a database of products, and you use an Auto-Enter calculation to copy the distributor's product code into your internal product code field. If you then change the internal product code to something unique to you, you probably *don't* want it to change again if you switch to a different distributor. In that case, you would leave the "Do not replace existing value (if any)" option turned on, ensuring that once you've put in your own special value, it never changes.

---

3. **From the View pop-up menu, choose "Text functions."**

   The function list updates to show just the text functions.

4. **In the function list, double-click "Length (text)."**

   The function appears in the calculation box. Notice that "text" is already highlighted, ready to be replaced. The Length function returns the length of a text value. You use it here to see how many characters are in the Zip Code field

5. **In the field list, double-click the Zip Code field.**

   FileMaker puts this field inside the parentheses, where it becomes the parameter to the Length function. Now that you have a function to tell you how long the Zip code is, you need to use the comparison operator to compare it to something.

---

6. **Click to the right of the closing parenthesis. Then, in the operators list, double-click =.**

FileMaker adds the comparison operator (=) to your calculation.

Validate Data Entry
with a Calculation

FREQUENTLY ASKED QUESTION

Validate Only if Field Has Been Modified

What is the "Validate only if field has been modified" checkbox for? I don't remember seeing this in the Specify Calculation window before. For that matter, where did the Result Type pop-up menu go?

Good eye. The Specify Calculation window can show up in lots of places—when defining a calculation field, when specifying an Auto-Enter calculation, and so on—and it can change slightly in each case.

First, the Result Type pop-up menu only shows up when you're defining a calculation field, since it can produce any data type. Since a validation calculation always has a Boolean result, there's no need to ask you here.

In place of this pop-up menu, you often see some new option specific to the calculation type—like the "Validate only if field has been modified" checkbox here.

Normally when you edit a record, FileMaker validates only the fields you actually change. Any field in the record that hasn't been changed is accepted even if it violates the validation rule. This can happen when you have your field set to validate "Only during data entry" and the records have been set some other way—from an import (page 623) or a script (page 639). If you want to validate this field whenever you edit the record, not just when the field itself changes, turn off this checkbox.

---

7. **After the = operator, type 5.**

Your calculation compares the length of the Zip code to the value 5. If they're equal, it returns True. But you also want to accept a Zip code with *10* characters.

8. **In the operator list, double-click *or*.**

The "or" operator is added to the end of the calculation. Remember that this operator connects two Boolean values and returns True if *either* value is true. Next, you set up the second value.

9. **Double-click the Length function again, then double-click the Zip Code function again, and then double-click the = operator.**

This second check should also compare the length to some other value.

10. **In the calculation box, type *10*.**

Your calculation is complete. It should look like the one in Figure 9-6.

11. **Click OK, then OK again, and then a third time.**

You're now back in your database and ready to test. Try giving a customer a few different Zip codes and make sure the validation works.

Most validations occur as soon as you leave the field, even if you're just moving to another field in the record. But some validation types—including most validation calculations—don't happen until you exit the *record*.

Figure 9-6:
Now you have two comparisons in your calculation. One comparison checks to see if the length is five, while the other looks for a length of 10. If either is True, your calculation is True as well, and FileMaker accepts the Zip code. If both conditions fail, the calculation result is False and FileMaker shows you an error message.

Tip: If you're dying to know what determines when your validation occurs, here's the skinny: If, when validating a field, FileMaker looks at the data only *in the field itself*, it performs the validation immediately. If it has to look at data in *other fields* or *other records*, then it waits until you commit the record before validating.

Replacing Data Using a Calculation

You can use calculations productively with the Records → Replace Field Contents command. This command tells FileMaker to visit every record in the found set, replacing the contents of one field with something new. When you first saw this command in Chapter 2, you entered a single value in every record. Sometimes, though, it's more useful to have FileMaker use a calculation to figure out what should go in each record.

Tip: Replace Field Contents is a huge time saver, but since it works on a found set of records, you can't undo it. Improperly used (bad calculation or the wrong found set), it can be destructive. See page 674 to learn how the Data Viewer in FileMaker Advanced helps you preview the results of a calculation before you make that one-way trip through the Replace Field Contents dialog box.

Imagine you attended the International Private Investigators conference in South Dakota, where you picked up 73 business cards you'd like to add to your database. Rather than type them yourself, you told your 13-year-old nephew you'd give him a gumball for each card he typed in. After the cards are tossed and the gum given, you discover he has an aversion to the Shift key—none of the names are capitalized.

You could go through all the records one by one, fixing the capitalization and regretting the cost of the gumballs. But if you use the Replace Field Contents command, you can do all your records with just one command, using a calculation. You use the Proper function, which capitalizes the first letter of each word it encounters. Here's how:

1. **From Browse mode, click the First Name field.**

   The Replace Field Contents command operates on the field you're in when you run it. So click to start in the correct field first.

2. **Choose Records → Replace Field Contents. In the Replace Field Contents window, select the "Replace with calculated result" radio button.**

   As soon as you make this choice, your old friend the Specify Calculation window appears.

3. **Choose "Text functions" from the View pop-up menu (above the function list).**

   The list updates to show only text functions.

4. **Double-click "Proper (text)" in the function list.**

   FileMaker inserts the Proper function in the calculation box. Since it has only one parameter, it's already selected. You just have to tell it what text to perform its magic on.

5. **Double click the First Name field in the field list.**

   FileMaker inserts *First Name* as the parameter for the Proper function.

6. **Click OK to close the Specify Calculation dialog box. Then, in the Replace Field Contents window, click Replace.**

   Notice—and beware—that the Cancel button in this dialog box is automatically highlighted. If you hit Enter too quickly, or accidentally click Cancel, you have to start all over, because the dialog box doesn't remember your calculation. It's worth taking an extra second to make sure you're clicking the appropriate button.

If you have a lot of records, you see a progress dialog box. Normally, though, the replacement happens quickly enough that you don't even notice.

Tip: FileMaker has two other functions for changing case: Upper and Lower. It probably goes without saying that Upper converts all the text to uppercase, and Lower converts it to lowercase.

Comments

Everything you can put in a calculation has some kind of value…unless it's a *comment*. Comments are chunks of text whose sole purpose is to help guide you through long calculations. Professional database developers, like all good programmers, provide lots of comments for the benefit of people who might work on the computer code months or years later. Once you've a few sets of parentheses or nested function calls, you may have trouble understanding even your *own* FileMaker calculation when you have to go back and make changes. When it evaluates the calculation, FileMaker ignores all comments completely—it's as if they weren't there. (But you'll be glad they are.)

You can use two different styles for your comments. First, any text that comes after two consecutive slash marks (//) is considered a comment. This kind of comment goes all the way to the end of the line.

```
// this is a comment
3.14 * Diameter // and so is this
```

A comment is also any text that comes between the symbols /* and */. This symbol pair comes in handy in two places. It saves typing if you need to type a long comment across multiple lines:

```
/* this is a comment that runs across multiple
lines. To make life easier, you can use the second
comment style */
```

Also, this comment style lets you add comments *within* a line:

```
3 /*sprocket size*/ * 10 /*sprocket count*/ * 57 /*tooth count*/
```

In addition to comments, you can—and should—use white space to make your calculations easier to read. Calculations don't have to be strung together in one long line, even though that's the way FileMaker does it in the Specify Calculation dialog box. Press the Return key or Space bar to add space anywhere, except in a field name, function name, text constant, or number. Comments and white space can make a world of difference. Here's a long calculation that doesn't make use of either:

```
Let([NewText = ":" & Path & ":"]; Case(Item < 0; Let( [TextLen =
Length(NewText); Pos = Position(NewText; ":"; TextLen; Item - 1) + 1; Len=
Position(NewText; ":"; TextLen; Item) - Pos ]; Middle(NewText; Pos; Len));
Let( [Pos = Position(NewText; ":"; 1; Item) + 1; Len= Position(NewText; ":";
1; Item + 1) - Pos ]; Middle(NewText; Pos; Len))))
```

Ten points to the first person who can make sense of that mess. Now here's the same calculation, written with more care:

```
// Parsing is easier if we can be sure we have delimiters
// on both ends of the text
Let( [NewText = ":" & Path & ":"];
   Case(

      // If the item number is negative, we count from the end
      Item < 0;
      Let( [TextLen = Length(NewText);
         Pos = Position(NewText; ":"; TextLen; Item - 1) + 1;
         Len= Position(NewText; ":"; TextLen; Item) - Pos ];
         Middle(NewText; Pos; Len)
      );

      // If the item number is positive, we count from the
      // beginning
      Let( [Pos = Position(NewText; ":"; 1; Item) + 1;
         Len= Position(NewText; ":"; 1; Item + 1) - Pos ];
         Middle(NewText; Pos; Len)
      )
   )
)
```

It may not be a picnic to run through in your head, but it's a lot easier to follow than before.

Calculations and Data Types

The last chapter introduced the terminology and concepts behind FileMaker's calculations. You learned how to create them using the Specify Calculation dialog box's tools. Functions, as you saw in the previous chapter, play a big role in good calculation construction. In this chapter, you'll learn the details about the most common functions for the various data types—text, number, date, time, timestamp, and container—and when to use them. As in your FileMaker design life, if you want to test a calculation, just create a calculation field and start building it using the techniques you've learned so far. If it doesn't work the way you expect, or if you don't need it after your experiment is done, just delete the field.

Number Crunching Calculations

Although they don't come first in the function list, number functions are the most obvious application of calculations. Since most people easily understand them, number functions are a logical place to start. A lot of the concepts you'll learn for number functions apply to other functions as well.

Number Operators

Operators, along with fields, constants, and functions, are one of the basic building blocks of a calculation. FileMaker has five operators that specifically apply to numerical calculations, the same five that you probably already know:

- + is for addition

- - is for subtraction

- * is for multiplication

- / is for division

- ^ is for exponentiation ("to the power of")

Page 386 explains how to use these operators in detail. In your day-to-day work with FileMaker, you usually use these operators to calculate the numerical values in your fields.

Note: If you're new to calculations, you'll want to get a handle on the material in this chapter before proceeding. But if you've worked with logical tests before, you can skip straight to Chapter 11.

Say you're an event planner and you always plan for 10 percent above the expected number of attendees. Use this calculation to find your fudge factor:

```
Sum ( Attendees::Confirmed ) * 1.1
```

Number Function Types

FileMaker also gives you dozens of functions that do special things to numbers. Because there are so many number functions, the function list breaks them up into smaller groups. The groups have descriptive names, so you can drive right to the group you need (or skim by them without looking, if you might be traumatized if you accidentally saw a sine or cosine function). The functions you use with your numeric data are:

- Number functions

- Aggregate functions

- Financial functions

- Trigonometric functions

As you saw on page 390, every number function expects one or more parameters, each a number value, and all the number functions return a number result. Here's how to put them to work:

Note: This book doesn't cover the financial and trigonometric functions, which have highly specialized uses. If you need to use these brawny functions, you probably have the mental muscle to decipher the technical terms in FileMaker's Help file, where you'll find them explained.

Precision

Some calculations demand a high degree of precision, like those that track radioactive isotopes or other scientific data with lots of places following the decimal point. FileMaker comes prepared with the SetPrecision function. This function extends FileMaker's default precision of 16 decimal places, up to a maximum of 400. If you need more precision, you add a SetPrecision function to the calculation that produces the value that requires precision. You can use SetPrecision with all other numeric functions, except trigonometric functions, which don't accept this extended precision. See Figure 10-1.

The SetPrecision function requires two parameters. The first parameter is a number, or any expression that results in a number. The second is the number of decimal places you want to see.

This calculation would return Pi with 3 decimal places:

```
SetPrecicion( Pi ; 3 )
```

This version would show 100 decimal places:

```
SetPrecision( Pi ; 100 )
```

Note: The SetPrecision function affects your calculation's result, but not the way FileMaker displays it. To save space on your layout, you can format a very precise calculation to show only a few decimal places until you click the field, when you see the stored value (Figure 10-1).

Going Beyond Basic Calculations

In the last chapter you created two very simple calculation fields using numbers: Extended Price and Invoice Total. But those calculations were very simple. Now, you build on those basic concepts to see how you can make a set of calculations that fit an upcoming sales promotion.

Preparing the Data

You've decided to start reselling personal security products to your customers. To help you keep track of things, you need to add a Products table to your database. The table should have these fields:

- A text field called *SKU*

- A text field called *Description*

- A number field called *Cost*

- A number field called *Price*

Note: See page 301 for advice on creating tables.

Once you've defined this new table, FileMaker automatically creates a layout—Products. Switch to that layout now and create a few product records. To help drive sales to your larger clients, you want to implement a volume discount scheme—they should get a 5 percent discount if they buy enough. But some of the products you sell don't have enough mark-up to justify these discounts. You want to be sure the discount never reduces your mark-up below 20 percent.

First, you add a line to your marketing materials: "Volume discounts not available for all products." You can make this line as small as humanly possible and hide it way down in the corner. Next, you need to fix your database so it tells you the discount price for each product.

Building the Calculation Fields

To implement this discount scheme, take what you need to know and translate it into calculation terms. You need three fields to carry out your sales promotion logic.

- First, calculate 95 percent of the price (a 5 percent discount):

    ```
    Price Each * .95
    ```

- Second, you also know the cost (in the Cost field) and you can figure out the lowest price by adding 20 percent to this cost:

    ```
    Cost * 1.2
    ```

- Finally, the discounted price is either the calculated discount price, *or* the cost + 20 percent price, whichever is *greater*. Put another way, you want the *maximum* of these two values:

    ```
    Max ( Price Each * .95 ; Cost * 1.2 )
    ```

Using the Max function, the previous calculation results in either the discounted price, or the minimum price, whichever is greater (see the box on page 415). That result's *almost* perfect. But suppose you have a product whose *normal* price is less than 20 percent above cost (hey, it's a competitive market). If you use the Max calculation as it is now, the new discounted price is *more* than the normal price. You need to go back and add to your calculation so that it takes the regular price into account, and uses *that price* if it's lower than the calculated discount. Read on to learn how to think through this calculation quandary.

UP TO SPEED

The Max and Min Functions

Many times, you need to know either the highest or lowest value in a series. The Max function and its twin sister, Min, fulfill these needs and you find them in the function list's Aggregate functions category. Like all the aggregate functions, they expect at least one parameter, and are glad to get more. Every parameter should be a number. Your parameters can be:

- Constant data

- Fields within a record

- Repeating fields

- Related fields

The Max function looks at every number referenced and returns whichever is largest. Min, on the other hand, returns the smallest value.

For example, look at this calculation:

```
Max ( 10 ; 3 ; 72 ; 19 ; 1 )
```

Its result is 72, since that's the largest of the parameters.

If you had a repeating field called Distances that held the distances from your office to each Krispy Kreme store, you could use this calculation to find the closest sugar fix:

```
Min ( Distances )
```

The same is true for *related* fields too. This calculation finds the most expensive line item:

```
Max ( Line Items::Price )
```

For another example of an aggregate function, Sum, see page 380.

Constructing the Calculation

When calculations start to get complicated like this discount price example, imagine that you have a field that contains the value you already want. You can use this pretend field in your new calculation, and then, when you're all finished, put the old calculation in place of the pretend field. In this case, just pretend you have a field called Calculated Discount that holds the discount price. With that imaginary field in mind, you can fix your problem with this calculation:

```
Min ( Calculated Discount ; Price Each )
```

The result of this calculation is either the calculated discount or the regular price, if it's lower. Now, just put the old calculation in place of the words "Calculated Discount" (since the old calculation *results in the calculated discount*):

```
Min ( Max ( Price Each * .95 ; Cost * 1.2 ) ; Price Each )
```

The entire Max function, complete with its two parameters, is now the Min function's first parameter. You might think it looks a little confusing at first, but with practice you become accustomed to looking at functions-inside-functions like this.

If it helps, you can add white space and comments to clarify the calculation, as Figure 10-2 shows.

Figure 10-2:
You may find it hard to write nested calculations, and hard to read them if you need to come back later and tweak them. In this case, though, a savvy person formatted the calculation with copious white space and plenty of comments. Chances are you'll understand this version better than the one shown on page 415.

To use the calculation, just create a new calculation field (call it *Discounted Price*) with the calculation above. It automatically adjusts and shows you an appropriate discounted price.

If you want to test a complicated calculation, spot-check a few records where you know the result. Sometimes the math is so complex that you just have to work it out on paper and enter dummy records to check the calculation. Usually, if a calculation isn't working, you can figure out how to fix it when you compare your math to the value in the field.

Text Parsing Calculations

Although most people think of functions for doing dry stuff like math in a spreadsheet, you can also use functions in your database's text fields. Just as you can add and subtract numbers with number functions, you can use text functions to slice and dice the words in your database. For example, you might receive data from an outside source that needs major cleanup before you can use it. This data has people's first and last names in the same field; it's even got entire email messages crammed into a field—address, subject, and body—when all you need is the email address. You can equip a temporary database with fields and text calculations to *parse* (think of it as sifting) the data into the form your better-designed database expects.

Tip: Fixing data this way usually means that you do a find for a certain kind of bad data—if only some records have two email addresses in the same field, say. Use a calculation with the Records → Replace-Field Contents command. Do a find first, and then do a calculated Replace Field Contents that fixes the error.

POWER USERS' CLINIC

Repeating Fields for Multiple Results

What if one discount price isn't enough? Suppose you want to give your customers 5 percent off on orders of five or more, 10 percent off on orders of 10 or more, 15 percent off on orders of 15 or more, and so on. You could create more calculation fields with slight variations on the calculations you've already defined:

- Discounted Price for 10:

  ```
  Min ( Max ( Price * .90 ; Cost * 1.2 ) ;
  Price)
  ```

- Discounted Price for 15:

  ```
  Min ( Max ( Price * .85 ; Cost * 1.2 ) ;
  Price)
  ```

If you want seven price breaks, you have to define seven fields. And if you want to change the calculation slightly (for example, to give an additional 2 percent discount per break instead of 5 percent). you have to change every single field's calculation.

This example is one of those cases where repeating fields come in handy. When you create a repeating calculation field, you have only *one* calculation, but you get multiple results. With only one calculation, though, FileMaker doesn't show you an obvious way to provide different discount rates. The secret ingredient is the Get(Calculation-RepetitionNumber) function. It returns the repetition number being calculated at the moment. For example, when FileMaker goes to calculate the *third* value in your repeating field, this function returns 3.

With this function in mind, you can devise a single calculation that uses different discount rates depending on the repetition number:

```
Min (
   Max (
      Price * (1 -
Get(CalculationRepetitionNumber) * .5) ;
      Cost * 1.2
   ) ;
   Price
)
```

In this calculation, you replace the constant discount rate by the expression:

```
(1 - Get(CalculatedRepetitionNumber) * .5)
```

If you test this calculation with a few numbers, you see it results in an extra 5 percent discount for each subsequent repetition. Once you've defined a field like this, a lot of things become really easy:

To add *more* price breaks, just change the number of repetitions in the Specify Calculation dialog box

- . Going from seven breaks to 20 is a 5-second change.

- To change the discount rates for *every* break, just change one number—the .5—and you affect every calculated value.

The Concatenation Operator

In contrast to the wide variety of mathematical operators for working with numbers, there's only one that pertains specifically to text—the *concatenation* operator. Represented by the & sign (ampersand), it strings bits of text together. (When you need to chop and divide your text in order to parse it, you use a function instead of an operator, as described on page 419.)

To use it, put it between units of text, as in the expression below:

```
"This is a " & "test"
```

The result of this calculation is *This is a test*.

The concatenation operator lets you combine text from two different fields and make them work better together. For example, when you set up the Jobs layout in your database in Chapter 8, you had to settle for a compromise. When creating the value list for the Customer pop-up menu (page 328), you could pick only *one* field to show along with the ID value. That example used the First Name field, but the full name would make the menu more useful. With a calculation, you can do just that.

Create a new field that shows what you want in your value list. Add a new calculation field to the Customers table, called *Full Name*. Use this calculation:

```
Last Name & ", " & First Name "
```

Some results might be "Gribble, Dale" or "Hill, Henry." Note that the calculation includes a comma and the appropriate spaces for separating data between your fields. Now you can modify the All Customers value list to take advantage of the new field. Just change it to use the new Full Name field instead of the First Name field. Figure 10-3 shows the result.

Figure 10-3:
The background window shows how the pop-up menu looked before the calculation field. In the front, you can see how it looks now. People often use calculations to combine multiple field values like this for display purposes.

Tip: Concatenating fields are great for simplifying the display of data, but they have other uses, too. Instead of setting up a two key sort to sort customers by last name, then first name, now you can just sort on your Full Name field. You can also make a subsummary part (page 273) that works when you sort on the Full Name field.

Text Function Types

FileMaker's text-handling functions come in two flavors: *Text functions* and *Text formatting functions*. Text functions handle tasks like the parsing mentioned above, or finding whether a particular string of characters occurs in a field. You can change all instances of specific characters within a field, or count text length, with text functions.

Text formatting functions change the way your text looks, like making a part of the text in a field bold and red. These functions are a lot more flexible than just making a field bold and red on your layout, because you can tell the calculation to search *inside* the field, find just the characters "Propane Sale!" and make them red, while it leaves all the surrounding text untouched.

Text Functions

Many of the text functions exist to help you *parse* text—split it apart in useful ways. Sometimes one text value contains multiple useful pieces of information, and you need to look at them individually. If you're lucky, the information comes in a form that FileMaker already understands. If you're not so lucky, you have to do some extra work to tell FileMaker exactly how to divide the text value.

FileMaker can automatically break text up three ways: by *characters*, *words*, or *values*. When it does the dividing, it gives you three ways to decide which parts you want: *Left*, *Middle*, or *Right*.

Character functions

Parsing by character comes in handy when you have data that's in a well-known format and you need to access pieces of it. You can use functions to grab the first three digits of a Social Security number, the last four digits of a credit card number, or the style code buried inside a product number.

FileMaker can work with individual characters inside a text value. The first letter in a text value is number one; the second is number two; and so on. Then you can ask for the first few characters, or the last few, or just the fifth, sixth, and seventh.

Note: Every letter, number, punctuation mark, space, tab, carriage return, or other symbol counts as a character.

POWER USERS' CLINIC

A Calculation in a Button

In Chapter 5, you learned how to create buttons on a layout and program them to perform all kinds of database duties at a click (page 246). The only problem is, the more features you give your database, the more buttons you have to make. And some of the folks using your database need a completely different assortment of buttons than others. Fortunately, most button commands have one or more options you can set with a calculation. The calculation can adjust what the button does based on field data, user information, the current date or time, and so forth.

Suppose you want a quick way to map your customer's location. Many Web sites provide free maps, and FileMaker has an Open URL button command that opens your Web browser and takes you to a specified Web page. With this command, and a calculation that produces the right Web address, you can add quick and easy mapping to your database.

First, you need to figure out what the URL should look like. You can make this decision by going to a Web page similar to the one you want. For example, this address shows a map of FileMaker Inc.'s home base using Map Quest:

http://www.mapquest.com/maps/map. adp?country=US&addtohistory=&address=5201+Patrick+ Henry+Drive&city=Santa+Clara&state=CA&zipcode=9505 2&homesubmit=Get+Map

At first these lines might look like garbage, but if you look closely you can see the street address, city, state, and zip code in there. It wouldn't be hard to make a text calculation that produces this same Web address for a customer, based on the right fields:

1. Add a button to the layout.

2. In the Specify Button dialog box, choose the Open URL command.

3. In the Options section of the window, turn on Perform without dialog, then click the Specify button.

4. When the Open URL Options window opens, click Specify in *that* window. A Specify Calculation window comes up.

You can now create the calculation. You probably want to paste a Web address, put quotes around it, and then set out inserting necessary fields in the right places. Be sure to end each section of the address with a quote, and use the & operator between each piece of text and each field. Here is a calculation from the address above:

```
"http://www.mapquest.com/maps/map.
adp?country=US&addtohistory=&address=" &
    Customers::Street Address &
"&city=" &
    Customers::City &
"&state=" &
    Customers::State &
"&zipcode=" &
    Customers::Zip Code &
"&homesubmit=Get+Map"
```

When you're finished, click OK a couple times until you're back on your layout. You can now test your button in Browse mode.

- The **Left** function returns the first few letters of a text value, eliminating the rest. You *pass* (that is, tell) the calculation the actual text value, and the number of letters you want. For example, to get a person's initials, you can use a calculation like this:

```
Left ( First Name ; 1 ) & Left ( Last Name ; 1 )
```

To get the first three digits of a Social Security number, you can use this calculation:

```
Left ( SSN ; 3 )
```

- The **Right** function does the same thing but starts from other end of the text value. If you want to record the last four digits of someone's credit card number, you can do it like this:

```
Right ( Credit Card Number ; 4 )
```

- If the information you want isn't on either end, you may need to use the **Middle** function instead. This function is a little different: It expects *three* parameters. Just as when using Left and Right, the first parameter is the text value FileMaker's inspecting. The second parameter is the starting position. Finally, you tell FileMaker how many characters you want.

For example, suppose you have a product database that uses a special coding system for each item. The code "SH-112-M" indicates shirt style 112, medium size. To pull out just the style number (that 112 in the middle of the product code), you want your calculation to grab three characters from the Product Number field, starting with the fourth character.

```
Middle ( Product Number ; 4 ; 3 )
```

Word functions

FileMaker also understands the concept of words. With word functions, you don't have to bother dealing with every single character.

In FileMaker's mind, a *word* is any stretch of letters, numbers, or periods that doesn't have any other spaces or punctuation in it. Most of the time, this definition means FileMaker does exactly what you expect: It sees the real words in the text. For example, each of the following is one word:

- FileMaker
- ABC123
- This.is.a.word

Any sequence of other characters isn't part of a word at all. Each of these has two words:

- FileMaker Pro
- ABC 123

- A-Test
- Two *** Words

Warning: If your text value doesn't have normal words (like a long URL, for example), you may have to pay special attention to the letters-numbers-periods rule to get the results you expect.

The Middle Way

It looks like you can tell the Middle function to isolate characters anywhere in a text field, just by telling it which characters to count. So why do we need Left and Right functions when you can do the same thing with Middle?

As the example on page 421 suggests, the Middle function indeed provides all the power you need to pick text values apart character by character. For example, instead of:

```
Left ( Model Number ; 3 )
```

You could do this:

```
Middle ( Model Number ; 1 ; 3 )
```

It gets a little tougher to mimic the Right function, but it's possible.

There are *lots* of places where one function can do the same thing as another (or a few others).

For example, you can use Left and Right instead of Middle if you want. This calculation:

```
Middle ( Product Number ; 4 ; 3 )
```

Can be rewritten like this:

```
Right ( Left ( Product Number ; 7 ) ; 3 )
```

The good new is, there's no *right answer*. You can write your calculations any way you want, as long as they work. In fact, FileMaker developers have a grand tradition of finding creative ways to do something with less typing. Bear in mind, though, that sometime in the future you'll probably have to figure out what you were doing in a calculation so you can change it, fix it, or use it somewhere else. If a few extra keystrokes makes the calculation easier to understand, they may well be worth it.

Along the same lines as the Character functions, FileMaker has three word-oriented functions called LeftWords, RightWords, and MiddleWords. Each takes two parameters, including the text value to examine, and a number or two to tell FileMaker which words you're interested in. You can use a LeftWords function to parse out a person's First and Middle Name if you ever get a file with all three names unceremoniously dumped into a single field.

- **LeftWords** returns all the text before the end of the specified word. For instance, this function:

```
LeftWords ( Preamble ; 3 )
```

Might return *We the People*. But if Preamble contained "This *** Is *** a *** Test" it would return *This *** Is *** A* instead. In other words, it doesn't just return the words. It returns *everything* before the end of the third word.

- Likewise, **RightWords** returns everything *after* the specified word's *beginning*, counting from the end. This calculation:

    ```
    RightWords ( Revelations ; 1 )
    ```

    Would return *Amen.*

- What would LeftWords and RightWords be without **MiddleWords**? You can probably guess how this function works: You pass in a text value, a starting word, and the number of words to return. It then returns everything from the beginning of the starting word through the end of the finishing word. The following calculation shows how it works; it returns "or not."

    ```
    MiddleWords ( "To be, or not to be" ; 3 ; 2 )
    ```

Text value functions

How can *text* have a *value*? Well, to FileMaker, values are what fields hold, so a field's text *is* its value. If a field holds more than one chunk of text, each on its own line, FileMaker considers each a separate value, hence the term *return-separated values*. You can think of these bits of text as *lines* or *paragraphs*. Text value functions let you use those line breaks to parse text. This trick comes in handy more often than you think.

Here's a simple example to show how it works. Suppose you have a field called Colors with lists like this:

Red
Green
Blue
Orange
Yellow

FileMaker tells you this field contains five values, and you can work with them just like characters and words. For example, this LeftValue function returns "Red" and "Green:"

```
LeftValues ( Colors ; 2 )
```

Use the GetValue function when you need to parse out just one value from a list. The value you need has to be in a predictable place in the list, as in the whole-email-slammed-into-one-field example at the beginning of this section. Say the email comes to you like this:

```
Email From
Email To
Subject
Body
```

You could grab the Email To address with this function:

```
Get Value ( Email ; 2 )
```

FileMaker has RightValues and MiddleValues functions, too. See the box below for ideas on how to use them.

Outsmarting the Smarties

LeftValues and RightValues are helpful when you need to pull some items from a return-separated list (page 219). But they're also helpful when you want to protect your database from people who know a few workarounds. Say you have a sales promotion going, where your best customers get to pick one free premium from a list of four items. So you've set up a field with a value list and a set of radio buttons. Everybody knows that you can choose only one item from a radio button set, right? Apparently not, because you've got some salespeople who know they can beat the system by Shift-clicking to select multiple radio buttons. (Those folks read page 219.)

All you have to do is add an Auto-Enter calculated value to your Premiums field. Make sure you uncheck the "Do not replace existing value (if any)" option. Here's how the calculation goes:

```
RightValues (Premiums ; 1 )
```

Now your savvy salespeople can wear out their Shift keys, but they still can't select more than one item in the premium field, because your calculation holds the field to a single value.

You can even add smarts to a Checkbox Set with a similar technique. Make this calculation:

```
LeftValues ( Premiums ; 2 )
```

People using the program can't select more than two checkboxes. FileMaker knows the first two items they selected, and just keeps putting those same two back into the field, no matter how many checkboxes the sales people try to select. For another twist, change the calculation to:

```
RightValues ( Premiums ; 2 )
```

Now FileMaker remembers the last two items that were selected and very cleverly deselects the oldest value, so that the field always contains the last two items selected from the Checkbox Set.

Text counting functions

Another way to parse text is to simply count its individual parts. FileMaker has three related functions for finding out *how much* text your fields contain:

- The **Length** function returns the length of a text value by counting characters.
- The **WordCount** function tells you how many words are in a text value.
- Using the **ValueCount** function, you can find out how many lines a field has.

These functions become powerhouses in combination with the various Left, Right, and Middle functions. When the fields you're parsing contain varying amounts of text, you can have FileMaker count each one so you don't have to. For example, to return all but the last letter in a field, you can use this calculation:

```
Left ( My Field ; Length ( My Field ) - 1 )
```

It uses the Left function to grab characters from the field, and the Length function (minus one) to find out how many to get. Just change the number on the end to chop off any number of junk characters from the end of a field. You're welcome.

Other text parsing functions

FileMaker includes dozens of text functions, but a few of them are worth special mention because you see them throughout the rest of this section, and because they're so useful for cleaning up messy data.

- The **Substitute** function performs a find-and-replace within a text value. For example, if you want to turn all the Xs to Os in your love letter (maybe you felt like you were coming on too strong), you can do this:

```
Substitute ( Love Letter ; "X" ; "O" )
```

A few FileMaker functions support a special *bracketed syntax* and Substitute is one of them. If you want to perform *several* replacements on a piece of text, you can do it with one Substitute function. Each pair in brackets represents one search value and its replacement value. Here's how you can show a field value with all the vowels removed. You can do this:

```
Substitute ( My Field ; ["a" ; "] ; ["e" ; ""] ; ["i" ; ""] ; ["o" ; ""] ;
["u" ; ""] )
```

Note: This example shows another nice fact about Substitute: You can use it to *remove* something. Just replace it with empty quotes: "".

WORKAROUND WORKSHOP

When Data Doesn't Comply

Sometimes the text you need to break up doesn't come in pieces that FileMaker automatically recognizes, like characters or words. For example, suppose you have a file path:

```
C:\My Documents\Product Shots\Tools\Large
Hammer.jpg
```

You need to get the name of the file (Large Hammer.jpg) and its parent folder (Tools). Unfortunately, this text value isn't divided into characters, words, or values. It's divided into *path components*, each with a backslash in between.

When you're faced with something like this, your best bet is to make it look like something FileMaker *can* deal with. If you can turn every backslash into a new line symbol (¶), then you can simply use the RightValues function to pull out the last two values. In other words:

```
Substitute ( File Path ; "\" ; "¶" )
```

The result of this expression is the list of path components, each on its own line:

```
C:
My Documents
Product Shots
Tools
Large Hammer.jpg
```

To get just the file name, you can do this:

```
RightValues ( Substitute ( File Path ; "\"
; "¶" ) ; 1 )
```

Unless your data already contains multiple lines, you can always use the Substitute function to turn any kind of delimited list into a list of values. Bear in mind, though, that the Substitute function is *case sensitive*. You can read more about case sensitivity on page 445.

• While Substitute can be used to change or remove what you specify, **Filter** can remove everything you *don't* specify. For example, suppose you want to strip any non-numeric characters from a credit card number. You can *try* to think of all the possible things a person might type in a Credit Card Number field (good luck!) or you can use Filter instead:

```
Filter ( Credit Card Number ; "0123456789" )
```

This calculation tells FileMaker to return the contents of the Credit Card Number field with everything except the numerals it removes. In other words, simply put the characters you'd like to *keep* in the second parameter.

Text Formatting Functions

Normally when you see data in a calculation field, it's displayed in the format (font, size, style, color, and so on) you applied in Layout mode. Every character in the field shares the same format, unless you want to manually search through all your records selecting the words "Limited Time Only" in your Promotion Notes field, so you can make that bold and red every time it appears. Not only does that method waste your precious time (especially if you're on salary), it also plays havoc with your design when you try to print the field.

FileMaker's Text Formatting functions let you specify exactly what bit of text you want in 18-point, boldfaced, red Verdana. And you don't have to visit a single record in person. You just write a calculation and FileMaker does the drudgework for you, without tampering with the real data.

FileMaker has six text formatting functions, as described below.

Tip: Since that big heading above clearly reads "*Text* Formatting Functions," any reasonable person would assume that this formatting applies only to text. Luckily, the unreasonable people rule the world. You can apply text formatting to any data type, as you'll see later in this chapter.

TextColor and RGB

The TextColor function takes two parameters: some text, and a color. It returns the text you send it in the right color. That's the text you specify using the companion function, RGB. Like many computer programs, FileMaker thinks of colors in RGB code, which defines all colors as combinations of red, green, and blue as expressed by numerical values.

This function returns a color based on three parameters—red, green, and blue. For example, if you want to change the Full Name field to show the first name in bright red, and the last name in bright blue, you use this calculation:

```
TextColor ( First Name ; RGB ( 255 ; 0 ; 0 ) )
   & " " &
TextColor ( Last Name ; RGB ( 0 ; 0 ; 255 ) )
```

Tip: For a crash course in RGB code—including how to avoid using it—see the box below.

**Text Parsing
Calculations**

Color My World (With 16M Colors)

FileMaker has a basic conflict over color. After all, it's a computer program that works with data, which comes in a limited number of types, like text value, number, date, and time. So what kind of data type is a *color*? The explanation isn't very, er, colorful. FileMaker understands 16,777,216 distinct colors, each subtly different from the one before, and each numbered from 0 to 16,777,215. Unfortunately, *learning* all those colors by number is beyond the reach of even the most bored developer. So FileMaker uses a standard (albeit entirely unintuitive) method of specifying a color as a mixture of component colors—red, green, and blue—with varying intensities.

Each parameter to the RGB function is a number, from zero to 255. The number says how intense—or bright—the component color should be. A zero in the first parameter means red doesn't enter into the equation at all. 255, on the other hand, means FileMaker should crank the red component to the max. The RGB function returns a number, identifying one of those 16-odd million choices. To make it doubly confusing for anyone who doesn't have a degree in computer programming or television repair, the RGB system deals with red, green, and blue as sources of *light*, not the more intuitive redyellow-blue primary colors of paints and pigments.

When colored lights mix (like those little pixels on a monitor), red and green make…yellow. In other words, to FileMaker and other RGB experts, it makes perfect sense to see bright yellow as the following:

```
RGB ( 255 ; 255 ; 0 )
```

So what's a person to do? Don't use RGB codes. Find some other tools.

If you use Mac OS X, you have just such a tool in the Utilities folder (in your Applications folder). It's called Digital Color Meter. Launch the application and choose RGB As Actual Value, 8-bit from the pop-up menu in its window. Now the little blue numbers show proper red (R), green (G), and blue (B) values for any color you point to on your screen. For example, in the status area (in Layout mode), pop open the Fill Color menu and point to any of the colors there to see the RGB equivalent.

On Microsoft Windows, you can see RGB colors in the standard color picker window. Just go to Layout mode, and in the status area, click the Fill Color button. Choose Other Color. When you click a color, you see the red, green, and blue values listed in the bottom-right corner of the window.

RGB Values in the Microsoft Windows color picker
RGB Values in the Mac OS X Digital Color Meter

TextFont

To change the font in a calculation result, use the TextFont function. In its simplest form, this function is…well…simple. You just pass it the text you want to format, and the name of the font to use. FileMaker returns the same text with the font applied:

```
TextFont ( "Dewey Defeats Truman!" ; "Times New Roman" )
```

TextFont also has a third optional parameter called fontScript. Most people can simply ignore this option. It tells FileMaker which *character set* you're interested in, and to select an appropriate font. (The character set determines which languages the font can be used for.) FileMaker accepts the following fontScript values:

- Roman
- Greek
- Cyrillic
- CentralEuropean
- ShiftJIS
- TraditionalChinese
- SimplifiedChinese
- OEM
- Symbol
- Other

Note: Unlike the font name, which is simply a text value, the script value shouldn't be in quotes. It's not a text value. Instead, you must specify one of the above values exactly, with no quotes.

If FileMaker can't find the specific font you've asked for, it selects another font in the specified script, so if you're on an English-based system and need to select a Chinese font, this parameter can help. (If you don't specify a script, FileMaker automatically uses the default script on your computer. That's why you rarely have to worry about it—you automatically get what you probably want.)

TextSize

The TextSize function is simple in every case. Just pass some text, and the point size you'd like (just like the sizes in the Format → Size menu in Browse mode). FileMaker returns the resized text.

TextStyleAdd and TextStyleRemove

Changing text *styles* (bold, italic, and so on) is a little more complicated. After all, a piece of text can only have *one* color, *one* font, or *one* size, but it can be bold, italic, and underlined all at the same time. With text styles, you don't just swap one style for another; you need to do things like take italic text and add bold formatting or even take bold-titlecase-strikethrough text and un-strikethrough it, leaving everything else in place.

To solve these problems, FileMaker gives you *two* functions for dealing with style: TextStyleAdd and TextStyleRemove. You use the first to add a style to a piece of text:

```
"Do it with " & TextStyleAdd ( "style" ; Italic )
```

Likewise, the TextStyleRemove function removes the specified style from the text.

```
TextStyleRemove ( My Text Field ; Italic )
```

The text style parameter goes in the calculation without quotes, just like the examples above. You can use any and every text style in FileMaker: Plain, Bold, Italic, Underline, Condense, Extend, Strikethrough, SmallCaps, Superscript, Subscript, Uppercase, Lowercase, Titlecase, WordUnderline, and DoubleUnderline. And then there's AllStyles. When you use the AllStyles parameter, it adds (or removes) *all* existing styles.

With these two functions and all these style options, you can do any kind of fancy formatting footwork imaginable. Here are some guidelines:

- When you add a style to some text using TextStyleAdd, it doesn't change any style that you've already applied. The new style's simply layered over the existing styles.

- Plain style's the notable exception to the above point. Adding Plain style effectively *removes* any other styling. This style comes in handy when you need to remove a mess of styling and apply something simpler. Say your fields contain the words "Past Due," styled in uppercase, bold, italic, and double underlined and you decide that modest italics would work just fine. Nesting the TextStyleAdd function with the Plain parameter does the trick:

```
TextStyleAdd ( TextStyleAdd ( "past due" ; Plain ) ; Italic )
```

Tip: As you may suspect, using TextStyleRemove with the AllStyles parameter does the exact same thing as TextStyleAdd with Plain. They both remove existing styling, but as you can see above, when you add Plain, you can write neater expressions.

- When you add more than one style parameter, FileMaker applies them all to the text. You can use nesting, as shown in the previous point, or simply stack them up with + signs:

```
TextStyleAdd ( "WARNING" ; Bold+Italic )
```

- If you take a bit of text that was formatted with a text formatting function, and then send it to another calculation as a parameter, the formatting goes along with the text. With the Substitute function, for example, you can format text that hasn't even been typed yet. If you add this function to a text field into which people can type letters to customers, it changes every occurrence of "for a limited time" to bold italics.

```
Substitute ( Letter ; "for a limited time" ; TextStyleAdd ( "for a limited
time" ; Bold+Italic )
```

Date and Time Calculations

FileMaker can be a little esoteric about dates and times. If you don't understand how they work, you can end up wasting a *lot* of time trying to do things that File-Maker can easily do for you. For example, you might need to know the first day of the month following the date an invoice is due. You can spend ages writing a calculation that takes leap years and the different number of days in each month into account. You'd be sweaty, tired, and proud when you were done...six hours after you started. But if you know how dates work in FileMaker, you can just type this single line:

```
Date ( Month ( Invoice Due Date ) + 1 ; 1 ; Year ( Invoice Due Date ) )
```

How FileMaker Looks at Time

Before you starting writing date and time calculations, you need to know how File-Maker actually keeps track of dates and times. FileMaker internally stores any date or time value as a single number that makes sense to it. Then, when it needs to display a date or time, it converts the number to a value people recognize as a date or time, like "11/7/2005" or "10:23 AM." As with other numbers that it stores one way and displays another, FileMaker does the math on the stored value, then converts it for your convenience. Here's how FileMaker keeps track of time:

- It stores a **date** as the number of days since the beginning of the year 1 A. D.
- It stores a **time** as the number of seconds since midnight.
- It stores a **timestamp** as the number of seconds since midnight at the beginning of the year 1 A. D. (a really big number).

This secret to date and time storage isn't just a technicality. It actually tells you a lot about how you can use dates and times in calculations. In the next few sections, you'll see how you can use simple math to do temporal magic.

Math with Dates and Times

Because FileMaker looks at dates and times as numbers, you're free to use them right along with other numbers and operators in all kinds of mathematical functions. By adding, subtracting, multiplying, and dividing dates, times, timestamps, and numbers, you can come up with meaningful results.

Dates

You can use the information in your database's date fields to have FileMaker figure out due dates, anniversaries, and so on. You can use date fields and numbers interchangeably. FileMaker's smart enough to figure out that you want to add whole days to the date value it's storing. Here are some general principles:

- To get a date in the future or past, add or subtract the number of days. For example, if your policy is that payments are due 10 days after invoices are presented, use this calculation:

  ```
  Invoice Date + 10
  ```

- Of course you aren't limited to adding constant numbers to dates. You can add a number field to a date field just as easily. If your video rental database holds the checkout date and the rental duration, you can find the due date with this calculation:

  ```
  Checkout Date + Rental Duration
  ```

- To get the number of days between two dates, subtract them.

  Imagine your registration database holds arrival and departure dates. You can find the duration of the stay (in days) using this calculation:

  ```
  Departure Date - Arrival Date
  ```

Note: When you're adding a number to a date, the result is a brand new date, and you should set the result type (page 400) of your calculation accordingly. On the other hand, if you're subtracting two dates, the result is a number—the number of days between the two dates. In this case, set your calculation to return a number result.

Times

Although FileMaker's internal clock counts time as the number of seconds since midnight, a time value doesn't always have to be a time of day. Depending on the field format (page 93), a time value can be a time of day, like 2:30 PM, or a *time* (as in duration, like 3 hours, 27 minutes).

Tip: FileMaker is savvy to the concept that time passes, but not all programs are. For instance, if you're exporting data to Excel, you should first convert time fields containing durations to plain old number fields.

In both cases, times have a numeric value, in hours:minutes:seconds format. 14:30:05 in a time of day field is 5 seconds after 2:30 PM, but in a time field, it's a duration of 14 hours, 30 minutes, and 5 seconds. If the time has fractional seconds (a decimal point), the numerical value does too.

You can record how long your 5-year-old takes to find her shoes (34:26:18), or how long she takes to find the Halloween candy (00:00:02.13).

The key to doing math with any kind of time value is to remember you're always adding and subtracting amounts of *seconds*. Here are the guidelines:

- To get a time in the future or past, add or subtract a number of seconds or a time value. If you know when a student finished her exam, and you know how long the exam took in minutes (1 minute = 60 seconds), you can figure out when she started.

  ```
  Finish Time - (Exam Duration * 60)
  ```

- To get the number of seconds between two times, subtract one from the other. Your Test Reporting database stores start and finish times for each exam. To find the duration, use this calculation:

  ```
  Finish Time - Start Time
  ```

- To get a time of day value in the future or past, add or subtract the number of seconds or a time value. Suppose you have a database of movie show times for your theater business. You use a timestamp field to record the date and time when each showing starts. You also use a time field to keep track of how long each movie is. Now you need to know when each movie *ends*:

  ```
  Showtime + Duration
  ```

Note: If you store the date and time the movie starts in separate date and time fields, the movie time calculation is much more difficult. Suppose a movie starts at 11:30 p.m. and runs for two hours. Adding these together, you get 25:30, which is a perfectly valid time value, but not a valid *time of day*. When you add to time values, they don't "roll over" after midnight. Timestamps, on the other hand, work as expected: You get 1:30 a.m. on the next day.

- To get the number of seconds between two timestamp values, subtract one from the other. For example, you use timestamps to record the date and time you start and finish a job. To find out how long the job took, in minutes, use this calculation:

  ```
  (Finish Time Stamp - Start Time Stamp) / 60
  ```

- To increase or decrease a time duration value, add or subtract the number of seconds, or another time duration. Say you use a repeating time field to hold the length of each song on a CD. This calculation tells you how long the entire CD is:

  ```
  Sum ( Songs::Song Lengths )
  ```

- To double, triple, halve, or otherwise scale a time duration, multiply or divide it by a number.

  If chilling your microbrew always takes twice as long as cooking, you can determine the chilling time with this calculation:

  ```
  Cooking Time * 2
  ```

Parsing Dates and Times

Just as you can parse out bits of text from text fields, FileMaker lets you pull out parts of a date or time value. For example, you might keep track of all your employee's birthdays in a normal date field, but you're trying to get statistical data from the year they were born, so you're not concerned about the month or date part of that value. You have six functions at your disposal to pick those individual components from a date, time, or timestamp value. They are:

- Year

- Month

- Day

- Hours

- Minutes

- Seconds

With a date value, you can use Year, Month, and Day. If you have a time, Hours, Minutes, and Seconds apply. You can use all six functions with a timestamp value.

These functions all have the same form. Each takes a single parameter—the value—and returns a numerical result. For example, the Day function returns the day portion of a date. This calculation returns 27:

```
Day ( GetAsDate ( "7/27/2006" ) )
```

UP TO SPEED

From Numbers to Times

If you can treat dates and times like numbers, it only makes sense that you can go the other way too. Suppose you have a field called Race Time that holds each athlete's race time as a number of seconds. If you'd rather view this time in the Hours:Minutes:Seconds (or Minutes:Seconds) format, you can easily use a calculation to convert it to a time value:

GetAsTime(Race Time)

The GetAsTime function, when you pass it a number value, converts it into the equivalent time.

(If you view this on a layout, you can use the time formatting options to display hours, minutes, and seconds in just about any way you want, as shown on page 240.) The GetAsTime function has another purpose as well: It can convert *text values* into times. If someone puts "3:37:03" into a text field, you can use GetAsTime to convert that text into a valid time value.

FileMaker has GetAsDate and GetAsTimestamp functions too, which work just the same.

Tip: For advice on how to display the results of month and day values in plain English, see the box below.

Name the Day (or Month)

Even when you're using the month number to group your data, you may prefer to *see* months by *name*. For example, if you produce a report of sales by month, you probably want the groupings labeled January, February, March, and so on, instead of 1, 2, and 3. You can use the MonthName function to get this effect:

    MonthName (Invoice Date)

This calculation returns "March."

You can still sort all your invoices by the date field to get them in order, but you use your new MonthName value to display in the sub-summary part. See page 273 for details on using sub-summary parts in reports.

Sometimes you need to see the day name (Monday, Tuesday, or Wednesday, for example). The DayName function does just that. To get its numerical equivalent, use DayOfWeek instead, which returns 1 for Sunday, 2 for Monday, and so forth.

Calculations that Create Dates and Times

Almost every database in existence has fields that create date and time values. Otherwise, folks would still sit around pecking out business forms with a typewriter, an adding machine, and a wall calendar. It sounds quaint, but there was one advantage—the human brain. Without even being aware of it, people do incredibly complex math every time they glance at a paper calendar or analog clock. When the boss said, "I want these invoices to go out two days after the end of next month," a human clerk knew exactly what to do.

When you work with dates and times in FileMaker, sometimes you can get away with just simple math as in the previous section, plugging date and time values into basic calculations. But how do you tell a computer to put "two days after the end of next month" in the Invoice Date field? FileMaker provides three functions to assist the translation:

- The **Date** function accepts three parameters—Month, Day, and Year—and returns the appropriate date value. For example, to put a date value of January 21, 2006 in a calculation, you use the date function like this:

      Date (1 ; 21 ; 2006)

- The **Time** function wants three parameters as well, this time Hours, Minutes, and Seconds. It returns the time value. (The Seconds parameter can have a decimal point if necessary.) For example, you can construct the time value "8:00 PM" like this:

      Time (20 ; 0 ; 0)

Note: For time-of-day values, the Time function doesn't let you specify a.m. or p.m., so you have to use 24-hour notation.

- The **Timestamp** function takes just two parameters: Date and Time. It combines the two into a single timestamp value. It shows January 10, 2006 at 8:30 p.m. like this:

```
Timestamp ( Date ( 1 ; 10 ; 2006) ; Time ( 20 ; 30 ; 0 ) )
```

In this example, you use all three functions: the date function to produce the correct date value, the time function for the time value, and the timestamp function to put them together.

FREQUENTLY ASKED QUESTION

Why Functions?

Why can't I just put "1/10/2006" in my calculation, just like I'd put it in a date field?

Because "1/10/2006" is a text value, not a date value. When you're entering data in a date field, FileMaker knows it's a date field, and is nice enough to convert text like this into a date for you. In a calculation, though, FileMaker may not know you want a date, so it treats what you put in as text instead.

You can use the GetAsDate() function to convert text values like this into dates:

```
GetAsDate ( "1/10/2006" )
```

But even this isn't advisable. Remember from page 93 that dates are interpreted depending on how you've configured your computer? On one computer, this calculation could produce the date value January 10, 2006, while on another machine it might result in October 1 instead. In other words, there's no safe way to ensure you get the date you really want when you use GetAsDate with a text value, unless you're using text the user supplied.

The Date function always expects the month, then the day, then the year. Computer settings don't affect it. So the date function is the safest way to record dates in calculations.

The secret powers of date

Although FileMaker doesn't look at calendars the way people do, that's not all bad. You see a calendar in absolute terms: April 30 belongs to April, May 1 belongs to May, and that's that. FileMaker, however, thinks of dates in relative terms and sees no such limitations. You can use this flexibility to your advantage in calculations— big time. You can give seemingly illogical parameters to the date function, and have FileMaker produce a valid date anyway.

For example, this calculation actually produces a valid date:

```
Date ( 5 ; 0 ; 2006 )
```

You see a nonsense result—May 0, 2006. But FileMaker looks at the same code and says, "No problem. Zero comes before 1, so you must mean the day that comes before May 1." And so it returns April 30, 2006.

These same smarts apply to the month as well:

```
Date ( 15 ; 11 ; 2006 )
```

Produces March 11, *2007*. In other words, three months into the next year, since 15 is three months more than one year.

This behavior comes in super-handy when you're trying to fiddle with dates in calculations. Suppose you have order records, each one with an order date. You bill on the last day of the month in which the order was placed, so your calculation needs to figure out that date, which could be 28, 30, or 31 depending on the month, or even 29 if it's February in a leap year. That calculation would take an entire page in this book. But here's a much easier approach: Instead of calculating which day each month ends, use the fact that the *last* day of *this* month is always the day *before* the *first* day of *next* month. To start with, you can calculate next month like this:

```
Month ( Order Date ) + 1
```

So the *date* of the first day of next month is:

```
Date ( Month(Order Date) + 1 ; 1 ; Year(Order Date) )
```

To get the day before, just subtract one from the whole thing:

```
Date (
    Month(Order Date) + 1;    // the _next_ month
    1;                        // the _first_ day
    Year(Order Date)          // the same year
) - 1                         // subtract 1 to get the day before
```

It may look a little confusing at first…but it's much shorter than a page. And it works perfectly every month of every year.

Containers in Calculations

Although it isn't a typical calculation data type, you can do a few interesting things with container fields in calculations. You don't have the same vast options you do with other types. It would be great if you could subtract Cousin Clem.jpg from Family Reunion.jpg to get the scoundrel out of the picture, but alas, the technology's not quite there yet. Nevertheless, FileMaker doesn't leave containers entirely out in the cold when it comes to calculations.

Calculations with Pictures, Sounds, Movies, and Files

When you create a calculation field (page 380), you can set its result type to Container. You can't *create* container data in a calculation, but you *can* refer to other container fields. When you do, the picture, sound, movie, or file in the referenced container field shows in the new calculation field.

You can, for example, make a calculation field that shows the contents of one container field when you're in Browse mode and another in Preview mode. This field lets you use low-resolution images when you view on the screen, and higher resolutions when you print. (You'll learn to do that in the next chapter, when you learn about calculations with that kind of decision-making ability.)

You might also want to use container fields in a calculated replace. Suppose you have a found set of 30 records that don't have a low-resolution image. You have to have something in that field, so you decide to take the hi-res image for those few records and plunk them down in the low-resolution image field. Choose Records → Replace Field Contents and perform this calculated replace:

```
Graphics::High Resolution Image
```

The entire calculation consists of a reference to a field of that name in the Graphics table. The calculation does the grunt work of copying the high-resolution image into the low-resolution field in each record.

Calculations with References

If a container field holds a reference to a picture, movie, sound, or file, instead of the object itself (page 71), you can do even more. When you treat such a field as *text*, FileMaker gives you some information about the referenced file.

If you have a field called Product Shot (see Figure 10-4) that holds a reference to a photograph file, you can use this calculation:

```
GetAsText ( Product Shot )
```

Figure 10-4:
FileMaker also includes two paths identifying the file's location. One's a relative path, starting from the location of the database file. The second's an absolute path, meaning it starts from the top level of your computer's system of files and folders.

The result of this calculation looks like this:

```
size:266,309
image:../../../../../quilt database/sale quilt pix/batik squares.jpg
imagemac:/babycakes/current work/quilt database/sale quilt pix/batik squares.
jpg
```

As shown in Figure 10-4, FileMaker tells you the size (width and height in pixels) and location of the file (if this weren't a picture, you wouldn't see the "size:" line).

You can use this calculation to help you keep track of a set of images that the whole company needs to use. You really need two container fields for this purpose. One holds the graphic itself, or a low-resolution copy, if you don't want the file size to balloon. Then, when you place the graphic as a reference in the second container field, the calculation stores the graphic's original location. The calculation's not dynamic, however, so the path serves as a reference of where the file *should* be, not where it really is. Company policy about putting things back where you found them has to reinforce your good data practices.

Advanced Calculations

In the previous two chapters, you've learned loads of ways calculations can make your databases work harder for you. But the functions you've learned so far can't make your databases work much *smarter*. For example, the TextColor function can display the balance due on an invoice in red. But suppose you want that to happen *only* if the invoice is past due? You could do it in any number of ways, from sorting invoice records to creating a special "past due balance" field. But they all either make extra work for the person using the database, or give you as designer yet another field to worry about every time you tweak, troubleshoot, or repurpose the database. The most elegant solution is to let the database figure out for itself when an invoice is past due. In other words, you want to create a calculation that makes a *decision* based on current data, whatever it may be. This chapter shows you how to give your calculations that brainpower by using logical functions and other advanced techniques.

Note: Before you read on, now's a good time to download a fresh copy of the working database. This chapter refers to some layouts and fields that your copy may not have. Head over to MissingManuals.com, as discussed on page xxiv.

Stored, Unstored, and Global Fields

When you defined calculation fields in Chapters 9 and 10, you may have wondered about the Specify Calculation dialog box's Storage Options button (Figure 11-1). You learned about indexing and other storage options back in

Chapter 3 (page 109). When you use similar options in your calculations, you exercise more control over the information your functions work with.

Figure 11-1:
When you click the Storage Options button in the Specify Calculation dialog box, you can set global storage and indexing options, just like any other field type. You also get a choice you haven't seen before: "Do not store calculation results." This exciting new option gives you control over when FileMaker recalculates the value in your formula. With this option, you can make your calculations either save information for later or use the most up-to-date information as your database changes.

Stored and Unstored Calculation Fields

Normally, a calculation field holds a value just like any other field. *You* can't edit the value, because FileMaker creates it for you from the calculation. When you use this field on a layout, for example, FileMaker simply displays its results. Depending on whether you turn on the "Do not store calculation result" option in Figure 11-1, FileMaker either grabs saved (stored) results from a table or calculates the value *on the fly* whenever necessary. For example, when you have an unstored calculation field on a layout, FileMaker recalculates the value as soon as you switch to the layout. In fact, whenever an unstored field is showing onscreen, FileMaker updates it automatically any time something causes its value to change.

At the same time, whenever the data in a field changes, FileMaker also works behind the scenes, finding all the *stored* calculation fields that depend on the changed field and *recalculates* them, storing the new value in the field. Whether it's stored or unstored, a calculation field usually changes because a field used in the calculation has changed, as you'll see next. Understanding *when* fields recalculate and how dependencies work can help you avoid future mistakes.

Note: When you use a field in a calculation, you can say the calculation *depends* on the field (or in other words, that it has a *dependency* on the field).

Field dependencies

Take a look at the example in Figure 11-2 to see how FileMaker knows when to recalculate fields. It's very common for calculation fields to use other calculation fields in complex arrangements, as this hierarchy of field dependencies illustrates.

First Name and Last Name are the only editable fields in Figure 11-2. When someone edits one of these fields, FileMaker looks at the field dependencies to see if it needs to do any extra work. The program sees that it needs to recalculate Full Name and then store that Full Name value, which in turn triggers more work. File-Maker must recalculate and store the Full Address value as well. In a sense, that one change trickles down through all the dependent fields as FileMaker calculates and stores, calculates and stores. All this recalculating happens as soon as the user exits the First Name field after making the change.

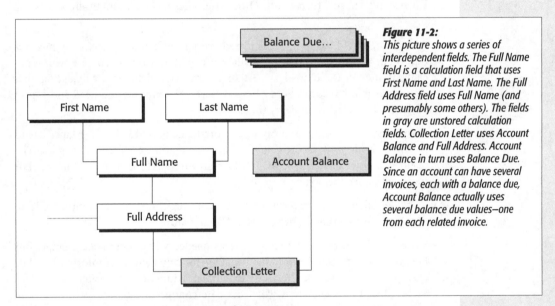

Figure 11-2:
This picture shows a series of interdependent fields. The Full Name field is a calculation field that uses First Name and Last Name. The Full Address field uses Full Name (and presumably some others). The fields in gray are unstored calculation fields. Collection Letter uses Account Balance and Full Address. Account Balance in turn uses Balance Due. Since an account can have several invoices, each with a balance due, Account Balance actually uses several balance due values—one from each related invoice.

By contrast, since Collection Letter is an *unstored field*, FileMaker *doesn't* recalculate it right away. (If it did, it would have no place to *store* the result.) Instead, the program waits until someone brings up the field onscreen, *then* it runs the calculation on the current data and displays the result.

Again, more things change. To calculate the Collection Letter value, FileMaker grabs the stored value for the Full Address field. But it also needs the Account Balance, which is not stored. As such, it has to first calculate *that* field. Doing so requires calculating the Balance Due on each invoice in turn, then adding them up to get an Account Balance. Finally, it has the values it needs to show you the Collection Letter. Thus, when you use *unstored* calculations, FileMaker pulls the data it needs down through the hierarchy of dependencies on an as-needed basis.

Deciding when to store

When you first create a calculation field, FileMaker makes it a stored field automatically, *if possible*. Some field values aren't eligible for storage. These are the situations when a calculation field must be unstored:

- If it depends on any other unstored fields.

- If it depends on any global fields.

- If it depends on any related fields.

- If it depends on any summary fields.

If your calculation meets any of these criteria, FileMaker automatically turns on the "Do not store calculation results – recalculate when needed" option on for you, and it doesn't let you turn it off. Otherwise, FileMaker automatically stores the field.

- An unstored field has to be recalculated every time it appears onscreen, in a layout, or in a report. All that recalculation can slow your database down, especially if the unstored field is part of a summary field or a calculation that aggregates many records. So it's best to store a field unless you need and expect a freshly calculated value every time.

- If you perform a find based on an unstored calculation field, FileMaker has to go through all your records one-by-one, calculating each one as it goes. The result is a slow search process. If you plan on searching a field, store it. (For more detail, see the box on page 443.)

Even if FileMaker can store a certain value, you might not always want it to. Here are some reasons you might turn *on* that "Do not store" box:

- Stored fields automatically recalculate as needed when *other fields* change. But FileMaker has no such automatic behavior for other kinds of information. For example, when you use the Get(CurrentDate) function in a calculation, FileMaker doesn't recalculate it when the date changes. In general, when you use any of the Get functions (page 390), you usually want to make your field unstored to "get" the most up-to-date information.

- A stored field takes up space on disk, while an unstored field doesn't. FileMaker 8 files can hold 8 terrabytes of data, so space isn't a major consideration for most people. But if you're into slim and trim files, you can save space by making calculations unstored.

- Lots of stored calculation fields can really slow down *record creation*. That's usually not a big deal, but if you often import data (Chapter 17) or use a script to regularly create lots of records, you can speed things up by reducing the number of stored calculations.

Tip: Obviously, there's some gray area here. When in doubt, store the field. You can always make it unstored later. Choose File → Define Database, then select your field from the list and click Options, and then Storage Options to find the "Do not store calculation results – recalculate as needed" option.

FREQUENTLY ASKED QUESTION

I *Want* to Store My Field

What if I want to search on a field that FileMaker won't let me store?

Just because you can't store a field doesn't mean you don't wish you could. For example, in your Invoices layout, you probably do want to be able to search for invoices with a balance due. But since that field uses related data, it's not storable.

The good news is, you don't have to store a field in order to search it; the search is just a little slower. You won't notice the slowdown until you've amassed *lots* of invoice records. Sadly, there's no easy way to speed it up.

One remedy is to change the way people work with your database. You have to make your Invoice Detail layout *read only*—meaning users can't change data on the invoice directly (see page 594). Instead, they use a special layout and a script to make invoice changes.

When they're finished, your script can calculate the balance due and update a number field on the invoice appropriately. This way, the Balance Due field is a normal, nonrelated field, eligible for indexing and quick searches.

Also, remember that FileMaker can't search a field based on related data very quickly, but it can search the related data *itself* with lightning speed. For example, to find an invoice that has payments applied to it, don't search the Amount Paid field in the invoice. Instead, search for invoices where Payments::Amount is greater than zero. That search turns up every invoice with a related payment record that's not negative. You get exactly what you want, and FileMaker can carry it out using indexed fields.

Note: With the exception of global fields and unstored fields, you can set indexing for calculation fields just like any other field, as discussed on page 109. The available options and their effects depend on the result type of the calculation—text, number, date, or time.

Global Calculation Fields

A calculation field can use *global storage* (page 109) just like any other field. When you're in the Storage Options window and you turn on "Use global storage," File-Maker calculates just one value for the entire table, rather than a value for each record. If your calculation uses other global fields—and *no* other fields—then it works just as you expect. That is, when you modify one of the global fields it depends on, FileMaker automatically recalculates its value.

If the calculation uses non-global fields, on the other hand, things get a little tricky. Whenever you change one of the fields referenced in the calculation, FileMaker recalculates the global calculation field using the values from the current record. For example, if you turn on "Use global storage" for your Full Name field, it shows the name of the person you're looking at when you dismiss the Define Database window. If you were on the first record, that's whose name you see in the field, just as expected. But as you flip through the records, you see that first user's name on every record. You're changing records, but with global storage, the Full Name value stays the same. That's because nothing it depends on has changed.

Now imagine you switch to the *last* record. If you then change the First Name field, Full Name recalculates. This new value displays the first and last name from the last record, since FileMaker reevaluates the calculation in its entirety.

This behavior may seem kind of odd, but there's a really cool use for it. If you need to track the data in the last record you *changed*—maybe you need an informal audit of which record just got changed while you're scanning through other records—throw a global calculation field on your data entry layout. Then, no matter which record you're looking at, you see the value of the last *edited* record in that field.

Logical Functions

The logical function group is a diverse and powerful lot. You get functions for making decisions (called *conditional functions*), learning about field values, and even evaluating calculations *inside* other calculations. This section covers all those possibilities. Along the way, you learn how to define and use *variables,* which act as placeholders while complex calculations go through their many steps.

Conditional Functions

This chapter began by posing an interesting challenge: You have a calculation field in the Invoices table called Total Due. It calculates the total amount due on an invoice by subtracting the sum of all payments from the total amount of the invoice. Can you modify the Total Due calculation to turn red when an invoice is past due?

The answer lies in the three conditional functions. Each one lets you specify more than one possible result. The function requires one or more parameters—called *conditions* or *conditional expressions*—that tell it which result to pick. The conditional functions—If, Case, and Choose—differ in how many possible results they support and what kind of condition they expect.

The If function

The first and most common conditional function is simply called If. The If function is the basic unit of decision making in FileMaker calculations. It's the ticket when you have to decide between two choices, based on some criteria.

It looks like this:

```
If ( Condition ; True Result ; False Result )
```

When you use the If function, FileMaker evaluates the condition looking for a Boolean result (true or false). If the condition has a true value, the function returns its second parameter (true result). If the condition is false, though, it returns the False Result instead. Here's an example:

```
If ( First Name = "Dominique" ; "Free" ; "$299.00" )
```

For example, this calculation returns Free if the First Name field matches "Dominique." If it *doesn't* match, then it returns $299.00 instead.

FREQUENTLY ASKED QUESTION

Matching Text Values

What do you mean by "First Name field matches 'Dominique'?" What constitutes a match?

When you use the = operator with text values, FileMaker compares the two values on each side letter-by-letter. If every letter, number, space, punctuation and so on matches, you get a True result. But the comparison isn't case sensitive. In other words, this expression has a True result:

```
"TEXT" = "text"
```

If this function is too forgiving for your needs, you can use the Exact function instead.

Exact takes two text parameters, compares them, and returns true if they match exactly—including case. This expression has a False result:

```
Exact ( "TEXT" ; "text" )
```

It's perfectly legal to use the Exact function (or any other function, field, or expression) as the first parameter of the If function, like this:

```
If ( Exact ( First Name ; "Dominique" ) ;
"Free" ; "$299.00" )
```

This version of the calculation would return "$299.00" if the First Name field contained "dominique," since the case on the letter D doesn't match.

The Case function

Sometimes you need to pick from more than just two choices. Luckily, If has a cousin named Case that simply excels at such problems. For example, suppose you want to show one of these four messages on the top of your layout:

• Good Morning

• Good Afternoon

• Good Evening

• Go To Bed

You obviously need to choose between these messages based on the time of day. The If function doesn't work very well for this problem because If only allows one condition and two possible results. You *can* nest If statements one inside the other, so that the false result is really another If statement. But nested If functions are really hard to read and even harder to tweak, so if you find that your business rules require a change in your calculation, you may rue the day you decided to use 12 nested Ifs to decide which discount your customers should get.

The Case function has this form:

```
Case ( Condition 1 ; Result 1 ; Condition 2 ; Result 2 ... )
```

You can add as many parameters as you want, in pairs, to represent a condition and the result to be returned if that condition is true. Because the conditions and results are sequential, and not nested, you can easily read a Case statement, no matter how many conditions you pile on. You can even add an optional parameter after the last result. This parameter represents the *default* result—the one File-Maker uses if none of the conditions were true.

Note: Since the Case function accepts several conditions, it's entirely possible that more than one condition is true at the same time. If so, FileMaker chooses the *first* true condition when it picks a result.

To implement the greeting message described on page 445, a calculation using the Case function might look like this:

```
Case (
    Get(CurrentTime) > Time(4;0;0) and Get(CurrentTime) < Time(12;0;0);
    "Good Morning";

     Get(CurrentTime) > Time(12;0;0) and Get(CurrentTime) < Time(18;0;0);
    "Good Afternoon";

    Get(CurrentTime) > Time(18;0;0) and Get(CurrentTime) < Time(22;0;0);
    "Good Evening";

    "Go To Bed"
)
```

In this calculation, the Case function checks first to see if the current time is between 4:00 a.m. and 12:00 p.m. If it is, the "Good Morning" value is returned. If not, it then checks whether the time is between 12:00 p.m. and 6:00 p.m., which would produce the "Good Afternoon" message. Finally, it checks to see if it's between 6:00 p.m. and 10:00 p.m. If so, the user sees "Good Evening."

You don't need to specify a condition for the last result—"Go To Bed"—because if all the previous conditions are false, it *must* be time for bed. In other words, if it *isn't* the morning, and it *isn't* the afternoon, and it *isn't* the evening, then it must be late at night. (If you need further help deciphering the above calculation, see the box on page 454. On the other hand, if you're so far ahead that you can see a better way to do it, see the box on page 448.)

The Choose function

The Choose function is sort of the forgotten third member of the conditional trio. People don't immediately grasp how to use it…so they don't. But if you think of it as a value list with the choices coded into a calculation, you see how Choose can turn an awfully ugly Case function into a specimen of neatness.

UP TO SPEED

A Complex Case

The Case function expresses a familiar concept—do thing #1 in one case, do thing #2 in a different case, and so on. But you might not immediately know how you get from that simple idea to the more complicated calculations shown int his chapter. Here's how it breaks down.

Remember that semicolons separate the parameters you pass to a function. So the first parameter is *all* of this:

```
Get(CurrentTime) > Time(4;0;0) and
Get(CurrentTime) < Time(12;0;0)
```

That whole expression forms the first condition. Remember from Chapter 9 that the *and* operator works on two Boolean values. It returns a true result if the values on each side are *both true*.

So really, you can split this condition in two. First, this must be true:

```
Get(CurrentTime) > Time(4;0;0)
```

If that's true, FileMaker checks to see if this expression is true too:

```
Get(CurrentTime) < Time(12;0;0)
```

These sub-expressions are much simpler. Each has the same form, comparing the current time to a time you construct with the Time function. The first makes sure it's after 4:00 a.m. The second makes sure it's *before* 12:00 p.m. The other two conditions in the calculation are exactly the same—except that they look at different times.

It looks like this:

```
Choose ( Condition ; Result Zero ; Result One ; Result Two ... )
```

Unlike the other conditional functions, Choose doesn't expect a Boolean expression for its condition. Instead, it looks for a *number*. The number tells it which of the results to choose: If Condition is zero, the function returns Result Zero; if it's one, it returns Result One; and so on.

Imagine you have a Student table, and one of its fields is called GPA. This field holds the student's current grade point average, as a number. You'd like to turn this number into a letter grade on the printed report.

Many FileMaker developers would immediately jump to the Case function to solve this problem. They'd do something like this:

```
Case (
    GPA < 0.5; "F";
    GPA < 1.5; "D";
    GPA < 2.5; "C";
    GPA < 3.5; "B";
    "A"
)
```

While this calculation gets the job done, you can do it more succinctly with the Choose function:

```
Choose ( Round(GPA; 0); "F"; "D"; "C"; "B"; "A" )
```

When you turn the GPA value into an integer (using Round), it becomes a candidate for the Choose function. When the GPA is 3.2, FileMaker rounds it to three, and selects result number three: "B." (Remember that the first result is for *zero*, so number three is actually the *fourth* result parameter. For more detail, see the box on page 449.)

Note: This calculation uses the Round function, which you haven't seen before. Round takes two numbers as parameters. It rounds the first value to the number of decimal places specified in the second parameter.

POWER USERS' CLINIC

Clever Case Conditions

If you're a logic-minded person with a healthy dose of schizophrenia, you might be jumping up and down in your chair right now, waving your hand in the air. What you're *dying* to say is that you "can make that Case function simpler!" Well, you're probably right. In fact, this calculation does the same job:

```
Case (
    Get(CurrentTime) <= Time(4;0;0) or
Get(CurrentTime) > Time(22;0;0);
    "Go To Bed";

    Get(CurrentTime) < Time(12;0;0);
    "Good Morning";

    Get(CurrentTime) < Time(18;0;0);
    "Good Afternoon";

    "Good Evening"
)
```

This version takes advantage of the fact that the Case function returns the result associated with the *first* true condition. FileMaker looks at the first condition, which checks to see if it's before 4:00 a.m. or after 10:00 p.m. If either's true (note the "or" operator), the function returns *Go To Bed*.

If both *aren't* true, FileMaker moves on to the second condition, which asks if it's earlier than 12:00 p.m. If so, it returns *Good Morning*. (What if it's three in the morning? That *is* earlier than 12:00 p.m., but you don't see "Good Morning" because FileMaker never gets this far. If it's 3:00 a.m., the search for truth stops after the first condition.)

If it still hasn't found a true condition, FileMaker moves on to the next: Is it before 6:00 p.m.? Again, the structure of the case statement *implies* that it must be after noon at this point since any time before noon would've been caught in the previous conditions. So this condition is *really* looking for a time between noon and six, even though it doesn't say so in so many words.

If you're comfortable with this kind of logic, you can save yourself some clicks and a little typing. (Technically you also make a more efficient calculation, but unless you're using the abacus version of FileMaker, that doesn't matter much.)

Many people, on the other hand, find a calculation like this one utterly confusing. In that case, just use the longer version and find something else in your life to brag about.

Constructing a Conditional Calculation

Now that you've seen the three conditional functions, it's time to take a stab at that calculation way back from the beginning of this chapter: Make the Total Due turn red when the due date has passed.

When you're trying to come up with a logical calculation, think about what information FileMaker needs to make the decision, and what action you want

FileMaker to take after it decides. Then consider how best to do that using your database's existing fields and structure. Your first decision is which conditional function to use.

FREQUENTLY ASKED QUESTION

No Zero

The Choose function insists that the first parameter should be for a zero condition. What if I don't want zero? My condition values start with 1.

This is a common question. Luckily you don't really have a problem at all. There are two equally easy ways to get what you want from Choose. Perhaps the most obvious is to simply add a dummy zero result:

```
Choose ( Door ; "" ; "European Vacation" ;
"New Car" ; "[Wah Wah Wah]" )
```

In this calculation, there is no Door number zero, so you just stick "" in the spot where the zero result belongs. You could just as well put "Henry Kissinger" there for all you care, since it never gets chosen anyway. Just make sure you put something in there, so your first real result is in the number-one spot.

If you just don't like having that dummy result in your calculation, you can take this approach instead:

```
Choose ( Door - 1 ; "European Vacation" ;
"New Car" ; "[Wah Wah Wah]" )
```

This version simply subtracts one from the Door number. Now Door number one gets the zero result, and Door number two gets the one result. This approach becomes more appealing when your choices begin with an even higher number:

```
Choose ( Year - 2000 ; "Dragon" ; "Snake"
; "Horse" ; "Sheep" )
```

Since this calculation uses the year as the condition, it would be a real drag to enter 2000 dummy values. Instead, you just subtract enough to get your sequence to start with zero.

Total Due calculation #1: using the If function

Most people's first thought would be the If function, since the calculation needs to check *if* one condition is true:

• Is the value of the Date Due field earlier than today's date?

The calculation then takes the result of the If function and returns one of two possible results:

• If it's *true* that the due date has passed, display the total due in red text.

• If it's *not true* that the due date has passed, display the total due in black text.

In plainer English, the If condition checks to see if the due date is passed. If so, it returns a red result; if not, it returns a black result. In addition, the calculation needs to find the value to display in black or red—the total due. The full calculation might look like the following:

```
If (
    // Condition
    Get(CurrentDate) > Date Due and
    // Calculate the total due here to make sure it's not zero
    Invoice Amount > Total Paid;
```

```
// True Result
TextColor (
    // Calculate the total due here for the red result
    Invoice Amount - Total Paid;
    RGB(255;0;0)
);

// False Result
// Calculate the black total due here
Invoice Amount - Total Paid
)
```

To put this calculation to work in your database, delete the calculation currently in the field definition for Total Due and type in this one. When the due date is passed, the value in your newly smarter Total Due field changes to red.

Note: Since the Total Due field already calculates the due balance, you may be tempted to take a short-cut: Create a *new* field that uses the If function to change the existing Total Due field to red, then plop that new field on the Invoices layout instead. But that would clutter your database with a superfluous field. And in a relational database especially, that kind of sloppy field swapping is only asking for trouble.

Total Due calculation #2: using the Case function

Lots of people like the Case function so much that they always use it, even in places where the If function is perfectly competent. You might choose to use Case if there's any chance you'll want to add some conditions to the statement later on. Instead of editing an If expression later, you can save time by using Case from the start (just in…case).

The same calculation using Case (and minus the helpful comments above) would look like this:

```
Case (

Get ( CurrentDate ) > Date Due and Invoice Amount > Total Paid ;

TextColor ( Invoice Amount - Total Paid ; RGB ( 255 ; 0 ; 0 ) ) ;

Invoice Amount - Total Paid

)
```

Tip: With a single condition and default result, the syntax for If and Case are the same. So if you do need to change an If statement to Case later, simply change the word "If" to "Case" and add the conditions.

This calculation works as advertised, but it has a couple of weak points. First, it has to calculate the total amount due *three times*. That makes for three times as many chances to introduce typos and three times as many places to edit the "Invoice Amount – Total Paid" expression if you change the calculation later.

Second, Total Paid is an unstored calculation based on the sum of related records. That's one of the slowest things you can ask a calculation to do. It may not matter much in this example, but in a more complicated situation, a calculation like this could slow FileMaker to a crawl.

In the next section, you'll learn how FileMaker helps you write leaner calculations that are easier for you to read—and quicker for FileMaker to work through.

The Let Function and Variables

The Let function creates a temporary holder for a value, called a *variable*, which can be plugged into a calculation over and over again. You'll do a little more work upfront to set up a variable, but that effort pays off with faster calculations that are easier to read, edit, and troubleshoot.

Defining Calculation Variables

In your Let function, you define a value and give it a name, and then use that name as often as you need throughout the calculation. In this case, you can calculate the amount due once, and store the result in a variable called Amount Due.

The Let function is unique among functions because it controls the way you write your calculation, not the result. Here's an example:

```
Let ( [ L = 5 ; W = 10 ; H = 3 ] ; L * W * H )
```

Like the Substitute function described on page 425, Let uses bracketed notation. It really takes just two parameters. The first is a list of variable definitions. Each variable gets a name and a value using this format:

```
Name = Value
```

Tip: FileMaker uses the terms "var" for Name and "expression" for Value in its manual and help files. The terms mean the same things, but "var" and "expression" sound much more impressive.

If you have more than one variable to define (as in the example above), put a semicolon between each one, and put them all in-between a pair of square brackets. You can use any calculation expression as the value.

In fact, the expression that determines the value of a variable can even use other variables that were defined earlier.

For example, the next calculation is perfectly legal. Its hours variable has a value of 240: 24 times the value of the Days variable:

```
Let (
    [ Days = 10 ;
    Hours = 24 * Days ;
    Minutes = 60 * Hours ];

    Minutes & " Minutes"
)
```

The second parameter can be any calculation expression. This parameter is special because you can use any of the variables you've defined inside the expression, just like fields. In the first example above, there are three defined variables (L, W, and H); the expression then multiplies them together.

When FileMaker evaluates the Let function, it determines the value of each variable just once, and then plugs this value into the expression every time that variable is used. The result of a Let function is simply the result of its expression.

Total Due calculation #3: using Let

Your Total Due calculation can use the Let function to solve all its problems. Just put the Amount Due in a variable and use it throughout the calculation:

```
Let ( Amount Due = Invoice Amount - Total Paid ;
    If ( Get(CurrentDate) > Date Due and Amount Due > 0;
        TextColor ( Amount Due ; RGB(255;0;0) );
        Amount Due
    )
)
```

This version of the calculation is simpler, easier to change, and more efficient. You can't beat that.

The Life of a Variable

Most variables last only as long as it takes FileMaker to work through the calculation, then they're gone. This type of variable is called a *local variable* because they aren't valid outside the Let function that calls them into existence. But you can also create a special variable, called a *global variable*, that lives beyond your calculation. Read on to see when to use each type.

Local variables

The variables you've written so far have all been local variables. Now it's time to learn that local variables having shockingly short memories.

Local variables can lose their values even before a calculation is finished. If you write:

```
Let ( Amount Due = Invoice Amount - Total Paid;
    If (
        Get ( CurrentDate ) > Date Due and Amount Due > 0;
        TextColor ( Amount Due ; RGB ( 255 ; 0 ; 0 ) );
        Amount Due
        )
) & If ( Amount Due < 0 ; "CR" ; "" )
```

The calculation tries to use the Amount Due variable after the end parenthesis in the Let function. Anything that happens after that in the calculation is outside the Let function's *scope*, so when you try to close the Specify Calculation dialog box on this calculation, FileMaker complains that it doesn't know what that last Amount Due is supposed to be. One way to rewrite that calculation using a local variable is:

```
Let ( Amount Due = Invoice Amount - Total Paid;
    Case (
        Get ( CurrentDate ) > Date Due and Amount Due > 0;
        TextColor ( Amount Due ; RGB ( 255 ; 0 ; 0 ) ;
        Amount Due < 0 ; "CR" ; ""
        )
)
```

In this example, you're including the last test condition within the scope of the Let function and you've switched to a Case function, so that you don't have to read a set of nested If functions.

If you want the local variables you set inside calculations to follow the same naming conventions as variables you set in scripts (see Chapter 15), prefix their names with "$." In that case, you'd write the calculation you just saw like this:

```
Let ( $Amount Due = Invoice Amount - Total Paid;
    Case (
        Get ( CurrentDate ) > Date Due and $Amount Due > 0;
        TextColor ( $Amount Due ; RGB ( 255 ; 0 ; 0 ) ;
        $Amount Due < 0 ; "CR" ; ""
        )
)
```

Notice that you have to include the prefix in the Let function *and* in the formula that follows it.

Global variables

But just as FileMaker gives you global fields, it also gives you *global variables*. Unlike local variables, global variables hold their results after the Let function is finished. To create a global variable, add a "$$" prefix to its name. Here's the same calculation rewritten with a global variable:

```
Let ( $$Amount Due = Invoice Amount - Total Paid;
   Case (
      Get ( CurrentDate ) > Date Due and $$Amount Due > 0;
      TextColor ( $$Amount Due ; RGB ( 255 ; 0 ; 0 ) ;
      $$Amount Due < 0 ; "CR" ; ""
      )
   )
```

The only difference you can see in the calculation is the $$ prefix. But the practical difference is vast: Global variable values remain until you change them (through another calculation or through a script), or until you close the file.

POWER USERS' CLINIC

Field Formatting Calculations

Now that you understand most of FileMaker's calculation power features, you're ready to see something really neat. Sometimes you have a field that lets you have free entry, but you want to be sure the end result is formatted properly.

The trick is to attach an Auto-Enter calculation to a field, and make the calculation depend on the field itself. Whenever the user changes the field, FileMaker recalculates the auto-enter calculation and updates the field. For example, imagine you want all customer phone numbers entered in this form:

> (555) 555-1212

Since Phone Number is a text field, there's nothing keeping the user from typing it this way instead:

> 555/555/1212

Or like this:

> 555-555-1212

Or like this:

> 55 55 55 12 12

To clean up the data when it's entered, just add an auto-enter calculation to the Phone Number field. This calculation does the trick:

```
Let(
   clean phone = Filter(Phone Number;
"0123456789");
   Case(
      Length(clean phone) = 10;

      "(" & Left(clean phone; 3) & ") " &
      Middle(clean phone; 4; 3) & "-" &
      Right(clean phone; 4);

      Phone Number
   )
)
```

First the calculation uses the Filter function to remove any non-numeric characters from the entered phone number, and puts the result in a variable called "clean phone." Then, if the clean phone has exactly 10 digits, the calculation breaks it apart according to the format you want. Otherwise it just returns the phone number the way the person entered it.

To make the calculation work properly, be sure you turn off "Do not replace existing value (if any)" in the Field Options dialog box.

Tip: FileMaker's Advanced Data Viewer (page 672) eliminates guesswork by letting you check the contents of local and global variables.

You could run a script that checks to see if a Payment was made within 10 days of the Invoice Date and if it was, apply a 1% discount to the $$Amount Due field. Sure, you can do something similar with a straightforward calculation field, but in that case, it gets a little trickier to apply the discount to some of the records, but not to others. With a script, you can find the records you want to give a spur-of-the-moment discount, run the script on that found set, and you're done.

Nesting Let Functions

As with other functions, you can nest Let functions inside one another. In fact, you can define a variable once, and then *redefine* it inside a nested Let function. The variable's value changes while inside the nested Let function, then changes back when it ends. By the same token, you can define a variable with the same name as a *field*, and FileMaker uses the variable's value while inside the Let function.

Here's a very simple example of a Let function *inside* another Let function:

```
Let ( X = 3 ;
    // only X is defined here
    Let ( Y = 4 ;
        // X and Y are both defined here
        X * Y
    )
    // Only X is defined here too
)
```

You can also use Let more than once in a single calculation without nesting:

```
Let ( [X = 3; Y = 4] ; X * Y ) &
Let ( units = "inches"; " " & units )
```

Extending Calculations

As you've seen in the past three chapters, FileMaker's calculation functions can do everything from text processing to financial analysis. Since calculations show up in so many different places in FileMaker, you might want to use the *same* calculation more than once. It would be a shame to have to type it in every time—and then make changes in several places the next time you need to modify it. In fact, a creative person like you may need a unique calculation to do something FileMaker, Inc. never thought of.

For these situations and more, FileMaker provides *two* ways to extend the calculation system. The first, called Custom Functions, lets you design your own calculation functions using the same syntax you use to create a calculation. You can then use these functions in any calculation in the same FileMaker file.

The second way is more complex, and thus more powerful. You (or someone you hire) can create a FileMaker *plug-in* in a programming language like C++. The plug-in also adds new functions to FileMaker's Specify Calculation window. The difference is that those functions can do *anything* a programmer wants them to do.

Note: To *create* custom functions *or* plug-ins, you need FileMaker Pro Advanced (a special version of FileMaker that has extra tools for developers). You can find out more here: *www.filemaker.com/products/ index.html*. Once you've defined a custom function, though, it can be *used* in any version of FileMaker. Read on to find out more.

Custom Functions

Often, you need to use a particular calculation more than once. Perhaps you have several tables that hold information about people and you want to write that "Full Address" calculation only *once*, then use it in each table. Or you might find yourself wondering why FileMaker doesn't have a function to do some incredibly useful thing. Maybe you frequently need to calculate your custom sprockets' weight, and FileMaker (for some reason) doesn't have a MySprocketWeight function. In all these cases, you can define your own functions to get the job done.

Defining a Custom Function

To get started, you add a new function that can calculate the radius of a circle. You may not actually need to calculate radii in your own databases much, but this example illustrates important concepts common to creating any custom function.

Note: If you don't have the FileMaker Advanced edition, you'll have to sit these next few exercises out, as explained in the previous Note.

---

1. **In FileMaker Pro Advanced, choose File → Define → Custom Functions.**

   You see the window shown in Figure 12-1. If you've never created your own function before, the list is blank, but not for long.

Figure 12-1:
The Define Custom Functions window is where you go to create your own functions. It shows a list of custom functions that are already defined. You also get buttons to edit, duplicate, or delete a custom function, or to make a new one. As usual, you can sort the list by making a choice from the "View by" pop-up menu. Finally, when you're all done, click OK to save all your changes, or Cancel to close the window and forget any changes you've made.

2. **Click the New button.**

   The Edit Custom Function window appears. You can see it in Figure 12-2.

3. **In the Function Name box, type *Circumference*.**

   You've just given your function a name, which you'll call upon later when you want to *use* this function in calculations.

---

4. **In the Function Parameters box, type** *diameter.*

Most functions need parameters (page 390), and this box is where you tell File-Maker which parameters your function needs. If you have more than one parameter, you must enter them one at a time.

5. **Click the Add Parameter button (see Figure 12-2).**

FileMaker moves "diameter" into the parameter list. This action means "diameter" is now officially a parameter of the Circumference function.

Parameter name
Edit parameter
Add parameter
Delete parameter

Parameter list   Function calculation   Function list

Figure 12-2:
The Edit Custom Fuction window is where you actually define the function. It looks a lot like the Specify Calculation dialog box you've seen so much of lately. But instead of fields, it has a list of Function Parameters (it's empty right now). Aside from this distinction, it also works a lot like the Specify Calculation dialog box.

Note: When you add more than one parameter to the parameter list, you can use the arrow icon by each item to move it up or down in the list. The order here is important: It determines the order in which you want the parameters to pass to the function (page 398).

6. **From the View pop-up menu (above the function list), choose "Trigonometric functions."**

The function list changes to show just the relevant options.

7. In the function list, double-click the *Pi* function, then click the * operator button (or type *).

The function calculation area now reads: *Pi *.*

8. Finally, in the parameter list, double-click *diameter.*

FileMaker adds the word *diameter* to the end of the calculation: *Pi * diameter.*

When you're done, click OK, and then OK again to close the Edit Custom Function and Define Functions dialog boxes. The database has a brand new function called Circumference. You can see your handiwork in the Specify Calculation dialog box's Functions list.

Editing Custom Functions

You probably feel like a pro at the Define Custom Functions window already, since it works a lot like other FileMaker dialog boxes. But even you could end up with a custom function that needs adjustment or repair. To edit an existing custom function, either double-click its name, or select it from the list and click Edit. In the Edit Custom Function window (Figure 12-2), you can modify the definition of a function as follows:

- To change its name, just type a new name in the Function Name box.

- You can also add new parameters, just like you added the "diameter" parameter in the Circumference function. If you no longer need a function parameter, select it and click the Delete Parameter button.

- To change a parameter's name, you must first select it in the parameter list. When you do, FileMaker puts the parameter in the Parameter Name box, where you can edit it. When you're done, click the Edit Parameter button to apply your change to the one in the list.

- You can also reorder parameters by dragging them up or down in the list.

If you click Duplicate, FileMaker makes an exact copy of the selected function. Finally, if you don't need a function anymore, select it and click Delete.

Warning: Be careful adding, reordering, or deleting parameters to an existing function. If the function is being used in a calculation somewhere, that calculation breaks because it no longer passes the right parameters back to the function. On the other hand, it's safe to *rename* a function or its parameters. FileMaker fixes any existing calculations when you do.

Recursion

As described in the box on page 461, you can create custom functions that call other custom functions, creating whole strings of mathematical wizardry that perform to your exact specifications. Even more interesting, a custom function can *use itself*, a technique known as *recursion*. With recursion, you can create calculations that repeat a process over and over again until they reach a result—called *iterative calculations*.

Tip: Recursion is a notoriously complicated topic, and many *very* capable FileMaker developers are stymied by it. Fortunately, recursion is rarely the only solution to a given problem, so you can certainly get by without it. (For example, consider using a script instead.)

Imagine you need a function that removes duplicate lines from a list. For example, if a field contains a list of colors, you want a new list with each *unique* color name, even if it appears in the original list several times. You can't do that with a normal calculation, because you just don't know how many words you need to pull out. A recursive function solves the problem by repeating its work until it takes care of all items (colors).

While the concept of a recursive function is simple, creating one can be tricky. To implement a recursive function, you're best off tackling the calculation in three distinct steps. First, solve the initial problem; second, call that first formula over and over again (that's the recursive part); and third, tell the formula how to stop.

Tip: If you're having trouble getting through the following recursion example on your own, you can download a sample database from the "Missing CD" page at *www.missingmanuals.com*.

Step 1: solve the first case

Rather than think about how to solve the entire problem, just figure out how to deal with the *first* line in the list. If you have a field called List, for example, and you want to make sure the *first* line appears only once in the list, you can use this calculation:

```
LeftValues ( List ; 1 ) & Substitute ( List ; LeftValues(List; 1) ; "" )
```

Suppose List contains:

```
Red
Green
Orange
Red
Orange
Yellow
```

The Substitute part of this expression does the lion's share of the work, so start with that to figure out how the formula works. The Substitute function sees that "Red" is the first item in List and takes it out of the field everywhere it occurs. If Substitute were the whole shooting match, "Red" would disappear entirely from List. But the "LeftValues (List ; 1) &" piece of the expression also notices that "Red" is the first item in List and it puts "Red" back at the top of the list, then repeats all the other items in List. Here's the result you'd see if you made a calculation field with the formula above:

```
Red
Green
Orange
Orange
Yellow
```

Now you're ready to move on to the rest of the function, where you call the same action over and over again, and things start to get interesting.

Step 2: assume your function already works, and use it

You're ready to take the *recursion leap of faith*. A recursive function, by definition, calls itself. So at some point, it depends on its own resources to work. But when you're *writing* the recursive custom function, it obviously doesn't work yet. You'll be at a total impasse if you don't *assume* it already works and just get on with writing.

So since you're writing a new custom function called RemoveDuplicates, write its syntax as if you already have a function called RemoveDuplicates that does what you want. If such a function did exist, you could use it in the above calculation like this:

```
LeftValues ( List ; 1 ) & RemoveDuplicates ( Substitute(List;
LeftValues(List; 1); "") )
```

This new version removes the first item from the list, then sticks it in front of the result of the RemoveDuplicates function, and then works its way through the list. Think of it this way: You removed duplicates of the first item from the list using the Substitute function, and RemoveDuplicates removed the rest.

So far, so good. Keep going to make sure RemoveDuplicates work for the rest of the calculation.

Step 3: find a stopping point

You now have two of the three critical components of a recursive function: You're manually doing the *first* part of the job, and you're telling recursion to do the rest. If you leave the function like this, though, you're in trouble. If RemoveDuplicates calls RemoveDuplicates, which in turn calls RemoveDuplicates (ad infinitum), you have a problem. This function just keeps going forever.

Note: When you work on recursive functions, you inevitably create such *loops* accidentally. When you do, you see FileMaker think for several seconds, then give up and return *invalid* (a question mark). If FileMaker seems to be hung, give it some time. It gives up eventually.

To avoid ending up in a loop, you need to figure out when to *stop* calling RemoveDuplicates. Think about what happens after this function calls itself several times. Each time it's called with a slightly smaller list than the time before (because the first item—along with any copies of it—have been removed). Eventually it's going to get called with just one item (or zero items). When that happens, you no longer need the services of RemoveDuplicates. Instead, you can just return that last word by itself since it obviously has no duplicates. You use an If function to help the recursion figure out when to stop. The final function looks like this (with comments added):

```
// Start the result with the first item in the list
LeftValues ( List ; 1 ) &

// If there are more items in List…
If ( ValueCount(List) > 1;
   // …then remove duplicates from the remaining items
   RemoveDuplicates ( Substitute(List; LeftValues(List; 1); "") );

   // …otherwise we're done
   ""
)
```

Now, all you have to do is create the RemoveDuplicates custom function shown above. RemoveDuplicates needs one parameter defined, which is a reference to the field from which you're sifting duplicates. A descriptive name, like "theField," helps you remember what this parameter does. Finally, create a calculation field using your new custom function and create a reference to the field containing the list of duplicated values.

Note: RemoveDuplicates works great for finding unique values in a list, so long as the last item in the list has a ¶ (paragraph return) following it. You can adjust for lists that don't have a trailing ¶ by adjusting your calculation field slightly:

```
RemoveDuplicates ( list & "¶" )
```

Figure 12-3 illustrates an example of a recursive calculation calling the RemoveDuplicates custom function to remove all duplicate colors it finds on the list. (It takes four iterations to remove all the duplicates and return a unique instance of each item in the list, in the order in which they occur.)

Figure 12-3:
The box in the top-left corner shows how RemoveDuplicates is first called. It receives a list of colors as its one parameter. It returns the first item in the list and the result of the second call. This time, though, Red has been removed from the list. The second call returns Green and the results of the third call. This progresses until the fourth call, when RemoveDuplicates is passed a single item. This time it simply returns the item without calling itself again. When it returns, the third call has all it needs, so it returns as well. This process goes back up the chain until the first call is reached, and the final result is returned. If you join up the results of each call, you see the correct list.

Plug-ins

Some things just can't be done (or can't be done well) using calculations and custom functions. When you run into this situation, you may consider looking into *plug-ins,* which are tiny applications that live inside FileMaker to help it do some specific task that it can't do on its own.

Many plug-ins focus on doing certain things: process a credit card transaction; create charts; perform certain jobs based on a schedule; or interact with special devices like cameras, barcode readers and so on. Although plug-ins work through calculation functions, scripts, which the next section covers, generally control them.

Some plug-ins, though, are perfect candidates for calculations. Plug-ins can convert, resize, and otherwise modify images in container fields; or perform complex mathematical, scientific, or financial calculations that would be difficult or inefficient in a calculation. Although this book doesn't cover any specific plug-ins, this section shows you how to access the functions any plug-in you install provides.

Installing Plug-ins

A plug-in comes in a file bearing a special FileMaker Plug-in icon (shown in Figure 12-4). In order to use plug-ins, FileMaker needs to *load* them (that is, it has to put the plug-in code into its own memory). Every time you launch the program, it searches for plug-ins in a folder called Extensions inside its own folder, and loads all that it finds.

AutoUpdate.fmplugin

Figure 12-4:
FileMaker plug-ins come in many varieties—with many names—but they all look like this. (Some plug-ins have a ".FMX" filename extension, some have ".FMPLUGIN," and some have no extension at all.) Your job is to put the file where FileMaker can find it.

Installing a plug-in is thus a simple matter of making sure it's in the right folder:

- On Windows, it's typically C: → Program Files → FileMaker → FileMaker Pro 8 → Extensions.

- On Mac OS X, it's usually here. Applications → FileMaker Pro 8 → Extensions.

Note: If you're using FileMaker Pro Advanced, the FileMaker folder is called FileMaker Pro 8 Advanced, not FileMaker Pro 8.

Once you've found the folder, just drag the plug-in file into it and restart FileMaker. You won't see anything on your screen to let you know it worked. To see which plug-ins FileMaker has actually loaded, you need to visit the application preferences (FileMaker Pro → Preferences on Mac OS X, Edit → Preferences on Windows). In the Preferences window, click the Plug-ins tab, or look to Figure 12-5.

Once you've installed plug-ins, you can use their functions from the External functions section of the list in the Specify Calculation dialog box (page 382). For details on how to use these functions, consult their developer's manuals or Web sites.

Figure 12-5:
The Plug-ins tab in FileMaker's Preferences dialog box shows you all the plug-ins you've installed. Disable a plug-in by deselecting the checkbox by its name. If a plug-in requires any configuration, select it in the list and click Configure. When you have a plug-in selected, you see a description of it below the list.

Old and New Plug-ins

There are actually two kinds of plug-ins for FileMaker: older FileMaker 4-style plug-ins and newer FileMaker 7/8-style plug-ins. FileMaker 8 works with *both* types of plug-ins, but it's a good idea to ask your plug-in provider which type you're getting, since the FileMaker 4 plug-ins have limited abilities:

• The functions provided by FileMaker 4 plug-ins always expect *one* parameter. Even if the function doesn't need a parameter, you have to pass "", which is just an empty parameter. If the function really needs more, consult the documentation that came with the plug-in to find out how to accommodate it.

• This single parameter's type is *always* text in a FileMaker 4 plug-in's function. If you want to pass a date, time, timestamp, or number, you have to convert it to text first, using GetAsText.

FileMaker 7/8 plug-ins give you a lot more options. Functions can have as many parameters as their creator cares to give them. They can also deal with all data types, including pictures, movies, and files stored in container fields.

Finding Plug-ins

Most FileMaker developers lack the know-how to build their own plug-ins. Although you can hire a programmer to make one to your specifications, you can often find one on the market that already does what you want. To help you hunt them down, FileMaker, Inc. has a plug-in registry on its Web site. Just visit *www.filemaker.com/plugins/index.html* to access the site.

You can also visit the more prolific FileMaker plug-in vendors' Web sites:

• 24U Software; *www.24usoftware.com*

• New Millennium Communications; *www.nmci.com*

• Troi Automatisering; *www.troi.com*

• Waves in Motion; *www.wmotion.com*

New vendors come up with great products all the time. Use your favorite search engine or try FileMaker's Web site for new plug-ins:

http://www.filemaker.com/plugins/all.html

Creating Your Own Plug-ins

If you're feeling adventurous (or have helpful programmer friends), you can create your own plug-ins. To do that, you first need FileMaker Advanced (it's the only version of FileMaker that includes the *Plug-in Software Development Kit* or SDK). You also need a C++ development environment. In Windows, you're best off with Visual C++ or Visual Studio.NET. On Mac OS X, you can use CodeWarrior (*www.codewarrior.com*) or XCode (included with Mac OS X 10.3). The Plug-in SDK includes sample projects for each of these environments—and sample plug-in code—to get you started.

Part Five: Scripting

5

Scripting Basics

Calculation fields let you tell FileMaker how to automatically update and validate the *data* in your database. But *working with the database* is still a manual affair. If you often need to print a summarized report, you have to perform a find, sort the records, switch layouts, print, and then switch back to the original layout manually. Once you've done it 27 times, you start wishing you could click a button and have the report print itself. Well, you can: Just tell FileMaker the same series of steps you've been doing over and over again, and attach the list to a button (page 246). That's the essence of scripting.

A *script* is a series of steps bundled together. When you run the script (by clicking a button, say), FileMaker carries out all the steps on your behalf, one after the other. Scripts can be simple—just the five steps necessary to print the report—or they can be much more complicated. Advanced scripts can even incorporate calculations (Chapter 9) to do different things in different situations by making simple decisions based on the data in your database, the current time or date, and so on.

Note: If you've worked with other scripting environments—like Visual Basic for Applications, AppleScript, or JavaScript—FileMaker's script-building tools are pleasantly familiar.

Your First Script

To get a feel for how scripting works, you'll create a really simple script. Suppose you want to find all invoices with a balance due and view them in a sorted list. The following pages show how to go about preparing your database, planning, creating and polishing the script, and finishing off with a way to run it.

Preparing the Database

FileMaker is flexible enough to let you create fields and layouts on the fly, at the same time as you write a script, but it's easier to focus on the script if you create all the supporting material you need before you even open ScriptMaker. In this example, you use a layout that shows a list of invoices, so create that first:

1. **Switch to Layout mode in your database and choose Layout → New Layout/ Report.**

   The New Layout/Report window appears.

2. **From the "Show records from" pop-up menu, choose *Invoices*. In the Layout Name box, enter *Invoice List*.**

   Since you'll tell the script which layout it needs to use, it helps to name the layout appropriately so that you can pick it from the list of layouts later.

3. **In the "Select a layout type" list, select *Columnar list/report*, and then click Next. Leave the "Columnar list/report" radio button turned on, and then click Next again.**

   Now you get to pick which fields to include in the list.

4. **Using the techniques described on page 143, add the following fields to the "Layout fields" list: Invoice ID, Jobs::Name, Date, Date Due, and Total Due. When you're finished, click Next.**

   FileMaker asks how you want the list sorted. Since this list isn't a report, you can simply ignore this setting. Click Next again.

5. **On the Themes screen, choose one that pleases you, and then click Next.**

   You now see the header and footer choices. You're ignoring these too, so click Next yet again. FileMaker then asks if it should create a script for you.

6. **Choose "Do not create a script" and click Next.**

   You're going to do that yourself, of course. The final screen asks if you'd like to view the layout in Preview mode or Layout mode.

7. **Select "View the report in Layout mode," and then click Finish.**

FileMaker creates your new layout and shows it to you. (Feel free to decorate the layout now if you want, using any of the features described in Chapter 4.)

Planning Your Script

Before you dive in and create the script, you should review what you think it's supposed to do. Everything you can do yourself in FileMaker, you can have a script do instead—and this instance is no exception. A script is just a series of steps. When you're planning a script, it often helps to actually *do* what you want the script to do, so you can see whether it works. So go through the steps necessary to find the balance due, and take notes. You probably end up with something like the following:

- **Switch to the Invoice List layout.** This layout has the fields the script needs to create the invoice list. It's also going to display the final list, so you want to make sure the script runs in this layout.

- **Choose View → Find Mode.** The script needs to *find* all invoices with a balance due. Scripts can't click a button or even choose a menu command, but you know that you need a script step that puts FileMaker into Find mode.

- **In the Total Due field, enter >0, then press Enter.** This step tells FileMaker what to find and puts it into action. When the script runs this step, FileMaker performs the find and shows the correct records, just as if you'd performed the find yourself.

Note: If none of your invoices has a balance due, just click Cancel when the error message pops up, and then choose Records → Show All Records so you can do the next step. Jot down that your script needs to account for this message box if it pops up when someone runs your script.

- **Choose Records → Sort and sort the records ascending by Date Due.** You should now see your final list, properly sorted. Once you have the results that you want the script to produce, you know everything you need to know to build it.

Now that you know all the steps involved, you're ready to get acquainted with ScriptMaker.

Creating Your Script

You create, edit, run, and delete scripts in FileMaker using *ScriptMaker*. It's *always* available as the first item in the Scripts menu. When you choose this item, you see the window shown in Figure 13-1.

Figure 13-1:
The Define Scripts window is more affectionately known as ScriptMaker and is accessed via the Scripts → ScriptMaker menu command. The window itself is dominated by an empty white space. As you add scripts, they're listed here. You use the buttons along the right edge to create, edit, run, and delete scripts (and a few other things). You'll learn all about these options in the next section.

Now it's time to build the script. FileMaker wants you to set up and name the script before adding the actual steps.

1. **Choose Scripts → ScriptMaker. When the Define Scripts window appears, click New.**

   The Edit Script window pops up (Figure 13-2).

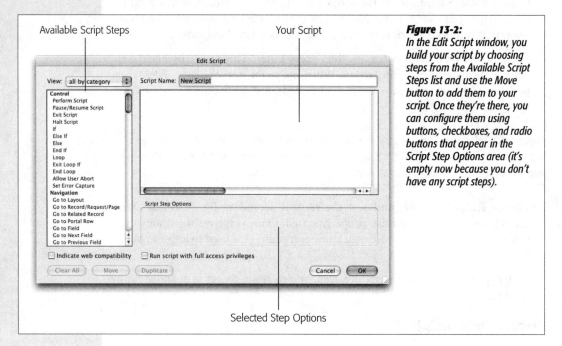

Available Script Steps   Your Script

Figure 13-2:
In the Edit Script window, you build your script by choosing steps from the Available Script Steps list and use the Move button to add them to your script. Once they're there, you can configure them using buttons, checkboxes, and radio buttons that appear in the Script Step Options area (it's empty now because you don't have any script steps).

Selected Step Options

2. **In the Script Name box, enter *Find Unpaid Invoices.***

   Your script's name is important. It's how you'll identify it when you want to run it later.

3. **From the View pop-up menu (top-left corner), choose *all by name.***

   The list of available script steps reorganizes to show you every step alphabetized by name.

   You're now ready to add steps to your script. You'll be adding a script step for each of the actions you performed when you manually created the list of unpaid invoices back on page 470.

4. **Scroll through the script step list (Figure 13-2) to *Go to Layout*, and then click to select it. Click the Move button, which is now available.**

   FileMaker adds (and selects) a "Go to Layout step to the list of current steps. This script step makes FileMaker go to a layout when the script is run. Your job is to choose *which* layout it should visit.

Tip: You can double-click a step in the list to avoid the trip to the Move button. For less mousing, you can type the first part of a step's name to scroll to it, and then press the Space bar to add it. You can also use the Tab key to move between the available step list, the current steps list, and the Script Name box.

5. **From the Specify pop-up menu (in the Script Step Options area), choose Invoice List. Click Move.**

   Now your script has just one step, or line. If you were to run it as is, it would simply take you to the Invoice List layout. (If you were *already* on the Invoice List layout, it wouldn't do anything.)

6. **From the available script step list, select Enter Find Mode, and then click Move.**

   FileMaker adds a second line to your script. The Script Step Options area now has new options (those that make sense with the Enter Find Mode step). Notice that the Pause option at the left side of the Script Step Options area is turned *on*.

7. **Turn off the Pause option.**

   Turning off this option tells the script not to wait for user input when it's run. (You'll learn more about pausing a script on page 517.)

8. **Add a Set Field script step to the script.**

   The procedure is similar to the previous two steps: Select *Set Field* in the available field list and click Move.

   The Set Field step lets you put (set) something into that field. You can use Set Field in Browse or Find mode. In Browse mode, it enters data; in Find mode it specifies find requests. In this case, you're specifying a find request for the invoices.

9. **In the Script Step Options area, turn on "Specify target field."**

   This tells FileMaker you want to indicate exactly *which* field to set. As soon as you turn this option on, FileMaker shows a slightly different Specify Field window (Figure 13-3).

Note: If you *don't* turn the Specify target field option on, the Set Field step modifies whichever field happens to be active when the step is carried out.

10. **In the field list, select *Total Due*, and then click OK.**

The Set Field step in your script (Figure 13-4) shows the option you've selected. In the Script Step Options area, click the bottom Specify button (the one beside "Calculated result.")

Figure 13-3:
This Specify Field dialog box looks almost exactly like the one you've seen in Layout mode. The only difference is the Repetition box at the bottom. If you select a repeating field (page 109), you can use this box to tell FileMaker exactly which repetition to set.

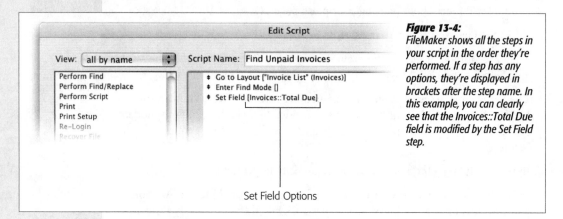

Figure 13-4:
FileMaker shows all the steps in your script in the order they're performed. If a step has any options, they're displayed in brackets after the step name. In this example, you can clearly see that the Invoices::Total Due field is modified by the Set Field step.

FileMaker shows you the Specify Calculation dialog box, the same one you used to build calculation fields in the previous few chapters. Here, though, you're using a calculation to tell FileMaker what to put in the Total Due field. When this step runs, you're in Find mode thanks to the second step in this script, so the next step tells FileMaker what to look for.

11. **In the Calculation box, enter ">0" (including the quotes), and then click OK.**

This bit of computerese sets the Total Due field to the appropriate value for finding unpaid invoices. FileMaker now shows the calculation beside the Set Field step as well. (Spoken out loud, this step reads, "Set the Invoices::Total Due field to greater than zero.")

12. **Add the Perform Find script step to your script.**

    This step carries out the find operation. It's the equivalent of clicking Find or pressing Enter if you were doing it yourself.

13. **Add the Sort Records script step to your script. Then, in the Script Step Options area (Figure 13-4), turn on "Perform without dialog."**

    This tells FileMaker you want the script to go ahead and sort, instead of opening the Sort dialog box every time it runs. Instead, since the sort's the same every time, you put it right here in the script.

14. **Turn on the "Specify sort order" checkbox.**

    Assuming you just went through the sort as described on page 471, the Sort dialog box is already configured properly. (When you add a Sort Records step to your script, FileMaker configures it to match the *last* sort you performed.)

15. **Click OK in the Sort Records window. Then, in the Edit Script window, click OK again.**

    FileMaker shows you the Define Scripts window again. This time, though, your new script—Find Unpaid Invoices—is in the otherwise empty list. Time to check your work.

16. **Click Perform.**

    FileMaker runs your script. You should immediately see the correct list of invoices, or—oops!—a message telling you no records were found. In the next section, you'll refine your script to help deal with these message boxes if they pop up when someone runs the script. (See the box on page 476.)

Note: You can adapt the basic structure of this script for a host of purposes. Just edit the script's find or sort criteria and specify a different layout.

Improving Your Script

On the preceding pages, you created a script that mimics what you would do to get an unpaid invoice list, step by step. But ScriptMaker has a lot of options to make writing scripts fast and easy. Often, a script can get the results you want with *fewer* steps than it would take to do it yourself. For example, to see your unpaid invoice list, the steps boil down to the following:

• Switch to the Invoice List layout.

• Find the right invoices.

• Sort the records.

This version has just *three* steps instead of five because it assumes you can "find the right invoices" in one step. Luckily, ScriptMaker's Perform Find script step *really can* find what you want in one step. Here's how to revise your script to use the simpler form:

1. **Choose Scripts → ScriptMaker. In the Define Scripts window, select the Find Unpaid Invoices script, and then click Edit.**

   The script you created earlier in this chapter pops up in the Edit Script window again.

2. **Select the *second and third* steps in your script (Enter Find Mode and Set Field).**

   You can select both by clicking Enter Find Mode in your script, then Shift-clicking Set Field.

Note: You should be selecting the steps in your script (in the window on the right), not the steps in the available script steps list (on the left side of the window).

To Be Continued

If your database has no unpaid invoices when you run the Find Unpaid Invoices script (page 472), you see the message shown here. The message is the same as the one you see if you perform the find manually, with one exception: This time you get a Continue button.

Since FileMaker was running a script when the error occurred, it gives you the choice to cancel the script (in other words, stop in the middle and return control to the user) or continue the script (or keep going and pretend nothing went wrong). In this case, Cancel and Continue do the same thing since the error happened on the *last* step in the script.

If you don't want the user to make this choice, you can tell FileMaker to *capture* the errors as they happen and let you deal with them inside the script. You'll learn about this process on page 549.

3. **Click the Clear button.**

   FileMaker removes the two selected steps from the script. It now has two steps that look a lot like the simplified process above. Also notice that the Perform Find step is already selected, since FileMaker automatically selects the *next* step when you clear one or more steps from the script.

4. **Turn on the "Specify find requests" checkbox in the Script Step Options area.**

   The Specify Find Requests dialog box (Figure 13-5) appears. Since the find request FileMaker created for you is exactly what you want, you don't need to do anything in the Specify Find Requests window.

---

5. **Click OK.**

   When you click OK, you see the Edit Script window again. Figure 13-6 shows how your script should look now. The script is now finished—and it's just three lines.

Figure 13-5:
This window opens whenever you attach specific find requests to a Perform Find script step. From here you can add new find requests to your script. If you look in the list, you see that FileMaker's already added a line for you. It has an Action of Find Records and Criteria that look like this: Invoices::Total Due: [>0]. Like the sort order, this is the last find you performed, and it's also just what you want.

Figure 13-6:
Your finished script should look like this. It wasn't too hard to build, and it's very easy to understand. No other scripting tool makes writing scripts this easy. And as you'll find out soon, this ease doesn't mean the scripts themselves have to be simple.

6. **Click OK again, and then click the Perform button.**

   You see your unpaid invoice list again.

This new, simpler script does everything the first script did. It's simpler because you didn't have to script all the steps involved in performing a find: Enter Find Mode; Set Field; Perform Find. Instead, you let FileMaker do all of that in one Perform Find step. You'll find that you can reduce *many* of FileMaker's common multi-step operations to a single step in ScriptMaker.

The Importance of the Layout

In a script, the active layout is very important, since it's what determines the script's *context*. Context is critical when you do things like delete records. If you write a script that simply deletes a record, it deletes the current record from whatever layout the user happens to be on—which may not be the right record at all. You could end up deleting a record from the Customer table instead of the single Invoice record you meant to delete!

Take the script you've created in this chapter, for example. Before it does anything else, your Find Unpaid Invoices script goes to the Invoice List layout—but what would happen if you left that step out? Figure 13-7 shows the options ScriptMaker gives you for the Perform Find script step. See if you can spot what's *missing*.

Figure 13-7:
The Perform Find scripts step gives you only one option–to specify a find request. When you click Edit in the Specify Find Request dialog box, you see the window in the front. To add requests, you can pick which fields to search in, and which tables those fields are in. Problem is…there's nowhere to tell FileMaker what kind of records to find: Invoices? Customers? Line Items? The answer to that question lies in the layout your script is running on.

Upon close examination of Figure 13-7, you can see that Perform Find—like every other script step—makes absolutely no mention of which table it should act upon. Just because you're asking it to "Find records when Invoices::Invoice ID > 0" doesn't mean you're looking for *invoice* records. You could be looking for customers whose attached invoices have a balance due. Or you could be looking for any line items that are on an unpaid invoice. The only way FileMaker can tell what you're looking for is by the context of the layout you're on. That's why the first step in the script goes to the Invoice List layout. That layout is attached to the Invoices table occurrence. This tells FileMaker which records to look through (those in the Invoices table) and from what perspective to resolve relationships (the Invoices table occurrence on the relationship graph).

When to Switch

Now that you've dutifully absorbed the lesson in the previous paragraphs, don't get lured into the idea that you *always* have to switch to a layout for your script to work. The fact that a script can do something useful from more than one context can be a good thing. In general, you have three choices when you write a script, and here are some guidelines on when to use each:

- **Switch to a layout associated with the table you want to work with.** The Go to Layout script step makes sense when you're showing certain results (like the Find Unpaid Invoices script) or when your script always makes sense, but only from one particular context. If necessary, you can then switch *back* to the original layout at the end of the script (Go to Layout has an Original Layout option).

- **Don't include a Go to Layout script step at all.** Just let the script go about its business, whatever the context. If you use this approach, you have to make sure the script works and makes sense from any perspective. For instance, a script could switch to Preview mode, resize the window to show the whole page, and then ask the user if he'd like to print. This script can run on nearly any layout and still do something useful—print. (See the box on page 483 for one example of context independent scripting.)

- **Prevent the script from running on the wrong layout.** As you'll see on page 486, you can make it so a script won't run at all if it's not designed to work properly on the current layout. This alternative is your best bet when switching layouts within the script isn't feasible. For example, suppose you have a Refund Invoice script that carries out the steps necessary to pay someone back. Using Go to Layout to switch to the Invoices layout would ensure the right layout, but not the right *invoice*. It's best if this script runs only when the user is *already* open to the Invoices layout—presumably looking at the invoice she wants to refund.

Tip: Anytime a script can do damage to your database when run from the wrong layout, you may want to use that last option even if you're the only person who uses your database. If your mouse hand slips when you're insufficiently caffeinated, the script can show you an error message rather than running at the wrong time (page 537).

Running Scripts

At this point you're probably starting to see how scripts could be really useful in your database. The fact is, most large database systems are *loaded* with scripts that do all kinds of things. But the only way you've seen to run a script is pretty tedious: Chose Scripts → ScriptMaker, select the script, and then click Perform. That's lots of clicks to run a script that's supposed to *save* you time! Thankfully, there are a few *other* ways to run scripts that are more convenient, and you can set them up when you first create a script. Here are the possibilities:

The Scripts Menu

You can choose to show some or all of your scripts right in the Scripts menu. If you have a script or two that you want quick access to from *anywhere*, then it makes sense to put it in the Scripts menu. That way, anyone can run it by simply choosing it from the menu. There are even keyboard shortcuts for the first 10 scripts in the Scripts menu: Ctrl+1 (⌘-1) through Ctrl+9 (⌘-9) for the first nine, and Ctrl+0 (⌘-0) for number 10. Figure 13-8 shows how to assign a script to this menu in the Define Scripts dialog box (page 471).

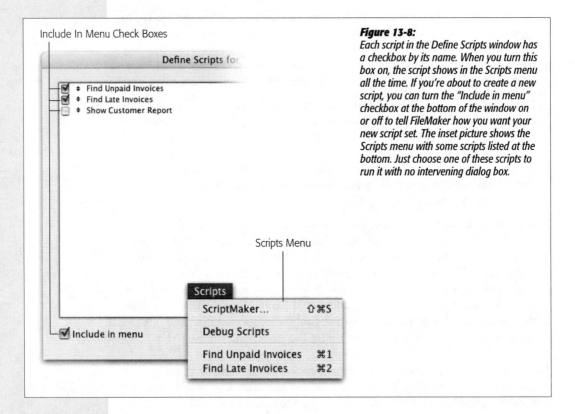

Figure 13-8:
Each script in the Define Scripts window has a checkbox by its name. When you turn this box on, the script shows in the Scripts menu all the time. If you're about to create a new script, you can turn the "Include in menu" checkbox at the bottom of the window on or off to tell FileMaker how you want your new script set. The inset picture shows the Scripts menu with some scripts listed at the bottom. Just choose one of these scripts to run it with no intervening dialog box.

Buttons

Throwing lots of scripts into the Scripts menu is a good way to give your users access to them no matter what context they're in. But what if you want to make a script available only on certain layouts? For scripts that apply only to the Invoices layout (like…oh…the Find Unpaid Invoices script), consider using *buttons* instead. When you add a button to the layout, FileMaker shows you the same Specify Button window you saw back on page 246. Perform Script is the very first command available in the list (aside from Do Nothing). You can see the options associated with this button in Figure 13-9.

Figure 13-9:
When you tell a button to execute the Perform Script command, you see the options shown in the background window. The Current Script pop-up menu lets you determine what FileMaker does when a script is already running. (You'll learn more about this option in Chapter 15.) When you click Specify, the foreground window appears. Here, you can choose a file from the pop-up menu (it shows all the files you have a file reference for, and lets you add a new file reference). The available scripts list then shows all the scripts in the selected file. You just select the script you want and click OK.

Using buttons, you can add one-click access to as many scripts as you want and you can place them *where you want them*. For example, you can put Invoice-related scripts on the Invoices layout and Payment-related scripts on the Payment layout. If you make sure your context-dependent scripts don't show up in the Scripts menu, you're adding another layer of assurance that FileMaker runs your scripts only from the right context.

Tip: If you want the ultimate in control over which of people get to see which scripts, and even which layout they can see them in, take a look at the Custom Menus section in Chapter 19. You need FileMaker Pro Advanced to create Custom Menus, but for many situations, this powerful feature alone is worth the price of admission.

Opening and Closing Scripts

Finally, you can tell FileMaker to automatically run a script when someone opens or closes the file. The opening script runs when you first open the file. You might use this script if you want to be greeted with the list of unpaid invoices first thing every morning. The closing script runs when you close the *last window* for an open file. This option is a little less common, but it has its uses: If you want to make sure other related files close whenever the main file closes (even if they have open windows), then you could write a script to close them all whenever you close the main file.

To make the selection, you need to visit the File Options dialog box (File → File Options). In the File Options window, make sure the Open/Close tab is selected. In this window, you first turn on one of the "Perform script" checkboxes (there's one under "When opening this file" and another under "When closing this file"). Then you can select one of your scripts from the associated pop-up menu. Figure 13-10 shows the result.

Figure 13-10:
The Open/Close tab of the File Options window (File → File Options) lets you tell FileMaker what to do when a user opens or closes a file. Most of this window is devoted to the things that are done when a file opens. Only the last checkbox (under "When closing this file") has to do with which script should run when the file closes.

Branching and Looping in Scripts

Now that you have a basic foundation in what scripts do and how you can run them, it's time to see some of ScriptMaker's more powerful features. The script you created at the beginning of this chapter was the simplest kind: It goes through a series of steps from start to finish every time. Sometimes your script needs more smarts. You can add steps to the script that cause it to take different actions depending on the situation (called *branching*) or make it do the same thing over and over again (called *looping*).

POWER USERS' CLINIC

Context Independence

You may be wondering why the Send Email to Customer script you created on these pages doesn't go to the Customers layout first. After all, doesn't it only make sense from this context?

Actually, this script is a perfect candidate for *context independence* (page 478). What happens if you run this script from the Jobs layout? It creates a new email message addressed to the *related customer*. That message sounds pretty useful. The same holds true from the Invoice layout. In fact, you can run this script from *any* layout and get a useful result: FileMaker finds the related Customer record and addresses the message to her.

But what if you have *multiple* related customer records? (Remember, the Send Email to Customer script is set to send only one email, even though the Send Mail script step lets you send multiple emails to all customers in a found set.)

If you just run the script from the Scripts menu, FileMaker automatically selects the *first* related customer based on the active record on the current layout. (If the relationship to Customers is sorted in the Relationships tab of Define Databases, it'll be the customer that sorts to the top. Otherwise you get the oldest customer record.)

But if your layout has a *portal* of related customers, you can put a button inside the portal row. Then, when you click this button, the script automatically addresses the email to the appropriate related customer, even if he's not the Customer in the *first* related record.

The point is you can put a button just about anywhere and tell it to run this script. FileMaker does something a little different depending on where the button is. So this example is one of those scripts that you *don't* want to associate with a specific layout.

Branching with If, Else If, Else, and End If

If you're comfortable with the If and Case functions in calculations (page 445), then you'll feel right at home with this topic. You've noticed that you often look someone up in the Customers layout, copy his email address, and then go to your mail program to send him an email. You'd like to add a button to the Customers layout that creates the email directly, saving you all the trouble of copying, switching, and pasting.

You can use FileMaker's Send Mail script step, which is just like the File → Send Mail command, to accomplish this task. First, create the script:

1. **Choose Scripts → ScriptMaker. Then, in the Define Scripts dialog box, click New.**

   The Edit Script window pops up.

2. **In the Script Name box, type *Send Email to Customer*.**

When you want to *run* this script, you choose this name from the Scripts menu.

3. **In the list of available script steps, select Send Mail, and then click Move.**

FileMaker adds the script step to the script.

Note: The Send Mail script step is under Miscellaneous near the bottom of the list. If you don't like looking through this long list, choose Miscellaneous from the View pop-up menu to see just the steps in this category. Whenever you're *not* sure which category holds the step you want, choose "all by name" from the menu to see every step in alphabetical order.

---

4. **In the Script Step Options area, turn on the "Perform without dialog" checkbox.**

This tells FileMaker you *don't* want a window that lets you enter or edit the Send Mail Options dialog box when the script runs. In this case, you just want it to do its work as you specify in the script step.

5. **Click Specify. Then, when the Send Mail Options dialog box appears, click the pop-up menu to the right of the To field. Choose Specify Field Name.**

You now see a Specify Field dialog box. Here, you *tell* FileMaker where to find your customer's email address. Make sure "One email using data from the current record" is selected or you could get some dicey results, like sending an email about a Customer's recent Invoice to all the Customers who happen to have records in your found set.

6. **Switch to the Customers table, if necessary, and then choose the Email address field. Click OK.**

FileMaker closes the Specify Field window and shows you the Send Mail Options window again. Now, though, it shows your Email Address field reference in the To field. You can also add field references or calculations for CC, BCC, Subject or even the body of your email message in those fields. This dialog box even lets you choose a file to attach to your email. But for now, just leave all these options blank.

Tip: Turn on the "Multiple emails (one for each record in found set)" option to use this script step to send email to more than one person at the time. But remember, use this option for good, never for evil. You'd never send spam emails, would you?

---

7. **Click OK again.**

You now see your single line script in the Edit Script dialog box again, with the Send Mail options [No dialog; To Customers::Email Address] listed as reference.

At this point you have a working script. If you run it, it indeed creates a new email addressed to the current customer. But what happens if you *don't* have an email address for this customer? If the Customers::Email Address field is *empty*, your script tries to send an email without a valid address to your email program, which complains mightily. Fortunately, you can head this problem off at the pass. If the Email Address field is empty, you'd rather have your script tell you about it and skip the Send Mail step entirely. This is a job for the If step, so add it as follows:

1. **In the Edit Script dialog box (page 472), add the If step to your script.**

    FileMaker adds this step *after* the Send Mail step. It also adds a third step: End If. You can't have an If without an End If, so you get both automatically.

Note: If you accidentally delete the End If step from your script, FileMaker shows an error message when you try to save the script. To fix the error, you need to add the End If step back to your script and drag it to its proper place.

---

2. **Using the little arrows to the left of the If step, drag the step up above the Send Mail step.**

    The process of moving a script step in a list is a familiar operation. It works just like moving fields, layouts, and so forth. By rearranging the steps in your script, you're telling FileMaker what order they should run in. (A script won't work if you've got a step above something that needs to happen *first*.)

    Also, notice that the Send Mail script step is now indented. Everything between If and End If indents automatically to remind you that you're inside an If condition.

3. **Select the If step and, in the Script Step Options area, click Specify.**

    FileMaker shows you a standard Specify Calculation dialog box like the one shown on page 382. You use a calculation to define the *condition* of this If step. If the calculation evaluates to True, FileMaker does the steps after the If. If the calculation evaluates to False, FileMaker skips to the End If and continues running the script from there.

4. **In the calculation box, type *Not IsEmpty(Customers::Email Address)*, and then click OK.**

    This calculation evaluates to *True* and sends your customer an email only if the Email Address field isn't empty. See the box on page 486 for details on how this calculation makes these decisions.

Your script now checks to see if the Email Address field has something in it before running off to create the email message. But what happens when you run the script and the Email Address field is empty? Right now, nothing at all. FileMaker evaluates the If condition, sees that it's false, and skips to the End If. There's nothing after the End If, so the script just stops and your user waits in suspense, until he finally realizes that the requested email message simply isn't coming and investigates the problem on his own...or chucks his computer out the window.

UP TO SPEED

Not What?

FileMaker lets you create calculations that involve layers of Boolean logic. In the script you wrote on page 485, the If script step runs the indented steps only when the whole calculation evaluates to True. To figure out when that happens, you have to deconstruct the calculation itself.

By itself, the IsEmpty function returns True when the value you pass to it is completely empty—in other words, when the Email Address field is empty:

```
IsEmpty (Customers::Email Address )
```

But that doesn't help you because you only want the email sent when there *is* data in the email field. If you have no email address entered, the calculation above returns True, and causes the Send Email step to run.

If the email address field is filled in, on the other hand, the calculation's result is False and FileMaker skips the Send Mail step.

This behavior is exactly the opposite of what you want. To flip the result of the calculation around, you use the Not operator. It looks at the Boolean value to its right, and turns a true to a false, or a false to a true. Here's the calculation you need:

```
Not IsEmpty ( Customers::Email Address )
```

You can easily tell if you've got the right construction by reading the If step like a sentence: "If not is empty Email Address." It may not be grammatical perfection, but it does get the logic right.

In the interest of preventing property damage, it's better for your script to tell the user *why* nothing's happening. For example, you can have your script open a message box when the If condition is false, saying, "You can't email this customer, since there's no email address on file," or whatever. You can get exactly what you want with the Else step:

1. **Return to your script in the Edit Script dialog box (page 472). Select the Send Mail script step in your script.**

   When you add a *new* step, FileMaker inserts it after the selected step. You want the Else step to go right after the Send Mail step, so you select that step first.

2. **Add the Else step to the script.**

   FileMaker inserts an Else step between Send Mail and End If.

Note: Don't click the Else If step by mistake. You want the step called just Else. If you added the wrong step, select it, click Clear, and try, try again.

---

3. **Right after the Else step, add the Show Custom Dialog script step to the script.**

   This step is also under Miscellaneous. Its job is to pop up a dialog box for the user. You get to decide what the box says, which buttons it includes, and which fields—if any—it should show.

4. **Click the Specify button in the Script Step Options area.**

   The Show Custom Dialog Options window (Figure 13-11) appears.

5. **In the Title box, type *No Email Address*.**

   This controls what shows in the title bar along the top of your custom dialog box.

6. **In the Message box, type *You can't email this customer, since there's no email address on file.***

   This tells FileMaker what to put *inside* the dialog box.

7. **From the Button 2 box, select and delete the word Cancel.**

   A custom dialog box can have up to three buttons. In this case, you want only one: an OK button. To keep the other buttons from showing up, just make sure there's nothing in the Button 2 and Button 3 boxes.

8. **Click OK.**

   Your script should now look like the one shown in Figure 13-12.

Just click OK twice to return to your database, and try your script out: Select a customer without an email address (enter Find mode, type ">0" in the Email address field, then click the Omit button), and choose Scripts → Send Email to Customer. If you look at a Customer record with an email address, the script creates a message in your mail program, ready for you to fill out. If the email address field is empty, you see an error message instead. You can create a button for this script and add it to the Customers layout for the ultimate in convenience (see page 246 for more detail on creating buttons for your scripts).

Figure 13-12:
The finished Send Email to Customer script looks like this. If you read it like a book, it says, "If the email address field is not empty, Send Mail. Otherwise show an error message to the user." The If/Else/End If steps create two branches in the script: one when the email address field is full, and one when it's empty.

POWER USERS' CLINIC

Testing Multiple Conditions

If you have more than one condition to consider, you can use the Else If script step. It works a lot like the Case function in a calculation. You could have a script like this, for instance:

```
If [ Get ( CurrentTime ) < Time ( 12 ; 0 ;
0 ) ]
    Show Custom Dialog [ "Good Morning!" ]
Else If [ Get ( CurrentTime ) < Time ( 18
; 0 ; 0 ) ]
    Show Custom Dialog [ "Good Afternoon!"
]
Else
    Show Custom Dialog [ "Good Evening!" ]
End If
```

When this script runs, it tests each condition in turn, deciding which custom dialog box to show your user, based on the actual current time. If the current time's before noon, your user sees a "Good morning" message and the script jumps to the end (the End If script step) without needing to test the second condition.

If it isn't before noon, the script does a second test to see if it's before 6 p.m. If it is, the user sees a "Good Afternoon" message and the script jumps to the end. But if both tests fail, no third condition is tested, and the Else just shows the "Good Evening" message, like a default condition in a Case statement. However, you can add other Else Ifs to test other conditions.

You can add as many Else If steps as you want, but they must come between the If and Else If steps. Each Else If can test a different condition. If you have an Else step, it should come after the If and every Else If, but before the End If.

For a really cool way to tell which of the conditions in your scripts are evaluating as True and which ones evaluate as False, see the section on Script Debugger on page 668.

Looping

Sometime you want to do the same thing over and over again, until you reach some kind of end point. For example, people often write a script that does something to every record in the found set, one after another. This kind of scripting is called *looping*. You make a script *loop through records* using the Loop script step.

Like the If step, the Loop step has a necessary partner called End Loop. When you put script steps between Loop and End Loop, FileMaker simply repeats them over and over, forever.

POWER USERS' CLINIC

Go to Record/Request/Page

Since looping through the records in the found set is such a common operation, FileMaker lets you do it with a simplified set of script steps. For example, if you want to delete the Email Address field in every record in the found set (say you no longer want to email local customers, just out-of-state ones), you might think you'd have to approach the problem like this:

```
Loop
    Set Field [ Email Address, "" ]
    Go to Record/Request/Page [ Next ]
    Exit Loop If [ Get ( FoundCount ) =
        Get (RecordNumber) ]
    End Loop
    Set Field [ Email Address, "" ]
```

This script first starts a loop. It then clears the Email Address field in the current record. Next, it moves to the next record (just like clicking the right-hand page in the Book icon). If the number of the record you're now on *equals* the current found count, FileMaker exits the loop. But when this loop exits, you still haven't cleared the last email address. The Exit Loop If step exits when you *first* reach the last record. You have to add the last step (a copy of the Set Field step in the loop) to clear the Email Address in this *last* record.

But the Go to Record/Request/Page script step has some special powers. When you choose the Next option (telling it to go to the *next* record), a new checkbox appears in the Script Step Options area (shown here).

This checkbox, called "Exit after last," tells FileMaker you want it to *automatically* exit the loop *after* the last record. (In other words, it happens when the Go To Record/Request/Page step is run and you're *already* on the last record.)

This kind of scripting is good for two reasons. First, you can save the Exit Loop If step in your script, since FileMaker exits the loop for you. Second, since the exit happens *after* the last record, there's no need to add the last Set Field script step. The revised script looks like this:

```
Loop
    Set Field [ Email Address, "" ]
    Go To Record/Request/Page [ Next,
        Exit after last ]
    End Loop
```

In the real world, you probably wouldn't clear an email address just to keep an email from being sent. You'd make a field with a checkbox, then mark the records that need to get an email. When you write your looping scripts, you'll probably have more steps than the single Set Field shown here, and your scripts will grow accordingly.

So how does a script like this end? Simple: You tell FileMaker to *exit the loop* at the right time. To this end, FileMaker has a script step called Exit Loop If. Like the If step, Exit Loop If has an associated calculation. If the calculation evaluates to True, FileMaker immediately skips ahead to the End Loop step, and continues with the step that follows. As such, a loop usually looks like this:

```
Loop
    # Do some stuff
    Exit Loop If [ // some condition ]
End Loop
```

Using what you've learned in this chapter and about calculations in Part 4, you can easily build a script like this. For "some condition," just use a calculation that describes the condition when the loop should stop repeating itself. In the box on page 489 you can see an example of a looping script that stops when every record in a found set has been used up.

Script Steps

Now that you know how to create scripts (you did read the previous chapter, didn't you?), it's time to expand your repertoire. FileMaker has a script step for just about everything you can do from the menus and status area. You can use any combination of these steps with script techniques like looping, branching, custom dialog boxes, and more to automate just about anything FileMaker can do. Major areas of scripting include working with field data and records, finding, sorting, working with windows and files, and printing. This chapter is a compendium of steps—and boatloads of scripting possibilities.

Go to Layout

The Go to Layout script step was introduced on page 472. Its purpose is simple: Change layouts. It works just like making a choice from the Layout pop-up menu in the status area, except that the script can go to *any* layout (even if it doesn't show in the menu).

Go to Layout has just one option, a pop-up menu labeled Specify. In addition to every layout in your database, this menu also has three special choices:

- The **original layout** option causes FileMaker to switch to the layout your user was on when the script started. After all, you can run lots of scripts anywhere, especially if they're on the Script menu. Since scripts often change layouts as they run, this option makes sure folks end up back where they started.

- The **Layout Name by calculation** option lets you specify a typical FileMaker calculation. The result of the calculation must be text, and it should match the *name* of one of the layouts in the database. When the script runs, FileMaker evaluates the calculation and switches to the layout with the correct name.

• The **Layout Number by calculation** option is similar. You specify a calculation with a *number* result. FileMaker numbers every layout sequentially, in the order in which they're listed in Layout mode. The result of the calculation determines which layout to visit by number.

Note: Layout numbers don't necessarily correspond to their position in the Layout pop-up menu. Remember that not all layouts show in this list and you can reorder them manually. To find out a layout's number reliably, switch to Layout mode first. Then go to the layout and look at the Layout box in the status area. It shows which layout number you're on.

See the box below to learn when to use Go to Layout with Layout Name and when to use Layout Number.

FREQUENTLY ASKED QUESTION

Specifying a Layout

There are three ways to tell the Go to Layout step which layout to visit. Which one should I use?

The easiest way is to choose the layout from the Specify pop-up menu (page 217). When the script runs, FileMaker goes to your chosen layout, period. (That is, unless somebody deletes the layout.)

The other two options—specifying a layout by name or number—are trickier, for a couple of reasons. First, they're a pain: You have to write a calculation when you could just pick from a menu. Second, both calculation methods have soft underbellies. If you specify a layout name using a calculation, and later rename the layout, the script can't find the layout anymore. If you use the layout number, and then add or delete a layout, or rearrange your layout list (page 203), the script goes to the wrong layout.

On the other hand, these options give you greater flexibility. For example, if you use Go to Layout and specify by Layout Name, you can use script parameters to name any layout in your database. With this technique, you can create a single navigation script and use it in all sorts of routine database tasks.

If you want to create a scripted process that's like a wizard or assistant in some programs, the Layout Number's a godsend. Create the layouts that control your process, and make one Next button that you copy onto each layout. The button gets a Go to Layout script step, specifying a Layout Number that's one more than the current layout number (Get(LayoutNumber) + 1). Now, no matter how you rearrange the layouts, the button always takes your user to the next one in the Set Layout Order list—and you've used only one script step.

Scripting for Fields

Most people using FileMaker spend *a lot* of their time working with field data, so it's no surprise that script steps devoted to fields abound. You can put the user in a specific field, select field text, and even play sounds and movies from container fields. You can perform a find and replace operation, run the Replace Field Contents command, and export field contents to a file. Finally, you get more than 10 ways to put data into a field.

Navigating Fields

FileMaker offers a couple of ways to field-hop—pressing Tab to move to the next field in order, or just clicking the desired field. It has script steps that mimic both techniques.

Go to Field

The simplest field navigation script step is called Go to Field. It's really a two-purpose step, with two checkboxes to prove it. In its simplest form, you turn on the "Go to target field" checkbox and pick the field you want to go to. When the script runs, FileMaker puts the user in the specified field (provided it's on the layout).

Tip: When you use Go to Field in a script, FileMaker dutifully ignores the field behavior specified on the layout and puts the user right into the field. Remember this point if you ever want a field that users can only get to by using your script.

The step also has a checkbox called "Select/perform." When this option is turned on, the script either *selects* the contents of the field it goes to or *does* what's in the field—if possible. For example, if the step goes to a *container* field that holds a sound or movie, FileMaker *plays* the contents instead. If the container field holds a *reference* to a picture or file, FileMaker *opens* the correct file, using the appropriate program.

The mildly weird thing about Go to Field is you can turn on "Select/perform" and *turn off* "Go to target field." With the options set this way, Go to Field doesn't go to a field at all. Instead, it simply selects or performs the contents of the field you happen to be in when the script runs.

Go to Next Field and Go to Previous Field

To mimic the process of tabbing through fields, FileMaker has two more script steps. The first, called Go to Next Field, just tabs to the next field in the tab order. You probably already figured out that Go to Previous Field goes to the *previous* field in the tab order. These steps don't have a "Select/perform" option—they just go to the field.

Tip: To get the effect of Select/Perform, use Go to Next Field or Go to Previous Field to get to the field you want, then use Go to Field to select/perform it. When you add the Go to Field step, don't turn on "Go to target field," and it acts on the field you're already in.

Editing Commands

FileMaker has all the classic commands in its Edit menu: Undo, Cut, Copy, Paste, and Clear. It also has a script step for each of these commands. The Undo step is the simplest. It has no options at all, and has exactly the same effect as choosing

Edit → Undo. It's rare that you want to Undo something you just scripted, so you'll rarely use this script step. It's quite handy, though, if you use Custom Menus (page 686) to control users' access to certain menu commands because you need to provide scripts for everything your users might want to do.

Cut, Copy, and Clear are slightly more complicated, with two options each. The first, "Select entire contents" lets you decide which part of a field's value gets copied and/or cleared. If you turn this option on, FileMaker selects the entire field before acting. If this option's turned off, FileMaker copies whatever happens to be selected in the field. You also get a "Go to target field" option, through which the script can tell FileMaker *which field* to act on. If it's not turned on, it uses the *current field*—the one the user's in when the step runs.

The Paste step is the most complicated of these four. In addition to specifying which field you want, and whether or not to select everything in the field before pasting, you get an option to "Paste without style." When you turn this option on, FileMaker pastes the text on the clipboard, but throws away any style information. If you're in Windows, you get a fourth option: "Link if available." If the data on the clipboard comes from a source that supports object linking, FileMaker embeds the linked object. Changes to the original data shows up in FileMaker. Turn this option off if you just want the script to paste a *copy* of the data.

Selecting Text

FileMaker has two script steps to help you select text. The first, called Select All, selects everything in the current field, just like the Edit → Select All command. If you need more control, use Set Selection instead. This step has two options. First, you can specify a target field so that FileMaker operates on the current field. The step also has a separate Specify button (below the one associated with "Go to target field") that brings up the Specify Set Selection window (Figure 14-1).

Figure 14-1:
This window lets you tell FileMaker exactly what text you want the script to select. You can type numbers directly in the Start Position and End Position boxes, or click either Specify button to bring up the Specify Calculation dialog box.

If you imagine the text in your field as a string of letters, numbers, spaces, and punctuation, then you can pretend each of these is numbered. For instance, the word "Missing" has letters numbered one through seven. You first tell FileMaker where the selection should *start* by putting the number of the first character in the Start Position box. Next, you put the number of the *last* character in the End

Position box. When the step runs, FileMaker selects these two characters and everything in between.

Scripting for Fields

POWER USERS' CLINIC

Positioning the Insertion Point

You can use the Set Selection script step to put the insertion point anywhere in a field too. The trick is to make sure *nothing* gets selected. When you specify a Start Position and an End Position, FileMaker selects the characters at each position, plus anything in between. If these two numbers are the same, FileMaker selects just one character.

But what if the End Position comes *before* the Start Position? When you set the End Position one number lower than the Start Position, FileMaker doesn't select anything. Instead, it puts the little flashing insertion point right before the Start Position. Using this technique, you can get your script to put the user anywhere you want inside a field.

Editing Field Data

Editing field data is such an important part of FileMaker that there are more than 10 ways to put stuff in fields with a script step. On page 475, you learned that the scripted process for creating a printed report could actually be shorter and more efficient than the manual process. Editing field data via scripts is also different from manually editing data, and the following sections cover those differences.

The first thing to understand is that most of these steps *work only if the field is on the current layout*. This property's no problem for scripts you use to structure a user's data entry, but it can be a roadblock in other cases. Suppose you have a script that sets a "Paid in Full" flag on an invoice. You want this script to work no matter what layout you're on (as long as it's one that shows Invoice records), and whether the field is on that layout or not. In that case, you need to understand the Set Field script step (page 496).

Using Cut, Copy, and Paste

Your first inclination might be to use Cut, Copy, and Paste in a script to move data from one field to another, and it works well. You can, for example, have a script copy the Customer ID field, then go to the Invoices layout, create a new invoice, and paste it into the Customer ID field there.

But most developers recommend against this approach for two reasons. First, many people consider the user's clipboard to be sacred ground. They argue you should *never* change what's on the clipboard unless the user asks you to. So it would be OK to have a Copy button by the Address fields, for example, that copies the address to the clipboard. But what if the user copies a long product description to the clipboard, and then runs the Create Invoice for Customer script? She then tries to paste the description in the invoice line item, only to find that the description's gone, replaced by the Customer ID for some odd reason. To keep from frustrating the user (or yourself), you should generally avoid Cut and Copy.

Also, these steps don't work if the field isn't on the layout. People often show the customer's *name* on an invoice, but not his *ID*. But if you delete the Customer ID field from the Invoice layout, any scripts that use Cut, Copy or Paste and the Customer ID field break. That's where Set Field steps in to save the day.

Set Field

The one field-editing power step that doesn't care a whit about what fields are on the layout is called Set Field. This step replaces the contents of a field with the result of a calculation. Its two options let you specify the field to set, and the calculation to use. The calculation result must be the same type as the field you've specified. For Text, Date, Time, and Timestamp fields, Set Field is usually the step of choice: It's flexible and reliable, no matter what's on the layout.

Like many of the steps you've seen so far, you can choose not to specify a field at all. When you do, Set Field changes the field it's in *at the moment the step runs*. (The current-field method works only with text results; otherwise, you have to specify the field so FileMaker knows what type you have in mind.)

Insert Calculated Result

Set Field's one weakness is that it *always* overwrites a field completely (but see the tip below). Another step, Insert Calculated Result, lets a script put data in a field while keeping the data that's already there. It has three options. First you can specify a target field. You can also choose "Select entire contents" in the field first (in which case it overwrites the entire field, just like Set Field). Finally, you get to specify the calculation. Here are some variations on these options:

- If you *don't* turn on the "Select entire contents" option, FileMaker inserts the calculation result *after* whatever's already in the field.

- If you *don't* specify a field at all, and you *don't* turn on "Select entire contents," then FileMaker inserts the result of the calculation into the current field. If you select data when the script step runs, the calculation result overwrites whatever's highlighted. Otherwise, the text goes in wherever the insertion point happens to be, just as though you'd typed it from the keyboard.

Tip: You can, if you wish, use Set Field to append results to existing data: Just include the field's data in the calculation. If you want to add "Esquire" to the end of the customer's last name (in the Last Name field), just use this calculation in your Set Field step:

```
Last Name & ", Esquire"
```

Inserting other values

FileMaker has six other *Insert* script steps that work like Insert Calculated Result. Each step lets you specify a target field and select the field contents if you want. They differ only in what gets inserted:

- **Insert Text** lets you specify any arbitrary text value and add it to the field verbatim. Use this if you know ahead of time what you want your script to put in the field, and don't need to calculate it.

- **Insert from Index** makes your script show the same View Index window just like choosing Insert → From Index in Browse or Find mode. The user picks a value from the list and FileMaker inserts it into the field. This option's especially valuable in Find mode, both to keep your user from having to type a value (and possibly making a typo) *and* to make sure that the search always finds records, since if a value's in the index, it's in a record somewhere.

- **Insert from Last Visited** is an interesting step. It grabs the value from the *same* field on the *last visited* record and inserts it. This step is particularly useful on data entry layouts. Imagine, for example, you have to enter 300 Person records from 15 different companies. You could use this step to create a button that pops in the *last* company you typed into the Company Name field, rather than type it over again.

- **Insert Current Date** and **Insert Current Time** do just as they say. Unfortunately, there's no Insert Current Timestamp step (use Insert Calculated Result and the Get(CurrentTimeStamp) function instead).

- **Insert Current User Name** puts the user name of the person using FileMaker into the field. Your operating system normally determines this user name, but you can easily change it from FileMaker's Preferences' General Tab.

See the box on page 498 for advice on when to use Set Field and when to use an insert step.

Putting data in container fields

In Part 4, you learned that calculations can work with container data. Set Field and Insert Calculated Result are no exception: You can use either of them to move pictures, movies, sounds, and files from one container field to another. You can also use Cut, Copy, and Paste to work with container fields, provided you're willing to live with the caveats for intruding on your user's Clipboard described on page 495.

But FileMaker has special commands in the Insert menu to get container data into your database in the first place, and these commands have script step equivalents:

- **Insert Picture** lets you specify the file to insert, and whether you want to "Store only a reference" (see page 71 for a refresher on references). If you don't specify a file, FileMaker asks the user to pick one when the step runs.

Note: The dialog box the user sees when he's asked to pick a picture file includes the "Store only a reference" checkbox, regardless of how you set this option on the script step itself. In a sense, your choice in the script becomes a *suggestion* to the user: It determines how the checkbox is set when the dialog box pops up. The user's free to change it.

POWER USERS' CLINIC

Set Field vs. Insert

FileMaker's field editing script steps have a lot of overlap (page 496). For example, Set Field with no target field does exactly the same thing as Insert Calculated Result with no target field and the "Select entire contents" checkbox turned on. And you can use Insert Calculated Result with the appropriate calculation to do the same thing as Insert Date, Insert Time, Insert Text, and Insert Current User Name. In general, it doesn't matter one bit which one you use.

But you should think twice about using the Insert script steps with a target field specified *and* the "Select entire contents" checkbox turned on. With both options set, these script steps simply overwrite the value in some field—exactly what Set Field does.

Since these steps need the field on the layout, though, they're more *fragile*: the script can break if you make changes to a layout. You'll probably save yourself a headache tomorrow if you just use Set Field today.

Of course, if you're inserting *into* a field (without "Select entire contents" turned on) then you *must* use an Insert step. Luckily, with settings like this one, a step makes sense only if the user's already in the field—and thus the field's obviously on the layout.

Finally, you can't accomplish some of the Insert steps from a calculation. Specifically, you can't access the last visited record or the View Index dialog box from a Set Field step.

- **Insert QuickTime** has only one option: the file you want to insert. Again, if no file is selected, the user gets to pick when the script runs. Since QuickTime files are *always* stored as a reference, you don't get that choice this time.

- **Insert File** has the most options of all. Of course you get to pick the file to be inserted. You also get a "Store only a reference" checkbox. This time, though, you also get a "Go to target field" checkbox. You can use it to tell FileMaker which field to put the file in.

Insert Picture and Insert QuickTime don't have an option to tell FileMaker *which field to use*, which probably seems odd. They're designed to put things in the current container field the user clicks before the script runs. If you want more control, just use Go to Field first, specifying the appropriate field. Then use Insert Picture or Insert QuickTime to insert into that field.

A Field Script in Action

Suppose you decide to add a Notes field to the Customer table in your database. You use this field to hold any arbitrary information you think is important about the customer. Unfortunately, you soon realize this field is a little *too* unorganized. You've no idea if the note that says, "Customer already paid" is from last Tuesday or last year. What you need is a consistent way to keep track of *who* left a note, and *when*. You decide everybody should record this information along with any note they leave. To make things even easier, you want to be sure people add *new* notes *above* older notes. Thus, when a customer record has been around for a while, the Notes field would look something like this:

```
--- 12/11/05 @ 3:30 PM by Summer ---
Called the customer, confirmed order was received.

--- 12/01/05 @ 1:25 PM by Stacey ---
Customer called saying he never got his order. I checked and we have no
record of shipment. I'm shipping again.

--- 11/03/05 @ 4:58 PM by Dave ---
Order came in really close to quittin' time. I'll deal with it later!
```

In this example, you create a script that "forces" all added comments into that format. This script adds a separator line with the date and time (plus a couple blank lines) and leaves the insertion point under the separator. You also create a button next to the Notes field that runs this script. All the user has to do is click and type.

Note: Like almost every problem you ever solve with a script, you can do this process in *about* 24,601 ways. One way's described below, and another in the box on page 500. You may prefer a different way, and that's OK.

Before you start creating your script, think about what you need to do in sequence. Here's a breakdown:

- Put the insertion point at the start (top) of the Notes field.
- Insert two blank lines—to create some space before the previous comment.
- Put the insertion point back at the start, and add the separator line with the date and time.
- At that point, the script ends and the user can start typing.

Your next mission is to translate these plain-English steps into ScriptMaker steps, which you'll do in the next section.

Building the script

If your Customers table doesn't already have a Notes field, create one before you write the script. Then proceed as follows:

1. **Choose Scripts → ScriptMaker. Create a new script called *Add Note Separator*.**

   Develop the habit of giving your scripts descriptive names so you can remember what you want them to do.

---

2. **Add a Set Selection script step to the script.**

   You can find this step under Editing in the list, or you can choose "all by name" from the View pop-up menu to see an alphabetical list. When you add the step, it appears in your script.

3. **Turn on the "Go to target field" checkbox. If necessary, choose *Customers* from the table pop-up menu, and then choose the *Notes* field and click OK.**

   The Set Field step in your script updates to show the target field.

GEM IN THE ROUGH

Fewer Steps, Bigger Calculations

The Add Note Separator script described on page 499 is easy to create, but it has one weakness: It uses four steps where two could accomplish the same thing. A more concise approach would be to first put the separator and a few blank lines at the top of the Notes field, *then* use the Set Selection script step to put the insertion point after the separator. The drawback here is that you have much more complex calculations to write. The choice is yours.

In the Set Selection step, you need a calculation that builds the separator line, adds two blank lines after it, and finally adds the *old* contents of the Notes field to the end:

```
"--- " & Get(CurrentDate) & " @ " &
Get(CurrentTime) & " by " & Get(UserName)
& " ---¶¶¶" & Customers::Notes
```

Once this process is done, you need to get the insertion point into place after the first line, using the Set Selection script step. Remember that when you use Set Selection with an End Position that's *smaller* than the Start Position, File-Maker puts the insertion point *before* the character at the Start Position. Since you want it *after* the end of the first line, you need to find the first new line symbol, add *1* to it, and put *that* in the Start Position. Here's the calculation that does the trick:

```
Position ( Customers::Notes, "¶", 1, 1 )
+ 1
```

You can use this script with or without the Go to Target Field option, as describe in step 3 of the "Building the script" section.

---

4. **In the Script Step Options area, click the second Specify button.**

   It's not labeled, but it's *below* the first Specify button. When you click it, the Specify Set Selection window appears.

5. **In *both* boxes (Start Position and End Position) type *0* (zero).**

   Zero in both boxes tells FileMaker you want the insertion point right at the start of the field, and you don't want any text selected. (Positioning at the start of a field is the single exception to the box on page 495, which discusses how to set the insertion point without selecting text.)

6. **Add an Insert Text step to the script and turn off the "Select entire contents" option.**

   You don't want the two blank lines you're about to insert to replace everything in the field.

7. Click the bottom Specify button.

A window called simply Specify appears (Figure 14-2).

Figure 14-2:
The Specify dialog for Insert Text seems puzzling, because there aren't any options for you to click. You just type the exact text you want the script step to insert. Note, this box isn't a calculation dialog box. It only allows the insertion of literal text. Use Insert Calculated Result if you need to insert dynamic text with a script step.

8. **In the Specify window, add two empty lines (press Return or Enter *twice*), and then click OK.**

That's the regular Enter key, not the one in the numerical keypad: In this dialog box, that key just clicks the OK button. Anyway, after pressing it twice, you don't see the returns you've typed in the dialog box, but you do see two blanks spaces inside quotes in the Insert Text script step. Those returns tell FileMaker to add two blank lines to the top of the Notes field.

9. **Select the Set Selection step at the top of the script, and then click the Duplicate button at the bottom of the window.**

FileMaker adds a second copy of the Set Selection step, right below the first.

10. **Drag either Set Selection step to the bottom of the script.**

Mouse junkies can use Ctrl+down arrow (⌘-down arrow) to move script steps.

The ultimate goal is to have a script with Set Selection, then Insert Text, and then Set Selection again. It doesn't matter *which* Set Selection step you drag, as long as one's on top and the other on the bottom when you're done.

11. **Add the Insert Calculated Result step to the script and turn off the "Select entire contents" option.**

Make sure the step lands *after* the last Set Selection script. If it doesn't, move it there. Turning off the selection option ensures that the calculation goes right in the middle of the text, not on top.

12. **Click the Specify button to the right of "Calculated result" and enter this calculation in the Specify Calculation window:**

```
"--- " & Get(CurrentDate) & " @ " & Get(CurrentTime) & " by " &
Get(UserName) & " ---¶"
```

You can use any method you want to enter the calculation, as long as it does the same thing as this one.

13. **Click OK until you're back in your database.**

Your new script is ready to run. Now you just need to add the Notes field to the Customers layout, and a button by it that runs the new script. When you click the button, FileMaker adds the separator to the field, and puts the insertion point in place. Your users can now type notes that are nicely organized and separated.

POWER USERS' CLINIC

A Reusable Notes Separator Script

The mark of a FileMaker power-scripter is someone always on the lookout for the opportunity to write *one* script that can be used in *several* places. After all, who wants to spend his life in ScriptMaker? The fact is, you're probably so happy with your new Notes field and its separator script that you want to use it in other places—on a Job, an Invoice, a Payment, and so forth.

It would be much nicer if the Add Note Separator script could add a note separator (and place the insertion point) in *any* field you wanted. You could then tell the user to click the Notes field before running the script.

The only thing tying your script to the Customers::Notes field is the "Go to target field" checkbox on the Set Selection steps. If you edit the script and turn this option off for *both* Set Selection steps, it works on whatever field is active when the script runs.

If you don't like to have to click the field before running the script, you can fix it in two ways, but both require information you haven't learned yet. See page 549 for a continuation of this technique.

Other Steps that Work with Fields

Lots of times, you want to be able to write scripts that work on multiple records. You might need to change values across a found set of records, or you might want to let FileMaker handle the serial numbering of all the records in a table. The next script steps let you manage data in lots of records without lots of hassle.

Perform Find/Replace

The Perform Find/Replace script step brings all the power of the Find/Replace command (page 51) to your scripts. You can include the find parameters in the script step, or create a calculation to determine the parameters on the fly, as shown in Figure 14-3.

When you use this step, you pick which action you want to perform from the Perform pop-up menu. Your choices are Find Next, Replace and Find, Replace, and Replace All (these correspond with the buttons you use to dismiss the normal Find/Replace dialog box). The "Find what" and "Replace with" boxes each have a Specify button by them. If you know exactly what you're looking for, you can type it right in these boxes. If you click Specify, you get to use a calculation to set these values instead.

For example, say your Notes field is such a smashing success, you find some customers have *pages* of notes—and it's becoming a problem to find what you want.

You'd like a quick way to search the material in the Notes fields. Figure 14-4 shows one solution—add a button to the Customers layout that runs a Find script.

Figure 14-3:
The window behind the Specify button on a Perform Find/Replace script step looks a lot like the normal Find/Replace window. But this version has a new pop-up menu (called Perform) and a couple new Specify buttons that let you specify calculated values for what you're looking for and what you want to replace the found results with.

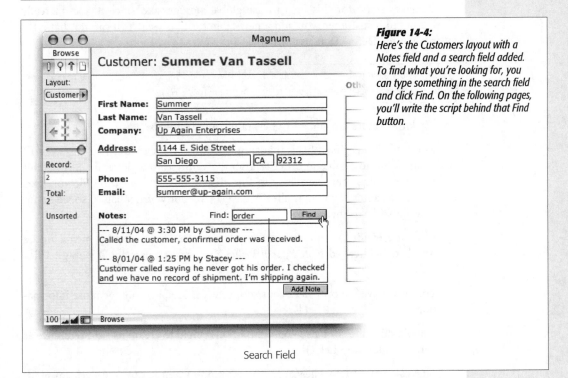

Figure 14-4:
Here's the Customers layout with a Notes field and a search field added. To find what you're looking for, you can type something in the search field and click Find. On the following pages, you'll write the script behind that Find button.

The script is simple. It just needs to go to the Notes field and use the Perform Find/Replace script step. You need a field to type the search value into, which you could create before opening ScriptMaker, but in real life you probably think of that after you start writing your script. FileMaker makes it easy to create fields without leaving the warmth and protection of ScriptMaker, as you'll see in the following steps.

Here's how to make the script. Call it *Search Notes Field*:

1. **Add Go to Field as your first script step. Set it to go to the Customers::Notes field.**

   First things first: You want to make sure the script searches the correct field. Now you create the Find script itself.

2. **Add the Perform Find/Replace step to the script, and turn on the "Perform without dialog" option. Click the Specify button.**

   You see the Perform Find/Replace Options window.

3. **Make sure the Perform pop-up menu is set to *Find Next*, then click the Specify button to the right of the "Find what" box.**

   The Specify Calculation window appears.

4. **From the pop-up menu above the field list, choose *Define Database*.**

   It makes sense for this field to use global storage, and since it doesn't really belong to a customer, you add a new table for it as well. You can do that right here in the Define Database window.

Note: Scripts often make use of global fields, so FileMaker lets you create a quick table to hold them without cluttering or interfering with your relationship graph (page 372).

---

5. **Click the Tables tab and add a new table called Globals.**

   This table holds global fields that aren't tied to specific tables. You don't need a relationship to a table in order to grab the value from a global field, so a table like this makes them very easy to find. If you're working in the file you used back in Chapter 8, you may already have a table for your globals. If so, add your new global fields there.

6. **Click the Fields tab, and select *Globals* from the Table pop-up menu. Add a new text field called *Note Search Value* and set it to use global storage. Click OK.**

   You now have the only field your script needs. See page 109 for more information on global storage fields.

7. **Double-click the Globals::Note Search Value field to create its field reference as your calculation. Click OK.**

   This calculation tells FileMaker where to look when it runs the Perform Find/ Replace step—whatever's in the new field, in this case. Clicking OK when you're done returns you to the Perform Find/Replace Options window.

8. **In the From the Direction pop-up menu, choose *All*.**

   This options tells FileMaker to look through the entire Notes field.

9. Turn on the "Current record/request" and "Current field" radio buttons. Click OK until you're back in your database.

You don't want the search to spill into different fields or records. These options restrict it to just the record the user's viewing. Since the script first goes to the Notes field, FileMaker searches only that field.

To finish the job, add the new global field and a Find button to the Customers layout (as shown in Figure 14-4 on page 503). Then type a value into the search field and click your script button to test your new script.

Replace Field Contents and Relookup Field Contents

It's probably no surprise to you that you can execute the Replace Field Contents and Relookup Field Contents commands from a script. These steps let you specify a specific field to act upon. If you *don't* specify a field, they act on the current field. You also get the typical "Perform without dialog" checkbox. When you turn this checkbox on, the action happens immediately when the step runs. If you leave this option off with the Replace Field Contents step, the user sees the typical Replace Field Contents dialog box (with all the settings you specified in the script). With the Relookup Field Contents step, the user just sees a confirmation message first, asking if she really wants to perform the relookup operation.

Set Next Serial Value

The Set Next Serial Value script step is invaluable—in the rare cases when anyone actually uses it. It's a one-trick pony: If a field auto-enters a serial number, this step changes the "next value" stored in the Field Options dialog box. In other words, if you want to start your customer ID values over again, you can use Set Next Serial Value to do it from a script. (See the box on page 506 for an example.)

Warning: Use extreme care when you change a field that's used as a key in a relationship. You risk leaving related records orphaned if you don't change their key fields, too. See the box on page 576 for a script that helps you change key fields without losing related records (or your sanity).

The step has two options. First, you can specify the field to update. As usual, if you don't specify a field, it works on the current field. You tell FileMaker what to set the "next value" to by entering a calculation.

Working with Records

You can get only so far with your scripts by working with field values. Eventually you need to deal with more than one *record*. Thankfully, FileMaker has script steps for creating, duplicating, and deleting records; navigating among existing records; and even managing the process of opening and editing a record, and saving (committing) or reverting the changes. You can also work directly with portal rows on the current layout—and the records they represent.

Why Set Next Serial Value

The prevously used Set Next Serial Value script step may seem odd to you. After all, if you want to set the next serial value for a field, you can just do it yourself from the Define Database window. But this step can come in very handy in some situations.

Imagine you're in the auto parts business and you have 200 stores around the country. Each office has its own copy of your database, which gets updated periodically. The main office sends a new empty database to each store with all the latest enhancements, and the folks at each store have to *import* all the data from their old database into the new one (you'll learn about importing and exporting data in Chapter 17).

Now suppose this database includes an Orders table with an Order ID field. After the old orders have been imported, the database may have orders with IDs from one to 1000. But since no *new* records have been created yet, the Order ID field still has a "next value" of *1*. The store's first thousand orders use IDs that are *already used by other records*. That's a big no-no.

The solution's obvious: You need to fix the "next value" on the Order ID field after the import's finished. To save the store manager the trouble, you can put a script in the database to fix this glitch for her. (In fact, you can make a script that does *all* the work of importing old data and fixing next serial values in every table.)

Creating, Duplicating, and Deleting Records

New Record/Request and Duplicate Record/Request have no options, and do exactly what you'd expect. The first script step creates a new record, just like the Records → New Record menu command. The second duplicates the current record. In either case, the *new* record becomes the current record, just like when you do it manually. You use these steps most often on buttons, when you're taking away menu commands from people and providing them with buttons that only appear on the layouts where you want your users to be able to create records.

The Delete Record/Request script step deletes the current record. If you turn on its "Perform without dialog" option, the delete happens automatically with no warning. When this option is turned off, the user sees the same "Are you sure" message box he'd see when deleting a record manually.

Note: Each of these three script steps also works for *find requests* when a script runs in Find mode.

Navigating Among Records

There are two ways to change to a different record. You can move to it with the Go to Record/Request/Page script step, which works a lot like the Book icon in the status area. Or you can switch to a related record, or a set of related records, using the Go to Related Record script step.

Go to Record/Request/Page

FileMaker has one script that handles changing *records*, *find requests*, and *pages*. This might seem strange at first, but it makes sense because it's exactly how the Book icon in the status area works: If you're in Browse mode, the step goes to a different record. If you're in Find mode, it switches find requests instead. Finally, if you're in Preview mode, it flips through pages.

Note: You can't run scripts when in Layout mode, and a script *can't* go to Layout mode, so it doesn't apply here.

The Go to Record/Request/Page step has just one option. You get to pick *which* record, request, or page to go to from a simple list:

• First

• Last

• Previous

• Next

• By Calculation

When you lock your users out of the usual interface and control everything they do through the script (see the box on page 529), the First, Last, Previous, and Next options let you provide your own customized replacement for the status area and Book icon. For example: Make four buttons and arrange them in a horizontal line (like those on a tape recorder or CD player). Give each button a Go to Record step and set them up in the follwoing order, so they mimic the tape recorder concept:

• Leftmost button – Go to Record/Request/Page [First]

• Second button – Go to Record/Request/Page [Previous]

• Third button – Go to Record/Request/Page [Next]

• Rightmost button – Go to Record/Request/Page [Last]

This visual concept is so common that your users are likely to know how the buttons work without any instructions. But you can add a tooltip (page 682) to each button if you want to provide that extra boost.

Another common, but more advanced use of this step is to provide a way for a looping script to end. When you choose the Next or Previous option, a new checkbox appears in the Script Step Options area, called "Exit after last." When it's turned on FileMaker knows to exit the loop after it's finished with the last record (when you choose Go to Record [next]) or after the first record (when you choose Go to Record [previous]). (When to exit a loop is no small matter, as page 489 explains.)

When you choose By Calculation, you get the chance to specify a calculation with a number result. FileMaker goes to exactly that record, request, or page. You could use this option if the record number's in a field, or if you want to skip ahead *10* records each time the script is run, for example.

Go to Related Record

You were first introduced to this power-step when learning about relationships (page 336). It can go to a different record, found set, layout, window, and even file; all in one step. This step's job is simple: It takes you to a related record. But carrying out that job *isn't* so simple. When you click the Specify button, you get a wealth of choices, as shown in Figure 14-5. To go to a related record, you first need to tell FileMaker which related table occurrence you're interested in, by selecting it from the "Get related record from" pop-up menu. For example, if you're on the Customer layout and you want to see a related invoice, you should choose Invoices from the menu.

With this done, FileMaker can find the right record. But how should it *show it to you*? If you're visiting related records, chances are you can't view them directly on the current layout (since the layout is associated with the wrong table occurrence). So a Go to Related Record command almost always involves changing layouts. You pick the layout you want from the "Show record using layout" pop-up menu.

Figure 14-5:
This window's the same one you saw when you attached a Go to Related Record script step to a button back on page 249 . But inside a script you wield a whole new level of power when you tie this command to other processes, like printing a report from a found set that changes based on whichever record a user's on when running the script.

At first you might be surprised by the menu choices. It shows all the layouts associated with the table occurrence in the first pop-up menu, as you might expect. But it *also* shows layouts associated with any *other* occurrence of the same table. FileMaker uses the specified table occurrence to find the right related record, and the specified layout to show it to you. You can show an Invoice record from any layout that shows records from the Invoices table, no matter what *occurrence* it uses:

- If the table occurrence you picked in the first menu is an occurrence of a table from a *different* file, you can turn on "Use external table's layout" to see layouts in the file the table comes from. When you use this option, FileMaker switches to a window for the other file instead of showing records in the current window.

- If you want a *new* window (whether you're using an external table or not), turn on the "Show in new window" checkbox. When you do, you see the New Window Options dialog box, which is explained alongside the New Window script step on page 524.

Finally, you get to decide how to deal with the found set when the script step finishes. See the box on page 510 to help you decide when each option makes sense.

- **If you don't turn on** "Show only related records," FileMaker goes to the related table, but you see all the records in the related table, not just those that are children of the formerly active record. The first related record is active in your new found set. So, from the Customer layout, GTRR without "Show only related records" shows all your invoices, and the active record is the first one for the Customer that you're viewing when the GTRR script step runs.

- **If you turn on** "Show only related records" and "Match current record only," FileMaker returns a found set of only those records that match the active parent record. From the Customers Invoice, GTRR set as described above shows you a found set of just the Invoices for the Customer record that was active when the script step ran. The first related record would be the active one.

- **Choosing** "Show only related records" and "Match all records in current found set," is most useful when you have a found set selected before the GTRR script step runs. In this scenario, FileMaker shows a new found set in which all the records are related to at least one of the records in the old found set. So, in the Customers layout, you've found your two highest volume customers. Use GTRR, matching all records in the current found set to find all the invoices related to either of these two customers. The first record that's related to the Customer record that's active when the GTRR script step runs is the active record in the new found set.

Opening, Reverting, and Committing Records

When you use your database in Browse mode, FileMaker does a lot of things automatically. When you start typing in a field, it locks the record. When you exit the record—click outside any field or press Enter—it commits the record. When you use a script, though, you're not really clicking fields and pressing Enter. So how does FileMaker know when to lock a record and when to commit? You have to tell it, by including the appropriate script steps: Open Record/Request, Revert Record/Request, and Commit Record/Request.

Open Record/Request

The Open Record/Request step simply tells FileMaker you're about to start editing a record. If the record is already open—or locked—it does nothing. That is, it doesn't automatically commit the record first. It just locks it if it isn't locked already.

Commit Record/Request

Whether you've used the Open Record/Request step or just let FileMaker lock the record for you, you can explicitly commit the record with the Commit Record/Request step. It has two options:

- The "Skip data entry validation" option tells FileMaker to commit the record even if it violates field validation. This option works only when you turn on the "Only during data entry" radio button in the Validation options for the field. If you have set the validation to happen "Always," then the script *can't* get around it.

- When the "Perform without dialog" option is turned off, and you turn *off* "Save record changes automatically" in the Layouts → Layout Setup window's General tab, FileMaker shows the message in Figure 14-6 when the step runs.

Tip: You know how to handle dialog boxes when they come up, but they often confuse and confound your users. Most database designers try to avoid requiring their users to interact with dialog boxes while scripts are running, especially when the user could make a choice that circumvents the purpose of their carefully crafted script.

Revert Record/Request

The Revert Record/Request step has only one option: "Perform without dialog." When this option is turned off, the user sees the message in Figure 14-7. Otherwise, FileMaker reverts the record directly when the script runs.

Figure 14-6:
If the layout is set not to save record changes (page 139), and you don't turn on the "Perform without dialog" checkbox you see this warning when the Commit Record/Request step runs. Click Save to commit the record. If you click Don't Save, FileMaker reverts the record instead. The Cancel button leaves the record open and locked.

Figure 14-7:
Unless you turn on the "Perform without dialog" option, your users see this dialog box when the Revert Record/Request step runs. If a user clicks Cancel, FileMaker leaves the record open and locked, which is probably not your intention.

These script steps are relatively easy to understand, but *when* to use them is hard to figure out. Here are some things to keep in mind when you're trying to decide when you need to open or commit a record in a script:

• When you use a script step that *inserts* data into a field (and leaves the user in the field), then FileMaker locks the record when the step runs, but doesn't commit the change. You can then do *more* work with fields if you want. FileMaker commits the record later, when the user exits the record.

• If your script changes to a different layout, switches to Find or Preview mode, or closes the window, FileMaker automatically commits the record if needed.

• If you use a script step that modifies several records—Replace Field Contents, for example—FileMaker locks, edits, and commits each record in turn, as it goes.

• If you perform a series of Set Field steps in a script, and you are *not* in the record when the script runs, FileMaker locks the record and makes the field changes. When the script is done, you're not in the record (no field is active), but the record's still locked and uncommitted. In other words, you can use the Records → Revert Record command to revert all the changes made by the script, which probably isn't what you want to happen. Add a Commit Records/Requests script step at the *end* of the script to prevent the loss of data your script enters.

• If your script changes some records and includes a step to revert them if something goes wrong, you should probably make sure to commit any changes your user was making before your script changes anything. That way, the script doesn't undo any of the user's work. Thus, put a Commit Records/Requests step at the *beginning* of your script.

And if you're still not sure if your script really needs an Open or Commit step, go ahead and open the record at the beginning of your script and commit it at the end. Sure it takes a nanosecond or two extra to run a couple of steps that might not strictly be needed. But what's a nanosecond on the grand scale of time when your data may be at risk?

FREQUENTLY ASKED QUESTION

Why Open a Record?

Why would I ever use the Open Record/Request step? Doesn't FileMaker automatically lock a record as soon as my script starts editing it?

For simple scripts, this step is almost always unnecessary. FileMaker does, indeed, just do the right thing. But as you'll learn in Chapter 18, you can set your FileMaker database up so that multiple people can use it at the same time, each on her own computer. When you set FileMaker up this way, lots of interesting things can start happening.

For example, a record can change while you're looking at it. Suppose a new area code is added in your area, and you write a script that looks at the phone number and decides, based on exchange code, whether or not to change the area code. The script might look like this:

```
If [ "Exchange Code = 555 or Exchange Code
= 377" ]
    Set Field [ Area Code, "602"]
End If
```

You probably find this hard to believe, but technically, someone could change the Exchange Code field after the If step runs, but before the Set Field happens. (Remember that other people are editing records on other computers, so they're free to make changes while the script is running on your computer.) If this scenario happens, you end up assigning the customer an incorrect phone number.

To fix this, you need to lock the record before you start looking at it:

```
Open Record/Request
If [ "Exchange Code = 555 or Exchange Code
= 377" ]
    Set Field [ Area Code, "602"]
    Commit Record/Request [No Dialog]
Else
    Revert Record/Request [No Dialog]
End If
```

Now, somebody else can't edit the Exchange Code field because the record is locked. In general, if your database has multiple users, you should open a record before you start looking at it in a script.

This script reverts the record when it didn't make any changes. FileMaker does this reverting for two reasons. First, committing a record means saving the data, and that's unnecessary here. Second, suppose a field has had validation turned on since this record was created. It's possible that this unmodified record has now-invalid data. If you try to commit this data back, you get a validation error. Reverting avoids this error since nothing's being saved. Moral of the story: Try to commit a record *only* when necessary.

Copying Records

FileMaker has two record-related script steps that do something you can't easily do manually in Browse mode: Copy an entire record to the clipboard. One version copies just the current record, while the other copies every record in the found set at once.

Copy Record/Request

The first, called Copy Record/Request, copies data from *every* field on the layout and puts it on the clipboard. FileMaker puts a tab character between each field value.

If any field has *more* than one line, FileMaker converts the new line character into a funny character called a Vertical Tab. Some programs, like Microsoft Word, convert these characters back into new lines when you paste in a copied record. Figure 14-8 shows the result of pasting a Customer record into Microsoft Word.

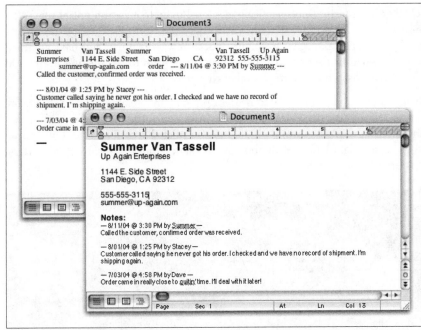

Figure 14-8:
The window in the back shows what it looks like when you copy a customer record, then paste it into a Word document. You see the first and last name twice because technically it appears on the layout twice (once in the header, and again in the editable fields). Although this block of text needs some serious cleanup, it's often easier to copy/paste it all in one shot than to copy each field value individually. You can see a cleaned-up version in the front most window.

Note: Some programs don't recognize vertical tab characters, so when you paste into them, you see boxes, vertical lines, or nothing at all. Your multi-line field values are strung together in one long line.

Copy All Records/Requests

While Copy Record/Request copies the entire *current* record, its brother—Copy All Records/Requests—copies *every* record in the found set. Each individual record is added to the clipboard in the same format as the Copy Record/Request command produces, and FileMaker puts one record on each line.

Suppose, for example, you want to get all the Invoice IDs for a particular customer and put them in an email to a coworker. Or perhaps you're compiling a list of all the zip codes in Phoenix where you have customers. Using Copy All Records/Requests, you can do this job with ease.

The trick is to create a *new* layout that has only one field on it. For example, make a new layout with just the Invoice ID field, or just the Zip Code field. Write a script that switches to this layout and run the Copy All Records/Requests command to get a simple list of values on the clipboard.

Working With Portals

FileMaker has a script step specifically designed to go to a certain portal row. Why would you want to do that? First, when you use the Go to Field script step to target a field in a portal, it goes to the *first* portal row, which may not have anything to do with what the user needs at that point. If you want to put the user in the field on a *different* row, you need to go to that row first.

When you use data from a related field, or put data in a related field, and there are *multiple* related records, FileMaker grabs the value form the *first* record. If you want to tell FileMaker to work with a different related record instead, use a portal and go to the right row. See the box below for tips (and a warning) on working with portals.

DIAMOND IN THE ROUGH

Beware the Portal

It's technically possible to do all kinds of things through a portal using a script—it's not always wise. For example, if you wanted to discount every line item on an invoice by 10 percent, you could write a looping script. It would start by visiting the first portal row and applying the invoice. It could then go to each additional row, applying the discount as it goes. In each pass through the loop, you'd be modifying the Line Items::Price field—the active portal row determines which line item is changed. Unfortunately, the active portal row is too transient to be relied upon. A script can do all kinds of things that make FileMaker forget which portal row you're on (change modes, change layouts, go to another field, commit or revert the record, and so forth).

If you accidentally do confuse FileMaker like this at some point inside your loop, you end up looping forever because you never reach the end of the portal.

It's much safer to find the appropriate records and work with them directly. You can get the same effect by using the Go to Related Records script step to find all the Line Item records, and then looping through the records directly with Go to Record/Request/Page, avoiding the perils of the portal.

Go to Portal Row

The Go to Portal Row script step works a lot like the Go to Record/Request/Page step. You can go to the First, Last, Previous, or Next portal row, or specify the row *number* with a calculation. It even has an "Exit after last" option to help when looping through portal rows.

This step includes an option you can use to make what's happening onscreen a little more obvious to your users—"Select entire contents." When you turn this checkbox on, FileMaker highlights the whole portal row. Otherwise, it goes to the portal row without highlighting it onscreen. (After all, you don't always want your user to see what's going on.)

One setting you *won't* find with Go to Portal Row is *which portal to use*. The guidelines below are how FileMaker knows which portal you have in mind:

- If the current layout only has one portal, FileMaker uses it automatically.

- If the layout has more than one portal, it assumes you want the portal that's currently active.

- If you're writing a script and you want to be sure you go to a row in the right portal, just use Go to Field first, targeting a field that's displayed in the portal.

Note: In general, a portal is active whenever a person (or a script) puts the cursor in one of its fields. If you aren't sure what your user will be doing before your script runs, throw in a Go to Field script step, just to be safe.

Finding Records

FileMaker has three nearly identical script steps to handle the grunt work of finding records. You can let your user tell the script what to find, you can decide what the script finds (a *hard-coded* find), or you can script a dynamic find using calculations. Deciding which one to use depends on whether your users know what they're looking for—or how much work you want to save them. The upcoming sections go into this topic in detail. You'll also see a find script in action, and learn how to make a script pause and wait for information.

Performing the User's Find Requests

The first, Perform Find, is the equivalent of a visit to Find mode, followed by a click of the Requests → Perform Find menu command. Perform Find's single option lets you specify what find requests to use, but, surprisingly, you can skip it entirely. If you *don't* turn this option on, then Perform Find assumes you're already in Find mode with one or more requests, and works just like the Requests → Perform Find menu command (and the Find button in the status area). It looks for records that match the already defined find requests. All the matching records become the new found set.

But where do those find requests *come from*? Either the user creates them, or your script does. For example, many developers like to add special "Find" layouts to their databases. These layouts can show just the right fields, along with helpful text, to make things easier for the user. Figure 14-9 shows a Find layout for the Customers table.

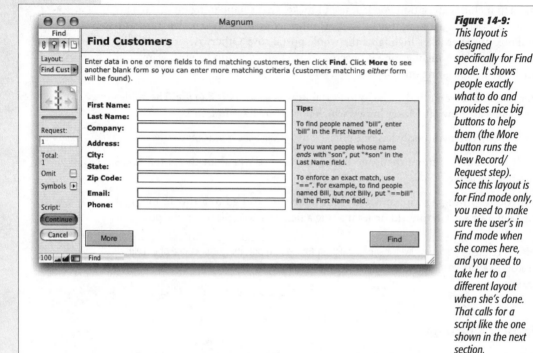

Figure 14-9:
This layout is designed specifically for Find mode. It shows people exactly what to do and provides nice big buttons to help them (the More button runs the New Record/ Request step). Since this layout is for Find mode only, you need to make sure the user's in Find mode when she comes here, and you need to take her to a different layout when she's done. That calls for a script like the one shown in the next section.

The best way to deal with a layout like this is to add a "Find" button on your normal Customers layout. When the user clicks this button, it runs a script that goes to the Find layout and puts the user in Find mode. The script then *pauses* (see the box on page 517), giving the user a chance to enter find requests. When she's done, she clicks a button to *Continue* the script, which performs the find and switches back to the Customers layout.

To set this process up yourself, first create a Find Customers layout like the one shown in Figure 14-9. Then visit the Define Scripts window, click New, and name the script appropriately. Then follow these steps to define the script itself:

1. **Add the Go to Layout script step, targeting the Find Customers layout.**

   After all, you want to make sure the user's in the right context—the new Find Customers layout—before the script enters Find mode.

2. **Add the Enter Find Mode script step to the script.**

   The step already has its Pause option turned on and its "Specify find requests" option turned off. That's just what you want. This step switches to Find mode *and* pause the script.

Pausing a Script

Normally when you run a script, FileMaker performs its steps one by one as fast as it can. When they're all finished, the script's done. But sometimes a script can *pause*. You can explicitly tell a script to pause. The Pause/Resume Script step, and some other steps (like Enter Find Mode) can pause the script automatically when their Pause option is turned on. When FileMaker gets to a step like this, it stops executing the script, but remembers where it left off. Later, the script continues, starting with the next step in line. While a script is paused, you're free to edit records, switch modes, change layouts, and so forth, You *can't* open the Define Database, Define Value Lists, Define Custom Functions, or Define Scripts windows, though, until the script finishes running.

While a script is paused, FileMaker adds two new buttons to the status area (shown in Figure 14-9). The Continue button causes the script to continue immediately (pressing the Enter key does the same thing). The Cancel button tells FileMaker you don't want to run the rest of the script. Your script stops and you get back full control of the program.

If you want to, you can tell FileMaker how long to pause by clicking the Specify button in the Script Step Options are when the Pause/Resume Script step is selected. The dialog box that appears has two choices, Indefinitely and For Duration. If you choose For Duration, you get to enter the number of seconds you want the script to pause, or click *another* Specify button to use a calculation to set the number of seconds. In either case, your pause duration can be fractional—like *4.5 seconds*—if needed. If you have set the script to pause for a specific duration, you can still do things with your database while the script is paused, including click the Continue or Cancel buttons.

With a name like "Pause/Resume Script" you'd think this step can also *resume* a paused script. But then again, if the script is paused, then how can the step possibly execute? Don't be fooled: This step can only pause.

Tip: If you want to start the user off with some basic criteria, you can specify them right in the Enter Find Mode step. FileMaker doesn't perform the find now. It just puts the user in Find mode and creates the requests you specify. The user's then free to *modify* or *delete* them as necessary.

---

3. **Add the Perform Find script step to the script.**

   Once the script continues, you assume the user has added the necessary find requests, so you're ready to use the Perform Find step with no find requests specified. (Be careful not to choose the Perform Find/*Replace* script step, which doesn't work in this script.)

4. **Add another Go to Layout script step to the script. This time, pick the Customers layout.**

   This step takes the user back to the Customers layout once FileMaker finds the correct records.

After you follow these steps, your completed Find Customer script should look like the one in Figure 14-10.

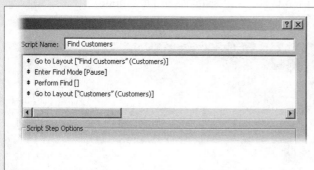

Figure 14-10:
This is how your Find Customer script should look if you've been following the steps on page 516. It first takes the user to the new Find Customers layout and switches to Find mode. Notice that the Enter Find Mode has its Pause option turned on—FileMaker automatically pauses the script after this step. When the user's finished adding find requests and continues the script, FileMaker runs the Perform Find step (with no find requests specified, so it uses the ones the user created) and switches back to the Customers layout.

To complete your layout, you need the to put Find button on the Find Customers layout. Since the user's always in the middle of a paused script when she sees this layout, you just need to wire this button to the Resume Script action.

Tip: It's probably a good idea to hide the Find Customers layout from the Layouts pop-up menu so users don't accidentally switch to it without running your script. In the Layout Setup dialog box, turn off the "Include in layouts menu" checkbox (page 137).

Static Find Requests

With the script you created on the previous few pages, your users can search for just about anything they want, by entering find requests. More often than not, you *don't* want to make users enter the find requests manually. After all, the whole point of a script is to have FileMaker do things so people don't have to. If you know ahead of time exactly what you want the script to find, use the Perform Find step all by itself: Just turn on the "Specify find requests" option and put those requests right in the dialog box and the search options stay the same each time the script runs. When you specify find requests in a script, you see the window shown in Figure 14-12.

This window is pretty straightforward. To add a new find request, click New. To edit an existing request, select it first, and then click Edit (Figure 14-11). You can also delete or duplicate the selected step using the Delete and Duplicate buttons. Using the Specify Find Requests and Edit Find Request windows, you can tell the Perform Find step to do any find you can do from Find mode.

Tip: The Edit Find Requests dialog box is confusing until you get used to it. But there's a way you can learn how it translates requests into its own particular syntax. Perform a find manually, then write a test script with a Perform Find script step. FileMaker sets the dialog box with the criteria for the search you just did.

Figure 14-11:
When you add a new find request or edit an existing one, you see this dialog box. It's just a more structured way to type data in fields in Find mode. Instead of using your layouts, you use this window, which gives you direct access to every field in the database (the Fields List) and makes it easy to see exactly what fields are being used in the Criteria List.

To define a particular find request, you first select a field from the Field list (if it's a repeating field, you can specify the repetition number in the Repetition box as well). Then you enter some text in the Criteria box. The Insert Symbol button gives you quick access to the same symbols you see in the status area in Find mode, and the Criteria box accepts all the standard symbols. Once you've finished entering the criteria, click Add to add it to the Criteria list.

- To edit an existing item in the criteria list, first select it. When you do, File-Maker automatically selects the matching field in the Field list and puts the criterion in the Criteria box. You can then make any changes necessary, and click Change.

- To remove a criterion from the list entirely, select it and click Remove.

- Finally, you get to choose whether this request should be used to *find* matching records, or to *omit* them (see page 37). To turn this into an omitting find request, choose Omit Records from the Action pop-up menu.

- When you're finished adding criteria, click OK. Just like Find mode, you can add more find requests if you want. In the Specify Find Requests window, just click the New button a second time. When you're all finished adding requests, click OK again.

Figure 14-12:
The Specify Find Requests window shows up when you tell FileMaker you want the Perform Find script step to perform a predetermined find. (Developers call this technique hard coding.) Right now the window's empty because nobody's added any requests. On your screen, it might not be empty; FileMaker automatically fills it with all the requests you used the last time you were in Find mode. If you have requests, select them all and click Delete.

Field List   Criteria List   Criteria Box

Dynamic Find Requests

As dependable as static finds are, you may not always be able to predict what the user wants to find. Or the criteria for finding the same thing over and over can change, like when you're searching in a date field. For example, suppose you want to find all the invoices created one week ago. You can easily do so in Find mode: Just put the date from a week ago in the Invoices::Date field. But what you put in that field *changes every day*. For example, if today's November 7, and you create a script to find invoices from a week ago, you could attach this request to the Perform Find step:

```
Invoices::Date = "10/31/2005"
```

Unfortunately, as soon as November 8 rolls around, this script *won't* find week-old invoices. It always finds invoices from October 31, 2005. When you're faced with a situation like this, you do have an option: Make the script build the find request the same way you would in Find mode. In other words, tell your script to go to Find mode, have *it* put the right date in the field, and then perform the find. You can use the Set Field script step to put the date in the Invoices::Date field since it conveniently lets you use a calculation to determine the actual date.

The script would look like the one in Figure 14-13.

Figure 14-13:
This script builds the find request itself since it needs to use a calculation to determine the proper date to search for. Notice that the second step uses the calculation Get(CurrentDate) - 7 to determine the date one week ago. The Perform Find step has no requests specified, so FileMaker uses the one the script created. This kind of find script, which changes as your data changes, is called a dynamic find.

Note: If your find request can be handled using the *symbols* supported by Find mode (page 40) then you can use Perform Find all by itself. For instance, to find invoices created today, tell Perform Find to find records with Invoices::Date = //. Since "//" stands for "today's date," it works on any day.

Constraining and Extending the Found Set

You may have already noticed that Perform Find doesn't have an option for the Requests → Constrain Found Set and Requests → Extend Found Set commands. That's because each of these is a separate script step. It makes sense really, because to Constrain or Extend a find, you have to *have* a find first. In other words, this process always takes two separate steps to complete.

The Extend Found Set and Constrain Found Set script step options work *exactly* like Perform Find. Everything you just learned about Perform Find still applies: You can hard-code the find requests, pause the script and let the user enter them, or build them in the script.

Omitting Records

The Omit Record script step lives a dual life. If you're in Browse mode when it runs, it simply omits the current record from the found set. If you're in Find mode, on the other hand, it turns on the Omit checkbox in the status area.

The Omit Multiple Records only works in Browse mode and does the same thing as the Records → Omit Multiple command. As usual, you can specify the number of records to omit in the script, either as a number or calculation. You also get a "Perform without dialog" option so you can decide whether or not the user gets to enter the number of records to omit.

Finally, the Show Omitted Only script step has the same effect as the Records →
Show Omitted menu command.

GEM IN THE ROUGH

Mix and Match

You've now seen that you have three options when performing a find in a script: You can let the user enter the find
requests, hard-code the requests right in the Perform Find
step, or build the requests bit by bit using script steps. But
these aren't mutually exclusive choices: You can mix and
match techniques.

For example, suppose you need a relatively complex set of
find requests that—for the most part—never change, but
one value in one field on just one request needs to be
based on the current date. It would be tedious to have to
add dozens of Set Field and New Record/Request steps to
your script when all but one use a hard-coded value.

Other times, it would be nice to let the user specify the find
requests, but add a little more to it when they're done. You
can start by turning on the "Specify find requests" option on
the Enter Find Mode script step. This step tells FileMaker to
go to Find mode *and* load it up with the requests you specify in a Specify Find Requests dialog box.

Once you're in Find mode, though, you're free to use Set
Field, New Record/Request and Go To Record/Request to
modify the prefab requests to your heart's content. Just go
to the right request and use Set Field to work the dynamic
date value into it.

Suppose you want to let the user search for invoices. You
create a Find Invoices layout and a script just like the one
for Find Customers. But this time, you want to restrict users
to invoices created only in the last year. Before the Perform
Find step, you can add these two steps:

```
New Record/Request
Omit
Set Field [Invoices::Date; "..." &
Get(CurrentDate) - 365]
```

Now the script finds just what the user asks for, but omit
records more than 365 days old. You've used the script to
add a new request to the ones the user defined. What's
more, your user doesn't even know you've controlled her
find.

Modify Last Find

The simplest find-related script step is Modify Last Find. It has exactly the same
effect as the Records → Modify Last Find command: It puts you in Find mode with
the same requests you created the *last* time you were in Find mode.

Save Records as...

Now that you've mastered the scripted find, you can keep right on going and automate the process of putting your found set to good use—outside of FileMaker. The
Save/Send Records commands (covered in full in Chapter 17) let you export
records into formats other programs can understand.

Save Records as Excel

As with its manual counterpart, your users will need export privileges (page 587)
to run the Save Records as Excel script step. (Actually, any user with full access
privileges can do it.) You need to make the same choices in this script step as you
do from the menu command, but the options are divided up amongst the various

---

dialog boxes a little bit differently. The Save Records as Excel script step has three options:

- **Perform without dialog** lets you control the step's options without input from your users. Don't turn on this option if you want users to be able to specify all the options they'd normally see in the Save Records as Excel dialog box.

- The **Specify output file** option lets you determine a where the file is saved. You can click the Browse button to select a location through the Open dialog box or simply type a file path. You also have access to the **Automatically open file** and **Create email with file as attachment** options.

- The **Specify Options** dialog is almost the same as the one you see when you chose this command manually and click the Options button. You can set a Worksheet name, document Title, Subject, and Author. Here's also where you specify whether you want to save the **Records being browsed** or just the **Current Record**.

Note: It'd be great if you could suppress one of these dialog boxes and leave the other one open for business…but you can't. If you tell the step to "Perform without dialog," *both* dialog boxes get shut down. You can, however, set up the options you want, show your users the dialog boxes, and instruct them that they should change only certain items. (Use of the phrase "under pain of reprisal" while you deliver these instructions is entirely optional.)

Save Records as PDF

Like its popular Excel twin, the Save Records as PDF script step is the automated version of a menu-driven counterpart. It requires printing privileges (page 587) or Full Access privileges to do its work. Similarly, you can control all the step's myriad options by choosing the "Perform without dialog" option, or you can open the script up to input from your users. Check out the full instructions for "Save/Send as PDF" on page 620 to see the ramifications of the full option set. The "Specify Options" button lets you choose output options appropriate to creating a PDF:

- The Save pop-up menu lets you choose between **Records being browsed** and the **Current Record**.

- The Options button produces a three-tabbed dialog box:

  - **Document.** Set the Title, Subject, Author, Keywords, Compatibility and page numbers here.

  - **Security.** Set passwords and access on this tab.

  - **Initial View.** Choose the setup your users see when the PDF is first opened.

Sorting Records

After all that fuss about finding records, the sorting script steps are refreshingly simple. There're only two of them, and you already know how to use both. The Sort Records script step behaves in a now-familiar way. All by itself, it brings up the Sort dialog box when the script runs. If you turn on its "Specify sort order" option, you can preload the sort dialog box with a specific sort order. Finally, turn on the "Perform without dialog" option to sort the records without bothering the user with a dialog box at all.

If the records are already sorted, you can *unsort* them from a script. For instance, you might sort records for a report, but you want to return them to their unsorted order when the report is finished so your users don't get confused. Just use the Unsort Records script step. It does its job with no options.

Working with Windows

Scripts give you complete control over the database windows on the screen. You can create new windows, close existing windows, bring any window to the front, and move or resize any window. (Why would a script need to monkey with someone's onscreen windows? See the box on page 526 for some ideas.)

Creating Windows

To make a new window on the screen, you use the New Window script step. With this step selected in your script, you see a Specify button in ScriptMaker's Script Step Options area. Clicking this button brings up the New Window Options dialog box, pictured in Figure 14-14.

The first box—Window Name—gives your script control over the name of the window. (Window name is something you can control *only* from a script. When you create the window from the Window menu, FileMaker assigns it a name for you.) You can also tell FileMaker how big the window should be (Height and Width), and where to put the window on the screen ("Distance from top" and "Distance from left").

Here are some tips on using the New Window Options dialog box:

- If you leave any of the values blank, FileMaker uses the same value from the *current* window (it adds a number to the end of the window name so the new name is different). For example, if the current window's called "My Database" and you run the New Window script step without specifying a name, the new window's name is "My Database – 2."

- If you also don't specify a size and position, FileMaker puts it right over the top of the current window (with the same size and position).

Tip: To avoid confusing your user, it's usually best to offset the new window at least a little so he can see that there's a new window on top of his old one.

- You can directly set each of the values by typing in the box in the New Window Options dialog box or set them from a calculation by clicking the Specify button by any box. See the box on page 526 for more detail.

Figure 14-14:
The Window Options dialog box lets your script open and close windows and move them around the screen. You can use it to make family members think they have poltergeists in their PCs, or just make windows behave properly when your scripts run. See the box on page 526 for advice.

Bringing a Window to the Front

In ScriptMaker parlance, you bring a window to the front by *selecting* it. As such, you use the Select Window script step. It has one option, which lets you specify a window by name, or select the current window, as shown in Figure 14-15. You also use the Select Window script step to show a hidden window and bring it to the front.

Figure 14-15:
This is the window you see when you click the Specify button with a Select Window script step selected. From here, you can specify the Current Window, or choose Window Name and put the name of the window you want in the box. As usual, you can use a calculation to determine the window name as well.

Note: Usually, the current window is already in the front, and you don't have to worry about this step. But when you run scripts that involve more than one database, as you'll learn in Chapter 15, you may need this step to bring forward the current window from *another file*.

Window Size and Position Calculations

The fact that you can set a new window's size and position using a calculation might seem a little strange. After all, do you really need a bigger window for someone named Bill? Do you want your windows in a different place on Thursdays?

In fact, though, you can do a lot of interesting things with window size and position calculations. FileMaker provides a handful of functions that let you find out about the size and position of the current window, and of the computer screen, and use that information in calculations:

- The Get (WindowHeight) function, for instance, returns the height of the current window, in screen pixels (the little dots on your screen). Its brother, Get (WindowContentHeight) returns the height of just the content area of the window; that is, the area inside the title bar, scroll bars, and status area.) The Get (WindowHeight) and Get (WindowContentHeight) functions are similar.

- Get (WindowTop) and Get (WindowLeft) functions tell you where the window is on the screen. The first returns the distance from the top of the window to the top of the screen. The second tells you the distance from the left edge of the window to the left side of the screen. Both distances are measured in pixels.

- The Get (WindowDesktopHeight) and Get (WindowDesktopWidth) functions tell you how much desktop space you have. On Windows, it's the area of FileMaker's main application window. On Mac OS X, it's the size of the desktop.

- Finally, Get (ScreenHeight) and Get (ScreenWidth) tell you how big the screen is. (If you have more than one screen, they tell you about the screen the current window is on.)

```
Let (
    [ Limit = Get ( WindowDesktopHeight ) -
Get ( WindowHeight ) ;
      Offset = Get ( WindowTop ) + 20 ;
      Best = Min ( Limit ; Offset ) ] ;

    Best
)
```

By combining these functions in creative ways, you can make your scripts smart about how they size and position windows. For example, to make the new window appear slightly offset from the current window, use these settings:

Distance from top: Get (WindowTop) + 20
Distance from left: Get (WindowLeft) + 20

If you're paranoid, and you want to make sure the new window never hangs off the bottom of the screen, use this calculation for the "Distance from top" value:

Similarly, you can use the "Distance from left" value to make sure it doesn't hang off the screen's right edge. Just substitute WindowDesktopWidth, WindowWidth, and WindowLeft for WindowDesktopHeight, WindowHeight, and WindowTop.

Closing a Window

The Close Window script step has the same options as Select Window. You tell FileMaker which window to close: the current window, or one you specify by name.

Moving and Resizing Existing Windows

FileMaker has three ways to move and resize a window. You can opt for one of its canned window maneuvers or you can set the exact pixel size and location of the window just like you can with the New Window step. You can also *hide* the current window.

Adjust Window

The Adjust Window script step always operates on the current window, and it gives you just five simple choices:

- Choose **Resize to Fit,** and FileMaker makes the window exactly the right size to fit its contents.

- Choose **Maximize** to make the window as large as possible.

- Choose **Minimize** to shrink the window to a little bar (Windows) or a Dock icon (Mac OS X).

- Choose **Restore** to switch a window back to the *last* size it was, just before it was most recently resized.

- Choose **Hide** to hide the window (just like the Window → Hide Window command).

Note: The Maximize options have slightly different behavior on Mac OS X and Windows. For example, when you maximize a window in Windows, and then select a different window, the second window also gets maximized. On Mac OS X, on the other hand, the second window keeps its original size. Also, a maximized window on Mac OS X fills as much of the screen as possible. On Windows, it fills FileMaker's outer application window, whatever size it may be, and there's no way to adjust the application window from a script.

Arrange All Windows

The Arrange All Windows script step is the equivalent of the four window arrangement options in the Window menu. You can choose to tile windows horizontally or vertically, or cascade them (see page 30). On Mac OS X, you can also choose to bring all FileMaker windows to the front.

Move/Resize Window

For the ultimate in window control, call upon the Move/Resize Window script step. It can move and/or resize any window with pixel-perfect precision. Its Specify

---

button shows the dialog box in Figure 14-16, where you can choose the window's size and position. As with New Window, you can leave any of the size or position values empty. When you do, FileMaker leaves that part of the window's size or position alone. For example, if you specify a new Width but leave Height blank, FileMaker makes the window wider or narrower, but its height doesn't change.

Figure 14-16:
The Move/Resize Window settings look like a combination of the Select Window settings and the New Window settings. First, you pick which window you want to work on (Current Window, or a window selected by name). You then specify the new size and position for the window.

Note: Move/Resize Window also *selects* the window it acts on, which always brings the window to the front, and, if it's a hidden window, shows it.

Other Window-Related Script Steps

FileMaker has a handful of other window-related script steps, listed below. They come in handy if you need to exert more control over what your users see. (Not to imply that you're a control freak or anything.)

- **Freeze Window** tells FileMaker to stop showing changes in the window while the script runs. For example, if your script is looping through all the records in the found set, you normally see each record on the screen as it runs. If you add a Freeze Window script step before the loop, the user sees only the first record while it runs. When the script is finished, FileMaker updates the window again. Looping scripts that have to visit lots of records run decidedly faster when the window is frozen.

- **Refresh Window** forces FileMaker to update what's inside the window when it normally wouldn't. This can be because you previously ran the Freeze Window step, or because FileMaker's simply being conservative. If you want to make sure the user sees a particular record or filed value on the screen while a script is running, add a Refresh Window step after making the change.

- **Scroll Window** lets you simulate a vertical scroll bar click in a window. You can scroll to the Home (top) or End of a window, or move up or down one screenful. You also get a To Selection option, which scrolls the window so that the selected record and field value both show. You'll design most of your window so that scrolling isn't necessary, which means you may never need this step.

- **Show/Hide Status Area** lets you decide if the user should see the status area or not. You can explicitly show or hide the status area, or ask that it be *toggled* (shown if it's hidden, and hidden if it's showing). You can also turn on the "Lock" option to prevent the user from manually changing the status area. For example, if you never want the user to see the status area at all, Hide and Lock it in the script that runs when your database opens. Then the status area is locked, its toggle icon and menu command are grayed out. More commonly, though, the status area's turned off and locked during a process, such as a scripted find. You don't want your users using the Cancel button during a Pause step to cancel a script and then end up dumped on a layout that you meant them to see only while a script is running.

Controlling the Interface

If you want to pull out all the stops, you can use a combination of layouts, custom menus (page 686), tooltips (page 682) and scripting to almost completely take over control of your database. You can hide and lock the status area, then give the user buttons to go to the next, previous, first, and last records. You can make it so that when you click a Customer on the list layout, a new Detail window pops up named after that particular customer. You can even make your script so smart that it selects an existing detail window for the customer if one exists, and makes a new one otherwise.

In this way, you give the user the impression that each customer has his own window, and you make comparing customers side by side a breeze.

This kind of high-level window management takes a fair amount of work, so most people stick with the normal every-layout-in-one-window approach and let the user create windows as needed. Which approach you use depends entirely on how much time you want to spend writing scripts and how important the multiple-window interface is to you.

- **Show/Hide Text Ruler** can toggle, show, or hide, the Text Ruler. Unlike Show/Hide Status Area, this step doesn't have a Lock option. The user can always override your setting, so this step is rarely worth the trouble.

- **Set Window Title** lets you change any window's name. You can specify the current window, or any window name, as well as the window's new name. FileMaker normally names a window with the file's name, but you can tailor each window to your user. Write a script that runs when the file is opened and use the Set Window Title script step with this calculation: Get (FileName & " " & Get (AccountName). See page 600 to learn about Account Names.

- **Set Zoom Level** sets the window zoom level, just like the zoom controls in the bottom-left corner of the window. You can pick a specific zoom level, or choose to zoom in or out to the next level. Again, you get a Lock option. If you set the zoom level and turn on the Lock checkbox, the user can't manually change the zoom level.

- **View As** step is in the Windows section of the script step list, but it isn't really a window-related step. It changes the view option for the current *layout*. You can pick Form View, List View, or Table View. You also get a choice called Cycle that tells FileMaker to switch to the *next* view setting in the list. If you really want to control how your users see your database, use Layout → Layout Setting (View Tab) to turn off the views you don't want them seeing. You can then let users override those settings with this script step.

Working with Files

The Files section in the Script Step list contains some of the *least often used* script steps in all of FileMaker. But if you work in a school, say, the day may come when you need to automate the process of formatting files or saving backup copies for every student in a class. You can also script the process of converting older databases to FileMaker 7/8 format and recovering damaged databases, but these are sensitive processes that are better handled manually.

Opening and Closing Files

The Open File script step lets you open another *FileMaker* file. You can pick any of your previously defined file references (see page 361) or define a new file reference if necessary. When the step runs, the specified file opens and appears in a new window. If the file has a script set to run when it opens, it runs.

If you want the file to open, but you don't want to see a window on the screen, turn on the "Open hidden" option for this step. The file opens, but it's listed in the Show Window submenu of the Window menu, with its name in parentheses.

The Close File script step closes an already open file. When you add the step, you get to pick any file reference or add a new one. You can also choose Current File to close the file the script is in. If the file is open when the script runs, all its windows close and its closing script runs.

Note: In general, FileMaker is very smart about when to open and close files. It opens a file when it needs to and closes it again when it no longer needs it. You usually don't need to open and close files from a script, but there's one important exception—when the file has an opening script that should run before the user can see the file. If you jump directly to a related record in another file, FileMaker bypasses the opening script, so use an Open File script step to ensure that the open script runs.

Save a Copy As

If you have a database you don't want to close, but you want to make a copy of it, you can do so with the Save a Copy As script step. It works just like the File → Save a Copy As command. You might want to script this command if you want to automatically back up several files at once without closing them.

Other File-Related Script Steps

The rest of the file-related script steps are almost never used...but that doesn't mean *you* won't find a good reason to use them.

- **Convert File** lets you convert an older FileMaker database to a FileMaker 7 database. There is very little reason to do this from a script.

- **Set User System Formats** toggles the Use System Formats file option on or off. When you first create a database, FileMaker remembers how your system expects dates, times, and numbers to be formatted. If someone opens the file on a computer with different settings (usually a different language), FileMaker has to decide if it should use the original format settings for the file, or those specified by the new system. You usually set this choice in the Edit → File Options window. Again, there's not much reason to change this from a script.

- **Recover File** runs FileMaker's automatic file repair process on a selected database. Recovering a file is a rare thing in general since FileMaker is careful to avoid damaging databases even when your computer crashes. It's even more rare to do this on the same database so often you'd need a script to do it for you.

Printing

Printing typically involves two specific commands on Windows or Mac OS X: File → Print Setup or File → Page Setup and File → Print. ScriptMaker sees it this way, too.

You use the Print Setup script step to set the options in the Print Setup or Page Setup dialog box. Turn on "Specify print setup" or "Specify page setup" to see the standard dialog box. You can pick the option you want to associate with the script step. When the script runs, FileMaker restores these same options. You can also turn on a "Perform without dialog" checkbox. When this option is off, the user sees—and gets a chance to configure—the dialog box when the script runs. If you just want to set the options without user intervention, turn "Perform without dialog" on.

The Print script step works very similarly. You can specify the exact print options (number of pages and so forth) or let the user make the choice. Either way, when the step runs, FileMaker prints the current record or found set.

Note: Many of the options you can set in the Print dialog box are specific to a particular printer model. For example, some printers let you pick color or black-and-white printing or have settings for different kinds of paper. If someone uses your database and script on a different printer, these options don't work.

Other Script Steps

You've now seen most of the often-used script steps (and a few of the not-so-often used ones). You'll see even more as they come up in the next few chapters. The rest of this chapter covers a few oddball steps that don't seem to fit in anywhere:

Open URL

You first saw the Open URL script step as a button command when learning about text calculations. When FileMaker runs this step, it asks the your computer's operating system to open the URL you specify. Most often the URL is a web address (HTTP), but it can be any URL type your computer supports, including FTP, MAILTO, SSH, and even FMP7 (to open a file on a network server). As usual, you can specify the URL or let the user do it, and you can use a calculation if needed.

Dial Phone

The Dial Phone script step tells your modem to dial the telephone using a phone number you provide. You can use a calculation to specify the phone number or enter it directly.

Note: This script step doesn't work on Mac OS X.

Send Email

If you have an email program set up on your computer, FileMaker can use it to send email from a script. The Send Email script step has two options, the standard "Perform without dialog" checkbox and a Specify button. Clicking Specify shows the Send Mail Options window in Figure 14-17.

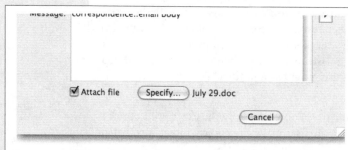

Figure 14-17:
These are the settings for an outgoing email message. You get to tell FileMaker whom to send the message to (using To, CC, and BCC) and what the Subject and Body of the message should be. Finally, you can pick a single file to include as an attachment.

Although you probably wouldn't guess it, you can use a calculation for each of the values in the Specify Mail dialog box. The little button to the right of each entry box shows a menu when clicked with two choices:

- Specify Field Name.

- Specify Calculation.

Whatever you specify for the To, CC, and BCC values, you can also select the associated "Get values from every record in found set" checkbox. When you turn any one of these boxes on, FileMaker creates one outgoing email message for each found record. Each message uses field data specific to one of the records. In this way, you can email all your customers in one shot, addressing each one individually, and including a custom-crafted email message for each.

The "Perform without dialog" option for this script step has an unexpected behavior. Instead of showing the user FileMaker's Specify Mail dialog box when this option is turned off, FileMaker opens her email program, creates the message, and opens it onscreen. The user can then modify the message as needed and send it. If you turn "Perform without dialog" on, FileMaker puts the message directly in your email program's outbox with no user interaction.

Flush Cache to Disk

Any time changes are made to a record, FileMaker records those changes in your computer's memory first, and writes the change to the hard drive later—when it gets some free time. If you want to *force* the changes to be written to disk immediately, you can run the Flush Cache to Disk script step. For instance, you might add this script step after a script that creates a new customer order. That way, if your computer crashes while you're busily taking orders, you lose only the last one you were working on.

Exit Application

Last but not least, you can have a script exit or quit the FileMaker application on your behalf. Of course this causes every open window and file to be closed as well. People usually use this when they have just one database, and they never use File-Maker unless they're in that database. They add the Exit Application step to the very end of their database's closing script so that when they close the last database window FileMaker goes away too. (Of course *you* find FileMaker so useful you *never* want to close it, right?)

Advanced Scripting

Familiarity with FileMaker's lengthy list of script steps is a great foundation, but putting together a workable script takes practice. Although some scripts are simple five-line affairs, sometimes a script requires a lot of forethought, planning, and organization. FileMaker gives you tools to help you write scripts and to troubleshoot them when they aren't working. Plus, you can organize and document your work as you go. In this chapter you'll pull these concepts together to learn how to write and manage complex scripts.

Commenting Scripts

When you look at a script someone else created—or you created a long time ago—it isn't always obvious what it's trying to do. To help keep things clear, add comments to your script. You add each comment via a Comment script step. This step has just one option: the text of the comment itself. The comment step is special for two reasons. First, it doesn't *do* anything except say whatever you tell it to say. Second, it shows in bold when you view your script in the Edit Script window. You can see a commented script in Figure 15-1.

Asking and Telling the User

Sometimes a script needs to tell your users something—"There are no records to include in this report"—or ask the user a question—"How many copies of the report do you want?" To this end, the Show Custom Dialog script step can display a dialog box that you control. Calling it a "Custom" dialog box might be a bit too

generous (you don't have much say in how it looks), but you do get to give information to people using your database, and ask them simple questions.

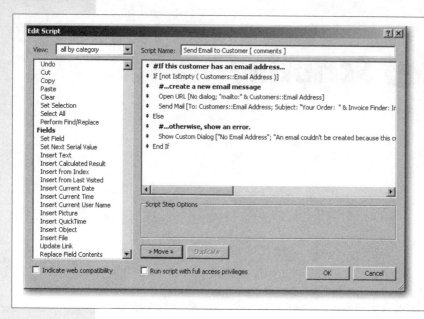

Figure 15-1:
This is the Send Email script you worked with in Chapter 14. Now, though, it has three comments explaining what it's supposed to do. The comment lines show up with a # symbol at the start, and in bold text.

When you add the Show Custom Dialog step to your script and click its Specify
button, you see the window shown in Figure 15-2.

Figure 15-2:
The Show Custom Dialog Options window has two tabs. Here you see what's under the General tab: Title, Message, and the buttons. In its most basic form, a custom dialog box shows a message with just one, two, or three buttons. Figure 15-3 shows how each of these settings affects the dialog box the user sees.

Note: There's another way to help people understand what your scripts are doing: Put comments in any embedded calculations. When a script has an If statement that uses a complex calculation for its condition, you're free to put comments in the calculation itself.

The Show Custom Dialog script step has three basic purposes. First, it can display a simple message. In a script that finds all overdue invoices, for example, you can have a message that says, "No invoices are overdue" if FileMaker finds nothing. Second, you can create a dialog box that asks a simple question. Say you have a script that posts a customer payment. Before launching into the process, your custom dialog box can ask, "Are you sure you want to post a payment?" and include Post Payment and Cancel buttons for your users' feedback. Finally, you can use this script step when you need to ask your users to enter some data, not just click a button. For example, a script that runs a sales report might start by asking what date range to report on. Here's how to create all three types:

Showing a Simple Message

In its simplest form, the Show Custom Dialog script step just delivers a message to the user. Figure 15-3 shows how to configure a box like this, and how the final result looks.

Figure 15-3:
If you simply need to tell users something, give your custom dialog box only a title, message, and one button. In this picture, you can see the resulting dialog box below the options set in the script step. The title appears along the top of the dialog box, the message inside, and the button at the bottom. The first button (called Default Button in the Show Custom Dialog Options window) is the one that users can "click" by simply pressing Enter or Return—or, if they insist, by clicking with the mouse.

You can generate the title and message from a calculation to make it more dynamic. For instance, if someone wants to see all open invoices for a particular client, but there aren't any, you can show a calculated custom message that says, "Lucy Pevensie's account is paid in full," instead of something equally true, but less helpful, like "No records were found."

Using a custom dialog box like this in a script is simple. Just use the Show Custom Dialog step wherever you want in your script. When the dialog box pops up, your script waits for the user to click the button, and then continues with the next step.

Asking a Simple Question

To ask the user a simple question (one with either two or three possible responses), just add more buttons to the dialog box by filling in the Button 2 and Button 3 boxes in the Show Custom Dialog Options window. You can see this process in action in Figure 15-4.

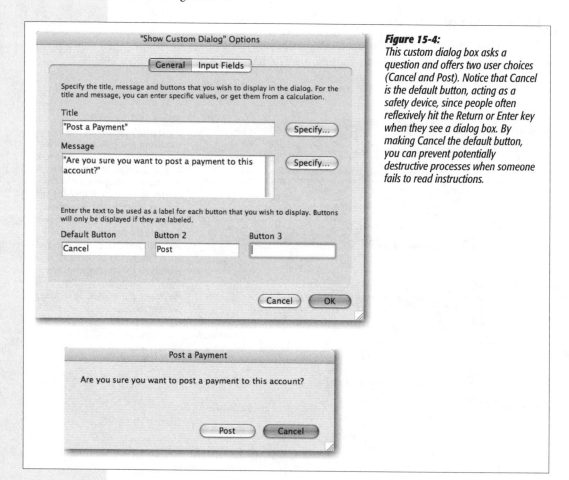

Figure 15-4:
This custom dialog box asks a question and offers two user choices (Cancel and Post). Notice that Cancel is the default button, acting as a safety device, since people often reflexively hit the Return or Enter key when they see a dialog box. By making Cancel the default button, you can prevent potentially destructive processes when someone fails to read instructions.

When a dialog box like this appears, your script waits for a click of one of its buttons, then continues. Although FileMaker knows whether button 1, 2, or 3 got clicked, you have to add logic to your script to tell the program what to *do* in each case. For that, you use the *Get (LastMessageChoice)* function and If statements based on its results. (The function returns *1* for the default button, *2* for Button 2, and *3* for Button 3.) The script in Figure 15-5 uses *Get (LastMessageChoice)* to take some steps only when someone clicks a custom dialog box's default button.

Figure 15-5:
This script uses the Show Custom Dialog script step to ask a question (the same question shown in Figure 15-4). If your user clicks Post, the script creates a new record and sets the Payments::Amount field appropriately. To make this decision, it uses an If step with the condition Get (LastMessageChoice) = 2.

Asking a Not-so-simple Question

If you need user input that goes beyond two or three simple choices, you can venture into the second tab—Input Fields—in the Show Custom Dialog script step (Figure 15-6). The Show Custom Dialog Options window's Input Fields tab lets you add fields to your custom dialog box. To add a field to a custom dialog box, turn on one of the "Show input field" checkboxes in the Input Fields tab of the Show Custom Dialog Options window. When you do, FileMaker shows a Specify Field dialog box, in which you can pick the field to use. (If you want to change the field later, click the Specify button).

You can also give the field a label (like Start Date and End Date in Figure 15-6). The label can be the result of a calculation. Finally, if you turn on "Use password character" for an input field, the field works like a typical Password box: It shows * or • instead of the letters you type, so someone watching over your shoulder can't see what you're entering.

The fields you add to a custom dialog box have some limitations, including the ones listed below. (For other alternatives, see the box on page 541.)

• As far as data entry goes, Show Custom Dialog can have only free-entry fields like those shown in Figure 15-6. You can't use radio buttons, checkboxes, or pop-up menus. You also have no control over the size of the field, so short fields for dates, or tall fields for lots of text, aren't an option.

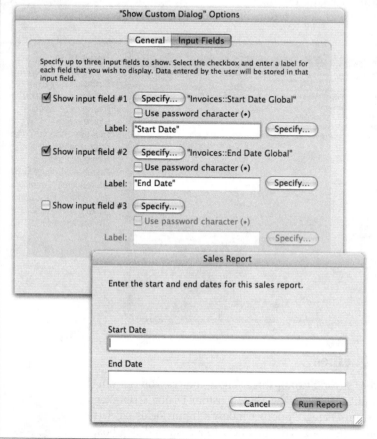

Figure 15-6:
You can have, at most, three fields, each of which corresponds to a real field in your database. The window in the front shows how the dialog box looks when the script runs. When the user types something in one of the fields and then clicks the default button, FileMaker puts the entered value into the real field on the current record. If the user clicks Button 2 or Button 3, on the other hand, FileMaker leaves your record's fields alone.

• "Data-entry only" validation doesn't apply to fields in custom dialog boxes. If you use a dialog box to gather data for a record, either use the Always option in the field validation, or check the validity of the data in your script (page 554).

• You must use the OK button as the default when you're using input fields in a custom dialog box. Consequently, you have to trust people to read the dialog box when they need to enter data in it.

Organizing Complex Scripts

Sometimes you need a script that does a *lot*. At the end of this chapter you'll build a script that generates an invoice for a selected job. As you'll see, this process involves a lot of steps across several tables. To do all this work in one long script can be cumbersome, especially when several levels of If and Loop steps get mixed up with one another.

In other situations, you might need two or more scripts that do similar things. In fact, sometimes entire sections of two scripts are identical. You might have a script that finds unpaid invoices so it can print a statement, and another that finds unpaid invoices to send email payment reminders.

WORKAROUND WORKSHOP

Really Custom Dialog Boxes

If the window created by the Show Custom Dialog script step (Figure 15-5) doesn't meet your needs, all is not lost. You have two options. For professional-level needs (*real, resizable* dialog boxes with text you can calculate, progress bars, multiple input fields), get a third-party plug-in made for the task. See page 464 for more information on how to use plug-ins and where to find them.

But for light duty, you can get the a similar effect by assembling your own dialog box from a window, a layout, and a script.

First, you need a layout that shows what you want. You can use text objects on the layout to show messages, fields of any kind to gather input, and layout buttons in any quantity and configuration. Once you've got the layout just the way you like it, you need a script to show it.

To get the effect of a typical dialog box, a few things need to happen. First, the new layout should appear in its own window. It probably shouldn't have the status area showing. And while the window is up, your users shouldn't be able to switch to a different window. Here's how to do all these things in a script:

- Use the New Window script step to make a new window. Then use Show/Hide Status Area to hide and lock the status area, and Adjust Window with the Resize to Fit option to make the new window just the right size.

- To keep the window front most, pause the script once the window is showing. When a script is paused, the user can't switch windows. For added assurance, add the Allow User Abort script step with the Off option before you pause the script. This step prevents the user from doing anything that would cancel the script.

- If the user presses Enter, FileMaker continues the script, so make one of the buttons look like a default button, and have the script take its action when it continues. To handle other buttons, you can have them set a variable (see page 565) and resume the script. The script can then check the variable when it continues to see what action it should take.

- After the pause script step, take any steps you need to deal with the user's input, and then close the window with the Close Window script step.

This layout-based approach has some drawbacks—most notably, it lacks the convenient default Cancel button of FileMaker's built-in custom dialog boxes. If you want this behavior in a layout-based box, you have to take special measures to avoid losing valuable data if someone clicks the wrong button. For instance, you could put entered data into global fields, and then move the entered data into the real fields only when the script continues.

If you build these two scripts independently, you have two problems. First, you have to write all the "find the unpaid invoices" stuff twice, which is a waste of time. More importantly, next month when you realize you need to exclude voided invoices from the list, you'll have to remember make the change in *both* places. A database that's been growing for years can be a real bear to manage if the same general business logic is implemented over and over in dozens of different scripts.

In both these situations, you can improve your prospects by dividing your scripts into smaller parts. That way, you can break up a complex script into four simpler scripts that each do part of the job. By the same token, you can make one script that finds unpaid invoices and use it both when you print a statement and when you send an email payment reminder.

The Perform Script Script Step

The key to each of these techniques is the *Perform Script* script step. It lets one script run another script—a *subscript*, in programming lingo. When you add the Perform Script step to your script, you get only one option: a Specify button. Figure 15-7 shows how to use the Specify Script dialog box to tell your script which subscript script you want to run and what file to find it in.

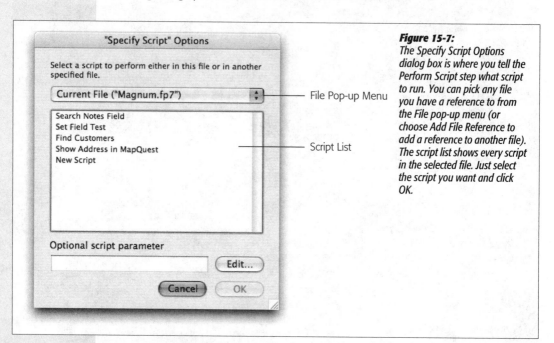

Figure 15-7:
The Specify Script Options dialog box is where you tell the Perform Script step what script to run. You can pick any file you have a reference to from the File pop-up menu (or choose Add File Reference to add a reference to another file). The script list shows every script in the selected file. Just select the script you want and click OK.

Halt Script and Exit Script

When one script runs another, it waits for the subscript to finish before continuing. Imagine you have a script called Find Unpaid Invoices and you want to make a new script to print statements for all your customers. The Print Statements script might start off by performing the Find Unpaid Invoices script. It would then go to the appropriate layout, sort the records, and print them. The script might look like the one shown in Figure 15-8, which performs the Find Unpaid Invoices script, goes to the Statement layout, and then sorts and prints the invoices.

Figure 15-8:
This script needs to find all the unpaid invoices before it can print statements. Luckily, you already have a script that finds unpaid invoices, so the first line in this script is the Perform Script step. That way, FileMaker first runs the Find Unpaid Invoices script, and waits for it to finish. By the time the second step (Go to Layout) runs, the find is finished and the found set includes the correct records.

When you perform a script in another file, FileMaker uses that file's front most window (which is behind the user's window). If it doesn't have any windows, FileMaker automatically creates one. In either case, you're in a unique scripting situation: The window you're working with in your script isn't the one in front. Here is where the Current Window option in the Select Window script step comes in handy.

Normally a script ends when its last step runs. For example, the script in Figure 15-8 ends as soon as the Print step finishes. But you can force a script to end early if you want to. FileMaker actually has *two* script steps that end a script prematurely: Exit Script and Halt Script. These two steps do exactly the same thing if you run a script yourself directly. But if the current script was run by *another script*—via the Perform Script step—then they do different things. The Exit Script step tells FileMaker to stop the current script and continue the script that ran it. Halt Script, on the other hand, causes *all* script execution to stop immediately, no matter how the current script was started. (To learn more about these ominously powerful steps and when to use them, see the box on page 544.)

Exit Script (Result)

Their behavior is different when subscripts are involved, but Exit Script also has a powerful option that Halt Script doesn't have. You can tie all the power of the calculation dialog box to Exit Script. Then your main script can check the script result and decide how to proceed based on the results of the test.

WORD TO THE WISE

The Dark Side of Halt Script and Exit Script

The Halt Script and Exit Script steps are convenient when you want to abort a script's execution because some problem has come up. But more often than not, you're better off without them. Take, for example, the two scripts shown here. The top script first performs a find. If no records are found, it shows a custom dialog box and moves on to an Exit Script step. The bottom version does the same thing, but doesn't exit the script afterwards. Instead, it puts all the remaining script steps in the *Else* section of the condition. The result is the same—the extra steps run only if some records were found—but the bottom script *always ends after the last step*. The top script, on the other hand, can end in two different places, depending on what it finds.

Suppose you revisit this script later and want to add some more steps to the end that you want to happen *last*, every time the script runs—not just when records are found.

If your script looks like the one on top, you have a problem. You either have to add your new steps to the script *twice* (once before the Exit Script, and again at the end of the script) or reorganize the entire script to support the changes. But the script on the bottom is easy to fix—just add the new steps to the end. In general, if a script ends in more than one place, it will come back to bite you later.

You're much better off organizing your script so that it always reaches the same ending place.

Halt Script has an even bigger downside. Since scripts can run other scripts, and most databases grow and change over time, you never know for sure if the script you're writing today is going to be run by another script some day in the future. But it's rarely acceptable to run another script that may potentially halt. It gives your new script no opportunity to recover if something goes wrong

---

Script Parameters

When a script or button runs a script, the Specify Script window shows a box labeled "Optional script parameter." As you can see in Figure 15-9, you can use script parameters to influence a script's behavior when you run it. For example, you might make a script that can sort the records in four different ways. The script parameter you specify when you run the script tells it which sort order to use.

Your script accesses its parameter using the *Get (ScriptParameter)* function. This function returns whatever value you specified in the "Optional script parameter" box in the button or Perform Script step.

Tip: A script can have only one parameter. If you really want to send it more than one value, you can put them all together in some way, and then pull them apart again in the script. For example, you could use this for a script parameter:

Stacey

Van Tassell

555-2121

stacey@mymail.com

The script could then use the MiddleValues function to grab each unique value.

Figure 15-9:
When specifying a script to run, you get the chance to supply an optional script parameter. This can be any value you type in the box, or you can click Edit and enter any FileMaker calculation. When the script runs, FileMaker evaluates this calculation and remembers the result. The script can ask for the result at any time, and use it anywhere it can use a calculation.

Suppose you wanted buttons to sort your Customer records by Name, City and State, or Zip Code. You might think each button needs its own script, but using script parameters, you can get the job done with just one script. Each button passes a different parameter to the script, which takes the appropriate action. Before you can create the buttons, you need to create the script they'll run:

1. **Create a new script called Sort Customers (see page 472 for a refresher on creating scripts). Add the If step to the script.**

   FileMaker adds two new lines (If and End If) to your script.

2. **Click the Specify button. From the View pop-up menu, choose *Get functions*.**

   The function list now shows all the Get functions.

3. **Find Get (Script Parameter) in the list and add it to your calculation.**

   You can choose "Get Functions" or "all functions by name" from the View menu to help you narrow the search. The Get (ScriptParameter) function returns the parameter value specified when this script was called. If the parameter was a calculation, it returns the *result* of the calculation. It's now in the calculation box.

4. **After *Get (ScriptParameter)* in the calculation box, type = "Name", and then click OK.**

   You're back in the Edit Script window, where the If step shows your calculation. Your calculation should look like this: *Get (ScriptParameter) = "Name"*. Its result is true if the parameter sent to this script is "Name" and false otherwise.

5. **Add the Sort Records script step to the script and turn on the "Perform without dialog" option.**

   Insert it *after* the If step and *before* the End If step. (If yours is somewhere else, move it between these two steps.)

Tip: New script steps are inserted just below any highlighted step. If no script step is highlighted, the new script step lands at the end of your script.

---

6. **Turn on the "Specify sort order" checkbox, add the Last Name, then First Name fields to the Sort Order list, and then click OK.**

   Your script now looks like the one shown in Figure 15-10.

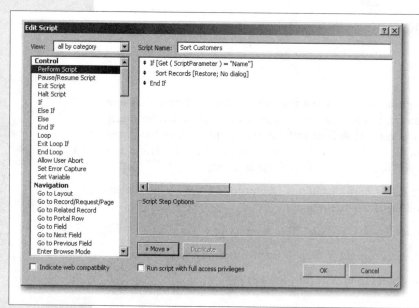

Figure 15-10:
This is how your sort script should look after you've added the Sort Records step and specified a sort order (step 5 above). In its current form, it sorts the records (by last name, then first name) if "Name" is given as a parameter when the script is run. As described on page 545, you need to add support for the other sort orders.

7. **Add the Else If script step to the script.**

   You want Else If to come after the Sort Records step. (If it doesn't land there, move it there.)

8. **Click Specify. In the Specify Calculation box, enter** *Get (ScriptParameter) =* **"City and State," and then click OK.**

   You're setting up a new test, this time checking to see if "City and State" is the script parameter. If so, you want a Sort step following this parameter to sort by—you guessed it—City and State.

9. **Add another copy of the Sort Records script step to the script. Turn on "Perform without dialog." Set the sort order to State, then City, and then click OK.**

   Your second test, and what to do if that test is true, is now complete.

10. **Add one more copy of the Else If script step, this time with** *Get (ScriptParameter) =* **"Zip Code" as the calculation.**

    If the first two tests fail, your script makes this third test.

11. **Add another Sort Record step, this time set to sort by the Zip Code field. Then click OK until you're back in the database.**

    Your finished script should look something like Figure 15-11.

Figure 15-11:
This is how your finished sort script should look. It has three branches (one for each of the possible sort orders). Now you just need to add buttons that run this script.

Note: When you're making a series of tests like the ones in this script, it's more efficient to put the condition that most often test as true at the top. That way, the script doesn't have to test conditions that usually fail.

Now it's time to add buttons to the Customers layout to make it easy for your users to run the script. You need three buttons, one for each sort in the script you just wrote.

1. **Add a new button to the Customers layout.**

   Quickest way: Use the button tool (you know, the one that looks like a finger pushing a button). FileMaker shows you the Specify Button dialog box.

2. **Choose the Perform Script button command, and then click Specify. In the "Specify Script" Options list, select *Sort Customers*.**

   This is the script you created on page 560.

3. **In the "Optional script parameter" box, type *Name*, and then click OK until you're back on the Customers layout.**

   The first test of the Sort Customers script (*Get (ScriptParameter) = "Name"*) is true when the users run it by clicking this button. Back on the layout, your button awaits its new name.

Note: If you check the text in the Optional script parameter box, you see that FileMaker put double quotes around Name for you. That's because it considers "Name" a text constant. If you click the Edit button beside the Optional script parameter field, you see the Specify Calculation dialog box, which signals that you can use any value you can calculate as a script parameter.

4. **Name the button *Sort by Name*.**

   You now have one button on your layout. Test it. It always sorts by name.

Time to work on the second button. To do so, you can save time by starting from a copy of the one you already have.

1. **Duplicate the Sort by Name button and double-click the new copy. In the dialog box's Options section, click the Specify button.**

   The Specify Script Options window pops up.

2. **Change the "Optional script parameter" box so it contains *City and State*.**

   Type carefully, since you're telling the script to exactly match what's in the Else If statement. The second test of the Sort Customers script (*Get (ScriptParameter) = "City and State"*) is true when the users run it by clicking this button.

3. **Click OK until you're back on the Customers layout and can rename your button.**

   Now you have two appropriately named buttons and you can switch the sort order back and forth by clicking each button in turn.

To add the third button, follow steps 1 through 3 again. This time, set the parameter to "Zip Code" and name the button *Sort by Zip Code*.

These three buttons each call the same script, but the script parameters attached to each button allow the script to do double, even triple duty. To make this script even more flexible, you could keep adding Else If and Sort steps, and then make a button with a script parameter that matches each new test. See the box below for a way to use script parameters to extend the flexibility of the Notes Separator script you wrote back in Chapter 14.

UP TO SPEED

Note Separators Revisited

In the previous chapter, you learned how to make the Insert Notes Separator script work with any field (page 502). The only drawback was that you had to click the field you wanted to work with before running the script. With script parameters, though, you can easily fix this problem. Just add a series of If and Else If script steps to the top of the script. Each one checks for one of the Notes field types (Invoice, Job, Customer, and so on) in the script parameter.

For instance, if the script parameter is "Invoice," then the script should use the Go to Field script step to go to the Invoices::Notes field first.

With these conditions in place, you just need to pass the right parameter from your Add Notes button. The picture here shows the finished script. Now if you want to add a new Notes field, you just need to add an Else If and a Go to Field step to this script. If you want to change the way the note separators look, you can change it in one place and the change applies to *every* Notes field in the database.

Handling Errors

As discussed on page 386, when an error occurs during a script (a Perform Find finds no records, for instance), FileMaker shows an error message almost like the one it would if you were doing the steps manually. The one difference is a button called Continue, as Figure 15-12 explains.

If the user clicks a Cancel button in an error message, the script stops immediately, and leaves the user wherever the script was when it stopped. If he clicks Continue instead, FileMaker ignores the error and moves on with the script. In the Perform Find example, for instance, the script continues with no records in the found set. Some errors (like the one in Figure 15-12) give the user a third choice. If the user clicks Modify Find, for instance, FileMaker takes him to Find mode on the current layout and pauses the script.

Figure 15-12:
The message on top is what you see when a script performs a find that doesn't find any records. The one on the bottom is what you see when you perform the same find manually (using Find mode). The only difference is the Continue button in the script version of the message. When an error occurs during a script, FileMaker gives the user all the normal choices, plus the option to ignore the error and continue the script.

Sometimes this error-handling approach is just fine. If the script is simple and everyone using it knows a little about FileMaker, it isn't too big a problem. But often, you simply need more control:

- If your system is complex and/or your users inexperienced with FileMaker, all sorts of confusion can result. First, the error message may make absolutely no sense to the user. The message complains, for instance, about not finding any records. But the user thinks, "I just wanted to create a new invoice for this job. Who said anything about finding records?" Even worse, if the user clicks Cancel, he could wind up just about anywhere: some layout in some window on some record. It could be a layout (like the Line Items layout) that he's never even seen before.

- If an error happens in the middle of a larger multi-step process, it might be really important that the script know about it and deal with it appropriately. But it's the *user*, not the *script*, which decides whether to continue or cancel. You might want to make sure the script *always* continues, so it can get on with important work.

Luckily, you can opt for more control over error handling if you want it. FileMaker gives you three functions for finding and dealing with errors that may occur when scripts run.

The Set Error Capture Script Step

The Set Error Capture script step lets you turn on *error capture*. That way, instead of displaying potentially confusing error messages to your database's users, File-Maker keeps track of error information (*captures* it) so you can pull it into your script and handle it there. Although error capturing is a great feature, it's not part of FileMaker's normal behavior. You have to activate it by adding the Set Error Capture step to your script, and choosing the On option. At any time in the script, you can turn it back off again by using the step a second time and switching the option off.

If a script turns error capture on, and then uses the Perform Script step to run another script, the second script also runs with error capture on. In other words, the error capture setting sticks around as long as scripts call other scripts. But as soon as script execution stops for good, FileMaker turns off error capture. Under-standing this behavior helps you determine when you need an Error Capture script step and when it would just be redundant. Figure 15-13 shows a script that turns error capture on before performing a find, then turns it back off when it's done.

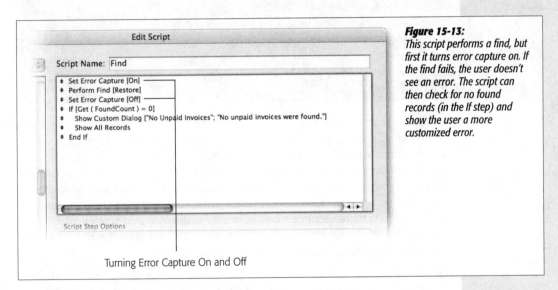

Figure 15-13:
This script performs a find, but first it turns error capture on. If the find fails, the user doesn't see an error. The script can then check for no found records (in the If step) and show the user a more customized error.

Turning Error Capture On and Off

As discussed in the box on page 552, you could just turn error capture on so that your script ignores any and all errors—but that's not good script writing. The best way to use Set Error Capture is hand-in-hand with the Get (LastError) function, described next, to achieve error-free results.

The Get (LastError) Function

When error capture is on, FileMaker doesn't just *ignore* the errors. Rather, it remembers which error occurred and gives you the chance to ask about it if you're interested. The script in Figure 15-13, for example, *isn't* interested. It doesn't ask if an error occurred at all. Instead, it just checks to see if the find worked by counting the records in the found set.

WORD TO THE WISE

Keep It Off

Using Set Error Capture to eliminate those pesky dialog boxes sounds so cool, you may be tempted to turn it on at the start of every script. You can't anticipate every error, but at least you can keep FileMaker from casting doubt on your database skills by throwing error messages in your users' faces. But if all your script does is turn on error capture, but then never checks to see which errors are happening, you're not doing your users—or yourself—any favors.

If odd error messages pop up, your users probably let you know about it (perhaps via cellphone), giving you a chance to figure out the problem and improve your script. With error capture turned on, a script might *seem* to be working because no warning dialog box shows up, but really, something's gone kablooie and error capture suppresses the dialog box that would have explained what happened.

You have little hope of figuring out what went wrong—especially if no one realizes there's been a problem until long after the script has run.

Usually, you find errors when you're developing your scripts, and you can use a custom dialog box (page 535) or error capture to deal with them. Don't turn error capture on unless you've already anticipated an error and figured out how your script can handle it; then turn it off again. That way, *unanticipated* errors don't get swept under the rug. In general, you should have just a few steps between Set Error Capture [On] and Set Error Capture [Off].

But sometimes you can use such error information within your script, much like any other value, to trigger other script steps. To check an error, use the Get (Last-Error) function to find out what happened. This function returns an *error code*, which is always a number. If there was no error in the previous step, Get (Last-Error) returns a zero. In other words, it doesn't return the number of the last error that occurred. Instead, it returns the error number for the *last step* that ran. You wouldn't, therefore, put a *comment* step before the step that checks the last error, since the comment step itself always sets the last error back to zero. The same goes for End If and even Set Error Capture [Off].

In FileMaker, just about everything that could possibly go wrong has its own error number. This feature gives you a lot of flexibility, but it also makes it a real pain to figure out which errors you should check for. A complete list of error numbers is found in Appendix B. Luckily, most of these errors are pretty obscure, and chances are you'll never have to worry about them. Here's a list of the more common error numbers you might actually be interested in:

- **Error 9, 200 - 211, 723 - 725:** Assorted security-related errors (see Chapter 16).

- **Error 112:** Window is missing (you get this error if you try to select, close, or move/resize a window that doesn't exist).

- **Error 301:** Record is in use by another user (you get this error when you try to modify a record that is locked in another window or by another user).

- **Error 400:** Find criteria are empty (if you let the user enter find criteria during a script, the Perform Script step gets this error if they don't enter anything).

- **Error 401:** No records match this request (this is the actual error that happens when no records are found; most people choose to check Get (FoundCount) instead since it's easier to understand).

- **Errors 500 - 507:** Assorted field validation errors (you get these errors when you try to modify a field in a way that violates its validation setting and it is set to "always" validate).

- **Errors 718 and 719:** XML processing errors (see Chapter 17).

- **Errors 1200 - 1219:** Calculation-related errors (you see these errors in conjunction with the *EvaluationError* and Evaulate functions).

- **Errors 1400 - 1408:** Assorted ODBC errors (see Chapter 17).

Tip: If you're seeing an error when you run a script, and you want to capture it instead, but you're unsure which error number it is, try this: Turn on error capture before the step that's producing the error. Then add a Show Custom Dialog step right after the offending step. Set the dialog box to show Get (LastError). When you run the script, instead of the error message you've been seeing, you'll see a custom dialog box with the real error number. You can then modify the script to handle this particular number.

The Allow User Abort Script Step

One more script step has ramifications when dealing with errors: Allow User Abort. This step lets you turn off a user's ability to cancel the script. Allow User Abort only has two options: on and off. Its normal state is to be turned on, unless you specifically turn it off with the script step. Like Set Error Capture, when you turn user abort off or back on within a script, the setting carries through any sub-scripts called by the main script. Allow User Abort always turns back on again when the script finishes running.

If you turn user abort off, but leave error capture on, the Cancel button in error messages is removed, so the user is forced to continue the script. Turning off user abort also prevents the user from pressing Escape (Windows) or ⌘-period (Mac OS X) to cancel a running script. Finally, if the script pauses, the user doesn't get a Cancel button in the status area. Instead, the only choice is to continue.

Note: When a script turns off user abort and pauses, the user also can't switch to a different window, close the window, or quit FileMaker.

Putting a Complex Script Together

Building a complicated script takes time and planning. Given the flexible nature of scripting, you could script a given process many different ways, and outside the artful application of your business's rules to your database, there is no one way. Your job is to find a *good* way.

In this section, you'll make a script that generates an invoice for a job. It gathers all the unbilled expenses and timeslips for the job and adds appropriate line items for them to the invoice. To make a script like this you need to cover all your bases:

- **Planning.** Without writing the actual script, what will your general approach be? Can you outline all the things your script will do, and in the right order? This process usually evolves from very general to somewhat specific. The most specific version is the script itself, when you'll tell FileMaker *exactly* what to do.

- **Exceptions.** What kinds of things can go wrong? How do you check for, and prevent, those problems?

- **Efficiency.** Are you doing the same things several places in the script? Are there other reasons to break your script into multiple smaller scripts?

Tip: The rest of this chapter is one long excercise. It's best digested if you work straight through from here to the end—without skipping parts or jumping around.

Planning the Script

Planning a big script is usually an iterative process. You start by outlining the steps the script will take in very general terms. You can then go in and fill in more and more detail with each pass. When you're done adding detail, you know exactly what steps your script will use. Using the invoicing script as an example, you'll see how FileMaker gives you the tools to plan and execute your new script.

You can do this planning on paper, or in a word processor, or any other tool you choose. But one good place you might *not* think of is ScriptMaker itself. Since the planning process involves a series of steps, and since it naturally produces the finished script when it's done, ScriptMaker is an ideal candidate. Just start with comments explaining each general step. You can then replace a comment line with some real script steps, and perhaps more comments. When you're done, the script is written. As an added bonus, you never get lost because you always have a comment to tell you exactly what you still need to add, and exactly where it should go.

For this script, begin your planning by creating the script in Figure 15-14.

Considering Exceptions

Many people forget one of the most critical steps in scriptwriting—planning for exceptions. The old saw, "A stitch in time saves nine," truly applies. Spend a few minutes now, thinking ahead to what might go wrong and planning how to prevent problems. These minutes can save you hours of troubleshooting and repair work on your data later.

Look at what your script is supposed to do and try to think of reasonable *exceptions*—situations where your script might not be able to do its job. Thinking of exceptions is important for two reasons:

- **If your script always assumes ideal circumstances, it can wreak havoc if your assumptions are wrong when it runs.** The last thing you need is a wild script running amok in your data, changing and deleting the wrong things.

- **If a script gets halfway through its job, and then discovers that it can't continue, you might be left with half-finished work.** It's usually best to look for the problems up front so the script can simply refuse to run if it won't be able to finish. (For more detail, see the box on page 558.)

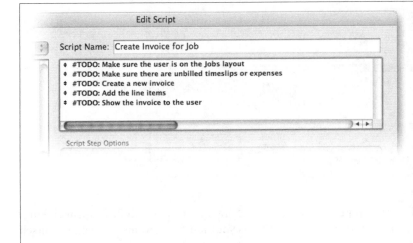

Figure 15-14:
This is the first rough-cut of your script. Of course, since it's all comments, it doesn't actually do anything yet. Instead, it just maps out, at the most general level, what the script is going to do. You'll add more and more details as you go. Since these comments are just placeholders for real steps and comments yet to come, each one starts with the word TODO. You're welcome to use any marker you want, but it helps if you can easily tell these placeholder comments apart from the real comments you'll add later.

For example, the Invoice creation script could run into two potential problems. The problems and fixes, if you haven't already guessed, are as follows:

- **How does the script know which job to create an invoice for?** This problem is easy to solve. You just make sure the user is on the Jobs layout when the script runs. Then the script runs on the current Job record. If another layout is selected, the script should just do nothing at all. Add an If script step and the Get (LayoutName) function. Since you don't want the script to do *anything* if the user's on a different layout, put all the other steps inside the If block.

• **What if the job has no timeslips or expenses that haven't been billed?** You'd wind up with an invoice that has no line items, and you don't want to send *that* to your customer. You could go ahead and create the invoice, and then delete it if it's empty. But this approach uses up an invoice number, and it means your script has to go through all the work of creating an invoice only to throw it away when it's done. Your script should check first to be sure there's something to bill. Then, it can show the user an informative message and skip all the hard work when there's nothing to bill. Here's how to add the If test, as shown in Figure 15-15.

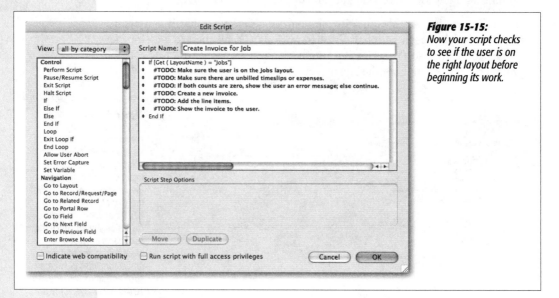

Figure 15-15:
Now your script checks to see if the user is on the right layout before beginning its work.

• **Add an If step just below the TODO item that finds unbilled expenses.** Put a commented calculation (page 408) as your test for now, just to remind yourself what needs to be tested. You can put the real test in later.

• **Add feedback for the user by putting a custom dialog step in the true part of the If step.** If you don't give the user feedback here, he may become confused, since nothing happens. The dialog box should tell your user why FileMaker doesn't create any invoice.

• **Add an Else step.** Since you don't want to create an invoice if there aren't any billable items for the Job, put the last three TODO items in an Else step. The End If for this test should be just above the final End If in the script.

After you've made these changes, the first three TODO comments now suggest that you find some records, then make a decision based on whether any records were found (Figure 15-16, top). In order to do this, you need to *store* the counts somewhere. In other words, you need a new tool called a *script variable*, which you'll learn about later in this chapter.

However, one of the remaining TODO comments is a bit broad. How are you going to "Add the line items?" Since you need to create line items from two different tables—expenses and timeslips—you handle them separately. First, you process expenses, and then you process timeslips. To "process" the expenses, you loop through the unbilled Expense records and add a line item for each one. Ditto for the timeslip records. Edit your script to match Figure 15-16, bottom.

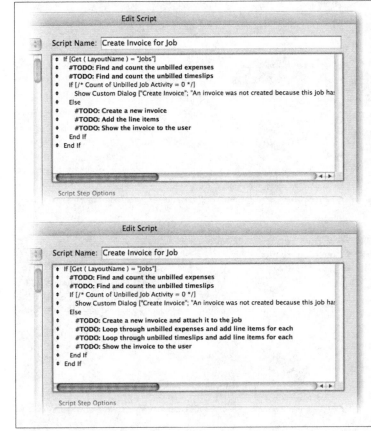

Figure 15-16:

Top: The script now has If and Else sections for the two possible outcomes: If there are no unbilled expenses or timeslips, it shows the user a custom dialog box that says, "An invoice was not created because this job has no unbilled activity." If the job does have unbilled activity, on the other hand, it creates the invoice, adds the line items, and shows the user the invoice. Of course, you still need to implement those steps.

Bottom: The script now explains in even more detail what it needs to do. You still have to add the necessary steps to find unbilled timeslips and expenses, to create a new invoice attached to the current job, and to add line items for the found expenses and timeslips. Finally, you'll go to the Invoices layout to show the new invoice to the user.

Creating Subscripts

Now that you've tested for exceptions in your script, you've come to a fork in the road. You could write a script containing all the necessary steps, but it would be long and hard to follow. For example, the End If steps at the end of the script would be a long way from their If and Else counterparts, making it hard to figure out where they belong. Alternatively, you might decide to break this script into pieces. Either way, you should make this decision before going any further.

You might consider a few other things: If you have several small scripts, you can run any one of them individually. This method gives you the chance to try out parts of the script to see if they work properly. Also, since you can pass parameters to scripts when you run them, using subscripts to do some jobs often saves you the trouble of adding another script variable. But in the end, either approach is perfectly valid. Some people really like short simple scripts, even if it means more of them and more opening and closing of the Edit Script window. Others find this multiple-script song and dance far worse than a script that needs a little scrolling.

DIAMOND IN THE ROUGH

The Problem with Problems

Although detecting problems up front is usually best, it isn't always possible. Sometimes you can't find out about problems until your script has run partway through.

Most database systems handle this problem with something called *transactions,* a chunk of work that's held in limbo until you tell the database to make it permanent. In a nutshell, you open a transaction, then you're free to do anything you want, but your changes don't get saved to the real data until you commit the record. If you decide you don't want the changes after all, you undo, the transaction.

FileMaker's uses this transaction concept under the hood to handle record changes, but unfortunately there's no easy way to tap in to the transaction system from a script. Here's why. When you first enter a record—using the Open Record/Request script step, for instance—FileMaker begins a transaction for you. When you exit the record—Commit Record/Request—FileMaker commits the transaction, writing all changes to the database. If you revert the record instead—Revert Record/Request—FileMaker essentially rolls back the transaction, leaving the database untouched. Just remember that each transaction is linked to a record. For example, you can't begin a transaction, then make changes to five different customer records and eleven invoices, and then roll back all those changes.

But if you create, edit, or delete records *in portal rows* while you're still in the record, all your changes happen in one transaction. Do this exercise in the Customers file to explore how this works. Have two windows open—one showing the Invoice layout and the other showing Line Items. Create a new Invoice record and add a few Line Items. Notice that FileMaker creates the new Line Item records when you add items to the Line Item portal on Invoice layout. Being very careful not to commit the record (that is, don't hit the Enter key or click anywhere outside the fields onto your layout), choose Records → Revert Record. The parent Invoice record disappears, *and* all the child Line Items disappear, too. You've just witnessed FileMaker's version of transactions.

Knowing this, you can use the Open Record/Request script step on an Invoice record, then make changes to dozens of line items. Then if your script detects a problem, you can revert the Invoice record, and all your line item changes are tossed out as well. If you absolutely positively must have control over your transactions, arrange your scripts so they do everything through relationships from one single record.

For this example, you'll be creating subscripts. Figure 15-17 shows a repeat of your script-in-progress with places for subscripts clearly identified. Each of these scripts are relatively short and easy to understand, but you'll have *five* scripts in all. (See the box on page 561 for some tips for breaking up long scripts into subscripts.)

Now that you know what subscripts you need, you can create them. And you already know how to do that because a subscript is just another script. To help you keep track of what you're doing, you should create all the subscripts you'll need first—but that doesn't mean writing them all yet. You just need to create scripts in the Define Scripts window and make some placeholder comments to remind you what they should do.

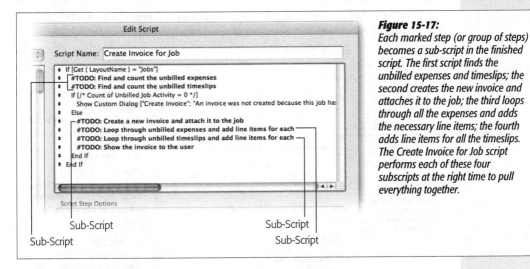

Figure 15-17:
Each marked step (or group of steps) becomes a sub-script in the finished script. The first script finds the unbilled expenses and timeslips; the second creates the new invoice and attaches it to the job; the third loops through all the expenses and adds the necessary line items; the fourth adds line items for all the timeslips. The Create Invoice for Job script performs each of these four subscripts at the right time to pull everything together.

Start by adding a new script called "- find unbilled activity." This script name starts with a dash, and is in all lowercase. These clues help to remind you later that this script is a subscript used by another script, and not one you should expect to work all by itself. You can see the "- find unbilled activity" script in its planning stage form in Figure 15-18.

Figure 15-18:
You'll create the "- find unbilled activity" subscript first. Since a subscript is just another script, approach it like you did the Create Invoice for Jobscript: Start with a plan. You can come back later and implement the actual script steps.

Tip: Using *naming conventions* like this can really help keep your script list organized and easy to work with. Which convention you use, though, is up to you. In this book, all subscripts start with a dash and use all lowercase.

The "- process unbilled expenses" and "- process unbilled timeslips" scripts are almost exactly the same. The only difference is that each script starts by going to a different layout, and sets a different Line Item ID field. It's more efficient to combine them, and use a script parameter to decide between the two sets of behavior. Figure 15-19 shows the new "- process unbilled items" script, which works equally well for expenses and timeslips. Create the two subscripts shown in Figure 15-19 now.

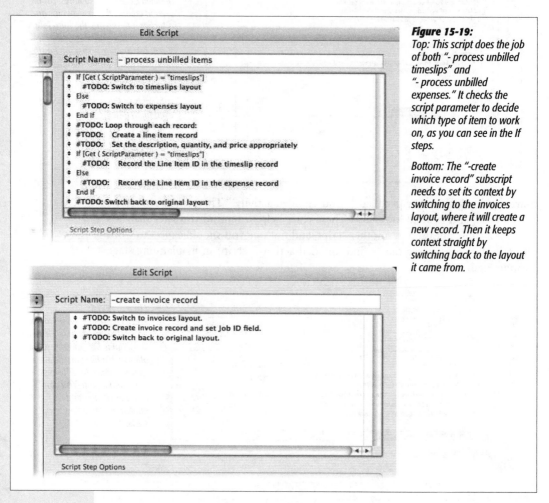

Figure 15-19:
Top: This script does the job of both "- process unbilled timeslips" and "- process unbilled expenses." It checks the script parameter to decide which type of item to work on, as you can see in the If steps.

Bottom: The "-create invoice record" subscript needs to set its context by switching to the invoices layout, where it will create a new record. Then it keeps context straight by switching back to the layout it came from.

With the three final subscripts defined, you're ready to revise the original Create Invoice for Job script. Now, you can delete the TODO comments that served as placeholders for your subscript and replace them with the new subscripts, even though they're made up of placeholder comments themselves.

The last TODO comment doesn't need a subscript. It can just use the Go to Layout script step. In Figure 15-20, you can see the result.

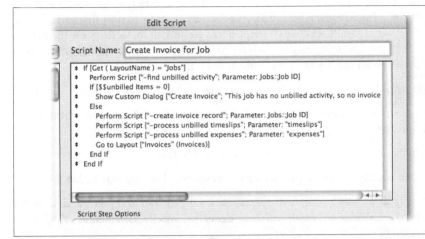

Figure 15-20:
This is the finished Create Invoice for Job script. You haven't finished writing the subscripts yet, but you can already see how easy this script is to follow: Just by reading the subscript names and parameters, you get a very good idea what this script is doing.

UP TO SPEED

The Right Way to Create Subscripts

When you think about ways to break your script into smaller pieces, you should be thinking about *tasks*. It makes good sense to create a smaller script to do one of the tasks needed in the larger script. It doesn't make sense to simply take a long script and break it in two, so that the last step in the first script simply performs the second script. Breaking scripts up that way has all the disadvantages of multiple scripts (more windows to work in, more scripts to scroll through) and none of the advantages (neither script is particularly simple or self-contained, and neither can be run individually for testing purposes). Also, as you look for places to use subscripts, you would also be looking for opportunities for reuse. In other words, you should look for things the script has to do more than once in two different places. It almost always makes sense to use a subscript in this situation.

In almost every case, the right way to subdivide a script is to create one master script that starts *and* finishes the process.

The Create Invoice for Job script does just that. It starts by checking what layout you're on, and finishes by showing the invoice. Along the way, it relies on other simple scripts to get the job done.

This isn't to say that a subscript should never have subscripts of its own. In fact, subscripts often do. But you should structure the entire set of scripts so that the top-level script implements the highest-level logic and behavior of the entire script itself. Each subscript should in turn do some particular task from start to finish. If the task is particularly complex, then the subscript itself might implement only the highest level of logic, calling upon more subscripts to handle parts of the task. In this way, the scripts themselves provide helpful overviews of what's going on. When the Create Invoice for Job script is finished, you see that even though it's somewhat complex, its structure makes it easy to follow. The script almost reads like a book, describing exactly what it's doing.

Adding a Script Parameter to a Perform Script Step

You already know that you can set a script parameter for a button as it runs a script. You can also set a script parameter when you run a script with a Perform Script step. Take a look at Figure 15-21 to see an example of how that can be helpful: The "-find unbilled activity" script needs to find all the activity for the *current* job. Since the Create Invoice for Job script is performing this script from the Jobs layout, it can set the Job ID in a script parameter.

Here's how to set a script parameter on a Perform Script step:

1. **In ScriptMaker, double-click the Create Invoice for Job script to edit it. Select the second script step, *Perform Script ["- find unbilled activity"]*.**

    The Script Step Options area shows a Specify button.

2. **Click Specify. In the "Optional script parameter" box, enter *Jobs::Job ID*.**

    If you don't like typing field names, click Edit instead and add the field in the Specify Calculation window. Then close the Specify Calculation window by clicking OK.

3. **Click OK until you're back in the database.**

    The first Perform Script step shows the proper parameter value.

The Create Invoice for Jobs script calls all the proper subscripts and sends script parameters to the subscripts where it's appropriate. Now it's time to finish writing your subscripts.

Finishing the Subscripts

You've created a series of subscripts that have placeholder comments to remind you what process the script will perform. Just as you did with the main Create Invoice for Job script, you'll finish each subscript and turn them into working scripts by replacing those comments with real script steps.

The "- find unbilled activity" subscript

Now that a script parameter is passing the Job ID to the "- find unbilled activity" script, you can write steps to find the right expense and timeslip records. The first TODO item is a cinch: Just use the Go to Layout script step to switch to the appropriate layout. Next, you need to find expenses for the current job that don't have a line item ID. This request is one of those find requests that you can't enter directly in the Perform Find script step because you need to use the script parameter, whose value you don't know until the script runs. Instead, you have to use Enter Find Mode, Set Field, and Perform Find together to build and perform the right find request:

1. **In ScriptMaker, double-click the "- find unbilled activity" script to edit it. Add the Go to Layout script step to the script.**

   If necessary, drag the Go to Layout step to the top of the script. If a script step is selected, any new step you create lands just below it. But there's no way to make a new step appear right at the top of a script that already has steps in it.

2. **From the Go to Layout Script Step Options area's Specify pop-up menu, choose Expenses. Select the first TODO comment, click Clear, and then click Go to Layout again.**

   FileMaker removes the step from the list. You select Go to Layout so the next script step you create lands below Go to Layout and becomes the second script step.

3. **Add the Enter Find Mode script step to the script. Turn off the Pause checkbox and turn on the "Specify find requests" option.**

   The Specify Find Requests dialog box pops up. One part of the find request you'll be using *is* the same every time: You need to find expenses with nothing in the Line Item ID field. You'll add this to the find request here, and then insert the Job ID in the next script step.

4. **If any requests are showing in the list, click Delete until they're all gone. Click the New button.**

   The Edit Find Request window appears.

5. **From the "Find records when" pop-up menu, choose Expenses, and then click the Line Item ID field.**

   The selected field is now highlighted.

6. **Click the Insert Symbol button and choose "== Field Content Match" from the resulting menu. Click the Add button. Then click OK, and then OK to get back to your script.**

   FileMaker puts "==" in the Criteria box. If you prefer, you can just type "==." Two equal signs, used alone, tell FileMaker you want records where the Line Item ID field matches *nothing*. These are all your expenses that haven't been billed.

7. **Add the Set Field script step to the script, and then turn on the "Specify target field" checkbox. Select the Expenses::Job ID field and click OK.**

   The step should appear after the Enter Find Mode step. If it doesn't, move it there now. Make sure you get the right Job ID field: You need to pick the Expenses table from the pop-up menu first.

8. **Click the Specify button to the right of "Calculated result." In the calculation box, enter "==" & Get (ScriptParameter). Click OK.**

This calculation puts the Job ID (from the script parameter) into the field, with "==" before it, telling FileMaker you want to find records that match this ID exactly. Together with the find request above, the script finds unbilled activity for the current Job.

9. **Add the Set Error Capture script step to the script and make sure its "On" option is selected.**

You're about to perform a find, and you don't want the user to see an error message if there are no unbilled expenses.

10. **Add the Perform Find script step to the script.**

The script step belongs below the Set Error Capture step. Make sure you don't select Perform Find/Replace by accident.

11. **Add another copy of the Set Error Capture step to the script, this time with the "Off" option selected.**

You can select the existing Set Error Capture step, then click the duplicate button, then drag the new step into place and set the option to "Off." Once the Perform Find step is finished, you want FileMaker to stop capturing error messages.

Your script should now look like the one in Figure 15-21.

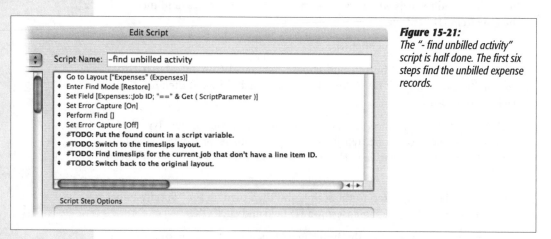

Figure 15-21:
The "- find unbilled activity" script is half done. The first six steps find the unbilled expense records.

Since it isn't exactly obvious what this script's doing, it's a good idea to add a comment to the top explaining it in plain English. So far, your script finds unbilled items in preparation for creating an invoice. But you need to count the number of records the script has found and store that value. That's where script variables come in.

Script variables

Global fields are great for storing a value that's not tied to a specific record in a table. Script variables are similar—you need to store a value for your script to use, usually when you're testing a condition. Use the Set Script Variable script step to set a variable. There are three options available for this script step:

- **Give your variable a name.** Choose a short, descriptive name. All script variable names require a "$" prefix. If you forget to type the prefix, ScriptMaker adds it for you. But you should get in the habit of typing the prefix because it determines how long the value in the variable is available. A single $ means that the variable is "local" and lasts only while your script is running. If you set a local variable, then perform a subscript, the local variable isn't sent to that subscript. But if you need a global variable, (the value persists through subscripts and even after all scripts have finished running), prefix the variable's name with "$$." Global variables are cleared when you close the file.

- **Assign a value.** This is the value you want to store in the variable. Values can be text or the result of a calculation.

- **Set a repetition.** Repetitions are optional. You can make a variable store multiple values, similar to the way a repeating field stores multiple values. Most of the time, though, you don't set a repetition.

Adding a Set Variable script steps is easy. Open your "- find unbilled activity" script in ScriptMaker:

1. **Select the second Set Error Capture script step, then create a Set Variable script step. Click its Specify button (Figure 15-22).**

   You want to capture the number of records the script just found, so it makes sense to set the script variable as soon as possible after the find was performed.

Figure 15-22:
The "Set Variable" Options dialog box lets you define variables that you can use in functions throughout your scripts. The two dollar signs at the beginning of "$$unbilled Items" in the name field indicate a global variable—one whose value persists until it's reset or until the file is closed.

2. **In the Name field, type *$$unbilled Items*.**

   You need to check this value after the current script is finished running, so use the "$$" prefix to make the variable available globally.

Tip: Don't make global variables without thinking about whether you really need the value to persist after the script is run. Although FileMaker purges variables when you close the file, it's bad housekeeping to clutter up your database by leaving unneeded values laying around in global variables.

3. **Click the Specify button beside the value field. In the View list, choose "Get Functions." Choose Get (FoundCount) from the list, and then click OK until you're back in your database.**

If you prefer not to rummage through the Specify Calculation dialog box, you can type Get (FoundCount) in the Value field. You're telling ScriptMaker to grab the found count from the find and hold it in a variable so you can test that value later on.

Your script finds all the unbilled expenses in your database and remembers how many records it's found. Now you have to repeat the process for timeslips. First, though, add a comment to the top of the script that says, "Find and count all unbilled expense records." In the next section, you'll see why this comment makes sense.

Tip: Script variables can be mysterious because unlike the Set Field script step, you can't really see the value that's set in them. But if you have FileMaker Pro Advanced, there's a great tool for monitoring variables. See page 672 to see how the Data Viewer can make your life a whole lot easier.

Copying and editing existing script steps

Since the timeslips half of the script is almost a duplication of what you've done in the past two tutorials, you could repeat all those steps above and you'd be done. But it's a lot faster to duplicate those steps, then make a few changes so that your duplicated steps operate on the timeslips table, not expenses. Here's how:

1. **Click the first line in the script (the comment you just added). With the Shift key held down, click the *last* Set Field step, and then click Duplicate.**

FileMaker creates an exact copy of the selected steps. They all wind up below the first set.

2. **Double-click the second comment step in the script (the first line of the new set of duplicated steps). Change the word *expense* in the comment to *timeslip*. Click OK when you're done.**

The comment shows that this section finds and counts unbilled *timeslips*. It's also an easy way to spot where the second half of your script starts.

3. **Select the next step—Go to Layout—and, from Script Step Options area's pop-up menu, choose Timeslips.**

This time you want to work with Timeslips records, so you need to go to the Timeslips layout.

4. Double-click the next step: Enter Find Mode. Double-click the find request in the list. Select the only criterion in the list. From the "Find records when" pop-up menu, choose Timeslips and in the field list, select Line Item ID. Finally, click Change.

You're changing the find request so that it searches for empty Line Item IDs in the Timeslips table instead of in Expenses. The line in the criteria list changes to show *Timeslips::Line Item ID* instead of *Expenses::Line Item ID*.

THINK LIKE A PROGRAMMER

Testing Multiple Conditions Redux

Back in the box on page 488, you learned how to write a script that tested multiple conditions. Now that you're familiar with setting variables, it's time to learn how to take a more advanced approach to the same problem. Instead of calling three different Custom Dialog boxes that are each hard coded, you can set your message in a *local variable*, then call a single Custom Dialog box that changes based on which condition tested as true.

Why go to all that trouble? It's certainly not because File-Maker gives you a limited number of Show Custom Dialog boxes and you have to ration their use.

The rational behind this little exercise is to give you a taste of the software engineer's approach to FileMaker's variables. By thinking in terms of storing data that doesn't need to last inside a local variable (which itself has a very short shelf-life), instead of as an option in a dialog box, you're well on the way to solving more advanced problems as they arise. And if you've come from another programming background, you'll be glad to see that FileMaker handles variable storage like some of the big toys in the programming world.

Here's how it looks:

```
If [ Get ( CurrentTime ) > Time ( 4 ; 0 ; 0 ) and Get ( CurrentTime ) < Time ( 12 ; 0 ; 0 ) ]
        Set Variable [ $customMessage ; Value:"Good morning!" ]
Else If [ Get ( CurrentTime ) > Time ( 12 ; 0 ; 0 ) and Get ( CurrentTime ) < Time ( 18 ; 0 ;
0 ) ]
        Set Variable [ $customMessage ; Value:"Good afternoon!" ]
Else
        Set Variable [ $customMessage ; Value:"Go to bed" ]
End If
Show Custom Dialog [ Title: "Greetings" ; Message: $customMessage ; Buttons: "Thanks" ]
```

---

5. Click OK, and then OK again.

These two clicks close the Edit Find Request and Specify Find Requests windows, respectively. You're back in the script.

6. Double-click the next Set Field step and change the targeted field to *Timeslips:: Job ID* instead of *Expenses::Job ID*.

The Set Error Capture and Perform Find steps don't need to be changed at all, so you skip ahead to the last step.

7. **Select the next Set Variable step (the last non-comment step), and click the Specify button. Change the value calculation to read: $\$\$Unbilled\ Items + Get\ (\ FoundCount\ )$. Then click OK.**

This time you don't want to *replace* the value in the script variable, so this calculation simply adds your new count to it.

8. **Select the remaining TODO calculation steps and clear them.**

You can do this in one shot by clicking the first one, Shift-clicking the last, and the clicking the Clear button.

9. **Add a Go to Layout step to the end of the script and set it to go to "original layout."**

Once the script is done finding things, it needs to return to the layout it started on so the script that ran this one won't be surprised by a layout change. It's usually best when a sub-script puts things back the way they were when it started. If you want, you can also add a comment before this step to separate it from the previous block of steps.

Whew! Finally, the "- find unbilled activity" script is finished. It should look just like the one in Figure 15-23. When you're done looking, click the OK button.

Figure 15-23:
This is the completed "- find unbilled activity" script. It finds and counts the expenses, and then the timeslips. This really serves two purposes in the final process: The $$unbilled items variable helps the Create Invoice for Job script decide if it should create an invoice or not, and FileMaker uses the found sets later to create line items.

The "- create invoice record" subscript

The "- create invoice record" script needs to switch to the Invoices layout, create a new record, attach it to the job (by filling in its Job ID field) and then switch back to the original layout. Just like the last script, you send it the right Job ID in its script parameter, so your first job is to edit the Create Invoice for Job script, and get it to send the Job ID when it performs the "- create invoice record" script.

Now you're ready to polish off the "- create invoice record" script itself:

1. **Double-click the "- create invoice record" script in ScriptMaker to edit it. Select the first line: "TODO: Switch to invoices layout."**

   The next step you add appears *after* this comment.

2. **Add the Go to Layout script step to the script. From the Specify pop-up menu, choose Invoices.**

   You can't add an invoice record from the Jobs layout, so you're switching to a layout attached to the Invoices table first.

3. **Select the second comment step: "TODO: Create invoice record and set Job ID field." Add the New Record/Request step to the script.**

   The step appears after the second comment.

4. **Add the Set Field step to the script. Turn on the "Specify target field" checkbox. From the pop-up menu at the top of the dialog box, choose Invoices. Then select the Job ID field in the list and click OK.**

   You want to be sure you're setting the *right-hand* Job ID field. When you make this choice, the fields from the Invoices table appear in the list.

5. **Click the Specify button to the right of "Calculated Result." Set the calculation to *Get (ScriptParameter)* and click OK.**

   You're matching the new Invoice to the Job number that was set as the script's parameter way back when the script began running.

6. **Add the Go to Layout step to the script.**

   Subscripts should always return the database to its previous state, so the main script doesn't get confused about its context.

7. **Clear the TODO comment steps from the script and click OK.**

   Your finished script creates a new Invoice record and sets the proper Job ID in it.

You can see the finished "- create invoice record" subscript in Figure 15-24. Now that your script creates a new invoice, you're ready to write the subscript that creates its line items.

The "- process unbilled items" script

Last up is the "- process unbilled items" script. It's time to look through its TODO steps and see what's in store. The first two—"Switch to timeslips layout" and

"Switch to expenses layout"—are easy. Just replace them with appropriately configured Go to Layout steps. Figure 15-25 shows how it should look. The *last* TODO
step is just as easy. You should replace it with a Go to Layout step, with the "original layout" option selected.

Figure 15-24:
*The finished "- create invoice record"
script is a simple one: just four steps.*

Figure 15-25:
*Once you've written the first
three subscripts, the whole
script looks like this. It checks
the script parameter and
goes to the right layout
accordingly. When the script
is finished with its real work,
it goes back to the original
layout as well. Now you need
to deal with the real meat of
the script: looping and
creating line items.*

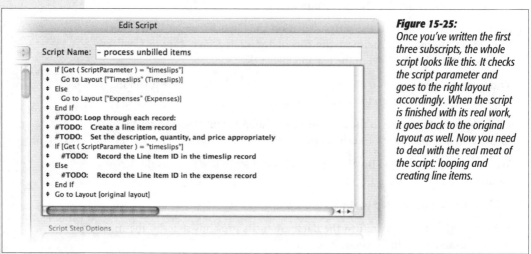

Retrofitting a prior subscript. The next item left in the TODO list is "Create a line
item record." This one requires some thinking about what your script knows and
when it knows it. Adding a record to the Line Items table is easy:

- Switch to a layout attached to the Line Items table.

- Create a record with a New Record/Request step.

But these two steps aren't enough. You need to make sure the new line item record
is related to the invoice created by the "- create invoice record" step. To do that,
you need to put the right Invoice ID in the Line Items::Invoice ID field.

So where can you find the Invoice ID? It's back there on the invoice record, but
when you're on the Line Items layout you can't see the current invoice record
because you don't have the right context.

Here's one approach. You could:

- Hop back to the Invoice table.
- Perform a find to make sure the current Invoice record didn't change while you were gone.
- Grab the Invoice ID (wait a minute—how did you find the right record if you didn't know what it was?).
- Then hop *back* to Line Items.
- Find the new record you just made (hope it's the *right* new record).
- Shove the Invoice ID into the new record.

It's possible to do all that hopping around reliably, but it'd be a mess. It's much easier to plan ahead and bring the proper Invoice ID with you when you first get to Line Items. This scenario happens often in scripting. You think you have a script completed, but in order to finish a *different* script, you've to come back to it and add a step or two. So, open the "- create invoice record" script" and add a Set Variable step so the Invoice ID is ready and waiting for you when you need it:

1. **Select the Set Field script step in the "- create invoice record" script. Add a Set Variable script step just below the Set Field step. Click the Specify button.**

   The value you're setting needs to persist past the end of this subscript, so you create a global variable, using the $$ prefix in the variable's name.

2. **Type *$$Invoice ID* in the Name field. Type Invoices::Invoice ID in the Value field, and then click OK until you're back in your database.**

   You can use the Specify button to pick the field from the list, but if you do, make sure you get the Invoice ID field from the *Invoices* table.

Now, as soon as your script creates a new invoice, it stores the Invoice ID in a script variable for later use.

Getting data from a script variable. The "- process unbilled items" script now has what it needs to add line items to the invoice. You can go back to it and add steps that create a Line Item and relate it to an Invoice now:

1. **Select the "TODO: Create a line item record" comment step, and then add the Go to Layout script step to the script.**

   The new step appears after the highlighted comment.

2. **From the Specify pop-up menu, choose Line Items.**

   This layout is associated with the table you want to add records to.

   In order, add a New Record/Request step and a Set Field step to the script. For Set Field, turn on the "Specify target field" checkbox.

   The Specify Field window makes another visit.

3. **From the pop-up menu above the field list, choose Line Items. Then select the Invoice ID field, and click OK.**

   The Set Field step shows it will set the Line Items::Invoice ID field.

4. **Click the Specify button to the right of "Calculated result." In the Specify Calculation window, set the calculation to *$$InvoiceID,* and then click OK.**

   This puts the invoice ID from the script variable into the new line item's Invoice ID field.

5. **Remove the "TODO: Create a line item record" comment step.**

   You're done with it, so clear it away.

Now the "- process unbilled items" script can create a Line Item that's related to the appropriate Invoice.

Making a script more efficient. When you're writing complex scripts, you often find that your game plan changes. The steps you outlined in the TODO comments made sense when you wrote them, but now that you're implementing the final script, you see things need to be changed. Take a look at your next TODO comment.

After it creates a Line Item, your script needs to return to the layout it came from. You might be tempted to use Go to Layout with the "original layout" setting, but that won't do it, because the "original layout" is the layout that was current when the *script* first started. You need to get back to the layout that the If test switched to at the beginning of this script.

You might decide to repeat the same logic you used at the top of the script: Switch layouts based on the script parameter. That method certainly works, but think about what happens when your script runs, using "timeslips" as its parameter:

- Switch to the Timeslips layout.

- Switch to the Line Items layout.

- Add a line item.

- Switch to the Timeslips layout.

You've discovered that it doesn't make sense to switch layouts at the top of the script after all. You can let the If test at the bottom handle the switching all by itself. Go ahead and remove those first five script steps (from If to End If). The script now looks like the one in Figure 15-26.

Pulling data through a relationship. The next TODO comment says you need to "Set the description, quantity, and price appropriately." That was good enough for a rough sketch, but now it's time to fill in the detail. You have to think about where that data's coming from and where it needs to go:

- **A new timeslip line item.** The line item description should match the timeslip description, and its start date and time. The quantity should be the number of *hours* worked, and the price should be your hourly rate (for now, pretend it is $20).

- **A new expense line item.** The description comes from the expense description. Add "Expense:" to the front, just to make it clear this is an expense. The price should be the amount of the expense, and the quantity should always be *1*.

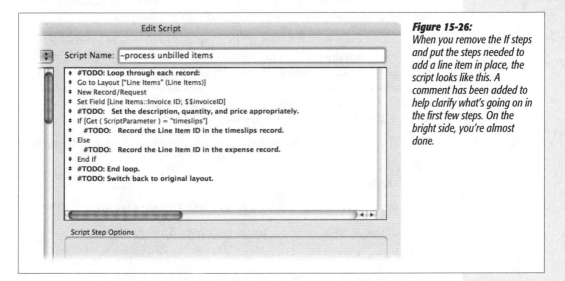

Figure 15-26:
When you remove the If steps and put the steps needed to add a line item in place, the script looks like this. A comment has been added to help clarify what's going on in the first few steps. On the bright side, you're almost done.

Clearly, then, you need access to two different tables and you may need to do a lot of layout hopping to get back and forth. You already have an If set that lets you update the right Line Item ID field, and there's no reason you can't update the line item record from inside this If block. To figure out the best way to move your data around, take a look at Figure 15-27. It shows the relevant portion of the relationship graph for your database.

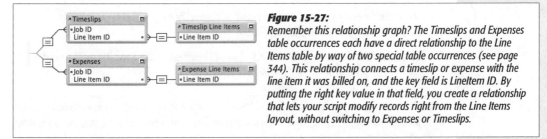

Figure 15-27:
Remember this relationship graph? The Timeslips and Expenses table occurrences each have a direct relationship to the Line Items table by way of two special table occurrences (see page 344). This relationship connects a timeslip or expense with the line item it was billed on, and the key field is LineItem ID. By putting the right key value in that field, you create a relationship that lets your script modify records right from the Line Items layout, without switching to Expenses or Timeslips.

If you were doing this process manually, it'd make perfect sense to switch layouts, so you could actually see the record you're modifying. But a script doesn't need to see a layout to edit data because it's using a field reference to make sure the data goes into the right field. Think of it this way: If your script's context has a relation-ship to the table you need to edit, then you can use the relationship to pull the data through without switching layouts. That's just what you do to finish this writing the "- process unbilled items" script:

1. **Select the Set Field script step in the script.**

   You need to grab the Line Item ID before you start the If test.

2. **Add a Set Variable script step. Click the Specify button. Type *$LineItemID* in the Name field and *Line Items::Line Item ID* in the value field.**

   You want to store the Line Item ID in a variable while you're here, so you can set in your Timeslips or Expenses record later on in the script. Since you won't need the value after the subscript has run, you can use a local variable (the kind with a single $ prefix). Now the script creates a new blank line item, attaches it to the right invoice, and puts the line item ID in a global field. Your next job is to get this line item ID into the expense or timeslip record.

3. **Select the "TODO: Record the Line Item ID in the timeslip record" comment step.**

   You'll tackle this one first.

4. **Add a Go to Layout step, and set it to go to the Timeslips layout.**

   You can't work on a timeslip if you're not on the Timeslips layout.

5. **Add another Set Field step to the script.**

   Set the options for the Set Field step so it targets the *Timeslips::Line Item ID* field and uses the calculation, *$LineItemID*.

6. **Click the Duplicate button. Drag that second copy of the Set Field step down and position it under the last TODO comment line.**

   It's now in the right place, but it sets the wrong field. Time to fix that. (You don't need to change the calculation because in both cases you're grabbing the value from the same global field.)

7. **Click the Specify button to the right of "Specify target field" and set it to target the Expenses::Line Item ID field.**

   If your field names match exactly, FileMaker keeps the Line Item ID field high-lighted for you. If it doesn't, select it yourself.

Tip: This saves you a little work, and a lot of hassle remembering which field you're supposed to be set-ting. So while you might have thought it was a little confusing to have fields with the same names in differ-ent tables, you get a payoff in increased efficiency when you're rummaging around in dialog boxes.

---

8. **Add another Go to Layout step, this time targeting the Expenses layout, and put it above the Set Field step you just added.**

Again, you need to make sure you're on the right layout.

9. **Delete the two TODO steps that start with "Record the Line Item ID."**

Isn't it nice to knock things off your to-do list? Figure 15-28 shows how your script should look now.

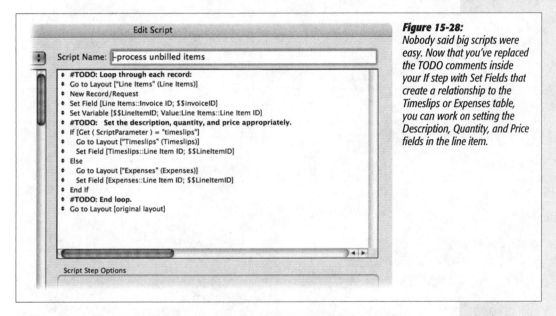

Figure 15-28:
Nobody said big scripts were easy. Now that you've replaced the TODO comments inside your If step with Set Fields that create a relationship to the Timeslips or Expenses table, you can work on setting the Description, Quantity, and Price fields in the line item.

You've now created a Line Item record that's related to another record in either Timeslips or Expenses (remember, that depended on your script parameter). Next, you need to pull three fields worth of data from the related record, so you need three set field steps. You need one set for Timeslips and one for Expenses, so you'll add *six* Set Field steps.

The only hard part—and it isn't that hard—is figuring out what to put in each field. Here goes:

1. **Select the Set Field step that targets the Timeslips::Line Item ID field (it's the one just after the If step).**

This step makes the link to the line item. So your new Set Field steps go after it.

2. **Add a Set Field step to the script. Turn on the "Specify target field" checkbox.**

The Specify Field window arrives on cue.

Note: You're about to set the Description field on the line item record. You're going to do this by accessing the line item related to the current timeslip. To accomplish it, you need to pick the Timeslip Line Items table occurrence, *not* Line Items itself. The relationship graph (as shown in Figure 15-28) tells you this.

---

3. **From the pop-up menu above the field list, choose Timeslip Line Items.**

The fields from the *Line Items* table show in the list. (Remember, this is just another *occurrence* of the same Line Items table.)

Referential Integrity

By now, it's ingrained in your developer's brain that relationships work because there's a match between key fields in the related tables. But what if you absolutely, positively *have* to change the value in a key field? You know it'll wreak havoc with your related records, because as soon as you change the value in the "one" side of the relationship, all the "to-many" records are no longer related to their parent records (or to any other record). In other words, they're orphaned.

If you changed the value in key fields manually, it'd be fairly easy to figure out how to keep this from happening. You use the existing relationship to find the child records, change their keys, and only then, go back to the parent record and change its key. The record family is reunited and everybody's happy.

There's still some brainwork that this script doesn't handle, like making sure that your NewCustomerID value is unique before you try to use it. If you're changing your key field value, it's probably not a surrogate key, so you'll have to know how your business policy creates and insures unique key values, and then apply that logic to your script. And you need to ensure that each related record is unlocked and available for your script to change. (See the box on page 647 for the scoop on record locking.) Only you can decide whether changing a key field is something you want to hand over to your users or if you'll manage this task yourself. Whichever way you go, this skeleton script will get you started.

Here's a script that handles that gruntwork for you:

```
Allow User Abort [ Off ]
Go to Layout [ "Customers" (Customers) ]
Set Variable [ $newID; Value:Customers::NewCustomerID ]
Go to Related Record [Show only related records ; From table: "Jobs"; Using layout: "Jobs"
(Jobs) ]
Loop
        Set Field [ Jobs::Customer ID; $newID ]
        Go to Record/Request/Page [ Next; Exit after last ]
End Loop
Go to Layout [ "Customers" (Customers) ]
Set Field [ Customers::Customer ID; $newID ]
```

4. **Select Description and click OK.**

You're now targeting the right field. As explained before, you want to put the timeslip date, time, and description in it.

5. **Set the calculation for this step to *Timeslips::Date Time & ": " & Timeslips:: Description.***

Don't worry if the box cuts off a bit of the end. Click the Duplicate button when you're done.

6. **For this next copy of the Set Field step, click Specify (to the right of "Specify target field"), and choose the Price Each field.**

   You want to set the price to $20.

7. **Set the calculation for this step to, simply, *20*. Click Duplicate again.**

8. **For this third Set Field step, target the *Timeslip Line Items::Quantity* field.**

   Since you duplicated the previous step, the Timeslip Line Items table occurrence is already selected; you just need to pick the field.

Note: Now you need to calculate the number of *hours* worked. The Timeslips::Duration field is a time field, so it holds the number of *seconds* worked. To convert seconds to hours, just divide by 60 twice (once gets you to minutes, the second gets you to hours). You should also round the result to two decimal places so you don't get ugly or truncated numbers on your invoice. The final calculation looks like this:

```
Round ( Timeslips::Duration / 60 / 60 ; 2 )
```

---

9. **Set the calculation for this step to *Round (Timeslips::Duration / 60 / 60 ; 2)*.**

   The three Set Field steps are in place for timeslip records. Now you need to add similar steps to the expenses half of the script.

10. **Select the Set Field step that is below the Else step in your script, and add another Set Field step to the script.**

    This is the same sort of maneuver you took in step 5.

11. **Set the step options to target the *Expense Line Items::Description* field and use this calculation: *"Expense: " & Expenses::Description*.**

    Easy enough. On to number two.

12. **Duplicate the script step, set it to target the *Price Each* field, and use this calculation: *Expenses::Amount*.**

    One more to go.

13. **Duplicate the step again. This time target the *Quantity* field and set the calculation to, simply, *1*.**

    Expenses always have a quantity of one.

Creating a looping script. Your script works great now—if you have only one Line Item to process. But you may have a dozen unbilled items that need to go on your invoice. So you'll create a loop that repeats for all your Line Items. The toughest thing about creating a loop is getting the steps in the right places:

1. **Add a Loop step to the script.**

   That's right: Both Loop *and* End Loop appear in the script. Your goal is to wrap the Loop and End Loop steps around everything that should happen over and over. That means everything except the Go to Layout step at the end.

2. Drag just the Loop step to the very top, so that it's first step. Drag the End Loop step down so that it's positioned between End If and the last Go to Layout step.

When you're done, you can remove the "TODO: Loop through each record" comment line.

3. Add a Go to Record/Request/Page step just before the End Loop step. In the Specify pop-up list, choose Next. Click the "Exit after last" option.

You don't have to use an Exit Loop If step in this script, because you have a finite set of records to flip through.

If you know ahead of time that you'll be processing a set of records, you can always start writing your script with a loop. But for testing a script, it's often easier to figure out what's happening if you don't add the loop until you know the core of the script works. Figure 15-29 shows the final script.

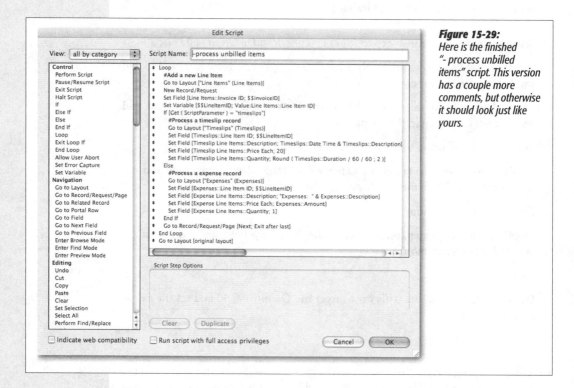

Figure 15-29:
*Here is the finished
"- process unbilled
items" script. This version
has a couple more
comments, but otherwise
it should look just like
yours.*

To test your script, first go to a job record that has unbilled timeslips and expenses (or create a new one if necessary). Once you're on the job record, run your Create Invoice for Job script. In a flash, you should see a new invoice, properly assigned to the customer and containing line items for each unbilled item. You might be a little miffed that it took you *hours* to build the script, and FileMaker runs the whole thing in seconds. Cheer up, though; think how much time it will save you *in the future*.

Tip: If the script doesn't work, you have a few options. First, you can look below to see the complete text of each script and make sure yours match. But if you have FileMaker Advanced, you should also read about the Debug Scripts and Data Viewer tools in Chapter 19. These gems can make hunting down script problems a breeze.

The Finished Scripts

To help you hunt down problems, here are the four scripts you just created, with all options fully specified (you can also get them at *www.missingmanuals.com*).

Create Invoice for Job

```
If [ Get ( LayoutName ) = "Jobs" ]
Perform Script [ Script: "- find unbilled activity";
Parameter: Jobs::Job ID ]
If [ $$unbilled Items  = 0 ]
Show Custom Dialog [ Title: "Create Invoice"; Message: "This job has no
unbilled activity, so no invoice was created."; Buttons: "OK" ]
Else
Perform Script [ Script: "- create invoice record"; Parameter: Jobs::Job ID ]
Perform Script [ Script: "- process unbilled items"; Parameter: "timeslips" ]
Perform Script [ Script: "- process unbilled items"; Parameter: "expenses" ]
Go to Layout [ "Invoices" ]
End If
End If
```

- find unbilled activity

```
#Find and count all unbilled expense records
Go to Layout [ "Expenses" (Expenses) ]
Enter Find Mode [ Specified Find Requests: Find Records; Criteria: Expenses::
Line Item ID: "==" ] [ Restore ]
Set Field [ Expenses::Job ID; "==" & Get ( ScriptParameter ) ]
Set Error Capture [ On ]
Perform Find [   ]
Set Error Capture [ Off ]
Set Variable [ $$Unbilled Items; Value:Get ( FoundCount ) ]
#Find and count all unbilled timeslip records
Go to Layout [ "Timeslips" (Timeslips) ]
Enter Find Mode [ Specified Find Requests: Find Records; Criteria: Timeslips:
:Line Item ID: "==" ] [ Restore ]
Set Field [ Timeslips::Job ID; "==" & Get ( ScriptParameter ) ]
Set Error Capture [ On ]
Perform Find [   ]
Set Error Capture [ Off ]
Set Variable [ $$Unbilled Items; $$Unbilled Items + Get ( FoundCount ) ]
#Return to the original layout
Go to Layout [ original layout ]
```

- create invoice record

```
Go to Layout [ "Invoices" (Invoices) ]
New Record/Request
Set Field [ Invoices::Job ID; Get ( ScriptParameter ) ]
Set Variable [ $$invoice ID; Invoices::Invoice ID ]
Go to Layout [ original layout ]
```

- process unbilled items

```
Loop
#Add a new empty line item
Go to Layout [ "Line Items" (Line Items) ]
New Record/Request
Set Field [ Line Items::Invoice ID; $$Invoice ID ]
Set Variable [ $LineItemID; Value:Line Items::Line Item ID ]
If [ Get ( ScriptParameter ) = "timeslips" ]
#Process a timeslip record
Go to Layout [ "Timeslips" (Timeslips) ]
Set Field [ Timeslips::Line Item ID; $LineItemID ]
Set Field [ Timeslip Line Items::Description; Timeslips::Date Time & ": " &
Timeslips::Description ]
Set Field [ Timeslip Line Items::Price Each; 20 ]
Set Field [ Timeslip Line Items::Quantity; Round ( Timeslips::Duration / 60 /
60 ; 2 ) ]
Else
#Process an expense record
Go to Layout [ "Expenses" (Expenses) ]
Set Field [ Expenses::Line Item ID; $LineItemID ]
Set Field [ Expense Line Items::Description; "Expense: " & Expenses::
Description ]
Set Field [ Expense Line Items::Price Each; Expenses::Amount ]
Set Field [ Expense Line Items::Quantity; 1 ]
End If
Go to Record/Request/Page [ Next; Exit after last ]
End Loop
Go to Layout [original layout]
```

Congratulations! You've just made it through a long, hard slog. Perhaps it seemed like you didn't know where you where going, but that's often the case when you're writing scripts. In this chapter, you learned a system for breaking down a complicated task into manageable pieces. When you're writing your first few complex scripts, you'll probably want to follow the same procedure fairly closely. But as you gain experience, you'll find that planning, finding exceptions, and subscripting will start to feel natural. You'll start envisioning scripts of increasing complexity and making them your own way, without following a rigid plan.

Part Six:
Security and Integration

6

Part Four
Security and Interaction

Security

Easy access to information is what FileMaker's all about. But that's a double-edged sword. As it stands now, every person who uses your database has unrestricted access. Of course, you can take all the usual precautions (give your computer a password, install virus protection software, lock your door, and so on). But eventually, you'll probably want to let other people work in your database, and that brings up all kinds of security challenges. Mike in Accounting is free to rename all your scripts if he so desires. And Kelly in Sales can delete all those "old" order records that are getting in her way. Fortunately, FileMaker has features of its own that give you a finer level of control, so you can let selected people use your database to the fullest, while keeping important information out of harm's way.

You may be tempted to think you don't have to worry about security. But the best time to think about protecting your data is *before* you have a problem. If you wait until your database grows big and complex before considering security, it'll take you longer to build in later.

How Security Works

FileMaker's security system has two levels of control: *who* can get into your database in the first place and *what* they can do once they're there. You determine who gets access to your database by setting up *user accounts*, and you control what each person can do by assigning *privilege sets* to each account.

Who Gets Access

FileMaker understands that different individuals access your database. The *who* part of security is important for several reasons. For instance, Malcolm and Lois each need access to the database, but their manager Craig doesn't. You get to decide *who* gets access. With individual accounts, you can keep track of who's in the file. If Lois leaves the company, you need to keep her from accessing the database in the future. Likewise, when Lois's replacement is hired, you need to give him access, too.

In FileMaker, you create an *account* for each person who accesses the database. Just like any password-protected document, an account has a user name and a password. When people open the database, they have to type a name and password to get in. If they don't know the right combination, they can't see your database. If they get the password right, FileMaker assumes they are who they say they are.

Note: When FileMaker asks for an account name and password, propeller-heads say it's *authenticating* the user. In other words, it's making sure the user's for real. The actual window that pops up on the screen is called the *Authentication dialog box*, and the whole process is called *authentication*. This book, for the most part, dispenses with this jargon.

POWER USERS' CLINIC

Spyware by Script

When you've set up database accounts, FileMaker remembers the account name of whoever's currently signed in. In fact, by using a script, you can find out who it is with the Get (AccountName) function. For example, if you want to record the account name in a Notes field when someone runs a particularly important script, you could include a script step like this:

```
Set Field [Notes;Notes & Get(AccountName)
& " ran THE script on " & Get
(CurrentDate) & " at " & Get (CurrentTime
)]
```

Then every time the script runs, FileMaker looks up the name and password of whoever's using the file at the moment, and puts the person's account name and the date and time in the Notes field.

Along with the account name, FileMaker remembers the name of the privilege set when someone logs in. You can use the Get (PrivilegeSetName) function to find out what it is.

What They Can Do

But who gets into your database is only half the story. You also control *what* they can do. Now then, while all people are unique, you probably don't need to grant each person the privilege to use individual layouts or scripts on a case-by-case basis. Instead, FileMaker assumes you have just a few different types of users, and lets you define *privilege sets* for each type. A privilege set is simply a list of things a user's allowed to do, and in effect it creates a *level* of privilege. For example, you might have one privilege set for Accounting and another for Sales. People with the

Accounting privilege set can run reports, but they can't enter new orders. People with the Sales privilege set can enter and edit data, but they can't run reports.

You can make as many—or as few—privilege sets as you need. And you can give 50 accounts the same privilege set, or make a privilege set just for one account. When you create a privilege set, you get lots of control over what it can do. A privilege set can prevent people from editing scripts, or it can let them edit just certain scripts. It can stop a sales person from editing any order entered more than five days ago, or prevent accountants from editing orders at all.

Privilege Sets

Generally, you create your privilege sets *first*, and then add accounts for each user, as you'll see in the following sections. When you add an account, FileMaker asks you to pick a privilege set to control that person's access. But true to the FileMaker way, if you start to create an account, and don't yet have an appropriate privilege set, you can easily create one right then and there, before you save the account.

All the work of creating and maintaining accounts and privilege sets is done in the Define Accounts & Privileges window (Figure 16-1). You can get there by way of the File → Define → Accounts & Privileges command.

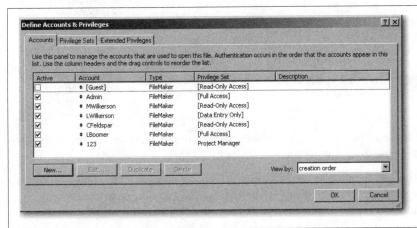

Figure 16-1:
The Define Accounts & Privileges window (File → Define → Accounts & Privileges) has three tabs: Accounts, Privilege Sets, and Extended Privileges. You'll learn about Extended Privileges on page 604, but the first two tabs are where you go to define accounts and privilege sets respectively.

When you're creating privilege sets, there's a big temptation to give people *too much power*. The more folks can do on their own, the less often they'll come bugging you, right? Unfortunately, this attitude invites trouble. For instance, if your database holds credit card numbers along with order records, and your Order Entry privilege set allows users to export data, you might one day find yourself the subject of an FBI investigation. To be on the safe side, if you aren't *sure* someone needs a privilege, don't give it to him.

There's a practical component to this rule as well. If someone has access to a feature he shouldn't have, it's very unlikely he'll complain. He probably won't even notice, and neither will you until someone abuses it. On the other hand, if you lock someone out of a capability she needs, you can bet you'll hear about it right away. You can easily add the needed power when it comes up. In other words, if your privilege sets start out too restrictive, they'll naturally grow to the right level of power over time based on user feedback.

Managing Privilege Sets

To create or edit privilege sets, click the Privilege Sets tab. The first thing you notice is that you already have some. Every FileMaker database has three built-in privilege sets: [Full Access], [Data Entry Only], and [Read-Only Access] (the brackets help to remind you that these privilege sets are special). You can see the Privilege Sets tab in Figure 16-2.

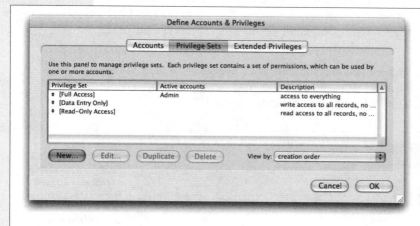

Figure 16-2:
The Privilege Sets tab of the Define Accounts & Privileges dialog box lists all the privilege sets in your database. Each privilege set has a name (in the Privilege Set column) and a description. The list also shows you all the accounts that are assigned each privilege set. In this case, only the [Full Access] privilege set is actually being used—by the Admin account.

The standard privilege sets cover three very common access levels, and you're welcome to use them if you want:

- Although you probably didn't know it, you've been using the **Full Access** privilege set all along. As the name says, it gives you full access to the file with absolutely no restrictions.

- The **Data Entry Only** privilege set is much less powerful. Accounts assigned to this privilege set can't create or modify tables, field definitions, scripts, or layouts. But they can add, edit, and delete records in any table.

- The least powerful built-in privilege set is **Read-Only Access**. Not only does it prevent developer activities, but it also prevents modification of the data. Accounts with this privilege set can't create, edit, or delete records. They can only *view* the data that's already there.

These built-in privilege sets provide basic security, but they don't give you a range of possibilities. Using just FileMaker's default privilege sets, you can't give

Malcolm full control of some tables, but let him just enter data in others. In developer's lingo, you don't get a lot of *granularity*.

Tip: Think of granularity as a medium for sculpture. If you're building a statue from boulders, you can't create delicate details like the nose or eyelashes. If you're building with grains of sand (get it?), you can work at a much finer level. Similarly, granularity in security lets you control specific access to very specific aspects of your database.

In FileMaker, you can exercise precise, granular control over security by creating your own privilege sets and assigning them to certain people or groups.

Creating a new privilege set

Before you create a new privilege set, you have a decision to make: Do you start from scratch, or do you take a shortcut? If you click New, FileMaker makes a new privilege set with absolutely no privileges. In other words, accounts attached to this set—if left alone—can't do *anything* in the database. You have to turn on exactly the privileges you think the user should have.

To save time, you can start by duplicating the [Data Entry Only] or [Read-Only Access] privilege set, and then add or remove privileges as necessary. This way is usually a little faster, but it does open up the possibility that you'll accidentally leave something turned on that shouldn't be.

Note: For some reason, you can't duplicate the [Full Access] privilege set. This is FileMaker's way of encouraging you to really think about the privileges you assign, and it should encourage you to give users the least access possible for them to do their jobs. If you want a privilege set that grants *almost* full access, you have to build it up by hand.

Other Privileges

Draw your attention to the Other Privileges area. Here is where you decide on some basic FileMaker features. Most of these are pretty self-explanatory:

- **Allow printing.** Turn this option on, and the user can print layouts. If you turn this option off, the Print menu command is grayed out and the Print script step fails.

- **Allow exporting.** This option lets people access the Export Records command. Again, if it's off, the menu command is grayed out, and the Export Records script step doesn't work.

Note: There's a workaround to let scripts do things the active privilege set doesn't let them do. See page 609.

- **Manage Extended Privileges.** Normally, only accounts with full access can manage security settings. But extended privileges are one exception. You'll learn about these shortly, but if this option's turned on, users can assign extended privileges to different privilege sets themselves.

- **Allow user to override data validation warnings.** When you use field validation, FileMaker shows displays an error message if people enter invalid data in a field. In the Field Options dialog box, you can turn on "Allow user to override during data entry" if you want to give folks the power to ignore this error. But you get one more layer of control with the "Allow user to override data validation warnings" checkbox in the Edit Privilege Set window. If you turn this option off, they can't override the errors even when the field options say they should be able to.

- **Disconnect user from FileMaker Server when idle.** This isn't actually a privilege. It's more of an *un-privilege*, and it's turned on when you create a new privilege set. When it's on, users are kicked out of a shared database if they don't use it for a while (you get to decide how long when you configure FileMaker Server). Turn it *off* if you want to give these users the power to stay connected right through lunch break.

- **Allow user to modify their own password.** FileMaker lets you implement some typical password management features. First, you get to decide if someone can change his account password at all. If you want to give him this power, turn this option on. Once it's on, you can choose "Must be changed every" and enter a number of days to *force* the user to change his password periodically. You can also enforce a minimum password length.

Note: You probably want to turn this option off if people *share* accounts in the same database. If you have just one account for each group, for instance, you don't want one wisenheimer changing the password on everybody else just for laughs.

- **Available menu commands.** A brand-new privilege set gets full access to the menu bar. Of course most menu commands don't actually *do* anything unless you turn on the appropriate privileges. If you don't want your users running menu commands willy-nilly, you can change the "Available menu commands" pop-up menu. Choose "Editing only" to give these people access only to the Edit menu and basic formatting commands. Choose "None" to turn off every menu command that affects the current database.

To develop a full understanding of how privilege sets work, why not try building one from scratch?

1. **Click New.**

   FileMaker pops up the Edit Privilege Set dialog box (Figure 16-3). First off, every privilege set needs a name, which can be anything you want. Call this one *Project Manager* by typing it in the Privilege Set Name box. While you're at it, in the Description box, type: *create and edit jobs, create new invoices.*

---

2. **For the Project Manager privilege set you're defining, turn on these check-boxes:**

   - Allow Printing

   - Allow user to override data validation warnings.

   - Disconnect user from FileMaker server when idle.

   - Allow user to modify their own password.

Figure 16-3:
When you create a new privilege set, FileMaker shows you a window where you can choose its settings. Notice how many things aren't turned on, or say "All no access." This set offers very few privileges.

3. **Then set the "Available menu commands" pop-up menu to "Editing only."**

   That's it for the "Other Privileges" part of the dialog box. But if you leave the Project Manager privilege set with these settings, your users can't do anything very useful. Next, you'll look at the section where all the granularity is hiding so you can start adding real privileges to the list.

Note: You may have noticed there's no checkbox for "Allow user to define the database," or "Allow user to create tables." Only accounts with full access can open the Define Database window and use its features. The same goes for the Accounts and Privilege Sets tabs in the Accounts & Privileges window.

Data Access and Design Privileges

The Data Access and Design section of the Edit Privilege Set dialog box is where you control access to your specific database elements. The window has a pop-up menu for Records, Layouts, Value Lists, and Scripts. Right now, the Project Manager privilege set doesn't allow access to any of these. To start adding privileges, click the Records pop-up menu. Figure 16-4 shows all your choices.

Record privileges

If the three built-in privilege sets form the first level of granularity in the security system, the options in this pop-up menu are part of the *second* level.

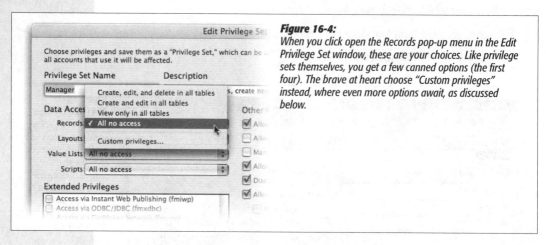

Figure 16-4:
When you click open the Records pop-up menu in the Edit Privilege Set window, these are your choices. Like privilege sets themselves, you get a few canned options (the first four). The brave at heart choose "Custom privileges" instead, where even more options await, as discussed below.

Without much fuss, you can pick one of the prebuilt options:

- **Create, edit, and delete in all tables** is the level you're accustomed to. It lets these people do anything they want with the records—including delete them all.

- **Create and edit in all tables** is almost as good. It just prevents the users from *deleting* records.

- **View only in all tables** is for the browsers among you. They can *see* anything they want, but they can't *change* anything.

- If, for some reason, you want to give somebody access to your *database* but not your *data*, then keep **All no access** selected.

Each of these options applies to *every* record in *every* table. But you might want to let some users "Create, edit, and delete" only in *some* tables, and let them "View only" in others. For instance, you can let part-timers create new customer records, but not tamper with the Expenses table. For that kind of control, choose "Custom privilege" (Figure 16-5).

To modify privileges for a particular table, you first have to select it. But don't waste time: You can select *several* tables if you want to, and then modify the settings for all of them at once. FileMaker even gives you a Select All button so you can easily make a change to *every* table.

For the Project Manager privilege set, you want to give *at least* View access to every table:

1. **From the Records pop-up list, choose Custom Privileges, and then click Select All.**

   FileMaker selects every table in the list.

2. **From the View pop-up menu, choose *yes*.**

The word "yes" appears in the View column for every table. Accounts with the Project Manager privilege set can see data in every table in the file.

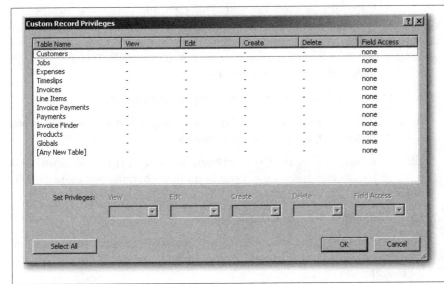

Figure 16-5:
Now you're starting to see some real granularity. The Custom Record Privileges window lets you control view, edit, create, and delete privileges on each individual table. You can also control exactly which fields the users have access to by choosing options from the Field Access pop-up menu.

3. **From the Field Access pop-up menu, choose *all*.**

This time, "all" appears in the Field Access column. Now Project Managers can see the contents of every field in all the tables. Project Managers need to work with customers, jobs, expenses, and timeslips, so you'll give them access to those tables next.

4. **Click in the list to deselect the group, then select the only the Customers, Jobs, Expenses, and Timeslips tables by holding the Control key (Windows) or ⌘ key (Mac OS X) while you click each one.**

Managers should be able to create, edit, and delete in those tables, not just view them.

5. **With all four tables selected, choose "yes" from the Edit pop-up menu, the Create pop-up menu, and the Delete pop-up menu.**

Creating record-level access

Invoice privileges are a little more complicated. You want Project Managers to be able to "create invoices," but invoices involve multiple tables and processes, which you have to translate into a set of privileges. They need to create invoice records, of course, but they also need to be able to create *line item* records. And once they've added items to an invoice, they should also be able to *edit* those items. You decide, however, that they *shouldn't* be able to edit items on invoices from last year. In fact, they probably shouldn't change any invoice that isn't dated today. You can handle even a complicated security requirement like this easily in FileMaker: Just add a simple calculation to the mix. (See Chapter 9 for a refresher on calculations.)

When you choose to limit access like this, FileMaker lets you use a calculation to decide *which* records the users can edit. This calculation gives you tremendous control over the security system. You can use data from the record itself, information about the current date, time, or account name, and even global field or global variable values. Your calculation must return a Boolean result: True if the record should be editable, and False if it shouldn't.

Here are the steps to set up the invoice privileges described above:

1. **In the Custom Record Privileges dialog box, select just the Invoices table. Then, from the Create pop-up menu, choose *yes*.**

   FileMaker puts "yes" in the Create column, meaning that managers with this privilege set can create invoice records. From here on, things get more complicated.

2. **From the Edit pop-up menu, choose *limited*.**

   You don't want the user to be able to edit *any* invoice record. Instead, you're giving them *limited* edit privileges. Your old friend, the Specify Calculation dialog box, appears.

3. **In the calculation box, enter *Date >= Get (CurrentDate)*.**

   This calculation returns a true result when the invoice date is on or after the current date. It's false for invoices dated before today, so that FileMaker allows Project Managers to edit only today's invoices.

   You're going to use the exact same calculation shortly, so why bother retyping?

4. **Select the entire calculation, and choose Edit → Copy, and *then* click OK to close the calculation box.**

   Unsurprisingly, you're back in the Custom Record Privileges window. The word "limited…" shows in the Edit column for Invoices.

5. **From the Delete pop-up menu, choose *limited*.**

   The Specify Calculation dialog box returns. This time, you're going to limit the managers' ability to delete invoice records. The rule is the same: They can only delete *new* invoices.

6. **Choose Edit → Paste to use the calculation from step 3 here.**

   FileMaker adds the calculation to the calculation box. Click OK when you're done.

Repeat the above steps for the Line Items table. In this case, though, you want to let managers edit or delete line items when the invoice they're attached to contains today's date. So use the following in steps 3 and 6:

```
Invoices::Date ≥ Get ( CurrentDate )
```

Project Managers at your company have no business creating or editing payments or products, so you can leave the Edit, Create, and Delete set to "no" for Invoice Payments, Payments, and Products.

Note: FileMaker shows a "–" instead of the word "no" when you turn off a privilege. The dashes make the denied privileges easier to spot when you're looking at a long list.

Field-level access

If you remember the original design requirements for this database, the Payments table has a field called Credit Card Number. This type of information falls into the *need-to-know* category: Unless someone *needs* it to do his job, he has no business seeing it. Even though Project Managers can view Payment records, you can still control access to individual *fields* in that table. You're about to exercise field-level granularity:

1. **Select the Payments table. Then, from the Field Access pop-up menu, choose**
   limited.

   The Custom Field Privileges window appears (Figure 16-6). FileMaker offers three field-level privileges: *modifiable* means users can see *and* edit the field data; *view only* means they can see the information in the field, but can't change it; and *no access* means they can't even see it.

Figure 16-6:
The Custom Field Privileges window lets you control access to individual fields. Select the fields you want to change, and then select one of the Privilege radio buttons. FileMaker dutifully changes every selected field accordingly. Click Select All to quickly select every field.

2. **Select the *Credit Card Number* and *Credit Card Expiry* fields. When they're both highlighted, select the *no access* radio button.**

   And indeed, the words "no access" appear in the Privilege column for the selected fields. Click OK.

Note: Even though the other fields in this list say "modifiable," the entire *record* isn't editable for these people, so they can't change field data. The record-level security settings effectively trump those at the field level.

The two tables whose privileges you haven't touched yet—Invoice Finder and Globals—have only global fields, so they don't need records at all. But you still need to turn on the Edit privilege, so the managers can change values in the globals. Select both tables and simply choose "yes" from the Edit pop-up menu. When you're finished, your Custom Record Privileges dialog box should look a lot like the one in Figure 16-7.

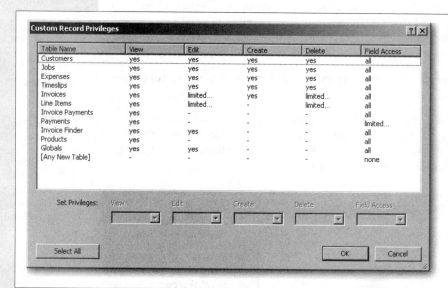

Figure 16-7:
The record privileges for the Project Manager privilege set look like this. Project Managers have wide-open access to some tables, limited access to others, and view-only access to a few. Record privileges represent the most granular level of FileMaker's security system.

When you're done looking, click OK to close this dialog box. Because you just made a set of complex choices, FileMaker sums up everything you just did by displaying "Custom privileges" in the Records pop-up menu in the Data Access and Design section of the Edit Privilege Set dialog box. To review or edit the record- or field-level access you've set, click "Custom Privileges" in the pop-up menu again.

Layout privileges

If you've been following along in this section, you've given Project Managers just the right access to the data in your database. But if you stop now, they still can't get very far. They don't have access to any *layouts* yet, and without layouts, a File-

---

Maker database isn't of much use. If someone were to open the database with this privilege set now, she'd see something like Figure 16-8.

Figure 16-8:
When people try to view a layout they don't have access to, this blank screen is what they see. FileMaker tries hard to avoid this, though; it removes layouts the user can't access from the Layouts pop-up menu. But your scripts can still put them somewhere the user doesn't belong. And in this case, they don't have access to any layout, so FileMaker doesn't have much choice.

FileMaker uses layouts to display your file's data, which means you'll need to add layout access to your privilege sets. To give your users all-important access to the various database layouts, use the Edit Privilege Set window's Layouts pop-up menu:

- **All modifiable** means the users can use *and* edit every layout. (Here, "edit," means, "add fields, delete portals, resize parts, and the whole nine yards.")

- **All view only** gives the users access to every layout, but won't let them change any.

- **All no access** prevents *any* layouts from showing, as shown in Figure 16-9.

Figure 16-9:
The Custom Layout Privileges window looks a lot like its records counterpart. You get a list of layouts and some privilege choices. Thankfully, there are fewer things to do here, and thus fewer things to learn. As usual, select the layout (or layouts) first, then make changes.

The final option, *Custom Privileges…* lets you exercise the most control over access to specific layouts. Because layouts are a vehicle for the other database items *on* the layout, there are two distinct layers of privilege.

- **Layout.** These privileges controls the users' ability to view or edit the layout itself. They're basically the same as the All layout privileges described above, but they apply only to the selected layout. Choose *modifiable* if you want to let people edit the layout (enter Layout mode and move fields and things around), *view only* if you want them only to see it, and *no access* if you want them to see that gray screen thing in Figure 16-8 instead.

- **Records via this layout.** Use this option to determine whether or not the users should be able to see or edit *data in fields* on a particular layout. If you make records from the Customer layout "view only," you can still edit them from the Customer List layout.

Tip: If you want to prevent editing of customer data altogether, it'd make more sense to use the record-level privileges instead. The "Records via this layout" setting is available just in case you want to restrict editing from one particular layout, even though the data in the table can be edited elsewhere.

UP TO SPEED

Any New Anything

Both the table list in the Custom Record Privileges window and the field list in the Custom Field Privileges window have an unusual last item: [Any New Table] and [Any New Field]. These items don't really exist in your database. Instead, when you set privileges for them, you're telling FileMaker how this privilege set should treat any new items that are added *later*.

Most FileMaker databases are living creatures that grow and adapt constantly. You might add new fields, layouts, scripts, and even tables at any time, so it would be foolhardy to give everybody access to any and every new item. Instead, you'll be more secure assuming that no one gets access to anything new, until you set the new privileges specifically. To implement this more strict security rule, turn off all privileges for the [Any New…] items. In fact, FileMaker already has "any new" turned off whenever you make a new privilege set.

Figure 16-9 shows the Custom Layout Privileges dialog box. This window has something else that didn't exist on the Custom Record Privileges dialog box: The "Allow creation of new layouts" checkbox lets you decide if these people can create their own new layouts. In fact, you can let users who can't even add or edit data, create layouts. For example, you might have a whole class of people—the Accounting Department, say—who shouldn't be editing customer records or adding product information, but they need to create monthly and annual reports (read: layouts) *from* that data.

In the current example, you want Project Managers to be able to use any layout (and edit records through them). But you also want them to be able to create their own layouts in case they need to do some custom reporting. These new layouts should of course be editable.

1. **If you're looking at the Custom Layout Privileges window, click OK to dismiss it and return to the Edit Privilege Set dialog box. Then, from the Layouts pop-up menu, choose "All view only."**

   You really intend to make custom privilege settings, but when you first visit the Custom Layout Privileges dialog box, everything is turned off. Since you want most options on, save your wrist by choosing "All view only," and FileMaker turns them all on for you. In the next step, you'll just turn a few options off.

2. **From the Layouts pop-up menu, choose "Custom privileges."**

   The Custom Layout Privileges window reappears. This time, though, every layout is set to "view only" with "modifiable" records.

3. **Turn on "Allow creation of new layout." Then select the [Any New Layout] item in the layout list.**

   You may have to scroll down to see it; it's always at the bottom of the list.

4. **Turn on the "modifiable" radio button under Layout.**

   This action tells FileMaker you want new layouts to be modifiable. Click OK when you're done.

If you had tried to click OK without making new layouts modifiable, FileMaker would complain that it doesn't make sense to let someone make a new layout he can't edit. Now, any user with the Project Manager privilege set can edit any new layouts he creates.

Value list privileges

Value lists may not seem as critical a security choice as records and layouts, but since value lists help your users enter consistent data, you want to pay attention to these choices. If you put a pop-up menu on a field to limit data input, but then you give those same users the ability to modify the value list underlying the pop-up menu, they have a way to circumvent your control.

You can see the Custom Value List Privileges window in Figure 16-10. This window lets you assign any of three privileges to each value list: modifiable, view only, or no access. You can also let the user create new value lists with an "Allow creation of new value lists" checkbox, and set the privileges to be assigned to any new value lists.

You can control access to value lists in much the same way you manage record and layout privileges. And like record and layout privileges, you have three canned choices in the pop-up menu, plus Custom privileges:

• **All modifiable** means the users can use and edit every value list.

- **All view only** lets the users see and select from your value lists, but not change them.

- **All no access** prevents the users from seeing value lists at all.

- **Custom privileges** gives you a dialog box where you can create your own set of privileges.

Figure 16-10:
The Custom Value List Privileges window is even simpler than the Custom Layout Privileges version. It works just like the others: Select a value list or two, and then choose a privilege.

In the business rules you're applying to your database, Project Managers should have view-only access to all value lists, so click Cancel and choose "All view only" from the Value Lists pop-up menu. The Value List access you assign to a privilege set overrides layout designs. That is, even if you set up a pop-up menu with the option of "Include 'Edit...' item to allow editing of value list," users with the Project Manager's privilege set can't edit values in the list.

Script privileges

The final option under Data Access and Design lets you control access to your scripts. As with layouts, it's possible to have a class of users who can create new scripts, but can't edit data. If it's the Accountants mentioned in the example on page 584, they need to write scripts to run the reports on the layouts you're letting them create. You could also create a privilege set that lets a level of users run most scripts, but doesn't let them run certain scripts that do destructive activities like deleting sets of records. You could save those scripts for higher-level users instead. Figure 16-11 shows the control choices you have.

Again, the pop-up menu gives you three canned choices and a Custom option:

- **All modifiable** means the users can run *and* edit any script.

- **All executable only** lets the users *run* scripts, but not edit them.

- **All no access** keeps them from running any scripts at all.

• **Custom Privileges** brings up the now-familiar Custom Privileges dialog box.

For the Project Managers set, choose "All executable only" from the Scripts pop-up menu. With this change, you've finished creating your privilege set. Your window should look just like Figure 16-12.

Figure 16-11:
The only thing unexpected in the Custom Script Privileges window is the Notes column in the script list. Since you can't assign notes to a script, you might wonder what exactly this column is for. In fact, it tells you when a script is set to "Run with full access privileges." You'll learn about this later in this chapter.

Figure 16-12:
When your privilege set is finished, it looks like this. Sadly, you can't see all your settings in one screen, but the "..." in the Records and Layouts pop-up menus lets you know there's more detail to be seen if you need it.

To save your new privilege set, click OK. FileMaker adds Project Manager to the list of privilege sets in the Define Accounts & Privileges window (Figure 16-1).

Note: When you give an element—a record, field, layout, value list, or script—the "no access" setting, it literally disappears from the user's view. Scripts disappear from the Scripts menu, layouts from the Layout pop-up menu, fields from sort dialog boxes, and records from lists and portals. Your users won't be tempted to run a script or go to a layout they don't have access to.

Editing a privilege set

If you need to make changes to this privilege set later, just come back to this window, select it in the list, and click Edit. You see the Edit Privilege Set window again, and you're free to change anything you want.

You can't edit FileMaker's built-in privilege sets. If you want to change one, duplicate it first and then change the duplicate. Remember, though, that you can't duplicate [Full Access].

Managing Accounts

At the start of this chapter, you learned that there are two facets to FileMaker security: *who* can get in and *what* they can do. So far, you've created a privilege set called Project Manager, which handles the *what* part of the security equation. But a privilege set has no effect until you tell FileMaker *who* gets those privileges. You handle the who part by assigning a privilege set to an account. As you can see in the Define Accounts & Privileges window's Privilege Sets tab, your new privilege set has no "Active accounts" assigned to it. This section covers creating and managing accounts.

Note: You can have privilege sets that don't have active accounts, but you can't create an account without assigning a privilege set to it. But if you start creating an account first, and then realize you need a custom privilege set for it, that's OK. Just choose "New Privilege Set…" and create it on the fly.

The Define Accounts & Privileges window's Accounts tab (Figure 16-13) shows you all the accounts in your database. You never knew it, but all this time you've been using an account called Admin. FileMaker added this account when you first created your database so you'd have full access to the file without a password. Unfortunately, so does the rest of the world. So your first job is to give the Admin account a password.

To assign a password to the Admin account, select it from the Define Accounts & Privileges list, then click Edit (or double-click the Admin account). The Edit Account window appears (Figure 16-14). Type any password in the Password field. Passwords can take any mix of alphanumeric characters and upper and lowercase characters you like. (Just remember, although account names aren't case sensitive, passwords are.) Click OK when you're done. Now that you've assigned a password to the Admin account, the next time you open this file, FileMaker will ask you for an account name and password.

If you want, you can change the name of the Admin account too. There's no reason you must have an account called Admin. On the other hand, you're required to have an account with full access. If you try to dismiss this dialog box without one, FileMaker complains. Finally, whenever you click OK in the Define Accounts & Privileges window, FileMaker wants to make sure you know an account name and password with full access, so it asks you to enter them. If you don't get it right, FileMaker doesn't let you save your changes. This password box is the final layer of protection from losing your file forever.

Figure 16-13:
The Account tab works a lot like the Privilege Sets tab. Click New to make a new account, or select an existing account and click Edit to change it. You can also duplicate or delete the selected account. Every account has a name (in the Account column), a type, an assigned privilege set (page 604), and an optional description.

Figure 16-14:
After creating a privilege set, the Edit Account window is refreshingly simple. It's even simpler when you consider that you can completely ignore the "Account is authenticated via" pop-up menu for now. You get to edit the account name and password, make an account inactive (when an account is inactive, FileMaker doesn't let users log in), assign a privilege set, and edit the description.

Warning: If you *forget* the password for your only full access account, you can kiss your database good-bye. FileMaker uses industry-standard and ultra-secure techniques to manage passwords, and there's simply no way to bypass them. As long as you know the password for an account with full access, you can change passwords for other accounts as needed. Just make sure you remember your full access password.

FREQUENTLY ASKED QUESTION

Automatic Login

If I've been using the Admin account all this time, how come FileMaker never asked me to log in? Does it just skip the authentication dialog box when some account has no password?

Actually, FileMaker's been logging in for you. Every new database is set up to log in automatically using the Admin account and a blank password. Once you give the Admin account a password for a given database, automatic login stops. But you can set your database to log in with any account automatically, or you can turn off automatic login entirely, which is a much more secure option.

The setting is behind the File → File Options (Mac OS X) or Edit → File Options (Windows) command. When you choose this command, you see the File Options dialog box shown here. Turn off the "Log in using" checkbox to stop the automatic login process. Alternately, you can type a different Account and/or Password in the appropriate box to log in a different way. Finally, you can have FileMaker automatically log into the file using the Guest account (see the box on page 603).

If you set your file to automatically log in with an account that doesn't have full access, including the Guest account, you can't come back to this window to turn it off. You might think you've just locked yourself out of your file completely. But you haven't. If you hold down the Shift key (Windows) or Option key (Mac OS X) while a file opens, FileMaker asks you for an account name and password even if the file's set to automatically log in.

Adding a New Account

Adding a new account is almost as easy as editing an existing one. Since it's so easy to add accounts, there's no reason not to follow best security practices and give everyone an individual account, complete with a unique name and password combination. It's even possible to give people more than one account. For example, you can designate some people as superusers who mostly do data entry and editing, but sometimes need to create layouts. As much as you trust them, you just want to make sure they don't inadvertently damage layouts and scripts while they're doing other work. So you require them to log in with higher-level access

---

when switching from data entry to tasks that require more care, like database design. (See page 611 for more detail on re-login.)

(See page 611 for more detail on re-login.)

UP TO SPEED

The Guest Account

FileMaker has one built-in account called [Guest] that you can't rename or delete. Normally it's assigned to the [Read-Only Access] privilege set, but you can change it to any privilege set you want. The [Guest] account is also normally *inactive*. In other words, it exists, but doesn't work until you turn it on.

If you want to let some people access your database even if they don't have an account, you should activate the guest account by turning on the checkbox by its name.

(Or you can bring up the Edit Account dialog box and, in the Account Status option, choose "Active," but that's a lot more work.) When FileMaker shows the authentication dialog box (shown here), it includes a Guest Account radio button.

Someone can choose this , and then click OK without entering an account name or password. FileMaker gives her access according to the privilege set you assigned to the guest account.

To create a new account, click New. In the Edit Account window, give the account a name and password and assign a privilege set. If you don't see a suitable privilege set, choose New Privilege Set from the Privilege Set pop-up menu. You can also edit the selected privilege set by clicking Edit.

If you let each person manage his or her own password, you can turn on "User must change password on next login." When you turn this option on, you can create an account for someone with a generic password and email the account information to her, with instructions to create to a more secret password when she first opens the database.

Note: If your colleague forgets her password, you can't retrieve it for her because FileMaker masks it as soon as you click OK in the Edit Account dialog box. You *can* change her password, though, so long as you have an account with full access to the file.

You can also make an account inactive. When you do, FileMaker keeps the account—and all its information—in the Accounts list, but it won't let the user open the database. You might make an account inactive if someone leaves the company for an extended period of time, but plans to return. You can easily reactivate the account when you need to. You can also use this option to create accounts for new employees before they start.

Create a new account with the name and password of your choosing. Assign it to the Project Manager privilege set, and then close and reopen the file. When prompted, enter the new account name and password. Now experiment. Try modifying or deleting old invoices, or editing product records. You should see your new security settings in action. When you're done, close the file again and open it one more time. This time use the Admin account to log in.

External authentication

If you work for a large organization that uses Windows Active Directory or Open Directory in Mac OS X, you can take advantage of the fact that your coworkers *already* log in to their computers each morning. With External Authentication, you can save yourself the trouble of creating scads of accounts in all your database files. You also save other people the trouble of entering account names and passwords in all the files they use.

Unlike the accounts discussed in the previous section, these accounts don't have names and passwords stored within FileMaker. To create an account that uses External Authentication, choose External Server from the "Account is authenticated via" pop-up menu. Instead of an individual name and password, you give it a *Group Name*, since you're creating an account for an entire group of users. The individual users (and their groups) are managed outside of FileMaker, on a directory server like Active Directory or Open Directory.

You can set up external authentication in two ways, but both require a working directory server and FileMaker Server (see Chapter 18):

- **Local accounts on your FileMaker server.** You can manage account names and passwords on the server itself, and have them apply to every database. This method saves you the trouble of creating individual FileMaker accounts in every file.

- **Domain accounts.** FileMaker Server communicates with the directory server on your company's network to authenticate users. This approach centralizes account management *and* lets people log in with the same account name and password they use for every other computer system on your network.

Both methods require coordination with your IT department. Consult them (or the documentation for your directory server) for more information on setting up and maintaining external authentication.

Extended Privileges

Extended privileges come in two flavors. There's a set of default extended privileges that let you determine how your users interact with shared databases. And you can create custom extended privileges to assign special privileges that can be turned off and on at will. All extended privileges are tied to privilege sets, to which you can add one or more Extended privileges.

Default Extended Privileges

The default extended privileges let you determine which method users are allowed to use to connect to your database. The default extended privileges are:

- **[fmiwp]** This privilege set allows users to connect to the database using Instant Web Publishing, which requires FileMaker Server Advanced. See page 644 for details on setting up IWP.

- **[fmxdbc]** This privilege set allows users to connect to the database ODBC/JDBC connections to other databases like SQL and Oracle. XDBC connections also require FMSA. See page 658 for details on configuring FileMaker Server to allow xDBC connections.

- **[fmapp]** This privilege set allows users to connect to the database when you're sharing it via FileMaker Server. See page 651 for details.

- **[fmmobile]** This privilege set allows users to connect to the database using File-Maker Mobile, a special version of the program used on PDA devices. File-Maker Mobile is not covered in this book. See FileMaker Mobile help file or manual for details.

- **fmxml** This privilege set allows users to connect to the database through the web, when you're creating custom XML pages, which requires FMSA. See the references on page 705 for details.

- **xmxslt** XSLT files work in conjunction with XML files to share data through custom web publishing.

Say you have 35 local users who need access to your database through FileMaker Server. Then you've got another 75 users in other locations who should use the internet to access your files. If these users need the same privileges, you can make sure your internal people don't use their browsers to access the files and the remote users can't login to the network files using the company WAN by setting up two Privilege Sets that are identical, except one has [fmapp] extended privileges and the other has [fmiwp] privileges.

Tip: You can have everything set perfectly on your FileMaker Server machine and people still can't get into the files over the network unless you remember to assign [fmapp] privileges to at least one privilege set and then assign that privilege set to an account.

On the other hand, the custom extended privileges you create don't actually add any privileges on their own. Instead, using scripts, you can check to see whether the active privilege set has an extended privilege before you allow the user to do anything important or irreversible. To use this feature fully, write your scripts with extended privileges in mind. Then, when you need to temporarily give extra power to a particular privilege set, you just turn on a checkbox in the Edit Privilege Set window and all your scripts do the right thing. The next section takes you through one example.

Creating an Extended Privilege

Suppose you've decided to let Project Managers delete records directly, and you give them that power in their privilege set. When *other* people try to delete a customer record, you want FileMaker to *flag* the record instead, so that a manager can find and delete the flagged records later. To automate the process, you write a Delete script, using the Get (PrivilegeSetName) function to check whether the person's a manager before deleting the records.

Here's how to set up the extended privileges so you can use them in the script. Open the Define Accounts & Privileges window and click the Extended Privileges tab. Then click New. You see the Edit Extended Privilege window on your screen. It's also in Figure 16-15. This extended privilege controls a user's ability to directly delete customer records, so put "Directly delete customer records" in the Description box. For the Keyword, enter *delcust* as an abbreviation. While you're here, turn on the checkbox next to [Full Access]. For now, only those people with full access can delete customer records. When you're done, click OK.

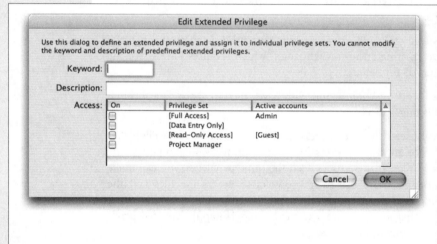

Figure 16-15:
The Edit Extended Privilege window lets you give your extended privilege a keyword and description. The description should say what the extended privilege is for. The keyword can be anything you want; it's wgat you'll look for in your scripts, so once you start using an extended privilege, you probably don't want to change its keyword. You can also tell FileMaker which privilege sets have this extended privilege turned on by clicking the Access list's checkboxes.

Checking for an Extended Privilege

Now you need to write your script. You'll use the Get (ExtendedPrivileges) function to ask FileMaker for the list of extended privileges turned on for the active privilege set. The script checks to see if this list includes "delcust," and takes the appropriate action. While creating this script, you need to add a new text field called Delete Flag to the Customers table. You can see the finished script in Figure 16-16.

Figure 16-16:
This script first checks to make sure you're on a layout associated with the Customers table occurrence. If not, it refuses to run. If you're on the right layout, it then checks your extended privileges to see if you have the "delcust" privilege turned on. If you do, it deletes the record. If you don't, it sets the Delete Flag field instead.

Try out your script by running it from the Customers layout. Assuming you're working in the Admin account, the script should delete the customer record, since you have the [Full Access] privilege set. Then close the database and open it again. This time, log in as someone assigned the Project Manager privilege set. Project Manager *doesn't* have the "delcust" extended privilege turned on, so when you run the script this time, it sets the Delete Flag field instead of deleting the record.

Assigning Extended Privileges

To give Project Managers the ability to delete customers directly, which is the whole point of the script you just wrote, you have two options: First, you can edit the Project Manager privilege set itself. The Edit Privilege Set window has a list of extended privileges in the bottom-left corner where you can control which extended privileges are turned on (see Figure 16-17). To give Project Managers the power to delete customer records, just turn on the checkbox next to "Directly delete customer records." If you're adding it to only a privilege set, editing the privilege set itself is the easiest way to turn on an Extended Privilege.

If you have a few Privilege Sets that need the same Extended Privilege, there's an alternate method: Go to the Define Accounts & Privileges window's Extended Privileges tab and edit the "delcust" extended privilege instead. This way, you see all the Privilege Sets in a list. In the Edit Extended Privilege window, you can turn the extended privilege off or on for any privilege set by clicking the checkboxes in the list of privilege sets.

To test the "delcust" Extended Privilege, turn it on for the Project Manager privilege set and close the database. Then open it, log in as a Project Manager, and run the Delete Customer script. This time it deletes the customer right away. (See page 611 to see how the Re-login script step can make testing security settings easier.)

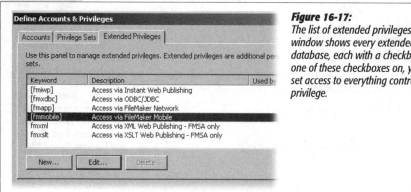

Figure 16-17:
The list of extended privileges in the Edit Privilege Set window shows every extended privilege defined in the database, each with a checkbox beside it. If you turn one of these checkboxes on, you're giving this privilege set access to everything controlled by that extended privilege.

Scripts and Security

Security and scriptwriting intersect in two areas. First, you need to take into account the level of access people have, and whether or not your scripts will override some or all of their privileges. (The previous section describes one way of doing so with extended privileges.) Second, FileMaker lets you automate some of the security features described earlier in this chapter with scripting. ScriptMaker has a handful of steps dedicated to security-related tasks, and this section shows you how to use them.

Detecting Privileges in a Script

The first way to handle security in your scripts is to deal with it directly. In the last section you learned how to check for extended privileges and take appropriate actions. If you want, you can check for specific privilege sets, or even specific account names.

- To check the privilege set, use the **Get (PrivilegeSetName)** function. It returns the name of the privilege set assigned to the current user. Bear in mind that if you change the name of a privilege set, you have to modify any scripts that use this function.

- If you must restrict an action to a particular account, use **Get (AccountName)** instead. As you probably expect, it returns the name of the account with which the user logged in. The same warning applies here: Beware of renamed accounts.

- Finally, FileMaker has one more tempting function: **Get (UserName)**. This function normally returns the user name from the computer's operating system (the name you use to log in to the computer itself). If you use shared accounts in FileMaker, you might want to use the user name to find out who's actually doing something.

These functions are easy to use, but they have some drawbacks. Chances are you'll need to change the account names, privilege sets, or users that can do certain things at some point in the future. Every time you do, you have to check and probably edit all your scripts.

Furthermore, the Get (UserName) function has a *severe* limitation: Anybody can change it at any time. In FileMaker's preferences window, under the General tab, FileMaker lets anyone type in any name they want. This characteristic means it's *easy* for someone to pretend to be someone else. For this reason, you should never rely on the user name for security purposes. If you want to secure a scripted process, the extended privilege feature described on page 606 is safer and makes it much easier to update accounts and privilege sets.

Handling Security Errors

If your script tries to do something that the user isn't allowed to do, FileMaker shows the error message in Figure 16-18. If you turn error capture on in your script, this error doesn't show on the screen. Instead, you can use the Get (Last-Error) function to check for an error (page 549). That way, you can have the script display a custom message box, or email you the name of the misbehaving person, or take some other action. The most common security-related error is number 200: Record Access is Denied. (If you're interested in learning more about error codes, check out the resources in Appendix B.)

Figure 16-18:
When someone tries something your security setup doesn't allow, he sees this message— even if it's a script that's breaking the rules. Unfortunately, FileMaker doesn't tell him—or you—what it's trying to do.

Running Scripts with Full Access Privileges

Sometimes you *want* the script to do its duty even though the user doesn't have the necessary privileges. For example, you may want to remove an accountant's ability to delete Invoice records since she's not supposed to delete any orders. But you may still want to let her run a script that finds old completed invoices, exports them to an archive, and then deletes them. Since this script is careful to delete only invoices that are ready to go, the accountants can safely run it when necessary.

For those kinds of circumstances, FileMaker lets you specify when a script should run with full access privileges for *anyone*. In other words, the script overrides the normal restrictions you set up in the user's privilege set. At the bottom of the Edit Script dialog box, just turn on the "Run script with full access privileges" option (page 472). With this option turned on, the script dutifully deletes the invoices even though the accountant running it isn't allowed to delete records in the Invoice or Line Item tables herself.

Even when you set a script to run with full access privileges in this way, you can still prevent some folks from running it by switching it to "no access" in the Custom Script Privileges window for a privilege set (page 598). You can also make the script check for an extended privilege and take appropriate actions for different people.

Managing Security with Scripts

ScriptMaker's Edit Script window (Figure 13-2) has an entire section called Accounts. It includes six steps that give you some control over the security system from your scripts. All of these steps require full access privileges to work. If you don't manage a lot of accounts in your database, you might not find much use for these steps. But if you have a large organization, or one that has lots of turnover—like a school system that's constantly adding new teachers or graduating a whole class of students who no longer need access to databases for class work—these script steps can save tons of time and effort.

Add Account

FileMaker actually lets you add new accounts to a database from a script—and for good reason. If you build a system that uses several databases, and you can't use external authentication, the Add Account step is your best friend. Instead of adding each account to all your files manually, try this: Write a script that asks for the account name and password with a custom dialog box, and stores them in global fields. Then use scripts in each file to add the same account to every file at once. When you're all done, be sure to clear the password from the global field to protect it from prying eyes.

Or, if you have to populate your brand-new file with a huge number of users when you're first installing your database, you save tons of time creating accounts if you have an electronic list of user names and passwords. Import them (page 623) into a table, and then use a looping script to create hundreds of accounts in a few seconds. The Add Account step lets you specify the account name and password using calculations, but you have to select a specific privilege set for all users in the loop. If you want to script the creation of accounts with different privilege sets, use the If/Else If steps and several copies of the Add Account step.

Delete Account

If you're going to create accounts with a script, why not delete them too? The Delete Account script needs only an account name—and you can supply it with a calculation. With this script, you can build the other half of your multi-file account management system.

Warning: If you write a script that adds or deletes accounts, pay special attention to its security settings. It's all too easy to give a database the tightest security FileMaker allows, then leave a gaping security hole through a script. Customize privilege sets so that only you (or a trusted few) can run it, and *don't* put it on the Scripts menu.

Reset Account Password

If lots of people use your database, forgotten passwords will undoubtedly become your worst nightmare. You could spend all day changing passwords for people. Why not write a script that can reset a password to something generic and then email it to the user? If you set the script to run with full access privileges, you can even delegate password resetting to someone else. The Reset Account Password step needs an account name and a new password to do its job.

Change Password

This odd step doesn't see the light of day very often. After all, folks can change their own passwords with the File → Change Password command (it only shows in accounts that don't have full access). You could use this step to create a Change Password button if you have users who aren't very good at remembering where menu commands are either.

Enable Account

Once you've created a bunch of new accounts using the Add Account step, this step lets you turn them on and off at will. That way, you can create accounts for, say, an entire class of students, and later turn on accounts for those who've arrived on campus. This step does the same thing as *make active* and *make inactive*) in the Edit Accounts dialog box, and it works only when there's a valid account name.

Re-Login

The most exciting step in the Accounts section is Re-Login. It provides a function that doesn't exist anywhere else in FileMaker. Namely, it lets you switch to a different account without closing the file, which gives you almost superhuman ability to test security settings. Instead of opening and closing the files until your mouse button wears out, just run a Re-Login script. Add steps in the script that set global fields on pertinent layouts to Get (AccountName) and Get (PrivilegeSet) so you can keep track of what you're testing as you Re-Login over and over.

You can also use Re-Login when someone inevitably calls you to his desk to show you a problem in the database. Just re-login as an account with full access and then you can poke around and find out what's happening *on his computer*. When you re-login, you're not just saving time not closing and reopening the file. You can actually work in the same window, on the same record, with the same found set and sort order without all the trouble of recreating the situation back at your desk. Again, since you can re-login only from a script, consider adding a Re-Login script to the Scripts menu in every database you create.

Exporting and Importing

You may have forgotten it by now—building a big database can make you feel like a slave to your computer—but the point of a database is to make managing information more efficient. Nothing illustrates this point more quickly than File-Maker's ability to suck data into your database from various sources, and dump it back out again in assorted ways.

If you have *data* of almost any kind—spreadsheets full of figures, lists of names and phone numbers, a vast corporate database, electronic orders in XML, folders full of pictures or text documents—FileMaker can *import* it directly into your database. On the other hand, if your data is already in FileMaker, you can *export* it to lists, other databases, XML, or almost any other format imaginable. FileMaker takes a wonderfully flexible approach: It lets you handle simple imports and exports with just a click or two, and provides the features to tackle the most complex cases as well—if you (or some hired help) are willing to do the necessary work.

Exporting a File

When you export data, FileMaker needs to know *what* data to export. You tell it with the Export dialog box (Figure 17-1). The Table pop-up menu shows you what FileMaker considers the *current table*—in this case, Customers. Below it, the Field list shows every field in the current layout for that table. But click the pop-up menu, and you'll see that you can choose Current Table ("Table Name"), which shows you all the fields defined in the current table. You're also welcome to pick other tables from the pop-up menu and see their fields. When you choose fields from other tables, you're still exporting Customer records. If you include fields from other tables, FileMaker gets the values from the first record related to each customer record.

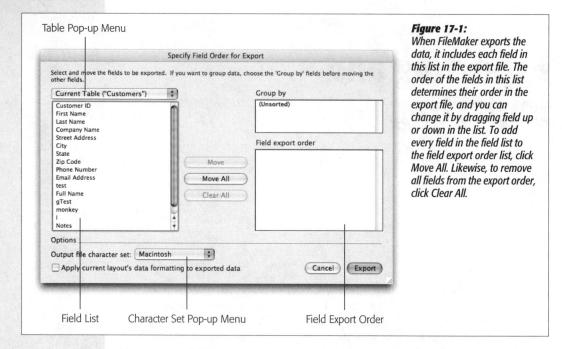

Table Pop-up Menu

Figure 17-1:
When FileMaker exports the data, it includes each field in this list in the export file. The order of the fields in this list determines their order in the export file, and you can change it by dragging field up or down in the list. To add every field in the field list to the field export order list, click Move All. Likewise, to remove all fields from the export order, click Clear All.

Field List   Character Set Pop-up Menu   Field Export Order

To choose a field for export, select it and click Move. FileMaker adds the field to the "Field export order" list, but doesn't actually move it there. Rather, the field stays in the list because you may want to export the same field *twice* in the same export file. Imagine, for example, you are creating an export file that needs the billing address info in the first four fields, and the shipping address info in the next four fields. Since your database has only one set of address fields, you can export them twice so the resulting file has the right number of fields. (Unfortunately, you can't ask FileMaker to export a blank field. If you often export to a format that needs fields you don't have, and leaving them blank is OK, just export an empty global field in each one's place.)

Tip: If a field isn't on the current layout, it doesn't show up in the export field list, so if you're wasting time scrolling through fields that you don't need, switch to a simpler layout from the same table. But if you can't find a field that you *know* is in the table, use the pop-up menu to choose Current Table. That way, you'll get a list of all the fields in the table, regardless of which ones are on the current layout.

At the bottom of the window, the Character Set pop-up menu lets you tell File-Maker how to *encode* characters in the export file so the receiving computer can read them properly. For instance, if you're using Mac OS X and you know the person receiving the export file is using Windows, it probably makes sense to choose the Windows (ANSI) choice. Unfortunately, the conversion from Macintosh to

Windows or Windows to Mac is imperfect, so some less common characters may be switched for others in the output file. Unicode is the best choice, assuming your recipient can accept it, because it can handle *all* the characters you might have in your database (even foreign language characters like Chinese and Korean).

Finally, the checkbox called "Apply current layout's data formatting to exported data" is a little misleading. It has nothing to do with font, size, style, or color. Rather, when you turn this option on, FileMaker formats numbers, dates, times, and timestamps according to the formatting options for each field on the layout—number of decimal places, date formats, and so forth. If you leave this option off, FileMaker exports the data exactly as it was originally entered.

Note: The "Group by" list lets you sort data as you export it. You'll learn how this feature works in the upcoming "grouped Export" section.

Here's an example of a typical database export. You've hired a printing company to print, address, and mail personalized cards to all your customers at holiday time. To do the job, the card company needs a list of names and addresses. Instead of typing all your customer info by hand, you can produce the list by exporting it from your database in the appropriate format. Often, plain text is fine, so that's what this example uses.

1. **Switch to the Customers layout.**

   Like many FileMaker features, the Export command is layout based. That is, it decides which table to export (and from which table occurrence to find related data) by looking at the current layout. To export customer records, you need to be on a layout associated with the Customers table.

2. **Choose Records → Show All Records.**

   If this command is dimmed, then all records are already showing. Otherwise, take this step to ensure that you export *every* customer.

3. **Choose File → Export Records. If the command isn't available, you're probably in Find mode, so switch to Browse mode.**

   You can also export from Layout and Preview modes, too, should the need arise. The Export Records to File dialog box appears. It looks a lot like a normal Save dialog box, except that it has a pop-up menu at the bottom called Type.

4. **Name the file *Holiday Card List.txt*, and choose any location you want.**

   When FileMaker exports data, it creates a new file and puts the data in it. You use this window to tell FileMaker what to call the file and where to put it.

5. **From the Type pop-up menu, choose Comma-Separated Text, and then click Save.**

   You'll learn what each of these types means in the next section. The Specify Field Order for Export window appears (Figure 17-2).

---

6. **While pressing Ctrl (Windows) or ⌘ (Mac), select these fields in the field list: *First Name, Last Name, Company Name, Street Address, City, State,* and *Zip Code*. Then click Move.**

   FileMaker adds the highlighted fields to the field export order list.

Tip: If you want to export most of your fields, but not quite all of them, it may be faster to click the Move All button, then clear the few you don't want from the Field export order list.

---

7. **Click Export.**

   FileMaker creates the file and returns you to your database.

So what just happened? If you open the Holiday Card List file you just created, you see names, company names, and addresses from your customers file. Dig a little deeper and you notice a few things:

- Each *record* is on its own line (if the program you're viewing the file in wraps lines, it might look like a record goes across two or more lines, but there's a return character at the *end* of each record).

- Each field value is in quotes, and there are commas between them.

These factors are important because this file conforms to a *standard*. Other programs—including the program used by the card printing company—that support files in the Comma-Separated Text format can read this file and grab the data.

Grouped Exports

When you were learning about exporting data above, you may have noticed the "Group by" list in the Specify Field Order for Export dialog box. Under normal circumstances, you see "(Unsorted)" in this list. But if you sort the records in the found set *before* choosing the Export Records command, you see instead a list of the fields in your sort order, each with a checkbox by its name. You can see this in action in Figure 17-2.

If you opt to group the data, you get just *one* record in the export file for each *unique* value in the "group by" field. For example, if you export 300 people records, grouped by state, you get one record for each state. Why would you ever want to do this? Because you can include *summary* fields in your export list and FileMaker properly summarizes all the records represented by each group. You could see, for example, *how many* people you have in each state.

You're free to select as many fields as you want in the "group by" list. If you select more than one, you get a hierarchical list of records, similar to a sub-summary report (Chapter 6). For example, if you sort first by state, then by city, and turn on the checkbox next to both fields in the "group by" list, you get a list of states, and below each state, you see one record for each city in that state. Again, summary fields included in your export show proper totals for both the state as a whole, and each city.

Figure 17-2:
When your data is sorted, FileMaker shows the sort fields in the "Group by" list. By turning on one or more of these checkboxes, you tell FileMaker you want to group the data in the export file.

Export Formats

When exporting data, you always create a file, but you get to decide what *format* the file should be. In the last example, you exported your data to a Comma-Separated Text file. This example is one of the many file formats FileMaker can produce when it exports. Most formats exist simply because computer software has put forth a lot of standards in the last 50 years, and FileMaker wants to be as flexible as possible. Some formats do have unique advantages, though.

The first question you need to ask is, "Where is the data going?" Your export format choice almost always depends on what the person you're sending it to needs, and most of the available formats are uncommon types you only use if the person on the other end asks for it. These include SYLK, DBF, DIF, WKS, and BASIC.

The remaining formats are explained below:

- **Tab-Separated Text** and **Comma-Separated Text** are very common formats for database data. They put each record on its own line. With Tab-Separated Text, you get a tab between each field value, while Comma-Separated Text has quotes around field values, and commas between them. Almost every program in the world that can import data supports one of these formats. If you're not sure, try Tab-Separated Text first—it's the most common.

- The **Merge** format is just like Comma-Separated Text, with one difference: The first line of the file shows individual field names. The advantage is that when you import this file in another program, you can see what each field is called, making it easier to get the right data. Unfortunately, most programs don't expect this extra line, and treat it as another record. People most often use this format for mail merge in word processing programs.

- If you want to put the data on a Web page, use **HTML Table**. The resulting file isn't suitable for importing into another program, but it can be displayed nicely in a Web browser. You can also open the file, copy the HTML table from inside it, and paste it into another Web page.

Where's My Style?

Most of FileMaker's export formats are *text based*. In other words, what gets produced is just a normal plain text file. The *structure* of this file determines which format it is, but you can open them all in Notepad or TextEdit and read them directly. A side effect of this reality is that none of them support *styles*. In other words, if you go to great lengths to change the first names in all your records so the font matches the customer's personality, you can kiss you hard work goodbye when you export.

In addition to the font, you lose the size, style, and color of the text. The notable exception to this rule is the FileMaker Pro format. Since this export format creates another FileMaker Pro database, all the formatting you painstakingly put in place is preserved.

If you *must* have text styles in your exported data, there is an option, but it ain't pretty. FileMaker has two calculation functions designed to aid this process: GetAsCSS and GetAsSVG.

Each function takes a single text parameter and returns a snippet of ordinary text with style information embedded using special *tags*. GetAsCSS produces text that can be put on a Web page. When viewed in a Web browser, the text takes on its original fonts, sizes, styles, and colors. GetAsSVG works the same way, but uses a different tagging scheme: the one used in the SVG, or Scalable Vector Graphics format.

To take advantage of these functions, you'd need to create a calculation field with a formula something like this:

```
GetAsCSS ( First Name )
```

You would then export *this* field instead of the First Name field. If you do this with the HTML Table export format, you get properly formatted text on your Web page. More realistically, you'd use these along with the XML format and a special XSLT style sheet that produces a Web page or SVG image. You'll learn more about this option at the end of this chapter.

- The **FileMaker Pro** format is your best choice if your data is destined to go back into FileMaker some day, or if you just want to view and work with the exported data directly. When you choose this format, FileMaker creates a brand new database with just one table and only the fields you choose to export. This format is the *only* one that preserves font, style, size, and color in field data (see the box above) and one of the few that supports repeating fields (page 109).

Tip: Usually, if you just want to export records from one FileMaker file to another, you don't have to export them first. Just go to the database where you want the data to *end up* and import them directly (page 623). Of course, if one database is in South Africa and the other is in Tibet, then by all means export them first.

- For the ultimate in flexibility, choose **XML**—the un-format. When you export XML, you get to apply something called an XSLT Style sheet. An XSLT Style sheet is a document written in a programming language all its own that tells FileMaker exactly how the exported data looks. If you need to produce an export format that FileMaker doesn't support directly, XSLT is the way to do it. But be forewarned: XSLT is *not* in the same league as FileMaker itself, ease-of-use-wise. Here is where you might need some hired help. XSLT is introduced briefly at the end of this chapter.

Tip: Although it applies to *one field value* and not a set of records, don't forget about the Edit → Export Field Contents command. This command lets you export the data in the current field to a file. Text, number, date, time, and timestamp fields are exported to a plain text file. Container fields create a file whose type is appropriate for the data in the field.

- Last but not least, you can choose **Excel** to create a bona fide spreadsheet. When you choose this format, FileMaker opens an extra dialog box, which lets you put FileMaker's field names in the first row of your new spreadsheet. You can even give your Excel file a worksheet Name, document Title, Subject, and Author if you so desire.

Regardless of which format you choose, the Export Records to File dialog box has two options that let you determine what happens to the file after FileMaker creates it. Choose "Automatically open file" to avoid hunting down the file on your hard drive and launching it yourself. And "Create email with file as attachment" does just what it promises—opens your email program and creates a new message with your fresh new document attached. To share your date, you just need to supply the email address, add a subject line, and click Send.

Save/Send Records As

After wading through the technical details about FileMaker's amazing flexibility in exporting to practically any format you might need, the following two export types should give you some breathing room. Forget about arcane formatting rules and settle into more familiar territory. Gone too, is the need to specify a field order for export. The File → Save/Send command lets you choose between an Excel spreadsheet and a PDF (Portable Document Format) document. Both commands grab whatever fields are on the current layout and whip them and their data into the shape you choose.

Excel

If people need to work with the data you send them, but they aren't lucky enough to have FileMaker, you can create an Excel file for them, as shown in Figure 17-3. Once you've sent the file, they're free to do anything to the data that Excel allows–make a table, create a chart, or run totals and summaries.

The Save option is a pop-up menu that lets you choose between the "Records being browsed" or the "Current Record" so you don't even have to do a find if all you want to do is send the current record. Like the other formats under the Export menu, you have the option to "Automatically open file" and "Create email with file as attachment," so it's easy to check your work and create a quick email with the data your boss just asked to email her.

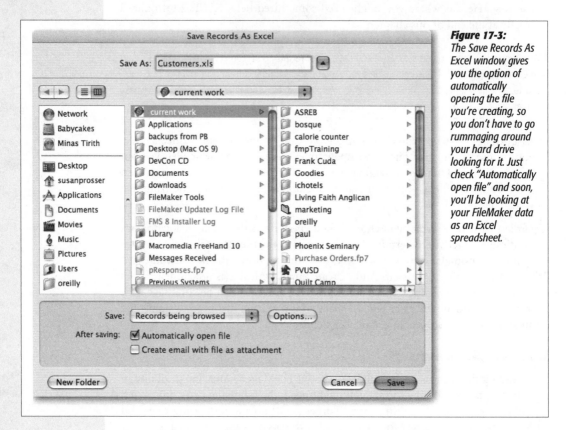

Figure 17-3:
The Save Records As Excel window gives you the option of automatically opening the file you're creating, so you don't have to go rummaging around your hard drive looking for it. Just check "Automatically open file" and soon, you'll be looking at your FileMaker data as an Excel spreadsheet.

If you click Options, you can set up some basic details for your new Excel file. For example, you can choose whether you want your FileMaker field names put in the first row of the spreadsheet. You can also type in a file name and a title, subject, and author (which appear in the Properties dialog box).

Portable Document Format (PDF)

PDF files are viewable by just about anybody with a computer. With PDF files, you get to choose exactly how the data looks, since this format preserves your beautifully crafted layouts. With FileMaker's layout tools, your keen design sense and the Save/Send Record as PDF command, you could use email to distribute invoices, product catalogs, sales brochures, or annual reports. You can even send vision impaired people a file their software can read out loud. Even if all you need to do is send people data they can see, but can't change, then a PDF file is just what the software engineer ordered.

FREQUENTLY ASKED QUESTION

Making It Fit

A lot of FileMaker's Export formats use special characters for important things. For instance, the Tab-Separated Text format uses a return character to separate records. What happens if I have a return character in my field?

Good question! Special characters are one of those problems with no ideal solution. But FileMaker does the best it can within the limitations of each export file type. For a file to be called Tab-Separated Text, for example, you simply *can't* have return characters inside records. It's just against the rules. In this particular case, FileMaker turns the return character into something else, called a *vertical tab*, which is a standard but rarely-used character left over from when computers had green screens. Presumably, you don't have any of these in your fields (you can't *type* them, so it is a pretty safe bet you don't), so it's easy enough to turn vertical tab characters back into return characters when you open the file in another program. In fact, that's exactly what happens when you *import* a Tab-Separated Text file into FileMaker.

Another character of concern is the quote mark. If you have these in your fields, and you export a Comma-Separated Text file, FileMaker has to do something with them so they don't interfere with the quotes around field values. In this case, FileMaker turns your quote mark into two quote marks together.

That doesn't *sound* like a solution, but it is. If you assume any quote mark that is *immediately* followed by a second one is really just data, and not the end quote mark for a field value, you can figure out which is which in the export file. Most programs that support Comma-Separated Text understand this convention. (You might think commas would also be a problem with Comma-Separated Text, but they're not. Since every field value is in quotes, commas are OK. Only the commas *between* quoted values are considered field separators.)

The HTML and XML formats have all kinds of special characters, but each has a special "entity" form that's used if they're supposed to be treated as ordinary data. FileMaker converts any such characters appropriately, and *every* program that processes these formats understands the conventions.

Finally, FileMaker has a data-structure concept that most formats simply don't understand: repeating fields. The idea that *one* field could hold *several* values is foreign to most database programs. When you export repeating fields, FileMaker pulls another freaky character out of its hat: It separates each value with a character called the Group Separator. Thankfully, this action is almost never a problem because you generally don't export repeating field data to a file that needs to be read by a program that doesn't understand repeating fields. One last note: The FileMaker Pro export format obviously *does* directly support repeating fields.

Tip: The most common PDF viewer, Adobe Acrobat, is a free download at *http://www.adobe.com/ products/acrobat/readstep2.html*. Mac OS X also comes preloaded with its own PDF viewer, called Preview.

The basic choices are the same as for Excel. You choose between sending just the current record or the whole found set. You can have the file opened in a PDF viewer or attached to a new, blank email just as soon as FileMaker's created it. But the PDF Option set is much richer. There are three tabs—Document, Security and Initial View. Starting with the Document tab, you can set:

- **Title.** This title isn't the name you give the file in the dialog box. It's an additional title that becomes part of the properties of the document. Most, but not all, PDF viewer programs let you see a file's properties.

- **Subject.** This document property helps you tell a series of similar documents apart from each other.

- **Author.** This document property is usually your name, but may also be the name of your company or department. Again, it helps you organize a bunch of similar files.

- **Keywords.** Some file management programs can search these keywords to locate documents.

- **Compatibility.** Choose from "Acrobat 5 and later" or "Acrobat 6 and later." Choose the lower number if you think your recipient might not have the latest and greatest PDF viewer.

- **Number pages from.** You can make a different numbering system than the one you have in FileMaker.

- **Include.** You can set a limited page number range with these options, so that only a part of the found set is included in the PDF file. You may have to go to Preview mode in FileMaker first, though, to help you set the page range properly.

Note: You can see the PDF file's Title, Subject, and Author in Adobe Acrobat's PDF viewer's Document Properties Summary window. For those on OS X, whose PDF viewer of choice is Preview, these items aren't available.

In the Security Tab, you can decide how much access you give your recipients when they receive your file. You can choose:

- **Require password to open the file.** Click the checkbox to turn this option on. Then enter a password. This checkbox is useful if you're selling a catalog and provide passwords only to people who've paid to receive it. Then, of course, there's the standard use; you just don't want every Malcolm, Reese, and Dewey poking around in your PDF files.

- **Require password to control printing, editing and security.** Click the checkbox to turn this option on and enter a password. You might want your PDF freely distributed, but not so freely used. If so, don't require a password to open the file, but lock it down so nobody without a password can use the material without your permission. With this option checked, a whole raft of new options become available. You can set:

- **Printing.** Choose from Not Permitted, Low Resolution (150 dpi) or High Resolution. These options would protect photographic or other artwork images that you want to send in a catalog, but don't want people to reprint freely.

- **Editing.** These options let your recipients interact with your document, but still allow you to protect your intellectual or business property. You can choose from **Not Permitted** for total control, restrict recipients to filling in form fields only, and so forth.

- **Enable copy of text, images and other content.** With this option checked, recipients can copy and paste material from your PDF file.

- **Allow text to be read by screen reading software.** This option allows people with vision or reading problems to let their screen reading programs read your document out loud.

The final tab in the PDF Options window is probably be the one you'll use the least. But if you like to control which PDF viewer options are visible when your recipient first opens your PDF file, then Initial View is the panel for you:

- **Show.** Your choices include **Page Only** (just the FileMaker layout, with no extra tools or panels), **Bookmarks Panel and Page**, or **Pages Panel and Page** to offer viewers some navigation options.

- **Page Layout.** Control the way the PDF viewer displays multipage documents. If you choose **Default**, your recipients' preferred view remains in force. But you can also specify **Single Page, Continuous,** or **Magnification**.

Importing Data

If you need to import information into FileMaker, you'll soon gain a whole new appreciation for the term *flexibility*. FileMaker can handle the most common data types—and quite a few lesser-known ones—with the same straightforward process. You tell FileMaker which file contains your incoming data, and then show it how you want to match the incoming data (the source) with the fields in your file (the target). This procedure is called *field mapping* and it's the trickiest part of any import. See Figure 17-4 for a preview of the Import Field Mapping dialog box.

The confusing part comes when you to try to match fields in the source with fields in the target. You can't rearrange the source, but you can drag the fields in your target table up and down. Your job is to line these fields up with the proper source data fields. For instance, you want to move the First Name field so it lines up horizontally with the first name shown at left. Although it's tempting to jump around and move fields as you happen to spot them, this place is one where a formal approach works best. Start at the top, with the first source field, match it, and then move along to the second one.

Between each source and destination field, you see one of two symbols: an arrow or a line. The arrow means FileMaker plans to import the data on the left side into the field on the right. A line tells FileMaker to ignore this particular piece of data in the import file. Click an arrow to change it to a line, or vice versa. (You sometimes see *other* symbols between fields, but they only show up when you change the Import Action setting. You'll learn about that on page 627.)

Tip: If you forget what the importing icons mean, never fear. The Import Field Mapping window has a legend at the bottom right.

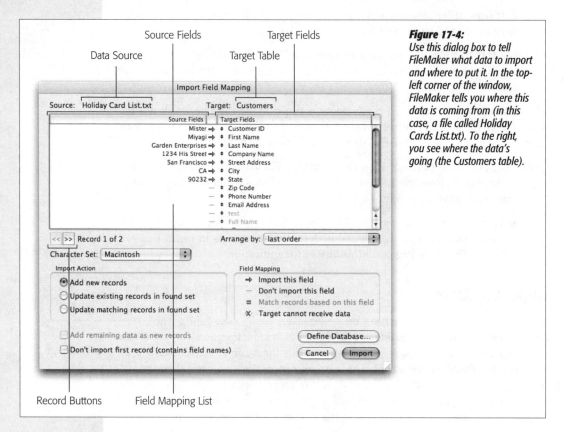

Source Fields   Target Fields

Data Source   Target Table

Figure 17-4:
Use this dialog box to tell FileMaker what data to import and where to put it. In the top-left corner of the window, FileMaker tells you where this data is coming from (in this case, a file called Holiday Cards List.txt). To the right, you see where the data's going (the Customers table).

Record Buttons   Field Mapping List

For the sake of illustration, here's the simple rundown on how importing works:

1. **Choose File → Import Records → File.**

   FileMaker can import data from all kinds of sources. In this case, you're telling it you want to import records from a *file*. When you choose this command, the standard Open File dialog box appears.

2. **Choose the Holiday Card List.txt file you just created, and then click Open.**

   The Import Field Mapping dialog box pops up.

3. **Drag the fields in the target field list so they line up properly with the input data.**

As you drag, you can ignore the arrows completely. You can fix them once you've got the fields in the right order.

Tip: If your data source has a field that doesn't match any existing field in your target table, just click the Define Database button to create a new field, and then return to your field mapping. See page 629 for how to handle an entire *table* that's missing.

Mapping Out Your Options

FileMaker's smart, but when it comes to something as pic-ayune as deciding which field to put where, there's no sub-stitute for human input. As you can see in Figure 17-4, the Import Field Mapping dialog box looks a trifle crowded, but every tool, button, and gizmo has saved a life (or career, anyway).

For example, your input data source may or may not include field names. If it doesn't, the Source Fields list shows you the first record in the import file instead. Or even if your data already has named fields, you may *want* to see some of the data being imported so you can catch (and repair) mix-ups and errors. Either way, FileMaker lets you check as many records as you wish before you import, by providing arrow buttons below the list. As you click, File-Maker replaces items in the source field list with data from the next (right) or previous (left) record. When field names are included, you see them as the *first* record. Occasionally, the format you're importing doesn't accommodate field names, but the import file has them anyway, as the first record. When this happens, turn on "Don't import first record" so FileMaker doesn't treat that record as data.

The "Arrange by" pop-up menu lets you bulk-reorder the target fields in the list. Most choices are obvious (alphabet-ical by field name, and by field type) but others aren't so clear. If you choose "matching names," FileMaker tries to match fields up by matching their names. If your input file has the same field names as your database, this option sets the right order for you. The "last order" choice restores the field order you used the last time you imported data. Choose "creation order" to see the fields in the order you created them. Finally, if you manually drag the fields in the list, FileMaker switches to the "custom import order" choice. If you decide to try one of the other arrangements, you can get back to the order you were working on by choosing "custom import order" yourself.

Finally, just like the export dialog box, this window lets you specify a character set (page 614). This time, though, you don't decide what you *want* it to be. Rather, you need to tell FileMaker what it *is*. If you're lucky, this pop-up menu is grayed out, meaning FileMaker was able to figure out the encoding itself. Otherwise, you need to make sure you make the right choice so special characters in the import file come through intact.

---

4. **Click the arrows or lines between fields until each matching field has an arrow, and each remaining field has a line.**

You can see the field mapping process in Figure 17-5. It also shows how it looks when you're done—although your import file may have different data, so your source field list looks different.

5. Make sure the "Add new records" radio button (in the Import Action area) is turned *on*.

This action tells FileMaker you want a new record created in the Customers table for each record in the import file. (The Import Field Mapping dialog box has more features, but you don't need them right now. See the box on page 625 for full detail.)

Figure 17-5:
This series of images shows the steps involved in setting the import field order (sometimes called "field mapping" or just "import order"). The first picture (top left) shows how the fields look when you first get here. To adjust the order, you drag fields on the right side up and down, as shown in the second picture (top right). When you drop a field somewhere in the list, it changes places with the one that's already there. In this example, the First Name field changes places with Customer ID. The third picture (bottom left) shows how things look once you've moved each field into place. Finally, you need to set the arrows between fields so FileMaker knows which fields to import (bottom right).

6. Click Import. When the Import Options dialog box appears (Figure 17-6), turn on "Perform auto-enter options while importing."

You want to make sure the new customers have valid customer IDs, and those come from auto-enter serial numbers.

Figure 17-6:
If you have any auto-enter fields, or you're importing repeating fields, you see this window after clicking Import. Turn off "Perform auto-enter options while importing" if you don't want FileMaker to auto-enter data in your records as they're created. When importing repeating fields, you usually want to choose "Keeping them in the original record." If you don't, FileMaker makes a new record for each repetition that has data in it.

Note: If you import into a field that has auto-enter options set, and you tell FileMaker to perform auto-enter options when importing, you might wonder *which* value will wind up in the field—the auto-entered data or the imported data. In *almost* every case, the imported data wins. The one exception: If a field is set to auto-enter a *looked up* value, FileMaker performs the lookup and thus overrides the imported value. Click Import one more time.

After a very short delay, the Import Records Summary dialog box appears (Figure 17-7). Click OK when you're done looking.

Figure 17-7:
This window appears after FileMaker completes the import operation. It tells you important information about your import, including how many records were imported. Sometimes problems can occur during import (for instance, some data in the import file might violate your field validation settings). When this happens, FileMaker may skip certain fields or whole records. This window also tells you when that happens (although it doesn't tell you which fields or records were skipped).

After the import's complete, FileMaker shows you a found set of just the records it imported. But don't reach for the Show All Records command yet: The fact that it's a found set is your safety net. If something goes wrong with your import (the wrong records came through, field mapping doesn't look right, or whatever), just delete the found set and start over. You can scan through the data and make sure you got what you wanted and that the data went into the fields you intended. You can also take this opportunity to perform other actions (like use the Replace Field Contents command) on every imported record.

Importing *Over* Existing Data

When you import data into a file that already has some records in it, the Import Action section of the Import Field Mapping dialog box (page 624) gives you three ways to specify how you want to deal with that existing data. Normally, it starts out with the "Add new records" setting turned on, meaning that FileMaker simply adds imported records to your database. Sometimes, though, you want to *update* existing records instead. For example, suppose your database holds shipping rates for every state you ship to. When your freight company updates its rates, it sends you a new file with one record for each state, and the new rates in a Rate field. If you add these records to your database, you end up with *two* records for each state, which is probably not what you want. So FileMaker gives you two other choices that let you update records as you import.

Update existing records in found set

To avoid creating duplicate records as in the shipping rates example, you can turn on "Update existing records in found set" and map just the Rate field to the appropriate field in your table. When you import, FileMaker takes the rate from the first record in the import file and puts it in the first record in the found set. It then copies the second rate into the second record. This process continues until it's imported every rate.

If your import file has more records than the found set, FileMaker simply skips the extra records. If you'd rather import *all* the records (adding new records once all those in the found set have been updated), turn on "Add remaining data as new records."

Warning: This import action is useful only if you're certain the records in the import file are in the *same order* as those in the export file. If they're not, FileMaker updates the wrong records, leaving you with incorrect data. If you aren't positive the records are in the right order, use "Update matching records in found set" instead.

Update matching records in found set

The "Update matching records in found set" works much the same way. When you import with this action, FileMaker updates data in existing records by copying it from the import file. This time, though, you get to tell FileMaker how to figure out which records in the import file match each record in the found set. You tell FileMaker this by specifying one or more *matching fields*, as described in Figure 17-8.

Figure 17-8:
When you turn on "Update matching records in found set," FileMaker lets you use a new symbol between source and target fields. In this picture, the Email Address field has an "=" symbol beside it. This symbol tells FileMaker to match records based on email address. In other words, when it imports the first record, it finds a record in the found set with the same email address. FileMaker then updates that record's data based on the import file. If FileMaker doesn't find a match, it skips the import record. It's safest to use a key field for import matching.

To get the new symbol in the field mapping list, just click the spot between fields. FileMaker now toggles between the *three* possible symbols: Import, Don't import, and Match. (If you forget what each symbol means, the "Field Mapping" area in the window reminds you.) Again, if you'd rather have FileMaker import every record in the import file, adding new records when no match is found, turn on "Add remaining data as new records."

Creating Tables on Import

All the importing you've learned about so far assumes that your tables and fields are already defined. In other words, your target table is already in place when you choose your source file. But when you're doing a big conversion job (say, moving a 35-file database system from FileMaker 6 format to FileMaker 7), it'll take quite some time to create all those tables and fields. And even though you have access to the Define Database dialog box while you're importing, this process isn't quick or easy when you've got hundreds of fields coming in from dozens of files. FileMaker's already thought of that, and offers to handle the tedious work of table and field creation for you.

Choose Import → File and select a data source. In the Import Field Mapping window, there's a handy pop-up menu called Target. Click it, and you see the current table (remember that's based on the layout that was active when you chose the Import command), all your other tables (grayed out, so you can't choose them), and a very useful command, New Table (Data Source). The stuff in parentheses is the name of your data source and the name FileMaker gives the new table it creates for you. If you already have a table with the same name as your data source, FileMaker appends a number to the end of the new table's name.

Choose New Table, then click Import. FileMaker creates a table and an appropriate set of fields for you, and then populates the new fields with data. You also get a simple form layout for your new table and a table occurrence on your relationships graph. You can treat this table just like one you created yourself. Start hooking it up to other table occurrences and you have a full-fledged related table.

Tip: See page 683 to see how FileMaker Pro Advanced lets you import tables and fields, *without* the data that normally comes with them.

When you let FileMaker create fields for you, it does its best to create the field types you want. For instance, if the data source is a FileMaker file, your new fields match the old file's field names and field types. But if the source is a plain text file with no formatting information to go by, FileMaker doesn't have any names to go by, so the new fields become text fields and get the prosaic names of f1, f2, f3, and so on. In either case, you should check the fields in your new table to make sure you get the names and field types you want. You have to manually define any calculations you need.

Finally, it pays off to think about the order in which you import your files. File-Maker can handle data from related files (lookup fields, and calculations based on relationships) for you if you import the file that contains the supporting records first, and then the file containing the dependent records. If you get the order mixed up, or if your relationships are so complicated that you can't import files in a perfectly clean order, then plan to spend some time cleaning up broken field references after your import.

Converting Files Without Importing

If using the import button is just too much trouble, or you don't need much control over how it's handled, FileMaker has an even simpler way of creating a File-Maker file from another data source, like an Excel file or a text file. Just choose File → Open and select the file you want to convert. (On the Mac, you can convert files by dragging them onto FileMaker's application icon.)

Tip: If you can see the file you want to convert, but you can't select it because it's grayed out, change the option in the "Files of Type" (Windows) or "Show" (Mac) pop-up list. If your file is one of the formats File-Maker supports, you can select it once you identify its type.

If FileMaker finds data with a first row that looks like field names, it asks you if you want to use those when FileMaker defines fields. If it can't find anything that looks like field names, you get those old standbys, f1, f2, f3. In addition to a single table and the appropriate number of fields (complete with data, of course), you get two very plain layouts. One is a generic form layout, showing one record at the time, and the other is a simple columnar list.

Use this same process (the Open file command), if you're converting files from older versions of FileMaker to the .fp7 format. Converting old files is a huge topic and most people find that conversion requires a certain amount of retrofitting, either to make scripts and other things that break during conversion whole again or to take full advantage of the .fp7 multiple-table-per-file power. (FileMaker offers two excellent white papers on this subject for download at *http://www.filemaker.com/support/whitepapers.html*. Look under Migration Topics.)

Import Data Sources

You've learned about the most common importing task—when your data's coming in from a single file. But you have other needs and FileMaker's got other choices. File → Import is an entire sub-menu, with commands to suit even the most demanding database manager. From there, you get to pick where the data should come from (the *data source*), and you get several choices.

File

The File → Import → File command shows an Open File dialog box. Select any file that matches one of the export formats explained earlier in this chapter. You see your old friend, the Import Field Mapping dialog box (Figure 17-5). Match your source to your target, and away you go.

You can also use a similar command when you have to move data from one table to another within the same file. Go to your target layout and choose File → Import Records → File. In the dialog box, choose the database you're in, and you see the Import Field Mapping dialog box. Select the table that's your data source from the Source pop-up menu and you're ready to go.

Folder

Using this command, you can pick any folder, and FileMaker imports the contents of each appropriate file in that folder. It creates *one* record for each file it imports, and puts the file into the field you specify. In other words, if you have a folder full of letters you've written in a folder, you can import them into a Letters database using this command. The complete text of each letter would go in a field, with one field per letter. (Remember, though, that FileMaker only supports pictures, movies, and plain text files when importing. If your letters are in Microsoft Word format, for example, you're out of luck.)

Choosing File → Import → Folder summons the Folder of Files Import Options dialog box shown in Figure 17-9.

Figure 17-9:
This window is what you see when you choose the import folder command. In the top part of the window, you get to choose which folder to import (click Specify). In the bottom half, you decide what kind of files you're interested in.

Normally, FileMaker finds only files directly inside the folder you pick—it ignores any *other folders* contained inside. You have to turn on "Include all enclosed folders" to make FileMaker look inside those folders, too. With this option turned on, it digs as deep as necessary to find every file.

Once you've picked a folder, you get to decide what kind of files to import. You have only two choices: "Picture and movie files" and "Text files." In the first case, FileMaker ignores every file that isn't a supported picture or movie type. You get to decide whether the files themselves are inserted in the container field, or just references to them. If you choose the "Text files" option instead, it seeks out only plain text files.

Importing a folder of pictures or movies

When you choose the "Pictures and movie files" option and click Continue, you might be in for a bit of a wait. Depending on the number of files FileMaker has to look through, you may see a progress dialog box for as long as several minutes. When the import is complete, you see the now-familiar Import Field Mapping dialog box. But the list of source fields looks entirely unfamiliar—in a good way. As outlined in Figure 17-10, FileMaker translates the file information into logical field types, perfect for database use.

Figure 17-10:
When you import a folder full of pictures, FileMaker practically reads your mind. It not only lets you dump the picture into a container field, but it also offers you the chance to put the file name and full path into text fields. Best of all, FileMaker can shrink the picture down to a thumbnail and put that into a container field too, which saves space by reducing size and resolution. The thumbnails appear even when the original images aren't available (if a network drive is unavailable, for instance). And the thumbnail's reduced in size and resolution, so it doesn't take up much space.

Importing a folder of text files

When you choose to import text files, you still get an Import Field Mapping dialog box. This time, the source field list includes Text Content, File Name, and File Path. Each expects to be imported into a text field.

Digital Camera

If you're using Mac OS X, the File → Import Records menu has a Digital Camera option. Unfortunately, this option relies on a feature unique to Mac OS X, so you can't import directly from a camera on Windows. You have to download the images to your computer first, and then import them. (There's a workaround, if you can set up your camera to show up as a USB disk on Windows, In that case, use the Import → Folder command to import images directly from the camera.)

When you first plug your camera into your Mac, chances are iPhoto launches and prepares to import the images. To avoid any potential confusion, quit iPhoto first (or be careful not to click Import in iPhoto while FileMaker's working with the camera).

Tip: If you import from your camera to FileMaker a lot, you can tell iPhoto to get out of the way: Just launch Image Capture (in your Applications folders) and in its Preferences → Camera tab, select File-Maker. If you use iPhoto sometimes, and FileMaker others, choose No Application in the pop-up menu instead. That way, you get to decide what program each time.

With the camera connected, choose File → Import Records → Digital Camera. The verbosely titled FileMaker Pro Photo Import Options dialog box appears (Figure 17-11).

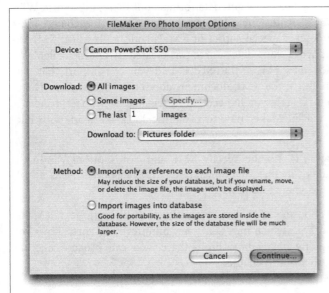

Figure 17-11:
This dialog box appears when you import from a digital camera in Mac OS X. The device pop-up menu lets you pick which camera to import from (on the off chance you have several connected). You also get to decide which images to import, where to put them (more on these options in a moment), and whether or not you want to store just references to the pictures.

If you want to import *everything* on the camera, turn on "All images." On the other hand, if you just want, for example, the last five shots you took, turn on the last radio button—"The last [blank] images"—and put the right number in its box. Finally, you can choose "Some images" and click Specify to see a list of image thumbnails to choose from.

Even if you want to import all the images, the "Some images" choice can come in handy. It's the only place you can *rotate* the images before you import them. There's no direct way to rotate an image once it's in the container field. You have to export it, rotate it in another program, and then insert it again.

Even if you're importing the images directly into FileMaker (rather than just a reference), it still puts them in the folder you specify in the "Download to" pop-up menu. If you want to, you can simply delete them when you're done. (If you're storing references, though, the folder you pick becomes very important. If you import the pictures and then move them to a different folder, the references are wrong, and the pictures don't display in FileMaker.)

When you're through making choices, click Continue. The Import Field Mapping window that appears next is loaded with source fields this time. FileMaker lets you import loads of image data along with the pictures, including dimensions, resolution, shot date and time, and all that photographer-speak stuff you see when you accidentally put your camera in advanced mode.

At this point you're in familiar territory. Just match up the fields and click Import. Be prepared for a wait as it takes FileMaker longer to import full-color digital pictures than, say, zip codes.

XML Data Source

Because there are so many programs and data formats out there, the World Wide Web Consortium (W3C) created the XML format to make data exchange more predictable. FileMaker uses a special subset of XML's code, called FMPXMLRESULT, to facilitate import. If your data source was created by another FileMaker Pro database, it already uses FMPXMLRESULT, and you can import that data straight up, no chaser. But if the XML document doesn't use FileMaker's Document Type Definition (DTD), you'll need an Extensible StyleSheet Language (XSLT) document to tell FileMaker how to make the XML file work with File-Maker.

As you can see in Figure 17-12, the Specify XML and XSL Options window is where you tell FileMaker whether or not your XML Data Source needs a style sheet, and if it needs one, where to find it.

When you're finished choosing XML and XSL options, click Continue. FileMaker processes the XML and XSL (which may take a few minutes), and then shows you the Import Field Mapping dialog box. From there, you can proceed like any import, as described earlier in this chapter.

Note: XML Data Source is a timesaver if you need data from a file that's in an older version of FileMaker (pre–version 7). Normally, FileMaker requires that you convert a file before you can import data from it. But if you export its data into an XML file, and then import it as XML, you skip conversion altogether.

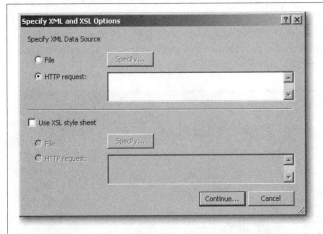

Figure 17-12:
When you import from an XML Data Source, FileMaker first asks you where to get the data from, and how to process it. You can instruct FileMaker to look in any XML file on your computer, or to fetch the XML data from a Web server (see the box on page 636).

XML and XSLT are complex languages and this book can't cover it in full. If you need to master XSLT, you can get whole books devoted to the subject. You can also find dozens of premade style sheets on FileMaker's Web site at *www.filemaker. com/technologies/xslt_library.html*.

XML Export

When you export to XML, FileMaker exports the data in the FMPXMLRESULT format, and then applies the style sheet. You create the style sheet to translate this XML into the appropriate format for your intended recipient. You have slightly more flexibility when exporting than when importing: XSLT can translate only XML documents, but it can *produce* any text-based format. So although you can *import* only XML files, you can *export* just about anything.

ODBC Data Source

The last import data source is called ODBC. This data source is a popular standard to allow programs to access information stored in database systems. For instance, if your company has an Oracle, Sybase, or Microsoft SQL Server database to manage orders, you can extract data directly from that database and import it into your FileMaker Pro database (perhaps you want to make your own reports with FileMaker).

ODBC is the most complex import data source to set up. It's a two-step process:

• First, you need to install an **ODBC Driver** for the kind of database you're connecting to. For example, if your corporate database is in Oracle, you need an

ODBC driver for Oracle. These drivers are platform specific, and most vendors only supply drivers for Microsoft Windows. If you're using Mac OS X, you can buy high-quality FileMaker compatible drivers from *www.openlinksw.com*.

- Next, you need to set up an **ODBC data source**. FileMaker doesn't connect to the database directly. Rather, it uses a data source that's been defined in the ODBC system on your computer. So you have to set up that data source first. In Microsoft Windows, you do this setting up in the ODBC control panel. In Mac OS X, you need to refer to the documentation that came with your driver (most drivers install their own data source management program).

POWER USERS' CLINIC

XML and HTTP

Sometimes the XML data you want to import is in a file on your computer. But a big part of the XML Data Source feature's power is that FileMaker can also get XML data from other computers using *HTTP*, or Hyper-Text Transport Protocol. You probably recognize this acronym because it usually sits in front of Web addresses (as in *http://www.missingmanuals.com*). HTTP is the way Web browsers talk to Web sites, but it's used for a lot more than that. Often, companies make important information available on HTTP servers in XML format. It's this kind of information that FileMaker wants to let you tap in to:

Many news-oriented Web sites make headlines and article excerpts available in XML formats called RSS or Atom. Using the XML Data Source feature in FileMaker, you could import news from *www.reuters.com* directly into your FileMaker database.

You can grab current or historical exchange rates from various sources to perform accurate currency conversions in FileMaker.

Some shippers let you track packages by downloading XML data. You can build package tracking right into FileMaker Pro.

FileMaker's XML import does have two significant limitations. First, it can't access data that's available only over a secure connection (in other words, it doesn't support HTTP over SSL, or HTTPS). If the data you need to access is only available in this form, you need to find another way.

Second, some XML data sources need information passed to them as *post arguments*—the equivalent of form fields on some Web pages. FileMaker can't send post arguments with the URL. Luckily, most data sources allow you to pass this information as part of the URL instead. Refer to the documentation for your data source for details.

Once you have a driver installed and a data source set up, you can use the File → Import Records → ODBC Data Source command. When you do, you see the Select ODBC Data Source window (Figure 17-13).

When you click Continue in this window, you probably need to enter a user name and password for the database you're connecting to. You need to get this information from the database administrator, unless you created it in the ODBC software yourself.

Next, FileMaker shows the SQL Query Builder dialog box (Figure 17-14). When you extract data from *most* databases (FileMaker being the notable exception), you have to use a special programming language called Structured Query Language, or SQL (often pronounced *sequel*). Writing an SQL *query* (or program) is a complicated affair. Luckily, in most cases, FileMaker can do it for you—you just make the right choices. (For more detail, see the box on page 638.)

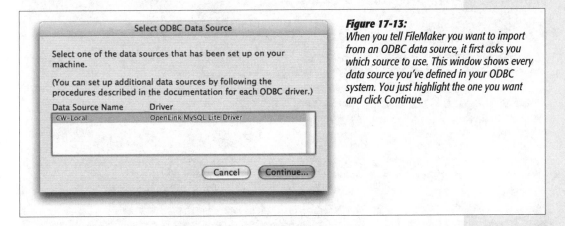

Figure 17-13:
When you tell FileMaker you want to import from an ODBC data source, it first asks you which source to use. This window shows every data source you've defined in your ODBC system. You just highlight the one you want and click Continue.

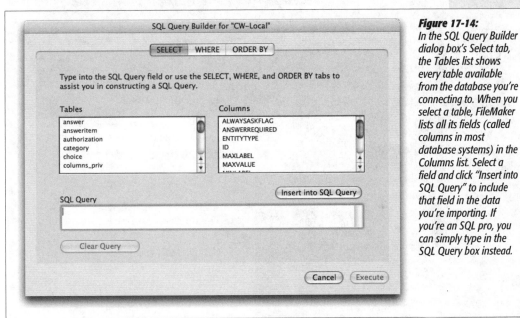

Figure 17-14:
In the SQL Query Builder dialog box's Select tab, the Tables list shows every table available from the database you're connecting to. When you select a table, FileMaker lists all its fields (called columns in most database systems) in the Columns list. Select a field and click "Insert into SQL Query" to include that field in the data you're importing. If you're an SQL pro, you can simply type in the SQL Query box instead.

When you're all finished building your query, click Execute. FileMaker performs the query, gathers the data from the data source, and shows the same Import Field Mapping dialog box you always see when importing data. If you find yourself doing a lot of ODBC imports, you might be well served by a good book on SQL.

Although the query builder supports only a little SQL, you can use *any* SQL commands supported by your database server if you type the query directly. And SQL can do *a lot.*

SQL Queries

To make use of FileMaker's query builder, you need to know just a little bit about SQL. An SQL query is made up of *clauses*, each of which influences the results you receive from the database server. Although SQL understands several clauses, the query builder window supports just three of them: SELECT, WHERE, and ORDER BY. The window has a tab for each of these.

The SELECT clause is where you tell the database what *fields* you want to import. You can include fields from more than one table if necessary. A SELECT clause alone imports *every* record in the table. If you include fields from more than one table, you get a result that might surprise you: Every record from each file is mixed in *every possible combination*. In other words, you import *lots* of records (multiply the record counts from each table to figure out how many).

The WHERE clause's job is to control which *records* get imported and how the tables are related. To specify certain records, you build find criteria into the WHERE clause. First, select a table and column from the pop-up menus. Then select something from the Operator pop-up menu. You can match this field with a value you type yourself (turn on the Value radio button) or with another field (turn on the Column radio button). Either way, enter or select the correct value. Finally, select either the And radio button or the Or radio button and turn on Not if you want to *omit* the matching records. When you're finished defining the criteria, click Insert into SQL Query.

Relationships in SQL are probably the most confusing. SQL databases don't have a relationship graph like FileMaker, so the database doesn't know how things relate to one another at all. Each time you build a query, it's your job to tell it how to relate records from one table to those in another. You do this job by matching field values in each table in the WHERE clause.

For instance, you might pick the Customer ID field from the Customers table, the "=" operator, and the Customer ID field from the Orders table. When you add a criteria like this to your WHERE clause, you've told the database how Order and Customer records relate. You can add as many criteria in this way as you need.

The last tab is called ORDER BY. This clause lets you specify a sort order for your data. It works just like FileMaker's normal Sort dialog box: Just add the fields to the Order By list, selecting Ascending or Descending as appropriate. When you've given it the order you want, click Insert into SQL Query again.

As you do these things, FileMaker builds the actual query in the SQL Query box at the bottom of the window so you can see how it comes together. If you feel adventurous, you can manually change this query at any time.

Importing and Exporting in a Script

Like almost everything else in FileMaker, you can completely control the import and export process from a script. You use the *Import Records* and *Export Records* script, which you can find in the Records section of the script steps list. You also find script steps for Save Records as Excel and Save Records as PDF, with similar options.

The Import Records Script Step

This script step has three options. First, you get to specify the data source to import from. Your choices match those in the File → Import Records menu: File, Folder, Digital Camera (Mac OS X only), XML Data, and ODBC Data. Whichever option you choose, FileMaker asks you for more information (*which* file to import, or *which* ODBC data source to use, for instance). When specifying a file, you get the standard path list dialog box. In other words, you can specify several paths if you want; FileMaker imports the first one it finds. (If you don't specify a source, your users have to do it as they run the script, in a potentially confusing series of dialog boxes. Since you're presumably providing a script to make things easier for people, it's best to store source files in a safe place and have the script escort your users to them.)

Once you've specified the source, you can turn on "Specify import order" to record the import field mapping, and other import options. Finally, you can turn on "Perform without dialog" if you want FileMaker to import the data directly, with no input from your users. If you leave this option off, FileMaker displays the Import Field Mapping dialog box when the script runs, so folks can make changes to any field mapping you specified.

The Export Records Script Step

The Export Records script step offers similar options. You can specify the output file and export order, and you can choose "Perform without dialog" if you don't want your users to see the export dialog box.

When you specify the output file, you may be surprised to see an Output File Path *List*. In other words, FileMaker lets you specify *more than one file*. This choice doesn't mean FileMaker exports more than one file, though. Instead, it exports to the first file path that is *valid*. If the first path in the list includes a folder name that doesn't exist, for example, FileMaker skips it and tries the next one.

Sharing Your Database

You've now got a solid foundation for building even the most complex database systems in FileMaker Pro. But your databases have so far been limited to just one user—you. Only the smallest small business, though, has only one person. Most databases are *multi-user databases,* used by lots of people, all at the same time. It's easy to set up any FileMaker database for lots of people to use; you simply turn on a checkbox or two. In this chapter, you'll learn about those settings, plus some of the things you can expect from FileMaker when you're sharing databases.

Before you dive in and start changing settings, consider where you're going to keep the shared file and how other people's computers connect to it. There are three types of sharing: Internet, Network, and FileMaker Server.

- **FileMaker Network.** This type of file sharing is also called *peer-to-peer.* That is, you don't use a server or any special software. You just use your ordinary computers to share files. Peer-to-peer sharing is limited to five guests. If more than five people need to use the database at the same time, use FileMaker Server.

- **Internet Sharing.** Internet sharing has its own set of benefits and tradeoffs. On the plus side, people who need access to your files don't need a copy of File-Maker. All they need is an Internet connection and a recent-model browser. On the downside, not everything you can do in FileMaker translates to the Web, so you may have to live with fewer features. FileMaker uses a type of Internet sharing called *Instant Web Publishing (IWP).* FileMaker translates your layouts to Web language according to settings you specify.

- **FileMaker Server** is the Big Daddy of FileMaker database sharing. FileMaker Server offers protection for your files in case of a crash, automated backups, and tremendous speed and stability boosts over peer-to-peer sharing.

Note: Another type of Internet sharing, called *Custom Web Publishing (CWP)*, offers more features than IWP. Using XML/XSLT, PHP, or Lasso, you can build incredibly powerful Web-based databases. But there are steep learning curves to these technologies—plus, they're beyond the scope of this book.

FileMaker Network Sharing

The easiest way to share your data is with *FileMaker Network Sharing*. If you already have a network in your office, and a few copies of FileMaker, you're ready to share your database. First, you put all your databases on one computer. Then open those files, change a few settings in each file, and call that computer the *host*. Every other computer that opens those files is called a *guest*, since it opens the same databases that are on the *host*. Up to five guests can connect to one host.

Once you're set up, all five people can work in the database at the same time, adding, editing, and deleting records, performing finds, printing, and running scripts. No two people can work in the same *record* at the same time, though. Once you're sharing files, you need to revisit the topic of record locking. See the box on page 647 for a refresher.

Setting Up a Host Computer

To set up the host, open the databases you want to share on one computer. Then choose Edit → Sharing → FileMaker Network (Windows) or FileMaker Pro → Sharing → FileMaker Network (Mac OS X). Either way, you see the FileMaker Network Settings dialog box: command central for all file sharing. Choose the database you're setting up from the list at left (if it's not there, make sure the file's open). Then, as described in Figure 18-1, turn sharing on.

Figure 18-1:
The FileMaker Network Settings dialog box lets you set up your database host. The first step is to turn on Network Sharing, by clicking the On radio button. When you do, FileMaker shows the computer's TCP/IP address, if it's connected to the network. (If you don't see a valid TCP/IP address, you may have network problems.)

Once you've turned Network Sharing on, turn your attention to the lower-right corner of the dialog box.

Choose one of the following three settings to control who gets access to the file:

- **All Users** means that anybody on your network with a copy of FileMaker and a valid account can get in, so long as only five people are on at a time.

- **Specify users by privilege set.** When you choose this option, you see a dialog box listing all your privilege sets. Click the checkbox to the left of each privilege set that should have access to the file.

- **No users.** If a file needs to be open on the host, but you don't want it shared, choose this option.

When you make changes to these settings, FileMaker is actually making changes to the privilege sets in the selected file (page 585). When you turn on "All users," File-Maker simply turns on the "Access via FileMaker Network" extended privilege for every privilege set. Likewise, if you choose "No users," it turns this extended privilege off for every set. When you specify people by privilege set, you get to decide which privilege sets have this extended privilege turned on. If you prefer, you can make these changes manually in Extended Privileges tab of the Define Accounts & Privileges window (File → Define → Accounts & Privileges). Look for the [fmapp] extended privilege if you're setting access manually (page 605).

Tip: You can control the access settings for each file even if you don't turn on network sharing. The settings you make to a file stick with that file even when you move it to another computer, so you can use this window to set the sharing options for a file *before* you send it to the host computer.

The "Don't display in Open Remote File dialog" option may seem odd at first, but it's actually very useful. Suppose you have a database system that's made up of several files, but you want your users to open only a specific one (because only one file has an interface and the others just hold data, for example). You want only that main file visible in the Open dialog box, so nobody opens the wrong one. Careful, though, you still need to *share* the other files. To share a file without showing it in the list, turn *on* the "Don't display in Open Remote File dialog" option in all the files you want hidden.

Opening a Shared File

Once you turn on network sharing and set it up to share at least one file, you can access that file from another computer. Just launch FileMaker Pro on another computer on the network, and then follow these steps:

1. **Choose File → Open → Remote.**

   If you're already looking at the Open File dialog box, click the Remote button instead. Either way, you see the Open Remote File dialog box (Figure 18-2).

2. **Select the appropriate host from the Hosts list.**

The shared files show in the Available Files list. (If the host computer you're looking for isn't listed, see the box on page 645 for advice.)

3. **Select the file you want to open from the Available Files list, and then click Open.**

If you've added accounts to the file, FileMaker asks you for an account name and password. When you give it what it needs, the database opens.

Figure 18-2:
The Open Remote File dialog box lets you find files that are shared on the network. This box lists all the hosts it can find in the Hosts list. Select a host to see all the available files in the list to the right. If you like the typing thing, you can enter exactly what FileMaker needs in the Network File Path box.

Note: When a database opens from a host, FileMaker puts the host name in parentheses in the window title bar to help you keep things straight. If you don't like seeing host names in your window's title bars, use the Set Window Title step to change that name in an open script.

Sharing Over the Internet

FileMaker Network sharing is the easiest way to share your database. Folks simply open the file, and it works *exactly* like a file on their hard drive. The catch is, they need a copy of FileMaker Pro on whatever computer they're using to connect. If you want to open up your database to people who don't have FileMaker—and you're willing to live with a less elegant interface—you can use Instant Web Publishing. This feature turns your computer into its own Web server. Like magic, it turns all your layouts into Web pages and lets anybody with an up-to-date Web browser search, sort, and edit your data directly.

Turning on Web Sharing

Enabling Instant Web Publishing (IWP for short) is just as easy as turning on File-Maker Network sharing. First, choose File → Sharing → Instant Web Publishing (Windows) or FileMaker Pro → Sharing → Instant Web Publishing (Mac OS X), and then click On. Once IWP starts up, FileMaker shows you the URL by which people access your databases. (You also get to pick a language for your Web pages. This action doesn't translate the information in your database, though. Instead, it controls what language all of FileMaker's buttons, labels, and links use in the Web browser.)

UP TO SPEED

Favorite Hosts

When you first visit the Open Remote File dialog box, File-Maker shows you *local hosts*. In general, FileMaker *discovers* only hosts that are on the same local network as the guest computer, but in the world of giant corporate networks, wireless nodes, and Internet connections everywhere, it's hard to guess where one network ends and the next one begins. If FileMaker *doesn't* show your host automatically, you have to add it to your Favorite Hosts list.

From the Open Remote File dialog box's View pop-up menu, choose *Favorite Hosts*. FileMaker adds three new buttons below the Hosts list: Add, Edit, and Remove. Click Add to add a new host to the list. When you do, you see the Edit Favorite Host dialog box (shown here).

In the Host's Internet Address box, type the TCP/IP Address or Host Name of the host computer. You can also give your host a nicer name (in the Favorite Host's Name box). Normally, FileMaker asks the host computer for a list of files and shows every available file. If your host often has lots of files, but you use only a few, you can turn on "Show only these files" and list the ones you want to see. When you're done, click Save. To remove an existing favorite, select its name and click Remove.

If you have a large network with lots of hosts and databases, you can use a Lightweight Directory Access Protocol (LDAP) server, like the ones used for email addresses, to centralize host management. Refer to your LDAP server's documentation for details.

Advanced Web Publishing Options

The Advanced Web Publishing Options window lets you configure FileMaker's built-in Web server. You get to pick a *port* (more on that next) and restrict access to only certain computers, among other settings. Clicking Advanced Options in the Instant Web Publishing window opens the dialog box (Figure 18-3).

Figure 18-3:
In the Advanced Web Options dialog box, you get to decide which information FileMaker records in log files (you can refer to these files if you have problems or are curious who's using the database). Also, you can tell FileMaker to forget about users who haven't clicked the Web page for a while by setting the "Disconnect inactive accounts" value (page 648).

Network servers set up shop at a *TCP/IP Port Number*, and once you turn on IWP, your computer is a network server, too. The usual web publishing port is 80 and, if you have no other Web services running on your computer, that's the one you'll usually use. But if you do need to set up your Web server with multiple services, you can change FileMaker's port number to avoid a conflict. As you can see in the figure above, FileMaker has registered its very own port number just for Web publishing (591). If you stick with port 591, chances are no other program's using it and you'll avoid conflicts even if you need to add other services later on. When you assign any other port number than 80, FileMaker automatically adds the port number to the URL it displays in the Instant Web Publishing dialog box, as a reminder of the link your browser uses to connect to your site.

Note: When you use port 80, links to your links don't need to include the port number, but if you're using any other port number, you'll have to make sure that your links include the port.

If you don't want just anybody trying to connect to your databases, you can turn on "Accessible only from these IP addresses." You then have to list the network address of each computer you want to allow (with commas in between). If you have a large intranet, you don't have to type dozens of IP addresses, though. You can specify a range of addresses using an asterisk. For example, 192.168.15.* lets everyone whose IP address matches the first three sets of numbers access the file.

UP TO SPEED

Record Locking Revisited

Back in Chapter 2, you learned about *record locking*. When you start editing a record, FileMaker locks it, so it can't be changed in another window until you commit it in the first. At the time, this scenario probably seemed like a pretty obscure situation: How often do you try to edit the same record in two different windows? But when several people start sharing the same database, record locking takes on a whole new meaning. Now, when you start editing a record, *nobody else* can edit it. If you type a few lines in the Notes field, and then go home sick without clicking out of the record, you keep it locked all day.

When you try to edit a locked record, FileMaker shows a message like this one. It tells you the record's locked, and *who* has it locked (including the user name on their computer, *and* the account name they've logged in with).

If you'd like to politely ask them to get out of the record, click Send Message. You see the Send Message to Conflicting Users window also shown here. Enter any message you want and click OK. The third window in this picture shows what the other user sees.

While record locking can be a minor annoyance to the user, it can be a real problem for the database developer. If you've designed all your scripts with the mistaken notion that you'll *always* be able to edit *any* record you want, you might get an unpleasant surprise the first time a script tries to modify a locked record.

Even worse, sometimes you build a process that simply doesn't work for multiple users. For example, suppose you expect people to flag a series of records, and then run a script that does something to all the ones they flagged. If the script *finds* the flagged records and loops through them, FileMaker gets utterly confused when two people try to use the same script at once. The script crashes, and it's anybody's guess how your poor records will wind up.

In general, you should think about how the script you write works if a record can't be edited, or if several people are using it at the same time. Or, to avoid the issue altogether, make it so only one person can use certain scripts, and use privilege sets to keep everybody else away from them.

While IWP is running, it can keep track of activity and errors. FileMaker keeps this information in log files in its Web Logs folder. The "Web activity" log records each time someone interacts with the database. The log includes the network address of the user, and the URL she requested. The "Script errors" log records errors in your FileMaker scripts. The "Web publishing errors" log holds other errors that occur in IWP, like invalid requests and missing databases. You can use these logs to see if you need to fix your scripts, or to see who's been using the databases and what problems they've encountered. On the other hand, if you use IWP a lot, these logs can get large. Turn any or all of them off to keep FileMaker from recording this information.

Web browsers don't work exactly like FileMaker itself. Someone has to explicitly log out to tell FileMaker he's disconnecting. If he doesn't—for example, if he just quits his browser or goes to a different Web site—FileMaker doesn't know he's left your site. To keep people from tying up connections forever, FileMaker automatically disconnects anyone who hasn't requested a page in a while. You get to decide how long "a while" is. A smaller setting (like 15 minutes) ensures that people don't hold connections long if they forget to log out. On the other hand, if they spend more than 15 minutes looking at a single record (reading a long Notes field, for instance) then they're disconnected even though they're still using the database. If you have situations like this one, set the "Disconnect inactive accounts" value to something larger (the maximum is 60 minutes).

Configuring file access

Just like FileMaker Network Sharing, you get to decide which files are shared by IWP, and which privilege sets have Web access. In fact, the settings are identical: Select an open file, and then choose the appropriate access level. Manage IWP access using the [fmiwp] extended privilege.

Connecting from a Web Browser

Not all Web browsers are created equal. They aren't all good at showing you Web sites that use Cascading Style Sheets (CSS). And since FileMaker translates your layouts into CSS when you share them via IWP, you must have a browser that understands CSS to use databases on the Web, like one of the following:

- Microsoft Internet Explorer 6.0 or higher in Windows

- Safari 1.2 or higher in Mac OS X 10.3

- Safari 2.0 or higher in Mac OS X 10.4

- Firefox 1.0 in Mac or Windows

To connect to the database from a Web browser, you need to know the URL in the Instant Web Publishing dialog box. Type this URL into the Location box in your Web browser. The resulting Web page looks like the one in Figure 18-4.

When you click a database link on the Web page, FileMaker asks you to log into the database—even if you haven't set up accounts on your database. If you've created accounts, enter a valid account name and password. Otherwise, enter Admin for the user name, and leave the password box blank. After you log in, you see what probably looks *a lot* like your real database displayed right inside the Web page (Figure 18-5).

The most noticeable difference is the status area: It's bigger and has more options, as Figure 18-6 attests. When you view your data in List view or Table view, the Web page shows only a few records at a time. To see more, click the pages in the book icon or type a record number in the Current Record box and click the Go to Record button in the status area. Since you're working on the Web, you *must* click this button to reload the page with the desired record.

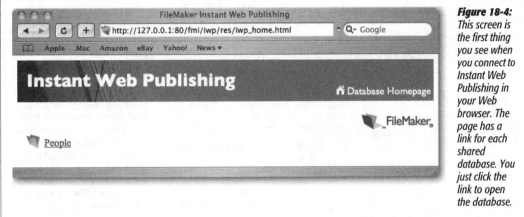

Figure 18-4:
This screen is the first thing you see when you connect to Instant Web Publishing in your Web browser. The page has a link for each shared database. You just click the link to open the database.

Figure 18-5:
If you hide the toolbars in your browser, and close the status area, the Web page (left) looks almost indistinguishable from the real FileMaker Pro window (right). FileMaker goes to heroic lengths to turn your layouts into real working Web pages so your IWP users get as much of your beautiful database as possible.

The process of editing records is also different in IWP. When you first click an editable field (or click the Edit Record button in the toolbar), FileMaker reloads the page in editable form. The status area also changes: Submit and Cancel buttons appear, while all other tools become unavailable. After you've made changes, you have to click Submit or FileMaker doesn't save them. If you don't want to keep your changes, click Cancel instead.

The toolbar in the status area has icons for common database activities. The icons change if you switch to Browse mode, and if you hold your mouse arrow over a button for a few seconds, a label pops up telling you what the button does. You can see the Browse mode and Find mode toolbars in Figure 18-7.

Custom Home Page

The IWP home page, shown in Figure 18-4, gets the job done, but it's not likely that it matches your corporate identity. And some users find it a bit confusing, since it doesn't provide them with a lot of clues about what your IWP database does. But you can make a Custom Home Page to replace it.

Figure 18-6:
Since FileMaker can't control the menu bar in your Web browser, it has to cram everything it thinks you'll ever need into the status area instead. Almost everything here has an exact counterpart in FileMaker Pro itself. Notable exceptions: the Home button, which returns you to the list of shared databases, and Log Out, which tells FileMaker you're done using the connection.

Your Custom Home Page will require a smidgeon of JavaScript to make sure the page loads properly. If you already have some JavaScript in your page, add this bit to the existing code:

```
If( window != window.top ) top.location = "/fmi/iwp/cgi?-home
```

If you don't have any existing JavaScript, add this:

```
<script type="text/JavaScript" language="JavaScript1.4">
    If( window != window.top ) top.location = "/fmi/iwp/cgi?-home
</script>
```

And if you can't stand the thought of dealing with JavaScript at all, you can just edit the sample copy of the home page that comes with FileMaker Pro.

Figure 18-7:
This picture shows what each toolbar button does. On the top you see the full toolbar in Browse mode (click the Show/Hide Extra Buttons arrow to show or hide the second row of buttons—they're hiding when you first arrive). If you switch to Find mode, you see the buttons on the bottom. Each button does the same thing as its namesake in FileMaker Pro.

Save the file with the name *iwp_home.html* and place it in the Web folder inside the FileMaker Pro folder. Now your users will see this page when they first click to your site and every time they reconnect to it.

FileMaker Server

Using FileMaker Pro on an ordinary desktop computer to host your files is easy and decidedly inexpensive, but it has some pretty severe drawbacks. First, it can handle no more than five guests at once. If you have more, you have to find a better way. There are some less obvious problems as well, including the following:

- If somebody's working on the host computer, chances are they're doing more than just FileMaker. The more you do on a computer, the more likely it is to crash—especially after you contract the next email virus. The host in a peer-to-peer setup can sometimes be unstable. You probably don't want your database server interrupting your office workflow. But more serious than that, databases that crash often are likely to get corrupted. And that's not safe for your data.

- FileMaker Pro is designed for *using* databases, not hosting them. It does an admirable hosting job, but it simply wasn't built for speed or large numbers of simultaneous users.

- As you remember from Chapter 1, you should close databases before you back them up. But if they're open on a host computer, you have to disconnect all the guests before closing the files. This necessity makes midday backups a little inconvenient.

The answer to all these problems—and more—is FileMaker Server. It's a special piece of software designed for one thing: turning a dedicated computer into a lean, mean, and *stable* database host. When FileMaker Server hosts your databases, you can have *250* guests connected at once. Since it runs on a dedicated server, it tends to be much more stable (and you can put it in the closet, where nobody will pull the plug or close the files accidentally). From a performance perspective, you *can't* launch FileMaker Server and use the database directly. In fact, it has no windows, menus, or dialog boxes at all (there is an administration tool through which you can monitor the server and make changes to it, though). Instead, it's a true *server* (sometimes called a *service*), designed specifically to share data over the network. Finally, it's loaded with special server-only features, including an automatic backup feature that can safely back up files while people are connected.

So what's the catch? Money. FileMaker Server costs $999, while another copy of FileMaker Pro is only $249. If you use Microsoft Windows, you've got a little more money to spend. FileMaker Server requires Windows 2000 *Server* or better. You can get Windows 2000 Server in several configurations, but they'll all set you back more than a copy of Windows XP. Don't be fooled, though. This cash is money well spent if your database is at all important to your business.

Tip: FileMaker Server comes in two flavors: *FileMaker Server 8* and *FileMaker Server 8 Advanced*. Both do a fine job with FileMaker Network sharing, but only the Advanced version does those *other* kinds of sharing—Instant Web Publishing, Custom Web Publishing, ODBC, and JDBC. If you're not sure you need Advanced just yet, don't sweat it. You can buy Server 7 today, and then trade it up to Advanced later if the need arises. This book doesn't cover the Advanced version. If you're interested in getting into big-time Web publishing, check out the resources in Appendix A.

File Compatibility

As you learned back near the beginning of this book, the file extension for database files created with version 7 and version 8 is "fp7." Therefore, you can do a fair amount of version mixing between FileMaker Server, FileMaker Developer and FileMaker Pro and still get good results. You could develop files on FileMaker Developer 7, but put them on a FileMaker Server 8 computer. People in your office with FileMaker Pro 7 or FileMaker Pro 8 (or FileMaker Developer 7 or FileMaker Pro Advanced 8) can each use the files.

Note: The files will open just fine across versions 7 and 8, however, some features, like Tab Controls and script variables won't work properly in version 7, so take care how you mix versions if you're using these 8-only features.

However, files prior to version 7 have to be converted before you can use them with any FileMaker product that's version 7 or above. But those good folks at File-Maker, Inc. have been careful to provide support for conversion. Both FileMaker 7 and 8 convert files from as far back as FileMaker 3. You *can* convert even older versions, but there's an intermediate step. Go to *http://www.filemaker.com/support/updaters.html* and download a trial version of FileMaker Pro version 5.0, then convert your old files to .fp5 format. Once the files have been updated, FileMaker Pro 8 can take over and get you up to .fp7-land.

If you have files to convert, be sure to check out two excellent documents on migration: "Migration foundations and methodologies" and "How to migrate existing solutions." Look for them in the Migration Topics section at *http://www.filemaker.com/support/whitepapers.html*.

Administering FileMaker Server

Once you install FileMaker Server, you can find its tools and other important files and folders on your hard drive. Normally this stuff is in C: → Program Files → File-Maker → FileMaker Server 8 in Windows and Hard Drive → Library → FileMaker Server 8 in Mac OS X. For FileMaker Server to host databases, they need to be installed on the server computer. You can put them in the Data → Databases folder inside FileMaker Server's folder, and FileMaker Server finds and shares them automatically when it starts up.

Tip: If you don't want to keep your databases in this folder, you can configure FileMaker Server to look somewhere else. See page 659 for details.

One of the nice things about FileMaker Server is that you can manage it from your own desktop, even though it runs on a different computer. Once you've installed FileMaker Server on the host computer, you can use the same CD to install the FileMaker Server Admin program on *your* computer. In fact, since FileMaker Server itself has *no* user interface, FileMaker (FM) Server Admin is the tool you use to configure and monitor it.

When you first install FileMaker Server, you can configure it only by running FM Server Admin on the same computer the server is installed on. This limitation prevents outsiders from configuring your server before you get a chance to. If you'd like to configure it from your desktop instead, you'll have to run FM Server Admin at least once on the host computer to turn on *remove administration* (you'll learn how in the next section). Once you've done that, you can run FM Server Admin on any computer and connect to the server. Sadly, unlike FileMaker Pro itself, FM

Server Admin doesn't look the same across platforms. The next section shows how it looks in Windows. If you use Mac OS X instead, skip to page 656.

Global Fields and Multiple Users

When many people share a single database, you might be worried about global fields. If one user changes a global field, does it change for *everybody*? In a word, "no." FileMaker keeps global field information on the *guest* computer. If you change what's in the global field, it has no effect on what's in that global field for other people.

This characteristic is, in general, a very good thing. But it does have an annoying side effect. Since everyone has his or her own globals, you *can't* change them for other people even when you want to. If you open a shared database, change a global, and then close it, you lose your changes. The next time you open the database, the globals have the same values as the *host* computer.

If you're using peer-to-peer sharing, you can change the globals on the host directly to make them stick. Since FileMaker Server has no real interface, there's no way to directly modify the initial value for a global field. You have to close the files on the server, move them to another computer, open them with FileMaker Pro, make the change, and then copy them back to the server. In other words, it's a pain.

If you have globals you often need to change permanently in a multi-user system, it's often easier to simply set them from a script that runs when the database opens. Then you're sure they have the right value, and you can always modify the script if you want to change the starting value while the databases are still hosted.

FileMaker Server Admin in Windows

Your first job is to run FM Server Admin (it's in your Start menu after you install FileMaker Server). Right now you're not connected to a FileMaker server. To remedy that, click the link shown in Figure 18-8, or right-click FileMaker Server in the console list on the left, and choose Connect to FileMaker Server.

Console list   Click to Connect to a Server

Figure 18-8:
When you first launch FM Server Admin in Windows, you get this welcome screen. FM Server Admin is actually a snap-in for Microsoft Management Console, so this interface may be familiar to you. On the left, you see your console list, including a new entry for FileMaker Server. Oddly, the words "FileMaker Server in the right-hand section are a link. You click them to get started.

When you do, the Connect to FileMaker Server window appears. The View pop-up menu reads Local Servers, which is the most common choice; select your server from the list. On a large network, you may have to choose Favorite Servers or LDAP first, as discussed in the box on page 645. Or, if you know the server's IP address, you can type it in the Address box at the bottom of the window. When you're done, click Connect.

If your desired server isn't running, FileMaker shows a message to that effect and offers to start it for you. Click Yes. (If the server's already running, you don't see this message). Once you've successfully connected, you see something like Figure 18-10.

To configure the server itself, select it from the console list on the left side of the window (it's automatically selected when you first connect). Server has six primary areas of configuration, each represented by a large icon, a label, and a description. When you click one of these, a wizard pops up and asks you a series of questions. You click your way through screen after screen trying to find the one setting you want. If you find that process too cumbersome, you can right-click the server name in the console list and choose Properties instead. When you do, you see the dialog box shown in Figure 18-9.

Figure 18-9:
If you don't like the big-button approach to application design, right-click the server name and choose Properties. Here, you can quickly access all the server settings without all the fuss.

In addition to these properties, you see six items listed under the server in the console list. These items give you access to other server features. You'll learn about the items, and the configuration options, below. But first, it's time to bring the Mac OS X users up to speed.

FileMaker Server Admin in Mac OS X

You can find FM Server Admin in the FileMaker Server 7 folder in your Applications folder (it's also in your Dock if you told the installer to make an icon for it there). Launch it, and behold the Connect to FileMaker Server window. The View pop-up menu reads Local Servers, which is the most common choice; Select your server from the list. On a large network, you may have to choose Favorite Servers or LDAP first, as discussed in the box on page 645. Or, if you know the server's IP address, you can type it in the Address box at the bottom of the window. When you're done, click Connect.

FM Server Admin attempts to connect to your server. (If the server isn't running, you see a message asking if you'd like to start it. Click Yes.) Once FM Server Admin has connected to the server, you see the FileMaker Server window shown in Figure 18-11.

Configuring FileMaker Server

Whether you're using Mac OS X or Windows, the general configuration options in FM Server Admin are the same. To configure the basic server features from Windows, right-click the server name in the console list and choose Properties. In Mac OS X, click the Configure toolbar button in the FileMaker Server window. In either case, you see a window full of tabs, similar to the one in Figure 18-12. This section explains how to fill them out.

Figure 18-10:
When Server Advanced is connected to a server, its window changes a lot. The server itself is added to the console list on the left. Under it, you see several new options. In the main section of the window, you see six prominent icons with names and descriptions. These icons are buttons that lead to various configuration options.

Remote administration

The first thing you should do when you connect to your new server is set a password so other people can't modify the configuration. In the server configuration window, click the Administration tab. Then turn on "Require password" and, when prompted, enter a secret password. The next time you connect to this server with FileMaker Server Admin, you have to type this password before you can make any changes.

Figure 18-11:
The FileMaker Server window starts off by showing you information about your server. The toolbar icons across the top of the window give you access to all the configuration options and features in FMSA. Click a button to see associated settings in the main window.

Once you've set a password, you probably want to turn on "Allow remote users to administer FileMaker Server." Once this option is on, you can run FileMaker Server Admin on *any* computer and connect to the FileMaker Server. This option saves you the trouble of walking over to the server to make changes—just run FileMaker Server Admin on the computer on your desk.

Clients tab

The next tab in the server configuration window is called Clients. In this tab, you can tell the server how many connections it should allow. You see *two* options: "FileMaker Pro and ODBC/JDBC connections" and "Web Publishing Engine sessions." But unless you have FileMaker Server Advanced, you can't make changes to the Web publishing option.

Warning: If you are installing and configuring FileMaker Server Advanced, be sure to refer to the installation manual that came with your software. This book doesn't cover configuration for the Web Publishing Engine. Configuration is easy if you follow those instructions, but painful if you decide you can go it alone.

The first option refers to how many people can connect to your server at the same time using an ordinary copy of FileMaker pro. You can also interact with FileMaker Server Advanced from other programs using ODBC or JDBC, and each of these connections also counts against the total number of connections. The second option controls how many people can connect to the server at the same time using a Web browser.

Figure 18-12:
The main server configuration looks something like this. (You can see the Windows version of this dialog box in Figure 18-9.) After you've gone through each tab the first time, setting the options the way you want them, you usually only have to revisit them to make specific changes, like specifying a new backup folder or changing the number of files Server can host.

For Server Advanced, you also see a checkbox called "Allow ODBC and JDBC connections." If you intend to connect to the server from programs other than FileMaker Pro, you need to turn this checkbox on. At the bottom of the window is an option to "Set maximum idle time allowed for FileMaker Pro clients." Turn this option on, and enter a time, to automatically disconnect guests if they haven't used FileMaker for the specified period of time.

Finally, the "Allow FileMaker Pro clients to download updates automatically" option lets you deploy FileMaker plug-ins to connected guest computers when they connect to the server. Contact your plug-in provider or see Auto Update in the FileMaker Pro documentation for more information.

Databases tab

From the Databases tab, you can tell the server how many files it should be able to host. The maximum is 125, but you should use a number appropriate for your installation so FileMaker Server doesn't waste memory for files you aren't serving. The rule of thumb is to set the number about 10 percent higher than the actual maximum number of files you'll be serving.

FileMaker Server performs consistency checks on all files that are opened for the first time on FMS8, and for FM07-v8 files that were closed improperly the last time they were running. If Server detects damage, it won't open the file, but it will create an error message in the Log File. This message contains instructions for repairing the file. Advanced users (those who know how to detect and repair file damage) can turn off the "Open files without consistency check" option, but this isn't recommended for mere mortals.

You can use the Database Cache settings to improve performance. When you increase the size reserved for the database cache, FileMaker can keep more information in memory, saving it the trouble of using the disk as often. You should make the cache as large as possible if you have lots of users and/or lots of data. But you can't assign more cache than you have available on your computer. FileMaker suggests a maximum cache setting for you based on 70 percent of available RAM.

Finally, you can tell FileMaker how to *distribute cache flush*. In general, if the cache setting is large, there's more new information in memory, where it can be lost if the server crashes. When FileMaker Server flushes its cache, it writes the new information to the disk to protect it. To increase performance, increase the time in the "Distribute cache flush over" box. To increase data integrity, decrease this time.

Tip: For help figuring out how to configure FileMaker Server's cache, see "Statistics" on page 664.

Runtime Solutions tab

As you'll learn in Chapter 19, FileMaker Developer lets you build *runtime solutions*. When you do, your databases have a unique file extension instead of the typical ".fp7," and FileMaker Server doesn't find and open them. To remedy this situation, you can add, edit, and remove runtime file extensions from the Runtime Solutions tab. Add a line for each extension you need FileMaker Server to open.

Default Folders tab

When FileMaker Server starts up, it automatically opens and shares every database in its "Default database folder." You can see the path to this folder in the Default Folders path. You can also add a second folder for FileMaker to search, if you want. Just turn on "Use additional database folder" and edit the associated path. Notice that the example file path ends with a "/" character. Don't forget that last slash or FM Server Admin tells you that you haven't created a valid path. Most people find the default folder works just fine, but you can change paths. If you installed FileMaker Server on your startup disk, for example, you may want to keep the databases on a different, faster disk.

Tip: Make sure the folder you're backing up to has permissions set properly! If they're not configured properly, your backups will fail and you won't get a warning dialog box. Set the owner to "fmserver" and the group to "fmsadmin." Both need read and write access.

When FileMaker Server backs up databases, it saves the backups in a different folder. You also get to specify the path to the backup folder from this tab. You can, for instance, have backups saved to a remote file server for added security, or you

---

can make alternating backups in different folders so that you have more than one set of backups.

Administration tab

Use the Administration tab to control your server's name, and who can connect to it with FM Server Admin. You can give the server a custom name (normally it takes the host name of the computer itself). This name appears in the Open Remote File dialog box when users connect to the server.

If you want to keep people from changing the server configuration, turn on "Require password" and create a password for yourself. Finally, if you want to be able to connect to the server with FM Server Admin from any computer on the network, turn on "Allow remote users to administer FileMaker Server." (See the box on page 661 for more detail.)

Logging tab

If you're trying to maximize your server performance, you can tell FileMaker to log *usage statistics*. You tell it how often to update its log, and how big the log file should be allowed to get. The usage statistics log contains information about server performance over time. You can use this information to help you understand how your server is being used and how to improve performance.

Directory Service tab

If you're managing several FileMaker Server computers, you can use an LDAP server to hold information about them and the files each one serves. This server makes it easier on your users, who use the list on the LDAP server to locate the FileMaker Server files they need. The main option on this tab tells this copy of File-Maker Server to register on your LDAP service. You have to specify the LDAP server's name and port. See your IT person or the LDAP manual to find out that server's name. The "Use Windows Authentication" option lets you access Windows Active Directory with an Account Name and Password set in this tab.

Security tab

In Chapter 16, you learned that you can separate your database accounts from the database itself using *external authentication*. If you plan on using external authentication, you need to tell the server. In the Security tab, turn on "FileMaker and External Server accounts." You also need to pick *which* accounts you want to use for authentication. Select "Use local user accounts and groups" if you intend to manage the accounts on the server computer itself. Turn on "Use domain user accounts and groups" if you want to manage accounts on your domain controller instead. Refer to Chapter 16 and your operating system documentation for more information.

From the Security tab, you can also tell FileMaker Server to show users only the files they have access to when they invoke the Open Remote File dialog box. When you turn on "Display only the databases each user is authorized to access," the server asks for a user name and password. Only databases that match this user name and password appear in the Available Files list.

POWER USERS' CLINIC

Local and Domain Accounts

If you have several FileMaker servers, or several people who all need to be able to configure the server, setting a single password for administration may be impractical. When an employee quits, you have to change the password on every server, and then let every administrator know about the change. And everybody has to share just one password for each server, which means they can't each set it to something they're familiar with (like the password they use to log into the computer in the morning). What's more, keeping track of the administrator passwords on several servers can be a real pain.

If you face this problem, you have some recourse. Instead of a single administrator password, you can essentially off-load the task of managing administrators to your operating system or directory server. Just create a group called "fmsadmin" on the server computer or on your network. Then add each user who needs administrator access to File-Maker Server to this group.

Finally, turn on the "Use local user accounts and 'fmsad-min' group" or "Use domain user accounts and 'fmsadmin' group" checkbox in the Administration tab of the server configuration window. Now, whenever someone tries to configure the server, FileMaker asks them for a user name and password. These user names and passwords are the same ones they use to log into their computer. If they're in the fmsadmin group, they're allowed in. Otherwise, they aren't.

Which of these checkboxes you turn on depends on where you add the group and how your network is configured. If you use local accounts on the server computer, choose the "Use local user accounts…" option. If you use a directory server like Active Directory in Windows or Open Directory in Mac OS X, choose "Use domain user accounts…" instead. Refer to your operating system documentation for more information.

Finally, turn on "Secure connections to FileMaker Server" if you want FileMaker to encrypt data as it transmits it over the network. Encryption helps keep sensitive data more secure by making it more difficult for people to intercept. On the other hand, it slows things down slightly.

Other Server Options

In addition to the server configuration options just explained, FMSA has six additional screens full of information and features. In Mac OS X, you access them by clicking the icons in the toolbar along the top of the FileMaker Server window. In Windows, each section's shown in the console list as an item underneath the server name.

Summary

Click the Summary icon to see basic information about your server. You can see what version of FileMaker server you're running, information about the computer and operating system it's running on, and license information for the server. You can also upgrade your server license from this window. If you've purchased a server upgrade (to support more users, for instance, or to upgrade to Server Advanced), enter the license information at the bottom of the window, and then click Update License.

Databases

When you select the Databases icon, you see all the databases the server's currently sharing, listed by file name. If you have your databases organized by folder, the folders are listed as well. In Windows, double-click Folders to see your databases organized by folder, or double-click Files instead to see an alphabetical list of files. Mac OS X shows the databases organized by folder automatically; if you'd rather see just the files, choose Action → Databases → Hide Folders.

Under Number of Clients, you can see how many people currently have a particular file open. If the database is open and ready to share, the Status column says Normal. When FileMaker's in the process of opening a database, and preparing to share it, this column may say Opening for a short time.

FileMaker Server normally opens all the files it finds in its Database folder. But sometimes you need to close a file while others are still running. You might close a file so you can work on it on a local computer (say you need to add a script or make a lot of changes to the file). Close a file by selecting it in the list, and then choosing Action → Databases → Close Database. The Status column changes to read Closed.

Warning: It's possible to do an amazing amount of database design work while your users are working in the database. But file corruption has been reported when many users (30 or more) are accessing a file while you're doing design tasks like defining fields or creating layouts. When in doubt, it's always safest to design locally, and then put your edited files back on the server for all to enjoy.

Clients

Under the Clients item, you find a list of connected users. You can see who's connected, what computer they're connecting from, how long they've been connected, and how many files they have open. For administrators connected to the server with FM Server Admin (including yourself), you see a zero in the Number of Files column.

Schedules

FileMaker Server can perform certain tasks on a schedule you set. Tasks include backing up the database, running a script, or sending a message to everyone who's connected. Click the Schedules item to see a list of the existing schedules. You can see the name of each schedule, when it last ran, and when it'll run next. Even after you've created a schedule, you can prevent it from running (*disable* it) temporarily and keep it on the list in case you want to activate it again later. In Mac OS X, turn on or off the checkbox by the schedule's name. In Windows, right-click the schedule and choose Disable or Enable.

To add a new schedule, in Windows choose Action → Schedule → New Schedule. In Mac OS X, click the New button below the schedule list. The interface you use to define a schedule is different in Windows and Mac OS X, but the information you provide is the same. First, you have to choose what kind of schedule to create: Back Up Databases, Run Script File, or Send Message.

- When you choose the **Back Up Databases** type, you next choose *which* databases to back up. You can opt to back up *all* databases, or just those in a particular folder. You also choose *where* to save the backups. FileMaker suggests you use the default backup folder set in the server configuration, but you're free to enter a different path if you want.

- The **Run Script File** option is available only after you've added a script to FileMaker's Scripts folder (C: → Program Files → FileMaker → FileMaker Server 7 → Data/Scripts in Windows, Hard Drive → Library → FileMaker Server 7 → Data/Scripts in Mac OS X). When you choose the Run Script File type, FM Server Admin lets you pick one of the files in this folder from a pop-up menu. The scripts can be batch files, shell scripts, runnable programs, or (in Mac OS X) AppleScripts.

- If you choose **Send Message**, you get to enter the text of the message you want FileMaker to send at the scheduled time.

Whichever type you choose, your next job is to tell FileMaker Server when to run the task, and how often. First, you pick a schedule type: Once, Daily, or Weekly. You also choose whether you want to turn on the schedule right away. When you're satisfied with your settings, click Accept, and the new schedule appears in the list. Here are your options in more detail:

- The simplest schedule type, **Once**, has only one option—the date and time you want the task to run.

- If you choose **Daily**, you first pick a start date. Then you decide how often you want the schedule to run (every day, every other day, every third day, and so forth). You can specify an end date and time if you want the schedule to stop running at a predetermined time in the future. If you don't enter an end date, the schedule runs until you manually disable, change, or delete it. Finally, if you want the schedule to run periodically throughout the day, you can tell FileMaker Server to repeat the task. You get to decide how often by specifying a number of minutes or hours.

- The **Weekly** type has even more options. You still get a start date and time, an optional end date and time, and the option to repeat the task throughout the day. But you also get to decide which days of the week the task should run (so you can skip weekends, for instance).

When you're trying to decide how often to backup, the main question you need to answer is "How much data am I willing to lose?" If your database does something critical—like track product orders for your business, or control your daily routine through tickler messages—you should back up a few times a day, at least.

When you're doing major development work, you also want frequent backups of your files, just in case. Since Server's usual behavior is to make all backups into the same folder, it's helpful to make an alternate backup location so that the first backup goes into the main folder and the second backup goes into the alternate folder.

But you might have data that changes infrequently, like your products' beauty shots or personnel files. Those files can be backed up weekly. If you have a mix of these data types—constantly changing data and relatively stable data—this might trigger a new design decision. Your stable data goes into one file and the dynamic data goes into another so that you don't have to slow your office down while large, stable files are backed up a few times each day.

Tip: Lots of designers work with their files mounted on Server even before there are multiple users working in them, since using Server to host the files creates a layer of protection in case of a crash. Think of it this way: If your computer crashes while you're designing a database, the file can become corrupted beyond repair. But if you're working in Server, the chances of corruption are much lower.

Plug-ins

If your database uses FileMaker plug-ins (page 464), you may have to install them on the server as well as on each guest computer for them to work. Check the documentation for your plug-in or contact the vendor if you're not sure whether the plug-in you need works from the server or locally. If you install a plug-in on FileMaker Server, be sure to then configure the server to use it by turning on the "Allow FileMaker Server to use plug-ins" option on this tab.

Note: Not all plug-ins that work on individual computers work with FileMaker Server, so it's very important to do your research before purchase. Fortunately, most vendors offer trial versions of their products and technical support.

Statistics

To help you understand how to get the best performance, FileMaker can show historical information about the server at any time. Just click the Statistics icon. You see the following facts and figures:

- **Network KB/sec** shows you how much data is being transferred over the host computer's network connection every second. By comparing these numbers to the speed of your network, you can decide if the speed of your network interface is limiting performance.

- **FileMaker Pro Clients** shows how many people have connected to the server. You can use these numbers to help you set the maximum number of users in the server configuration window.

- **Files** shows how many open databases you've had, which can help you set the server's maximum number of hosted files.

- **Disk KB/sec** tells you how much data FileMaker is writing to and reading from the disk each second. In conjunction with disk benchmarking tools, this information can help you decide if a faster disk system will improve performance.

- **Cache Unsaved %** indicates what percentage of the new data in the disk cache has not yet been flushed to disk. Ideally this number should be low (under 5 percent). If it's often higher, you might want to decrease the cache flush interval to reduce the likelihood of lost data if the system crashes.

- **Cache Hit %** tells you how often FileMaker can find what it needs in its cache. Every time it looks for data from the database, it checks the cache first. If it can't find what it's looking for, it reads data from the disk instead. Ideally, increase the cache size and/or add more memory to the server computer to keep this number above 90 percent.

Server Hardware

While you're spending money, why not get a better *computer* too? If you have lots of users or lots of data (or both), your database server needs all the power you can give it. After all, FileMaker Server performs finds, edits records, sorts, imports, exports, and otherwise constantly busies itself with the work of *every user*.

The most important thing you can do to make FileMaker Server faster is give it faster access to the data on the disk. At the very least, this increased speed means you should *never* store the files on a file server. Instead, they should always be on a hard drive in the host computer. If you still find things aren't as fast as you'd like them, your best upgrade is often a faster disk system—something called a RAID, or Redundant Array of Inexpensive Disks. You can ignore the "Redundant" part and the "Inexpensive" part, though. A RAID is an *array* of hard disks. By putting several disks together, you can get faster access to your data than you would with just one disk. As important, you can get *more reliable* access as well, since the same data can be stored in more than one place in case a disk drive fails, as outlined in the box on page 666.

In addition to a fast disk system, you should consider adding plenty of RAM to the host computer. The least important component is the CPU speed itself (but that's not to say it doesn't matter; don't expect a fast server with a 75 MHz Pentium processor).

If you find all this terribly confusing, be comforted by the fact that most major computer companies sell specially configured server computers. Let them know you're setting up a database server, and you can probably buy a fantastic host computer with RAID, lots of RAM, and a fast CPU all in one box.

POWER USERS' CLINIC

RAID Overview

RAID is just a generic term for any assemblage of several disks that look, to the computer, like just one disk. But the devil is in the details. It turns out there are several different *kinds* of RAID out there, and each serves a different purpose.

If speed is all you care about, there's something called *striping*. With striping, the data's spread across all disks so that when FileMaker Server reads or writes, it can usually do it to every disk at once. In general, a four-disk array with striping can shuffle data four times faster than just one disk. The trouble with striping is that every doubling of performance also produces a halving of reliability. In other words, if you expect one drive to fail sometime in the next four years, then one of the drives in your array will fail in the next year, on average.

On the other end of the spectrum is *mirroring*. This model gives you *maximum* reliability, but with very little speed benefit. In a mirrored array, every piece of data is written to every drive at the same time. If one drive fails, the system can simply switch to another drive without losing any data. But you often need more performance than a mirrored array can give.

Generally the best bet is a combination of mirroring and striping. Ideally, you'd create a few mirrored sets of disks, and then connect these sets into a striped super-set. If you use RAID, you should look for a system that lets you set up this kind of *striping over mirroring* configuration for the maximum in reliability and performance. You get to decide how much reliability you want (by picking the number of disks in each mirrored set) and how much speed you want (by choosing the number of mirrored sets to create).

Developer Utilities

FileMaker Pro takes you from your first simple database all the way into power-user territory. It lets you create complex relational databases with ease, design virtually any layout imaginable, and add features of your own invention with buttons and scripts. With it, you can create any database you might need for a small business or organization. Once you have more than a handful of people using your database, you may eventually outgrow even FileMaker Pro's abilities and need to buy another FileMaker product. In Chapter 18, for example, you can see how File-Maker Server lets more than five users work in a database at once—something FileMaker Pro simply can't handle. When you learned about Custom Functions in Chapter 11, you got a hint of some of the extras in the Advanced version of File-Maker.

In this chapter, you'll learn about FileMaker Pro Advanced 8. For a couple hundred dollars more ($299 for Pro versus $499 for Advanced), you get a whole raft of developer tools that will make your life easier and your databases better. If you find yourself troubleshooting long, complex scripts, Script Debugger may save your sanity and your valuable time. The analysis tools are indispensable if you're in a consultant role, working on databases that other people created. And most File-Maker developers have longed for an easy way to keep their more adventuresome users away from potentially destructive menu commands (including but not limited to Delete All Records). Finally, a new feature called Custom Menus gives them—and you—the godlike power to determine which commands are available to a database's users.

Script Debugger

When you write a script using FileMaker Pro, your testing and troubleshooting routine is pretty simple. You perform the script and wait to see what happens at the end. In a simple script, like one that prints a report, it's easy enough to see what went wrong and fix it: Your script just went to the wrong layout, perhaps. But when you're creating a complex script that sets variables and works with different sets of records that you can't verify before the next script step whizzes past, it's devilishly hard to figure out where your script veers off course. Even simple scripts can go wrong in puzzling ways that you can't detect by reading over your steps. That's where Script Debugger comes in. When you run scripts with Script Debugger turned on, FileMaker performs scripts at human speed, so you can see exactly what's happening, each step of the way.

Note: To run Script Debugger, you must be logged into the file with a password that has script-editing privileges (page 598). If a script for which you have editing privileges calls a subscript for which you don't, the subscript will execute but you won't be able to see the steps in the debugger.

The Script Debugger Window

To run a script using Script Debugger, choose Tools → Debug Scripts. It's a toggle command, so a checkmark appears when the debugger's on and disappears when it's off. While the debugger's on, FileMaker shows the Script Debugger window any time you run a script (Figure 19-1).

Debugger toolbar   Script steps

Figure 19-1:
The Script Debugger window's loaded with information about the current script. But even better, it gives you complete control over the script while it runs. You can run just one line of the script at a time, dig into subscripts or back out to the calling script, skip over some steps completely, back up and run some steps over again, or stop the script completely.

Current position   Active script(s) information

Break point

Unlike most dialog boxes, Script Debugger stays on top of your work while your script is running, giving you constant feedback. Because you often need to see what's happening on your layout, you may find yourself moving the debugger window around on your screen so you can keep tabs on data that's being created or edited, changing found sets and the context in which script steps are performed.

You may find that debugging is a whole lot easier on a desktop's monitor, preferably one with a whole lot of screen real estate. Often, you need to see two or more FileMaker windows and Debugger at the same time. (Now that most laptop computers have higher resolutions, though, you may be able to arrange a laptop's screen so that you can see at least one FileMaker window that's unobscured by Debugger.) For instance, when you're pushing or pulling data from one table to another (page 572) you may need to see the layout for the source table as well as the target table, so you can see if the data's moving into the proper fields. Or, if you're using lots of Go to Related Record steps to create your found sets, one layout can show the parent records and another can show the child records. See the box on page 676 for more debugger tips.

Tip: You can resize the debugger window by dragging the handle in the bottom right corner. Make it smaller so you can see more of your database in the background or make it larger if you have long script names, lots of indented If or Loop steps, or subscripts with script parameters.

Debugger toolbar

The most important part of the debugger is its toolbar: Its nine buttons give you all the control you could ever want over running scripts. Unfortunately, the buttons don't have names, so you have to either learn what each icon means, or spend a lot of time pointing at things and waiting for the little yellow tooltip to appear. For reference, Figure 19-2 shows the debugger's tools.

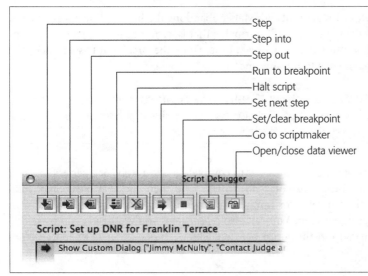

Step
Step into
Step out
Run to breakpoint
Halt script
Set next step
Set/clear breakpoint
Go to scriptmaker
Open/close data viewer

Script Debugger

Script: Set up DNR for Franklin Terrace

Show Custom Dialog ["Jimmy McNulty"; "Contact Judge a

Figure 19-2:
With this picture, you get up-close and personal with the toolbar in the Script Debugger window. Each of these buttons is explained in more detail throughout this chapter. If you've ever used a debugger in another development environment, then you probably feel right at home.

Stepping through a script. The first three buttons on the debugger toolbar all have "step" in their names. When you first start a script with the debugger, it doesn't start running. Instead, you see all the steps in the script, and the Current Position arrow (see Figure 19-1) points to the first step. This arrow always points to the *next* step that will run. If you just want to run that single step, click Step. The step runs, FileMaker moves the arrow to the next step in the list, and everything stops again, waiting for you to do something else. With this behavior in mind, you can easily *step* through the script line by line. You can see how your If and Loop steps work (by following the arrow), and you can watch things happen in your database windows while the script runs.

When the Current Position arrow points to a Perform Script step, the Step button runs the subscript as one unit. In other words, it run the whole subscript without stopping and then moves the arrow to the next line in *this* script. Click Step Into instead if you want to move *into* the subscript and step through it line by line. The last Step button is called Step Out. When you click this button, FileMaker *finishes* the current script, and returns you to the one that called it. Then you can step through that script line by line. If you click Step Out from a script that wasn't called by another script, FileMaker just finishes the script and closes the debugger window.

Breakpoints. If clicking a button for each step starts to wear on you—say you've got a looping script with a whole slew of steps—you can use Run to Breakpoint instead. Often when you debug a script, you know the first several lines work fine, and you want to fast-forward to the part that seems to be broken. You can tell the debugger where to stop and pause—a *breakpoint*. Just select the line you want to get to, and click Set/Clear Breakpoint (you can also just click the gray bar to the left of the script step). FileMaker adds a breakpoint symbol by the step name. (To remove a breakpoint, click it or select the step and click Set/Clear Breakpoint again.)

Then click Run to Breakpoint. FileMaker abandons the line-by-line approach and starts running through the script normally; that is, as fast as it can. The script runs until it ends, or until it hits a breakpoint. Once the breakpoint is reached, the debugger switches back to line-by-line mode.

Note: When you click Run to Breakpoint, FileMaker stops at the *first* breakpoint it finds. If your script calls *other* scripts, and they have breakpoints, it may stop inside another script before it gets back to your breakpoint. If that happens, click Run to Breakpoint again to move to the next one.

Skipping and repeating. If you want to completely *skip* a step (or a series of steps), simply select the next step you *want* to run, and then click Set Next Step. FileMaker moves the Current Position arrow down to the new step, but doesn't run any of the steps in between. You can also *repeat* steps you've already run by selecting a line higher up in the script before clicking Set Next Step. Either way, File-

Maker stops at the new line so you can use the Step buttons to go line by line from there.

Stopping. If you get halfway through a script and then spot the problem, you can stop the script right away without stepping to the end. Just click Stop Execution and the debugger window disappears, leaving you wherever the script left off.

Once you've been debugging for a while, you may forget you have it on. To your chagrin, the debugger window pops up when you expect to see the script running. Don't feel bad—it happens to professional developers all the time. Just click Stop Execution right away, turn off the debugger, and then run the script again. When the debugger first appears, *nothing has happened yet*, so it's always safe to stop before you step. (If you have breakpoints set throughout your scripts, you can use Stop Execution rather than repeatedly clicking Run to Breakpoint to get to the end of the script.)

Editing. More often than not, you want to edit the script you're debugging once you've found the problem. Normally you'd have to switch to the right file, open ScriptMaker, and then scroll to the right script. But the Go to ScriptMaker button can do all this for you. Click it, and FileMaker opens ScriptMaker with the right script already selected.

The Go to ScriptMaker button is useful even when you don't necessarily need to debug. Suppose you have a button on a layout, and you want to edit the script it runs. Trouble is, you're not exactly sure *which* script that is. The quickest way to find out—and get to the script—is to turn on the debugger, click the Go to Script-Maker button, and then click ScriptMaker's Edit button. You go directly to the script in just three clicks.

Script steps

Most of the debugger window is devoted to showing you the steps in the script that's running. You can't edit the steps here, but you can select them, and scroll up, down, right, or left to see more. The gray bar running along the left side of the list of steps is just a place for the Current Position arrow and breakpoints to live. You can click this bar to set or remove breakpoints directly. (This same bar appears in the Edit Script window when you're creating or editing scripts using FileMaker Advanced, so you can add breakpoints there, too.)

Active script(s) information

The bottom part of the window shows you detail about the *active* script—in other words, the script that's running right now. It shows the name of the script, the file it lives in, and the value, if any, of the script parameter it had when it started.

But why's this box so big if it just shows a few facts about one script? Because it can actually show a few bits about *lots* of scripts. Every time a script performs another script, it moves down in the list to make room for the new script's information. FileMaker puts the top-most—and current—script in boldface at the top of the list. Below it, you see the script that came before. If *that* script was itself run by another script, that first script's then third in the list. You can see how this looks in Figure 19-3.

Click on a script in the list to switch the debugger's view to the new script. The Current Position arrow changes color (white with blue outline) to indicate that you're viewing a script that doesn't include the current script step.

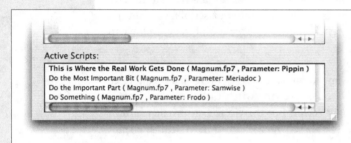

Figure 19-3:
When scripts call other scripts, FileMaker stacks the script names up in the Active Scripts list. On top—and in bold lettering—you see the name of the script you're currently looking at. Directly below each script is the name of the script that called it. If you have scripts calling scripts with more than four levels, you have to scroll the list to see the oldest ones.

Data Viewer

The last button on Script Debugger's toolbar shows you the Data Viewer, a handy little window that lets you see the current values in script variables, fields, and calculations. You create a list of values that you want to keep an eye on—a *watch list*—and then use this box to see exactly what happens to them as you debug. Make heavy use of this little gem and you may find that you rarely need to switch layouts while Debugger's running because you can monitor all your data through the Data Viewer. Before the viewer can show you any data, you have to tell it what to watch. Figure 19-4 shows you the Data Viewer window and its tools.

Figure 19-4:
The Data Viewer has some standard buttons on its toolbar. The + sign lets you specify a new value to monitor, the double plus signs duplicate an existing one that you can edit, the pencil opens the dialog box for editing an expression, and the trash can lets you delete an expression from Data Viewer's watch list.

When you open the Data Viewer for the first time, there's nothing in its watch list yet. To add a watch item, click the + sign. In the window that opens, you tell File-Maker what fields and calculations you want to inspect. It works much like the Specify Calculation dialog box (page 382), but with a few changes and a couple of extras:

- The **Expression** field is where you type your calculation.

- Click **Evaluate Now** to see a live evaluation of the calculation you're building in the **Result** field.

- The "OK" button says **Monitor** instead. When you click it, the new item appears in the watch list's Expressions column.

In all other respects, this dialog box works just like Specify Calculation. If you're using Data Viewer in conjunction with Script Debugger, you want it to monitor the fields and variables in the script you're troubleshooting. For example, if you wanted to troubleshoot the Create Invoice for Job script, you'd need to add its variables to the Data Viewer. The formula for watching a variable is just the variable's name. Since variables aren't tied to tables, they don't appear in the Fields list, so you have to manually type in the names. But if you want to monitor a function, like Get (ScriptParameter), you pick it from the function list.

Items in your watch list may or may not show values when you tell Data Viewer to monitor them. Their behavior is determined by *what* you're monitoring and *when* you add the item to the watch list. Here are some guidelines:

- Local script variables are usually blank when you first create them, since they're set only when a script step runs.

- Global variables set by scripts may or may not have values in them when they're created. You see a value if you run the script that sets a global variable after you open the file, but *before* you monitor the global variable. If you haven't run a script that sets the global variable since the last time the file was closed, the value's blank.

- Local and global variables set by calculations display their values upon creation.

- Functions that monitor continually evaluated processes (like Get (Account-Name)) show their current value when you create them. These values don't update unless you click the Refresh Values button, though.

- Field values, like Customers::Last Name, have values based on the record that's active when you add the item to the watch list. Field values don't update automatically when you scroll through records. Like functions, click Refresh Values to see the updated value.

Once you've added all the items you want to monitor to Data Viewer's watch list, run your script with the debugger turned on. As a script steps sets a variable or runs a function, you see the updated value in the Value column. By watching your layouts, running Script Debugger, and monitoring Data Viewer, you've got plenty of help troubleshooting misbehaving scripts.

Warning: Anybody with FileMaker Pro Advanced can fire up Data Viewer and monitor the values in local and global variables, even if their privilege set doesn't allow them to peek into certain fields or layouts. Using local variables doesn't alleviate the security problem entirely, but it makes it a little harder for folks to peek at the data, since the script that sets a local variable has to be running in order to see the value in it.

Data Viewer isn't attached to any particular file, so its watch list contents don't change when you open and close files. The viewer can even be open while you have no databases open. Since all files and scripts share the same watch list, it can quickly get long and hard to monitor. Select items you aren't using, then click the trash can icon to delete them.

You can also use Data Viewer to test a calculation *before* you define a field for it, or add it to a testing step in a script. Click the Evaluate Now button to see the calculation's value, and then tweak the formula and reevaluate it until you get it working. Then just copy the formula and paste it into a field definition or script step.

Unlooping the Loop

If you're familiar with debuggers for other systems, you might have noticed that FileMaker's debugger is missing a *conditional breakpoint*. In other words, you can't set a breakpoint that stops the script sometimes but lets it continue other times.

If you have a long script that does a lot of looping, and you want to see what's going wrong the 237th time through the loop, then you find yourself in debugger hell.

If you set a breakpoint *in* the loop, you have to click Run to Breakpoint 236 times to get where you want to start stepping. If you put it *outside* the loop, then FileMaker runs right past the problem and you don't get a chance to see what's happening.

To solve this problem, add an If step inside the loop with a comment inside. Make sure the comment is reached only when you want to stop, and then set a breakpoint on the comment itself, as pictured here. Now FileMaker runs through the loop until it gets right where you want, and only *then* does it find the breakpoint.

Debugging Controls submenu

If you prefer menus to toolbars, or keyboard shortcuts to mouse clicks, then the Tools → Debugging Controls menu is tailor-made for you. This menu's grayed out until you start running a script with the debugger. Then the menu becomes active, with all your tools (complete with shortcuts), represented in the submenu. Plus,

---

you get a new command, Remove Breakpoints, which does just what it promises, removes all the breakpoints in the script that's currently running.

The ScriptMaker command in the Debugging Controls submenu is different from the ScriptMaker command on the *Scripts* menu, which does nothing but open ScriptMaker, with no scripts highlighted. Choosing ScriptMaker from the Debugging Controls submenu stops the script that's running in the debugger, closes the debugger window and opens ScriptMaker, with the now-stopped script highlighted. Just double-click the highlighted script to edit it.

Disable Script Steps

The Set Next Step button (page 675) lets you skip script steps manually, but it's not much help unless *you* remember to click it at the right time. Instead, FileMaker Advanced lets you specify which steps you want to disable whenever the script runs. For example, looping scripts can take a long time to run in large databases, so temporarily disable your Loop and End Loop steps while you're checking other parts of the script. After one loop, the script continues on its merry way so you can continue debugging. (See the box on page 674 for another cool way to get out of a loop.) You should also disable script steps that may do something destructive to your data—relying on Set Next Step and your mouse button is leaving an awful lot to chance.

To disable a script step (see Figure 19-5), open the script in ScriptMaker, then highlight the step you want to disable. Click the Disable button in the Edit Script dialog box. FileMaker puts two slashes in front of disabled script steps so you can identify them. To enable a step again, select it. The Disable button changes to Enable; click it and the step is back in business.

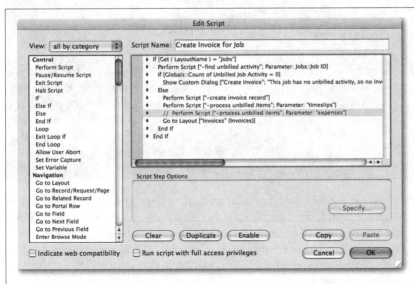

Figure 19-5:
The last Perform Script step, which is highlighted, is disabled in this illustration. When a disabled script step is highlighted the Disable button reads "Enable." You need FileMaker Advanced and script editing privileges to enable or disable a script step.

Disabling script steps is useful for debugging, but it can have long-term use, too. Any step that you disable in FileMaker Advanced gets skipped whenever someone runs it—even in FileMaker Pro. So say your company has a semi-regular promotion, that creates discounts for a limited period.

You don't have to write two different scripts, one with the discount and one without, and then worry about some kind of test to make them available on a button or in the script menu at the proper times. Write one script, making sure the discount creation steps are separate from the main process. Then you can enable the pertinent steps when the promotion starts and disable them when it's over, with very little fuss or muss.

The Database Design Report

Sometimes you inherit a large database from somebody else, and you simply don't see how it comes together. (OK, be honest. Sometimes *you* create a large database and still don't understand how it's put together.) While FileMaker's point-and-click interface makes it easy to *build* databases, teasing things out later is a different story. You can look at a script, field, layout, table occurrence, or even an entire table in FileMaker Pro, and have no idea whether the database actually uses or needs it.

GEM IN THE ROUGH

View Through a Window

Like most people, you may not realize you're free to move or resize your database windows, and even switch layouts, *while* you're debugging a script. Don't be shy; it's perfectly safe. Just bear in mind that changing layouts mid-script changes *context*, so it can also change the way your script works. Be careful to switch *back* to the original layout before you step further through the script.

Switching layouts is an invaluable technique when there are processes you want to check as the script is running ("Did I get the right found set?" "Is my script going to the right layout?" "Is the loop running through the found set properly?"). As powerful a tool as Data Viewer is, it can't show you two fields, or two layouts, side-by-side.

So, drop any fields you want on this developer-only layout, or use Table view and the fields you're working with (or any other setup that works for you). Then make a new window and switch it to this layout before you start debugging. Often, you can tuck this window off to the side and glance at it, or switch layouts as needed.

Finally, even if you prefer to use Data Viewer instead of a custom layout, it can still be helpful to open a new window before you start debugging. Although you can switch layouts while Script Debugger's running, you can't create a new one once it's started. Having that spare window open can keep you from having to stop the script, open a new window and start over again.

If you've shelled out for FileMaker Advanced, however, you've got help. Its built-in internal analysis tool, the Database Design Report (affectionately called DDR), gives you an overview of your database, where you can easily see how database items are connected and other details all in one place. You run the report, tell it what kinds of things you're interested in, and FileMaker presents the information in a series of Web pages.

Unlike the reports discussed in Chapter 6, the DDR is a report about the structure of your database, not about the data inside. It tells you what tables and fields you have, which fields are used on each layout, and so on, but nothing about the information in your records and fields.

Generating the DDR

The Database Design Report window lets you tell FileMaker exactly what you want it to report on. You get to pick which files and table occurrences to include, what kinds of things you want to report on, and what format you want the report to use. You also get to decide whether you want to open the report right away, or just save it for later use. To get started, choose Tools → Database Design Report. Up pops the Database Design report dialog box (Figure 19-6).

Figure 19-6:
Turn on "Automatically open report when done" if you want to see your Database Design Report right away. If you're running this report because you want to look at it right now, turn this option on. Sometimes, though, you just run the report to have around in case you need it later. If that's the case, turn this option off to save a few clicks.

The Available Files list in this window shows every open file. To include a file in the report, turn on the checkbox by its name. FileMaker assumes you want every file at first, so you may have to do more turning off than on.

In the DDR window, you tell FileMaker which files to examine by turning on their checkboxes. Select one in the list to see all its fields in the "Include fields from tables in selected file" list. Again, you can use the checkboxes in this list to tell FileMaker which tables you want included in the report.

In the "Include in Report" section, there's a checkbox for each kind of database element the DDR can report on. Again, FileMaker assumes you want everything, but you're free to limit the report to just certain information. The less you report on, the faster the report runs, and the smaller the final files.

Normally, FileMaker saves the report in HTML format so you can read and navigate it in any Web browser, but it also offers a more structured XML format. XML files aren't easy for *humans* to read, but with the help of other software, you can process the XML and integrate information about your database into other systems. Furthermore, several companies make DDR analysis tools that process the XML version of your DDR and provide extra tools for browsing, finding, and reporting on the information it contains. (See the box on page 680 for more information on these third-party tools.)

When you're done making decisions, click Create. FileMaker asks you where to save the report. The DDR is made up of several files, so you probably want to make a new folder to hold the report. The more complex your files, the longer it takes to create the DDR. In a file with dozens of tables, each of which may have dozens or even hundreds of fields, this could take a minute or more. FileMaker displays a progress bar for you, so you can gauge how long the process will take.

Note: A DDR is a snapshot of the database at the moment you create it. So it's good to make periodic DDRs as your database evolves. You can create a record of when you added or changed various parts of the database. A DDR can also help with troubleshooting broken elements (page 681).

Using the DDR

If you checked "Automatically open report when done," when you created the DDR, FileMaker launches your browser and shows you the DDR Report Overview (Figure 19-7) as soon as the progress bar disappears.

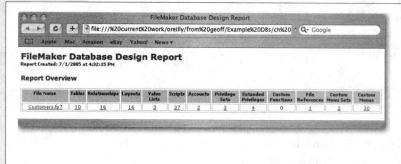

Figure 19-7:
Report Overview is the first thing you see when you open a DDR is . It's a table, with one row for every file you included in the report, and a column for each option you checked when you created the DDR. Each "cell" contains a link leading to more information. Each DDR lists the time/ and date of its creation, so you can tell if the report matches the current state of your database.

This file is the main report file, and it has URL links that bring up the detail pages. To view the DDR later, go to where you saved it and open the file called Summary, or Summary.html. (You also see a folder named for each file you selected when you created the DDR.)

On the overview page, the DDR tells you which elements you chose when you created the DDR. If you click a file name, you see the file detail page (Figure 19-8), with lots of information about that file. The links in each column go to the same file detail page, but each link scrolls you to the relevant section. On large databases, with lots of fields, this option can save you a lot of time scrolling through the page, looking for what you want. For instance, if you click the number in the Relationships column, you see the Relationships section of the file detail page.

Figure 19-8:
When you click the File Name link on the Overview page, you see this page. The top link on the left leads back to the Overview page. All the others just scroll the page to various important parts. The report itself is also loaded with links. You can click any link to go to more details about that item.

Use the DDR to help you figure out what parts of your database can safely be edited or deleted. Since it's so easy to create tables, fields, and layouts in FileMaker, you may well end up with extras that you don't need when your database reaches completion. You can make your database easier to understand and more efficient by deleting these extra elements. But even if a database is the last word in efficiency, running a DDR is one of the best ways to trace the designer's thinking process.

To see if—and how—a particular element is used, look at its detail. Suppose you have a bunch of fields you'd like to delete from your database, and you want to find out whether it's safe to do so. First, click the Tables link—fields are part of tables. You see a list of tables, with information about how many fields each table contains, along with a list of occurrences of each table in the Relationship Graph (Figure 19-8). Click the link for a table's fields, and you see a list of all the fields defined for that table.

POWER USERS' CLINIC

Getting the Most from the DDR

At first glance, you may not appreciate the true value of the DDR. It appears to tell you the same things you can find out in other FileMaker windows, like Define Database, Script-Maker, and so on. But once you run your first DDR, you understand it has powers those flimsy boxes never dreamed of.

For example, the DDR information for a script helps you determine how the script functions in and interacts with the rest of the database. In a neat chart, you can see every field, layout, table, table occurrence, and custom function the script uses. More importantly, you can see every script or layout button that runs this script. That kind of information would be very hard to nail down without the DDR. You'd basically have to go to each layout in your database, click anything that might be a button, and see if the script you're interested in is attached to it.

If you've created Custom Menus , you'd have to check them individually, too. The DDR gathers up all that information for you; not just for scripts but for tables, layouts, value lists, and other kinds of database elements as well.

If you want even more power, consider acquiring a DDR analysis tool. One such tool—Analyzer from Waves in Motion—can let you search your DDR, quickly hotlink from element to element (with forward, back, and history), and print trace reports that show *everything* a script does, including the things its subscripts do.

It's also worth mentioning that some tools can analyze your database *without* using the DDR. They tend to be faster than DDR analysis tools, but somewhat less comprehensive. Two excellent choices are MetaData Magic (for Version 7 and 8 files) by New Millennium Communications (*www.nmci. com*) and Brushfire (for v7 only) by Chaparral Software (*www.chapsoft.com*).

Details appear in the Field Name, Type, and Options columns for every field. Comments, if there are any, show up in the Comments column. Any layouts or scripts that use the field are listed in the Layout and Script columns, respectively. You see the information in the Relationship column only if it's a key field. Fields used in layouts, relationships, and scripts are called *dependencies* of those elements.

Note: Even if you don't use a Go to Field script step for a specific field, a key field may be listed in the scripts column. Go to Related Record, or any other step that uses a relationship, also requires the use of that relationship's key field, so it also has that field as a dependency.

A DDR is also very useful if you're upgrading a file from a previous version of File-Maker. You can figure out which elements of the old database are crucial and which ones you don't have to bother recreating when you build your new database.

Finding Broken Elements with the DDR

Suppose you've deleted a field, unaware that it's a dependency for a script, as described in the previous section. Later, you run that script and notice an error, but you're not sure what you did wrong. The DDR is the best way to track down the error—which is the first step in fixing it. Take, for example, the "-find unbilled activity" script you wrote back in Chapter 15 (page 562). It searched in the Expenses::Job ID field for all unbilled expenses...but you've deleted the Job ID field.

If you examine that script in ScriptMaker, you can see the words "<Field Missing>" right in the script.

```
Set Field [Expenses::<Field Missing>; "==" & Get (ScriptParameter)]
```

You might be able to find the error, but then again you might not, because the "<Field Missing>" error isn't bold, or red, or highlighted in any way. And as great as Script Debugger is, it doesn't lead you to the broken script step either. But a DDR can help you find all the trouble spots that arise from the deleted Expenses:: Job ID field.

To do this kind of sleuthing, search the DDR page for a character string, using your browser's Find tool (pressing Ctrl+F or ⌘-F does the trick in most programs). Type the text you're looking for in the Find field, then click Next (or whatever button your browser uses) to start the search. You see the first instance of your search criteria highlighted. Click the button again to find other instances.

The whole list of errors you might search for appears below. If you have any inkling what kind of error you're looking for, start with that one:

- **<Missing Field>**. Referenced field is missing.

- **<Missing Table Occurrence>**. Referenced table occurrence set is missing.

- **<Missing Base Table>**. Referenced base table is missing.

- **<Missing File Reference>**. Referenced file reference is missing.

- **<Missing Layout>**. Referenced layout is missing.

- **<Missing Valuelist>**. Referenced value list is missing.

- **<Missing Custom Function>**. Referenced custom function is missing.

- **<Missing Script>**. Referenced script is missing.

- **<Missing Account>**. Referenced account is missing.

- **<Missing Privilege Set>**. Referenced privilege set is missing.

- **<Missing Extended Privilege>**. Referenced extended privilege is missing.

- **<Missing Custom Menu>**. Referenced custom menu is missing.

- **<Missing Custom Menu Set>**. Referenced custom menu set is missing.

Once you find a broken element, return to your database and fix it manually. The DDR won't update itself to show your fix until you run another one. And since you can't mark the electronic version of your DDR, a good way to keep track of your work is to print it out, then mark off each item as you fix it. Then, when all the broken elements are fixed (or you've deleted all the unused stuff), run another DDR. This time it should be clean, but if it's not, you've got the tools to fix it.

Tooltips

Training people, either when you first launch a new database, or when new employees come into your workforce, is a big part of making your database successful. You can have beautiful layouts, bulletproof privilege sets and complex, well-thought-out scripts, but if folks don't know how and when to use them, they'll miss out on the benefits. To spare you the wrath of confused (or worse, frustrated) users, FileMaker Advanced has a feature called *tooltips*. Like the onscreen labels that pop up in Windows and many other programs, tooltips can help guide people through the features you've created for them, maybe even cut down on training time.

You can attach tooltips to any object, or group of objects, that you can select on a layout: fields, text, or graphics. Tooltips are visible in FileMaker Pro Advanced, FileMaker Pro, runtimes (page 695), and on databases that use Instant Web Publishing. You can create, edit, or delete tooltips only with FileMaker Pro Advanced.

To create a tooltip, go to Layout mode and choose the object you want to have a tooltip. Then choose Format → Set Tooltip. Create your tooltip, and then click OK. Now people see the tooltip when the mouse hovers over the object in Browse Mode. Just like tooltips in other applications, the tooltip doesn't appear immediately, so as not to inconvenience more advanced users.

The tooltip for a report button could give users the name of the report that the button runs. Or you could make field labels into tooltips, and let people know about the format the field needs. But the Set Tooltip dialog box gives you the power of calculations, so you might as welll make full use of them. Using the GetNthRecord () function, you could put a tooltip on a button that takes your users to the next record. But *before* they click, the tooltip shows content from the next record. Now your users don't need to go to the next record to see if it's the one they want. See Figure 19-9 to see this calculation and tooltip in action.

Copying Database Structure

Since a large percentage of a database designer's work is fairly repetitive, File-Maker Advanced provides some tools that let you take shortcuts through the tedious process of creating tables, fields, and scripts. By copying work you've already done, you can spend less time defining fields or recreating complex scripts and more time doing the creative work of designing a database.

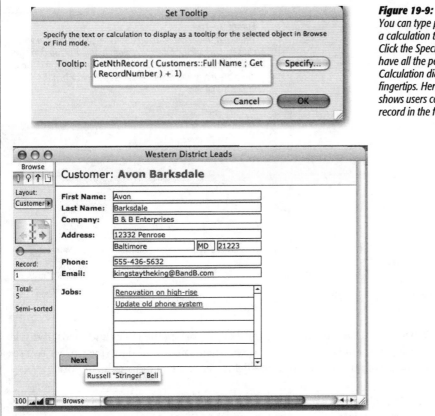

Figure 19-9:
Figure 19-9:
You can type plain text, or create a calculation to display a tooltip. Click the Specify button and you have all the power of the Specify Calculation dialog box at your fingertips. Here, a claculation shows users content from the next record in the found set.

As this section describes, you can import tables and fields without copying data between tables in the same file and between different files. FileMaker also provides Copy and Paste buttons in several major dialog boxes so that you can reuse fields, scripts and script steps. (You need full access privileges in both the source file and the target file to import or copy and paste elements from file to file.)

Importing Tables and Fields

Back on page 629, you learned how to have FileMaker create tables and fields as you import data. But FileMaker Advanced is even cleverer. It lets you import tables and fields *without* the accompanying data, so you can copy the framework and fill in the information later. Start by choosing File → Define Database and clicking the Table tab. Click Import, and then locate the file that contains the table you want to copy.

You can even choose the current file, effectively copying an entire table or set of tables within the same file. Next, you tell FileMaker which specific tables to import in the dialog box shown in Figure 19-10.

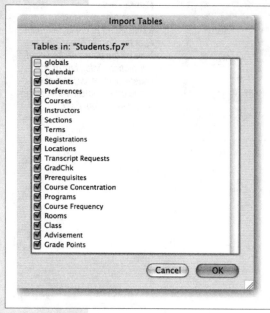

Figure 19-10:
You see a simple list of all tables in the source file you've chosen. Click all the tables you want to import. You don't get to specify which fields are imported – they all come in. So if there are a few you don't need, delete them when the import's finished.

When FileMaker Advanced has finished importing the tables and fields, it displays a dialog box similar to the one you see when you import data (page 627). You see a summary of how many tables and fields were created during the import.

Tip: When FileMaker Advanced builds your new tables and fields, it saves a record of its progress in a log file. If you see an error in the summary window, click the Open Log File button to see what went wrong.

Copying Fields

If you have complex calculations that you want to reuse in another table within the same file, or in a different file, use the Copy and Paste buttons on the Fields tab in Define Database dialog box. Use the Shift key to select items next to each other in the field list. Use the ⌘ key (Mac) or the Ctrl key (Windows) to select fields that aren't next to each other in the list. When you've selected the fields you need, click Copy. Then open the table where you want to create the new fields, and finally click Paste to do the deed.

When you copy *calculation* fields, your results may vary depending on whether you also copy the field's calculations reference (page 384). It usually saves time to plan ahead and make sure the field references already exist in the target table before you copy and paste. But you can always paste the calculation fields and clean up the references later, especially if you intend to use different field names anyway. Here are some general rules:

- If fields matching the references in your copied calculation don't exist in the target table, FileMaker pastes the calculation as a comment (/*Amount * Quantity*/), since it can't find matching fields in the new table. Simply edit the calculations with the new field references, and then click OK.

- To save yourself some editing work, *first* paste into the target table (or create) fields with names that match the ones in the calculation you're transferring. Then, when you paste the calculation, FileMaker resolves the field references automatically.

- If the field references are local (that is, they refer to other fields within the same table), you can copy the fields referenced in the calculation *and* the calculation field at the same time. When you paste the set of fields, FileMaker resolves the field references automatically, and you have nothing to edit.

- If you're copying a calculation field that contains a fully qualified field reference (containing both a table name and a field name, like Expenses::Job ID), the calculation again transfers just fine.

Copying Scripts and Script Steps

You can use the Import button in the Define Scripts dialog box to import whole scripts from other files, but if you have FileMaker Advanced, you can avoid that cumbersome process. Simply open the file that contains the scripts you want to copy, then use the Copy and Paste buttons in the Define Scripts dialog box. Copy the scripts you want to reuse, then open the Define Scripts dialog box in the *target* file, and finally click Paste. Check all pasted scripts to see if any field, layout, or other reference needs to be pointed to another element in its new location. Copying or importing scripts works best when you need the whole script *and* all the elements referenced in your script were already in place, so that no script steps break on the way in.

You can also copy script steps individually or in chunks. In the Edit Script dialog box, select just the script steps you want, then click Copy. Then you either create a new script or open the script that needs your copied steps. Highlight the script step just *above* where you want the next steps to land, and then click Paste. Your recycled steps appear in your script. Fix any broken references as needed.

You don't even have to move to a new script to find Copy and Paste useful. If you have a script in which a series of steps could be duplicated, and then edited so that they work slightly differently, just copy and paste them. Sure, you could use the Duplicate button, but then you have to move each step down into place one by one. With Copy and Paste, you get to place the new steps right where you want them.

Note: FileMaker doesn't include break points when you Import or Copy/Paste scripts or script steps.

Custom Menus

FileMaker's menus are all about power. Through them, you can control—and limit—your users' access to the whole feature set. As the developer, you need all those commands to do your design and development of your database, but there are plenty of commands that give too much power to your users, particularly folks who don't much computer experience or who aren't shy about experimenting with commands...even if they aren't sure what might happen at the other end of a dialog box.

Brand new to version 8 is the power to customize FileMaker's menus. You can remove the Delete All Records and the Replace Field Contents commands for all your users, or you can remove them only from certain users' privilege sets. If you're the type of developer who likes to take charge of the user interface (see the box on page 529, Custom Menus are your dream come true.

Here are just a few of the things you can do:

- Remove potentially destructive items from menus (Delete All Records, for example).

- Edit menu commands: Change Modify Last Find to read Repeat Last Find, perhaps.

- Add, edit, or remove keyboard shortcuts: If you can't remember that Ctrl+S (Windows) or ⌘-S (Mac) does *not* mean Save in FileMaker, you can at least prevent that pesky Sort dialog box from popping up every time.

- Remove entire menus, like the Window menu, which can be confusing for folks new to FileMaker Pro.

- Run a script from a new or edited menu item: Substitute a custom Delete Record script (complete with a custom warning), for FileMaker's normal Delete Record command.

- Change menus when a user changes layout: Create a special menu that runs commands or scripts that pertain to invoices and only shows up on the Invoice layout.

- Make one set of menus for Mac and another for Windows. For example, you may want to suppress the Window → New Window command in Windows, since it bafflingly resizes *all* windows whenever someone uses it.

- Make menu sets that match privilege sets: Give Admin-level users a special menu showing the scripts only they can run.

You can create and edit Custom Menus only in FileMaker Advanced, but anyone can use them with FileMaker Pro or in a runtime version of your database. These menus don't transfer to files you publish on the Web, though (page 644). When you create Custom Menus for a database, be sure to provide a User Guide or similar documentation explaining what your custom commands do.

You can use Custom Menus to supplement, and even go beyond, privilege set features. For example, if you want to limit data entry people to using the copy and paste buttons that run *your* scripts, remove the Edit menu for users with that privilege set. They won't be able to use keyboard shortcuts to cut, copy, or paste. Removing the View menu prevents the Mode pop-up menu, toolbar, and all related keyboard shortcuts from working. (But you'll need to do some work providing replacement commands in your buttons and menus.)

Note: As powerful as Custom Menus are, they're no substitute for good security practices, as discussed in Chapter 16.

Editing a Menu

All new files you create use FileMaker's standard menu set unless you tell them to use a custom set. Just as each new file contains three default privilege sets, you get one set of custom menus that you can edit to suit your needs. And as with privilege sets, some items are in brackets and cannot be edited or duplicated, but you're free to create new menus with the same name and customize them.

Your goal for this exercise in customizing menus is to remove menu items that might confuse your users. When people are just learning FileMaker, simplified menus are less intimidating than masses of unfamiliar commands. You can also help protect your database from damage by someone unwittingly choosing the wrong command. You start the process by editing the View menu so that only a few items show up.

1. **In FileMaker Advanced, choose File → Define → Custom Menus.**

   The Define Custom Menus dialog box appears (Figure 19-11).

Figure 19-11:
You can reorder the items in the Custom Menu list with the "View by" pop-up menu. You can also click each of the four column heads to sort the list. Probably this window's most important item is the small pop-up menu at the bottom. You can do all the editing of custom menus you like, but unless you remember to switch to your custom set, you don't see any change in your file.

2. **Click "View copy" in the Custom Menu list, and then click Edit.**

   Or you can double-click an item to edit it. The Edit Custom Menu window appears (Figure 19-12). This where you tell the custom menu what it should look like and how it should behave.

Figure 19-12:
This dialog box has many splendors. You can specify that a menu appears only when your user's on a Mac, or only when she's in Find mode. You can even make specific menu commands appear only on Windows computers, but not on Macs. You can add, change or remove keyboard shortcuts. You can even take the liberty of replacing a command's normal action with a script.

3. **Click the checkbox beside the Override Title field, and then type *Switch* in the field.**

   The Override Title option changes what the user sees in his menu bar. You changed it to Switch since the word "View" is too vague for beginning users. Plus, you don't want them getting confused if they pick up FileMaker's manual (or this book) for help. The changed menu name should clue people in that they need to look at your custom documentation for help.

   The menu's name *in this dialog box* remains View Copy; that's how you know it originated from the normal View menu, not from scratch.

Warning: If you customize menus even in the slightest, consider turning off the built-in Help menu as well. It opens FileMaker's online Help file, which can't answer people's questions about *your* custom menus.

---

4. **Select the first hyphen below "Go to Layout >" in the Menu Items list, and then press Shift as you select the last item in the list. Click the trash can Icon. Then select Layout Mode and delete it.**

   All highlighted items disappear when you click the trash can icon (those hyphens represent divider lines in menus). You should have only three mode

---

menu items, a hyphen and a Go to Layout menu (a total of five items) remaining in the list.

5. **Click the Browse Mode menu item. As with View mode in step 2, turn on the override checkbox and change the title to "Browse".**

   This menu item title replaces the text that appears in the list. Your users will see a command called Browse, not Browse Mode. Notice the quotation marks around "Browse." If you forget (or refuse) to type the quotes, FileMaker obstinately puts them back in for you. That's your indication that FileMaker considers that text a character string, and that's a further cue that the Specify button gives you access to the calculation dialog box.

6. **Repeat the previous step for Find Mode, Preview Mode and Go to Layout>. Change Find Mode's title to "Find," change Preview Mode's title to "Print Preview," and change Go to Layout>'s title to "Show." When you've made these changes, click OK.**

   Use terms that are easy for folks to comprehend. Most people already understand what Print Preview does, but the meaning of Preview Mode is a little murky.

7. **Choose "Custom Menu Set 1" from the Default menu set for this file pop-up menu, and then click OK.**

   You've just told FileMaker to display the customized version of your View menu.

   The View menu now says "Switch." When you click it, there are only four items. Notice that the Layout tool is grayed out, and Layout Mode has disappeared from the Layout pop-up menu at the bottom of your screen. Also, the commands in the pop-up menu match the changes you made in the View custom menu.

By editing menus to suppress items that might confuse those who haven't had in-depth FileMaker training, you've made your database a friendlier place to work. But don't stop there: In the next section, you'll learn how to create menus that show lists of commands you *do* want people to see, like your scripts.

Creating a New Menu

Using the steps described in the previous tutorial, you can edit FileMaker's menus to your heart's content, renaming them, and deleting extraneous commands to make room for new ones. If you don't necessarily want to delete any existing menus or commands, or even if you do, you can always create *additional* menus from scratch.

1. **In Define Custom Menus, click Create. In the Create Custom Menu window that appears, choose "Start with an empty menu." Click OK.**

   If an existing menu is similar to what you need, you can use it as a template when you create new menus. But in this case, you don't need any existing menu commands because you'll attach your scripts to a new menu. When you click OK, the Edit Custom Menu window appears, just as in Figure 19-12. This time, though, you won't edit it, you'll build the menu from the ground up.

2. **Type "Invoices" in the Custom Menu Name fields. Also type "Invoices" in the Override Title field.**

   Since you started with an empty menu, FileMaker assumes you want a custom name. If you don't type a name, the word "Untitled" appears in your menu bar.

3. **Turn off the Menu Mode options for Find and Preview modes.**

   You don't want your scripts run from either Find or Preview modes, so by telling the menu not to even *show up* in those modes, you're adding another layer of security.

4. **Click the Command button. In the Specify FileMaker Command dialog box, choose the "No command assigned" option above the list of available commands, and then click OK**

   This action creates a new command, but doesn't use one of FileMaker's canned actions. You could use this method to build a new menu that picks and chooses from various default menus, but in this instance, you're going to run your scripts from the new Invoices menu.

5. **In the Title field, type *Create invoice for unbilled expenses*, and then click Specify (to the right of the Action pop-up menu). From the list in the Specify Script Options window, choose the "Create Invoice for Job" script, and then click OK.**

   The Specify Script Options shows all the scripts you've created in this database file. To add more scripts to this menu, repeat the last two steps until you've created new commands for all the scripts you want. The arrows to the left of each item let you rearrange them. Click the Separator button to create a divider line in the menu.

6. **Click the Menu Sets tab of the Define Custom Menus dialog box. If necessary, select "Custom Menu Set 1" in the list, and then click Edit.**

   The Edit Menu Set window appears.

7. **Scroll through the list of Available Custom Menus until you see Invoices. Select it, and then click the Move button. Click the arrow to the left of the Invoices menu and move it up, so that it appears above [Scripts]. Click OK until you're back in your database.**

   The Invoices custom menu is now a part of the new custom menu set and it appears between the Records and Scripts Menu.

So far, you've simplified one of FileMaker's menus and created a custom menu from scratch. Now you need to get rid of a menu that strikes fear even in the hearts of experienced FileMaker users: You're going to *completely* suppress the Windows menu.

Removing a Menu

At first glance through the Define Custom Menus dialog box, you might think that you just click an item in the Custom Menu list, and then click Delete to remove it. But you'll run into problems if you do. First, if you highlight menus with brackets around their names, the Delete button is inactive. And if you select an item where the Delete button remains active (Help), and then delete it, you get a nasty surprise when you click OK and return to your file. You see the text "Missing Menu" inserted in the menu bar, and the Help menu stays right where it was. Despite these obstacles, you *can* remove an entire menu; you just have to dig a little deeper to do it.

Tip: Troubleshoot a file for missing menu items by running a DDR (page 676), or by checking Get (LastError) after you load a menu set in a script.

As mentioned previously (page 30), the Window menu can cause problems for new users. For example, the Show command lists files that they may not know are open. Hiding and showing windows is also perilous for new users if they don't understand how FileMaker manages windows. Instead of bothering people with stuff they don't need to know, you can just suppress this menu entirely by removing it from the menu bar.

1. **In the Define Custom Menus dialog box, click the Menu Sets tab. Select Custom Menu Set 1, and then click Edit.**

   The Edit Menu Set dialog box appears.

2. **In the Menus Set Name field, type "Data Entry."**

   This descriptive name helps you remember the menu set's purpose. If you like, type additional information in the Comment box.

3. **In the "Menus in 'Data Entry'" list, click the [Window] menu. Click Clear, and then click OK until you're back in your database.**

   Usually brackets on a list item indicate you can't delete it. But you *can* delete it from the display list, as you've just done. The [Window] menu remains in the Available Custom Menus list at left. If you change your mind, you can move it back into the display list to restore it.

Back in your database, the Window menu is gone entirely from the menu bar. This menu configuration is ideal for your data entry people, but not so great for administrative users, who understand the Window menu and use it all the time. Read on to find out how to tailor *sets* of menus for people with different privilege levels.

Installing Custom Menu Sets

FileMaker Pro Advanced lets you create a set of custom menus (see Figure 19-13) and use it as the *default* for a file, meaning that everyone who uses your database sees it, every time. But since the people using your database may have different levels of skill (and trust), you may want your custom menus to adapt accordingly. In fact, if you've read this book's chapters on layouts and privilege sets, you have all the tools you need to make the right menus appear to the right people at the right time. It's a simple matter of assigning menu sets to these existing features. You can conceal certain menus and commands from people who don't need them, but keep them available for everybody else. Or maybe you just want menu items to show up when they make sense for the active layout.

Figure 19-13:
The field on the left lists the Custom Menus attached to the current set. Look in the list to see your edited View menu. The list on the right is a subset of the list on the left. Menus that aren't in the right-hand list are not displayed when this custom menu set is active. The Move, Clear, and Clear All buttons are similar to the ones in the Sort dialog box.

Once you've created menu sets using the steps outlined earlier in this chapter, you can install them in any of several ways:

- **As the default for a file.** That's what you did in the tutorial in the "Editing a Menu" section on page 687. Unless you tell FileMaker otherwise, everybody gets the same custom menus. This option works great for a runtime file, or any situation where all users are at the same level.

- **On individual layouts.** In this scenario, when someone switches layouts, either by menu command or via a script, the menu set changes to a layout-specific one of your choosing. Choose Layout → Layout Setup to attach a custom menu set to a layout.

- **By mode.** This option offers the ultimate in elegance. It lets you do things like create a set with only one menu and just a few items, and make it the *only* menu people see when they're in Find mode. Instead of a gaggle of buttons to perform and cancel finds, write the appropriate scripts and display them in the one menu, short and sweet.

- **When a script is run.** By checking the privilege set in a script that runs when someone logs into your file, you can load a set of menus customized to that person's level of privilege. Use the Get (PrivilegeSetName) step to check privileges (page 585) and the Install Menu Set script step to specify which menu set installs. (If you have a Re-login script, you need to make sure that the right menu set is installed each time users re-login.)

Warning: Since you're effectively removing features for your users when you customize menus, thorough testing is a critical part of the process. Be sure to test menus with all affected layouts, privilege sets, scripts and across platforms. In FileMaker Pro Advanced, choose Tools → Custom Menus to switch among sets as you test them.

Developer Utilities

The Tools → Developer Utilities command looks so insignificant and benign to the unsuspecting person, but behind it lurks a vast array of powerful features. There are developer utilities for all of the following techniques:

- Rename one file in a system of interconnected files, and have every file reference in the *other* files automatically update to the new name.

- Turn your database into a *kiosk* system. You can use this feature to make interactive programs that run on publicly accessible computers. In this setup, FileMaker hides the menu bars, the Windows taskbar or Macintosh Dock, and every other screen decoration that's not a part of your layouts.

- Create a *runtime solution*—a special version of your database that anyone can use, even if they don't have FileMaker Pro.

- Permanently remove full access to files so you can send your database to people you don't know, and be sure they can't tamper with your hard work, including your scripts, table and field definitions, and relationship graph.

- Create an error log to help you troubleshoot problems that occur when FileMaker generates runtimes.

In fact, you can (and often want to) do *several* of these things at once. Here's an example: You build a beautiful interactive product catalog, complete with pictures and an easy-to-use ordering screen. You then want to set up a kiosk computer at a trade show where attendees can use the database to see what you have and place their orders. Using the developer utilities, you could do all this:

- Add "Kiosk" to the end of every file name, so you can keep this copy separate from the one you use in the office.

- Make the database run in Kiosk mode so users at the trade show won't be able to exit FileMaker, switch to other programs, or otherwise cause mischief.

• Make the whole thing run by itself so you don't have to bother installing File-Maker on the computer you're renting just for this job.

• Lock out full access so if someone manages to steal a copy of your database while you're not looking, they can't see how it works or steal your product's beauty shots.

Using the Developer Utilities

The most confusing thing about the developer utilities is that you have to *close* your files before you work with them—just the opposite of every other command in FileMaker. So close the files you want to modify, and *then* choose File → Developer Utilities. You behold the Developer Utilities dialog box (Figure 19-14).

Figure 19-14:
The Developer Utilities window (File → Developer Utilities) lets you gather the files you want to change, and then tell FileMaker what changes to make. When you're done, you click Create, and FileMaker builds new versions of your files (in a new location) with all the changes in place.

In the Developer Utilities window, you first choose which files you want to work with. Click Add to put a file on the list. In Mac OS X, you can select several files at once in the Open File dialog box using your Shift and ⌘ keystrokes. Alas, in Windows, you have to pick just one file, and then click Add again to add the next one. Keep on adding until every file you want to change is in the list. If you accidentally add the wrong file, select it and click Remove.

You have to pick one file to be your *main* file. This file is the one that opens first if you create a runtime solution, for example. To set the main file, just double-click it in the list. FileMaker shows a red square—it looks surprisingly like a script breakpoint—by the main file.

Renaming files

Of course, you can always rename a file in Window Explorer or the Mac's Finder. But those interfaces let you change *only* the file name. Developer Utilities makes that look like child's play. When it changes a file name, it also looks *inside* the file and updates any internal file references to match the file's new name. If you've ever tried to open two versions of a multiple file solution at the same time (to test some scripts that delete data and on a copy of the files, say), you know that FileMaker sometimes gets confused and keeps multiple copies open even after you try to close one set. You can eliminate the crossover problem by renaming one set in Developer Utilities. You can test your scripts without a problem, since the scripts in the copy files automatically inherit the correct new file names.

To rename a file or set of files, add them to the Solution File list (Figure 19-14). Select a file, type the new name in the "Rename file" box, and then click Change. FileMaker shows the new name in the New Name column.

Next, you need to pick the *project folder*. This folder is the one where FileMaker saves the finished files. Just click the Specify button under "Project Folder" and pick any folder you wish. If the folder already contains files with the same names as the ones you're about to create, you get an error message—unless you turn on "Overwrite matching files within the Project Folder." When you click Create, FileMaker Advanced makes copies of the files with their new names, leaving the originals untouched.

To complete the example above (your kiosk product catalog), you would turn on "Create Runtime solution application(s)," "Remove admin access from files permanently," and "Enable Kiosk mode for non-admin accounts." Only the first option needs to be configured.

Create Runtime Solution application(s)

To create Runtime Solutions, add the files to the Solution Files list, and then select a project folder, just as you did above. Don't type a new name for the Runtime in this window, though. Click the Specify button under Solution Options. You see the Specify Solution Options dialog box, as shown in Figure 19-15.

When you tell FileMaker you want to build a runtime solution, it generates a special program that you need to include with your databases. This program can do most of what FileMaker Pro can do, but it can't modify tables, fields, layouts, or scripts. You get to decide what this program is called—just type it in the Runtime Name box. Along with the runtime program, FileMaker creates new copies of each of your files to go with it, and changes all the file name extensions to something other than .fp7. Tell FileMaker what extension to use in the Extension field.

Warning: Your computer's operating system uses file name extensions to figure out which program files belong to. The Developer Utilities let you assign *any* extension you want, but you should avoid common extensions like .doc, .jpg, .mp3, and so on. You know computers—they get confused easily.

The new files don't just have a new name; they are also modified internally so they're *bound* to the runtime program, and the runtime program in turn can open only properly bound files. In other words, when you send people a runtime program, they can't use it to open any old FileMaker Pro file.

Figure 19-15:
The Specify Solution Options window lets you tell FileMaker what you want done to the files. Turn on a checkbox in the Options list to tell FileMaker you want that thing done to your files. Most options need to be configured, and when you select an item in the list, the bottom half of the window lets you change the appropriate settings.

To facilitate the binding process, FileMaker asks you to provide a *bindkey*. File-Maker stores this value in both the runtime program and any database files in the Developer Utilities window. The value you use for the bindkey is entirely unimportant, and there's no need to keep it secret. But if you later want to bind *new* databases to the same runtime program, you'll have to use the same bindkey.

Finally, when users exit the runtime program (in other words, when they close your database system), they see a "Made with FileMaker" splash screen. Normally, this screen looks like the one in Figure 19-16. You can also control how long the splash screen shows by putting the number of seconds in the Delay box. Unfortunately, you can't make it go away entirely.

Remove admin access from files permanently

The "Remove admin access from files permanently" option doesn't actually remove the accounts that have full access. Instead, it modifies the [Full Access] privilege set so that it no longer truly has full access. If you log in with an account that normally has full access, it doesn't have access to the Define Database window, Layout mode, or ScriptMaker, and its access to Accounts & Privileges is limited to the Extended Privileges tab. This option has no settings.

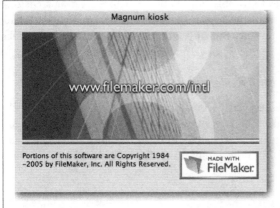

Figure 19-16:
When you quit a runtime solution, this window pops up for a few seconds. You can't get rid of the "Made with FileMaker" logo, but you can change the big FileMaker graphic to anything you want. Just turn on "Custom image" and pick a picture file from your hard drive. FileMaker stretches the picture to fit in the window, so to avoid distortion, you should create a picture that is exactly 382 pixels wide and 175 pixels high.

Enable Kiosk mode for non-admin accounts

If you turn on Kiosk mode and then open the new file using an account that has full access, you don't see any changes. But if you log in with a lesser account, *everything* changes. The screen goes completely black, except for the content area of your database window. You can see an example in Figure 19-17.

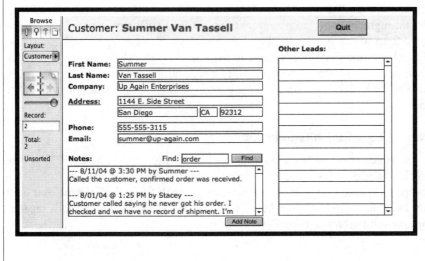

Figure 19-17:
When you open a database in Kiosk mode (with an account that doesn't have full access) it looks like this. Everything on the screen is completely black outside your layout. You can still switch layouts and otherwise interact with your database, but you can't make new windows, resize the window, exit FileMaker, or switch to other programs. You also can't print, enter Find mode, or otherwise use FileMaker's features unless buttons on the layout let you.

When you use Kiosk mode, you typically hide the status area and let people control everything from buttons on layouts. Alternatively, you can use custom menus (page 686) to hide all the menus and commands that would let nosy people poke around in your file. Remember to troubleshoot your file before creating a custom runtime from it, because any problems in your file (broken links, missing data, bad scripts) also show up in the runtime. But once you've suppressed all the normal FileMaker commands, folks have no way of getting around these problems.

Databases must have a FileMaker file extension

Sometimes people, Mac types especially, create databases without the .fp7 file extension, only to regret that decision later. An extension is computers' most accurate way to identify a file. So turn on "Database must have a FileMaker file extension," and FileMaker adds ".fp7" to the end of every file name that doesn't already have it.

Create error log for any processing errors

While FileMaker processes your files, applying your options, building runtime programs, or renaming files, it might encounter problems. Turn on "Create error log for any processing errors" so you can see what went wrong. FileMaker saves error messages in a file on your hard drive (you get to pick where it goes and what it's called).

Loading and saving settings

If you maintain a database system that other people use, you may well run your files through developer utilities every time you send out a new version. To save you the tedium of configuring the Database Utilities dialog box again and again, FileMaker lets you save all your settings to a special file—just click Save Settings. Later, when you're ready to process your files again, click Load Settings and select the same file. FileMaker sets up everything in the dialog box for you. All you have to do is click Create.

Delivering a Runtime Solution

If you build a runtime solution with FileMaker Advanced in Mac OS X, it runs *only* in Mac OS X. Likewise, if you build from Windows, your runtime solution is limited to Windows. If you need a runtime solution for *both* platforms, you must buy FileMaker Advanced for Mac OS X *and* for Windows and build a separate runtime solution on each kind of computer.

File Maintenance

The File Maintenance utility doesn't come into play as you're developing a database. Instead, you use it periodically on existing, actively used databases—with good reason. As people add, remove, and modify records in a database, FileMaker has to go to great lengths to make room for things in the file on your hard drive. For the sake of speed, the program avoids actions that require massive reorganization of the data on disk. As FileMaker shuffles things around, information from one record can spread to different parts of the file, and sections of the file can be wasted—too small to hold anything useful, but stuck there in the middle of the file anyway.

The Tools → File Maintenance command tidies up such scattered data and frees unused disk space. When you choose it, you see the File Maintenance dialog box (Figure 19-18).

Figure 19-18:
The File Maintenance window (File → File Maintenance) lets you do two things: Compact and Optimize your files. You get to decide which to do by turning on or off the appropriate checkboxes. You're free to do either of these, or to do both at once. Each takes quite a bit of time on a large file, so plan ahead.

The Compact File option goes through the file from top to bottom seeking out the wasted space. When it finds some, it moves everything *else* in the file a little bit so the wasted space is gone. In the end, you have a file that's as small as possible.

The Optimize File option works differently. It goes through the records, layouts, scripts, and other elements of your database and makes sure all the information for each element is together. Instead of searching all over your large file to get the entire Customer list, FileMaker can stay within a consecutive block of information in a small area of the file. Everything in the database works just a little bit faster.

Warning: Running File Maintenance on a damaged file can actually make the problem worse. If you have any doubt about the stability of your file, choose File → Save a Copy As → Compressed Copy instead. This command rebuilds the database's internal structure and can fix many minor problems.

Part Seven:
Appendixes

7

Appendix A: Getting Help

Appendix B: FileMaker Error Codes

Getting Help

This book provides a solid foundation in FileMaker and takes you well into power-user territory, but it doesn't cover everything there is to know about this vastly versatile program. (You wouldn't be able to lift it if it did.) This appendix is a guide to the many resources available to help you plumb the depths of FileMaker database design and development.

Getting Help from FileMaker Itself

The installation CDs for FileMaker Pro and FileMaker Pro Advanced include online help files, electronic documentation, templates, and example files. The installer program *always* installs Online help, but the others are optional. When you choose the Easy Install option in the Install panel of the installation wizard, you get *everything* installed. Choose Custom Install instead to pick and choose which of the optional files you want installed. And if FileMaker's already installed on your computer, but the helpers listed below are missing, you can perform a Custom Install and choose the helper files you need without having to uninstall and reinstall FileMaker itself.

On Windows you can find these helpers at C: → Program Files → FileMaker → File-Maker Pro 8 → English Extras. And on the Mac, look in Macintosh HD → Applications → FileMaker Pro 8 → English Extras.

FileMaker Pro Help

To access FileMaker's onboard help files, choose Help → FileMaker Pro Help. You can also simply press F1 (Windows) or ⌘-? (Mac). If you launch Help while no dialog boxes are open, it opens to the Contents page (Figure A-1).

If what you need help with is the dialog box that's open in front of you, whatever you do don't close it! Instead, leave the dialog box open, which tells FileMaker you want context-sensitive help. For example, if you choose File → Define Database, then click the Relationships tab, and *then* choose Help → FileMaker Pro Help, the file opens to the detail page called "Working with related tables and files."

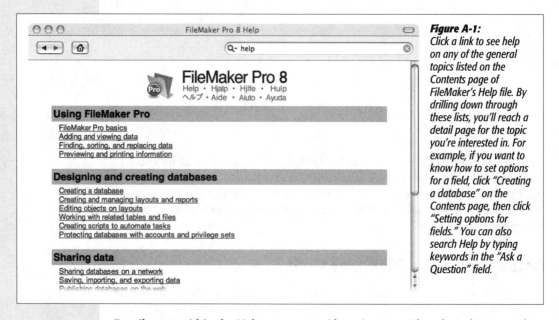

Figure A-1:
Click a link to see help on any of the general topics listed on the Contents page of FileMaker's Help file. By drilling down through these lists, you'll reach a detail page for the topic you're interested in. For example, if you want to know how to set options for a field, click "Creating a database" on the Contents page, then click "Setting options for fields." You can also search Help by typing keywords in the "Ask a Question" field.

Detail pages within the Help system provide assistance with technical terms. When you see underlined words or phrases, click those links for a short definition. At the bottom of each page is a list of related topics for further reading.

One of the most useful parts of the Help file is a comprehensive list of FileMaker's functions. As in the Specify Calculation dialog box, the functions are listed two ways: by type and alphabetically. The detail page for each function gives you the function name, parameter(s), data type returned, and a description of what the function does. Use these pages to help you when you're using a function for the first time.

Templates

You got a glimpse of these starter solutions in Chapter 1, when you created your first new file from the Contact Management template. You see all these template files listed in the New Database dialog box—unless you've previously checked that dialog box's option to "No longer show this dialog." If you've turned this option on, but want to see the templates listed again, choose FileMaker Pro → Preferences (Mac) or Edit → Preferences (Windows), then turn on the "Show templates in new Database dialog box" option on the General tab of the Preferences dialog box. The next time you choose File → New Database, FileMaker's templates will be listed. Pick the template you want, and FileMaker creates a new copy of the file for you. You can add data, create and edit scripts, or delete objects you don't need without affecting the original template.

Tip: If you prefer, you can navigate to the Templates folder and launch the template you want just like any other file. When you launch a template file directly, though, you're opening the *original* template file, and any changes you make to the template will be reflected in any new copies you make when you choose File → New Database.

These basic file templates are great for getting you up and running with basic data management tasks without wasting time figuring out how things work in File-Maker's universe. But they also serve another purpose—as an introduction to good database design. They have a clean, uncluttered look you can adapt for your own purposes. Feel free to copy the design as is or use it as a jumping-off point for your new database.

Each template stores different kinds of data, so it's helpful to explore several templates to get ideas for arranging and grouping your data effectively. In general, there's usually an easy-to-read name at the top of the layout, which serves to orient your users to the task at hand. Underneath the name, you'll find a couple of rows of navigation tools and buttons grouped together by function. The largest portion of the layout is dedicated to a logical arrangement of data fields.

Finally, FileMaker's templates contain ideas you can use for creating relationships, buttons and scripts that will make your own databases more powerful. For instance, the Contact Management template contains a script that allows you to swap a contact's main address data with the secondary address data. By studying these files, you can pick up tips about how the pros use FileMaker's power to make data management easier.

Electronic Documentation

The Electronic Documentation folder on the installation CD contains PDF (Portable Document Format) manuals in specific FileMaker topics. A User's Guide is included with both FileMaker Pro and FileMaker Pro Advanced. FileMaker Pro Advanced has a special PDF called the "Developer's Guide" with help on the developer tools included only in that product. Some other guides included in the product line are:

- **FileMaker Pro User's Guide.** At 115 pages (or more), this manual provides an overview to FileMaker's features, with some step-by-step instructions.

- **Installation Guide for FileMaker Pro and FileMaker Pro Advanced.** This short guide tells you about registration and support options, hardware and software requirements, and walks you through the steps for installing FileMaker on Mac and on Windows.

- **FileMaker Instant Web Publishing Guide.** This manual tells you how to design databases that are suitable for web publishing using FileMaker's Instant Web Publishing feature.

- **Customizing Starter Solutions.** If you want to customize FileMaker's templates, use this guide to learn more about their structure and features.

- **Installing FileMaker ODBC and JDBC Client Drivers.** Learn how to install xDBC drivers.

- **FileMaker ODBC and JDBC Developer's Guide.** Use this guide to get up to speed on sharing FileMaker data with xDBC sources.

Note: The document names given above are the official titles of the guides. They may not exactly match the PDF file names, but they're close enough so you can find the one you're looking for.

XML Examples

Example files, including a database and sample XML and XSLT files, are in a folder aptly titled Examples. These simple files serve as a primer for working with File-Maker and XML. To get started, open the database file ("xml example.fp7"), then run each script to see how XML import and export works. Then take a look at the steps that make up each script, paying particular attention to the options set for the Import Records and Export Records steps. Finally, take a look at the files that are imported and the files that are created by the export scripts. In them you'll see how your XML pages should be structured.

Getting Help from FileMaker, Inc.

FileMaker's Web site has the usual marketing materials you'd expect from a great software company. But there's lots of substance there, too. Look for "Support" in its main navigation menu, where you'll find free and fee-based help.

Updaters & Downloads

Like most programs, FileMaker's latest software versions are those found on the software company's Web site. You'll find Software Updates and support files, like localized language packs at *www.filemaker.com/support/downloads/index.html*. Trial software and development tools, including an XLST library and a list of recently released plug-ins, are also available from this page.

If your installation is missing some (or all) of its templates, click the Starter Solutions link to download new copies. You can also download a free, ready-made business solution called FileMaker Business Tracker. It's an invoicing system that lets you track sales, contacts, and product data. Even if your business doesn't do sales, you'll find this product useful for study purposes. It was written as a demo file for FileMaker 7, and it's full of developer tricks of the trade you can analyze. When you've mastered all the secrets there, you're ready to leave the monastery, Grasshopper.

Documentation and Publications

You can reach this list from the Downloads page above, but it's so jammed-packed that it deserves a headline all its own.

- **Product Documentation.** You'll find all the documentation that came with your product here, plus any updates to those guides. There are also tutorial files and some extra guides on topics like security, Windows 2000 Terminal Services, and Citrix.

- **White Papers.** Here you'll find shorter papers on specific subjects, like migrating your older files to .fp7 format and custom Web publishing with server-side scripting. If you want to make the case for FileMaker's power and simplicity to higher-ups in your organization, check out the Industry sections, where you'll find such topics as Information Management and Cost of Ownership studies on FileMaker.

- **Technical Briefs.** These are usually longer documents than the white papers, so they cover similar topics in more depth. Unlike product documentation, which has explanations and step-by-step instructions, these works focus more on methods and benefits of FileMaker's newest technologies, like improved security and the new server and web publishing models.

- **FileMaker Resource Guide.** The Resource Guide lists FileMaker's complete product line, third-arty products, trainers, and consultants.

- **Knowledge Base.** Find FAQs, bug alerts, workarounds, errata, and the official word on topics that don't fit into FileMaker's other document categories. You can either search the Knowledge Base with keywords, or peruse the most recent topics to see what's new. A button at the bottom of each page lets you request email notification if the page is updated, so you can stay on top of developments with ease. A clickable list of related topics helps you wander around in case the main topic didn't fit the bill.

Technical Support

FileMaker supports the current version of its software and one version prior. If your files are older than that, you'll need to get help from a third party, usually a

---

consultant or a user group. See the section below to find out how to find those animals.

You can't start making databases until FileMaker's installed, so everybody who purchases FileMaker gets unlimited tech support phone calls regarding installation. Plus, you get one free troubleshooting call for each product you buy, which is helpful when you have a bunch of staffers on FileMaker Pro, a copy or two of Server and your very own copy of FileMaker Pro Advanced. The tech support is free, but you'll pay for the phone call, so break out those free long-distance minutes. Dial (408) 727-9004 for the free stuff.

Paid tech support is available by calling (800) 965-9090. Get out your credit card when you call, then decide how you want to pay. You can choose a $45 flat fee and they'll solve a single issue for you or you can roll the dice (and get multiple problems solved at once) by choosing the $3 per minute rate, with a $75 maximum. Phone tech support is available 7 a.m. to 5 p.m. PT weekdays.

Premium 800 Support lets you pre-pay $180 for a five-pack of access codes that let you make the calls when the trouble arises. Codes are good for one year. Call (800) 325-2747 for the bulk discount.

Professional Support costs $899 per year. You nominate one person from your company who can call a special toll-free number as many times as needed for twelve months. Add $699 for each additional person who needs the same access. Download the order form at *www.filemaker.com/support/prof_support_info.html*.

Note: Technical Support deals with technical problems, like when a feature isn't working as advertised and you need help figuring out why. Teaching you how to create databases or writing your calculations and scripts for you are not considered technical support issues.

File corruption isn't common with FileMaker, but it's devastating when it happens. FileMaker offers file recovery services at $100 per table. Go to *www.filemaker. com/support/technical_support.html* and scroll to the bottom of the page for more information.

FileMaker Applications

If you find yourself without the time or inclination to create a new database, you may be able to purchase one of these ready-made systems, professionally designed by FileMaker staff. Like FileMaker's Starter Solutions (aka templates), FileMaker Applications are fully unlocked and customizable. But they go a lot further than the Starter Solutions, and you may find that they meet many of your needs straight out of the box. Prices range from $69 to $448. These applications let you manage tasks like employment recruiting, tracking donors and donations, managing meetings, and work requests. See *www.filemaker.com/products/applications/index.html* for a complete list. Click the link for each solution to get more information about each product and to see online demos.

FileMaker Solutions Alliance (FSA)

The FSA is a bit of a hybrid. It's run by FileMaker, Inc. and to be sure, you pay annual dues to be a member, but you become a part of the developer community when you do. For the casual or in-house developer, one of the most practical benefits is TechTalk, a members-only email list where you can ask questions and share your own experiences. The old hands are willing to share their wisdom with newcomers. The list is very active, with upwards of a hundred messages a day, particularly when a topic sparks developers' interest. (The list is moderated, so it rarely veers off track.)

Other FSA benefits include access to exclusive technical information, invitations to exclusive technical briefings and the annual meeting at the developer's convention, and discounted or even free products. There are four levels of membership, with increasing benefits (you can be listed in the FSA Directory, and a free copy of FileMaker Pro Advanced, for example). If you're planning to become an independent consultant, membership in the FSA is invaluable.

Getting Help from the Community

Even outside of the members-only FSA, the FileMaker developer community is a congenial bunch. There are lots of resources on the Internet, including free newsgroups and Web sites. Lots of independent consultants' sites have free or low-cost resources, too, like lists of custom functions free for the taking or sample files that demonstrate specific techniques.

Mail Lists and Newsgroups

A list of email lists is available at *www.filemaker.com/support/mailinglists.html*, but new sites are cropping up all the time and URLs change even on established sites, so use the link above, or check your favorite search engine to get the latest link for these groups. To get your feet wet, try general lists, like the one run by Dartmouth University or FileMaker Today, New kid on the block fmpug.com is a membership-based, online user group with forums, reviews, resources, including podCast interviews with subject-matter experts. For more specialized topics, have a look at FileMaker XML Talk, FileMaker Pro CGI Talk, and Troi FileMaker Plug-in Talk.

Training/Consultants

FileMaker's Web site lists trainers and consultants who are members of the FSA. And the FileMaker Resource Guide also lists the FSA group, plus it takes paid advertisements. Your favorite search engine will yield hundreds of results. FileMaker has a certification program, so look for the FileMaker Certified Developer logo or ask the consultant if they've been certified as part of your selection process.

DevCon

If total FileMaker immersion is what you seek, the annual Developer's Convention (DevCon) is the way to go. Each day you can attend as many as seven sessions on about 30 different topics, ranging from running a FileMaker consulting firm to Web publishing, so you're sure to come away from the three-day conference with a brain-pan full of new ideas: *www.filemaker.com/devcon*.

FileMaker Error Codes

The following table lists the error codes that might pop up when FileMaker detects something out-of-whack in your database, especially when youre writing or running a script. Like many things written by and for computer programmers, these official descriptions may not make much sense in English, but they may provide a little more guidance than the error number alone.

Error codes marked with an asterisk (*) pertain only to Web-published databases.

Error Number	Description
-1	Unknown error
0	No error
1	User canceled action
2	Memory error
3	Command is unavailable (for example, wrong operating system, wrong mode, and so on)
4	Command is unknown
5	Command is invalid (for example, a Set Field script step does not have a calculation specified)
6	File is read-only
7	Running out of memory
8	Empty result
9	Insufficient privileges
10	Requested data is missing
11	Name is not valid

Error Number	Description
12	Name already exists
13	File or object is in use
14	Out of range
15	Can't divide by zero
16	Operation failed, request retry (for example, a user query)
17	Attempt to convert foreign character set to UTF-16 failed
18	Client must provide account information to proceed
19	String contains characters other than A–Z, a–z, 0–9 (ASCII)
100	File is missing
101	Record is missing
102	Field is missing
103	Relationship is missing
104	Script is missing
105	Layout is missing
106	Table is missing
107	Index is missing
108	Value list is missing
109	Privilege set is missing
110	Related tables are missing
111	Field repetition is invalid
112	Window is missing
113	Function is missing
114	File reference is missing
115	Specified menu set is not present
130	Files are damaged or missing and must be reinstalled
131	Language pack files are missing (such as template files)
200	Record access is denied
201	Field cannot be modified
202	Field access is denied
203	No records in file to print, or password doesn't allow print access
204	No access to field(s) in sort order
205	User does not have access privileges to create new records; import will overwrite existing data
206	User does not have password change privileges, or file is not modifiable
207	User does not have sufficient privileges to change database schema, or file is not modifiable
208	Password does not contain enough characters
209	New password must be different from existing one

Error Number	Description
210	User account is inactive
211	Password has expired
212	Invalid user account and/or password; please try again
213	User account and/or password does not exist
214	Too many login attempts
215	Administrator privileges cannot be duplicated
216	Guest account cannot be duplicated
217	User does not have sufficient privileges to modify administrator account
300	File is locked or in use
301	Record is in use by another user
302	Table is in use by another user
303	Database schema is in use by another user
304	Layout is in use by another user
306	Record modification ID does not match
400	Find criteria are empty
401	No records match the request
402	Selected field is not a match field for a lookup
403	Exceeding maximum record limit for trial version of FileMaker Pro
404	Sort order is invalid
405	Number of records specified exceeds number of records that can be omitted
406	Replace/Reserialize criteria are invalid
407	One or both match fields are missing (invalid relationship)
408	Specified field has inappropriate data type for this operation
409	Import order is invalid
410	Export order is invalid
412	Wrong version of FileMaker Pro used to recover file
413	Specified field has inappropriate field type
414	Layout cannot display the result
415	One or more required related records are not available
500	Date value does not meet validation entry options
501	Time value does not meet validation entry options
502	Number value does not meet validation entry options
503	Value in field is not within the range specified in validation entry options
504	Value in field is not unique as required in validation entry options
505	Value in field is not an existing value in the database file as required in validation entry options
506	Value in field is not listed on the value list specified in validation entry option

Error Number	Description
507	Value in field failed calculation test of validation entry option
508	Invalid value entered in Find mode
509	Field requires a valid value
510	Related value is empty or unavailable
511	Value in field exceeds maximum number of allowed characters
600	Print error has occurred
601	Combined header and footer exceed one page
602	Body doesn't fit on a page for current column setup
603	Print connection lost
700	File is of the wrong file type for import
706	EPSF file has no preview image
707	Graphic translator cannot be found
708	Can't import the file or need color monitor support to import file
709	QuickTime movie import failed
710	Unable to update QuickTime file reference because the database file is read-only
711	Import translator cannot be found
714	Password privileges do not allow the operation
715	Specified Excel worksheet or named range is missing
716	A SQL query using DELETE, INSERT, or UPDATE is not allowed for ODBC import
717	There is not enough XML/XSL information to proceed with the import or export
718	Error in parsing XML file (from Xerces)
719	Error in transforming XML using XSL (from Xalan)
720	Error when exporting; intended format does not support repeating fields
721	Unknown error occurred in the parser or the transformer
722	Cannot import data into a file that has no fields
723	You do not have permission to add records to or modify records in the target table
724	You do not have permission to add records to the target table
725	You do not have permission to modify records in the target table
726	There are more records in the import file than in the target table. Not all records were imported
727	There are more records in the target table than in the import file. Not all records were updated
729	Errors occurred during import. Records could not be imported
730	Unsupported Excel version. (Convert file to Excel 7.0 [Excel 95], Excel 97, 2000, or XP format and try again)
731	The file you are importing from contains no data

Error Number	Description
732	This file cannot be inserted because it contains other files
733	A table cannot be imported into itself
734	This file type cannot be displayed as a picture
735	This file type cannot be displayed as a picture. It will be inserted and displayed as a file
736	Too much data to export to this format. It will be truncated
800	Unable to create file on disk
801	Unable to create temporary file on System disk
802	Unable to open file
803	File is single user or host cannot be found
804	File cannot be opened as read-only in its current state
805	File is damaged; use Recover command
806	File cannot be opened with this version of FileMaker Pro
807	File is not a FileMaker Pro file or is severely damaged
808	Cannot open file because access privileges are damaged
809	Disk/volume is full
810	Disk/volume is locked
811	Temporary file cannot be opened as FileMaker Pro file
813	Record Synchronization error on network
814	File(s) cannot be opened because maximum number is open
815	Couldn't open lookup file
816	Unable to convert file
817	Unable to open file because it does not belong to this solution
819	Cannot save a local copy of a remote file
820	File is in the process of being closed
821	Host forced a disconnect
822	FMI files not found; reinstall missing files
823	Cannot set file to single-user, guests are connected
824	File is damaged or not a FileMaker file
900	General spelling engine error
901	Main spelling dictionary not installed
902	Could not launch the Help system
903	Command cannot be used in a shared file
905	No active field selected; command can only be used if there is an active field
920	Can't initialize the spelling engine
921	User dictionary cannot be loaded for editing
922	User dictionary cannot be found

Error Number	Description
923	User dictionary is read-only
951	An unexpected error occurred (*)
954	Unsupported XML grammar (*)
955	No database name (*)
956	Maximum number of database sessions exceeded (*)
957	Conflicting commands (*)
958	Parameter missing (*)
1200	Generic calculation error
1201	Too few parameters in the function
1202	Too many parameters in the function
1203	Unexpected end of calculation
1204	Number, text constant, field name or "(" expected
1205	Comment is not terminated with "*/"
1206	Text constant must end with a quotation mark
1207	Unbalanced parenthesis
1208	Operator missing, function not found or "(" not expected
1209	Name (such as field name or layout name) is missing
1210	Plug-in function has already been registered
1211	List usage is not allowed in this function
1212	An operator (for example, +, -, *) is expected here
1213	This variable has already been defined in the Let function
1214	AVERAGE, COUNT, EXTEND, GETREPETITION, MAX, MIN, NPV, STDEV, SUM and GETSUMMARY: expression found where a field alone is needed
1215	This parameter is an invalid Get function parameter
1216	Only Summary fields allowed as first argument in GETSUMMARY
1217	Break field is invalid
1218	Cannot evaluate the number
1219	A field cannot be used in its own formula
1220	Field type must be normal or calculated
1221	Data type must be number, date, time, or timestamp
1222	Calculation cannot be stored
1223	The function is not implemented
1224	The function is not defined
1300	The specified name can't be used
1400	ODBC driver initialization failed; make sure the ODBC drivers are properly installed
1401	Failed to allocate environment (ODBC)
1402	Failed to free environment (ODBC)

Error Number	Description
1403	Failed to disconnect (ODBC)
1404	Failed to allocate connection (ODBC)
1405	Failed to free connection (ODBC)
1406	Failed check for SQL API (ODBC)
1407	Failed to allocate statement (ODBC)
1408	Extended error (ODBC)

Index

G

Colophon

Philip Dangler was the production editor and proofreader for *FileMaker Pro 8: The Missing Manual*. Sohaila Abdulali was the copyeditor. Sarah Sherman and Marlowe Shaeffer provided quality control. Julie Hawks wrote the index.

Marcia Friedman designed the cover of this book, based on a series design by David Freedman. Rose Cassano created the cover illustration with Adobe Illustrator CS. Marcia Friedman produced the cover layout with Adobe InDesign CS using Adobe's Minion and Gill Sans fonts.

David Futato designed the interior layout, based on a series design by Phil Simpson. This book was converted by Andrew Savikas to FrameMaker 5.5.6 with a format conversion tool created by Erik Ray, Jason McIntosh, Neil Walls, and Mike Sierra that uses Perl and XML technologies. The text font is Adobe Minion; the heading font is Adobe Formata Condensed; and the code font is LucasFont's TheSans Mono Condensed. The illustrations that appear in the book were produced by Robert Romano, Jessamyn Read, and Lesley Borash using Macromedia FreeHand MX and Adobe Photoshop CS.

Related Titles from O'Reilly

Missing Manuals

Access: The Missing Manual, *Startup Edition*

AppleWorks 6: The Missing Manual

Creating Web Sites: The Missing Manual

Dreamweaver MX 2004: The Missing Manual

eBay: The Missing Manual

Excel: The Missing Manual

Excel for Rookies: The Missing Manual

FileMaker Pro: The Missing Manual

FrontPage 2003: The Missing Manual

GarageBand: The Missing Manual

Google: The Missing Manual, *2nd Edition*

Home Networking: The Missing Manual

iLife '04: The Missing Manual

iMovie HD & iDVD 5: The Missing Manual

iPhoto 5: The Missing Manual

iPod & iTunes: The Missing Manual, *3rd Edition*

iWork '05: The Missing Manual

Mac OS X: The Missing Manual, *Tiger Edition*

Office 2004 for Macintosh: The Missing Manual

Windows 2000 Pro: The Missing Manual

Windows XP: The Missing Manual, *Startup Edition*

Windows XP Pro: The Missing Manual, *2nd Edition*

Windows XP Home Edition: The Missing Manual, *2nd Edition*

Pogue Press

Mac OS X Panther Power Hound

Switching to the Mac, *Tiger Edition*

Windows XP Power Hound

O'REILLY®

Our books are available at most retail and online bookstores.

To order direct: 1-800-998-9938 • *order@oreilly.com* • *www.oreilly.com*

Online editions of most O'Reilly titles are available by subscription at *safari.oreilly.com*

Keep in touch with O'Reilly

Download examples from our books

To find example files from a book, go to: *www.oreilly.com/catalog* select the book, and follow the "Examples" link.

Register your O'Reilly books

Register your book at *register.oreilly.com* Why register your books? Once you've registered your O'Reilly books you can:

- Win O'Reilly books, T-shirts or discount coupons in our monthly drawing.
- Get special offers available only to registered O'Reilly customers.
- Get catalogs announcing new books (US and UK only).
- Get email notification of new editions of the O'Reilly books you own.

Join our email lists

Sign up to get topic-specific email announcements of new books and conferences, special offers, and O'Reilly Network technology newsletters at:

elists.oreilly.com

It's easy to customize your free elists subscription so you'll get exactly the O'Reilly news you want.

Get the latest news, tips, and tools

www.oreilly.com

- "Top 100 Sites on the Web"—PC Magazine
- CIO Magazine's Web Business 50 Awards

Our web site contains a library of comprehensive product information (including book excerpts and tables of contents), downloadable software, background articles, interviews with technology leaders, links to relevant sites, book cover art, and more.

Work for O'Reilly

Check out our web site for current employment opportunities:

jobs.oreilly.com

Contact us

O'Reilly Media, Inc.
1005 Gravenstein Hwy North
Sebastopol, CA 95472 USA
Tel: 707-827-7000 or 800-998-9938
  (6am to 5pm PST)
Fax: 707-829-0104

Contact us by email

For answers to problems regarding your order or our products:
order@oreilly.com

To request a copy of our latest catalog:
catalog@oreilly.com

For book content technical questions or corrections: **booktech@oreilly.com**

For educational, library, government, and corporate sales: **corporate@oreilly.com**

To submit new book proposals to our editors and product managers:
proposals@oreilly.com

For information about our international distributors or translation queries:
international@oreilly.com

For information about academic use of O'Reilly books:
adoption@oreilly.com
or visit:
academic.oreilly.com

For a list of our distributors outside of North America check out:
international.oreilly.com/distributors.html

Order a book online

www.oreilly.com/order_new

O'REILLY®

Our books are available at most retail and online bookstores.
To order direct: 1-800-998-9938 • *order@oreilly.com* • *www.oreilly.com*
Online editions of most O'Reilly titles are available by subscription at *safari.oreilly.com*